UNCLOS 1982 COMMENTARY

Center for Oceans Law and Policy
University of Virginia School of Law

UNCLOS 1982 COMMENTARY

Supplementary Documents

Myron H. Nordquist
Series Editor-in-Chief

Satya N. Nandan, C.F., C.B.E.
Series General Editor

James Kraska
Associate Editor

MARTINUS
NIJHOFF
PUBLISHERS

LEIDEN . BOSTON
2012

This book is printed on acid-free paper.

Library of Congress Cataloging-in-Publication Data

United Nations Convention on the Law of the Sea, 1982 : a commentary / Myron N. Nordquist, editor-in-chief, Sataya N. Nandan, general editor, and James Kraska, associate editor.
p. cm.
At head of title: Center for Oceans Law and Policy, University of Virginia.
ISBN 9789004215634 (supplementary documents)
1. United Nations Convention on the Law of the Sea (1982)
2. Maritime law. I. Nordquist, Myron H. II. Nandan, Sataya N.
III. Kraska, James. IV. University of Virginia. School of Law. Center for Oceans Law and Policy.
JX4421.U55 1989
341.4'5—dc19

88 - 12691

ISBN 978 90 04 21563 4

CONTENTS

Part V. Other Supplementary Documents and Materials

INTRODUCTION

Supplementary Documents complements the seven-volume *Commentary* on the United Nations Convention on the Law of the Sea, a scholarly endeavor that has unfolded over the course of three decades under the sponsorship of the Center for Oceans Law and Policy, University of Virginia School of Law. The United Nations Convention on the Law of the Sea (Convention) was opened for signature at Montego Bay, Jamaica, on 10 December 1982. The conclusion of the Convention was a momentous occasion in the history of international law and international relations. That event was all the more significant in that Convention, for the most part, was the result of consensus or broad agreement among about 160 States which participated in the Third United Nations Conference on the Law of the Sea (Conference). Taken as a whole, the Convention provides for an equitable relationship among States in their use of the oceans based on their respective geographical characteristics, economic circumstances, political imperatives and global responsibilities. It establishes certainty in the international law of the sea in place of the instability created by the proliferation of unilateral claims that prompted the General Assembly to convene the Conference on the Law of the Sea in 1973.

The Convention achieves a delicate balance between competing interests in the world's maritime zones. It establishes 12 nautical miles as the breadth of the territorial sea with a guaranteed right of passage for international navigation in those waters; it ensures unhampered passage of all kinds of vessels and aircraft through archipelagic sea lanes and vital straits around the world; it secures for coastal States resource jurisdiction in a 200-nautical-mile exclusive economic zone (EEZ); it provides for an extended continental shelf jurisdiction of coastal States beyond the EEZ; it guarantees access to and from the sea for land-locked States; it provides for a regime for archipelagic States; it establishes a regime for the development of the mineral resources of the deep seabed; it sets out rules for the conduct of marine scientific research; it imposes a duty on all States to ensure, through proper conservation and management measures, the long-term sustainability of fish resources; it contains the most comprehensive rules yet agreed for the protection and preservation of the marine environment and imposes a duty on States to protect the oceans from all sources of pollution; and it promotes peaceful settlement of disputes arising from the interpretation and application of the provisions of the Convention.

The Convention entered into force after 12 years of negotiations, on 16 November 1994. A subsequent Agreement relating to the implementation of Part XI of the Convention was adopted on 28 July 1994 and entered into force on 28 July 1996, about which more is said in what follows in this introduction. The 1994 Agreement and the Convention are to be interpreted and applied together as a single instrument.

The documents in this volume provide additional material to the *Commentary* series, including associated legal authorities, guidelines and agreements. Since adoption of the Convention it has attracted 161 Parties as of June 2011. While the Convention itself is recognized as an authoritative guide to humankind's activities and future progress in the oceans, it is also an umbrella agreement whose detailed implementation is found in supplementary authorities and agreements. Much of the work under the Convention going forward will unfold within the ambit of the three independent institutions established by the Convention—the International Seabed Authority, the International Tribunal of the Law of the Sea and the Commission on the Limits of the Continental Shelf. Each of these institutions has individually promulgated codes and guidelines that serve to implement its mandate. The editors decided to select the most important of such documents to reproduce in this *Supplementary Documents* volume. In addition, we have included a few other documents that we felt would be useful to users of the Virginia *Commentary* series.

The origins of the Convention may be traced to two parallel initiatives. In 1966, the United States and the Soviet Union drew a package of proposals for a 12-mile territorial sea that took account of their interests in unimpeded passage through and over straits used for international navigation. The Soviet Union together with its East European allies followed this initiative with a proposal to add to the agenda of the Sixth (Legal) Committee of the UN General Assembly an item limited to the question of the breadth of the territorial sea. The other initiative came on 1 November 1967 when, inspired by the work of J. Mero in his book *The Mineral Resources of the Sea* (1964),[1] Ambassador Arvid Pardo of Malta addressed the General Assembly of the United Nations and called for "an effective international regime over the seabed and the ocean floor beyond a clearly defined national jurisdiction." This proposal did not deal with the breadth of the territorial sea or any other aspects of the traditional law of the sea. Eventually, the Soviet and Maltese items were merged into a single agenda item, which was examined in the First Committee of the UN General Assembly. That led to Resolution 2750C (XXV) of 17 December 1970. In that resolution it was decided to convene the Third UN Conference on the Law of the Sea to draft a comprehensive convention on the law of the sea.[2] After nine years of intensive negotiations, the Convention was adopted albeit with differences remaining over Part XI dealing with the deep seabed regime. These differences were resolved through an Implementing Agreement in 1994. The Convention establishes a comprehensive legal framework to regulate all ocean space, its uses and resources with provisions relating to the territorial sea, the contiguous zone, the continental shelf, the EEZ and the high seas. It also provides for the protection and preservation of the marine environment, for marine scientific research and for the development and transfer of marine technology.

---

[1] For more details see volume six of the *Commentary* series.

[2] For more details see volume one at 178 and the introduction to volume two of the *Commentary* series.

THE INTERNATIONAL SEABED AUTHORITY

One of the most important parts of the Convention concerns the exploration for and exploitation of the resources of the seabed and ocean floor and subsoil thereof, beyond the limits of national jurisdiction (the Area). The Convention declares the Area and its resources to be "the common heritage of mankind". The International Seabed Authority (ISA), established by the Convention, administers the resources of the Area. The ISA is an autonomous international organization established under the Convention and the 1994 Agreement relating to the Implementation of Part XI of the United Nations Convention on the Law of the Sea [1994 Agreement]. When differences in seabed mining began to undermine the treaty as a whole, a number of states opened a dialogue to find a mutually agreeable solution. The dialogue to resolve the outstanding issues that ensued concerning seabed mining was based on two fundamental premises: first, the integrity of the Convention must not be eroded—all issues in the Convention are interrelated and must remain part of the whole, there can be no reservation on any part of the Convention, and all parts must be subject to compulsory dispute settlement procedures as provided for in the Convention; and second, the specific issues in Part XI which created difficulties for industrialized countries should be clearly identified and addressed in the context of Part XI. The progress that has been made in the negotiations among States since 1990 was due to adherence to these two premises which were clearly reflected in the 1994 Agreement adopted by the UN General Assembly in July, 1994.

At the Conference, informal private negotiating groups were critical to the resolution of the most intractable issues. The negotiations which led to the 1994 Agreement were no exception to this well-established practice. Thus, at a crucial stage in the Secretary-General's informal consultations, when negotiations were heading towards an impasse, a group of representatives from both developed and developing States who held similar views in the discussion on procedural approaches to an agreement, developed an informal and anonymous paper which was dated August 1993. The paper came to be known as the "Boat Paper" because of an illustration of a seabed mining vessel on the cover.[3]

The "Boat Paper," which was presented first simply as a contribution to the process of consultations, soon became the basic paper in the negotiations. It contained a draft resolution for adoption by the General Assembly to which was appended a draft agreement with annexes. Subsequent revisions of the paper were undertaken in an expanded Boat Paper Group in which all key delegations and interest groups were represented. These revisions took into account the discussions in the Secretary-General's consultations and in the

---

[3] Satya N. Nandan chaired the informal group which resolved the outstanding issues concerning Part XI of the Convention.

Boat Paper Group itself. The final text as developed by the Group is contained in an annex of the Secretary-General's report (A/48/950) and in document A/48/L.60.

The Chairman of the informal group introduced the draft resolution A/48/L.60 entitled "Agreement relating to the implementation of Part XI of the United Nations Convention on the Law of the Sea of 10 December 1982." The Implementing Agreement was adopted by the General Assembly on 28 July 1994. In adopting the resolution, the General Assembly also adopted the Agreement relating to the Implementation of Part XI of the United Nations Convention on the Law of the Sea of 10 December 1982, which was appended to it. The General Assembly, *inter alia*, affirmed that the 1994 Agreement would be interpreted and applied together with Part XI of the Convention as a single instrument.

By adopting the 1994 Agreement, the General Assembly expressed its satisfaction at the entry into force of the Convention on 16 November 1994. The Assembly also requested the Secretary-General to open the 1994 Agreement for signature immediately after its adoption. It urged all States and entities to apply the Agreement provisionally and become parties to it at the earliest possible date. In addition, it urged those who had not already done so to become parties to the Convention as a whole in order to ensure universal participation in it.

In the 1994 Agreement, which was appended to the resolution, States *inter alia*, recognized the important contribution of the 1982 Convention to the maintenance of peace, justice and progress for all peoples of the world. The 1994 Agreement referred to the report of the Secretary-General on the results of the informal consultations among States held from 1990 to 1994 on the outstanding issues relating to Part XI and related provisions of the Convention. It noted that political and economic changes, including market-oriented approaches, had affected the implementation of Part XI since the adoption of the Convention in 1982. It also indicated that States consider that the 1994 Agreement relating to the implementation of Part XI—as appended to the draft resolution—would best meet the objective of facilitating universal participation in the Convention.

Section 1 dealt with costs to States Parties and institutional arrangements. It provided, *inter alia*, that a cost-effective and evolutionary approach should be taken in the establishment of all organs and subsidiary bodies under the Convention and the 1994 Agreement in order to minimize costs to States Parties. Consistent with this approach, it identified the early functions on which the International Seabed Authority would concentrate. It set out the procedures for the approval of plans of work, and, in particular, it dealt with the plans of work that were to be submitted to the Authority by those identified as being eligible for pioneer investor status under Resolution II of the Convention. It prescribed special procedures to facilitate the integration into the Convention system of the pioneer investors registered by the Preparatory Commission for the ISA and for the International Tribunal for the Law of the Sea [Tribunal or ITLOS]. It also provided that any plan of work submitted to the Authority was to be accompanied by an assessment of the potential environmental impact of the proposed activities and by a description of a program for oceanographic and baseline environmental studies in accordance with the rules, regulations and procedures to be adopted by the Authority. Finally, the section provided that the Authority might, at any time, elaborate and adopt rules, regulations and procedures based on the principles contained in the annex to the 1994 Agreement, as well as any additional rules, regulations and procedures necessary to facilitate the approval of plans of work for exploration or exploitation as seabed mining activities develop.

Section 2 of the annex dealt with the Enterprise, the operating arm of the Authority. It provided that the initial functions of the Enterprise would be undertaken by the Secretariat of the Authority. More importantly, the initial deep-seabed mining operations of the Enterprise were to be through joint ventures. If joint-venture arrangements with the Enterprise accord with sound commercial principles, the Council was required to issue a directive for the independent functioning of the Enterprise from the Secretariat of the Authority. The obligation of States Parties to fund one mine site for the Enterprise as provided for in the Convention would not apply, and States Parties were under no obligation to finance any operation of the Enterprise. The Enterprise was to be subject to the same rules and regulations as any other deep-seabed mining operator.

Section 3 dealt with decision-making. The procedure for decision-making in the Council of the Authority was considerably streamlined and simplified. This section provides that voting would take place only when all efforts to reach a decision on substantive matters by consensus had been exhausted. This section set out a system of voting by chambers. The practical effect of the chamber system of voting was to promote decisions by consensus. In cases other than those for which the Convention provides for decisions by consensus, decisions on substantive matters in the Council were to be taken by a two-thirds majority, provided such decisions were not opposed by a majority in any one of the chambers. The Council would have 36 members and consist of four chambers for this purpose. These chambers would ensure that important interests were assured representation in the Council.

In order to ensure that a duly qualified applicant was assured of a contract with the Authority, a special procedure was prescribed for the approval of an application for a plan of work. Such plans of work can only be disapproved by the Council of the Authority by a two-thirds majority, provided such majority includes a majority of members in each chamber. Further, a plan of work would be deemed to have been approved if the Council did not act within 60 days following the recommendation of its approval by the Legal and Technical Commission, which is a technical body composed of experts that advises the Council.

Section 4 deals with the Review Conference and provides that such a review may take place at any time, but not until after 15 years from the date of the first commercial production, as was stated in the Convention. Furthermore, any amendments arising from such a Review Conference shall be subject to the amendment procedures set out in the Convention.

Section 5 deals with the transfer of technology. In the light of the approach taken for the operations of the Enterprise, the requirement for a possible mandatory transfer of technology by a contractor as provided for originally in the Convention does not apply. The Enterprise and developing States are to obtain the required technology through joint venture arrangements or from the open market. If this is not possible, the Authority may request the cooperation of States whose nationals may have such technology to facilitate their acquisition on fair and reasonable commercial terms and conditions consistent with the protection of intellectual property rights. For this purpose, the cooperation of all States Parties is urged.

Section 6 deals with production policy. The Convention had provided for a mathematical formula to control the level of production of minerals from the seabed. This formula was based on historical data on the growth of consumption of minerals, in particular, nickel. However, the prolonged downturn in the world metal market in the more than two decades since the adoption of the Convention in 1982 had rendered the formula inoperative. The Agreement therefore provides that the production policy of the Authority shall be based on market forces and that the provisions of the General Agreement on Tariffs and Trade (GATT), its relevant codes and successor or superseding agreements shall apply to activities in the deep seabed. To ensure that minerals produced from land-based sources and those from the seabed compete on a level playing field, it is provided that there shall be no subsidization of mining activities in the seabed, except as permitted under the GATT rules. Further, there shall be no discrimination between minerals derived from the deep seabed and from other sources in their access to markets or for imports of commodities produced from such minerals.

Section 7 deals with economic assistance to developing land-based producer countries. It anticipates that some land-based producers of the same minerals that are to be produced from the seabed may suffer serious adverse effects on their export earnings or economies. In cases where such effects may be attributed to mining from the deep seabed, the Authority is required to provide assistance to the affected developing countries. For this purpose, the Authority is to establish an economic assistance fund from a portion of the proceeds from mining in excess of those necessary to cover the administrative expenses of the Authority. This is a significant improvement, in that there is a clear indication of the source from which such assistance would be provided.

Section 8 deals with the financial terms of contracts. This relates to the system of payment to the Authority for the mineral resources recovered by an operator from the deep seabed. The Agreement sets out the principles on which the financial terms of a contract shall be established. In essence, the rates of payment under the system shall be within the range of those prevailing in respect of land-based mining of similar minerals in order to avoid giving deep seabed minerals an artificial competitive advantage or imposing on them a competitive disadvantage. The system, however, must be fair to the operator and to the Authority.

Section 9 establishes a Finance Committee within the Authority which is essentially a technical body charged with the responsibility of overseeing the financial implications of the decisions of the Authority. The Committee is to include nationals of the highest contributors in its membership. In particular, the Council and the Assembly are obliged to take into account the recommendations of this technical body. On this issue of finance, it is also prescribed that no decisions having financial implications shall be adopted by the Assembly without first receiving a recommendation on the financial implications from the Council, and in cases where the Assembly does not agree with a recommendation of the Council, the matter shall be referred to the Council for its further consideration and recommendation, taking into account the views expressed in the Assembly.

As a consequence of the Agreement, the regime for the mining of the deep seabed was considerably streamlined and simplified. It takes a functional approach towards the establishment of the administrative institutions under Part XI; it provides for a stable environment for investors in deep-seabed minerals under a market-oriented regime; it guarantees access to the resources of the seabed to all qualified investors; it provides for the establishment of a system of taxation which is fair to the seabed miner and from which the international community as a whole may benefit; and it makes provisions for assistance to developing land-based producers of minerals whose economies may be affected as a consequence of deep seabed mining. Thus the 1994 Agreement provides a practical and realistic basis for the realization of the principle of the common heritage of mankind.

Today the Authority is a functioning organization through which States Parties to the Convention administer the resources of the deep seabed in accordance with the regime for the seabed and ocean floor and subsoil thereof beyond the limits of national jurisdiction (the Area) established in Part XI and the 1994 Agreement. The Authority has the function of organizing and controlling certain clearly identified activities in the Area, particularly with a view to administering the resources of the Area.

The Authority, which has its headquarters in Kingston, Jamaica, came into existence on 16 November 1994, upon the entry into force of the 1982 Convention. The Authority became fully operational as an autonomous international organization in June 1996, when it took over the premises and facilities in Kingston, Jamaica, which were previously used by the United Nations Kingston Office for the Law of the Sea. Meetings of the Authority are held at the Jamaica Conference Centre in Kingston. The Authority has an Observer status in the UN General Assembly. In 2004, at the tenth anniversary of the Authority, Ambassador Felipe Paolillo Permanent representative of Uruguay to the United Nations in New York traced the history of the International Seabed Authority back to the years before its establishment in 1994. He described the Authority's ten years of existence as "a happy childhood and adolescence," in stark contrast to the "lengthy and tormented period of its conception and birth." What made the early years so difficult was the reality of what was at stake – the access to and control of the tremendous wealth of the world's oceans – and predictions that if the exploitation of polymetallic nodules did not begin before the end of the twentieth century, the demand for certain metals would exceed the production capacity of land-based sources and the world would face a terrible crisis.

From the outset, Ambassador Paolillo explained, there were two positions, which seemed irreconcilable. The industrialized nations envisioned an Authority with functions limited to ensuring that activities in the international seabed area were conducted in an orderly fashion, while issuing, almost automatically, the required licenses for these activities to be carried out. However, the developing countries saw an opportunity to establish a regime for exploiting the sea's wealth, which would be based on the principle of the "common heritage of mankind", and which would be the foundation of a new world economic order. After many years of dispute, debate and negotiation, the application of the laws, which govern the Area was now the clear responsibility of the Authority.

Supplementary Documents includes selected basic texts from the International Seabed Authority, including the Regulations on Prospecting and Exploration for Polymetallic Nodules in the Area (The "Mining Code"), Notification of Intention to engage in Prospecting, a sample Application for Approval of a Plan of Work for Exploration to Obtain a Contract, a Model Contract for Exploration and Standard Clauses, the Rules of Procedure of the Assembly of the International Seabed Authority, the Rules of Procedure of the Council of the International Seabed Authority, an agreement on the relationship between the United Nations and the International Seabed Authority and the Memorandum of Understanding between the Intergovernmental Oceanographic Commission of UNESCO and the International Seabed Authority.

THE INTERNATIONAL TRIBUNAL FOR THE LAW OF THE SEA

The International Tribunal for the Law of the Sea (ITLOS) is the second international organization established by the Convention and *Supplementary Documents* includes selected basic texts pertaining to ITLOS. ITLOS is an independent judicial body established by the Convention to adjudicate disputes arising out of the interpretation or application of the Convention. The Tribunal is composed of 21 independent members, elected from among persons enjoying the highest reputation for fairness and integrity and of recognized competence in the field of the law of the sea. Part XV of the Convention sets forth a comprehensive system for the settlement of disputes that might arise with respect to the interpretation or application of the Convention. The mechanism established by the Convention provides for four alternative means for the settlement of disputes: the International Tribunal for the Law of the Sea, the International Court of Justice, an arbitral tribunal constituted in accordance with Annex VII to the Convention, and a special arbitral tribunal constituted in accordance with Annex VIII to the Convention.

A State Party is free to choose one or more of these means by a written declaration to be made under article 287 of the Convention and deposited with the Secretary-General of the United Nations (declarations made by States Parties under article 287). It requires States Parties to settle their disputes concerning the interpretation or application of the Convention by peaceful means indicated in the Charter of the United Nations. However, if parties to a dispute fail to reach a settlement by peaceful means of their own choice, they are obliged to resort to the compulsory dispute settlement procedures entailing binding decisions, subject to limitations and exceptions contained in the Convention. If the parties to a dispute have not accepted the same settlement procedure, the dispute may be submitted only to arbitration in accordance with Annex VII, unless the parties otherwise agree.

Pursuant to the provisions of its Statute, the Tribunal has formed the following Chambers: the Chamber of Summary Procedure, the Chamber for Fisheries Disputes, the Chamber for Marine Environment Disputes and the Chamber for Maritime Delimitation Disputes. At the request of Chile and the European Community, the Tribunal also formed a special chamber to deal with the Case concerning the Conservation and Sustainable Exploitation of Swordfish Stocks in the South-Eastern Pacific Ocean (Chile/European Community). Disputes relating to activities in the International Seabed Area are submitted to the Seabed Disputes Chamber of the Tribunal, consisting of 11 judges. Any party to a dispute over which the Seabed Disputes Chamber has jurisdiction may request the Seabed Disputes Chamber to form an *ad hoc* chamber composed of three members of the Seabed Disputes Chamber. On February 1, 2011, the Seabed Disputes Chamber unanimously adopted an historic opinion, the Advisory Opinion on the "Responsibilities and Obligations of States Sponsoring Persons and Entities with respect to Activities in the Area." This is the first time that the advisory jurisdiction of ITLOS had been invoked and the first time that the Seabed Disputes Chamber had been called upon. It is also the first time that the Tribunal—whose jurisprudence has to date been marked by a multiplicity of dissenting and separate opinions—reached a completely unanimous ruling in a case referred to it.

The Tribunal is open to States Parties to the Convention and, in certain cases, to entities other than States Parties (such as international organizations and natural or legal persons). The jurisdiction of the Tribunal comprises all disputes submitted to it in accordance with the Convention. It also extends to all matters specifically provided for in any other agreement, which confers jurisdiction on the Tribunal. Unless the parties otherwise agree, the jurisdiction of the Tribunal is mandatory in cases relating to the prompt release of vessels and crews under article 292 of the Convention and to provisional measures pending the constitution of an arbitral tribunal under article 290, paragraph 5, of the Convention.

The Seabed Disputes Chamber is competent to give advisory opinions on legal questions arising within the scope of the activities of the International Seabed Authority. The Tribunal may also give advisory opinions in certain cases under international agreements related to the purposes of the Convention. The General Assembly of the United Nations, at its fifty-first session, granted Observer status to the Tribunal (General Assembly resolution A/RES/51/204 of 17 December 1996). Observer status enables the

Tribunal to participate in the meetings and the work of the General Assembly when matters of relevance to the Tribunal are being considered. Disputes before the Tribunal are instituted either by written application or by notification of a special agreement. The procedure to be followed for the conduct of cases submitted to the Tribunal is defined in its Statute and Rules.

The relevant documents contained in this volume include the Statute for the International Tribunal of the Law of the Sea, the Rules of the Tribunal (ITLOS/8) and Guidelines concerning the Preparation and Presentation of Cases before the Tribunal (ITLOS/9), Guidelines concerning the Preparation and Presentation of Cases before the Tribunal (ITLOS/10) and Guidelines Concerning the Posting of a Bond or other Financial Security with the Registrar. The Agreement between the International Tribunal for the Law of the Sea and the Government of the Federal Republic of Germany on the Occupancy and Use of the Premises of the International Tribunal for the Law of the Sea in the Free and Hanseatic City of Hamburg (Additional Agreement) of 18 October 2000 establishes the terms and conditions under which the premises are made available by the Government to the Tribunal.

COMMISSION ON THE LIMITS OF THE CONTINENTAL SHELF

Finally, *Supplementary Documents* contains documents from the Commission on the Limits of the Continental Shelf. The purpose of the Commission on the Limits of the Continental Shelf (the Commission or CLCS) is to facilitate the implementation of the Convention in respect of the establishment of the outer limits of the continental shelf beyond 200 nautical miles from the baselines from which the breadth of the territorial sea is measured. Under the Convention, the coastal State shall establish the outer limits of its continental shelf where it extends beyond 200 nautical miles on the basis of the recommendation of the Commission. The Commission shall make recommendations to coastal States on matters related to the establishment of those limits; its recommendations and actions shall not prejudice matters relating to the delimitation of boundaries between States with opposite or adjacent coasts.

Annex II to the Convention contains the provisions governing the Commission. As set forth in article 3 of Annex II, the functions of the Commission are:

> (a) To consider the data and other material submitted by coastal States concerning the outer limits of the continental shelf in areas where those limits extend beyond 200 nautical miles, and to make recommendations in accordance with article 76 and the Statement of Understanding adopted on 29 August 1980 by the Third United Nations Conference on the Law of the Sea;
>
> (b) To provide scientific and technical advice, if requested by the coastal State concerned during preparation of such data. In accordance with article 76(8), the Commission shall make recommendations to

> coastal States on matters related to the establishment of the outer limits of their continental shelf. The limits of the shelf established by a coastal State on the basis of these recommendations shall be final and binding. The Commission ordinarily meets twice a year, in the spring and fall, at United Nations Headquarters in New York. The convening of these sessions and services to be provided are subject to approval by the General Assembly of the United Nations in its annual resolutions on oceans and the law of the sea.

The meetings of the Commission, its subcommissions and subsidiary bodies are held in private, unless the Commission decides otherwise (Rule 23 - Public and private meetings - of the Rules of Procedure of the Commission). During its second session (September 1997), the Commission set up a number of technical working groups to formulate scientific and technical guidelines with respect to the data and information to be included in the submission by a coastal State. After the initial work was accomplished, the Commission established an Editorial Working Group on its Scientific and Technical Guidelines at its third session (May 1998).

The Guidelines are aimed at assisting coastal States to prepare their submissions regarding the outer limits of their continental shelf. The determination of these criteria involves complex technical and scientific data, which must be considered by the Commission. The Scientific and Technical Guidelines were finally adopted by the Commission on 13 May 1999 and published in document CLCS/11. An extensive exchange of views took place, particularly on those parts of the text on which consensus had not yet been reached. It was also determined that all issues raised at the 1993 and 1995 meetings of experts on the continental shelf were addressed in the Guidelines.

Several States had addressed letters to the Commission containing comments to the Guidelines. The comments were translated and issued as conference room papers intended only for the internal use of the Commission so that its members might consider them before taking a decision on the Guidelines. Some substantive amendments proposed by various members of the Commission to ensure a final consensus text were accepted and incorporated in the revised version. Among them were amendments on the issues of baselines, selection of straight lines to delineate the outer limit of the continental shelf, some aspects of geodetic methodologies, sources of data for bathymetric measurements, foot of the continental slope determined as the point of maximum change of gradient, foot of the continental slope determined on the basis of evidence to the contrary, ridges and sediment thickness. Annex II to the Guidelines, containing flowcharts and illustrations to assist States in the preparation of their submissions, was not adopted at the same time as the remainder of the Guidelines, as it was felt that further elaboration was needed. Annexes II to IV (CLCS/11/Add.1) were adopted at the following (sixth) session on 3 September 1999.

The Commission also decided to convene an open meeting for the first day of its seventh session (1-5 May 2000), with a view to raising the awareness of States of the necessity of implementing the provisions of article 76 relating to the establishment of the outer limits of the continental shelf beyond 200 nautical miles, bearing in mind the requirement of the Convention to submit particulars of such limits to the Commission in accordance with the 10-year rule. In order to provide additional scientific and technical guidance to help coastal States throughout the process of preparation of a submission, the Commission also decided to continue its work on a flowchart, which was adopted provisionally at its seventh session on 5 May 2000 (CLCS/22). An Open Meeting was held by the Commission on 1 May 2000, which was intended to point out to policymakers and legal advisors the benefits coastal States may derive from implementing the provisions of article 76, as well as to explain to the experts in marine sciences who are involved in the preparation of submissions how the Commission considers that the Scientific and Technical Guidelines should be applied in practice.

Selected basic CLCS texts in *Supplementary Documents* include the Rules of Procedure of the Commission on the Limits of the Continental Shelf (CLCS/40/Rev.1), Scientific and Technical Guidelines of the Commission on the Limits of the Continental Shelf (CLCS/11, CLCS/11/Corr.1, CLCS/11/Corr.2), Scientific and Technical Guidelines of the Commission on the Limits of the Continental Shelf - Annexes II-IV to the Guidelines of 3 September 1999 (CLCS/11/Add.1, and CLCS/11/Add.1/Corr.1) and the Internal Code of Conduct (CLCS/47). The section also includes a Legal Opinion on submission of additional materials (CLCS/46).

As the law and policy of the international law of the sea continues to mature and evolve, these institutions—and perhaps others—will create additional agreements, codes and guidelines that help to implement the provisions of the United Nations Convention on the Law of the Sea. Thus, with the introduction of this softcover *Supplementary Documents*, our aim is to provide a tool for scholars, policy makers and experts that complements the bound Virginia *Commentary* series, providing recent updates to the body of authority for humankind's activities on the global oceans.

The editors wish to acknowledge the assistance given in preparing the *Supplementary Documents* provided by David Balton, Michael Lodge and George Walker. Particular recognition must be acknowledged to J. Ashley Roach who authored Part V (B) and kindly consented to the inclusion of the charts in that section. Judith A. Ellis of the Center for Oceans Law and Policy assembled the documents and was the technical editor for *Supplementary Documents*.

Myron H. Nordquist/ Satya N. Nandan/James Kraska

PART I

THE INTERNATIONAL SEABED AUTHORITY

INTERNATIONAL SEABED AUTHORITY **ISBA**

Assembly

Distr.
GENERAL

ISBA/A/6
7 July 1994

ORIGINAL: ENGLISH

INTERNATIONAL SEABED AUTHORITY
First session of the Assembly
Kingston, Jamaica

RULES OF PROCEDURE OF THE ASSEMBLY OF THE INTERNATIONAL SEABED AUTHORITY

(adopted at its 15th meeting, on 17 March 1995)

CONTENTS

CONTENTS (continued)

CONTENTS (continued)

CONTENTS (continued)

CONTENTS (continued)

Introductory note

On 28 July 1994 the General Assembly of the United Nations adopted the Agreement relating to the implementation of Part XI of the United Nations Convention on the Law of the Sea, and the Agreement has been provisionally applied since 16 November 1994.

According to the Agreement, its provisions and Part XI of the Convention are to be interpreted and applied together as a single instrument; the present rules and references in these rules to the Convention are to be interpreted and applied accordingly.

I. SESSIONS

Regular sessions

Rule 1

Regular annual sessions

The Assembly shall meet in regular annual sessions unless it decides otherwise.

Rule 2

Date and duration

The date of commencement and the duration of each such session shall be decided by the previous session of the Assembly.

Rule 3

Notification of members

The Secretary-General shall notify the members of the Assembly at least sixty days in advance of the opening of a regular session.

Special sessions

Rule 4

Convening of special sessions

1. The Assembly may convene special sessions and shall fix the date of commencement and the duration of each such session.

2. At the request of the Council or of a majority of the members of the Authority, the Secretary-General shall convene a special session of the Assembly and it shall meet no earlier than thirty days and no later than ninety days after the receipt of such a request unless the request has stipulated otherwise.

3. Any member of the Authority may request the Secretary-General to convene a special session of the Assembly. The Secretary-General shall immediately inform the other members of the Authority of the request and inquire whether they concur in it. If within thirty days of the date of communication by the Secretary-General a majority of the members of the Assembly concur in the request, a special session of the Assembly shall be convened by the Secretary- General and it shall meet no earlier than thirty days and no later than ninety days after the receipt of such concurrence.

Rule 5

Notification of members

The Secretary-General shall notify the members of the Assembly at least thirty days in advance of the opening of a special session.

Regular and special sessions

Rule 6

Place of meeting

The Assembly shall meet at the seat of the Authority unless it decides otherwise.

Rule 7

Notification to observers

Copies of the notice convening each session of the Assembly shall be addressed to observers referred to in rule 82.

Rule 8

Temporary adjournment of session

The Assembly may decide at any session to adjourn temporarily and resume its meetings at a later date. A regular session shall not normally be adjourned beyond the end of the year.

II. AGENDA

Regular sessions

Rule 9

Provisional agenda

The provisional agenda for a regular session shall be drawn up by the Secretary-General and communicated to the members of the Assembly and to observers referred to in rule 82 at least sixty days before the opening of the session.

Rule 10

Drawing up of the provisional agenda

The provisional agenda of a regular session shall include:

(a) The report of the Secretary-General on the work of the Authority;

(b) Reports from the Council and the Enterprise,[1] and special reports requested from the Council or any other organs;

(c) Items the inclusion of which has been ordered by the Assembly at a previous session;

(d) Items proposed by the Council;

(e) Items proposed by any member of the Assembly;

(f) Items pertaining to the budget for the next financial period and the report on the accounts for the last financial period;

(g) Items which the Secretary-General deems it necessary to put before the Assembly.

Rule 11

Supplementary items

Any member of the Assembly, the Council or the Secretary-General may, at least thirty days before the date fixed for the opening of a regular session, request the inclusion of supplementary items in the agenda. Such items shall be placed on a supplementary list, which shall be communicated to the members of the Assembly and to observers referred to in rule 82 at least twenty days before the opening of the session.

Rule 12

Additional items

Additional items of an important and urgent character, proposed for inclusion in the agenda less than thirty days before the opening of a regular session or during a regular session, may be placed on the agenda if the Assembly so decides by a majority of the members of the Assembly present and voting. No additional item may, unless the Assembly decides otherwise by a two-thirds majority of the members of the Assembly present and voting, be considered until seven days have elapsed since it was placed on the agenda.

---

[1] See footnote 2.

Special sessions

Rule 13

Communication of the provisional agenda

The provisional agenda of a special session shall be communicated to the members of the Assembly and to observers referred to in rule 82 at least fourteen days before the opening of the session.

Rule 14

Provisional agenda

The provisional agenda for a special session shall consist only of those items proposed for consideration in the request for the holding of the session.

Rule 15

Supplementary items

Any member of the Assembly, the Council or the Secretary-General may, at least seven days before the date fixed for the opening of a special session, request the inclusion of supplementary items in the agenda. Such items shall be placed on a supplementary list, which shall be communicated to the members of the Assembly and to observers referred to in rule 82 as soon as possible.

Rule 16

Additional items

During a special session, items on the supplementary list and additional items may be added to the agenda by a two-thirds majority of the members of the Assembly present and voting.

Regular and special sessions

Rule 17

Explanatory memorandum

Any item proposed for inclusion in the agenda shall be accompanied by an explanatory memorandum and, if possible, by basic documents or by a draft resolution.

Rule 18

Adoption of the agenda

At each session, the provisional agenda and the supplementary list shall be submitted to the Assembly for approval as soon as possible after the opening of the session.

Rule 19

Amendment and deletion of items

Items on the agenda may be amended or deleted by the Assembly by a majority of the members of the Assembly present and voting.

Rule 20

Debate on inclusion of items

Debate on the inclusion of an item in the agenda shall be limited to three representatives of the members of the Assembly in favour of, and three against, the inclusion. The President may limit the time to be allowed to speakers under this rule.

Rule 21

Modification of the allocation of expenses

No proposal for a modification of the allocation of expenses for the time being in force shall be placed on the agenda unless it has been communicated to the members of the Assembly at least ninety days before the opening of the session.

III. REPRESENTATION

Rule 22

Representation

1. Each member of the Assembly shall be represented by an accredited representative and such alternate representatives and advisers as may be required.

2. Observers referred to in rule 82 shall be represented by accredited or designated representatives, as the case may be, and by such alternate representatives and advisers as may be required.

3. The representative may designate an alternate representative or an adviser to act in his capacity.

IV. CREDENTIALS

Rule 23

Submission of credentials

The credentials of representatives and the names of alternate representatives and advisers shall be submitted to the Secretary-General if possible not later than twenty-four hours after the opening of the session. The credentials shall be issued either by the Head of the State or Government, by the Minister for Foreign Affairs or person authorized by him or, in the case of entities referred to in article 305, paragraph 1 (f) of the United Nations Convention on the Law of the Sea, by another competent authority.

Rule 24

Credentials Committee

A Credentials Committee shall be appointed at the beginning of each session. It shall consist of nine members of the Assembly, who shall be appointed by the Assembly on the proposal of the President. The Committee shall elect its own officers. It shall examine the credentials of representatives of members and report to the Assembly without delay.

Rule 25

Provisional admission to a session

Pending a decision of the Assembly upon their credentials, representatives shall be entitled to participate provisionally in the Assembly.

Rule 26

Objection to the representation

If an objection is raised against a representative, such objection shall be considered by the Credentials Committee forthwith. The report thereon shall be submitted to the Assembly without delay for its decision.

V. PRESIDENT AND VICE-PRESIDENTS

Rule 27

Temporary President

At the opening of each regular session of the Assembly, the President of the previous session or, in his absence, the head of the delegation from which the President of the previous session was elected shall preside until the Assembly has elected a President for the session.

Rule 28

Elections

At the beginning of each regular session the Assembly shall elect its President and four Vice-Presidents in such a way as to ensure the representative character of the Bureau. They shall hold office until a new President and other officers are elected at the next regular session.

Rule 29

Acting President

If the President finds it necessary to be absent during a meeting or any part thereof, he shall designate one of the Vice-Presidents to take his place.

Rule 30

Powers of the Acting President

A Vice-President acting as President shall have the same powers and duties as the President.

Rule 31

Replacement of the President

If the President is unable to perform his functions, a new President shall be elected for the unexpired term.

Rule 32

General powers of the President

In addition to exercising the powers conferred upon him elsewhere by these rules, or by the United Nations Convention on the Law of the Sea, the President shall declare the opening and closing of each plenary meeting of the session, direct the discussions in plenary meeting, ensure observance of these rules, accord the right to speak, put questions and announce decisions. He shall rule on points of order and, subject to these rules, shall have complete control of the proceedings at any meeting and over the maintenance of order thereat. The President may, in the course of the discussion of an item, propose to the Assembly the limitation of the time to be allowed to speakers, the limitation of the number of times each representative may speak, the closure of the list of speakers or the closure of the debate. He may also propose the suspension or the adjournment of the meeting or the adjournment of the debate on the item under discussion.

Rule 33

Limitation of the powers of the President

The President, in the exercise of his functions, remains under the authority of the Assembly.

Rule 34

Voting of the President and Acting President

The President, or a Vice-President acting as President, shall not vote but shall designate another member of his delegation to vote in his place.

VI. BUREAU

Rule 35

The President and Vice-Presidents shall constitute the Bureau which shall meet periodically throughout each session to review the progress of the Assembly and its subsidiary organs and to make recommendations for furthering such progress. It shall also meet at such other times as the President deems necessary or upon the request of any other of its members. The Bureau shall assist the President in the general conduct of the work of the Assembly which falls within the competence of the President. The Chairmen of the subsidiary organs of the Assembly may be invited to attend meetings of the Bureau.

VII. SECRETARIAT

Rule 36

Duties of the Secretary-General

1. The Secretary-General shall act in that capacity in all meetings of the Assembly and its subsidiary organs. He may designate a member of the Secretariat to act in his place at these meetings. He shall discharge such other responsibilities as are assigned to him by the Assembly in the conduct of its business.

2. The Secretary-General shall provide and direct the staff required by the Assembly and its subsidiary organs.

Rule 37

Duties of the Secretariat

The Secretariat shall receive, translate, reproduce and distribute documents, reports and resolutions of the Assembly and its subsidiary organs; interpret speeches made at the meetings; prepare and circulate, if so decided by the Assembly in accordance with rule 42, the records of the session; have the custody and proper preservation of the documents in the archives of the Authority; distribute all documents of the Assembly to the members of the Authority and observers referred to in rule 82; and, generally, perform all other work which the Assembly may require.

Rule 38

Report of the Secretary-General on the work of the Authority

The Secretary-General shall make an annual report, and such supplementary reports as are necessary, to the Assembly at its regular session on the work of the Authority. He shall communicate the annual report to the members of the Authority and observers referred to in rule 82 at least forty-five days before the opening of the regular session.

VIII. LANGUAGES

Rule 39

Languages

Arabic, Chinese, English, French, Russian and Spanish shall be the languages of the Assembly and its subsidiary organs.

Rule 40

Interpretation

1. Speeches made in a language of the Assembly shall be interpreted into the other such languages.

2. Any representative may make a speech in a language other than a language of the Assembly. In that case he shall himself provide for interpretation into one of the languages of the Assembly. Interpretation into the other languages of the Assembly by the interpreters of the Secretariat may be based on the interpretation given in the first such language.

Rule 41

Languages of resolutions and other documents

All resolutions and other documents shall be published in the languages of the Assembly.

IX. RECORDS

Rule 42

Records and sound recordings of meetings

1. The Assembly may keep summary records of plenary meetings if it so decides. As a general rule, such records shall be circulated as soon as possible, simultaneously in all languages of the Assembly, to all representatives, who shall inform the Secretariat within five working days after the circulation of the summary record of any changes they wish to have made.

2. The Secretariat shall make and retain sound recordings of meetings of the Assembly, and of its subsidiary organs when they so decide.

X. PUBLIC AND PRIVATE MEETINGS OF THE ASSEMBLY AND ITS SUBSIDIARY ORGANS

Rule 43

Public and private meetings

1. The meetings of the Assembly shall be held in public unless the Assembly decides that exceptional circumstances require that the meeting be held in private.

2. As a general rule, meetings of subsidiary organs shall be held in private.

3. All decisions of the Assembly taken at a private meeting shall be announced at an early public meeting of the Assembly. At the close of a private meeting of a subsidiary organ, the Chairman may issue a communiqué through the Secretary-General.

XI. MINUTE OF SILENT PRAYER OR MEDITATION

Rule 44

Invitation to silent prayer or meditation

Immediately after the opening of the first plenary meeting and immediately preceding the closing of the final plenary meeting of each session of the Assembly, the President shall invite the representatives to observe one minute of silence dedicated to prayer or meditation.

XII. PLENARY MEETINGS

Conduct of business

Rule 45

Quorum

The President may declare a meeting open and permit the debate to proceed when at least a majority of the members of the Assembly are present.

Rule 46

Speeches

No representative may address the Assembly without having previously obtained the permission of the President. The President shall call upon speakers in the order in which they signify their desire to speak. The President may call a speaker to order if his remarks are not relevant to the subject under discussion.

Rule 47

Precedence

The Chairman of a subsidiary organ may be accorded precedence for the purpose of explaining the conclusions arrived at by that organ.

Rule 48

Statement by the Secretariat

The Secretary-General or a member of the Secretariat designated by him as his representative may at any time make either oral or written statements to the Assembly concerning any question under consideration by it.

Rule 49

Points of order

During the discussion of any matter, a representative of a member of the Assembly may rise to a point of order, and the point of order shall be immediately decided by the President in accordance with these rules of procedure. A representative of a member of the Assembly may appeal against the ruling of the President. The appeal shall be immediately put to the vote, and the President's ruling shall stand unless overruled by a majority of the members of the Assembly present and voting. A representative rising to a point of order may not speak on the substance of the matter under discussion.

Rule 50

Time-limit on speeches

The Assembly may limit the time to be allowed to each speaker and the number of times each representative may speak on any question. Before a decision is taken, two representatives of members of the Assembly may speak in favour of, and two against, a proposal to set such limits. When the debate is limited and a representative exceeds his allotted time, the President shall call him to order without delay.

Rule 51

Closing of list of speakers, right of reply

During the course of the debate, the President may announce the list of speakers and, with the consent of the Assembly, declare the list closed. He may, however, accord the right of reply to any representative if a speech delivered after he has declared the list closed makes this desirable.

Rule 52

Adjournment of debate

During the discussion of any matter, a representative of a member of the Assembly may move the adjournment of the debate on the item under discussion. In addition to the proposer of the motion, two representatives of members of the Assembly may speak in favour of, and two against, the motion, after which the motion shall be immediately put to the vote. The President may limit the time to be allowed to speakers under this rule.

Rule 53

Closure of debate

A representative of a member of the Assembly may at any time move the closure of the debate on the question under discussion, whether or not any other representative has signified his wish to speak. Permission to speak on the motion shall be accorded only to two representatives of members of the Assembly opposing the closure, after which the motion shall be immediately put to the vote. If the Assembly is in favour of the closure, the President shall declare the closure of the debate. The President may limit the time to be allowed to speakers under this rule.

Rule 54

Suspension or adjournment of the meeting

During the discussion of any matter, a representative of a member of the Assembly may move the suspension or the adjournment of the meeting. Such motions shall not be debated, but shall be immediately put to the vote. The President may limit the time to be allowed to the speaker moving the suspension or adjournment of the meeting.

Rule 55

Order of procedural motions

Subject to rule 49, the following motions shall have precedence in the following order over all other proposals or motions before the meeting:

(a) To suspend the meeting;

(b) To adjourn the meeting;

(c) To adjourn the debate on the item under discussion;

(d) To close the debate on the item under discussion.

Rule 56

Proposals and amendments

Proposals and amendments shall normally be submitted in writing to the Secretary-General, who shall circulate copies to the delegations. As a general rule, no proposal shall be discussed or put to the vote at any meeting of the Assembly unless copies of it have been circulated to all delegations in the languages of the Assembly not later than the day preceding the meeting. The President may, however, permit the discussion and consideration of amendments, or of motions as to procedure, even though such amendments and motions have not been circulated or have only been circulated the same day.

Rule 57

Decisions on competence

Subject to rule 55, any motion calling for a decision on the competence of the Assembly to adopt a proposal submitted to it shall be put to the vote before a vote is taken on the proposal in question.

Rule 58

Withdrawal of motions

A motion may be withdrawn by its proposer at any time before voting on it has commenced, provided that the motion has not been amended. A motion thus withdrawn may be reintroduced by any member.

Rule 59

Reconsideration of proposals

When a proposal has been adopted or rejected, it may not be reconsidered at the same session unless the Assembly, by a two-thirds majority of the members of the Assembly present and voting, so decides. Permission to speak on a motion to reconsider shall be accorded only to two representatives of members of the Assembly opposing the motion, after which it shall be immediately put to the vote.

XIII. DECISION-MAKING

Rule 60

Voting rights

Each member of the Assembly shall have one vote. Participation in decision-making by entities referred to in article 305, paragraph 1 (f), of the United Nations Convention on the Law of the Sea shall be in accordance with Annex IX of the Convention.

Rule 61

Decision-making

1. As a general rule, decision-making in the Assembly should be by consensus.

2. If all efforts to reach a decision by consensus have been exhausted, decisions by voting in the Assembly on questions of procedure shall be taken by a majority of members present and voting, and decisions on questions of substance shall be taken by a two-thirds majority of members present and voting, as provided for in article 159, paragraph 8, of the Convention.

3. Decisions of the Assembly on any matter for which the Council also has competence or on any administrative, budgetary or financial matter shall be based on the recommendations of the Council. If the Assembly does not accept the recommendation of the Council on any matter, it shall return the matter to the Council for further consideration. The Council shall reconsider the matter in the light of the views expressed by the Assembly.

4. Decisions by the Assembly having financial or budgetary implications shall be based on the recommendations of the Finance Committee.

Rule 62

Decisions on amendments to proposals relating to questions of substance

Decisions of the Assembly on amendments to proposals relating to questions of substance, and on parts of such proposals put to the vote separately, shall be made by a two-thirds majority of the members of the Assembly present and voting, provided that such majority includes a majority of the members participating in the session.

Rule 63

Use of terms

1. For the purpose of these rules, the phrase "members of the Assembly present and voting" means members of the Assembly present and casting an affirmative or negative vote. Members of the Assembly who abstain from voting shall be considered as not voting.

2. Subject to the provisions of rules 23 to 26 and without prejudice to the powers and functions of the Credentials Committee, the term "members of the Assembly participating" in relation to any particular session of the Assembly means any member of the Assembly whose representatives have registered with the Secretariat as participating in that session and which has not subsequently notified the Secretariat of its withdrawal from that session or part of it. The Secretariat shall keep a register for this purpose.

Rule 64

Deferment of voting on questions of substance coming up for voting for the first time

When a question of substance comes up for voting for the first time, the President may, and shall, if requested by at least one fifth of the members of the Assembly, defer the issue of taking a vote on that question for a period not exceeding five calendar days. This rule may be applied only once to any question, and shall not be applied so as to defer the question beyond the end of the session.

Rule 65

Deferment of voting upon request for an advisory opinion

Upon a written request addressed to the President and sponsored by at least one fourth of the members of the Assembly for an advisory opinion on the conformity with the United Nations Convention on the Law of the Sea of a proposal before the Assembly on any matter, the Assembly shall request the Seabed Disputes Chamber of the International Tribunal for the Law of the Sea to give an advisory opinion thereon and shall defer voting on that proposal pending receipt of the advisory opinion by the Chamber. If the advisory opinion is not received before the final week of the session in which it is requested, the Assembly shall decide when it will meet to vote upon the deferred proposal.

Rule 66

Method of voting

1. The Assembly shall, in the absence of mechanical means for voting, vote by show of hands or by standing but a representative of any member of the Assembly may request a roll-call. The roll-call shall be taken in the English alphabetical order of the names of the members of the Assembly

participating in that session, beginning with the member whose name is drawn by lot by the President. The name of each member of the Assembly shall be called in any roll-call, and one of its representatives shall reply “yes”, “no” or “abstention”. The result of the voting shall be inserted in the record in the English alphabetical order of the names of the members.

2. When the Assembly votes by mechanical means, a non-recorded vote shall replace a vote by show of hands or by standing and a recorded vote shall replace a roll-call vote. A representative of any member of the Assembly may request a recorded vote. In the case of a recorded vote, the Assembly shall, unless a representative of a member of the Assembly requests otherwise, dispense with the procedure of calling out the names of the members; nevertheless, the result of the voting shall be inserted in the record in the same manner as that of a roll-call vote.

Rule 67

Conduct during voting

After the President has announced the commencement of voting, no representative of a member of the Assembly may interrupt the voting, except that representatives of members of the Assembly may interrupt on a point of order in connection with the actual conduct of voting.

Rule 68

Explanation of vote

Representatives of members of the Assembly may make brief statements consisting solely of explanations of their votes before the voting has commenced or after the voting has been completed. The President may limit the time to be allowed for such statements. The representative of a member of the Assembly sponsoring a proposal or motion shall not speak in explanation of vote thereon, except if it has been amended.

Rule 69

Division of proposals and amendments

A representative of a member of the Assembly may move that parts of a proposal or of an amendment should be voted on separately. If objection is made to the request for division, the motion for division shall be voted upon. Permission to speak on the motion for division shall be given only to two speakers in favour and two speakers against. If the motion for division is carried, those parts of the proposal or of the amendment which are approved shall then be put to the vote as a whole. If all operative parts of the proposal or of the amendment have been rejected, the proposal or the amendment shall be considered to have been rejected as a whole.

Rule 70

Order of voting on amendments

When an amendment is moved to a proposal, the amendment shall be voted on first. When two or more amendments are moved to a proposal, the Assembly shall first vote on the amendment furthest removed in substance from the original proposal and then on the amendment next furthest removed therefrom, and so on until all the amendments have been put to the vote. Where, however, the adoption of one amendment necessarily implies the rejection of another amendment, the latter amendment shall not be put to the vote. If one or more amendments are adopted, the amended proposal shall then be voted upon. A motion is considered an amendment to a proposal if it merely adds to, deletes from or revises part of the proposal.

Rule 71

Order of voting on proposals

If two or more proposals relate to the same question, the Assembly shall, unless it decides otherwise, vote on the proposals in the order in which they have been submitted. The Assembly may, after each vote on a proposal, decide whether to vote on the next proposal.

Rule 72

Elections

All elections shall be held by secret ballot.

Rule 73

Restricted balloting for one elective place

1. When one person or a member of the Assembly is to be elected and no candidate obtains in the first ballot the votes of a majority of the members of the Assembly present and voting, a second ballot restricted to the two candidates obtaining the largest number of votes shall be taken. If in the second ballot the votes are equally divided, the President shall decide between the candidates by drawing lots.

2. In the case of a tie in the first ballot among more than two candidates obtaining the largest number of votes, a second ballot shall be held. If on that ballot a tie remains among more than two candidates, the number shall be reduced to two by lot and the balloting, restricted to them, shall continue in accordance with the preceding paragraph.

3. If a two-thirds majority is required, the balloting shall be continued until one candidate secures two thirds of the votes cast; provided that, after the third inconclusive ballot, votes may be cast for any eligible person or

member. If three such unrestricted ballots are inconclusive, the next three ballots shall be restricted to the two candidates who obtained the greatest number of votes in the third of the unrestricted ballots, and the following three ballots thereafter shall be unrestricted, and so on until a person or member of the Assembly is elected.

4. The above provisions of this rule shall not prejudice the application of rules 83, 84 and 96.

Rule 74

Restricted balloting for two or more elective places

When two or more elective places are to be filled at one time under the same conditions, those candidates, not exceeding the number of such places, obtaining in the first ballot the majority required shall be elected. If the number of candidates obtaining such a majority is less than the number of persons or members of the Assembly to be elected, there shall be additional ballots to fill the remaining places, the voting being restricted to the candidates obtaining the greatest number of votes in the previous ballot to a number not more than twice the places remaining to be filled; provided that, after the third inconclusive ballot, votes may be cast for any eligible person or member of the Assembly. If three such unrestricted ballots are inconclusive, the next three ballots shall be restricted to the candidates who obtained the greatest number of votes in the third of the unrestricted ballots, to a number not more than twice the places remaining to be filled, and the following three ballots thereafter shall be unrestricted, and so on until all the places have been filled. The above provisions of this rule shall not prejudice the application of rules 83, 84 and 96.

Rule 75

Equally divided votes on matters other than elections

If a vote is equally divided on matters other than elections, a second vote shall be taken at a subsequent meeting which shall be held within 48 hours of the first vote; and it shall be expressly mentioned in the agenda that a second vote will be taken on the matter in question. If this vote also results in equality, the proposal shall be regarded as rejected.

XIV. SUBSIDIARY ORGANS

Rule 76

Establishment

The Assembly may establish such subsidiary organs as it finds necessary for the exercise of its functions.

Rule 77

Composition

In the composition of subsidiary organs due account shall be taken of the principle of equitable geographical distribution and of special interests and the need for members qualified and competent in the relevant technical questions dealt with by such organs.

Rule 78

Statements by non-members of a subsidiary organ

Any member of the Assembly that is not a member of a subsidiary organ shall have the right to explain its views to that organ when a matter particularly affecting it is under consideration.

Rule 79

Officers, conduct of business and voting

The rules relating to officers, conduct of business and voting of the Assembly apply, mutatis mutandis, to the proceedings of subsidiary organs except that the Chairman of a subsidiary organ may exercise the right to vote.

XV. SUSPENSION OF RIGHTS

Rule 80

Suspension of the exercise of voting rights

A member of the Assembly which is in arrears in the payment of its financial contributions to the Authority shall have no vote if the amount of its arrears equals or exceeds the amount of the contributions due from it for the preceding two full years. The Assembly may, nevertheless, permit such a member of the Assembly to vote if it is satisfied that the failure to pay is due to conditions beyond the control of the member.

Rule 81

Suspension of the exercise of rights and privileges of membership

1. A member of the Authority which has grossly and persistently violated the provisions of Part XI of the United Nations Convention on the Law of the Sea may be suspended from the exercise of the rights and privileges of membership by the Assembly upon the recommendation of the Council.

2. No action may be taken under paragraph 1 until the Seabed Disputes Chamber of the International Tribunal for the Law of the Sea has found that a member of the Authority has grossly and persistently violated the provisions of Part XI of the Convention.

XVI. OBSERVERS

Rule 82

1. The following may participate as observers in the Assembly:

(a) States and entities referred to in article 305 of the United Nations Convention on the Law of the Sea which are not members of the Authority;

(b) National liberation movements which in their respective regions are recognized by the Organization of African Unity or by the League of Arab States;

(c) Observers to the Third United Nations Conference on the Law of the Sea who have signed the Final Act and who are not referred to in article 305, paragraph 1 (c), (d), (e) and (f), of the United Nations Convention on the Law of the Sea;

(d) The United Nations, its specialized agencies, the International Atomic Energy Agency and other intergovernmental organizations invited by the Assembly;

(e) Non-governmental organizations with which the Secretary-General has entered into arrangements in accordance with article 169, paragraph 1, of the United Nations Convention on the Law of the Sea, and other non-governmental organizations invited by the Assembly which have demonstrated their interest in matters under the consideration by the Assembly.

2. Observers referred to in paragraph 1 (a), (b) and (c) of this rule may participate subject to the provisions of these rules in the deliberations of the Assembly and its subsidiary organs but shall not be entitled to participate in the taking of decisions.

3. Observers referred to in paragraph 1 (d) of this rule may participate in the deliberations of the Assembly upon the invitation of the President on questions within the scope of their competence.

4. Written statements submitted by observers referred to in paragraph 1 (d) of this rule shall be distributed by the Secretariat to the members of the Assembly.

5. Observers referred to in paragraph 1 (e) of this rule may sit at public meetings of the Assembly, and upon the invitation of the President and subject to the approval by the Assembly may make oral statements on questions within the scope of their activities.

6. Written statements submitted by observers referred to in paragraph 1 (e) of this rule within the scope of their activities which are relevant to the work of the Assembly should be made available by the Secretariat in the quantities and in the languages in which the statements are submitted.

XVII. ELECTIONS TO ORGANS

Members of the Council

Rule 83

Nominations

1. Before electing the members of the Council, the Assembly shall establish lists of countries fulfilling the criteria for membership in the groups of States referred to in rule 84 (a) to (d). If a State fulfils the criteria for membership in more than one group it will be included in the lists of all relevant groups but it may only be proposed by one group for election to the Council and it shall represent only that group in voting in the Council.

2. Each group of States referred to in rule 84 (a) to (d) shall be represented in the Council by those members nominated by that group. Each group shall nominate only as many candidates as the number of seats required to be filled by that group. When the number of potential candidates in each of the groups referred to in rule 84 (a) to (e) exceeds the number of seats available in each of those respective groups, as a general rule, the principle of rotation shall apply. States members of each of those groups shall determine how this principle shall apply in those groups.

Rule 84

Elections

The Council shall consist of 36 members of the Authority elected by the Assembly in the following order:

(a) Four members from among those States Parties which, during the last five years for which statistics are available, have either consumed more than 2 per cent in value terms of total world consumption or have had net imports of more than 2 per cent in value terms of total world imports of the commodities produced from the categories of minerals to be derived from the Area, provided that the four members shall include one State from the Eastern European region having the largest economy in that region in terms of gross domestic product and the State, on the date of entry into force of the Convention, having the largest economy in terms of gross domestic product, if such States wish to be represented in this group;

(b) Four members from among the eight States Parties which have made the largest investments in preparation for and in the conduct of activities in the Area, either directly or through their nationals;

(c) Four members from among States Parties which, on the basis of production in areas under their jurisdiction, are major net exporters of the categories of minerals to be derived from the Area, including at least two developing States whose exports of such minerals have a substantial bearing upon their economies;

(d) Six members from among developing States Parties, representing special interests. The special interests to be represented shall include those of States with large populations, States which are land-locked or geographically disadvantaged, island States, States which are major importers of the categories of minerals to be derived from the Area, States which are potential producers of such minerals and least developed States;

(e) Eighteen members elected according to the principle of ensuring an equitable geographical distribution of seats in the Council as a whole, provided that each geographical region shall have at least one member elected under this subparagraph. For this purpose, the geographical regions shall be Africa, Asia, Eastern Europe, Latin America and the Caribbean and Western Europe and Others.

Rule 85

Terms of office

Each member of the Council shall be elected for four years. At the first election, however, the term of one half of the members of each group referred to in rule 84 shall be for two years. Determination of the members whose terms are to expire at the end of two years shall, as a general rule, be left to the agreement of each group. If no agreement can be reached, the members whose terms are to expire at the end of two years shall be chosen by lot to be drawn by the President of the Assembly immediately after the first election.

Rule 86

Eligibility for re-election

Members of the Council shall be eligible for re-election, but due regard should be paid to the desirability of rotation of membership. Members of the Council which were elected upon the nomination by one of the groups referred to in rule 84 (a) to (d) but which fulfil the criteria for membership in other groups, may be re-elected to the Council upon the nomination by one of those groups.

Rule 87

By-elections

Should a member cease to belong to the Council before its term of office expires, a by-election shall be held separately at the next session of the Assembly to elect a member for the unexpired term.

The Secretary-General of the Authority

Rule 88

Election of the Secretary-General

The Secretary-General shall be elected for four years by the Assembly from among the candidates proposed by the Council and may be re-elected.

The Enterprise[2]

Rule 89

Elections

1. The Assembly shall elect, upon the recommendation of the Council, the fifteen members of the Governing Board of the Enterprise.

2. In the election of the members of the Board, due regard shall be paid to the principle of equitable geographical distribution. In submitting nominations of candidates for election to the Board, members of the Authority shall bear in mind the need to nominate candidates of the highest standard of competence, with qualifications in relevant fields, so as to ensure the viability and success of the Enterprise.

Rule 90

Terms of office

1. Members of the Board shall be elected for four years and may be re-elected; due regard shall be paid to the principle of rotation of membership.

2. Members of the Board shall continue in office until their successors are elected.

Rule 91

By-elections

If the office of a member of the Board becomes vacant, the Assembly shall, in accordance with rule 89, elect a new member for the remainder of his predecessor's term.

Rule 92

The Director-General of the Enterprise

The Assembly shall, upon the recommendation of the Council and the nomination of the Governing Board, elect the Director-General of the Enterprise, who shall not be a member of the Board. The Director-General shall hold office for a fixed term, not exceeding five years, and may be re-elected for further terms.

---

[2] According to the Agreement relating to the implementation of Part XI of the United Nations Convention on the Law of the Sea, the Secretariat of the Authority shall perform the functions of the Enterprise until it begins to operate independently of the Secretariat. Upon the approval of a plan of work for exploitation for an entity other than the Enterprise, or upon receipt by the Council of an application for a joint-venture operation with the Enterprise, the Council shall take up the issue of the functioning of the Enterprise independently of the Secretariat of the Authority. If joint-venture operations with the Enterprise accord with sound commercial principles, the Council shall issue a directive pursuant to article 170, paragraph 2, of the Convention providing for such independent functioning.

XVIII. ADMINISTRATIVE AND BUDGETARY QUESTIONS

Rule 93

Proposed annual budget

The Assembly shall consider and approve the proposed annual budget of the Authority submitted by the Council taking into account the recommendations of the Finance Committee.

Rule 94

Financial implications of resolutions

No resolution involving expenditure shall be recommended for approval by the Assembly unless it is accompanied by an estimate of expenditures prepared by the Secretary-General and any recommendations of the Finance Committee.

Rule 95[3]

Contributions

The Assembly shall assess the contributions of members of the Authority to the administrative budget of the Authority in accordance with an agreed scale of assessment based upon the scale used for the regular budget of the United Nations until the Authority shall have sufficient income from other sources to meet its administrative expenses.

XIX. FINANCE COMMITTEE

Rule 96

Finance Committee

1. The Assembly shall elect 15 members of the Finance Committee from the candidates nominated by the States Parties by taking into due account the need for equitable geographical distribution and the representation of special interests. Members of the Finance Committee shall have appropriate qualifications relevant to financial matters.

2. Candidates for the election to the Finance Committee shall be nominated by the States Parties. They shall be of the highest standards of competence and integrity.

3. No two members of the Finance Committee shall be nationals of the same State Party.

---

[3] According to the Agreement relating to the implementation of Part XI of the United Nations Convention on the Law of the Sea, the administrative expenses of the Authority shall be met through the budget of the United Nations until the end of the year following the year during which that Agreement enters into force.

4. Each group of States referred to in rule 84 (a) to (d) shall be represented on the Finance Committee by at least one member. Until the Authority has sufficient funds other than assessed contributions to meet its administrative expenses, the membership of the Finance Committee shall include representatives of the five largest financial contributors to the administrative budget of the Authority. Thereafter, the election of one member from each group shall be on the basis of nomination by the members of the respective group, without prejudice to the possibility of further members being elected from each group.

5. Members of the Finance Committee shall hold office for a term of five years. They shall be eligible for re-election for a further term.

6. In the event of the death, incapacity or resignation of a member of the Finance Committee prior to the expiration of the term of office, the Assembly shall elect for the remainder of the term a member from the same geographical region or group of States.

XX. AMENDMENTS

Rule 97

Method of amendment

These rules of procedure may be amended by a decision of the Assembly, taken by a simple majority of the members of the Assembly present and voting, after a committee has considered the proposed amendment.

INTERNATIONAL SEABED AUTHORITY **ISBA**

Council

Distr.
GENERAL

ISBA/C/12
3 December 1996

ORIGINAL: ENGLISH

Resumed second session
Kingston, Jamaica
5–16 August 1996

RULES OF PROCEDURE OF THE COUNCIL OF THE INTERNATIONAL SEABED AUTHORITY

(Adopted at its 10th meeting, on 16 August 1996)

CONTENTS

CONTENTS (continued)

CONTENTS (continued)

CONTENTS (continued)

Introductory note

On 28 July 1994 the General Assembly of the United Nations adopted the Agreement relating to the Implementation of Part XI of the United Nations Convention on the Law of the Sea of 10 December 1982. The Agreement has been provisionally applied since 16 November 1994 and entered into force on 28 July 1996.

According to the Agreement, its provisions and Part XI of the Convention are to be interpreted and applied together as a single instrument; these rules and references in these rules to the Convention are to be interpreted and applied accordingly.

I. SESSIONS

Regular sessions

Rule 1

Frequency of sessions

The Council shall meet in regular annual sessions unless it decides otherwise.

Rule 2

Date of commencement and duration

Before the end of each session the Council shall decide on the date of commencement and the approximate duration of the next session.

Rule 3

Notification of members

The Secretary-General shall notify the members of the Council as early as possible but at least thirty days in advance of the opening of a regular session. On the same date he shall notify other members of the Authority.

Rule 4

Alteration of the date of a regular session

1. Any member of the Council or the Secretary-General may request an alteration of the date of a regular session.

2. A request coming from a member of the Council shall be submitted to the Secretary-General at least forty-five days before the date originally scheduled and thirty days before the proposed new date. The Secretary-General shall immediately communicate the request to the members of the Council, together with all appropriate observations, including, if any, a statement on financial implications.

3. A request coming from the Secretary-General shall be subject to the same conditions.

4. If, within fifteen days of the request, a majority of the members of the Council concurs, the Secretary-General shall convene the session of the Council on the date indicated in the request.

Special sessions

Rule 5

Convening of special sessions

When the urgent business of the Authority so requires, special sessions of the Council shall be held at the request of:

(a) The Assembly;

(b) The Council;

(c) Any member of the Council supported by a majority of the members of the Council;

(d) The President of the Council in consultation with the Vice-Presidents of the Council;

(e) The Secretary-General in consultation with the President of the Council.

Rule 6

Notification of members

The Secretary-General shall notify the members of the Council as early as possible, but no later than twenty-one days in advance of the opening of the special session. On the same date he shall notify other members of the Authority. When a special session is convened to consider an emergency matter under article 162, paragraph 2 (w), of the United Nations Convention on the Law of the Sea, such notification shall be sent as early as possible.

Regular and special sessions

Rule 7

Place of meeting

The Council shall meet at the seat of the Authority.

Rule 8

Notification of observers

In accordance with the timetable envisaged in rules 3 and 6, copies of the notice convening each session of the Council shall be addressed to observers referred to in rule 82 of the rules of procedure of the Assembly.

Rule 9

Temporary adjournment of session

The Council may decide to adjourn any session temporarily and resume it at a later date.

II. AGENDA

Regular sessions

Rule 10

Drawing up of the provisional agenda

The provisional agenda of a regular session shall include:

(a) Items proposed by the Assembly;

(b) Reports of the Enterprise,[1] reports and proposals of the Economic Planning Commission,[2] the recommendations of the Legal and Technical Commission and reports of the Finance Committee;

(c) Items proposed by the Council;

(d) Items proposed by any member of the Council;

(e) Items proposed by the Secretary-General.

Rule 11

Communication of the provisional agenda

The provisional agenda for a regular session shall be drawn up by the Secretary-General and communicated to the members of the Council and to the members and observers of the Authority as early as possible but at least thirty days before the opening of the session. Any subsequent change in or addition to the provisional agenda shall be brought to the notice of the members and observers of the Authority at least ten days before the opening of the session.

---

[1] According to the Agreement relating to the Implementation of Part XI of the United Nations Convention on the Law of the Sea of 10 December 1982, the Secretariat of the Authority shall perform the functions of the Enterprise until it begins to operate independently of the Secretariat. Upon the approval of a plan of work for exploitation for an entity other than the Enterprise, or upon receipt by the Council of an application for a joint-venture operation with the Enterprise, the Council shall take up the issue of the functioning of the Enterprise independently of the Secretariat of the Authority. If joint-venture operations with the Enterprise accord with sound commercial principles, the Council shall issue a directive pursuant to article 170, paragraph 2, of the Convention providing for such independent functioning.

[2] According to the Agreement relating to the Implementation of Part XI of the United Nations Convention on the Law of the Sea of 10 December 1982, the functions of the Economic Planning Commission shall be performed by the Legal and Technical Commission until such time as the Council decides otherwise or until the approval of the first plan of work for exploitation.

Special sessions

Rule 12

Drawing up of the provisional agenda

The provisional agenda for a special session shall consist only of those items proposed for consideration in the request for the holding of the session.

Rule 13

Communication of the provisional agenda

The provisional agenda for a special session shall be communicated to the members of the Council as early as possible, but at least twenty-one days before the opening of the session. It shall be communicated to other members and observers of the Authority on the same date. When a special session is convened to consider an emergency matter under article 162, paragraph 2 (w), of the United Nations Convention on the Law of the Sea, the provisional agenda shall be sent as early as possible.

Regular and special sessions

Rule 14

Adoption of the agenda

At the beginning of each session, the Council shall adopt its agenda for the session on the basis of the provisional agenda. The Council may, however, in urgent circumstances, make additions to the agenda at any time during a session.

Rule 15

Allocation of items

The Council may allocate items for its consideration or for consideration by any of its organs or any of its subsidiary organs and may refer items without preliminary debate to:

(a) One or more of its organs or subsidiary organs for examination and report at a subsequent session of the Council;

(b) The Secretary-General for study and report at a subsequent session of the Council; or

(c) The proposer of the item, for further information or documentation.

III. REPRESENTATION AND CREDENTIALS

Rule 16

Composition of delegations

Each member of the Council shall be represented at the meetings of the Council by an accredited representative, who may be accompanied by such alternate representatives and advisers as may be required by the delegation.

Rule 17

Submission of credentials

The credentials of representatives and the names of alternate representatives and advisers shall be submitted to the Secretary-General if possible not later than twenty-four hours after they take their seats on the Council. The credentials shall be issued either by the Head of State or Government, by the Minister for Foreign Affairs or person authorized by him or, in the case of entities referred to in article 305, paragraph 1 (f), of the United Nations Convention on the Law of the Sea, by another competent authority.

Rule 18

Submission of credentials by the members of the Authority not represented on the Council

Any member of the Authority not represented on the Council, attending a meeting of the Council in accordance with rule 74, shall submit credentials for the representative appointed by it for this purpose. The credentials of such a representative shall be communicated to the Secretary-General not less than twenty-four hours before the first meeting which he attends.

Rule 19

Examination of credentials

The credentials of representatives on the Council and of any representative appointed in accordance with rule 18 shall be examined by the Secretary-General, who shall submit a report to the Council for approval.

Rule 20

Provisional admission to the session

Pending the approval of the credentials of a representative on the Council in accordance with rule 19, such representative shall be seated provisionally with the same rights as other representatives.

Rule 21

Objection to representation

Any representative on the Council, to whose credentials objection has been made within the Council, shall continue to sit with the same rights as other representatives until the Council has decided the matter.

IV. OFFICERS

Rule 22

Elections

1. Each year at its first regular session, the Council shall elect a President and four Vice-Presidents from among its members, so that every regional group is represented by one officer.

2. In the election of the President the principle of rotation between regional groups shall be observed, and every effort shall be made to elect the President without a vote.

3. Vice-Presidents shall be eligible for re-election.

Rule 23

Term of office

The President and the Vice-Presidents shall, subject to rule 26, hold office until their successors are elected.

Rule 24

Acting President

1. If the President finds it necessary to be absent during a meeting or any part thereof, he shall designate one of the Vice-Presidents to take his place.

2. If the President ceases to hold office pursuant to rule 26, one of the Vice-Presidents shall act in his place until the election of a new President.

Rule 25

Powers of the Acting President

A Vice-President acting as President shall have the same powers and duties as the President.

Rule 26

Replacement of the President or Vice-President

If the President or a Vice-President ceases to be able to carry out his functions or ceases to be a representative of a member of the Council, or if a member of which he is a representative ceases to be a member of the Council, he shall cease to hold such office and a new President or Vice-President shall be elected for the unexpired term.

Rule 27

General powers of the President

In addition to exercising the powers conferred upon him elsewhere in these rules or by the United Nations Convention on the Law of the Sea, the President shall declare the opening and closing of each meeting of the Council, direct the discussions, ensure observance of these rules, accord the right to speak, put questions for decisions and announce decisions. He shall rule on points of order and, subject to these rules, shall have complete control of the proceedings of the Council and over the maintenance of order at its meetings. The President may, in the course of discussion of an item, propose to the Council the limitation of time to be allowed to speakers, the limitation of the number of times each representative may speak on any question, the closure of the list of speakers or the closure of the debate, and the suspension or the adjournment of the meeting or of the debate on the question under discussion.

Rule 28

Functions of the President

1. The President shall preside over the meetings of the Council and shall represent it in its capacity as the executive organ of the Authority.

2. The President, in the exercise of his functions, remains under the authority of the Council.

Rule 29

Voting of the President and Acting President

The President, or a Vice-President acting as President, shall not vote, but may designate another member of his delegation to vote in his place.

V. SECRETARIAT

Rule 30

Duties of the Secretary-General

1. The Secretary-General, as the chief administrative officer of the Authority, shall act in that capacity in all meetings of the Council and of its organs and subsidiary organs. He may designate an officer of the Secretariat to act as his representative. He shall discharge such other responsibilities as are assigned to him under Part XI of the United Nations Convention on the Law of the Sea.

2. The Secretary-General shall provide and direct, with due regard to the principles of economy and efficiency, the staff required by the Council, its organs and its subsidiary organs.

3. The Secretary-General shall keep the members of the Council informed of any questions which may be of interest to the Council.

Rule 31

Submission of the annual budget

The Secretary-General shall draft the proposed annual budget of the Authority and submit it together with the recommendations of the Finance Committee to the Council for its consideration. The Council shall consider the proposed annual budget taking into account the recommendations of the Finance Committee and submit it to the Assembly, together with its own recommendations thereon.

Rule 32

Duties of the Secretariat

1. The Secretariat shall receive, translate, reproduce and distribute documents of the Council and its organs to the members and observers of the Authority; interpret speeches made at the meetings; prepare and circulate, if so decided by the Council in accordance with rule 37, the records of the session; have the custody and proper preservation of the documents in the archives of the Authority; and, generally, perform all other work which the Council may require.

2. The Secretary-General may distribute to members of the Authority written reports submitted by the non-governmental organizations referred to in article 169, paragraph 1, of the United Nations Convention on the Law of the Sea. Such reports submitted by non-governmental organizations within the scope of their competence which are relevant to the work of the Council shall be distributed by the Secretariat in the quantity and in the languages in which the reports are available.

Rule 33

Estimate of expenditures

1. Before any proposal which involves expenditures from the Authority's funds is approved by the Council, the Secretary-General shall prepare, as early as possible, a report on the estimated costs involved as well as on administrative and budgetary implications with reference to existing financial authorizations and budgetary appropriations and submit it to the Finance Committee. After consideration by the Finance Committee, the report shall be circulated to all members of the Council together with the recommendations of the Finance Committee thereon.

2. The Council shall take into account the estimates and recommendations referred to in paragraph 1 before adopting any proposal involving expenditure from the Authority's funds. If the proposal is adopted, the Council shall indicate, whenever appropriate, the priority or degree of urgency which it attaches to the proposal.

3. The Council may, in accordance with the procedures established for the operation of a contingency fund to be set up, recommend withdrawals from the contingency fund to meet unanticipated emergencies that may arise before the next regular session of the Assembly.

VI. LANGUAGES

Rule 34

Languages

Arabic, Chinese, English, French, Russian and Spanish shall be the languages of the Council.

Rule 35

Interpretation

1. Speeches made in a language of the Council shall be interpreted into the other such languages.

2. Any representative may make a speech in a language other than the language of the Council. In that case, he shall himself provide for interpretation into one of the languages of the Council. Interpretation into the other languages of the Council by the interpreters of the Secretariat may be based on the interpretation given in the first such language.

Rule 36

Languages of resolutions and documents

All resolutions and other documents shall be published in the languages of the Council.

VII. RECORDS

Rule 37

Records and sound recordings of meetings

1. The Council may decide to keep summary records of plenary meetings; but all decisions taken by the Council and all statements made for the record shall be duly included in the published records of the Council. As a general rule, they shall be circulated as soon as possible, simultaneously in all the languages of the Council, to all representatives, who shall inform the Secretariat within five working days after the circulation of the summary record of any changes they wish to have made.

2. The Secretariat shall make and retain sound recordings of the meetings of the Council, and of its subsidiary organs when they so decide. The Secretariat shall provide appropriate facilities to enable members of the Authority to have access to such sound recordings of public meetings upon request.

Rule 38

Communication of decisions

Decisions adopted by the Council shall be communicated by the Secretary-General to the members of the Authority within fifteen days after the close of the session.

VIII. PUBLIC AND PRIVATE MEETINGS OF THE COUNCIL AND ITS SUBSIDIARY ORGANS

Rule 39

Public and private meetings

1. The meetings of the Council shall be held in public unless otherwise decided.

2. As a general rule, meetings of subsidiary organs shall be held in private.

3. All decisions of the Council taken at a private meeting shall be announced at the earliest possible public meeting of the Council. At the close of each private meeting of a subsidiary organ, the Chairman may issue a communiqué through the Secretary-General.

IX. CONDUCT OF BUSINESS

Rule 40

Quorum

A majority of the members of the Council shall constitute a quorum.

Rule 41

Speeches

No representative may address the Council without having previously obtained the permission of the President. The President shall call upon speakers in the order in which they signify their desire to speak. The President may call a speaker to order if his remarks are not relevant to the subject under discussion.

Rule 42

Precedence

The Chairman of an organ of the Council, or of a subsidiary organ of the Council, may be accorded precedence in speaking for the purpose of explaining the conclusion arrived at by that organ.

Rule 43

Statements by the Secretariat

The Secretary-General, or a member of the Secretariat designated by him as his representative, may at any time make either oral or written statements to the Council concerning any question under consideration by it.

Rule 44

Points of order

During the discussion of any matter, a representative of a member of the Council may rise to a point of order, and the point of order shall be immediately decided by the President in accordance with the rules of procedure. A representative of a member of the Council may appeal against the ruling of the President. The appeal shall be immediately put to the vote, and the President's ruling shall stand unless overruled by a majority of the members of the Council present and voting. A representative rising to a point of order may not speak on the substance of the matter under discussion.

Rule 45

Time limit on speeches

The Council may limit the time to be allowed to each speaker and the number of times each representative may speak on any question. Before a decision is taken, two representatives of members of the Council may speak in favour of, and two against, a proposal to set such limits. When the debate is limited and a representative exceeds his allotted time, the President shall call him to order without delay.

Rule 46

Closing of list of speakers, right of reply

During the course of a debate, the President may announce the list of speakers and, with the consent of the Council, declare the list closed. The President may, however, accord the right of reply to any representative if a speech delivered after he has declared the list closed makes this desirable.

Rule 47

Adjournment of debate

During the discussion of any matter, a representative of a member of the Council may move the adjournment of the debate on the item under discussion. In addition to the proposer of the motion, two representatives of members of the Council may speak in favour of, and two against, the motion, after which the motion shall be immediately put to the vote. The President may limit the time to be allowed to speakers under this rule.

Rule 48

Closure of the debate

A representative of a member of the Council may at any time move the closure of the debate on the question under discussion, whether or not any other representative has signified his wish to speak. Permission to speak on the motion shall be accorded only to two representatives of members of the Council opposing the closure, after which the motion shall be immediately put to the vote. If the Council is in favour of the closure, the President shall declare the closure of the debate. The President may limit the time to be allowed to speakers under this rule.

Rule 49

Suspension or adjournment of the meeting

During the discussion of any matter, a representative of a member of the Council may move the suspension or the adjournment of the meeting. Such motions shall not be debated, but shall be immediately put to the vote. The President may limit the time to be allowed to the speaker moving the suspension or adjournment of the meeting.

Rule 50

Order of procedural motions

Subject to rule 44, the following motions shall have precedence in the following order over all other proposals or motions before the meeting:

(a) To suspend the meeting;

(b) To adjourn the meeting;

(c) To adjourn the debate on the item under discussion;

(d) To close the debate on the item under discussion.

Rule 51

Proposals and amendments

Proposals and amendments shall normally be submitted in writing to the Secretary-General, who shall circulate copies to the delegations. As a general rule, no proposal shall be discussed or put to the vote at any meeting of the Council unless copies of it have been circulated to all delegations not later than the day preceding the meeting. The President may, however, permit the discussion and consideration of amendments, or of motions as to procedure, even though such amendments and motions have not been circulated or have only been circulated the same day.

Rule 52

Decision on competence

Subject to rule 50, any motion calling for a decision on the competence of the Council to adopt a proposal submitted to it shall be put to the vote before a vote is taken on the proposal in question.

Rule 53

Withdrawal of proposals and motions

A proposal or a motion may be withdrawn by its proposer at any time before voting on it has commenced, provided that the proposal or motion has not been amended. A proposal or a motion thus withdrawn may be reintroduced by any member.

Rule 54

Reconsideration of proposals

When a proposal has been adopted or rejected, it may not be reconsidered at the same session unless the Council, by a two-thirds majority of the members of the Council present and voting and subject to the requirement referred to in rule 56, paragraph 2, so decides. Permission to speak on a motion to reconsider shall be accorded only to two representatives of members of the Council opposing the motion, after which it shall be immediately put to the vote.

X. DECISION-MAKING

Rule 55

Voting rights

Each member of the Council shall have one vote.

Rule 56

Decision-making

1. As a general rule, decision-making in the Council should be by consensus.

2. If all efforts to reach a decision by consensus have been exhausted, decisions by voting in the Council on questions of procedure shall be taken by a majority of members present and voting, and decisions on questions of substance, except where the United Nations Convention on the Law of the Sea provides for decisions by consensus in the Council, shall be taken by a two-thirds majority of members present and voting, provided that such decisions are not opposed by a majority in any one of the chambers referred to in paragraph 5 below. To facilitate the determination of a majority in chambers, ballot papers distributed to the members of each of the chambers should be distinctly marked.

3. The Council may defer the taking of a decision in order to facilitate further negotiation whenever it appears that all efforts at achieving consensus have not been exhausted.

4. Decisions by the Council having financial or budgetary implications shall be based on the recommendations of the Finance Committee.

5. Each group of States elected under paragraphs (a) to (c) of rule 84 of the rules of procedure of the Assembly shall be treated as a chamber for the purposes of voting in the Council. The developing States elected under paragraphs (d) and (e) of rule 84 of the rules of procedure of the Assembly shall be treated as a single chamber for the purposes of voting in the Council.

Rule 57

Use of terms

1. For the purposes of these rules, the phrase "members present and voting" means members of the Council present and casting an affirmative or negative vote. Members of the Council who abstain from voting shall be considered as not voting.

2. Subject to the provisions of rules 16 and 21, the term "members participating" in relation to any particular session of the Council means any member of the Council whose representatives have registered with the Secretariat as participating in that session and which has not subsequently notified the Secretariat of its withdrawal from that session or part of it. The Secretariat shall keep a register for this purpose.

Rule 58

Decisions requiring a consensus

Decisions on questions of substance arising under the following provisions of the United Nations Convention on the Law of the Sea shall be taken by consensus: article 162, paragraph 2 (m) and (o); adoption of amendments to Part XI.

Rule 59

Use of term "consensus"

For the purposes of these rules, "consensus" means the absence of any formal objection.

Rule 60

Method of voting

1. The Council shall, in the absence of mechanical means for voting, vote by show of hands, but a representative of any member of the Council may request a roll-call. The roll-call shall be taken in the English alphabetical order of the names of the members of the Council participating in that session, beginning with the member of the Council whose name is drawn by lot by the President. The name of each member of the Council shall be called in any roll-call, and one of its representatives shall reply "yes" or "no" or "abstention". The result of the voting shall be inserted in the record in the English alphabetical order of the names of the members of the Council.

2. When the Council votes by mechanical means, a non-recorded vote shall replace a vote by show of hands and a recorded vote shall replace a roll-call vote. A representative of any member of the Council may request a recorded vote. In the case of a recorded vote, the Council shall, unless a representative of any member of the Council requests otherwise, dispense with the procedure of calling out the names of the members of the Council; nevertheless, the result of the voting shall be inserted in the record in the same manner as that of a roll-call vote.

Rule 61

Conduct during voting

After the President has announced the beginning of voting, no representative of any member of the Council shall interrupt the voting, except that representatives of members of the Council may interrupt on a point of order in connection with the actual conduct of the voting.

Rule 62

Explanation of vote

Representatives of members of the Council may make brief statements consisting solely of explanations of their votes before the voting has commenced or after the voting has been completed. The President may limit the time to be allowed for such statements. The representative of any member of the Council sponsoring a proposal or motion shall not speak in explanation of vote thereon, unless it has been amended.

Rule 63

Division of proposals and amendments

A representative of a member of the Council may move that parts of a proposal or of an amendment should be voted on separately. If objection is made to the request for division, the motion for division shall be voted upon. Permission to speak on the motion for division shall be given only to two speakers in favour and to two speakers against. If the motion for division is carried, those parts of the proposal or of the amendment which are approved shall then be put to the vote as a whole. If all operative parts of the proposal or of the amendment have been rejected, the proposal or the amendment shall be considered to have been rejected as a whole.

Rule 64

Order of voting on amendments

When an amendment is moved to a proposal, the amendment shall be voted on first. When two or more amendments are moved to a proposal, the Council shall first vote on the amendment furthest removed in substance from the original proposal and then on the amendment next furthest removed therefrom, and so on until all the amendments have been put to the vote. Where, however, the adoption of one amendment necessarily implies the rejection of another amendment, the latter amendment shall not be put to the vote. If one or more amendments are adopted, the amended proposal shall then be voted upon. A motion is considered an amendment to a proposal if it merely adds to, deletes from or revises part of the proposal.

Rule 65

Order of voting on proposals

If two or more proposals relate to the same question, the Council shall, unless it decides otherwise, vote on the proposals in the order in which they have been submitted. The Council may, after each vote on a proposal, decide whether to vote on the next proposal.

Rule 66

Elections

All elections shall be held by secret ballot.

Rule 67

Restricted balloting for one elective place

If, when a person or a member of the Council is to be elected, no candidate obtains in the first ballot the required majority provided for in rule 56, paragraph 2, the balloting shall be continued until one candidate secures the required majority of the votes cast, provided that, after the third inconclusive ballot, votes may be cast for any eligible person or member of the Council. If three such unrestricted ballots are inconclusive, the next three ballots shall be restricted to the two candidates who obtained the greatest number of votes in the third of the unrestricted ballots, and the following three ballots thereafter shall be unrestricted, and so on until a person or member of the Council is elected.

Rule 68

Restricted balloting for two or more elective places

When two or more elective places are to be filled at one time under the same conditions, those candidates, not exceeding the number of such places, obtaining in the first ballot the majority required shall be elected. If the number of candidates obtaining such majority is less than the number of persons or members to be elected, there shall be additional ballots to fill the remaining places, the voting being restricted to the candidates obtaining the greatest number of votes in the previous ballot to a number not more than twice the places remaining to be filled, provided that, after the third inconclusive ballot, votes may be cast for any eligible person or member. If three such unrestricted ballots are inconclusive, the next three ballots shall be restricted to the candidates who obtained the greatest number of votes in the third of the unrestricted ballots, to a number not more than twice the places remaining to be filled, and the following three ballots thereafter shall be unrestricted, and so on until all the places have been filled.

Rule 69

Equally divided votes on matters other than elections

If a vote is equally divided on matters other than elections, a second vote shall be taken at a subsequent meeting which shall be held within forty-eight hours of the first vote, and it shall be expressly mentioned in the agenda that a second vote will be taken on the matter in question. If this vote also results in equality, the proposal shall be regarded as rejected.

XI. SPECIAL PROCEDURES

Rule 70

Approval of plans of work

The Council shall approve a recommendation by the Legal and Technical Commission for approval of a plan of work unless by a two-thirds majority of its members present and voting, including a majority of members present and voting in each of the chambers of the Council, the Council decides to disapprove a plan of work. If the Council does not take a decision on a recommendation for approval of a plan of work within a prescribed period, the recommendation shall be deemed to have been approved by the Council at the end of that period. The prescribed period shall normally be 60 days unless the Council decides to provide for a longer period. If the Commission recommends the disapproval of a plan of work or does not make a recommendation, the Council may nevertheless approve the plan of work in accordance with its rules of procedure for decision- making on questions of substance.

XII. SUBSIDIARY ORGANS

Rule 71

Establishment

The Council may establish, as appropriate, and with due regard to economy and efficiency, such subsidiary organs as it finds necessary for the exercise of its functions.

Rule 72

Composition

In the composition of subsidiary organs, emphasis shall be placed on the need for members qualified and competent in relevant technical matters dealt with by those organs, provided that due account shall be taken of the principle of equitable geographical distribution and of special interests.

Rule 73

Rules of procedure

These rules of procedure of the Council apply, mutatis mutandis, to the proceedings of subsidiary organs unless the Council decides otherwise.

XIII. PARTICIPATION BY NON-MEMBERS OF THE COUNCIL

Rule 74[3]

Participation by members of the Authority

Any member of the Authority not represented on the Council may send a representative to attend a meeting of the Council. Such a representative shall be entitled to participate in the deliberations but not to vote.

---

[3] This rule is without prejudice to the understanding reached by the Assembly, at the first part of the second session held in March 1996, which provides the following: "The regional group which relinquishes a seat will have the right to designate a member of that group in the Assembly to participate in the deliberations of the Council without the right to vote during the period the regional group relinquishes the seat" (ISBA/A/L.8, note 2, and ISBA/A/L.9, para. 11).

Rule 75

Participation by observers

Observers referred to in rule 82 of the rules of procedure of the Assembly may designate representatives to participate, without the right to vote, in the deliberations of the Council, upon the invitation of the Council, on questions affecting them or within the scope of their activities.

Rule 76

Cooperation with international and non-governmental organizations

The Secretary-General shall, on matters within the competence of the Authority, make suitable arrangements, with the approval of the Council, for consultation and cooperation with international and non-governmental organizations recognized by the Economic and Social Council of the United Nations.

XIV. ELECTIONS TO THE ECONOMIC PLANNING COMMISSION AND LEGAL AND TECHNICAL COMMISSION[4]

Rule 77

Composition

1. Each Commission shall be composed of fifteen members, elected by the Council from among the candidates nominated by the members of the Authority.

2. However, if necessary, the Council may decide to increase the size of either Commission, having due regard to economy and efficiency.

3. In accordance with rule 56, paragraph 2, decisions of the Council on matters referred to in paragraphs 1 and 2 above shall be taken by a two-thirds majority of members present and voting, provided that such decisions are not opposed by a majority in any one of the chambers referred to in rule 56, paragraph 5.

Rule 78

Equitable geographical distribution and the representation of special interests

In the election of members of the Commissions, due account shall be taken of the need for equitable geographical distribution and the representation of special interests.

---

[4] See note 2 above.

Rule 79

Nominations

No State Party may nominate more than one candidate for the same Commission. No person shall be elected to serve on more than one Commission.

Rule 80

Term of office

1. Members of the Commissions shall hold office for a term of five years. They shall be eligible for re-election for a further term.

2. A member of a Commission shall begin his term of office on the date of election.

3. In the event of the death, incapacity or resignation of a member of a Commission prior to the expiration of his term of office, the Council shall elect for the remainder of the term, a member from the same geographical region or area of interest.

Rule 81

General qualifications for membership of a Commission

Members of a Commission shall have appropriate qualifications in the area of competence of that Commission. Members of the Authority shall nominate candidates of the highest standards of competence and integrity with qualifications in relevant fields so as to ensure the effective exercise of the functions of the Commissions.

Rule 82

Qualifications for membership of the Economic Planning Commission

Members of the Economic Planning Commission shall have appropriate qualifications, such as those relevant to mining, management of mineral resources activities, international trade or international economics. The Council shall endeavour to ensure that the membership of the Commission reflects all appropriate qualifications. The Commission shall include at least two members from developing States whose exports of the categories of minerals to be derived from the Area have a substantial bearing upon their economies.

Rule 83

Qualifications for membership of the Legal and Technical Commission

Members of the Legal and Technical Commission shall have appropriate qualifications, such as those relevant to exploration for and exploitation and processing of mineral resources, oceanology, protection of the marine environment, or economic or legal matters relating to ocean mining and related fields of expertise. The Council shall endeavour to ensure that the membership of the Commission reflects all appropriate qualifications.

XV. AMENDMENTS

Rule 84

Method of amendment

These rules of procedure may be amended by a decision of the Council, taken by a majority of the members present and voting, after a committee has considered the proposed amendment.

AGREEMENT BETWEEN THE INTERNATIONAL SEABED AUTHORITY AND THE GOVERNMENT OF JAMAICA REGARDING THE HEADQUARTERS OF THE INTERNATIONAL SEABED AUTHORITY

The International Seabed Authority and the Government of Jamaica,

Having regard to the United Nations Convention on the Law of the Sea of 10 December 1982, which establishes the International Seabed Authority;

Taking into account article 156, paragraph 4, of the Convention, which provides that the seat of the International Seabed Authority shall be in Jamaica;

Recognizing the need to ensure the availability of all necessary facilities to enable the International Seabed Authority to perform its functions as required by the Convention;

Desiring to conclude an agreement for the purpose of regulating, in accordance with the Convention, questions relating to the establishment and functioning of the International Seabed Authority in Jamaica;

Have agreed as follows:

Article 1

Use of terms

For the purposes of this Agreement:

(a) “archives” includes records and correspondence, documents, manuscripts, maps, still and moving pictures, films, computer-based communications and sound recordings belonging to or held by the Authority in Jamaica;

(b) “Authority” means the International Seabed Authority as defined in the Convention;

(c) “competent authorities” means such government, municipal or other authorities in Jamaica as may be appropriate in the context and in accordance with the laws applicable in Jamaica;

(d) “Convention” means the United Nations Convention on the Law of the Sea of 10 December 1982 together with the Agreement relating to the Implementation of Part XI of the United Nations Convention on the Law of the Sea of 10 December 1982;

(e) “Director-General” means the Director-General of the Enterprise;

(f) “domestic staff” means the persons employed exclusively in the domestic service of the representatives of members of the Authority, of the representatives of observers of the Authority and the officials of the Authority;

(g) "Enterprise" means the organ of the Authority as provided for in the Convention;

(h) "experts" means experts performing missions for the Authority;

(i) "Government" means the Government of Jamaica;

(j) "Headquarters" means the area occupied by the Authority in Jamaica, as specified in article 2;

(k) "laws of Jamaica" means the Constitution of Jamaica, statute law and regulations made pursuant to statutes and includes common law;

(l) "members of the Authority" means all States Parties to the Convention;

(m) "members of the permanent mission" or "members of the permanent observer mission" means the head of the mission and the members of the staff;

(n) "observer State" means a State which enjoys observer status with the Authority;

(o) "observers of the Authority" means States and intergovernmental and non-governmental organizations which enjoy such status with the Authority;

(p) "officials of the Authority" means the Secretary-General and all members of the staff of the Authority, except those who are locally recruited and assigned to hourly rates;

(q) "permanent mission" means a mission of permanent character, representing a member of the Authority;

(r) "permanent observer mission" means a mission of permanent character, representing an observer State;

(s) "Protocol" means the Protocol on the Privileges and Immunities of the Authority;

(t) "representatives of members of the Authority" means delegates, deputy delegates, advisers and any other accredited members of delegations;

(u) "representatives of observer States" means delegates, deputy delegates, advisers and any other accredited members of delegations;

(v) "Secretary-General" means the Secretary-General of the International Seabed Authority or his authorized representative; and

(w) "States Parties" has the same meaning as defined in article 1 of the Convention.

Article 2

The seat of the Authority

1. The seat of the Authority shall be in Jamaica.

2. Jamaica undertakes to grant to the Authority, for the permanent use and occupation by the Authority, such area and facilities as may be specified in supplementary agreements to be concluded for the purpose.

3. Any building or buildings in Jamaica outside the Headquarters which may, with the concurrence of the Government, be temporarily used for meetings convened by the Authority shall be considered as included in the Headquarters. Requests by the Authority requiring the concurrence of the Government shall not be unreasonably withheld.

Article 3

Legal personality and capacity of the Authority

The Authority shall have international legal personality and such legal capacity as may be necessary for the exercise of its functions and the fulfilment of its purposes in accordance with the Convention; consequently it has, in particular, the capacity:

(a) To contract;

(b) To acquire and dispose of immovable and movable property; and

(c) To be a party to legal proceedings.

Article 4

Law and authority in the Headquarters

1. The Headquarters shall be under the authority and control of the Authority in accordance with this Agreement.

2. The Authority shall have the power to adopt regulations, operative within the Headquarters, for the purpose of establishing therein the conditions in all respects necessary for the full and independent exercise of its functions.

3. The Authority shall promptly inform the Government of regulations adopted by it in accordance with paragraph 2.

4. Except as otherwise provided in this Agreement and subject to the provisions of paragraphs 2 and 5, the laws of Jamaica shall apply in the Headquarters.

5. No law of Jamaica which is inconsistent with a regulation of the Authority authorized by paragraph 2 shall, to the extent of such inconsistency, be applicable in the Headquarters.

6. Any dispute between the Authority and Jamaica as to whether a regulation of the Authority is authorized by paragraph 2, or as to whether a law of Jamaica is inconsistent with any regulation of the Authority authorized by paragraph 2, shall be promptly settled by the procedure set out in article 49. Pending such settlement, the regulation of the Authority shall apply and the law of Jamaica shall be inapplicable in the Headquarters to the extent that the Authority claims it to be inconsistent with the regulation of the Authority.

7. Except as otherwise provided in this Agreement, the courts of Jamaica or other competent authorities shall have jurisdiction, as provided in applicable laws, over acts done and transactions taking place in the Headquarters.

8. The courts of Jamaica or other competent authorities, when dealing with cases arising out of or relating to acts done or transactions taking place in the Headquarters, shall take into account the regulations adopted by the Authority under paragraph 2.

9. The Authority may expel or exclude persons from the Headquarters for violation of its regulations adopted under this article, or for any other proper cause.

10. Without prejudice to the provisions of this article, the regulations of the competent authorities relating to fire protection and sanitation shall be respected.

Article 5

Inviolability of the Headquarters

1. The Headquarters shall be inviolable. No officer or official of Jamaica, or other person exercising any public authority within Jamaica, shall enter the Headquarters to perform any duties therein except with the express consent of, or at the request of, the Secretary-General, and under conditions approved by him.

2. The service of legal process, including the seizure of private property, shall not take place within the Headquarters except with the express consent of, and under conditions approved by, the Secretary-General.

3. Without prejudice to the provisions of this Agreement, the Authority shall prevent the Headquarters from being used as a refuge from justice by persons who are avoiding arrest under any law of Jamaica, or who are required by the Government for extradition, expulsion or deportation to another country, or who are endeavouring to avoid service of legal process.

4. In case of fire or other emergency requiring prompt protective action or in the event that the competent authorities have reasonable cause to believe that such an emergency has occurred, the consent of the Secretary-General to entry of the Headquarters by the competent authorities shall be presumed if the Secretary-General cannot be reached in time. Every effort shall be made to seek such consent.

5. Subject to paragraphs 1 and 2, nothing in this article shall preclude the official delivery by the postal service of Jamaica of letters and documents to the Headquarters.

Article 6

Protection of the Headquarters

1. The competent authorities shall exercise due diligence to ensure that the tranquillity of the Headquarters and free access thereto are not disturbed by the unauthorized entry of any person or group of persons from outside or by disturbances in its immediate vicinity, and shall provide the Headquarters with such appropriate protection as may be required.

2. If so requested by the Secretary-General, the competent authorities shall provide a sufficient number of police for the preservation of law and order in the Headquarters, and for the removal therefrom of persons as requested.

3. The competent authorities shall take all necessary measures to ensure that the Authority shall not be dispossessed of all or any part of the Headquarters without the express consent of the Authority.

Article 7

Vicinity of the Headquarters

1. The competent authorities shall take all necessary steps to ensure that the amenities of the Headquarters are not prejudiced and that the purposes for which the Headquarters is intended are not obstructed by the use made of the land and buildings in the vicinity of the Headquarters.

2. The Authority shall take all necessary steps to ensure that the Headquarters is not used for other purposes than those for which it is intended and to ensure that the land and buildings in its vicinity are not unreasonably obstructed.

Article 8

Flag and emblem

The Authority shall be entitled to display its flag and emblem in the Headquarters and on vehicles used for official purposes.

Article 9

Public services in the Headquarters

1. The competent authorities shall do their utmost to ensure that the Authority shall be provided, on fair and equitable terms but in any case not less favourable than those accorded to the agencies of the Government, with necessary utilities and public services, including but not limited to

electricity, water, gas, sewerage, collection of waste, fire protection and local transportation.

2. In case of any interruption or threatened interruption of any such services, the competent authorities shall consider the needs of the Authority as being of equal importance with those of essential agencies of the Government, and shall take steps accordingly to ensure that the work of the Authority is not prejudiced.

3. Upon the request of the competent authorities, the Secretary-General shall make suitable arrangements to enable duly authorized representatives of the appropriate public services to inspect, repair, maintain, reconstruct and relocate utilities, conduits, mains and sewers within the Headquarters under conditions which shall not unreasonably disturb the carrying out of the functions of the Authority.

4. In cases where gas, electricity or water is supplied by the competent authorities, or where the prices thereof are under their control, the Authority shall be supplied at rates which shall not exceed the lowest comparable rates accorded to the agencies of the Government.

5. The Government shall do its utmost to ensure that the Authority is provided at all times with gasoline or other fuels and lubricating oils for each automobile operated by the Authority on such terms and conditions as may be established for diplomatic missions in Jamaica.

Article 10

Communications facilities

1. For the purposes of its official communications, the Authority shall enjoy as far as is compatible with international agreements, regulations and arrangements to which Jamaica is a party, treatment at least as favourable as that which is accorded to diplomatic missions in Jamaica and to international organizations in the matter, inter alia, of priorities, rates and taxes applicable to mail and different forms of telecommunications.

2. The competent authorities shall secure the inviolability of all communications and correspondence directed to the Authority, or to any of the officials of the Authority in the Headquarters, as well as all outgoing communications and correspondence of the Authority, by whatever means or in whatever form transmitted, and they shall be immune from censorship and from any other form of interception or interference with their privacy. Such inviolability shall extend, without limitation by reason of this enumeration, to publications, still and moving pictures, films, computer-based communications and sound or videotape recordings dispatched to or by the Authority.

3. The Authority shall have the right to use codes and to dispatch and receive its correspondence and other materials by courier or in sealed bags,

which shall have the same privileges and immunities as diplomatic couriers and bags.

4. (a) The Authority may establish and operate at the Headquarters:

(i) Its own short-wave sending and receiving radio broadcasting facilities, including emergency link equipment which may be used on the same frequencies, within the tolerances prescribed for the broadcasting service by applicable Jamaican regulations, for radiotelegraph, radiotelephone, satellite and similar services;

(ii) Such other radio facilities as may be specified by supplementary agreement between the Authority and the competent authorities;

(b) The Authority shall make arrangements for the operation of the services referred to in this paragraph with the International Telecommunication Union, the appropriate agencies of the Government and the appropriate agencies of other affected Governments with regard to all frequencies and similar matters.

5. The facilities provided for in paragraph 4 may, to the extent necessary for efficient operation, be established and operated outside the Headquarters with the consent of the Government.

6. If so requested by the Secretary-General, the competent authorities shall provide for the official purposes of the Authority appropriate radio and other telecommunication facilities in conformity with the regulations of the International Telecommunication Union. These facilities may be specified by supplementary agreement between the Authority and the competent authorities.

Article 11

Freedom of publication and broadcasting

The Government recognizes the right of the Authority freely to publish and broadcast within Jamaica in the fulfilment of its purposes set out in the Convention. It is, however, understood that the Authority shall respect any laws of Jamaica or any international agreements to which Jamaica is a party, relating to publications and broadcasting.

Article 12

Freedom of assembly

1. The Government recognizes the right of the Authority to convene meetings within the Headquarters or, with the concurrence of the Government, elsewhere in Jamaica.

2. To ensure full freedom of assembly and discussion, the Government shall take all proper steps to guarantee that no impediment is placed in

the way of conducting the proceedings of any meeting convened by the Authority.

Article 13

Inviolability of archives

1. The archives of the Authority, wherever located, shall be inviolable.

2. The location of the archives of the Authority shall be made known to the competent authorities if it is at a place other than in the Headquarters.

Article 14

Immunity and exemptions of the Authority, its property and assets

1. The Authority, its property and assets shall enjoy immunity from legal process except to the extent that the Authority expressly waives this immunity in a particular case.

2. The property and assets of the Authority, wherever located and by whomsoever held, shall be immune from search, requisition, confiscation, expropriation or any other form of seizure by executive or legislative action.

3. The property and assets of the Authority shall be exempt from restrictions, regulations, controls and moratoria of any nature.

Article 15

Exemption from taxes and customs duties

1. Within the scope of its official activities, the Authority, its assets and property, its income, and its operations and transactions, authorized by the Convention, shall be exempt from all direct taxation, and goods imported or exported for its official use shall be exempt from all customs duties. The Authority shall not claim exemption from taxes which are no more than charges for services rendered.

2. When purchases of goods or services of substantial value necessary for the official activities of the Authority are made by or on behalf of the Authority and when the price of such goods or services includes taxes or duties, appropriate measures shall, to the extent practicable, be taken by the Government to grant exemption from such taxes or duties or provide for their reimbursement. With respect to such taxes or duties, the Authority shall at all times enjoy at least the same exemptions as are granted to the heads of diplomatic missions in Jamaica.

3. Goods imported or purchased under an exemption provided for in this article shall not be sold or otherwise disposed of in the territory of Jamaica, except under conditions agreed with the Government.

Article 16

Financial facilities

1. Without being subject to any financial controls, regulations or moratoria of any kind, the Authority may freely:

(a) Purchase any currencies through authorized channels and hold and dispose of them;

(b) Operate accounts in any currencies;

(c) Purchase through authorized channels, hold and dispose of, funds, securities and gold;

(d) Transfer its funds, securities, gold and foreign currencies to or from Jamaica, to or from any other country, or within Jamaica; and

(e) Raise funds through the exercise of its borrowing power or in any other manner which it deems desirable, except that with respect to the raising of funds within Jamaica, the Authority shall obtain the concurrence of the Government.

2. The Government shall employ its best endeavours to enable the Authority to obtain the most favourable conditions as regards exchange rates, banking commissions in exchange transactions and the like.

3. The Authority shall, in exercising its rights under this article, pay due regard to any representations made by the Government in so far as effect can be given to such representations without detriment to the interests of the Authority.

Article 17

Principal office of the Enterprise

The Enterprise shall have its principal office at the seat of the Authority.

Article 18

Legal status of the Enterprise

The Enterprise shall, within the framework of the international legal personality of the Authority, have such legal capacity as is necessary for the exercise of its functions and fulfilment of its purposes and, in particular, the capacity:

(a) To enter into contracts, joint arrangements or other arrangements, including agreements with States and international organizations;

(b) To acquire, lease, hold and dispose of immovable and movable property;

(c) To be a party to legal proceedings.

Article 19

Position of the Enterprise with regard to judicial process

1. Actions may be brought against the Enterprise in a court of competent jurisdiction in Jamaica.

2. The property and assets of the Enterprise, wherever located and by whomsoever held, shall be immune from all forms of seizure, attachment or execution before the delivery of final judgement against the Enterprise.

Article 20

Immunity of the property and assets of the Enterprise

1. The property and assets of the Enterprise, wherever located and by whomsoever held, shall be immune from requisition, confiscation, expropriation or any other form of seizure by executive or legislative action.

2. The property and assets of the Enterprise, wherever located and by whomsoever held, shall be free from discriminatory restrictions, regulations, controls and moratoria of any nature.

Article 21

Respect for laws of Jamaica by the Enterprise

The Enterprise shall respect the laws of Jamaica.

Article 22

Rights, privileges and immunities of the Enterprise

1. The Government shall ensure that the Enterprise enjoys all rights, privileges and immunities accorded by it to entities conducting commercial activities in its territory. These rights, privileges and immunities shall be accorded to the Enterprise on no less favourable a basis than that on which they are accorded to entities engaged in similar commercial activities. If special privileges are provided by Jamaica for developing States or their commercial entities, the Enterprise shall enjoy those privileges on a similarly preferential basis.

2. The Government may provide special incentives, rights, privileges and immunities to the Enterprise without the obligation to provide such incentives, rights, privileges and immunities to other commercial entities.

Article 23

Exemption from direct and indirect taxation

The Government and the Enterprise shall enter into special agreements concerning the exemption of the Enterprise from direct and indirect taxation.

Article 24

Financial facilities for the Enterprise

The Enterprise shall have the power to borrow funds and to furnish such collateral or other security as it may determine. Before making a public sale of its obligations in the financial markets or currency of Jamaica, the Enterprise shall obtain the approval of the Government.

Article 25

Waiver of immunity by the Enterprise

The Enterprise may waive any of the privileges and immunities conferred under articles 18, 19, 20, 21, 22 and 23 of this Agreement or in the special agreements provided for in article 51 to such extent and upon such conditions as it may determine.

Article 26

Freedom of access and residence

1. The Government shall take all necessary measures to facilitate the entry into and residence in Jamaican territory and shall place no impediment in the way of the departure from Jamaican territory of the persons listed below; it shall ensure that no impediment is placed in the way of their transit to or from the Headquarters and shall afford them any necessary protection in transit:

(a) Representatives of members of the Authority and of observers of the Authority, including alternate representatives, advisers, experts and staff, as well as their spouses, dependent members of their families and domestic staff;

(b) Officials of the Authority, as well as their spouses, dependent members of their families and domestic staff;

(c) Officials of the United Nations or of any of its specialized agencies or the International Atomic Energy Agency, attached to the Authority and who have official business with the Authority, as well as their spouses, dependent members of their families and domestic staff;

(d) Representatives of other organizations with which the Authority has established official relations and who have official business with the Authority as well as their spouses and dependent members of their families;

(e) Persons on mission for the Authority but who are not officials of the Authority, as well as their spouses and dependent members of their families;

(f) Representatives of the press, radio, film, television or other information media, who have been accredited to the Authority at its discretion after consultation with the Government;

(g) All persons invited by the Authority to the Headquarters on official business. The Secretary-General shall communicate the names of such persons to the Government before their intended entry.

2. This article shall not apply in the case of general interruptions of transportation, which shall be dealt with as provided in article 9, paragraph 2, and shall not impair the effectiveness of generally applicable laws relating to the operations of means of transportation.

3. Visas, where required for persons referred to in paragraph 1, shall be granted without charge and as promptly as possible.

4. No activity performed by any person referred to in paragraph 1 in his official capacity with respect to the Authority shall constitute a reason for preventing his entry into or his departure from the territory of Jamaica or for requiring him to leave such territory.

5. No person referred to in paragraph 1 shall be required by the Government to leave Jamaica save in the event of an abuse of the right of residence, in which case the following procedures shall apply:

(a) No proceeding shall be instituted to require any such person to leave Jamaica except with the prior approval of the Minister for Foreign Affairs of Jamaica;

(b) In the case of the representative of a member of the Authority or observer State, such approval shall be given only after consultation with the Government of the member or observer State concerned;

(c) In the case of any other person mentioned in paragraph 1, such approval shall be given only after consultation with the Secretary-General, and if expulsion proceedings are taken against any such person, the Secretary-General shall have the right to appear or to be represented in such proceedings on behalf of the person against whom such proceedings are instituted; and

(d) Officials of the Authority who are entitled to diplomatic privileges and immunities under article 34 shall not be required to leave Jamaica otherwise than in accordance with the customary procedure applicable to members, having comparable rank, of diplomatic missions in Jamaica.

6. It is understood that persons referred to in paragraph 1 shall not be exempt from the reasonable application of quarantine and other health regulations.

7. This article shall not prevent the requirement of reasonable evidence to establish that persons claiming the rights granted by this article come within the classes described in paragraph 1.

8. The Secretary-General and the competent authorities shall, at the request of either of them, consult as to methods of facilitating entry in Jamaica by persons coming from abroad who wish to visit the Headquarters and

do not enjoy the privileges and immunities provided by articles 33, 34, 35 and 36.

Article 27

Establishment of missions

1. A member of the Authority may establish a permanent mission and an observer State may establish a permanent observer mission in Jamaica for the purposes of the representation of that State to the Authority. Such mission shall be accredited to the Authority.

2. A member of the Authority and an observer State shall notify the Secretary-General of their intention to establish a permanent mission or observer mission.

3. The Secretary-General shall notify the Government of the intention of a member of the Authority or an observer State to establish a permanent mission or a permanent observer mission upon receipt of such notification.

4. The permanent mission or the permanent observer mission shall notify the Secretary-General of the names of the members of their missions, as well as the names of spouses and dependent members of their families.

5. The Secretary-General shall communicate to the Government a list of persons referred to in paragraph 4 and shall revise such list from time to time as may be necessary.

6. The Government shall provide the members of the permanent mission or the permanent observer mission and their spouses and dependent members of their families with an identity card certifying that they are enjoying the privileges, immunities and facilities specified in this Agreement. This card shall serve to identify the holder in relation to the competent authorities.

Article 28

Privileges and immunities of missions

The permanent mission or the permanent observer mission shall enjoy the same privileges and immunities as are accorded to a diplomatic mission in Jamaica.

Article 29

Privileges and immunities of members of missions

Members of the permanent mission or of the permanent observer mission shall be entitled to the same privileges and immunities as the Government accords to the members, having comparable rank, of a diplomatic mission in Jamaica.

Article 30

Notification

1. The members of the Authority or the observer States shall notify the Authority of the appointment, position and title of the members of the permanent mission or of the observer mission, their arrival, final departure or the termination of their functions with the mission and any other changes affecting their status that occur in the course of their service with the mission.

2. The Authority shall provide the Government with the information referred to in paragraph 1.

Article 31

Assistance by the Authority in respect of privileges and immunities

1. The Authority shall, where necessary, assist the members of the Authority or the observer States, their permanent missions and the members of such mission in securing the enjoyment of the privileges and immunities provided for under this Agreement.

2. The Authority shall, where necessary, assist the Government in securing the discharge of the obligations of the members of the Authority and of the observer States, their missions and members of such missions in respect of the privileges and immunities provided for under this Agreement.

Article 32

Privileges and immunities of the officials of the Authority

1. Without prejudice to article 34, the officials of the Authority, regardless of their nationality and rank, shall enjoy in the territory of Jamaica the following privileges and immunities:

(a) Immunity from legal process in respect of words spoken and written, and of acts performed by them in their official capacity; such immunity to continue notwithstanding that the persons concerned may have ceased to be officials of the Authority;

(b) Immunity from personal arrest or detention in relation to acts performed by them in their official capacity;

(c) Immunity from inspection and seizure of personal and official baggage, except in case of flagrante delicto. In such cases the competent authorities shall immediately inform the Secretary-General. Inspections shall, in the case of personal baggage, be conducted only in the presence of the official concerned or his authorized representative, and in the case of official baggage, in the presence of the Secretary-General or his authorized representative;

(d) Exemption from taxation in respect of salaries and emoluments paid or any other form of payment made by the Authority;

(e) Exemption from any form of taxation on income derived by them from sources outside Jamaica;

(f) Exemption from registration fees in respect of their automobiles;

(g) Exemption from immigration restrictions and alien registration procedures;

(h) Exemption from national service obligations, provided that, with respect to Jamaican nationals, such exemption shall be confined to officials of the Authority whose names have, by reason of their duties, been placed upon a list compiled by the Secretary-General and approved by the Government; provided further that, should officials of the Authority, other than those listed, who are Jamaican nationals be called up for national service, the Government shall, upon request of the Secretary-General, grant such temporary deferments in the call-up of such officials of the Authority as may be necessary to avoid interruption of the essential work of the Authority;

(i) The right to purchase petrol free of duty for their vehicles on similar terms as are accorded to members of diplomatic missions in Jamaica;

(j) Exemption for themselves for the purpose of official business from any restrictions on movements and travel inside Jamaica;

(k) In regard to foreign exchange, including holding accounts in foreign currencies, enjoyment of the same facilities as are accorded to members of diplomatic missions in Jamaica;

(l) Enjoyment of the same protection and repatriation facilities as are accorded to members of diplomatic missions in Jamaica, in time of international crisis;

(m) The right to import for personal use, free of duty and other levies, prohibitions and restrictions on imports:

(i) Their furniture, household and personal effects, in one or more separate shipments, and thereafter to import necessary additions to the same;

(ii) In accordance with the relevant laws of Jamaica, one automobile, every three years, and in cases where the official is accompanied by dependants, a second automobile on the basis of representations to the Government by the Secretary-General; however, where the Secretary-General and the Government agree, in particular cases, replacement may take place at an earlier date in the event of loss, extensive damage or otherwise; automobiles may be sold in Jamaica after their importation, subject to the laws concerning the payment of customs duties and established diplomatic practice in Jamaica during his or her assignment. After three years such automobiles can be sold without payment of customs duties;

(iii) Reasonable quantities of certain articles including liquor, tobacco, cigarettes and foodstuffs, for personal use or consumption and not for gift or sale. The Authority may establish a commissary for the sale of such articles to the officials of the Authority and members of delegations. A supplementary agreement shall be concluded between the Secretary-General and the Government to regulate the exercise of these rights.

2. The facilities, privileges and immunities granted to the officials of the Authority in paragraphs 1 (g), 1 (h), 1 (j), and 1 (l) shall extend to their spouses and to dependent family members.

Article 33

Additional privileges and immunities of the Secretary-General and other senior officials of the Authority

1. The Secretary-General and the Director-General shall be accorded the same privileges and immunities as are accorded to heads of diplomatic missions in Jamaica.

2. Officials of the Authority at the P-4 level and above, and such additional categories of officials of the Authority as may be designated in an agreement with the Government by the Secretary-General on the ground of the responsibilities of their positions in the Authority regardless of their nationality, shall enjoy the privileges and immunities as the Government accords to the members, having comparable rank, of a diplomatic mission in Jamaica.

Article 34

Application of the Agreement to officials of other international organizations

The provisions of articles 32, 33, paragraph 2, and 36 shall apply to the officials of the United Nations and of its specialized agencies and the International Atomic Energy Agency, attached to the Authority on a continuing basis.

Article 35

Privileges and immunities of experts

1. Experts, other than the officials of the Authority, while performing the functions assigned to them by the Authority or in the course of their travel to take up those functions or perform those duties, shall enjoy the following privileges, immunities and facilities that are necessary for the effective exercise of their duties:

(a) Immunity from legal process in respect of words spoken and written and all acts performed by them in their official capacity, such immunity to continue notwithstanding that the persons concerned may have ceased to exercise their functions with the Authority;

(b) Immunity from personal arrest or detention in relation to acts performed by them in their official capacity;

(c) Immunity from inspection and seizure of personal and official baggage, except in case of flagrante delicto. In such cases the competent authorities shall immediately inform the Secretary-General. Inspections shall, in the case of personal baggage, be conducted only in the presence of the official concerned or his authorized representative, and in the case of official baggage, in the presence of the Secretary-General or his authorized representative;

(d) Exemption from taxation in respect of the salaries and emoluments paid or any other form of payment made by the Authority, provided that nationals of Jamaica may enjoy such exemptions as may be accorded by the Government;

(e) Inviolability of all papers, documents and other official material;

(f) The right, for the purpose of all communications with the Authority, to use codes and to dispatch or receive papers, correspondence or other official material by courier or in sealed bags;

(g) Exemption from immigration restrictions, alien registration and national service obligations;

(h) Enjoyment of the same protection and repatriation facilities as are accorded to the members of diplomatic missions in Jamaica;

(i) The same privileges with respect to currency and exchange restrictions as are accorded to representatives of foreign Governments on temporary official missions.

2. The facilities, privileges and immunities granted to experts in paragraphs 1 (g) and (h) shall extend to their spouses and dependent family members.

Article 36

Waiver of immunity of the officials of the Authority and experts

Privileges and immunities are granted to the officials of the Authority and experts in the interests of the Authority and not for their own personal benefit. The Secretary-General shall have the right and the duty to waive the immunity of any official of the Authority or expert in any case where, in his opinion, the immunity would impede the course of justice and can be waived without prejudice to the interests of the Authority. In the case of the Secretary-General, the Council shall have the right to waive the immunity.

Article 37

List of officials of the Authority and experts

The Secretary-General shall communicate to the Government a list of persons referred to in articles 32, 33, 34 and 35 and shall revise such list from time to time as may be necessary.

Article 38

Abuse of privilege or immunity

1. The Secretary-General shall take every precaution to ensure that no abuse of a privilege or immunity conferred by this Agreement shall occur and, for this purpose, the Council shall adopt rules and regulations as may be deemed necessary and expedient for officials of the Authority.

2. Should the Government consider that an abuse of a privilege or immunity conferred by this Agreement has occurred, the Secretary-General shall, upon request, consult with the Government to determine whether any such abuse has occurred. If such consultations fail to achieve a result satisfactory to the Secretary-General and to the Government, the matter shall be determined in accordance with the procedure set out in article 48.

Article 39

Identity card

The Government shall provide the officials of the Authority and the experts with an identity card certifying that they are enjoying the privileges, immunities and facilities specified in this Agreement. This card shall also serve to identify the holder in relation to the competent authorities.

Article 40

Cooperation with the competent authorities

The Authority shall cooperate at all times with the competent authorities to facilitate the proper administration of justice, secure the observance of police regulations and avoid the occurrence of any abuse in connection with the privileges, immunities and facilities mentioned in this Agreement.

Article 41

Respect for the laws of Jamaica

Without prejudice to the privileges, immunities and facilities accorded by this Agreement, it is the duty of all persons enjoying such privileges, immunities and facilities to respect the laws of Jamaica. They also have the duty not to interfere in the internal affairs of Jamaica.

Article 42

Laissez-passer

1. The Government shall recognize and accept laissez-passer issued to the officials of the Authority as a valid travel document equivalent to a passport.

2. The Government shall recognize and accept certificates issued to experts and other persons travelling on the business of the Authority. The Government agrees to issue any required visas based on such certificates.

3. Applications for visas from the holders of laissez-passer, when accompanied by a certificate that they are travelling on the business of the Authority, shall be dealt with as speedily as possible.

4. Similar facilities to those specified in paragraph 3 shall be accorded to experts and other persons who, though not holders of laissez-passer, have a certificate that they are travelling on the business of the Authority.

Article 43

Social security and pension funds

1. The United Nations Joint Staff Pension Fund shall, when the Authority is a member, enjoy legal capacity in Jamaica and shall enjoy the same exemptions, privileges and immunities as the Authority itself.

2. The Authority shall be exempt from all compulsory contributions to, and officials of the Authority shall not be required by the Government to participate in, any social security scheme of Jamaica.

3. The Government shall make such provision as may be necessary to enable any official of the Authority who is not afforded social security coverage by the Authority to participate, if the Authority so requests, in any social security scheme of Jamaica, to the extent that such scheme exists. The Authority shall, insofar as possible, arrange, under conditions to be agreed upon, for the participation in any Jamaican social security system, to the extent that such a system exists, of those locally recruited members of its staff who do not participate in the United Nations Joint Staff Pension Fund or to whom the Authority does not grant social security protection at least equivalent to that offered under the laws of Jamaica.

Article 44

Responsibility, liability and insurance

1. Jamaica shall not incur by reason of the location of the Headquarters within its territory any international responsibility for acts or omissions of the Authority or of its officials acting or abstaining from acting within the scope of their functions, other than the international responsibility which Jamaica would incur as a member of the Authority.

2. Without prejudice to its immunities under this Agreement, the Authority shall carry insurance to cover liability for any injury or damage arising from activities of the Authority in Jamaica or from its use of the Headquarters that may be suffered by persons other than the officials of the Authority, or by the Government. To this end, the competent authorities shall make every reasonable effort to secure for the Authority, at reasonable rates, insurance coverage permitting claims to be submitted directly to the insurer by parties suffering injury or damage. Such claims and liability shall, without prejudice to the privileges and immunities of the Authority, be governed by the laws of Jamaica.

Article 45

Security

Without prejudice to the performance of its functions by the Authority in a normal and unrestricted manner, the Government may take every preventive measure to preserve the national security of Jamaica after consultation with the Secretary-General.

Article 46

Responsibility of the Government

Whenever this Agreement imposes obligations on the competent authorities, the ultimate responsibility for the fulfilment of such obligations shall rest with the Government.

Article 47

Special agreement relating to the Enterprise

The provisions of this Agreement relating to the Enterprise may be supplemented by a special agreement to be concluded between the Enterprise and the Government in accordance with Annex IV, article 13, paragraph 1, of the Convention.

Article 48

Settlement of disputes

1. The Authority shall make suitable provisions for the proper settlement of:

(a) Disputes arising out of contracts, or disputes of a private law character to which the Authority is a party;

(b) Disputes involving an official of the Authority or any person who by reason of his official position enjoys immunity, if such immunity has not been waived.

2. Any dispute between the Authority and the competent authorities concerning the interpretation or application of this Agreement or of any

supplementary agreement, or any question affecting the Headquarters or the relationship between the Authority and the Government which is not settled by consultation, negotiation or other agreed mode of settlement within three months following such a request by one of the parties to the dispute, shall be referred, at the request of either party to the dispute, for a final and binding decision to a panel of three arbitrators: one to be nominated by the Secretary-General, one to be nominated by the Government. If either or both of the nominations are not made within three months following the request for arbitration, the President of the International Tribunal for the Law of the Sea shall proceed to make the appointment. The third arbitrator, who shall be the chairman of the panel, shall be chosen by the first two arbitrators. Should the first two arbitrators fail to agree upon the appointment of the third arbitrator within three months following the nomination or appointment of the first two arbitrators, such third arbitrator shall be chosen by the President of the International Tribunal for the Law of the Sea at the request of the Authority or the Government.

Article 49

Application of the Agreement

This Agreement shall apply irrespective of whether the Government maintains diplomatic relations with a member of the Authority or an observer State. It shall be applied to all persons entitled to privileges and immunities under this Agreement, regardless of their nationality and irrespective of whether their State grants a similar privilege or immunity to diplomatic agents or nationals of Jamaica.

Article 50

Relationship between the Agreement and the Protocol

The provisions of this Agreement shall be complementary to the provisions of the Protocol. Insofar as any provision of this Agreement and any provisions of the Protocol relate to the same subject matter, the two provisions shall, wherever possible, be treated as complementary, so that both provisions shall be applicable and neither shall narrow the effect of the other; but in any case of conflict, the provisions of this Agreement shall prevail.

Article 51

Supplementary agreements

1. The Authority and the Government may enter into such supplementary agreements as may be necessary.

2. If and to the extent that the Government shall enter into any agreement with any intergovernmental organization containing terms or conditions more favourable to that organization than similar terms or conditions of this Agreement, the Government shall extend such more favourable terms or conditions to the Authority, by means of a supplemental agreement.

3. Paragraph 2 shall not apply to any terms or conditions granted by the Government pursuant to any agreement establishing a customs union, free-trade area or economic integration organization.

Article 52

Amendments

Consultations with respect to amendments to this Agreement shall be entered into at the request of either party. Any such amendment shall be by mutual consent and shall be expressed in an exchange of letters or an agreement concluded by the Authority and the Government.

Article 53

Termination of the Agreement

This Agreement shall cease to be in force by mutual consent of the Authority and the Government, except for such provisions as may be applicable in connection with the orderly termination of the operations of the Authority at its Headquarters in Jamaica and the disposal of its property therein.

Article 54

Final provisions

1. This Agreement shall enter into force on its approval by the Assembly of the Authority and the Government of Jamaica.

2. This Agreement shall be applied provisionally by the Authority and the Government upon signature by the Secretary-General of the Authority and on behalf of the Government of Jamaica.

INTERNATIONAL SEABED AUTHORITY **ISBA**

Assembly

Council

Distr.
LIMITED

ISBA/3/A/L.2
ISBA/3/C/L.2
24 February 1997

ORIGINAL: ENGLISH

INTERNATIONAL SEABED AUTHORITY
Third session
Kingston, Jamaica
17–27 March 1997

Agreement concerning the relationship between the United Nations and the International Seabed Authority

1. At the resumed second session of the Authority, held at Kingston from 5 to 16 August 1996, the Council requested the Secretary-General to negotiate with the Secretary-General of the United Nations a relationship agreement, taking into account the draft of such an agreement prepared by the Preparatory Commission for the International Seabed Authority and for the International Tribunal for the Law of the Sea (ISBA/C/10).

2. The Council also decided that the agreement should be provisionally applied upon its signature and that it would enter into force on its approval by the Assembly of the Authority and the General Assembly of the United Nations.

3. In January 1997, in accordance with the Council's directive, negotiations took place between officials of the Authority and officials of the United Nations. The outcome of these negotiations was the Agreement concerning the relationship between the United Nations and the International Seabed Authority, contained in the annex to the present document.

4. The Council is invited to recommend to the Assembly that it approve the Agreement concerning the relationship between the United Nations and the International Seabed Authority.

Annex

AGREEMENT CONCERNING THE RELATIONSHIP BETWEEN THE UNITED NATIONS AND THE INTERNATIONAL SEABED AUTHORITY

The United Nations and the International Seabed Authority,

Bearing in mind that the General Assembly of the United Nations in its resolution 3067 (XXVIII) of 16 November 1973 decided to convene the Third United Nations Conference on the Law of the Sea for the adoption of a convention dealing with all matters relating to the law of the sea and that the Conference adopted the United Nations Convention on the Law of the Sea, which, inter alia, establishes the International Seabed Authority,

Recalling that the General Assembly of the United Nations in its resolution 48/263 of 28 July 1994 adopted the Agreement relating to the Implementation of Part XI of the United Nations Convention on the Law of the Sea of 10 December 1982,

Mindful of the entry into force of the United Nations Convention on the Law of the Sea on 16 November 1994 and the entry into force of the Agreement relating to the Implementation of Part XI of the United Nations Convention on the Law of the Sea of 10 December 1982 on 28 July 1996,

Noting General Assembly resolution 51/6 of 24 October 1996 inviting the International Seabed Authority to participate in the deliberations of the General Assembly in the capacity of observer,

Noting further article 162, paragraph 2 (f), of the United Nations Convention on the Law of the Sea of 10 December 1982, General Assembly resolution 51/34 of 9 December 1996 and decision ISBA/C/10 of 12 August 1996 of the Council of the International Seabed Authority calling for the conclusion of a relationship agreement between the United Nations and the International Seabed Authority,

Desiring to make provision for an effective system of mutually beneficial relationship whereby the discharge of their respective responsibilities may be facilitated,

Taking into account for this purpose the provisions of the Charter of the United Nations, the provisions of the United Nations Convention on the Law of the Sea and the provisions of the Agreement relating to the Implementation of Part XI of the United Nations Convention on the Law of the Sea of 10 December 1982,

Have agreed as follows:

Article 1

Purpose of the Agreement

This Agreement, which is entered into by the United Nations and the International Seabed Authority (hereinafter referred to as "the Authority"), pursuant to the provisions of the Charter of the United Nations (hereinafter referred to as "the Charter") and the provisions of the United Nations Convention on the Law of the Sea (hereinafter referred to as "the Convention") and the Agreement relating to the Implementation of Part XI of the United Nations Convention on the Law of the Sea of 10 December 1982 (hereinafter referred to as "the Agreement") respectively, is intended to define the terms on which the United Nations and the Authority shall be brought into relationship.

Article 2

Principles

1. The United Nations recognizes the Authority as the organization through which States Parties to the Convention shall, in accordance with Part XI of the Convention and the Agreement, organize and control activities in the seabed and ocean floor and subsoil thereof, beyond the limits of national jurisdiction (hereinafter referred to as "the Area"), particularly with a view to administering the resources of the Area. The United Nations undertakes to conduct its activities in such a manner as to promote the legal order for the seas and oceans established by the Convention and the Agreement.

2. The United Nations recognizes that the Authority, by virtue of the Convention and the Agreement, shall function as an autonomous international organization in the working relationship with the United Nations established by this Agreement.

3. The Authority recognizes the responsibilities of the United Nations under the Charter and other international instruments, in particular in the fields of international peace and security and economic, social, cultural and humanitarian development, protection and preservation of the environment.

4. The Authority undertakes to conduct its activities in accordance with the purposes and principles of the Charter to promote peace and international cooperation and in conformity with the policies of the United Nations furthering these purposes and principles.

Article 3

Cooperation and coordination

1. The United Nations and the Authority recognize the desirability of achieving effective coordination of the activities of the Authority with those of the United Nations and the specialized agencies, and of avoiding unnecessary duplication of activities.

2. The United Nations and the Authority agree that, with a view to facilitating the effective discharge of their respective responsibilities, they will cooperate closely with each other and consult each other on matters of mutual interest.

Article 4

Assistance to the Security Council

1. The Authority shall cooperate with the Security Council by providing to it at its request such information and assistance as may be required in the exercise of its responsibility for the maintenance or restoration of international peace and security. In case confidential information is provided, the Security Council shall preserve its confidential character.

2. At the invitation of the Security Council, the Secretary-General of the Authority may attend its meetings to supply it with information or give it other assistance with regard to matters within the competence of the Authority.

Article 5

International Court of Justice

The Authority agrees, subject to the provisions of this Agreement relating to the safeguarding of confidential material, data and information, to provide any information which may be requested by the International Court of Justice in accordance with the Statute of that Court.

Article 6

Reciprocal representation

1. Without prejudice to the decision of the General Assembly in resolution 51/6 of 4 November 1996 granting observer status to the Authority, and subject to such decisions as may be taken concerning the attendance of their meetings by observers, the United Nations shall, subject to the rules of procedure and practice of the bodies concerned, invite the Authority to send representatives to meetings and conferences of other competent bodies, whenever matters of interest to the Authority are discussed.

2. Subject to such decisions as may be taken by its competent bodies concerning the attendance of their meetings by observers, the Authority shall, subject to the rules of procedure and practice of the bodies concerned, invite the United Nations to send representatives to all its meetings and conferences, whenever matters of interest to the United Nations are discussed.

3. Written statements submitted by the United Nations to the Authority for distribution shall be distributed by the secretariat of the Authority to all members of the appropriate organ or organs of the Authority in accordance with the relevant rules of procedure. Written statements presented by the Authority to the United Nations for distribution shall be distributed by the Secretariat of the United Nations to all members of the appropriate organ or organs of the United Nations in accordance with the relevant rules of procedure. Such written statements will be circulated in the quantities and languages in which they are made available to the respective secretariat.

Article 7

Cooperation between the two secretariats

The Secretary-General of the United Nations and the Secretary-General of the Authority shall consult from time to time regarding the implementation of their respective responsibilities under the Convention and the Agreement. They shall consult, in particular, regarding such administrative arrangements as may be necessary to enable the two organizations effectively to carry out their functions and to ensure effective cooperation and liaison between their secretariats.

Article 8

Exchange of information, data and documents

1. The United Nations and the Authority shall arrange for the exchange of information, publications and reports of mutual interest.

2. In fulfilment of the responsibilities entrusted to him under article 319, subparagraphs 2 (a) and (b) of the Convention and assumed by him pursuant to General Assembly resolution 37/66 of 3 December 1982, the Secretary-General of the United Nations shall report to the Authority from time to time on issues of a general nature that have arisen with respect to the Convention and shall regularly notify the Authority of ratifications and formal confirmations of and accessions to the Convention and amendments thereto, as well as of denunciations of the Convention.

3. The United Nations and the Authority shall cooperate in obtaining from States Parties to the Convention copies of charts or lists of geographical coordinates of the outer limit lines of their continental shelf as referred to in article 84 of the Convention. They will exchange copies of such lists of coordinates or, to the extent practicable, charts.

4. Where the outer limits of the national jurisdiction of a State Party are defined by the outer limit of the exclusive economic zone, the United Nations shall provide to the Authority copies of such lists of geographical coordinates or, to the extent practicable, charts, indicating the outer limit lines of the

exclusive economic zone of such State Party as may be deposited with the Secretary-General of the United Nations pursuant to article 75, paragraph 2, of the Convention.

5. The Authority, to the extent practicable, shall furnish special studies or information requested by the United Nations. The submission of such reports, studies and information shall be subject to conditions set forth in article 14.

6. The United Nations and the Authority are subject to necessary limitations for the safeguarding of confidential material, data and information furnished to them by their members or others. Subject to article 4, paragraph 1, nothing in this Agreement shall be construed to require either the United Nations or the Authority to furnish any material, data and information the furnishing of which could, in its judgement, constitute a violation of the confidence of any of its members or anyone from whom it shall have received such information, or which would otherwise interfere with the orderly conduct of its operation.

Article 9

Statistical services

The United Nations and the Authority, recognizing the desirability of maximum cooperation in the statistical field and of minimizing the burdens placed on Governments and other organizations from which information may be collected, undertake to avoid undesirable duplication between them with respect to the collection, analysis and publication of statistics, and agree to consult with each other on the most efficient use of resources and of technical personnel in the field of statistics.

Article 10

Technical assistance

The United Nations and the Authority undertake to work together in the provision of technical assistance in the fields of marine scientific research in the Area, transfer of technology and the prevention, reduction and control of pollution of the marine environment from activities in the Area. In particular, they agree to take such measures as may be necessary to achieve effective coordination of their technical assistance activities within the framework of existing coordinating machinery in the field of technical assistance, taking into account the respective roles and responsibilities of the United Nations and the Authority under their constitutive instruments, as well as those of other organizations participating in technical assistance activities.

Article 11

Personnel arrangements

1. The United Nations and the Authority agree to apply, in the interests of uniform standards of international employment and to the extent feasible, common personnel standards, methods and arrangements designed to avoid unjustified differences in terms and conditions of employment and to facilitate interchange of personnel in order to obtain the maximum benefit from their services.

2. To the end, the United Nations and the Authority agree:

(a) To consult together from time to time concerning matters of common interest relating to the terms and conditions of employment of the officers and staff, with a view to securing as much uniformity in these matters as may be feasible;

(b) To cooperate in the interchange of personnel when desirable, on a temporary or a permanent basis, making due provision for the retention of seniority and pension rights;

(c) To cooperate in the establishment and operation of suitable machinery for the settlement of disputes arising in connection with the employment of personnel and related matters.

3. Pursuant to decision ISBA/A/15 of 15 August 1996 of the Assembly of the International Seabed Authority, and upon the approval of the General Assembly of the United Nations, the Authority shall participate in the United Nations Joint Staff Pension Fund in accordance with the Regulations of the Fund and shall accept the jurisdiction of the United Nations Administrative Tribunal in matters involving applications alleging non-observance of those Regulations.

4. The terms and conditions on which any facilities or services of the Authority or the United Nations in connection with the matters referred to in this article are to be extended to the other shall, where necessary, be the subject of supplementary arrangements concluded for this purpose.

Article 12

Conference services

1. Unless the General Assembly of the United Nations, after giving reasonable notice to the Authority, decides otherwise, the United Nations will make available to the Authority, on a reimbursable basis, such facilities and services as may be required for the meetings of the Authority, including translation and interpretation services, documentation and conference services.

2. The terms and conditions on which any facilities or services of the United Nations in connection with the matters referred to in this article may be extended to the Authority shall, where necessary, be the subject of separate arrangements concluded for this purpose.

Article 13

Budgetary and financial matters

The Authority recognizes the desirability of establishing close budgetary and financial cooperation with the United Nations aimed at benefiting from the experience of the United Nations in this field.

Article 14

Financing of services

The costs and expenses resulting from the provision of services pursuant to this Agreement shall be the subject of separate arrangements between the Authority and the United Nations.

Article 15

United Nations laissez-passer

Without prejudice to the right of the Authority to issue its own travel documents, officials of the Authority shall be entitled, in accordance with such special arrangements as may be concluded between the Secretary-General of the United Nations and the Secretary-General of the Authority, to use the laissez-passer of the United Nations as a valid travel document where such use is recognized under the Protocol on the Privileges and Immunities of the International Seabed Authority or other agreements defining the privileges and immunities of the Authority.

Article 16

Implementation of the Agreement

The Secretary-General of the United Nations and the Secretary-General of the Authority may enter into such supplementary arrangements for the implementation of this Agreement as may be found desirable.

Article 17

Amendments

This Agreement may be amended by agreement between the United Nations and the Authority. Any such amendment agreed upon shall enter into force on its approval by the General Assembly of the United Nations and the Assembly of the Authority.

Article 18

Entry into force

1. This Agreement shall enter into force on its approval by the General Assembly of the United Nations and the Assembly of the Authority.

2. This Agreement shall be applied provisionally by the United Nations and the Authority upon signature by the Secretary-General of the United Nations and the Secretary-General of the Authority.

INTERNATIONAL SEABED AUTHORITY

Assembly

Distr.
GENERAL

ISBA/4/A/8
30 March 1998

ORIGINAL: ENGLISH

INTERNATIONAL SEABED AUTHORITY
Fourth session
Kingston, Jamaica
16–27 March 1998

DECISION OF THE ASSEMBLY OF THE INTERNATIONAL SEABED AUTHORITY RELATING TO THE PROTOCOL ON THE PRIVILEGES AND IMMUNITIES OF THE INTERNATIONAL SEABED AUTHORITY

The Assembly of the International Seabed Authority

1. Adopts the Protocol on the Privileges and Immunities of the International Seabed Authority, which is annexed to the present document;

2. Notes that the provisions of article 8, paragraph 3, of the Protocol will apply to the Director-General of the Enterprise, when elected;

3. Decides that the Protocol, in accordance with article 15 thereof, shall be open for signature at the headquarters of the Authority from 17 to 28 August 1998 and subsequently until 16 August 2000 at United Nations headquarters in New York;

4. Encourages those members of the Authority which intend to ratify, approve, accept or accede to the Protocol to apply the Protocol provisionally in accordance with article 19 thereof as soon as possible after it is opened for signature.

54th Meeting
26 March 1998

Annex

PROTOCOL ON THE PRIVILEGES AND IMMUNITIES OF THE INTERNATIONAL SEABED AUTHORITY

The States Parties to this Protocol,

Considering that the United Nations Convention on the Law of the Sea establishes the International Seabed Authority,

Recalling that article 176 of the United Nations Convention on the Law of the Sea provides that the Authority shall have international legal personality and such legal capacity as may be necessary for the exercise of its functions and the fulfilment of its purposes,

Noting that article 177 of the United Nations Convention on the Law of the Sea provides that the Authority shall enjoy in the territory of each State Party to the Convention the privileges and immunities set forth in section 4, subsection G of Part XI of the Convention and that the privileges and immunities of the Enterprise shall be those set forth in annex IV, article 13,

Recognizing that certain additional privileges and immunities are necessary for the exercise of the functions of the International Seabed Authority,

Have agreed as follows:

Article 1

Use of terms

For the purposes of this Protocol:

(a) "Authority" means the International Seabed Authority;

(b) "Convention" means the United Nations Convention on the Law of the Sea of 10 December 1982;

(c) "Agreement" means the Agreement relating to the Implementation of Part XI of the United Nations Convention on the Law of the Sea of 10 December 1982. In accordance with the Agreement, its provisions and Part XI of the Convention are to be interpreted and applied together as a single instrument; this Protocol and references in this Protocol to the Convention are to be interpreted and applied accordingly;

(d) "Enterprise" means the organ of the Authority as provided for in the Convention;

(e) "member of the Authority" means:

- (i) any State Party to the Convention; and
- (ii) any State or entity which is a member of the Authority on a provisional basis pursuant to paragraph 12(a) of section 1 of the annex to the Agreement;

(f) "representatives" means representatives, alternate representatives, advisers, technical experts and secretaries of the delegations;

(g) "Secretary-General" means the Secretary-General of the International Seabed Authority.

Article 2

General provision

Without prejudice to the legal status, privileges and immunities accorded to the Authority and the Enterprise set forth in section 4, subsection G, of Part XI and Annex IV, article 13, of the Convention respectively, each State Party to this Protocol shall accord to the Authority and its organs, the representatives of members of the Authority, officials of the Authority and experts on mission for the Authority such privileges and immunities as are specified in this Protocol.

Article 3

Legal personality of the Authority

The Authority shall possess legal personality. It shall have the legal capacity:

(a) to contract;

(b) to acquire and dispose of immovable and movable property;

(c) to be a party in legal proceedings.

Article 4

Inviolability of the premises of the Authority

The premises of the Authority shall be inviolable.

Article 5

Financial facilities of the Authority

1. Without being restricted by financial controls, regulations or moratoriums of any kind, the Authority may freely:

(a) purchase any currencies through authorized channels and hold and dispose of them;

(b) hold funds, securities, gold, precious metals or currency of any kind and operate accounts in any currency;

(c) transfer its funds, securities, gold or currency from one country to another or within any country and convert any currency held by it into any other currency.

2. The Authority shall, in exercising its rights under paragraph 1 of this article, pay due regard to any representations made by the Government of any member of the Authority in so far as it is considered that effect can be given to such representations without detriment to the interests of the Authority.

Article 6

Flag and emblem

The Authority shall be entitled to display its flag and emblem at its premises and on vehicles used for official purposes.

Article 7

Representatives of members of the Authority

1. Representatives of members of the Authority attending meetings convened by the Authority shall, while exercising their functions and during their journey to and from the place of meeting, enjoy the following privileges and immunities:

(a) immunity from legal process in respect of words spoken or written, and all acts performed by them in the exercise of their functions, except to the extent that the member which they represent expressly waives this immunity in a particular case;

(b) immunity from personal arrest or detention and the same immunities and facilities in respect of their personal baggage as are accorded to diplomatic envoys;

(c) inviolability for all papers and documents;

(d) the right to use codes and to receive papers or correspondence by courier or in sealed bags;

(e) exemption in respect of themselves and their spouses from immigration restrictions, alien registration or national service obligations in the State they are visiting or through which they are passing in the exercise of their functions;

(f) the same facilities as regards exchange restrictions as are accorded to representatives of foreign Governments of comparable rank on temporary official missions.

2. In order to secure, for the representatives of members of the Authority, complete freedom of speech and independence in the discharge of their duties, the immunity from legal process in respect of all acts done by them in discharging their functions shall continue to be accorded, notwithstanding that the persons concerned are no longer representatives of members of the Authority.

3. Where the incidence of any form of taxation depends upon residence, periods during which the representatives of members of the Authority attending the meetings of the Authority are present in the territory of a member of the Authority for the discharge of their duties shall not be considered as periods of residence.

4. Privileges and immunities are accorded to the representatives of members of the Authority, not for the personal benefit of the individuals themselves, but in order to safeguard the independent exercise of their functions in connection with the Authority. Consequently, a member of the Authority has the right and the duty to waive the immunity of its representative in any case where in the opinion of the member of the Authority the immunity would impede the course of justice, and it can be waived without prejudice to the purpose for which the immunity is accorded.

5. Representatives of members of the Authority shall have insurance coverage against third-party risks in respect of vehicles owned or operated by them, as required by the laws and regulations of the State in which the vehicle is operated.

6. The provisions of paragraphs 1, 2 and 3 are not applicable as between a representative and the authorities of the member of the Authority of which he or she is a national or of which he or she is or has been a representative.

Article 8

Officials

1. The Secretary-General will specify the categories of officials to which the provisions of paragraph 2 of this article shall apply. The Secretary-General shall submit these categories to the Assembly. Thereafter these categories shall be communicated to the Governments of all members of the Authority. The names of the officials included in these categories shall from time to time be made known to the Governments of members of the Authority.

2. Officials of the Authority, regardless of nationality, shall:

(a) be immune from legal process in respect of words spoken or written and all acts performed by them in their official capacity;

(b) be immune from personal arrest or detention in relation to acts performed by them in their official capacity;

(c) be exempt from tax in respect of salaries and emoluments paid or any other form of payment made by the Authority;

(d) be immune from national service obligations provided that, in relation to States of which they are nationals, such immunity shall be confined to officials of the Authority whose names have, by reason of their duties, been placed upon a list compiled by the Secretary-General and approved by the State concerned; should other officials of the Authority be called up for national service, the State concerned shall, at the request of the Secretary-General, grant such temporary deferments in the call-up of such officials as may be necessary to avoid interruption in the continuation of essential work;

(e) be exempt, together with their spouses and relatives dependent on them, from immigration restrictions and alien registration;

(f) be accorded the same privileges in respect of exchange facilities as are accorded to the officials of comparable ranks forming part of diplomatic missions to the Governments concerned;

(g) have the right to import free of duty their furniture and effects at the time of first taking up their post in the country in question;

(h) be exempt from inspection of personal baggage, unless there are serious grounds for believing that the baggage contains articles not for personal use or articles the import or export of which is prohibited by the law or controlled by the quarantine regulations of the Party concerned; and inspection in such a case shall be conducted in the presence of the official concerned, and in the case of official baggage, in the presence of the Secretary-General or his or her authorized representative;

(i) be given, together with their spouses and relatives dependent on them, the same repatriation facilities in time of international crises as are accorded to diplomatic agents.

3. In addition to the privileges and immunities specified in paragraph 2, the Secretary-General or any official acting on his behalf during his absence from duty and the Director-General of the Enterprise shall be accorded in respect of themselves, their spouses and minor children the privileges and immunities, exemptions and facilities accorded to diplomatic envoys, in accordance with international law.

4. Privileges and immunities are accorded to officials, not for the personal benefit of the individuals themselves, but in order to safeguard the independent exercise of their functions in connection with the Authority. The Secretary-General has the right and the duty to waive the immunity of any official where, in the opinion of the Secretary-General, the immunity would impede the course of justice, and it can be waived without prejudice to the interests of the Authority. In the case of the Secretary-General, the Assembly shall have the right to waive immunity.

5. The Authority shall cooperate at all times with the appropriate authorities of members of the Authority to facilitate the proper administration of justice, secure the observance of police regulations and prevent the occurrence of any abuse in connection with the privileges, immunities and facilities referred to in this article.

6. Pursuant to the laws and regulations of the State concerned, the officials of the Authority shall be required to have insurance coverage against third-party risks in respect of vehicles owned or operated by them.

Article 9

Experts on mission for the Authority

1. Experts (other than officials coming within the scope of article 8) performing missions for the Authority shall be accorded such privileges and immunities as are necessary for the independent exercise of their functions during the period of their missions, including the time spent on journeys in connection with their missions. In particular they shall be accorded:

(a) immunity from personal arrest or detention and from seizure of their personal baggage;

(b) in respect of words spoken or written and acts done by them in the exercise of their functions, immunity from legal process of every kind. This immunity shall continue notwithstanding that the persons concerned are no longer employed on missions for the Authority;

(c) inviolability for all papers and documents;

(d) for the purposes of their communications with the Authority, the right to use codes and to receive papers or correspondence by courier or in sealed bags;

(e) exemption from tax in respect of salaries and emoluments paid or any other form of payment made by the Authority. This provision is not applicable as between an expert and the member of the Authority of which he or she is a national;

(f) the same facilities in respect of currency or exchange restrictions as are accorded to representatives of foreign Governments on temporary official missions.

2. Privileges and immunities are accorded to experts, not for the personal benefit of the individuals themselves, but in order to safeguard the independent exercise of their functions in connection with the Authority. The Secretary-General shall have the right and the duty to waive the immunity of any expert where, in the opinion of the Secretary-General, the immunity would impede the course of justice, and it can be waived without prejudice to the interests of the Authority.

Article 10

Respect for laws and regulations

Without prejudice to their privileges and immunities, it is the duty of all persons referred to in articles 7, 8 and 9 to respect the laws and regulations of the member of the Authority in whose territory they may be on the business of the Authority or through whose territory they may pass on such business. They also have a duty not to interfere in the internal affairs of that member.

Article 11

Laissez-passer and visas

1. Without prejudice to the possibility for the Authority to issue its own travel documents, the States Parties to this Protocol shall recognize and accept the United Nations laissez-passer issued to officials of the Authority.

2. Applications for visas (where required) from officials of the Authority shall be dealt with as speedily as possible. Applications for visas (where required) from officials of the Authority holding United Nations laissez-passer shall be accompanied by a document confirming that they are travelling on the official business of the Authority.

Article 12

Relationship between the Headquarters Agreement and the Protocol

The provisions of this Protocol shall be complementary to the provisions of the Headquarters Agreement. Insofar as any provision of this Protocol relates to the same subject matter, the two provisions shall, wherever possible, be treated as complementary, so that both provisions shall be applicable and neither shall narrow the effect of the other; but in any case of conflict, the provisions of that Agreement shall prevail.

Article 13

Supplementary agreements

This Protocol shall in no way limit or prejudice the privileges and immunities which have been, or may hereafter be, accorded to the Authority by any member of the Authority by reason of the location in the territory of that member of the Authority's Headquarters or regional centres or offices. This Protocol shall not be deemed to prevent the conclusion of supplementary agreements between the Authority and any member of the Authority.

Article 14

Settlement of disputes

1. In connection with the implementation of the privileges and immunities granted under this Protocol, the Authority shall make suitable provision for the proper settlement of:

(a) disputes of a private law character to which the Authority is a party;

(b) disputes involving any official of the Authority or any expert on mission for the Authority who by reason of his or her official position enjoys immunity, if immunity has not been waived by the Secretary-General.

2. Any dispute between the Authority and a member of the Authority concerning the interpretation or application of this Protocol which is not settled by consultation, negotiation or other agreed mode of settlement within three months following a request by one of the parties to the dispute shall, at the request of either party, be referred for a final and binding decision to a panel of three arbitrators:

(a) one to be nominated by the Secretary-General, one to be nominated by the other party to the dispute and the third, who shall be Chairman of the panel, to be chosen by the first two arbitrators;

(b) if either party has failed to make its appointment of an arbitrator within two months of the appointment of an arbitrator by the other party, the President of the International Tribunal for the Law of the Sea shall proceed to make such appointment. Should the first two arbitrators fail to agree upon the appointment of the third arbitrator within three months following the appointment of the first two arbitrators, the third arbitrator shall be chosen by the President of the International Tribunal for the Law of the Sea upon the request of the Secretary-General or the other party to the dispute.

Article 15

Signature

This Protocol shall be open for signature by all members of the Authority at the Headquarters of the International Seabed Authority in Kingston, Jamaica, from 17 August until 28 August 1998 and subsequently until 16 August 2000 at United Nations Headquarters in New York.

Article 16

Ratification

This Protocol is subject to ratification, approval or acceptance. The instruments of ratification, approval or acceptance shall be deposited with the Secretary-General of the United Nations.

Article 17

Accession

This Protocol shall remain open for accession by all members of the Authority at any time. The instruments of accession shall be deposited with the Secretary-General of the United Nations.

Article 18

Entry into force

1. The Protocol shall enter into force 30 days after the date of deposit of the tenth instrument of ratification, approval, acceptance or accession.

2. For each member of the Authority which ratifies, approves or accepts this Protocol or accedes thereto after the deposit of the tenth instrument of ratification, approval, acceptance or accession, this Protocol shall enter into force on the thirtieth day following the deposit of its instrument of ratification, approval, acceptance or accession.

Article 19

Provisional application

A State which intends to ratify, approve, accept or accede to this Protocol may at any time notify the depositary that it will apply this Protocol provisionally for a period not exceeding two years.

Article 20

Denunciation

1. A State Party may, by written notification addressed to the Secretary-General of the United Nations, denounce this Protocol. The denunciation shall take effect one year after the date of receipt of the notification, unless the notification specifies a later date.

2. The denunciation shall not in any way affect the duty of any State Party to fulfil any obligation embodied in this Protocol to which it would be subject under international law independently of this Protocol.

Article 21

Depositary

The Secretary-General of the United Nations shall be the depositary of this Protocol.

Article 22

Authentic texts

The Arabic, Chinese, English, French, Russian and Spanish texts of this Protocol are equally authentic.

IN WITNESS WHEREOF, the undersigned Plenipotentiaries, being duly authorized thereto, have signed this Protocol.

OPENED FOR SIGNATURE at Kingston, the ________ day of ________ one thousand nine hundred and ninety-eight, in a single original, in the Arabic, Chinese, English, French, Russian and Spanish languages.

\- - - - - - -

INTERNATIONAL SEABED AUTHORITY

Council

Distr.
GENERAL

ISBA/6/C/9
13 July 2000

ORIGINAL: ENGLISH

INTERNATIONAL SEABED AUTHORITY
Resumed sixth session
Kingston, Jamaica
3–14 July 2000

DECISION OF THE COUNCIL OF THE AUTHORITY CONCERNING THE RULES OF PROCEDURE OF THE LEGAL AND TECHNICAL COMMISSION

The Council of the International Seabed Authority,

Recalling that, at its 58th meeting on 26 August 1999, the Council approved the rules of procedure of the Legal and Technical Commission, as contained in document ISBA/5/C/L.1/Rev.2, with the exception of rules 6 and 53,

Having examined the aforementioned rules 6 and 53 during the resumed sixth session of the Authority,

Noting that the rules of procedure of the Legal and Technical Commission shall enter into force on the date of their approval by the Council,

Approves the rules of procedure of the Legal and Technical Commission as contained in the annex to the present document.

68th meeting
13 July 2000

Annex

RULES OF PROCEDURE OF THE LEGAL AND TECHNICAL COMMISSION

Introductory Note

1. On 28 July 1994, the General Assembly of the United Nations adopted the Agreement relating to the Implementation of Part XI of the United Nations Convention on the Law of the Sea of 10 December 1982 (hereafter referred to as "the Agreement"). The Agreement has been provisionally applied since 16 November 1994 and entered into force on 28 July 1996.

2. According to the Agreement, its provisions and Part XI of the United Nations Convention of the Law of the Sea of 10 December 1982 (hereinafter referred to as "the Convention") are to be interpreted and applied together as a single instrument; the present rules and references in the rules to the Convention are to be interpreted and applied accordingly.

3. The Legal and Technical Commission, established under article 163 of the Convention, shall function in accordance with the provisions of the Convention and the Agreement.

I. SESSIONS

Rule 1

Frequency of sessions

The Legal and Technical Commission (hereinafter referred to as "the Commission") shall meet as often as required, including in emergency sessions, for the efficient exercise of its functions, taking into account the requirement of cost-effectiveness.

Rule 2

Place of sessions

The Commission shall normally meet at the seat of the Authority. Whenever circumstances warrant or the business of the Commission so requires, the Commission may, in consultation with the Secretary-General, and taking into account section 1, paragraph 2 of the annex to the Agreement, decide to meet elsewhere.

Rule 3

Convening of sessions

Taking into account the provisions of rule 1, the Commission shall be convened at the request of:

(a) The Council;

(b) A majority of the members of the Commission;

(c) The Chairman of the Commission; or

(d) The Secretary-General.

Rule 4

Notification of the members

The Secretary-General shall notify the members of the Commission and the members of the Authority as early as possible of the date and duration of each session, and shall seek confirmation of their attendance.

Rule 5

Temporary adjournment of session

The Commission may decide to adjourn any session temporarily and resume it at a later date.

Rule 6

Meetings

The meetings of the Commission shall be held in private unless the Commission decides otherwise. The Commission shall take into account the desirability of holding open meetings when issues of general interest to members of the Authority, which do not involve the discussion of confidential information, are being discussed.

II. AGENDA

Rule 7

Communication of the provisional agenda

The provisional agenda for each session of the Commission shall be drawn up by the Secretary-General and communicated to the members of the Commission and the members of the Authority as early as possible but at least thirty days before the opening of the session. Any subsequent change in or addition to the provisional agenda shall be brought to the notice of the members of the Commission and to the members of the Authority sufficiently in advance of the session.

Rule 8

Drawing up of the provisional agenda

The provisional agenda of each session shall consist of:

(a) All items proposed by the Council;

(b) All items proposed by the Commission;

(c) All items proposed by the Chairman of the Commission;

(d) All items proposed by any member of the Commission;

(e) All items proposed by the Secretary-General.

Rule 9

Adoption of the agenda

At the beginning of each session, the Commission shall adopt its agenda for the session on the basis of the provisional agenda. The Commission may, if necessary, amend the agenda at any time during a session.

III. ELECTIONS AND FUNCTIONS

Rule 10

Elections

The members of the Commission shall be elected by the Council in accordance with the Convention and the rules of procedure of the Council.

Rule 11

Conflict of interest

1. Members of the Commission shall have no financial interest in any activity relating to exploration and exploitation in the Area.

2. Before assuming his or her duties, each member of the Commission shall make the following written declaration witnessed by the Secretary-General or his authorized representative:

"I solemnly declare that I will perform my duties as a member of the Legal and Technical Commission, honourably, faithfully, impartially and conscientiously.

"I further solemnly declare and promise that I shall have no financial interest in any activity relating to exploration and exploitation in the Area. Subject to my responsibilities to the Legal and Technical Commission, I shall not disclose, even after the termination of my functions, any industrial secret, proprietary data which are transferred to the Authority in accordance with the Convention and the Agreement, or any other confidential information coming to my knowledge by reason of my duties for the Authority.

"I shall disclose to the Secretary-General and to the Commission any interest in any matter under discussion before the Commission which might constitute a conflict of interest or which might be incompatible with the requirements of integrity and impartiality expected of a member of the Commission and I shall refrain from participating in the work of the Commission in relation to such matter."

Rule 12

Confidentiality

1. Subject to their responsibilities to the Commission, members of the Commission shall not disclose, even after the termination of their functions, any industrial secret, proprietary data which are transferred to the Authority in accordance with annex III, article 14, of the Convention, or any other confidential information coming to their knowledge by reason of their duties for the Authority.

2. The Commission shall recommend to the Council, for approval, procedures on the handling of confidential data and information coming to the knowledge of members of the Commission by reason of their duties for the Commission. Such procedures shall be based upon the relevant provisions of the Convention, the rules, regulations and procedures of the Authority and the procedures established by the Secretary-General pursuant thereto in order to carry out his responsibility to maintain the confidentiality of such data and information.

3. The duty of the members of the Commission not to disclose confidential information constitutes an obligation in respect of that member and shall remain an obligation after the expiration or termination of that member's functions for the Commission.

Rule 13

Enforcement of rules relating to conflict of interest and confidentiality

1. The Secretary-General shall provide the Commission and the Council with all necessary assistance in enforcing the rules on conflict of interest and confidentiality.

2. In the event of an alleged breach of the obligations relating to conflict of interest and confidentiality by a member of the Commission, the Council may institute appropriate proceedings and shall make known its findings and recommendations.

Rule 14

Exercise of functions

The Commission shall exercise its functions in accordance with these Rules and such guidelines as the Council may adopt from time to time.

Rule 15

Consultations

In the exercise of its functions, the Commission may, where appropriate, consult another commission, any competent organ of the United Nations or of its specialized agencies or any international organizations with competence in the subject-matter of such consultation.

IV. OFFICERS

Rule 16

Election and term of Chairman

1. Each year at the first session, the Commission shall elect a Chairman and a Vice-Chairman from among its members.

2. The Chairman and the Vice-Chairman shall be elected for a term of one year. They shall be eligible for re-election.

Rule 17

Acting Chairman

In the absence of the Chairman, the Vice-Chairman shall take the place of the Chairman. If the Chairman ceases to hold office pursuant to rule 18, the Vice-Chairman shall take his or her place until the election of a new Chairman.

Rule 18

Replacement of the Chairman

If the Chairman ceases to be able to carry out his or her functions or ceases to be a member of the Commission, a new Chairman shall be elected for the remainder of the term.

Rule 19

Functions of the Chairman

1. The Chairman shall preside over the meetings of the Commission as provided for under rule 29 of these Rules.

2. The Chairman, or any other member designated by the Commission, shall represent the Commission in that capacity in the Council and, at the invitation of the Council, shall attend meetings of the Council and respond to questions when a matter of particular relevance or complexity relating to the work of the Commission is under consideration by the Council.

3. Such attendance shall not preclude the holding of concurrent meetings of the Council and the Commission.

Rule 20

Exercise of the Chairman's functions

The Chairman, in the exercise of his or her functions and powers as provided for under rules 19 and 29, remains under the authority of the Commission.

V. SECRETARIAT

Rule 21

Duties of the Secretary-General

1. The Secretary-General shall act in that capacity in all meetings of the Commission. The Secretary-General may designate a member of the Secretariat to act as his or her representative. The Secretary-General shall perform such other administrative functions as are requested of him or her by the Commission.

2. The Secretary-General shall provide and direct the staff required by the Commission, taking into account to the greatest extent possible the requirements of economy and efficiency, and be responsible for all the arrangements that may be necessary for its meetings.

3. The Secretary-General shall keep the members of the Commission informed of any matter which is dealt with by other organs of the Authority and which may be of interest to the Commission.

4. The Secretary-General shall provide to the Commission, at its request, reports on questions specified by the Commission.

Rule 22

Duties of the Secretariat

The Secretariat shall receive, translate, reproduce and distribute recommendations, reports and other documents of the Commission; interpret speeches made at the meeting; prepare and circulate, if so decided by the Commission in accordance with rule 23, the records of the session; have custody and proper preservation of the documents in the archives of the Commission; and, generally, perform all other administrative functions which the Commission may require.

Rule 23

Records and sound recordings of meetings

1. The Commission may decide to keep summary records of its meetings; but all decisions taken by the Commission shall be duly included in the published records of the Commission. As a general rule they shall be circulated as soon as possible to all members of the Commission, who shall inform the Secretariat within five working days after the circulation of the summary record of any changes they wish to have made.

2. The Secretariat shall make and retain sound recordings of the meetings of the Commission when it so decides.

VI. LANGUAGES

Rule 24

Languages of the Commission

Arabic, Chinese, English, French, Russian and Spanish shall be the languages of the Commission.

Rule 25

Interpretation

Speeches made in any of the six languages of the Commission shall be interpreted into the other five languages.

Rule 26

Interpretation from a language other than the languages of the Commission

Any member may make a speech in a language other than the languages of the Commission. In this case, he or she shall himself or herself provide for interpretation into one of the languages of the Commission. Interpretation into the other languages of the Commission by the interpreters of the Secretariat may be based on the interpretation given in the first such language.

Rule 27

Languages of recommendations and reports

All recommendations and reports of the Commission shall be published in the languages of the Commission.

VII. CONDUCT OF BUSINESS

Rule 28

Quorum

A majority of the members of the Commission shall constitute a quorum.

Rule 29

Powers of the Chairman

In addition to exercising the powers conferred upon him or her elsewhere in these Rules, the Chairman shall declare the opening and closing of each meeting of the Commission, direct the discussions, ensure observance of these Rules, accord the right to speak, put questions to the vote and announce decisions. The Chairman shall rule on points of order and, subject to these Rules, shall have complete control of the proceedings of the Commission and over the maintenance of order at its meetings. The Chairman may, in the course of the discussion of an item, propose to the Commission the limitation of time to be allowed to speakers, the limitation of the number of times each member may speak on any question, the closure of the list of speakers or the closure of the debate. The Chairman may also propose the suspension or the adjournment of the meeting or of the debate on the question under discussion.

Rule 30

Speeches

The Chairman shall call upon speakers in the order in which they signify their desire to speak. The Chairman may call a speaker to order if his or her remarks are not relevant to the subject under discussion.

Rule 31

Statements by the Secretariat

The Secretary-General, or a member of the Secretariat designated by the Secretary-General as his or her representative, may at any time make either oral or written statements to the Commission concerning any questions under consideration by it.

Rule 32

Points of order

During the discussion of any matter, a member may rise to a point of order, and the point of order shall be immediately decided by the Chairman in accordance with the rules of procedure. A member may appeal against the ruling of the Chairman. The appeal shall be immediately put to the vote, and the Chairman's ruling shall stand unless overruled by a majority of the members present and voting. A member rising to a point of order may not speak on the substance of the matter under discussion.

Rule 33

Time limit on speeches

The Commission may limit the time to be allowed to each speaker and the number of times each member may speak on any question. Before a decision is taken, two members may speak in favour of, and two against, a proposal to set such limits. When the debate is limited and a member exceeds his or her allocated time, the Chairman shall call him or her to order without delay.

Rule 34

Closing of list of speakers

During the course of a debate, the Chairman may announce the list of speakers and, with the consent of the Commission, declare the list closed. The Chairman may, however, accord the right of reply to any member if a speech delivered after he or she has declared the list closed makes this desirable.

Rule 35

Adjournment of debate

During the discussion of any matter, a member may move the adjournment of the debate on the item under discussion. In addition to the proposer of the motion, two members may speak in favour of, and two against, the motion, after which the motion shall be immediately put to the vote. The Chairman may limit the time to be allowed to speakers under this rule.

Rule 36

Closure of debate

A member may at any time move the closure of the debate on the question under discussion, whether or not any other member has signified his wish to speak. Permission to speak on the motion shall be accorded only to two members opposing the closure, after which the motion shall be immediately put to the vote. If the Commission is in favour of the closure, the Chairman shall declare the closure of the debate. The Chairman may limit the time to be allowed to members under this rule.

Rule 37

Suspension or adjournment of the meeting

During the discussion of any matter, a member may move the suspension or the adjournment of the meeting. Such motions shall not be debated, but shall be immediately put to the vote. The Chairman may limit the time to be allowed to the speaker moving the suspension or adjournment of the meeting.

Rule 38

Order of procedural motions

Subject to rule 32, the following motions shall have precedence in the following order over all other proposals or motions before the meeting:

(a) To suspend the meeting;

(b) To adjourn the meeting;

(c) To adjourn the debate on the item under discussion;

(d) To close the debate on the item under discussion.

Rule 39

Proposals and amendments

Proposals and amendments shall normally be submitted in writing to the Secretary-General, who shall circulate copies to the members of the Commission. As a general rule, no proposal shall be discussed or put to the vote at any meeting of the Commission unless copies of it have been circulated to all members not later than twenty-four hours before the meeting. The Chairman may, however, permit the discussion and consideration of amendments, or of motions as to procedure, even though such amendments and motions have not been circulated or have only been circulated the same day.

Rule 40

Decision on competence

Subject to rule 38, any motion calling for a decision on the competence of the Commission to adopt a proposal submitted to it shall be put to the vote before a decision is taken on the proposal in question.

Rule 41

Withdrawal of proposals and motions

A proposal or a motion may be withdrawn by its proposer at any time before voting on it has commenced, provided that it has not been amended. A proposal or a motion thus withdrawn may be reintroduced by any member.

Rule 42

Reconsideration of proposals

When a proposal has been adopted or rejected, it may not be reconsidered at the same meeting unless the Commission, by a majority of the members present and voting, so decides. Permission to speak on a motion to reconsider shall be accorded only to two speakers opposing the motion, after which it shall be immediately put to the vote.

VIII. DECISION-MAKING

Rule 43

Voting rights

Each member of the Commission shall have one vote.

Rule 44

Decision-making by consensus and voting

1. As a general rule, decision-making in the Commission should be by consensus.

2. If all efforts to reach a decision by consensus have been exhausted, decisions by voting shall be taken by a majority of members present and voting.

3. For the purpose of this rule, "consensus" means the absence of any formal objection.

Rule 45

Meaning of the phrase "members present and voting"

For the purposes of these Rules, the phrase "members present and voting" means members present at the meeting and casting an affirmative or negative vote. Members who abstain from voting shall be considered as not voting.

Rule 46

Recommendations to the Council

Recommendations to the Council shall, wherever necessary, be accompanied by a summary on the divergences of opinion in the Commission.

Rule 47

Method of voting

1. The Commission shall, in the absence of mechanical means for voting, vote by show of hands, but any member may request a roll-call. The roll-call shall be taken in the English alphabetical order of the names of the members participating in that session, beginning with the member whose name is drawn by lot by the Chairman. The name of each member shall be called in any roll-call, and the member shall reply "yes" or "no" or "abstention". The result of the voting shall be inserted in the record in the English alphabetical order of the names of the members.

2. When the Commission votes by mechanical means, a non-recorded vote shall replace a vote by show of hands and a recorded vote shall replace a roll-call vote. Any member may request a recorded vote. In the case of a recorded vote, the Commission shall, unless a member requests otherwise, dispense with the procedure of calling out the names of the members; nevertheless, the result of the voting shall be inserted in the record in the same manner as that of a roll-call vote.

Rule 48

Conduct during voting

After the Chairman has announced the beginning of voting, no member shall interrupt the voting, except on a point of order in connection with the actual process of the voting.

Rule 49

Explanation of vote

Members may make brief statements consisting solely of explanations of their votes before the voting has commenced or after the voting has been completed. The member sponsoring a proposal or motion shall not speak in explanation of vote thereon, except if it has been amended.

Rule 50

Division of proposals and amendments

A member may move that parts of a proposal or of an amendment should be voted upon separately. If objection is made to the request for division, the motion for division shall be voted upon. Permission to speak on the motion for division shall be given only to two speakers in favour and two speakers against. If the motion for division is carried, those parts of the proposal or of the amendments which are approved shall then be put to the vote as a whole. If all operative parts of the proposal or of the amendments have been rejected, the proposal or the amendments shall be considered to have been rejected as a whole.

Rule 51

Order of voting on amendments

When an amendment is moved to a proposal, the amendment shall be voted upon first. When two or more amendments are moved to a proposal, the Commission shall first vote on the amendment furthest removed in substance from the original proposal and then on the amendment next furthest removed therefrom, and so on until all the amendments have been put to the vote. Where, however, the adoption of one amendment necessarily implies the rejection of another amendment, the latter amendment shall not be put to the vote. If one or more amendments are adopted, the amended proposal shall then be voted upon. A motion is considered an amendment to a proposal if it merely adds to, deletes from or revises part of the proposal.

Rule 52

Order of voting on proposals

If two or more proposals relate to the same question, the Commission shall, unless it decides otherwise, vote on the proposals in the order in which they have been submitted. The Commission may, after each vote on a proposal, decide whether to vote on the next proposal.

IX. PARTICIPATION BY NON-MEMBERS OF THE COMMISSION

Rule 53

Participation by members of the Authority and entities carrying out activities in the Area

1. Any member of the Authority may, with the permission of the Commission, send a representative to attend a meeting of the Commission when a matter particularly affecting such member is under consideration. For the purpose of facilitating the work of the Commission, such representative shall be allowed to express his or her views on any such matter being considered by the Commission.

2. The Commission may invite any State or entity carrying out activities in the Area for the purposes of consultation and collaboration, where the Commission considers appropriate.

3. The members of the Commission shall, upon request by any member of the Authority or other party concerned, be accompanied by a representative of such member or other party concerned when carrying out their function of supervision and inspection.

4. Any member of the Authority may make a request to the Secretary-General to convene a meeting of the Commission in order to consider a matter of particular concern to that member involving an environmental emergency. The Secretary-General shall convene the Commission which shall give urgent consideration to such matter and report to the Council as soon as possible with its findings and recommendations. Any member concerned with such matter has the right to send a representative to the meeting of the Commission to express its views on the matter without participation in decision-making, although the Commission may determine that such presence be limited at certain stages when confidential information is being discussed.

Rule 54

Entry into force

These Rules of Procedure shall enter into force on the date of their approval by the Council.

INTERNATIONAL SEABED AUTHORITY

Assembly

Distr.
GENERAL

ISBA/6/A/18
20 July 2000

ORIGINAL: ENGLISH

INTERNATIONAL SEABED AUTHORITY
Resumed sixth session
Kingston, Jamaica
3–14 July 2000

DECISION OF THE ASSEMBLY OF THE INTERNATIONAL SEABED AUTHORITY RELATING TO THE REGULATIONS ON PROSPECTING AND EXPLORATION FOR POLYMETALLIC NODULES IN THE AREA

The Assembly of the International Seabed Authority

Having considered the regulations on prospecting and exploration for polymetallic nodules, as provisionally adopted by the Council at its 69th Meeting, on 13 July 2000,[1]

Approves the regulations on prospecting and exploration for polymetallic nodules in the Area, as contained in the annex to the present document.

13 July 2000
76th Meeting

[1] ISBA/6/C/12.

Annex

REGULATIONS ON PROSPECTING AND EXPLORATION FOR POLYMETALLIC NODULES IN THE AREA

Preamble

In accordance with the United Nations Convention on the Law of the Sea ("the Convention"), the seabed and ocean floor and the subsoil thereof beyond the limits of national jurisdiction, as well as its resources, are the common heritage of mankind, the exploration and exploitation of which shall be carried out for the benefit of mankind as a whole, on whose behalf the International Seabed Authority acts. The objective of this first set of Regulations is to provide for prospecting and exploration for polymetallic nodules.

PART I - INTRODUCTION

Regulation 1

Use of terms and scope

1. Terms used in the Convention shall have the same meaning in these Regulations.

2. In accordance with the Agreement relating to the Implementation of Part XI of the United Nations Convention on the Law of the Sea of 10 December 1982 ("the Agreement"), the provisions of the Agreement and Part XI of the United Nations Convention on the Law of the Sea of 10 December 1982 shall be interpreted and applied together as a single instrument. These Regulations and references in these Regulations to the Convention are to be interpreted and applied accordingly.

3. For the purposes of these Regulations:

(a) "exploitation" means the recovery for commercial purposes of polymetallic nodules in the Area and the extraction of minerals therefrom, including the construction and operation of mining, processing and transportation systems, for the production and marketing of metals;

(b) "exploration" means searching for deposits of polymetallic nodules in the Area with exclusive rights, the analysis of such deposits, the testing of collecting systems and equipment, processing facilities and transportation systems, and the carrying out of studies of the environmental, technical, economic, commercial and other appropriate factors that must be taken into account in exploitation;

(c) "marine environment" includes the physical, chemical, geological and biological components, conditions and factors which interact and determine the productivity, state, condition and quality of the marine ecosystem, the waters of the seas and oceans and the airspace above those waters, as well as the seabed and ocean floor and subsoil thereof;

(d) "polymetallic nodules" means one of the resources of the Area consisting of any deposit or accretion of nodules, on or just below the surface of the deep seabed, which contain manganese, nickel, cobalt and copper;

(e) "prospecting" means the search for deposits of polymetallic nodules in the Area, including estimation of the composition, sizes and distributions of polymetallic nodule deposits and their economic values, without any exclusive rights;

(f) "serious harm to the marine environment" means any effect from activities in the Area on the marine environment which represents a significant adverse change in the marine environment determined according to the rules, regulations and procedures adopted by the Authority on the basis of internationally recognized standards and practices.

4. These Regulations shall not in any way affect the freedom of scientific research, pursuant to article 87 of the Convention, or the right to conduct marine scientific research in the Area pursuant to articles 143 and 256 of the Convention. Nothing in these Regulations shall be construed in such a way as to restrict the exercise by States of the freedom of the high seas as reflected in article 87 of the Convention.

5. These Regulations may be supplemented by further rules, regulations and procedures, in particular on the protection and preservation of the marine environment. These Regulations shall be subject to the provisions of the Convention and the Agreement and other rules of international law not incompatible with the Convention.

PART II - PROSPECTING

Regulation 2

Prospecting

1. Prospecting shall be conducted in accordance with the Convention and these Regulations and may commence only after the prospector has been informed by the Secretary-General that its notification has been recorded pursuant to regulation 4, paragraph 2.

2. Prospecting shall not be undertaken if substantial evidence indicates the risk of serious harm to the marine environment.

3. Prospecting shall not be undertaken in an area covered by an approved plan of work for exploration for polymetallic nodules or in a reserved area; nor may there be prospecting in an area which the Council has disapproved for exploitation because of the risk of serious harm to the marine environment.

4. Prospecting shall not confer on the prospector any rights with respect to resources. A prospector may, however, recover a reasonable quantity of minerals, being the quantity necessary for testing, and not for commercial use.

5. There shall be no time limit on prospecting except that prospecting in a particular area shall cease upon written notification to the prospector by the Secretary-General that a plan of work for exploration has been approved with regard to that area.

6. Prospecting may be conducted simultaneously by more than one prospector in the same area or areas.

Regulation 3

Notification of prospecting

1. A proposed prospector shall notify the Authority of its intention to engage in prospecting.

2. Each notification of prospecting shall be in the form prescribed in Annex 1 to these Regulations, addressed to the Secretary-General, and shall conform to the requirements of these Regulations.

3. Each notification shall be submitted:

(a) in the case of a State, by the authority designated for that purpose by it;

(b) in the case of an entity, by its designated representative; and

(c) in the case of the Enterprise, by its competent authority.

4. Each notification shall be in one of the languages of the Authority and shall contain:

(a) the name, nationality and address of the proposed prospector and its designated representative;

(b) the coordinates of the broad area or areas within which prospecting is to be conducted, in accordance with the most recent generally accepted international standard used by the Authority;

(c) a general description of the prospecting programme, including the proposed date of commencement and its approximate duration;

(d) a satisfactory written undertaking that the proposed prospector will:

(i) comply with the Convention and the relevant rules, regulations and procedures of the Authority concerning:

a. cooperation in the training programmes in connection with marine scientific research and transfer of technology referred to in articles 143 and 144 of the Convention; and

b. protection and preservation of the marine environment; and

(ii) accept verification by the Authority of compliance therewith.

Regulation 4

Consideration of notifications

1. The Secretary-General shall acknowledge in writing receipt of each notification submitted under regulation 3, specifying the date of receipt.

2. The Secretary-General shall review and act on the notification within 45 days of its receipt. If the notification conforms with the requirements of the Convention and these Regulations, the Secretary-General shall record the particulars of the notification in a register maintained for that purpose and shall inform the prospector in writing that the notification has been so recorded.

3. The Secretary-General shall, within 45 days of receipt of the notification, inform the proposed prospector in writing if the notification includes any part of an area included in an approved plan of work for exploration or exploitation of any category of resources, or any part of a reserved area, or any part of an area which has been disapproved by the Council for exploitation because of the risk of serious harm to the marine environment, or if the written undertaking is not satisfactory, and shall provide the proposed prospector with a written statement of reasons. In such cases, the proposed prospector may, within 90 days, submit an amended notification. The Secretary-General shall, within 45 days, review and act upon such amended notification.

4. A prospector shall inform the Secretary-General in writing of any change in the information contained in the notification.

5. The Secretary-General shall not release any particulars contained in the notification except with the written consent of the prospector. The Secretary-General shall, however, from time to time inform all members of the Authority of the identity of prospectors and the general areas in which prospecting is being conducted.

Regulation 5

Annual report

1. A prospector shall, within 90 days of the end of each calendar year, submit a report to the Authority on the status of prospecting. Such reports shall be submitted by the Secretary-General to the Legal and Technical Commission. Each such report shall contain:

(a) a general description of the status of prospecting and of the results obtained; and

(b) information on compliance with the undertakings referred to in regulation 3, paragraph (4)(d).

2. If the prospector intends to claim expenditures for prospecting as part of the development costs incurred prior to the commencement of commercial

production, the prospector shall submit an annual statement, in conformity with internationally accepted accounting principles and certified by a duly qualified firm of public accountants, of the actual and direct expenditures incurred by the prospector in carrying out prospecting.

Regulation 6

Confidentiality of data and information from prospecting contained in the annual report

1. The Secretary-General shall ensure the confidentiality of all data and information contained in the reports submitted under regulation 5 in accordance with the provisions of regulations 35 and 36.

2. The Secretary-General may, at any time, with the consent of the prospector concerned, release data and information relating to prospecting in an area in respect of which a notification has been submitted. If the Secretary-General determines that the prospector no longer exists or cannot be located, the Secretary-General may release such data and information.

Regulation 7

Notification of incidents causing serious harm to the marine environment

A prospector shall immediately notify the Secretary-General in writing, using the most effective means, of any incident arising from prospecting which causes serious harm to the marine environment. Upon receipt of such notification the Secretary-General shall act in a manner consistent with regulation 32.

Regulation 8

Objects of an archaeological or historical nature

A prospector shall immediately notify the Secretary-General in writing of any finding in the Area of an object of an archaeological or historical nature and its location. The Secretary-General shall transmit such information to the Director-General of the United Nations Educational, Scientific and Cultural Organization.

PART III - APPLICATIONS FOR APPROVAL OF PLANS OF WORK FOR EXPLORATION IN THE FORM OF CONTRACTS

SECTION 1. GENERAL PROVISIONS

Regulation 9

General

Subject to the provisions of the Convention, the following may apply to the Authority for approval of plans of work for exploration:

(a) the Enterprise, on its own behalf or in a joint arrangement;

(b) States Parties, state enterprises or natural or juridical persons which possess the nationality of States Parties or are effectively controlled by them or their nationals, when sponsored by such States, or any group of the foregoing which meets the requirements of these Regulations.[2]

SECTION 2. CONTENT OF APPLICATIONS

Regulation 10

Form of applications

1. Each application for approval of a plan of work for exploration shall be in the form prescribed in Annex 2 to these Regulations, shall be addressed to the Secretary-General, and shall conform to the requirements of these Regulations.[3]

2. Each application shall be submitted:

(a) in the case of a State Party, by the authority designated for that purpose by it;

(b) in the case of an entity, by its designated representative or the authority designated for that purpose by the sponsoring State or States; and

(c) in the case of the Enterprise, by its competent authority.

3. Each application by a state enterprise or one of the entities referred to in subparagraph (b) of regulation 9 shall also contain:

(a) sufficient information to determine the nationality of the applicant or the identity of the State or States by which, or by whose nationals, the applicant is effectively controlled; and

(b) the principal place of business or domicile and, if applicable, place of registration of the applicant.

4. Each application submitted by a partnership or consortium of entities shall contain the required information in respect of each member of the partnership or consortium.

---

[2] A request by a registered pioneer investor for approval of a plan of work for exploration under paragraph 6(a)(ii) of section 1 of the annex to the Agreement shall be submitted within 36 months of the entry into force of the Convention.

[3] A request by a registered pioneer investor for approval of a plan of work for exploration under paragraph 6(a)(ii) of section 1 of the annex to the Agreement shall consist of documents, reports and other data submitted to the Preparatory Commission both before and after registration and shall be accompanied by a certificate of compliance, consisting of a factual report describing the status of fulfilment of obligations under the registered pioneer investor regime, issued by the Preparatory Commission in accordance with resolution II, paragraph 11(a). The registered pioneer investor shall, where such information has not already been provided, update the information, using, as far as possible, the provisions of regulation 18 as a guide, and submit its programme of activities for the immediate future, including a general assessment of the potential environmental impacts of the proposed activities.

Regulation 11

Certificate of sponsorship

1. Each application by a state enterprise or one of the entities referred to in subparagraph (b) of regulation 9 shall be accompanied by a certificate of sponsorship issued by the State of which it is a national or by which or by whose nationals it is effectively controlled.[4] If the applicant has more than one nationality, as in the case of a partnership or consortium of entities from more than one State, each State involved shall issue a certificate of sponsorship.

2. Where the applicant has the nationality of one State but is effectively controlled by another State or its nationals, each State involved shall issue a certificate of sponsorship.

3. Each certificate of sponsorship shall be duly signed on behalf of the State by which it is submitted and shall contain:

(a) the name of the applicant;

(b) the name of the sponsoring State;

(c) a statement that the applicant is:

(i) a national of the sponsoring State; or

(ii) subject to the effective control of the sponsoring State or its nationals;

(d) a statement by the sponsoring State that it sponsors the applicant;

(e) the date of deposit by the sponsoring State of its instrument of ratification of, or accession or succession to, the Convention;

(f) a declaration that the sponsoring State assumes responsibility in accordance with article 139, article 153, paragraph 4, and Annex III, article 4, paragraph 4, of the Convention.

4. States or entities in a joint arrangement with the Enterprise shall also comply with this regulation.

Regulation 12

Financial and technical capabilities

1. Each application for approval of a plan of work for exploration shall contain specific and sufficient information to enable the Council to determine whether the applicant is financially and technically capable of carrying out

---

[4] In the case of a request by a registered pioneer investor for approval of a plan of work for exploration, the certifying State or States at the time of registration or their successors shall be deemed to be the sponsoring State or States provided such State or States are States Parties to the Convention or are provisional members of the Authority at the time of the request.

the proposed plan of work for exploration and of fulfilling its financial obligations to the Authority.[5]

2. An application for approval of a plan of work for exploration submitted on behalf of a State or entity, or any component of such entity, referred to in resolution II, paragraph 1(a)(ii) or (iii), other than a registered pioneer investor, which has already undertaken substantial activities in the Area prior to the entry into force of the Convention, or its successor in interest, shall be considered to have met the financial and technical qualifications necessary for approval of a plan of work for exploration if the sponsoring State or States certify that the applicant has expended an amount equivalent to at least US$ 30 million in research and exploration activities and has expended no less than 10 per cent of that amount in the location, survey and evaluation of the area referred to in the plan of work for exploration.

3. An application for approval of a plan of work for exploration by the Enterprise shall include a statement by its competent authority certifying that the Enterprise has the necessary financial resources to meet the estimated costs of the proposed plan of work for exploration.

4. An application for approval of a plan of work for exploration by a State or a state enterprise, other than a registered pioneer investor or an entity referred to in resolution II, paragraph 1(a)(ii) or (iii), shall include a statement by the State or the sponsoring State certifying that the applicant has the necessary financial resources to meet the estimated costs of the proposed plan of work for exploration.

5. An application for approval of a plan of work for exploration by an entity, other than a registered pioneer investor or an entity referred to in resolution II, paragraph 1(a)(ii) or (iii), shall include copies of its audited financial statements, including balance sheets and profit-and-loss statements, for the most recent three years, in conformity with internationally accepted accounting principles and certified by a duly qualified firm of public accountants; and

(a) if the applicant is a newly organised entity and a certified balance sheet is not available, a pro forma balance sheet certified by an appropriate official of the applicant;

(b) if the applicant is a subsidiary of another entity, copies of such financial statements of that entity and a statement from that entity, in conformity with internationally accepted accounting principles and certified by a duly qualified firm of public accountants, that the applicant will have the financial resources to carry out the plan of work for exploration;

---

[5] A registered pioneer investor requesting approval of a plan of work for exploration under paragraph 6(a)(ii) of section 1 of the annex to the Agreement shall be considered to have satisfied the financial and technical qualifications necessary for approval of a plan of work.

(c) if the applicant is controlled by a State or a state enterprise, a statement from the State or state enterprise certifying that the applicant will have the financial resources to carry out the plan of work for exploration.

6. Where an applicant referred to in paragraph 5 intends to finance the proposed plan of work for exploration by borrowings, its application shall include the amount of such borrowings, the repayment period and the interest rate.

7. Except as provided for in paragraph 2, all applications shall include:

(a) a general description of the applicant's previous experience, knowledge, skills, technical qualifications and expertise relevant to the proposed plan of work for exploration;

(b) a general description of the equipment and methods expected to be used in carrying out the proposed plan of work for exploration and other relevant non-proprietary information about the characteristics of such technology; and

(c) a general description of the applicant's financial and technical capability to respond to any incident or activity which causes serious harm to the marine environment.

8. Where the applicant is a partnership or consortium of entities in a joint arrangement, each member of the partnership or consortium shall provide the information required by this regulation.

Regulation 13

Previous contracts with the Authority

Where the applicant or, in the case of an application by a partnership or consortium of entities in a joint arrangement, any member of the partnership or consortium, has previously been awarded any contract with the Authority, the application shall include:

(a) the date of the previous contract or contracts;

(b) the dates, reference numbers and titles of each report submitted to the Authority in connection with the contract or contracts; and

(c) the date of termination of the contract or contracts, if applicable.

Regulation 14

Undertakings

Each applicant, including the Enterprise, shall, as part of its application for approval of a plan of work for exploration, provide a written undertaking to the Authority that it will:

(a) accept as enforceable and comply with the applicable obligations created by the provisions of the Convention and the rules, regulations and procedures of the Authority, the decisions of the relevant organs of the Authority and the terms of its contracts with the Authority;

(b) accept control by the Authority of activities in the Area, as authorized by the Convention; and

(c) provide the Authority with a written assurance that its obligations under the contract will be fulfilled in good faith.[6]

Regulation 15

Total area covered by the application

Each application for approval of a plan of work for exploration shall define the boundaries of the area under application by a list of coordinates in accordance with the most recent generally accepted international standard used by the Authority. Applications other than those under regulation 17 shall cover a total area, which need not be a single continuous area, sufficiently large and of sufficient estimated commercial value to allow two mining operations. The applicant shall indicate the coordinates dividing the area into two parts of equal estimated commercial value. The area to be allocated to the applicant shall be subject to the provisions of regulation 25.

Regulation 16

Data and information to be submitted before the designation of a reserved area

1. Each application shall contain sufficient data and information, as prescribed in Section II of Annex 2 to these Regulations, with respect to the area under application to enable the Council, on the recommendation of the Legal and Technical Commission, to designate a reserved area based on the estimated commercial value of each part. Such data and information shall consist of data available to the applicant with respect to both parts of the area under application, including the data used to determine their commercial value.

2. The Council, on the basis of the data and information submitted by the applicant pursuant to Section II of Annex 2 to these Regulations, if found satisfactory, and taking into account the recommendation of the Legal and Technical Commission, shall designate the part of the area under application which is to be a reserved area. The area so designated shall become a reserved area as soon as the plan of work for exploration for the non-reserved area is approved and the contract is signed. If the Council determines that additional information, consistent with these Regulations and Annex 2,

---

[6] Such undertaking shall also be provided by a registered pioneer investor requesting approval of a plan of work for exploration under paragraph 6(a)(ii) of section 1 of the annex to the Agreement.

is needed to designate the reserved area, it shall refer the matter back to the Commission for further consideration, specifying the additional information required.

3. Once the plan of work for exploration is approved and a contract has been issued, the data and information transferred to the Authority by the applicant in respect of the reserved area may be disclosed by the Authority in accordance with article 14, paragraph 3, of Annex III to the Convention.

Regulation 17

Applications for approval of plans of work with respect to a reserved area

1. Any State which is a developing State or any natural or juridical person sponsored by it and effectively controlled by it or by any other developing State, or any group of the foregoing, may notify the Authority that it wishes to submit a plan of work for exploration with respect to a reserved area. The Secretary-General shall forward such notification to the Enterprise, which shall inform the Secretary-General in writing within six months whether or not it intends to carry out activities in that area. If the Enterprise intends to carry out activities in that area, it shall, pursuant to paragraph 4, also inform in writing the contractor whose application for approval of a plan of work for exploration originally included that area.

2. An application for approval of a plan of work for exploration in respect of a reserved area may be submitted at any time after such an area becomes available following a decision by the Enterprise that it does not intend to carry out activities in that area or where the Enterprise has not, within six months of the notification by the Secretary-General, either taken a decision on whether it intends to carry out activities in that area or notified the Secretary-General in writing that it is engaged in discussions regarding a potential joint venture. In the latter instance, the Enterprise shall have one year from the date of such notification in which to decide whether to conduct activities in that area.

3. If the Enterprise or a developing State or one of the entities referred to in paragraph 1 does not submit an application for approval of a plan of work for exploration for activities in a reserved area within 15 years of the commencement by the Enterprise of its functions independent of the Secretariat of the Authority or within 15 years of the date on which that area is reserved for the Authority, whichever is the later, the contractor whose application for approval of a plan of work for exploration originally included that area shall be entitled to apply for a plan of work for exploration for that area provided it offers in good faith to include the Enterprise as a joint-venture partner.

4. A contractor has the right of first refusal to enter into a joint venture arrangement with the Enterprise for exploration of the area which was included in its application for approval of a plan of work for exploration and which was designated by the Council as a reserved area.

Regulation 18

Data and information to be submitted for approval of the plan of work for exploration[7]

After the Council has designated the reserved area, the applicant, if it has not already done so, shall submit, with a view to receiving approval of the plan of work for exploration in the form of a contract, the following information:

(a) a general description and a schedule of the proposed exploration programme, including the programme of activities for the immediate five-year period, such as studies to be undertaken in respect of the environmental, technical, economic and other appropriate factors that must be taken into account in exploration;

(b) a description of the programme for oceanographic and environmental baseline studies in accordance with these Regulations and any environmental rules, regulations and procedures established by the Authority that would enable an assessment of the potential environmental impact of the proposed exploration activities, taking into account any recommendations issued by the Legal and Technical Commission;

(c) a preliminary assessment of the possible impact of the proposed exploration activities on the marine environment;

(d) a description of proposed measures for the prevention, reduction and control of pollution and other hazards, as well as possible impacts, to the marine environment;

(e) data necessary for the Council to make the determination it is required to make in accordance with regulation 12, paragraph 1; and

(f) a schedule of anticipated yearly expenditures in respect of the programme of activities for the immediate five-year period.

SECTION 3. FEES

Regulation 19

Fee for applications

1. The fee for processing applications for approval of a plan of work for exploration shall be US$ 250,000 or its equivalent in a freely convertible currency. The fee shall be paid to the Authority by the applicant at the time of submitting an application.[8]

---

[7] In the case of a request by a registered pioneer investor for approval of a plan of work for exploration under paragraph 6(a)(ii) of section 1 of the annex to the Agreement, this Regulation shall be implemented in the light of regulation 10.

[8] In the case of a registered pioneer investor requesting approval for a plan of work for exploration under paragraph 6(a)(ii) of section 1 of the annex to the Agreement, the fee

2. The amount of the fee shall be reviewed from time to time by the Council in order to ensure that it covers the administrative costs incurred by the Authority in processing the application.

3. If the administrative costs incurred by the Authority in processing the application are less than the fixed amount, the Authority shall refund the difference to the applicant.

SECTION 4. PROCESSING OF APPLICATIONS

Regulation 20

Receipt, acknowledgement and safe custody of applications

1. The Secretary-General shall:

(a) acknowledge in writing receipt of every application for approval of a plan of work for exploration submitted under this Part, specifying the date of receipt;

(b) place the application together with the attachments and annexes thereto in safe custody and ensure the confidentiality of all confidential data and information contained in the application; and

(c) notify the members of the Authority of the receipt of such application and circulate to them information of a general nature which is not confidential regarding the application.

Regulation 21

Consideration by the Legal and Technical Commission[9]

1. Upon receipt of an application for approval of a plan of work for exploration, the Secretary-General shall notify the members of the Legal and

---

of US$ 250,000 paid pursuant to resolution II, paragraph 7(a), shall be deemed to be the fee referred to under paragraph 1 relating to the exploration phase.

[9] In the case of a request by a registered pioneer investor for approval of a plan of work for exploration under paragraph 6(a)(ii) of section 1 of the annex to the Agreement, the Secretary-General shall ascertain whether:

(a) the documents, reports and other data submitted to the Preparatory Commission both before and after registration are available;

(b) the certificate of compliance, consisting of a factual report describing the status of fulfilment of obligations under the registered pioneer investor regime, issued by the Preparatory Commission in accordance with resolution II, paragraph 11(a), has been produced;

(c) the registered pioneer investor has updated the information provided in the documents, reports and other data submitted to the Preparatory Commission both before and after registration and has submitted its programme of activities for the immediate future, including a general assessment of the potential environmental impacts of the proposed activities; and

(d) the registered pioneer investor has given the undertakings and assurances specified in regulation 14.

Technical Commission and place consideration of the application as an item on the agenda for the next meeting of the Commission.

2. The Commission shall examine applications in the order in which they are received.

3. The Commission shall determine if the applicant:

(a) has complied with the provisions of these Regulations;

(b) has given the undertakings and assurances specified in regulation 14;

(c) possesses the financial and technical capability to carry out the proposed plan of work for exploration; and

(d) has satisfactorily discharged its obligations in relation to any previous contract with the Authority.

4. The Commission shall, in accordance with the requirements set forth in these Regulations and its procedures, determine whether the proposed plan of work for exploration will:

(a) provide for effective protection of human health and safety;

(b) provide for effective protection and preservation of the marine environment;

(c) ensure that installations are not established where interference may be caused to the use of recognized sea lanes essential to international navigation or in areas of intense fishing activity.

5. If the Commission makes the determinations specified in paragraph 3 and determines that the proposed plan of work for exploration meets the requirements of paragraph 4, the Commission shall recommend approval of the plan of work for exploration to the Council.

6. The Commission shall not recommend approval of the plan of work for exploration if part or all of the area covered by the proposed plan of work for exploration is included in:

(a) a plan of work for exploration approved by the Council for polymetallic nodules; or

(b) a plan of work approved by the Council for exploration for or exploitation of other resources if such proposed plan of work for exploration for polymetallic nodules might cause undue interference with activities under such an approved plan of work for such other resources; or

---

If the Secretary-General informs the Commission that the provisions of (a), (b), (c) and (d) have been satisfied by a registered pioneer investor, the Commission shall recommend approval of the plan of work.

(c) an area disapproved for exploitation by the Council in cases where substantial evidence indicates the risk of serious harm to the marine environment; or

(d) if the proposed plan of work for exploration has been submitted or sponsored by a State that already holds:

(i) plans of work for exploration and exploitation or exploitation only in non-reserved areas that, together with either part of the area covered by the application, exceed in size 30 per cent of a circular area of 400,000 square kilometres surrounding the centre of either part of the area covered by the proposed plan of work;

(ii) plans of work for exploration and exploitation or exploitation only in non-reserved areas which, taken together, constitute 2 per cent of that part of the Area which is not reserved or disapproved for exploitation pursuant to article 162, paragraph (2)(x), of the Convention.

7. Except in the case of applications by the Enterprise, on its own behalf or in a joint venture, and applications under regulation 17, the Commission shall not recommend approval of the plan of work for exploration if part or all of the area covered by the proposed plan of work for exploration is included in a reserved area or an area designated by the Council to be a reserved area.

8. If the Commission finds that an application does not comply with these Regulations, it shall notify the applicant in writing, through the Secretary-General, indicating the reasons. The applicant may, within 45 days of such notification, amend its application. If the Commission after further consideration is of the view that it should not recommend approval of the plan of work for exploration, it shall so inform the applicant and provide the applicant with a further opportunity to make representations within 30 days of such information. The Commission shall consider any such representations made by the applicant in preparing its report and recommendation to the Council.

9. In considering a proposed plan of work for exploration, the Commission shall have regard to the principles, policies and objectives relating to activities in the Area as provided for in Part XI and Annex III of the Convention and the Agreement.

10. The Commission shall consider applications expeditiously and shall submit its report and recommendations to the Council on the designation of the areas and on the plan of work for exploration at the first possible opportunity, taking into account the schedule of meetings of the Authority.

11. In discharging its duties, the Commission shall apply these Regulations and the rules, regulations and procedures of the Authority in a uniform and non-discriminatory manner.

Regulation 22

Consideration and approval of plans of work for exploration by the Council[10]

The Council shall consider the reports and recommendations of the Commission relating to approval of plans of work for exploration in accordance with paragraphs 11 and 12 of section 3 of the annex to the Agreement.

PART IV - CONTRACTS FOR EXPLORATION

Regulation 23

The contract

1. After a plan of work for exploration has been approved by the Council, it shall be prepared in the form of a contract between the Authority and the applicant as prescribed in Annex 3 to these Regulations. Each contract shall incorporate the standard clauses set out in Annex 4 in effect at the date of entry into force of the contract.

2. The contract shall be signed by the Secretary-General on behalf of the Authority and by the applicant. The Secretary-General shall notify all members of the Authority in writing of the conclusion of each contract.

3. In accordance with the principle of non-discrimination, a contract with a State or entity or any component of such entity referred to in paragraph 6(a)(i) of section 1 of the annex to the Agreement shall include arrangements that shall be similar to and no less favourable than those agreed with any registered pioneer investor. If any of the States or entities or any components of such entities referred to in paragraph 6(a)(i) of section 1 of the annex to the Agreement are granted more favourable arrangements, the Council shall make similar and no less favourable arrangements with regard to the rights and obligations assumed by the registered pioneer investors provided that such arrangements do not affect or prejudice the interests of the Authority.

Regulation 24

Rights of the contractor

1. The contractor shall have the exclusive right to explore an area covered by a plan of work for exploration in respect of polymetallic nodules. The Authority shall ensure that no other entity operates in the same area for resources other than polymetallic nodules in a manner that might interfere with the operations of the contractor.

---

[10] In the case of a request by a registered pioneer investor for approval of a plan of work for exploration under paragraph 6(a)(ii) of section 1 of the Agreement, once the Commission recommends approval of the plan of work and submits its recommendation to the Council, the plan of work shall be considered approved by the Council in accordance with paragraph 6(a)(ii) of section 1 of the annex to the Agreement.

2. A contractor who has an approved plan of work for exploration only shall have a preference and a priority among applicants submitting plans of work for exploitation of the same area and resources. Such preference or priority may be withdrawn by the Council if the contractor has failed to comply with the requirements of its approved plan of work for exploration within the time period specified in a written notice or notices from the Council to the contractor indicating which requirements have not been complied with by the contractor. The time period specified in any such notice shall not be unreasonable. The contractor shall be accorded a reasonable opportunity to be heard before the withdrawal of such preference or priority becomes final. The Council shall provide the reasons for its proposed withdrawal of preference or priority and shall consider any contractor's response. The decision of the Council shall take account of that response and shall be based on substantial evidence.

3. A withdrawal of preference or priority shall not become effective until the contractor has been accorded a reasonable opportunity to exhaust the judicial remedies available to it pursuant to Part XI, section 5, of the Convention.

Regulation 25

Size of area and relinquishment

1. The total area allocated to the contractor under the contract shall not exceed 150,000 square kilometres. The contractor shall relinquish portions of the area allocated to it to revert to the Area, in accordance with the following schedule:

(a) 20 per cent of the area allocated by the end of the third year from the date of the contract;

(b) an additional 10 per cent of the area allocated by the end of the fifth year from the date of the contract; and

(c) an additional 20 per cent of the area allocated or such larger amount as would exceed the exploitation area decided upon by the Authority, after eight years from the date of the contract,

provided that a contractor shall not be required to relinquish any portion of such area when the total area allocated to it does not exceed 75,000 square kilometres.

2. In the case of a registered pioneer investor, the contract shall take into account the schedule of relinquishment, where applicable, in accordance with the terms of its registration as a registered pioneer investor.

3. The Council may, at the request of the contractor, and on the recommendation of the Commission, in exceptional circumstances, defer the schedule of relinquishment. Such exceptional circumstances shall be determined by the Council and shall include, <u>inter alia</u>, consideration of prevailing

economic circumstances or other unforeseen exceptional circumstances arising in connection with the operational activities of the Contractor.

Regulation 26

Duration of contracts

1. A plan of work for exploration shall be approved for a period of 15 years. Upon expiration of a plan of work for exploration, the contractor shall apply for a plan of work for exploitation unless the contractor has already done so, has obtained an extension for the plan of work for exploration or decides to renounce its rights in the area covered by the plan of work for exploration.

2. Not later than six months before the expiration of a plan of work for exploration, a contractor may apply for extensions for the plan of work for exploration for periods of not more than five years each. Such extensions shall be approved by the Council, on the recommendation of the Commission, if the contractor has made efforts in good faith to comply with the requirements of the plan of work but for reasons beyond the contractor's control has been unable to complete the necessary preparatory work for proceeding to the exploitation stage or if the prevailing economic circumstances do not justify proceeding to the exploitation stage.

Regulation 27

Training

1. Pursuant to article 15 of Annex III to the Convention, each contract shall include as a schedule a practical programme for the training of personnel of the Authority and developing States and drawn up by the contractor in cooperation with the Authority and the sponsoring State or States. Training programmes shall focus on training in the conduct of exploration, and shall provide for full participation by such personnel in all activities covered by the contract. Such training programmes may be revised and developed from time to time as necessary by mutual agreement.

2. In the case of a registered pioneer investor, the contract shall take into account the training provided in accordance with the terms of its registration as a registered pioneer investor.

Regulation 28

Periodic review of the implementation of the plan of work for exploration

1. The contractor and the Secretary-General shall jointly undertake a periodic review of the implementation of the plan of work for exploration at intervals of five years. The Secretary-General may request the contractor to submit such additional data and information as may be necessary for the purposes of the review.

2. In the light of the review, the contractor shall indicate its programme of activities for the following five-year period, making such adjustments to its previous programme of activities as are necessary.

3. The Secretary-General shall report on the review to the Commission and to the Council. The Secretary-General shall indicate in the report whether any observations transmitted to him by States Parties to the Convention concerning the manner in which the contractor has discharged its obligations under these Regulations relating to the protection and preservation of the marine environment were taken into account in the review.

Regulation 29

Termination of sponsorship

1. Each contractor shall have the required sponsorship throughout the period of the contract.

2. If a State terminates its sponsorship it shall promptly notify the Secretary-General in writing. The sponsoring State should also inform the Secretary-General of the reasons for terminating its sponsorship. Termination of sponsorship shall take effect six months after the date of receipt of the notification by the Secretary-General, unless the notification specifies a later date.

3. In the event of termination of sponsorship the contractor shall, within the period referred to in paragraph 2, obtain another sponsor. Such sponsor shall submit a certificate of sponsorship in accordance with regulation 11. Failure to obtain a sponsor within the required period shall result in the termination of the contract.

4. A sponsoring State shall not be discharged by reason of the termination of its sponsorship from any obligations accrued while it was a sponsoring State, nor shall such termination affect any legal rights and obligations created during such sponsorship.

5. The Secretary-General shall notify the members of the Authority of the termination or change of sponsorship.

Regulation 30

Responsibility and liability

Responsibility and liability of the contractor and of the Authority shall be in accordance with the Convention. The contractor shall continue to have responsibility for any damage arising out of wrongful acts in the conduct of its operations, in particular damage to the marine environment, after the completion of the exploration phase.

PART V - PROTECTION AND PRESERVATION OF THE MARINE ENVIRONMENT

Regulation 31

Protection and preservation of the marine environment

1. The Authority shall, in accordance with the Convention and the Agreement, establish and keep under periodic review environmental rules, regulations and procedures to ensure effective protection for the marine environment from harmful effects which may arise from activities in the Area.

2. In order to ensure effective protection for the marine environment from harmful effects which may arise from activities in the Area, the Authority and sponsoring States shall apply a precautionary approach, as reflected in Principle 15 of the Rio Declaration,[11] to such activities. The Legal and Technical Commission shall make recommendations to the Council on the implementation of this paragraph.

3. Pursuant to article 145 of the Convention and paragraph 2 of this regulation, each contractor shall take necessary measures to prevent, reduce and control pollution and other hazards to the marine environment arising from its activities in the Area as far as reasonably possible using the best technology available to it.

4. Each contract shall require the contractor to gather environmental baseline data and to establish environmental baselines, taking into account any recommendations issued by the Legal and Technical Commission pursuant to regulation 38, against which to assess the likely effects of its programme of activities under the plan of work for exploration on the marine environment and a programme to monitor and report on such effects. The recommendations issued by the Commission may, inter alia, list those exploration activities which may be considered to have no potential for causing harmful effects on the marine environment. The contractor shall cooperate with the Authority and the sponsoring State or States in the establishment and implementation of such monitoring programme.

5. The contractor shall report annually in writing to the Secretary-General on the implementation and results of the monitoring programme referred to in paragraph 4 and shall submit data and information, taking into account any recommendations issued by the Commission pursuant to regulation 38. The Secretary-General shall transmit such reports to the Commission for its consideration pursuant to article 165 of the Convention.

---

[11] Report of the United Nations Conference on Environment and Development, Rio de Janeiro, 3–14 June 1991 (United Nations publication, Sales No. E.91.I.8 and corrigenda), vol. I: Resolutions adopted by the Conference, resolution 1, Annex I.

6. Contractors, sponsoring States and other interested States or entities shall cooperate with the Authority in the establishment and implementation of programmes for monitoring and evaluating the impacts of deep seabed mining on the marine environment.

7. If the Contractor applies for exploitation rights, it shall propose areas to be set aside and used exclusively as impact reference zones and preservation reference zones. "Impact reference zones" means areas to be used for assessing the effect of each contractor's activities in the Area on the marine environment and which are representative of the environmental characteristics of the Area. "Preservation reference zones" means areas in which no mining shall occur to ensure representative and stable biota of the seabed in order to assess any changes in the flora and fauna of the marine environment.

Regulation 32

Emergency orders

1. When the Secretary-General has been notified by a contractor or otherwise becomes aware of an incident resulting from or caused by a contractor's activities in the Area that has caused, or is likely to cause, serious harm to the marine environment, the Secretary-General shall issue a general notification of the incident, shall notify in writing the contractor and the sponsoring State or States, and shall report immediately to the Legal and Technical Commission and to the Council. A copy of the report shall be circulated to all members of the Authority, to competent international organizations and to concerned subregional, regional and global organizations and bodies. The Secretary-General shall monitor developments with respect to all such incidents and shall report on them as appropriate to the Commission and to the Council.

2. Pending any action by the Council, the Secretary-General shall take such immediate measures of a temporary nature as are practical and reasonable in the circumstances to prevent, contain and minimize serious harm to the marine environment. Such temporary measures shall remain in effect for no longer than 90 days, or until the Council decides what measures, if any, to take pursuant to paragraph 5 of this regulation, whichever is the earlier.

3. After having received the report of the Secretary-General, the Commission shall determine, based on the evidence provided to it and taking into account the measures already taken by the contractor, which measures are necessary to respond effectively to the incident in order to prevent, contain and minimize the serious harm, and shall make its recommendations to the Council.

4. The Council shall consider the recommendations of the Commission.

5. The Council, taking into account the recommendations of the Commission and any information provided by the Contractor, may issue emergency

orders, which may include orders for the suspension or adjustment of operations, as may be reasonably necessary to prevent, contain and minimize serious harm to the marine environment arising out of activities in the Area.

6. If a contractor does not promptly comply with an emergency order to prevent serious harm to the marine environment arising out of its activities in the Area, the Council shall take by itself or through arrangements with others on its behalf, such practical measures as are necessary to prevent, contain and minimize any such serious harm to the marine environment.

7. In order to enable the Council, when necessary, to take immediately the practical measures to prevent, contain and minimize serious harm to the marine environment referred to in paragraph 6, the contractor, prior to the commencement of testing of collecting systems and processing operations, will provide the Council with a guarantee of its financial and technical capability to comply promptly with emergency orders or to assure that the Council can take such emergency measures. If the contractor does not provide the Council with such a guarantee, the sponsoring State or States shall, in response to a request by the Secretary-General and pursuant to articles 139 and 235 of the Convention, take necessary measures to ensure that the contractor provides such a guarantee or shall take measures to ensure that assistance is provided to the Authority in the discharge of its responsibilities under paragraph 6.[12]

Regulation 33

Rights of coastal States

1. Nothing in these Regulations shall affect the rights of coastal States in accordance with article 142 and other relevant provisions of the Convention.

2. Any coastal State which has grounds for believing that any activity in the Area by a contractor is likely to cause serious harm to the marine environment under its jurisdiction or sovereignty may notify the Secretary-General in writing of the grounds upon which such belief is based. The Secretary-General shall provide the Contractor and its sponsoring State or States with a reasonable opportunity to examine the evidence, if any, provided by the coastal State as the basis for its belief. The contractor and its sponsoring State or States may submit their observations thereon to the Secretary-General within a reasonable time.

3. If there are clear grounds for believing that serious harm to the marine environment is likely to occur, the Secretary-General shall act in accordance with regulation 32 and, if necessary, shall take immediate measures of a temporary nature as provided for in paragraph 2 of regulation 32.

---

[12] See ISBA/6/C/12 (Decision of the Council relating to the regulations on prospecting and exploration for polymetallic nodules in the Area).

Regulation 34

Objects of an archaeological or historical nature

The contractor shall immediately notify the Secretary-General in writing of any finding in the exploration area of an object of an archaeological or historical nature and its location. The Secretary-General shall transmit such information to the Director-General of the United Nations Educational, Scientific and Cultural Organization. Following the finding of any such object of an archaeological or historical nature in the exploration area, the contractor shall take all reasonable measures to avoid disturbing such object.

PART VI - CONFIDENTIALITY

Regulation 35

Proprietary data and information and confidentiality

1. Data and information submitted or transferred to the Authority or to any person participating in any activity or programme of the Authority pursuant to these Regulations or a contract issued under these Regulations, and designated by the contractor, in consultation with the Secretary-General, as being of a confidential nature, shall be considered confidential unless it is data and information which:

(a) is generally known or publicly available from other sources;

(b) has been previously made available by the owner to others without an obligation concerning its confidentiality; or

(c) is already in the possession of the Authority with no obligation concerning its confidentiality.

2. Confidential data and information may only be used by the Secretary-General and staff of the Secretariat, as authorized by the Secretary-General, and by the members of the Legal and Technical Commission as necessary for and relevant to the effective exercise of their powers and functions. The Secretary-General shall authorize access to such data and information only for limited use in connection with the functions and duties of the staff of the Secretariat and the functions and duties of the Legal and Technical Commission.

3. Ten years after the date of submission of confidential data and information to the Authority or the expiration of the contract for exploration, whichever is the later, and every five years thereafter, the Secretary-General and the contractor shall review such data and information to determine whether they should remain confidential. Such data and information shall remain confidential if the contractor establishes that there would be a substantial risk of serious and unfair economic prejudice if the data and information were to be released. No such data and information shall be released until the contractor has been accorded a reasonable opportunity to exhaust the judicial remedies available to it pursuant to Part XI, section 5, of the Convention.

4. If, at any time following the expiration of the contract for exploration, the contractor enters into a contract for exploitation in respect of any part of the exploration area, confidential data and information relating to that part of the area shall remain confidential in accordance with the contract for exploitation.

5. The contractor may at any time waive confidentiality of data and information.

Regulation 36

Procedures to ensure confidentiality

1. The Secretary-General shall be responsible for maintaining the confidentiality of all confidential data and information and shall not, except with the prior written consent of the contractor, release such data and information to any person external to the Authority. To ensure the confidentiality of such data and information, the Secretary-General shall establish procedures, consistent with the provisions of the Convention, governing the handling of confidential information by members of the Secretariat, members of the Legal and Technical Commission and any other person participating in any activity or programme of the Authority. Such procedures shall include:

(a) maintenance of confidential data and information in secure facilities and development of security procedures to prevent unauthorized access to or removal of such data and information;

(b) development and maintenance of a classification, log and inventory system of all written data and information received, including its type and source and routing from the time of receipt until final disposition.

2. A person who is authorized pursuant to these Regulations to have access to confidential data and information shall not disclose such data and information except as permitted under the Convention and these Regulations. The Secretary-General shall require any person who is authorized to have access to confidential data and information to make a written declaration witnessed by the Secretary-General or his or her authorized representative to the effect that the person so authorized:

(a) acknowledges his or her legal obligation under the Convention and these Regulations with respect to the non-disclosure of confidential data and information;

(b) agrees to comply with the applicable regulations and procedures established to ensure the confidentiality of such data and information.

3. The Legal and Technical Commission shall protect the confidentiality of confidential data and information submitted to it pursuant to these Regulations or a contract issued under these Regulations. In accordance with the provisions of article 163, paragraph 8, of the Convention, members of the Commission shall not disclose, even after the termination of their functions, any industrial secret, proprietary data which are transferred to the Authority

in accordance with Annex III, article 14, of the Convention, or any other confidential information coming to their knowledge by reason of their duties for the Authority.

4. The Secretary-General and staff of the Authority shall not disclose, even after the termination of their functions with the Authority, any industrial secret, proprietary data which are transferred to the Authority in accordance with Annex III, article 14, of the Convention, or any other confidential information coming to their knowledge by reason of their employment with the Authority.

5. Taking into account the responsibility and liability of the Authority pursuant to Annex III, article 22, of the Convention, the Authority may take such action as may be appropriate against any person who, by reason of his or her duties for the Authority, has access to any confidential data and information and who is in breach of the obligations relating to confidentiality contained in the Convention and these Regulations.

PART VII – GENERAL PROCEDURES

Regulation 37

Notice and general procedures

1. Any application, request, notice, report, consent, approval, waiver, direction or instruction hereunder shall be made by the Secretary-General or by the designated representative of the prospector, applicant or contractor, as the case may be, in writing. Service shall be by hand, or by telex, facsimile or registered airmail to the Secretary-General at the headquarters of the Authority or to the designated representative.

2. Delivery by hand shall be effective when made. Delivery by telex shall be deemed to be effective on the business day following the day when the "answer back" appears on the sender's telex machine. Delivery by facsimile shall be effective when the "transmit confirmation report" confirming the transmission to the recipient's published facsimile number is received by the transmitter. Delivery by registered airmail shall be deemed to be effective 21 days after posting.

3. Notice to the designated representative of the prospector, applicant or contractor shall constitute effective notice to the prospector, applicant or contractor for all purposes under these Regulations, and the designated representative shall be the agent of the prospector, applicant or contractor for the service of process or notification in any proceeding of any court or tribunal having jurisdiction.

4. Notice to the Secretary-General shall constitute effective notice to the Authority for all purposes under these Regulations, and the Secretary-General shall be the Authority's agent for the service of process or notification in any proceeding of any court or tribunal having jurisdiction.

Regulation 38

Recommendations for the guidance of contractors

1. The Legal and Technical Commission may from time to time issue recommendations of a technical or administrative nature for the guidance of contractors to assist them in the implementation of the rules, regulations and procedures of the Authority.

2. The full text of such recommendations shall be reported to the Council. Should the Council find that a recommendation is inconsistent with the intent and purpose of these Regulations, it may request that the recommendation be modified or withdrawn.

PART VIII – SETTLEMENT OF DISPUTES

Regulation 39

Disputes

1. Disputes concerning the interpretation or application of these Regulations shall be settled in accordance with Part XI, section 5, of the Convention.

2. Any final decision rendered by a court or tribunal having jurisdiction under the Convention relating to the rights and obligations of the Authority and of the Contractor shall be enforceable in the territory of each State Party to the Convention.

PART IX - RESOURCES OTHER THAN POLYMETALLIC NODULES

Regulation 40

Resources other than polymetallic nodules

If a prospector or contractor finds resources in the Area other than polymetallic nodules, the prospecting and exploration for and exploitation of such resources shall be subject to the rules, regulations and procedures of the Authority relating to such resources in accordance with the Convention and the Agreement.

Annex 1

NOTIFICATION OF INTENTION TO ENGAGE IN PROSPECTING

1. Name of prospector:

2. Street address of prospector:

3. Postal address (if different from above):

4. Telephone number:

5. Facsimile number:

6. Electronic mail address:

7. Nationality of prospector:

8. If prospector is a juridical person, identify prospector's

   (a) place of registration; and

   (b) principal place of business/domicile.

and attach a copy of the prospector's certificate of registration.

9. Name of prospector's designated representative:

10. Street of prospector's designated representative (if different from above):

11. Postal address (if different from above):

12. Telephone number:

13. Facsimile number:

14. Electronic mail address:

15. Attach the coordinates of the broad area or areas in which prospecting is to be conducted (in accordance with the World Geodetic System WGS 84).

16. Attach a general description of the prospecting programme, including the date of commencement and the approximate duration of the programme.

17. Attach a written undertaking that the prospector will:

(a) comply with the Convention and the relevant rules, regulations and procedures of the Authority concerning:

- (i) cooperation in the training programmes in connection with marine scientific research and transfer of technology referred to in articles 143 and 144 of the Convention; and
- (ii) protection and preservation of the marine environment; and

(b) accept verification by the Authority of compliance therewith.

18. List hereunder all the attachments and annexes to this notification (all data and information should be submitted in hard copy and in a digital format specified by the Authority):

Date: ______________ ______________________________

Signature of prospector's designated representative

ATTESTATION:

____

Signature of person attesting

____

Name of person attesting

____

Title of person attesting

Annex 2

APPLICATION FOR APPROVAL OF A PLAN OF WORK FOR EXPLORATION TO OBTAIN A CONTRACT

Section I

Information concerning the applicant

1. Name of applicant:

2. Street address of applicant:

3. Postal address (if different from above):

4. Telephone number:

5. Facsimile number:

6. Electronic mail address:

7. Name of applicant's designated representative:

8. Street address of applicant's designated representative (if different from above):

9. Postal address (if different from above):

10. Telephone number:

11. Facsimile number:

12. Electronic mail address:

13. If the applicant is a juridical person, identify applicant's

    (a) place of registration; and

    (b) principal place of business/domicile.

and attach a copy of the applicant's certificate of registration.

14. Identify the sponsoring State or States.

15. In respect of each sponsoring State, provide the date of deposit of its instrument of ratification of, or accession or succession to, the 1982 United Nations Convention on the Law of the Sea and the date of its consent to be bound by the Agreement relating to the Implementation of Part XI of the United Nations Convention on the Law of the Sea of 10 December 1982.

16. A certificate of sponsorship issued by the sponsoring State must be attached with this application. If the applicant has more than one nationality, as in the case of a partnership or consortium of entities from more than one State, certificates of sponsorship issued by each of the States involved must be attached.

Section II

Information relating to the area under application

17. Define the boundaries of the area under application by attaching a list of geographical coordinates (in accordance with the World Geodetic System WGS 84).

18. Attach a chart (on a scale and projection specified by the Authority) and a list of the coordinates dividing the total area into two parts of equal estimated commercial value.

19. Include in an attachment sufficient information to enable the Council to designate a reserved area based on the estimated commercial value of each part of the area under application. Such attachment must include the data available to the applicant with respect to both parts of the area under application, including:

(a) data on the location, survey and evaluation of the polymetallic nodules in the areas, including:

(i) a description of the technology related to the recovery and processing of polymetallic nodules that is necessary for making the designation of a reserved area;

(ii) a map of the physical and geological characteristics, such as seabed topography, bathymetry and bottom currents and information on the reliability of such data;

(iii) data showing the average density (abundance) of polymetallic nodules in kg/m^2 and an associated abundance map showing the location of sampling sites;

(iv) data showing the average elemental content of metals of economic interest (grade) based on chemical assays in (dry) weight per cent and an associated grade map;

(v) combined maps of abundance and grade of polymetallic nodules;

(vi) a calculation based on standard procedures, including statistical analysis, using the data submitted and assumptions made in the calculations that the two areas could be expected to contain polymetallic nodules of equal estimated commercial value expressed as recoverable metals in mineable areas;

(vii) a description of the techniques used by the applicant.

(b) information concerning environmental parameters (seasonal and during test period) including, inter alia, wind speed and direction, wave height, period and direction, current speed and direction, water salinity, temperature and biological communities.

20. If the area under application includes any part of a reserved area, attach a list of coordinates of the area which forms part of the reserved area and indicate the applicant's qualifications in accordance with regulation 17 of the Regulations.

Section III

Financial and technical information[a]

21. Attach sufficient information to enable the Council to determine whether the applicant is financially capable of carrying out the proposed plan of work for exploration and of fulfilling its financial obligations to the Authority.

(a) If the application is made by the Enterprise, attach certification by its competent authority that the Enterprise has the necessary financial resources to meet the estimated costs of the proposed plan of work for exploration.

(b) If the application is made by a State or a state enterprise, attach a statement by the State or the sponsoring State certifying that the applicant has the necessary financial resources to meet the estimated costs of the proposed plan of work for exploration.

(c) If the application is made by an entity, attach copies of the applicant's audited financial statements, including balance sheets and profit-and-loss statements, for the most recent three years in conformity with internationally accepted accounting principles and certified by a duly qualified firm of public accountants; and

(i) if the applicant is a newly organized entity and a certified balance sheet is not available, a pro forma balance sheet certified by an appropriate official of the applicant;

(ii) if the applicant is a subsidiary of another entity, copies of such financial statements of that entity and a statement from that entity in conformity with internationally accepted accounting practices and certified by a duly qualified firm of public accountants that the applicant will have the financial resources to carry out the plan of work for exploration;

(iii) if the applicant is controlled by a State or a state enterprise, a statement from the State or state enterprise certifying that the

---

[a] An application for approval of a plan of work for exploration submitted on behalf of a State or entity, or any component of such entity, referred to in resolution II, paragraph 1(a)(ii) or (iii), other than a registered pioneer investor, which has already undertaken substantial activities in the Area prior to the entry into force of the Convention, or its successor in interest, shall be considered to have met the financial and technical qualifications necessary for approval of a plan of work if the sponsoring State or States certify that the applicant has expended an amount equivalent to at least US$ 30 million in research and exploration activities and has expended no less than 10 per cent of that amount in the location, survey and evaluation of the area referred to in the plan of work.

applicant will have the financial resources to carry out the plan of work for exploration.

22. If it is intended to finance the proposed plan of work for exploration by borrowings, attach a statement of the amount of such borrowings, the repayment period and the interest rate.

23. Attach sufficient information to enable the Council to determine whether the applicant is technically capable of carrying out the proposed plan of work for exploration, including:

(a) a general description of the applicant's previous experience, knowledge, skills, technical qualifications and expertise relevant to the proposed plan of work for exploration;

(b) a general description of the equipment and methods expected to be used in carrying out the proposed plan of work for exploration and other relevant non-proprietary information about the characteristics of such technology; and

(c) a general description of the applicant's financial and technical capability to respond to any incident or activity which causes serious harm to the marine environment.

Section IV

The plan of work for exploration

24. Attach the following information relating to the plan of work for exploration:

(a) a general description and a schedule of the proposed exploration programme, including the programme of activities for the immediate five-year period, such as studies to be undertaken in respect of the environmental, technical, economic and other appropriate factors which must be taken into account in exploration;

(b) a description of a programme for oceanographic and environmental baseline studies in accordance with the Regulations and any environmental rules, regulations and procedures established by the Authority that would enable an assessment of the potential environmental impact of the proposed exploration activities, taking into account any recommendations issued by the Legal and Technical Commission;

(c) a preliminary assessment of the possible impact of the proposed exploration activities on the marine environment;

(d) a description of proposed measures for the prevention, reduction and control of pollution and other hazards, as well as possible impacts, to the marine environment;

(e) a schedule of anticipated yearly expenditures in respect of the programme of activities for the immediate five-year period.

Section V

Undertakings

25. Attach a written undertaking that the applicant will:

(a) accept as enforceable and comply with the applicable obligations created by the provisions of the Convention and the rules, regulations and procedures of the Authority, the decisions of the relevant organs of the Authority and the terms of its contracts with the Authority;

(b) accept control by the Authority of activities in the Area as authorized by the Convention;

(c) provide the Authority with a written assurance that its obligations under the contract will be fulfilled in good faith.

Section VI

Previous contracts

26. Has the applicant or, in the case of an application by a partnership or consortium of entities in a joint arrangement, any member of the partnership or consortium previously been awarded any contract with the Authority?

27. If the answer to 26 is "yes", the application must include:

(a) the date of the previous contract or contracts;

(b) the dates, reference numbers and titles of each report submitted to the Authority in connection with the contract or contracts; and

(c) the date of termination of the contract or contracts, if applicable.

Section VII

Attachments

28. List all the attachments and annexes to this application (all data and information should be submitted in hard copy and in a digital format specified by the Authority):

Date: ____________________ ______________________________

Signature of applicant's designated representative

ATTESTATION:

____

Signature of person attesting

____

Name of person attesting

____

Title of person attesting

Annex 3

CONTRACT FOR EXPLORATION

THIS CONTRACT made the day of between the INTERNATIONAL SEABED AUTHORITY represented by its SECRETARY-GENERAL (hereinafter referred to as "the Authority") and represented by (hereinafter referred to as "the Contractor") WITNESSETH as follows:

Incorporation of clauses

A. The standard clauses set out in Annex 4 to the Regulations on Prospecting and Exploration for Polymetallic Nodules in the Area shall be incorporated herein and shall have effect as if herein set out at length.

Exploration area

B. For the purposes of this contract, the "exploration area" means that part of the Area allocated to the Contractor for exploration, defined by the coordinates listed in schedule 1 hereto, as reduced from time to time in accordance with the standard clauses and the Regulations.

Grant of rights

C. In consideration of:

(1) their mutual interest in the conduct of exploration activities in the exploration area pursuant to the Convention and the Agreement;

(2) the responsibility of the Authority to organize and control activities in the Area, particularly with a view to administering the resources of the Area, in accordance with the legal regime established in Part XI of the Convention and the Agreement and Part XII of the Convention respectively; and

(3) the interest and financial commitment of the Contractor in conducting activities in the exploration area and the mutual covenants made herein,

the Authority hereby grants to the Contractor the exclusive right to explore for polymetallic nodules in the exploration area in accordance with the terms and conditions of this contract.

Entry into force and contract term

D. This contract shall enter into force on signature by both parties and, subject to the standard clauses, shall remain in force for a period of fifteen years thereafter unless:

(1) the Contractor obtains a contract for exploitation in the exploration area which enters into force before the expiration of such period of fifteen years; or

(2) the contract is sooner terminated, provided that the term of the contract may be extended in accordance with standard clauses 3.2 and 17.2.

Schedules

E. The schedules referred to in the standard clauses, namely section 4 and section 8, are for the purposes of this contract schedules 2 and 3 respectively.

Entire agreement

F. This contract expresses the entire agreement between the parties, and no oral understanding or prior writing shall modify the terms hereof.

IN WITNESS WHEREOF the undersigned, being duly authorized thereto by the respective parties, have signed this contract at ...., this .... day of ....

SCHEDULE 1

[Coordinates and illustrative chart of the exploration area]

SCHEDULE 2

[The current five-year programme of activities as revised from time to time]

SCHEDULE 3

[The training programme shall become a schedule to the contract when approved by the Authority in accordance with section 8 of the standard clauses.]

Annex 4

STANDARD CLAUSES FOR EXPLORATION CONTRACT

Section 1

Definitions

1.1 In the following clauses:

(a) "exploration area" means that part of the Area allocated to the Contractor for exploration, described in schedule 1 hereto, as the same may be reduced from time to time in accordance with this contract and the Regulations;

(b) "programme of activities" means the programme of activities which is set out in schedule 2 hereto as the same may be adjusted from time to time in accordance with sections 4.3 and 4.4 hereof;

(c) "Regulations" means the Regulations for Prospecting and Exploration for Polymetallic Nodules in the Area, adopted by the Authority.

1.2 Terms and phrases defined in the Regulations shall have the same meaning in these standard clauses.

1.3 In accordance with the Agreement relating to the Implementation of Part XI of the United Nations Convention of the Law of the Sea of 10 December 1982, its provisions and Part XI of the Convention are to be interpreted and applied together as a single instrument; this contract and references in this contract to the Convention are to be interpreted and applied accordingly.

1.4 This contract includes the schedules to this contract, which shall be an integral part hereof.

Section 2

Security of tenure

2.1 The Contractor shall have security of tenure and this contract shall not be suspended, terminated or revised except in accordance with sections 20, 21 and 24 hereof.

2.2 The Contractor shall have the exclusive right to explore for polymetallic nodules in the exploration area in accordance with the terms and conditions of this contract. The Authority shall ensure that no other entity operates in the exploration area for a different category of resources in a manner that might unreasonably interfere with the operations of the Contractor.

2.3 The Contractor, by notice to the Authority, shall have the right at any time to renounce without penalty the whole or part of its rights in the exploration area, provided that the Contractor shall remain liable for all obligations accrued prior to the date of such renunciation in respect of the area renounced.

2.4 Nothing in this contract shall be deemed to confer any right on the Contractor other than those rights expressly granted herein. The Authority reserves the right to enter into contracts with respect to resources other than polymetallic nodules with third parties in the area covered by this contract.

Section 3

Contract term

3.1 This contract shall enter into force on signature by both parties and shall remain in force for a period of fifteen years thereafter unless:

(a) the Contractor obtains a contract for exploitation in the exploration area which enters into force before the expiration of such period of fifteen years; or

(b) the contract is sooner terminated,

provided that the term of the contract may be extended in accordance with sections 3.2 and 17.2 hereof.

3.2 Upon application by the Contractor, not later than six months before the expiration of this contract, this contract may be extended for periods of not more than five years each on such terms and conditions as the Authority and the Contractor may then agree in accordance with the Regulations. Such extensions shall be approved if the Contractor has made efforts in good faith to comply with the requirements of this contract but for reasons beyond the Contractor's control has been unable to complete the necessary preparatory work for proceeding to the exploitation stage or if the prevailing economic circumstances do not justify proceeding to the exploitation stage.

3.3 Notwithstanding the expiration of this contract in accordance with section 3.1 hereof, if the Contractor has, at least 90 days prior to the date of expiration, applied for a contract for exploitation, the Contractor's rights and obligations under this contract shall continue until such time as the application has been considered and a contract for exploitation has been issued or refused.

Section 4

Exploration

4.1 The Contractor shall commence exploration in accordance with the time schedule stipulated in the programme of activities set out in schedule 2 hereto and shall adhere to such time periods or any modification thereto as provided for by this contract.

4.2 The Contractor shall carry out the programme of activities set out in schedule 2 hereto. In carrying out such activities the Contractor shall spend in each contract year not less than the amount specified in such programme, or any agreed review thereof, in actual and direct exploration expenditures.

4.3 The Contractor, with the consent of the Authority, which consent shall not be unreasonably withheld, may from time to time make such changes in the programme of activities and the expenditures specified therein as may be necessary and prudent in accordance with good mining industry practice, and taking into account the market conditions for the metals contained in polymetallic nodules and other relevant global economic conditions.

4.4 Not later than 90 days prior to the expiration of each five-year period from the date on which this contract enters into force in accordance with section 3 hereof, the Contractor and the Secretary-General shall jointly undertake a review of the implementation of the plan of work for exploration under this contract. The Secretary-General may require the Contractor to submit such additional data and information as may be necessary for the purposes of the review. In the light of the review, the Contractor shall indicate its programme of activities for the following five-year period, including a revised schedule of anticipated yearly expenditures, making such adjustments to its previous programme of activities as are necessary. Schedule 2 hereto shall be adjusted accordingly.

Section 5

Environmental monitoring

5.1 The Contractor shall take necessary measures to prevent, reduce and control pollution and other hazards to the marine environment arising from its activities in the Area as far as reasonably possible using the best technology available to it.

5.2 The Contractor shall, in accordance with the Regulations, gather environmental baseline data as exploration activities progress and develop and shall establish environmental baselines against which to assess the likely effects of the Contractor's activities on the marine environment.

5.3 The Contractor shall, in accordance with the Regulations, establish and carry out a programme to monitor and report on such effects on the marine environment. The Contractor shall cooperate with the Authority in the implementation of such monitoring.

5.4 The Contractor shall, within 90 days of the end of each calendar year, report to the Secretary-General on the implementation and results of the monitoring programme referred to in section 5.3 hereof and shall submit data and information in accordance with the Regulations.

5.5 Prior to the commencement of testing of collecting systems and processing operations, the Contractor shall submit to the Authority:

(a) a site-specific environmental impact statement based on available meteorological, oceanographic and environmental data collected during the preceding phases of exploration and containing data that could be used to establish an environmental baseline against which to assess the likely effect of the mining tests;

(b) an assessment of the effects on the marine environment of the proposed tests of collecting systems;

(c) a proposal for a monitoring programme to determine the effect on the marine environment of the equipment that will be used during the proposed mining tests.

Section 6

Contingency plans and emergencies

6.1 The Contractor shall, prior to the commencement of its programme of activities under this contract, submit to the Secretary-General a contingency plan to respond effectively to incidents that are likely to cause serious harm to the marine environment arising from the Contractor's activities at sea in the exploration area. Such contingency plan shall establish special procedures and provide for adequate and appropriate equipment to deal with such incidents and, in particular, shall include arrangements for:

(a) the immediate raising of a general alarm in the area of the exploration activities;

(b) immediate notification to the Secretary-General;

(c) the warning of ships which might be about to enter the immediate vicinity;

(d) a continuing flow of full information to the Secretary-General relating to particulars of the contingency measures already taken and further actions required;

(e) the removal, as appropriate, of polluting substances;

(f) the reduction and, so far as reasonably possible, prevention of serious harm to the marine environment, as well as mitigation of such effects;

(g) as appropriate, cooperation with other contractors with the Authority to respond to an emergency; and

(h) periodic emergency response exercises.

6.2 The Contractor shall promptly report to the Secretary-General any incident arising from its activities that has caused or is likely to cause serious harm to the marine environment. Each such report shall contain the details of such incident, including, inter alia:

(a) the coordinates of the area affected or which can reasonably be anticipated to be affected;

(b) the description of the action being taken by the Contractor to prevent, contain, minimize and repair the serious harm to the marine environment;

(c) a description of the action being taken by the Contractor to monitor the effects of the incident on the marine environment; and

(d) such supplementary information as may reasonably be required by the Secretary-General.

6.3 The Contractor shall comply with emergency orders issued by the Council and immediate measures of a temporary nature issued by the Secretary-General in accordance with the Regulations, to prevent, contain, minimize or repair serious harm to the marine environment, which may include orders to the Contractor to immediately suspend or adjust any activities in the exploration area.

6.4 If the Contractor does not promptly comply with such emergency orders or immediate measures of a temporary nature, the Council may take such reasonable measures as are necessary to prevent, contain, minimize or repair any such serious harm to the marine environment at the Contractor's expense. The Contractor shall promptly reimburse the Authority the amount of such expenses. Such expenses shall be in addition to any monetary penalties which may be imposed on the Contractor pursuant to the terms of this contract or the Regulations.

Section 7

Objects of an archaeological or historical nature

The Contractor shall immediately notify the Secretary-General in writing of any finding in the exploration area of an object of an archaeological or historical nature and its location. Following the finding of any such object of an archaeological or historical nature in the exploration area, the Contractor shall take all reasonable measures to avoid disturbing such object.

Section 8

Training

8.1 In accordance with the Regulations, the Contractor shall, prior to the commencement of exploration under this contract, submit to the Authority for approval proposed training programmes for the training of personnel of the Authority and developing States, including the participation of such personnel in all of the Contractor's activities under this contract.

8.2. The scope and financing of the training programme shall be subject to negotiation between the Contractor, the Authority and the sponsoring State or States.

8.3 The Contractor shall conduct training programmes in accordance with the specific programme for the training of personnel referred to in section 8.1 hereof approved by the Authority in accordance with the Regulations, which programme, as revised and developed from time to time, shall become a part of this contract as schedule 3.

Section 9

Books and records

The Contractor shall keep a complete and proper set of books, accounts and financial records, consistent with internationally accepted accounting principles. Such books, accounts and financial records shall include information which will fully disclose the actual and direct expenditures for exploration and such other information as will facilitate an effective audit of such expenditures.

Section 10

Annual reports

10.1 The Contractor shall, within 90 days of the end of each calendar year, submit a report to the Secretary-General covering its programme of activities in the exploration area and containing, as applicable, information in sufficient detail on:

(a) the exploration work carried out during the calendar year, including maps, charts and graphs illustrating the work that has been done and the results obtained;

(b) the equipment used to carry out the exploration work, including the results of tests conducted of proposed mining technologies, but not equipment design data; and

(c) the implementation of training programmes, including any proposed revisions to or developments of such programmes.

10.2 Such reports shall also contain:

(a) the results obtained from environmental monitoring programmes, including observations, measurements, evaluations and analyses of environmental parameters;

(b) a statement of the quantity of polymetallic nodules recovered as samples or for the purpose of testing;

(c) a statement, in conformity with internationally accepted accounting principles and certified by a duly qualified firm of public accountants, or, where the Contractor is a State or a state enterprise, by the sponsoring State, of the actual and direct exploration expenditures of the Contractor in carrying out the programme of activities during the Contractor's accounting year. Such expenditures may be claimed by the contractor as part of the contractor's development costs incurred prior to the commencement of commercial production; and

(d) details of any proposed adjustments to the programme of activities and the reasons for such adjustments.

10.3 The Contractor shall also submit such additional information to supplement the reports referred to in sections 10.1 and 10.2 hereof as the

Secretary-General may from time to time reasonably require in order to carry out the Authority's functions under the Convention, the Regulations and this contract.

10.4 The Contractor shall keep, in good condition, a representative portion of samples of the polymetallic nodules obtained in the course of exploration until the expiration of this contract. The Authority may request the Contractor in writing to deliver to it for analysis a portion of any such sample obtained during the course of exploration.

Section 11

Data and information to be submitted on expiration of the contract

11.1 The Contractor shall transfer to the Authority all data and information that are both necessary for and relevant to the effective exercise of the powers and functions of the Authority in respect of the exploration area in accordance with the provisions of this section.

11.2 Upon expiration or termination of this contract the Contractor, if it has not already done so, shall submit the following data and information to the Secretary-General:

(a) copies of geological, environmental, geochemical and geophysical data acquired by the Contractor in the course of carrying out the programme of activities that are necessary for and relevant to the effective exercise of the powers and functions of the Authority in respect of the exploration area;

(b) the estimation of mineable areas, when such areas have been identified, which shall include details of the grade and quantity of the proven, probable and possible polymetallic nodule reserves and the anticipated mining conditions;

(c) copies of geological, technical, financial and economic reports made by or for the Contractor that are necessary for and relevant to the effective exercise of the powers and functions of the Authority in respect of the exploration area;

(d) information in sufficient detail on the equipment used to carry out the exploration work, including the results of tests conducted of proposed mining technologies, but not equipment design data; and

(e) a statement of the quantity of polymetallic nodules recovered as samples or for the purpose of testing.

11.3 The data and information referred to in section 11.2 hereof shall also be submitted to the Secretary-General if, prior to the expiration of this contract, the Contractor applies for approval of a plan of work for exploitation or if the Contractor renounces its rights in the exploration area to the extent that such data and information relates to the renounced area.

Section 12

Confidentiality

Data and information transferred to the Authority in accordance with this contract shall be treated as confidential in accordance with the provisions of the Regulations.

Section 13

Undertakings

13.1 The Contractor shall carry out exploration in accordance with the terms and conditions of this contract, the Regulations, Part XI of the Convention, the Agreement and other rules of international law not incompatible with the Convention.

13.2 The Contractor undertakes:

(a) to accept as enforceable and comply with the terms of this contract;

(b) to comply with the applicable obligations created by the provisions of the Convention, the rules, regulations and procedures of the Authority and the decisions of the relevant organs of the Authority;

(c) to accept control by the Authority of activities in the Area as authorized by the Convention;

(d) to fulfil its obligations under this contract in good faith; and

(e) to observe, as far as reasonably practicable, any recommendations which may be issued from time to time by the Legal and Technical Commission.

13.3 The Contractor shall actively carry out the programme of activities:

(a) with due diligence, efficiency and economy;

(b) with due regard to the impact of its activities on the marine environment; and

(c) with reasonable regard for other activities in the marine environment.

13.4 The Authority undertakes to fulfil in good faith its powers and functions under the Convention and the Agreement in accordance with article 157 of the Convention.

Section 14

Inspection

14.1 The Contractor shall permit the Authority to send its inspectors on board vessels and installations used by the Contractor to carry out activities in the exploration area to:

(a) monitor the Contractor's compliance with the terms and conditions of this contract and the Regulations; and

(b) monitor the effects of such activities on the marine environment.

14.2 The Secretary-General shall give reasonable notice to the Contractor of the projected time and duration of inspections, the name of the inspectors and any activities the inspectors are to perform that are likely to require the availability of special equipment or special assistance from personnel of the Contractor.

14.3 Such inspectors shall have the authority to inspect any vessel or installation, including its log, equipment, records, facilities, all other recorded data and any relevant documents which are necessary to monitor the Contractor's compliance.

14.4 The Contractor, its agents and employees shall assist the inspectors in the performance of their duties and shall:

(a) accept and facilitate prompt and safe boarding of vessels and installations by inspectors;

(b) cooperate with and assist in the inspection of any vessel or installation conducted pursuant to these procedures;

(c) provide access to all relevant equipment, facilities and personnel on vessels and installations at all reasonable times;

(d) not obstruct, intimidate or interfere with inspectors in the performance of their duties;

(e) provide reasonable facilities, including, where appropriate, food and accommodation, to inspectors; and

(f) facilitate safe disembarkation by inspectors.

14.5 Inspectors shall avoid interference with the safe and normal operations on board vessels and installations used by the Contractor to carry out activities in the area visited and shall act in accordance with the Regulations and the measures adopted to protect confidentiality of data and information.

14.6 The Secretary-General and any duly authorized representatives of the Secretary-General, shall have access, for purposes of audit and examination, to any books, documents, papers and records of the Contractor which are necessary and directly pertinent to verify the expenditures referred to in section 10.2(c).

14.7 The Secretary-General shall provide relevant information contained in the reports of inspectors to the Contractor and its sponsoring State or States where action is necessary.

14.8 If for any reason the contractor does not pursue exploration and does not request a contract for exploitation, it shall, before withdrawing from the exploration area, notify the Secretary-General in writing in order to permit the Authority, if it so decides, to carry out an inspection pursuant to this section.

Section 15

Safety, labour and health standards

15.1 The Contractor shall comply with the generally accepted international rules and standards established by competent international organizations or general diplomatic conferences concerning the safety of life at sea, and the prevention of collisions and such rules, regulations and procedures as may be adopted by the Authority relating to safety at sea. Each vessel used for carrying out activities in the Area shall possess current valid certificates required by and issued pursuant to such international rules and standards.

15.2 The Contractor shall, in carrying out exploration under this contract, observe and comply with such rules, regulations and procedures as may be adopted by the Authority relating to protection against discrimination in employment, occupational safety and health, labour relations, social security, employment security and living conditions at the work site. Such rules, regulations and procedures shall take into account conventions and recommendations of the International Labour Organization and other competent international organizations.

Section 16

Responsibility and liability

16.1 The Contractor shall be liable for the actual amount of any damage, including damage to the marine environment, arising out of its wrongful acts or omissions, and those of its employees, subcontractors, agents and all persons engaged in working or acting for them in the conduct of its operations under this contract, including the costs of reasonable measures to prevent or limit damage to the marine environment, account being taken of any contributory acts or omissions by the Authority.

16.2 The Contractor shall indemnify the Authority, its employees, subcontractors and agents against all claims and liabilities of any third party arising out of any wrongful acts or omissions of the Contractor and its employees, agents and subcontractors, and all persons engaged in working or acting for them in the conduct of its operations under this contract.

16.3 The Authority shall be liable for the actual amount of any damage to the Contractor arising out of its wrongful acts in the exercise of its powers and functions, including violations under article 168, paragraph 2, of the Convention, account being taken of contributory acts or omissions by the Contractor, its employees, agents and subcontractors, and all persons engaged in working or acting for them in the conduct of its operations under this contract.

16.4 The Authority shall indemnify the Contractor, its employees, subcontractors, agents and all persons engaged in working or acting for them in the conduct of its operations under this contract, against all claims and liabilities of any third party arising out of any wrongful acts or omissions in the exercise of its powers and functions hereunder, including violations under article 168, paragraph 2, of the Convention.

16.5 The Contractor shall maintain appropriate insurance policies with internationally recognized carriers, in accordance with generally accepted international maritime practice.

Section 17

Force majeure

17.1 The Contractor shall not be liable for an unavoidable delay or failure to perform any of its obligations under this contract due to force majeure. For the purposes of this contract, force majeure shall mean an event or condition that the Contractor could not reasonably be expected to prevent or control; provided that the event or condition was not caused by negligence or by a failure to observe good mining industry practice.

17.2 The Contractor shall, upon request, be granted a time extension equal to the period by which performance was delayed hereunder by force majeure and the term of this contract shall be extended accordingly.

17.3 In the event of force majeure, the Contractor shall take all reasonable measures to remove its inability to perform and comply with the terms and conditions of this contract with a minimum of delay; provided that the Contractor shall not be obligated to resolve or terminate any labour dispute or any other disagreement with a third party except on terms satisfactory to it or pursuant to a final decision of any agency having jurisdiction to resolve the dispute.

17.4 The Contractor shall give notice to the Authority of the occurrence of an event of force majeure as soon as reasonably possible, and similarly give notice to the Authority of the restoration of normal conditions.

Section 18

Disclaimer

Neither the Contractor nor any affiliated company or subcontractor shall in any manner claim or suggest, whether expressly or by implication, that the Authority or any official thereof has, or has expressed, any opinion with respect to polymetallic nodules in the exploration area and a statement to that effect shall not be included in or endorsed on any prospectus, notice, circular, advertisement, press release or similar document issued by the Contractor, any affiliated company or any subcontractor that refers directly or indirectly to this contract. For the purposes of this section, an "affiliated company" means any person, firm or company or State-owned entity controlling, controlled by, or under common control with, the Contractor.

Section 19

Renunciation of rights

The Contractor, by notice to the Authority, shall have the right to renounce its rights and terminate this contract without penalty, provided that the Contractor shall remain liable for all obligations accrued prior to the date of such renunciation and those obligations required to be fulfilled after termination in accordance with the Regulations.

Section 20

Termination of sponsorship

20.1 If the nationality or control of the Contractor changes or the Contractor's sponsoring State, as defined in the Regulations, terminates its sponsorship, the Contractor shall promptly notify the Authority forthwith.

20.2 In either such event, if the Contractor does not obtain another sponsor meeting the requirements prescribed in the Regulations which submits to the Authority a certificate of sponsorship for the Contractor in the prescribed form within the time specified in the Regulations, this contract shall terminate forthwith.

Section 21

Suspension and termination of contract and penalties

21.1 The Council may suspend or terminate this contract, without prejudice to any other rights that the Authority may have, if any of the following events should occur:

(a) if, in spite of written warnings by the Authority, the Contractor has conducted its activities in such a way as to result in serious persistent and wilful violations of the fundamental terms of this contract, Part XI of the Convention, the Agreement and the rules, regulations and procedures of the Authority; or

(b) if the Contractor has failed to comply with a final binding decision of the dispute settlement body applicable to it; or

(c) if the Contractor becomes insolvent or commits an act of bankruptcy or enters into any agreement for composition with its creditors or goes into liquidation or receivership, whether compulsory or voluntary, or petitions or applies to any tribunal for the appointment of a receiver or a trustee or receiver for itself or commences any proceedings relating to itself under any bankruptcy, insolvency or readjustment of debt law, whether now or hereafter in effect, other than for the purpose of reconstruction.

21.2 Any suspension or termination shall be by notice, through the Secretary-General, which shall include a statement of the reasons for taking such action. The suspension or termination shall be effective 60 days after such notice, unless the Contractor within such period disputes the Authority's right to suspend or terminate this contract in accordance with Part XI, section 5, of the Convention.

21.3 If the Contractor takes such action, this contract shall only be suspended or terminated in accordance with a final binding decision in accordance with Part XI, section 5, of the Convention.

21.4 If the Council has suspended this contract, the Council may by notice require the Contractor to resume its operations and comply with the terms and conditions of this contract, not later than 60 days after such notice.

21.5 In the case of any violation of this contract not covered by section 21.1(a) hereof, or in lieu of suspension or termination under section 21.1 hereof, the Council may impose upon the Contractor monetary penalties proportionate to the seriousness of the violation.

21.6 The Council may not execute a decision involving monetary penalties until the Contractor has been accorded a reasonable opportunity to exhaust the judicial remedies available to it pursuant to Part XI, section 5, of the Convention.

21.7 In the event of termination or expiration of this contract, the Contractor shall comply with the Regulations and shall remove all installations, plant, equipment and materials in the exploration area and shall make the area safe so as not to constitute a danger to persons, shipping or to the marine environment.

Section 22

Transfer of rights and obligations

22.1 The rights and obligations of the Contractor under this contract may be transferred in whole or in part only with the consent of the Authority and in accordance with the Regulations.

22.2 The Authority shall not unreasonably withhold consent to the transfer if the proposed transferee is in all respects a qualified applicant in accordance with the Regulations and assumes all of the obligations of the Contractor and if the transfer does not confer to the transferee a plan of work, the approval of which would be forbidden by Annex 3, article 6, paragraph 3(c), of the Convention.

22.3 The terms, undertakings and conditions of this contract shall inure to the benefit of and be binding upon the parties hereto and their respective successors and assigns.

Section 23

No waiver

No waiver by either party of any rights pursuant to a breach of the terms and conditions of this contract to be performed by the other party shall be construed as a waiver by the party of any succeeding breach of the same or any other term or condition to be performed by the other party.

Section 24

Revision

24.1 When circumstances have arisen or are likely to arise which, in the opinion of the Authority or the Contractor, would render this contract inequitable or make it impracticable or impossible to achieve the objectives set out in this contract or in Part XI of the Convention or the Agreement, the parties shall enter into negotiations to revise it accordingly.

24.2 This contract may also be revised by agreement between the Contractor and the Authority to facilitate the application of any rules, regulations and procedures adopted by the Authority subsequent to the entry into force of this contract.

24.3 This contract may be revised, amended or otherwise modified only with the consent of the Contractor and the Authority by an appropriate instrument signed by the authorized representatives of the parties.

Section 25

Disputes

25.1 Any dispute between the parties concerning the interpretation or application of this contract shall be settled in accordance with Part XI, section 5, of the Convention.

25.2 Any final decision rendered by a court or tribunal having jurisdiction under the Convention relating to the rights and obligations of the Authority and of the Contractor shall be enforceable in the territory of each State Party to the Convention.

Section 26

Notice

26.1 Any application, request, notice, report, consent, approval, waiver, direction or instruction hereunder shall be made by the Secretary-General or by the designated representative of the Contractor, as the case may be, in writing. Service shall be by hand, or by telex, facsimile or registered airmail to the Secretary-General at the headquarters of the Authority or to the designated representative.

26.2 Either party shall be entitled to change any such address to any other address by not less than ten days' notice to the other party.

26.3 Delivery by hand shall be effective when made. Delivery by telex shall be deemed to be effective on the business day following the day when the "answer back" appears on the sender's telex machine. Delivery by facsimile shall be effective when the "transmit confirmation report" confirming the transmission to the recipient's published facsimile number is received by the transmitter. Delivery by registered airmail shall be deemed to be effective 21 days after posting.

26.4 Notice to the designated representative of the Contractor shall constitute effective notice to the Contractor for all purposes under this contract, and the designated representative shall be the Contractor's agent for the service of process or notification in any proceeding of any court or tribunal having jurisdiction.

26.5 Notice to the Secretary-General shall constitute effective notice to the Authority for all purposes under this contract, and the Secretary-General shall be the Authority's agent for the service of process or notification in any proceeding of any court or tribunal having jurisdiction.

Section 27

Applicable law

27.1 This contract shall be governed by the terms of this contract, the rules, regulations and procedures of the Authority, Part XI of the Convention, the Agreement and other rules of international law not incompatible with the Convention.

27.2 The Contractor, its employees, subcontractors, agents and all persons engaged in working or acting for them in the conduct of its operations under this contract shall observe the applicable law referred to in section 27.1 hereof and shall not engage in any transaction, directly or indirectly, prohibited by the applicable law.

27.3 Nothing contained in this contract shall be deemed an exemption from the necessity of applying for and obtaining any permit or authority that may be required for any activities under this contract.

Section 28

Interpretation

The division of this contract into sections and subsections and the insertion of headings are for convenience of reference only and shall not affect the construction or interpretation hereof.

Section 29

Additional documents

Each party hereto agrees to execute and deliver all such further instruments, and to do and perform all such further acts and things as may be necessary or expedient to give effect to the provisions of this contract.

International Seabed Authority ISBA/16/A/12/Rev.1

Assembly

Distr: General
15 November 2000

Original: English

Sixteenth session
Kingston, Jamaica
26 April–7 May 2010

Decision of the Assembly of the International Seabed Authority relating to the regulations on prospecting and exploration for polymetallic sulphides in the Area

The Assembly of the International Seabed Authority,

Having considered the Regulations on prospecting and exploration for polymetallic sulphides in the Area, as provisionally adopted by the Council at its 161st meeting, on 6 May 2010 (ISBA/16/C/L.5),

Approves the Regulations on prospecting and exploration for polymetallic sulphides in the Area as contained in the annex to the present document.

130th meeting
7 May 2010

Annex

Regulations on prospecting and exploration for polymetallic sulphides in the Area

Preamble

In accordance with the United Nations Convention on the Law of the Sea ("the Convention"), the seabed and ocean floor and the subsoil thereof beyond the limits of national jurisdiction, as well as its resources, are the common heritage of mankind, the exploration and exploitation of which shall be carried out for the benefit of mankind as a whole, on whose behalf the International Seabed Authority acts. The objective of this set of Regulations is to provide for prospecting and exploration for polymetallic sulphides.

Part I
Introduction

Regulation 1
Use of terms and scope

1. Terms used in the Convention shall have the same meaning in these Regulations.

2. In accordance with the Agreement relating to the Implementation of Part XI of the United Nations Convention on the Law of the Sea of 10 December 1982 ("the Agreement"), the provisions of the Agreement and Part XI of the United Nations Convention on the Law of the Sea of 10 December 1982 shall be interpreted and applied together as a single instrument. These Regulations and references in these Regulations to the Convention are to be interpreted and applied accordingly.

3. For the purposes of these Regulations:

(a) "exploitation" means the recovery for commercial purposes of polymetallic sulphides in the Area and the extraction of minerals therefrom, including the construction and operation of mining, processing and transportation systems, for the production and marketing of metals;

(b) "exploration" means searching for deposits of polymetallic sulphides in the Area with exclusive rights, the analysis of such deposits, the use and testing of recovery systems and equipment, processing facilities and transportation systems, and the carrying out of studies of the environmental, technical, economic, commercial and other appropriate factors that must be taken into account in exploitation;

(c) "marine environment" includes the physical, chemical, geological and biological components, conditions and factors which interact and determine the productivity, state, condition and quality of the marine ecosystem, the waters of the seas and oceans and the airspace above those waters, as well as the seabed and ocean floor and subsoil thereof;

(d) "polymetallic sulphides" means hydrothermally formed deposits of sulphides and accompanying mineral resources in the Area which contain concentrations of metals including, inter alia, copper, lead, zinc, gold and silver;

(e) "prospecting" means the search for deposits of polymetallic sulphides in the Area, including estimation of the composition, size and distribution of deposits of polymetallic sulphides and their economic values, without any exclusive rights;

(f) "serious harm to the marine environment" means any effect from activities in the Area on the marine environment which represents a significant adverse change in the marine environment determined according to the rules, regulations and procedures adopted by the Authority on the basis of internationally recognized standards and practices.

4. These Regulations shall not in any way affect the freedom of scientific research, pursuant to article 87 of the Convention, or the right to conduct marine scientific research in the Area pursuant to articles 143 and 256 of the Convention. Nothing in these Regulations shall be construed in such a way as to restrict the exercise by States of the freedom of the high seas as reflected in article 87 of the Convention.

5. These Regulations may be supplemented by further rules, regulations and procedures, in particular on the protection and preservation of the marine environment. These Regulations shall be subject to the provisions of the Convention and the Agreement and other rules of international law not incompatible with the Convention.

Part II
Prospecting

Regulation 2
Prospecting

1. Prospecting shall be conducted in accordance with the Convention and these Regulations and may commence only after the prospector has been informed by the Secretary-General that its notification has been recorded pursuant to regulation 4, paragraph 2.

2. Prospectors and the Secretary-General shall apply a precautionary approach, as reflected in principle 15 of the Rio Declaration.[1] Prospecting shall not be undertaken if substantial evidence indicates the risk of serious harm to the marine environment.

3. Prospecting shall not be undertaken in an area covered by an approved plan of work for exploration for polymetallic sulphides or in a reserved area; nor may there be prospecting in an area which the Council has disapproved for exploitation because of the risk of serious harm to the marine environment.

4. Prospecting shall not confer on the prospector any rights with respect to resources. A prospector may, however, recover a reasonable quantity of minerals, being the quantity necessary for testing and not for commercial use.

5. There shall be no time limit on prospecting, except that prospecting in a particular area shall cease upon written notification to the prospector by the Secretary-General that a plan of work for exploration has been approved with regard to that area.

6. Prospecting may be conducted simultaneously by more than one prospector in the same area or areas.

Regulation 3
Notification of prospecting

1. A proposed prospector shall notify the Authority of its intention to engage in prospecting.

2. Each notification of prospecting shall be in the form prescribed in annex 1 to these Regulations, addressed to the Secretary-General, and shall conform to the requirements of these Regulations.

3. Each notification shall be submitted:

(a) In the case of a State, by the authority designated for that purpose by it;

(b) In the case of an entity, by its designated representative;

(c) In the case of the Enterprise, by its competent authority.

4. Each notification shall be in one of the languages of the Authority and shall contain:

---

[1] *Report of the United Nations Conference on Environment and Development, Rio de Janeiro, 3–14 June 1991* (United Nations publication, Sales No. E.91.1.8 and corrigenda), vol. 1: *Resolutions adopted by the Conference*, resolution 1, annex 1.

(a) The name, nationality and address of the proposed prospector and its designated representative;

(b) The coordinates of the broad area or areas within which prospecting is to be conducted, in accordance with the most recent generally accepted international standard used by the Authority;

(c) A general description of the prospecting programme, including the proposed date of commencement and its approximate duration;

(d) A satisfactory written undertaking that the proposed prospector will:

(i) Comply with the Convention and the relevant rules, regulations and procedures of the Authority concerning:

a. Cooperation in the training programmes in connection with marine scientific research and transfer of technology referred to in articles 143 and 144 of the Convention; and

b. Protection and preservation of the marine environment;

(ii) Accept verification by the Authority of compliance therewith; and

(iii) Make available to the Authority, as far as practicable, such data as may be relevant to the protection and preservation of the marine environment.

Regulation 4
Consideration of notifications

1. The Secretary-General shall acknowledge in writing receipt of each notification submitted under regulation 3, specifying the date of receipt.

2. The Secretary-General shall review and act on the notification within 45 days of its receipt. If the notification conforms with the requirements of the Convention and these Regulations, the Secretary-General shall record the particulars of the notification in a register maintained for that purpose and shall inform the prospector in writing that the notification has been so recorded.

3. The Secretary-General shall, within 45 days of receipt of the notification, inform the proposed prospector in writing if the notification includes any part of an area included in an approved plan of work for exploration or exploitation of any category of resources, or any part of a reserved area, or any part of an area which has been

disapproved by the Council for exploitation because of the risk of serious harm to the marine environment, or if the written undertaking is not satisfactory, and shall provide the proposed prospector with a written statement of reasons. In such cases, the proposed prospector may, within 90 days, submit an amended notification. The Secretary-General shall, within 45 days, review and act upon such amended notification.

4. A prospector shall inform the Secretary-General in writing of any change in the information contained in the notification.

5. The Secretary-General shall not release any particulars contained in the notification except with the written consent of the prospector. The Secretary-General shall, however, from time to time inform all members of the Authority of the identity of prospectors and the general areas in which prospecting is being conducted.

Regulation 5
Protection and preservation of the marine environment during prospecting

1. Each prospector shall take necessary measures to prevent, reduce and control pollution and other hazards to the marine environment arising from prospecting, as far as reasonably possible, applying a precautionary approach and best environmental practices. In particular, each prospector shall minimize or eliminate:

(a) Adverse environmental impacts from prospecting; and

(b) Actual or potential conflicts or interference with existing or planned marine scientific research activities, in accordance with the relevant future guidelines in this regard.

2. Prospectors shall cooperate with the Authority in the establishment and implementation of programmes for monitoring and evaluating the potential impacts of the exploration for and exploitation of polymetallic sulphides on the marine environment.

3. A prospector shall immediately notify the Secretary-General in writing, using the most effective means, of any incident arising from prospecting which has caused, is causing or poses a threat of serious harm to the marine environment. Upon receipt of such notification the Secretary-General shall act in a manner consistent with regulation 35.

Regulation 6
Annual report

1. A prospector shall, within 90 days of the end of each calendar year, submit a report to the Authority on the status of prospecting.

Such reports shall be submitted by the Secretary-General to the Legal and Technical Commission. Each such report shall contain:

(a) A general description of the status of prospecting and of the results obtained;

(b) Information on compliance with the undertakings referred to in regulation 3, paragraph 4 (d); and

(c) Information on adherence to the relevant guidelines in this regard.

2. If the prospector intends to claim expenditures for prospecting as part of the development costs incurred prior to the commencement of commercial production, the prospector shall submit an annual statement, in conformity with internationally accepted accounting principles and certified by a duly qualified firm of public accountants, of the actual and direct expenditures incurred by the prospector in carrying out prospecting.

Regulation 7
Confidentiality of data and information from prospecting contained in the annual report

1. The Secretary-General shall ensure the confidentiality of all data and information contained in the reports submitted under regulation 6 applying mutatis mutandis the provisions of regulations 38 and 39, provided that data and information relating to the protection and preservation of the marine environment, in particular those from environmental monitoring programmes, shall not be considered confidential. The prospector may request that such data not be disclosed for up to three years following the date of their submission.

2. The Secretary-General may, at any time, with the consent of the prospector concerned, release data and information relating to prospecting in an area in respect of which a notification has been submitted. If, after having made reasonable efforts for at least two years, the Secretary-General determines that the prospector no longer exists or cannot be located, the Secretary-General may release such data and information.

Regulation 8
Objects of an archaeological or historical nature

A prospector shall immediately notify the Secretary-General in writing of any finding in the Area of an object of actual or potential archaeological or historical nature and its location. The Secretary-General shall transmit such information to the Director-General of the United Nations Educational, Scientific and Cultural Organization.

Part III
Applications for approval of plans of work for exploration in the form of contracts

Section 1
General provisions

Regulation 9
General

Subject to the provisions of the Convention, the following may apply to the Authority for approval of plans of work for exploration:

(a) The Enterprise, on its own behalf or in a joint arrangement;

(b) States Parties, State enterprises or natural or juridical persons which possess the nationality of States or are effectively controlled by them or their nationals, when sponsored by such States, or any group of the foregoing which meets the requirements of these Regulations.

Section 2
Content of applications

Regulation 10
Form of applications

1. Each application for approval of a plan of work for exploration shall be in the form prescribed in annex 2 to these Regulations, shall be addressed to the Secretary-General, and shall conform to the requirements of these Regulations.

2. Each application shall be submitted:

(a) In the case of a State, by the authority designated for that purpose by it;

(b) In the case of an entity, by its designated representative or the authority designated for that purpose by the sponsoring State or States; and

(c) In the case of the Enterprise, by its competent authority.

3. Each application by a State enterprise or one of the entities referred to in subparagraph (b) of regulation 9 shall also contain:

(a) Sufficient information to determine the nationality of the applicant or the identity of the State or States by which, or by whose nationals, the applicant is effectively controlled; and

(b) The principal place of business or domicile and, if applicable, place of registration of the applicant.

4. Each application submitted by a partnership or consortium of entities shall contain the required information in respect of each member of the partnership or consortium.

Regulation 11
Certificate of sponsorship

1. Each application by a State enterprise or one of the entities referred to in subparagraph (b) of regulation 9 shall be accompanied by a certificate of sponsorship issued by the State of which it is a national or by which or by whose nationals it is effectively controlled. If the applicant has more than one nationality, as in the case of a partnership or consortium of entities from more than one State, each State involved shall issue a certificate of sponsorship.

2. Where the applicant has the nationality of one State but is effectively controlled by another State or its nationals, each State involved shall issue a certificate of sponsorship.

3. Each certificate of sponsorship shall be duly signed on behalf of the State by which it is submitted, and shall contain:

(a) The name of the applicant;

(b) The name of the sponsoring State;

(c) A statement that the applicant is:

(i) A national of the sponsoring State; or

(ii) Subject to the effective control of the sponsoring State or its nationals;

(d) A statement by the sponsoring State that it sponsors the applicant;

(e) The date of deposit by the sponsoring State of its instrument of ratification of, or accession or succession to, the Convention;

(f) A declaration that the sponsoring State assumes responsibility in accordance with article 139, article 153, paragraph 4, and annex III, article 4, paragraph 4, of the Convention.

4. States or entities in a joint arrangement with the Enterprise shall also comply with this regulation.

Regulation 12
Total area covered by the application

1. For the purposes of these Regulations, a "polymetallic sulphide block" means a cell of a grid as provided by the Authority,

which shall be approximately 10 kilometres by 10 kilometres and no greater than 100 square kilometres.

2. The area covered by each application for approval of a plan of work for exploration for polymetallic sulphides shall be comprised of not more than 100 polymetallic sulphide blocks which shall be arranged by the applicant in at least five clusters, as set out in paragraph 3 below.

3. Each cluster of polymetallic sulphide blocks shall contain at least five contiguous blocks. Two such blocks that touch at any point shall be considered to be contiguous. Clusters of polymetallic sulphide blocks need not be contiguous but shall be proximate and confined within a rectangular area not exceeding 300,000 square kilometres in size and where the longest side does not exceed 1,000 kilometres in length.

4. Notwithstanding the provisions in paragraph 2 above, where an applicant has elected to contribute a reserved area to carry out activities pursuant to article 9 of annex III to the Convention, in accordance with regulation 17, the total area covered by an application shall not exceed 200 polymetallic sulphide blocks. Such blocks shall be arranged in two groups of equal estimated commercial value and each such group of polymetallic sulphide blocks shall be arranged by the applicant in clusters, as set out in paragraph 3 above.

Regulation 13
Financial and technical capabilities

1. Each application for approval of a plan of work for exploration shall contain specific and sufficient information to enable the Council to determine whether the applicant is financially and technically capable of carrying out the proposed plan of work for exploration and of fulfilling its financial obligations to the Authority.

2. An application for approval of a plan of work for exploration by the Enterprise shall include a statement by its competent authority certifying that the Enterprise has the necessary financial resources to meet the estimated costs of the proposed plan of work for exploration.

3. An application for approval of a plan of work for exploration by a State or a State enterprise shall include a statement by the State or the sponsoring State certifying that the applicant has the necessary financial resources to meet the estimated costs of the proposed plan of work for exploration.

4. An application for approval of a plan of work for exploration by an entity shall include copies of its audited financial statements,

including balance sheets and profit-and-loss statements, for the most recent three years, in conformity with internationally accepted accounting principles and certified by a duly qualified firm of public accountants; and

(a) If the applicant is a newly organized entity and a certified balance sheet is not available, a pro forma balance sheet certified by an appropriate official of the applicant;

(b) If the applicant is a subsidiary of another entity, copies of such financial statements of that entity and a statement from that entity, in conformity with internationally accepted accounting principles and certified by a duly qualified firm of public accountants, that the applicant will have the financial resources to carry out the plan of work for exploration;

(c) If the applicant is controlled by a State or a State enterprise, a statement from the State or State enterprise certifying that the applicant will have the financial resources to carry out the plan of work for exploration.

5. Where an applicant referred to in paragraph 4 intends to finance the proposed plan of work for exploration by borrowings, its application shall include the amount of such borrowings, the repayment period and the interest rate.

6. Each application shall include:

(a) A general description of the applicant's previous experience, knowledge, skills, technical qualifications and expertise relevant to the proposed plan of work for exploration;

(b) A general description of the equipment and methods expected to be used in carrying out the proposed plan of work for exploration and other relevant non-proprietary information about the characteristics of such technology;

(c) A general description of the applicant's financial and technical capability to respond to any incident or activity which causes serious harm to the marine environment.

7. Where the applicant is a partnership or consortium of entities in a joint arrangement, each member of the partnership or consortium shall provide the information required by this regulation.

Regulation 14
Previous contracts with the Authority

Where the applicant or, in the case of an application by a partnership or consortium of entities in a joint arrangement, any member of the partnership or consortium, has previously been awarded any contract with the Authority, the application shall include:

(a) The date of the previous contract or contracts;

(b) The date, reference number and title of each report submitted to the Authority in connection with the contract or contracts; and

(c) The date of termination of the contract or contracts, if applicable.

Regulation 15
Undertakings

Each applicant, including the Enterprise, shall, as part of its application for approval of a plan of work for exploration, provide a written undertaking to the Authority that it will:

(a) Accept as enforceable and comply with the applicable obligations created by the provisions of the Convention and the rules, regulations and procedures of the Authority, the decisions of the organs of the Authority and the terms of its contracts with the Authority;

(b) Accept control by the Authority of activities in the Area, as authorized by the Convention; and

(c) Provide the Authority with a written assurance that its obligations under the contract will be fulfilled in good faith.

Regulation 16
Applicant's election of a reserved area contribution or equity interest in a joint venture arrangement

Each applicant shall, in the application, elect either to:

(a) Contribute a reserved area to carry out activities pursuant to Annex III, article 9, of the Convention, in accordance with regulation 17; or

(b) Offer an equity interest in a joint venture arrangement in accordance with regulation 19.

Regulation 17
Data and information to be submitted before the designation of a reserved area

1. Where the applicant elects to contribute a reserved area to carry out activities pursuant to article 9 of annex III to the Convention, the area covered by the application shall be sufficiently large and of sufficient estimated commercial value to allow two mining operations and shall be configured by the applicant in accordance with regulation 12, paragraph 4.

2. Each such application shall contain sufficient data and information, as prescribed in section II of annex 2 to these Regulations, with respect to the area under application to enable the Council, on the recommendation of the Legal and Technical Commission, to designate a reserved area based on the estimated commercial value of each part. Such data and information shall consist of data available to the applicant with respect to both parts of the area under application, including the data used to determine their commercial value.

3. The Council, on the basis of the data and information submitted by the applicant pursuant to section II of annex 2 to these Regulations, if found satisfactory, and taking into account the recommendation of the Legal and Technical Commission, shall designate the part of the area under application which is to be a reserved area. The area so designated shall become a reserved area as soon as the plan of work for exploration for the non-reserved area is approved and the contract is signed. If the Council determines that additional information, consistent with these Regulations and annex 2, is needed to designate the reserved area, it shall refer the matter back to the Commission for further consideration, specifying the additional information required.

4. Once the plan of work for exploration is approved and a contract has been issued, the data and information transferred to the Authority by the applicant in respect of the reserved area may be disclosed by the Authority in accordance with article 14, paragraph 3, of annex III to the Convention.

Regulation 18
Applications for approval of plans of work with respect to a reserved area

1. Any State which is a developing State or any natural or juridical person sponsored by it and effectively controlled by it or by any other developing State, or any group of the foregoing, may notify the Authority that it wishes to submit a plan of work for exploration with respect to a reserved area. The Secretary-General shall forward such notification to the Enterprise, which shall inform the Secretary-General in writing within six months whether or not it intends to carry out activities in that area. If the Enterprise intends to carry out activities in that area, it shall, pursuant to paragraph 4, also inform in writing the contractor whose application for approval of a plan of work for exploration originally included that area.

2. An application for approval of a plan of work for exploration in respect of a reserved area may be submitted at any time after such an area becomes available following a decision by the Enterprise

that it does not intend to carry out activities in that area or where the Enterprise has not, within six months of the notification by the Secretary-General, either taken a decision on whether it intends to carry out activities in that area or notified the Secretary-General in writing that it is engaged in discussions regarding a potential joint venture. In the latter instance, the Enterprise shall have one year from the date of such notification in which to decide whether to conduct activities in that area.

3. If the Enterprise or a developing State or one of the entities referred to in paragraph 1 does not submit an application for approval of a plan of work for exploration for activities in a reserved area within 15 years of the commencement by the Enterprise of its functions independent of the Secretariat of the Authority or within 15 years of the date on which that area is reserved for the Authority, whichever is the later, the contractor whose application for approval of a plan of work for exploration originally included that area shall be entitled to apply for a plan of work for exploration for that area provided it offers in good faith to include the Enterprise as a joint-venture partner.

4. A contractor has the right of first refusal to enter into a joint venture arrangement with the Enterprise for exploration of the area which was included in its application for approval of a plan of work for exploration and which was designated by the Council as a reserved area.

Regulation 19
Equity interest in a joint venture arrangement

1. Where the applicant elects to offer an equity interest in a joint venture arrangement, it shall submit data and information in accordance with regulation 20. The area to be allocated to the applicant shall be subject to the provisions of regulation 27.

2. The joint venture arrangement, which shall take effect at the time the applicant enters into a contract for exploitation, shall include the following:

(a) The Enterprise shall obtain a minimum of 20 per cent of the equity participation in the joint venture arrangement on the following basis:

(i) Half of such equity participation shall be obtained without payment, directly or indirectly, to the applicant and shall be treated *pari passu* for all purposes with the equity participation of the applicant;

(ii) The remainder of such equity participation shall be treated *pari passu* for all purposes with the equity participation of the applicant except that the Enterprise shall not receive any profit distribution with respect to such participation until the applicant has recovered its total equity participation in the joint venture arrangement;

(b) Notwithstanding subparagraph (a), the applicant shall nevertheless offer the Enterprise the opportunity to purchase a further thirty per cent of the equity in the joint venture arrangement, or such lesser percentage as the Enterprise may elect to purchase, on the basis of *pari passu* treatment with the applicant for all purposes;[2]

(c) Except as specifically provided in the agreement between the applicant and the Enterprise, the Enterprise shall not by reason of its equity participation be otherwise obligated to provide funds or credits or issue guarantees or otherwise accept any financial liability whatsoever for or on behalf of the joint venture arrangement, nor shall the Enterprise be required to subscribe for additional equity participation so as to maintain its proportionate participation in the joint venture arrangement.

Regulation 20
Data and information to be submitted for approval of the plan of work for exploration

1. Each applicant shall submit, with a view to receiving approval of the plan of work for exploration in the form of a contract, the following information:

(a) A general description and a schedule of the proposed exploration programme, including the programme of activities for the immediate five-year period, such as studies to be undertaken in respect of the environmental, technical, economic and other appropriate factors that must be taken into account in exploration;

(b) A description of the programme for oceanographic and environmental baseline studies in accordance with these Regulations and any environmental rules, regulations and procedures established by the Authority that would enable an assessment of the potential environmental impact including, but not restricted to, the impact on biodiversity, of the proposed exploration activities, taking into account any recommendations issued by the Legal and Technical Commission;

(c) A preliminary assessment of the possible impact of the proposed exploration activities on the marine environment;

---

[2] The terms and conditions upon which such equality participation may be obtained would need to be further elaborated.

(d) A description of proposed measures for the prevention, reduction and control of pollution and other hazards, as well as possible impacts, to the marine environment;

(e) Data necessary for the Council to make the determination it is required to make in accordance with regulation 13, paragraph 1; and

(f) A schedule of anticipated yearly expenditures in respect of the programme of activities for the immediate five-year period.

2. Where the applicant elects to contribute a reserved area, the data and information relating to such area shall be transferred to the Authority by the applicant after the Council has designated the reserved area in accordance with regulation 17, paragraph 3.

3. Where the applicant elects to offer an equity interest in a joint venture arrangement, the data and information relating to such area shall be transferred to the Authority by the applicant at the time of the election.

Section 3
Fees

Regulation 21
Fee for applications

1. The fee for processing a plan of work for exploration for polymetallic sulphides shall be:

(a) A fixed fee of 500,000 United States dollars or its equivalent in a freely convertible currency, payable by the applicant at the time of submitting an application; or

(b) At the election of the applicant, a fixed fee of 50,000 United States dollars or its equivalent in a freely convertible currency, payable by the applicant at the time of submitting an application, and an annual fee calculated as set out in paragraph 2.

2. The annual fee shall be calculated as follows:

(i) 5 United States dollars multiplied by the area factor from the date of the first anniversary of the contract;

(ii) 10 United States dollars multiplied by the area factor from the date of the first relinquishment in accordance with regulation 27(2); and

(iii) 20 United States dollars multiplied by the area factor from the date of the second relinquishment in accordance with regulation 27(3).

3. The "Area Factor" means the number of square kilometres comprised in the exploration area at the date upon which the periodic payment in question becomes due.

4. Upon notification by the Secretary-General that the amount of the fee has been insufficient to cover the administrative costs incurred by the Authority in processing an application, the fee set out in paragraph 1 (a) of this regulation shall be reviewed by the Council.

5. If the administrative costs incurred by the Authority in processing an application are less than the fixed amount, the Authority shall refund the difference to the applicant.

Section 4
Processing of applications

Regulation 22
Receipt, acknowledgement and safe custody of applications

The Secretary-General shall:

(a) Acknowledge in writing within 30 days receipt of every application for approval of a plan of work for exploration submitted under this Part, specifying the date of receipt;

(b) Place the application together with the attachments and annexes thereto in safe custody and ensure the confidentiality of all confidential data and information contained in the application; and

(c) Notify the members of the Authority of the receipt of such application and circulate to them information of a general nature which is not confidential regarding the application.

Regulation 23
Consideration by the Legal and Technical Commission

1. Upon receipt of an application for approval of a plan of work for exploration, the Secretary-General shall notify the members of the Legal and Technical Commission and place consideration of the application as an item on the agenda for the next meeting of the Commission. The Commission shall only consider applications in respect of which notification and information has been circulated by the Secretary-General in accordance with regulation 22 (c) at least 30 days prior to the commencement of the meeting of the Commission at which they are to be considered.

2. The Commission shall examine applications in the order in which they are received.

3. The Commission shall determine if the applicant:

(a) Has complied with the provisions of these Regulations;

(b) Has given the undertakings and assurances specified in regulation 15;

(c) Possesses the financial and technical capability to carry out the proposed plan of work for exploration and has provided details as to its ability to comply promptly with emergency orders; and

(d) Has satisfactorily discharged its obligations in relation to any previous contract with the Authority.

4. The Commission shall, in accordance with the requirements set forth in these Regulations and its procedures, determine whether the proposed plan of work for exploration will:

(a) Provide for effective protection of human health and safety;

(b) Provide for effective protection and preservation of the marine environment including, but not restricted to, the impact on biodiversity;

(c) Ensure that installations are not established where interference may be caused to the use of recognized sea lanes essential to international navigation or in areas of intense fishing activity.

5. If the Commission makes the determinations specified in paragraph 3 and determines that the proposed plan of work for exploration meets the requirements of paragraph 4, the Commission shall recommend approval of the plan of work for exploration to the Council.

6. The Commission shall not recommend approval of the plan of work for exploration if part or all of the area covered by the proposed plan of work for exploration is included in:

(a) A plan of work for exploration approved by the Council for polymetallic sulphides; or

(b) A plan of work approved by the Council for exploration for or exploitation of other resources if the proposed plan of work for exploration for polymetallic sulphides might cause undue interference with activities under such approved plan of work for other resources; or

(c) An area disapproved for exploitation by the Council in cases where substantial evidence indicates the risk of serious harm to the marine environment.

7. The Legal and Technical Commission may recommend approval of a plan of work if it determines that such approval would not permit a State Party or entities sponsored by it to monopolize the conduct of activities in the Area with regard to polymetallic sulphides or to preclude other States Parties from activities in the Area with regard to polymetallic sulphides.

8. Except in the case of applications by the Enterprise, on its own behalf or in a joint venture, and applications under regulation 18, the Commission shall not recommend approval of the plan of work for exploration if part or all of the area covered by the proposed plan of work for exploration is included in a reserved area or an area designated by the Council to be a reserved area.

9. If the Commission finds that an application does not comply with these Regulations, it shall notify the applicant in writing, through the Secretary-General, indicating the reasons. The applicant may, within 45 days of such notification, amend its application. If the Commission after further consideration is of the view that it should not recommend approval of the plan of work for exploration, it shall so inform the applicant and provide the applicant with a further opportunity to make representations within 30 days of such information. The Commission shall consider any such representations made by the applicant in preparing its report and recommendation to the Council.

10. In considering a proposed plan of work for exploration, the Commission shall have regard to the principles, policies and objectives relating to activities in the Area as provided for in part XI and annex III of the Convention and the Agreement.

11. The Commission shall consider applications expeditiously and shall submit its report and recommendations to the Council on the designation of the areas and on the plan of work for exploration at the first possible opportunity, taking into account the schedule of meetings of the Authority.

12. In discharging its duties, the Commission shall apply these Regulations and the rules, regulations and procedures of the Authority in a uniform and non-discriminatory manner.

Regulation 24
Consideration and approval of plans of work for exploration by the Council

The Council shall consider the reports and recommendations of the Commission relating to approval of plans of work for exploration in accordance with paragraphs 11 and 12 of section 3 of the annex to the Agreement.

Part IV
Contracts for exploration

Regulation 25
The contract

1. After a plan of work for exploration has been approved by the Council, it shall be prepared in the form of a contract between the Authority and the applicant as prescribed in annex 3 to these Regulations. Each contract shall incorporate the standard clauses set out in annex 4 in effect at the date of entry into force of the contract.

2. The contract shall be signed by the Secretary-General on behalf of the Authority and by the applicant. The Secretary-General shall notify all members of the Authority in writing of the conclusion of each contract.

Regulation 26
Rights of the contractor

1. The contractor shall have the exclusive right to explore an area covered by a plan of work for exploration in respect of polymetallic sulphides. The Authority shall ensure that no other entity operates in the same area for other resources in a manner that might interfere with the operations of the contractor.

2. A contractor who has an approved plan of work for exploration only shall have a preference and a priority among applicants submitting plans of work for exploitation of the same area and resources. Such preference or priority may be withdrawn by the Council if the contractor has failed to comply with the requirements of its approved plan of work for exploration within the time period specified in a written notice or notices from the Council to the contractor indicating which requirements have not been complied with by the contractor. The time period specified in any such notice shall not be unreasonable. The contractor shall be accorded a reasonable opportunity to be heard before the withdrawal of such preference or priority becomes final. The Council shall provide the reasons for its proposed withdrawal of preference or priority and shall consider any contractor's response. The decision of the Council shall take account of that response and shall be based on substantial evidence.

3. A withdrawal of preference or priority shall not become effective until the contractor has been accorded a reasonable opportunity to exhaust the judicial remedies available to it pursuant to part XI, section 5, of the Convention.

Regulation 27
Size of area and relinquishment

1. The contractor shall relinquish the area allocated to it in accordance with paragraph 2 of this regulation. Areas to be relinquished need not be contiguous and shall be defined by the contractor in the form of sub-blocks comprising one or more cells of a grid as provided by the Authority.

2. The total area allocated to the contractor under the contract shall not exceed 10,000 square kilometres. The contractor shall relinquish parts of the area allocated to it in accordance with the following schedule:

(a) By the end of the eighth year from the date of the contract, the contractor shall have relinquished at least 50 per cent of the original area allocated to it;

(b) By the end of the tenth year from the date of the contract, the contractor shall have relinquished at least 75 per cent of the original area allocated to it; or

3. The contractor may at any time relinquish parts of the area allocated to it in advance of the schedule set out in paragraph 2, provided that a contractor shall not be required to relinquish any additional part of such area when the remaining area allocated to it after relinquishment does not exceed 2,500 square kilometres.

4. Relinquished areas shall revert to the Area.

5. At the end of the fifteenth year from the date of the contract, or when the contractor applies for exploitation rights, whichever is the earlier, the contractor shall nominate an area from the remaining area allocated to it to be retained for exploitation.

6. The Council may, at the request of the contractor, and on the recommendation of the Commission, in exceptional circumstances, defer the schedule of relinquishment. Such exceptional circumstances shall be determined by the Council and shall include, inter alia, consideration of prevailing economic circumstances or other unforeseen exceptional circumstances arising in connection with the operational activities of the contractor.

Regulation 28
Duration of contracts

1. A plan of work for exploration shall be approved for a period of 15 years. Upon expiration of a plan of work for exploration, the contractor shall apply for a plan of work for exploitation unless the contractor has already done so, has obtained an extension for the

plan of work for exploration or decides to renounce its rights in the area covered by the plan of work for exploration.

2. Not later than six months before the expiration of a plan of work for exploration, a contractor may apply for extensions for the plan of work for exploration for periods of not more than five years each. Such extensions shall be approved by the Council, on the recommendation of the Commission, if the contractor has made efforts in good faith to comply with the requirements of the plan of work but for reasons beyond the contractor's control has been unable to complete the necessary preparatory work for proceeding to the exploitation stage or if the prevailing economic circumstances do not justify proceeding to the exploitation stage.

Regulation 29
Training

Pursuant to article 15 of annex III to the Convention, each contract shall include as a schedule a practical programme for the training of personnel of the Authority and developing States and drawn up by the contractor in cooperation with the Authority and the sponsoring State or States. Training programmes shall focus on training in the conduct of exploration, and shall provide for full participation by such personnel in all activities covered by the contract. Such training programmes may be revised and developed from time to time as necessary by mutual agreement.

Regulation 30
Periodic review of the implementation of the plan of work for exploration

1. The contractor and the Secretary-General shall jointly undertake a periodic review of the implementation of the plan of work for exploration at intervals of five years. The Secretary-General may request the contractor to submit such additional data and information as may be necessary for the purposes of the review.

2. In the light of the review, the contractor shall indicate its programme of activities for the following five-year period, making such adjustments to its previous programme of activities as are necessary.

3. The Secretary-General shall report on the review to the Commission and to the Council. The Secretary-General shall indicate in the report whether any observations transmitted to him by States Parties to the Convention concerning the manner in which the contractor has discharged its obligations under these Regulations relating to the protection and preservation of the marine environment were taken into account in the review.

Regulation 31
Termination of sponsorship

1. Each contractor shall have the required sponsorship throughout the period of the contract.

2. If a State terminates its sponsorship it shall promptly notify the Secretary-General in writing. The sponsoring State should also inform the Secretary-General of the reasons for terminating its sponsorship. Termination of sponsorship shall take effect six months after the date of receipt of the notification by the Secretary-General, unless the notification specifies a later date.

3. In the event of termination of sponsorship the contractor shall, within the period referred to in paragraph 2, obtain another sponsor. Such sponsor shall submit a certificate of sponsorship in accordance with regulation 11. Failure to obtain a sponsor within the required period shall result in the termination of the contract.

4. A sponsoring State shall not be discharged by reason of the termination of its sponsorship from any obligations accrued while it was a sponsoring State, nor shall such termination affect any legal rights and obligations created during such sponsorship.

5. The Secretary-General shall notify the members of the Authority of the termination or change of sponsorship.

Regulation 32
Responsibility and liability

Responsibility and liability of the contractor and of the Authority shall be in accordance with the Convention. The contractor shall continue to have responsibility for any damage arising out of wrongful acts in the conduct of its operations, in particular damage to the marine environment, after the completion of the exploration phase.

Part V
Protection and preservation of the marine environment

Regulation 33
Protection and preservation of the marine environment

1. The Authority shall, in accordance with the Convention and the Agreement, establish and keep under periodic review environmental rules, regulations and procedures to ensure effective protection for the marine environment from harmful effects which may arise from activities in the Area.

2. In order to ensure effective protection for the marine environment from harmful effects which may arise from activities in the

Area, the Authority and sponsoring States shall apply a precautionary approach, as reflected in principle 15 of the Rio Declaration, and best environmental practices.

3. The Legal and Technical Commission shall make recommendations to the Council on the implementation of paragraphs 1 and 2 above.

4. The Commission shall develop and implement procedures for determining, on the basis of the best available scientific and technical information, including information provided pursuant to regulation 20, whether proposed exploration activities in the Area would have serious harmful effects on vulnerable marine ecosystems, in particular hydrothermal vents, and ensure that, if it is determined that certain proposed exploration activities would have serious harmful effects on vulnerable marine ecosystems, those activities are managed to prevent such effects or not authorized to proceed.

5. Pursuant to article 145 of the Convention and paragraph 2 of this regulation, each contractor shall take necessary measures to prevent, reduce and control pollution and other hazards to the marine environment arising from its activities in the Area as far as reasonably possible, applying a precautionary approach and best environmental practices.

6. Contractors, sponsoring States and other interested States or entities shall cooperate with the Authority in the establishment and implementation of programmes for monitoring and evaluating the impacts of deep seabed mining on the marine environment. When required by the Council, such programmes shall include proposals for areas to be set aside and used exclusively as impact reference zones and preservation reference zones. "Impact reference zones" means areas to be used for assessing the effect of activities in the Area on the marine environment and which are representative of the environmental characteristics of the Area. "Preservation reference zones" means areas in which no mining shall occur to ensure representative and stable biota of the seabed in order to assess any changes in the biodiversity of the marine environment.

Regulation 34
Environmental baselines and monitoring

1. Each contract shall require the contractor to gather environmental baseline data and to establish environmental baselines, taking into account any recommendations issued by the Legal and Technical Commission pursuant to regulation 41, against which to assess the likely effects of its programme of activities under the plan of work for exploration on the marine environment and a programme to monitor and report on such effects. The recommendations issued by the Commission may, inter alia, list those exploration

activities which may be considered to have no potential for causing harmful effects on the marine environment. The contractor shall cooperate with the Authority and the sponsoring State or States in the establishment and implementation of such monitoring programme.

2. The contractor shall report annually in writing to the Secretary-General on the implementation and results of the monitoring programme referred to in paragraph 1 and shall submit data and information, taking into account any recommendations issued by the Commission pursuant to regulation 41. The Secretary-General shall transmit such reports to the Commission for its consideration pursuant to article 165 of the Convention.

Regulation 35
Emergency orders

1. A contractor shall promptly report to the Secretary-General in writing, using the most effective means, any incident arising from activities which have caused, are causing, or pose a threat of, serious harm to the marine environment.

2. When the Secretary-General has been notified by a contractor or otherwise becomes aware of an incident resulting from or caused by a contractor's activities in the Area that has caused, is causing or poses a threat of, serious harm to the marine environment, the Secretary-General shall cause a general notification of the incident to be issued, shall notify in writing the contractor and the sponsoring State or States, and shall report immediately to the Legal and Technical Commission, to the Council and to all other members of the Authority. A copy of the report shall be circulated to competent international organizations and to concerned subregional, regional and global organizations and bodies. The Secretary-General shall monitor developments with respect to all such incidents and shall report on them as appropriate to the Commission, the Council and all other members of the Authority.

3. Pending any action by the Council, the Secretary-General shall take such immediate measures of a temporary nature as are practical and reasonable in the circumstances to prevent, contain and minimize serious harm or the threat of serious harm to the marine environment. Such temporary measures shall remain in effect for no longer than 90 days, or until the Council decides at its next regular session or a special session, what measures, if any, to take pursuant to paragraph 6 of this regulation.

4. After having received the report of the Secretary-General, the Commission shall determine, based on the evidence provided to it and taking into account the measures already taken by the

contractor, which measures are necessary to respond effectively to the incident in order to prevent, contain and minimize serious harm or the threat of serious harm to the marine environment, and shall make its recommendations to the Council.

5. The Council shall consider the recommendations of the Commission.

6. The Council, taking into account the recommendations of the Commission, the report of the Secretary-General, any information provided by the Contractor and any other relevant information, may issue emergency orders, which may include orders for the suspension or adjustment of operations, as may be reasonably necessary to prevent, contain and minimize serious harm or the threat of serious harm to the marine environment arising out of activities in the Area.

7. If a contractor does not promptly comply with an emergency order to prevent, contain and minimize serious harm or the threat of serious harm to the marine environment arising out of its activities in the Area, the Council shall take by itself or through arrangements with others on its behalf, such practical measures as are necessary to prevent, contain and minimize any such serious harm or threat of serious harm to the marine environment.

8. In order to enable the Council, when necessary, to take immediately the practical measures to prevent, contain and minimize the serious harm or threat of serious harm to the marine environment referred to in paragraph 7, the contractor, prior to the commencement of testing of collecting systems and processing operations, will provide the Council with a guarantee of its financial and technical capability to comply promptly with emergency orders or to assure that the Council can take such emergency measures. If the contractor does not provide the Council with such a guarantee, the sponsoring State or States shall, in response to a request by the Secretary-General and pursuant to articles 139 and 235 of the Convention, take necessary measures to ensure that the contractor provides such a guarantee or shall take measures to ensure that assistance is provided to the Authority in the discharge of its responsibilities under paragraph 7.

Regulation 36
Rights of coastal States

1. Nothing in these Regulations shall affect the rights of coastal States in accordance with article 142 and other relevant provisions of the Convention.

2. Any coastal State which has grounds for believing that any activity in the Area by a contractor is likely to cause serious harm or a threat of serious harm to the marine environment under its

jurisdiction or sovereignty may notify the Secretary-General in writing of the grounds upon which such belief is based. The Secretary-General shall provide the Contractor and its sponsoring State or States with a reasonable opportunity to examine the evidence, if any, provided by the coastal State as the basis for its belief. The contractor and its sponsoring State or States may submit their observations thereon to the Secretary-General within a reasonable time.

3. If there are clear grounds for believing that serious harm to the marine environment is likely to occur, the Secretary-General shall act in accordance with regulation 35 and, if necessary, shall take immediate measures of a temporary nature as provided for in paragraph 3 of regulation 35.

4. Contractors shall take all measures necessary to ensure that their activities are conducted so as not to cause serious harm to the marine environment, including, but not restricted to, pollution, under the jurisdiction or sovereignty of coastal States, and that such serious harm or pollution arising from incidents or activities in its exploration area does not spread beyond such area.

Regulation 37
Human remains and objects and sites of an archaeological or historical nature

The contractor shall immediately notify the Secretary-General in writing of any finding in the exploration area of any human remains of an archaeological or historical nature, or any object or site of a similar nature and its location, including the preservation and protection measures taken. The Secretary-General shall transmit such information to the Director-General of the United Nations Educational, Scientific and Cultural Organization and any other competent international organization. Following the finding of any such human remains, object or site in the exploration area, and in order to avoid disturbing such human remains, object or site, no further prospecting or exploration shall take place, within a reasonable radius, until such time as the Council decides otherwise after taking account of the views of the Director-General of the United Nations Educational, Scientific and Cultural Organization or any other competent international organization.

Part VI
Confidentiality

Regulation 38
Confidentiality of data and information

1. Data and information submitted or transferred to the Authority or to any person participating in any activity or programme of

the Authority pursuant to these Regulations or a contract issued under these Regulations, and designated by the contractor, in consultation with the Secretary-General, as being of a confidential nature, shall be considered confidential unless it is data and information which:

(a) Is generally known or publicly available from other sources;

(b) Has been previously made available by the owner to others without an obligation concerning its confidentiality; or

(c) Is already in the possession of the Authority with no obligation concerning its confidentiality.

Data and information that is necessary for the formulation by the Authority of rules, regulations and procedures concerning protection and preservation of the marine environment and safety, other than proprietary equipment design data, shall not be deemed confidential.

2. Confidential data and information may only be used by the Secretary-General and staff of the Secretariat, as authorized by the Secretary-General, and by the members of the Legal and Technical Commission as necessary for and relevant to the effective exercise of their powers and functions. The Secretary-General shall authorize access to such data and information only for limited use in connection with the functions and duties of the staff of the Secretariat and the functions and duties of the Legal and Technical Commission.

3. Ten years after the date of submission of confidential data and information to the Authority or the expiration of the contract for exploration, whichever is the later, and every five years thereafter, the Secretary-General and the contractor shall review such data and information to determine whether they should remain confidential. Such data and information shall remain confidential if the contractor establishes that there would be a substantial risk of serious and unfair economic prejudice if the data and information were to be released. No such data and information shall be released until the contractor has been accorded a reasonable opportunity to exhaust the judicial remedies available to it pursuant to Part XI, section 5, of the Convention.

4. If, at any time following the expiration of the contract for exploration, the contractor enters into a contract for exploitation in respect of any part of the exploration area, confidential data and information relating to that part of the area shall remain confidential in accordance with the contract for exploitation.

5. The contractor may at any time waive confidentiality of data and information.

Regulation 39
Procedures to ensure confidentiality

1. The Secretary-General shall be responsible for maintaining the confidentiality of all confidential data and information and shall not, except with the prior written consent of the contractor, release such data and information to any person external to the Authority. To ensure the confidentiality of such data and information, the Secretary-General shall establish procedures, consistent with the provisions of the Convention, governing the handling of confidential information by members of the Secretariat, members of the Legal and Technical Commission and any other person participating in any activity or programme of the Authority. Such procedures shall include:

(a) Maintenance of confidential data and information in secure facilities and development of security procedures to prevent unauthorized access to or removal of such data and information;

(b) Development and maintenance of a classification, log and inventory system of all written data and information received, including its type and source and routing from the time of receipt until final disposition.

2. A person who is authorized pursuant to these Regulations to have access to confidential data and information shall not disclose such data and information except as permitted under the Convention and these Regulations. The Secretary-General shall require any person who is authorized to have access to confidential data and information to make a written declaration witnessed by the Secretary-General or his or her authorized representative to the effect that the person so authorized:

(a) Acknowledges his or her legal obligation under the Convention and these Regulations with respect to the non-disclosure of confidential data and information;

(b) Agrees to comply with the applicable regulations and procedures established to ensure the confidentiality of such data and information.

3. The Legal and Technical Commission shall protect the confidentiality of confidential data and information submitted to it pursuant to these Regulations or a contract issued under these Regulations. In accordance with the provisions of article 163, paragraph 8, of the Convention, members of the Commission shall not disclose, even

after the termination of their functions, any industrial secret, proprietary data which are transferred to the Authority in accordance with Annex III, article 14, of the Convention, or any other confidential information coming to their knowledge by reason of their duties for the Authority.

4. The Secretary-General and staff of the Authority shall not disclose, even after the termination of their functions with the Authority, any industrial secret, proprietary data which are transferred to the Authority in accordance with Annex III, article 14, of the Convention, or any other confidential information coming to their knowledge by reason of their employment with the Authority.

5. Taking into account the responsibility and liability of the Authority pursuant to Annex III, article 22, of the Convention, the Authority may take such action as may be appropriate against any person who, by reason of his or her duties for the Authority, has access to any confidential data and information and who is in breach of the obligations relating to confidentiality contained in the Convention and these Regulations.

Part VII
General procedures

Regulation 40
Notice and general procedures

1. Any application, request, notice, report, consent, approval, waiver, direction or instruction hereunder shall be made by the Secretary-General or by the designated representative of the prospector, applicant or contractor, as the case may be, in writing. Service shall be by hand, or by telex, facsimile, registered airmail or electronic mail containing an authorized electronic signature to the Secretary-General at the headquarters of the Authority or to the designated representative.

2. Delivery by hand shall be effective when made. Delivery by telex shall be deemed to be effective on the business day following the day when the "answer back" appears on the sender's telex machine. Delivery by facsimile shall be effective when the "transmit confirmation report" confirming the transmission to the recipient's published facsimile number is received by the transmitter. Delivery by registered airmail shall be deemed to be effective 21 days after posting. An electronic document is presumed to be received by the addressee when it enters an information system designated or used by the addressee for the purpose of receiving documents of the type sent and is capable of being retrieved and processed by the addressee.

3. Notice to the designated representative of the prospector, applicant or contractor shall constitute effective notice to the prospector, applicant or contractor for all purposes under these Regulations, and the designated representative shall be the agent of the prospector, applicant or contractor for the service of process or notification in any proceeding of any court or tribunal having jurisdiction.

4. Notice to the Secretary-General shall constitute effective notice to the Authority for all purposes under these Regulations, and the Secretary-General shall be the Authority's agent for the service of process or notification in any proceeding of any court or tribunal having jurisdiction.

Regulation 41
Recommendations for the guidance of contractors

1. The Legal and Technical Commission may from time to time issue recommendations of a technical or administrative nature for the guidance of contractors to assist them in the implementation of the rules, regulations and procedures of the Authority.

2. The full text of such recommendations shall be reported to the Council. Should the Council find that a recommendation is inconsistent with the intent and purpose of these Regulations, it may request that the recommendation be modified or withdrawn.

Part VIII
Settlement of disputes

Regulation 42
Disputes

1. Disputes concerning the interpretation or application of these Regulations shall be settled in accordance with Part XI, section 5, of the Convention.

2. Any final decision rendered by a court or tribunal having jurisdiction under the Convention relating to the rights and obligations of the Authority and of the Contractor shall be enforceable in the territory of each State Party to the Convention.

Part IX
Resources other than polymetallic sulphides

Regulation 43
Resources other than polymetallic sulphides

If a prospector or contractor finds resources in the Area other than polymetallic sulphides, the prospecting and exploration for and exploitation of such resources shall be subject to the rules, regulations and procedures of the Authority relating to such resources in accordance with the Convention and the Agreement. The prospector or contractor shall notify the Authority of its find.

Part X
Review

Regulation 44
Review

1. Five years following the approval of these Regulations by the Assembly, or at any time thereafter, the Council shall undertake a review of the manner in which the Regulations have operated in practice.

2. If, in the light of improved knowledge or technology, it becomes apparent that the Regulations are not adequate, any State Party, the Legal and Technical Commission, or any contractor through its sponsoring State may at any time request the Council to consider, at its next ordinary session, revisions to these Regulations.

3. In the light of the review, the Council may adopt and apply provisionally, pending approval by the Assembly, amendments to the provisions of these Regulations, taking into account the recommendations of the Legal and Technical Commission or other subordinate organs concerned. Any such amendments shall be without prejudice to the rights conferred on any Contractor with the Authority under the provisions of a contract entered into pursuant to these Regulations in force at the time of any such amendment.

4. In the event that any provisions of these Regulations are amended, the Contractor and the Authority may revise the contract in accordance with section 24 of annex 4.

Annex 1

Notification of intention to engage in prospecting

1. Name of prospector:

2. Street address of prospector:

3. Postal address (if different from above):

4. Telephone number:

5. Facsimile number:

6. Electronic mail address:

7. Nationality of prospector:

8. If prospector is a juridical person, identify prospector's

   (a) Place of registration; and

   (b) Principal place of business/domicile.

and attach a copy of the prospector's certificate of registration.

9. Name of prospector's designated representative:

10. Street address of prospector's designated representative (if different from above):

11. Postal address (if different from above):

12. Telephone number:

13. Facsimile number:

14. Electronic mail address:

15. Attach the coordinates of the broad area or areas in which prospecting is to be conducted (in accordance with the World Geodetic System WGS 84).

16. Attach a general description of the prospecting programme, including the date of commencement and the approximate duration of the programme.

17. Attach a written undertaking that the prospector will:

(a) Comply with the Convention and the relevant rules, regulations and procedures of the Authority concerning:

> (i) Cooperation in the training programmes in connection with marine scientific research and transfer of technology referred to in articles 143 and 144 of the Convention; and
>
> (ii) Protection and preservation of the marine environment; and

(b) Accept verification by the Authority of compliance therewith.

18. List hereunder all the attachments and annexes to this notification (all data and information should be submitted in hard copy and in a digital format specified by the Authority):

Date:__________ ________________________________

Signature of prospector's designated representative

ATTESTATION:

____

Signature of person attesting

____

Name of person attesting

____

Title of person attesting

Annex 2

Application for approval of a plan of work for exploration to obtain a contract

Section I
Information concerning the applicant

1. Name of applicant:

2. Street address of applicant:

3. Postal address (if different from above):

4. Telephone number:

5. Facsimile number:

6. Electronic mail address:

7. Name of applicant's designated representative:

8. Street address of applicant's designated representative (if different from above):

9. Postal address (if different from above):

10. Telephone number:

11. Facsimile number:

12. Electronic mail address:

13. If the applicant is a juridical person, identify applicant's

    (a) Place of registration; and

    (b) Principal place of business/domicile.

and attach a copy of the applicant's certificate of registration.

14. Identify the sponsoring State or States.

15. In respect of each sponsoring State, provide the date of deposit of its instrument of ratification of, or accession or succession to, the 1982 United Nations Convention on the Law of the Sea and the date of its consent to be bound by the Agreement relating to the Implementation of Part XI of the United Nations Convention on the Law of the Sea of 10 December 1982.

16. A certificate of sponsorship issued by the sponsoring State must be attached with this application. If the applicant has more than one nationality, as in the case of a partnership or consortium of entities from more than one State, certificates of sponsorship issued by each of the States involved must be attached.

Section II
Information relating to the area under application

17. Define the boundaries of the blocks under application by attaching a chart (on a scale and projection specified by the Authority) and a list of geographical coordinates (in accordance with the World Geodetic System WGS 84).

18. Indicate whether the applicant elects to contribute a reserved area in accordance with regulation 17 or offer an equity interest in a joint venture arrangement in accordance with regulation 19.

19. If the applicant elects to contribute a reserved area:

(a) Attach a chart (on a scale and projection specified by the Authority) and a list of the coordinates dividing the total area into two parts of equal estimated commercial value; and

(b) Include in an attachment sufficient information to enable the Council to designate a reserved area based on the estimated commercial value of each part of the area under application. Such attachment must include the data available to the applicant with respect to both parts of the area under application, including:

(i) Data on the location, survey and evaluation of the polymetallic sulphides in the areas, including:

a. A description of the technology related to the recovery and processing of polymetallic sulphides that is necessary for making the designation of a reserved area;

b. A map of the physical and geological characteristics, such as seabed topography, bathymetry and bottom currents and information on the reliability of such data;

c. A map showing the remotely sensed data (such as electromagnetic surveys) and other survey data used to determine the lateral extent of each polymetallic sulphide bodies;

d. Drill core and other data used to determine the third dimension of the deposits and therefore used to determine the grade and tonnage of the polymetallic sulphide bodies;

e. Data showing the distribution of active and inactive polymetallic sulphide sites and the age that activity ceased in inactive sites and was initiated at active sites;

f. Data showing the average tonnage (in metric tonnes) of each polymetallic sulphide body that will comprise the mine site and an associated tonnage map showing the location of sampling sites;

g. Data showing the average elemental content of metals of economic interest (grade) based on chemical assays in (dry) weight per cent and an associated grade map for data among and within the polymetallic sulphide bodies;

h. Combined maps of tonnage and grade of polymetallic sulphides;

i. A calculation based on standard procedures, including statistical analysis, using the data submitted and assumptions made in the calculations that the two areas could be expected to contain polymetallic sulphides of equal estimated commercial value expressed as recoverable metals in mineable areas;

j. A description of the techniques used by the applicant;

(ii) Information concerning environmental parameters (seasonal and during test period) including, inter alia, wind speed and direction, water salinity, temperature and biological communities.

20. If the area under application includes any part of a reserved area, attach a list of coordinates of the area which forms part of the reserved area and indicate the applicant's qualifications in accordance with regulation 18 of the Regulations.

Section III
Financial and technical information

21. Attach sufficient information to enable the Council to determine whether the applicant is financially capable of carrying out the proposed plan of work for exploration and of fulfilling its financial obligations to the Authority:

(a) If the application is made by the Enterprise, attach certification by its competent authority that the Enterprise has the necessary financial resources to meet the estimated costs of the proposed plan of work for exploration;

(b) If the application is made by a State or a State enterprise, attach a statement by the State or the sponsoring State certifying that the applicant has the necessary financial resources to meet the estimated costs of the proposed plan of work for exploration;

(c) If the application is made by an entity, attach copies of the applicant's audited financial statements, including balance sheets and profit-and-loss statements, for the most recent three years in conformity with internationally accepted accounting principles and certified by a duly qualified firm of public accountants; and

(i) If the applicant is a newly organized entity and a certified balance sheet is not available, a pro forma balance sheet certified by an appropriate official of the applicant;

(ii) If the applicant is a subsidiary of another entity, copies of such financial statements of that entity and a statement from that entity in conformity with internationally accepted accounting practices and certified by a duly qualified firm of public accountants that the applicant will have the financial resources to carry out the plan of work for exploration;

(iii) If the applicant is controlled by a State or a State enterprise, a statement from the State or State enterprise certifying that the applicant will have the financial resources to carry out the plan of work for exploration.

22. If it is intended to finance the proposed plan of work for exploration by borrowings, attach a statement of the amount of such borrowings, the repayment period and the interest rate.

23. Attach sufficient information to enable the Council to determine whether the applicant is technically capable of carrying out the proposed plan of work for exploration, including:

(a) A general description of the applicant's previous experience, knowledge, skills, technical qualifications and expertise relevant to the proposed plan of work for exploration;

(b) A general description of the equipment and methods expected to be used in carrying out the proposed plan of work for exploration and other relevant non-proprietary information about the characteristics of such technology;

(c) A general description of the applicant's financial and technical capability to respond to any incident or activity which causes serious harm to the marine environment.

Section IV
The plan of work for exploration

24. Attach the following information relating to the plan of work for exploration:

(a) A general description and a schedule of the proposed exploration programme, including the programme of activities for the immediate five-year period, such as studies to be undertaken in respect of the environmental, technical, economic and other appropriate factors which must be taken into account in exploration;

(b) A description of a programme for oceanographic and environmental baseline studies in accordance with the Regulations and any environmental rules, regulations and procedures established by the Authority that would enable an assessment of the potential environmental impact including, but not restricted to, the impact on biodiversity, of the proposed exploration activities, taking into account any recommendations issued by the Legal and Technical Commission;

(c) A preliminary assessment of the possible impact of the proposed exploration activities on the marine environment;

(d) A description of proposed measures for the prevention, reduction and control of pollution and other hazards, as well as possible impacts, to the marine environment;

(e) A schedule of anticipated yearly expenditures in respect of the programme of activities for the immediate five-year period.

Section V
Undertakings

25. Attach a written undertaking that the applicant will:

(a) Accept as enforceable and comply with the applicable obligations created by the provisions of the Convention and the rules, regulations and procedures of the Authority, the decisions of the relevant organs of the Authority and the terms of its contracts with the Authority;

(b) Accept control by the Authority of activities in the Area as authorized by the Convention;

(c) Provide the Authority with a written assurance that its obligations under the contract will be fulfilled in good faith.

Section VI
Previous contracts

26. Has the applicant or, in the case of an application by a partnership or consortium of entities in a joint arrangement, any member of the partnership or consortium previously been awarded any contract with the Authority?

27. If the answer to 26 is "yes", the application must include:

(a) The date of the previous contract or contracts;

(b) The date, reference number and title of each report submitted to the Authority in connection with the contact or contracts; and

(c) The date of termination of the contract or contracts, if applicable.

Section VII
Attachments

28. List all the attachments and annexes to this application (all data and information should be submitted in hard copy and in a digital format specified by the Authority):

Date:__________ ________________________________

Signature of applicant's designated representative

ATTESTATION:

____
Signature of person attesting

____
Name of person attesting

____
Title of person attesting

Annex 3

Contract for exploration

THIS CONTRACT made the day of between the INTERNATIONAL SEABED AUTHORITY represented by its SECRETARY-GENERAL (hereinafter referred to as "the Authority") and represented by (hereinafter referred to as "the Contractor") WITNESSETH as follows:

Incorporation of clauses

A. The standard clauses set out in annex 4 to the Regulations on Prospecting and Exploration for Polymetallic Sulphides in the Area shall be incorporated herein and shall have effect as if herein set out at length.

Exploration area

B. For the purposes of this contract, the "exploration area" means that part of the Area allocated to the Contractor for exploration, defined by the coordinates listed in schedule 1 hereto, as reduced from time to time in accordance with the standard clauses and the Regulations.

Grant of rights

C. In consideration of:

(1) Their mutual interest in the conduct of exploration activities in the exploration area pursuant to the Convention and the Agreement;

(2) The responsibility of the Authority to organize and control activities in the Area, particularly with a view to administering the resources of the Area, in accordance with the legal regime established in Part XI of the Convention and the Agreement and Part XII of the Convention respectively; and

(3) The interest and financial commitment of the Contractor in conducting activities in the exploration area and the mutual covenants made herein, the Authority hereby grants to the Contractor the exclusive right to explore for polymetallic sulphides in the exploration area in accordance with the terms and conditions of this contract.

Entry into force and contract term

D. This contract shall enter into force on signature by both parties and, subject to the standard clauses, shall remain in force for a period of fifteen years thereafter unless:

(1) The Contractor obtains a contract for exploitation in the exploration area which enters into force before the expiration of such period of fifteen years; or

(2) The contract is sooner terminated provided that the term of the contract may be extended in accordance with standard clauses 3.2 and 17.2.

Schedules

E. The schedules referred to in the standard clauses, namely section 4 and section 8, are for the purposes of this contract schedules 2 and 3 respectively.

Entire agreement

F. This contract expresses the entire agreement between the parties, and no oral understanding or prior writing shall modify the terms hereof.

IN WITNESS WHEREOF the undersigned, being duly authorized thereto by the respective parties, have signed this contract at …, this … day of …

Schedule 1

[Coordinates and illustrative chart of the exploration area]

Schedule 2

[The current five-year programme of activities as revised from time to time]

Schedule 3

[The training programme shall become a schedule to the contract when approved by the Authority in accordance with section 8 of the standard clauses.]

Annex 4

Standard clauses for exploration contract

Section 1
Definitions

1.1 In the following clauses:

(a) "exploration area" means that part of the Area allocated to the Contractor for exploration, described in schedule 1 hereto, as the same may be reduced from time to time in accordance with this contract and the Regulations;

(b) "programme of activities" means the programme of activities which is set out in schedule 2 hereto as the same may be adjusted from time to time in accordance with sections 4.3 and 4.4 hereof;

(c) "regulations" means the Regulations on Prospecting and Exploration for Polymetallic Sulphides in the Area, adopted by the Authority.

1.2 Terms and phrases defined in the Regulations shall have the same meaning in these standard clauses.

1.3 In accordance with the Agreement relating to the Implementation of Part XI of the United Nations Convention on the Law of the Sea of 10 December 1982, its provisions and Part XI of the Convention are to be interpreted and applied together as a single instrument; this contract and references in this contract to the Convention are to be interpreted and applied accordingly.

1.4 This contract includes the schedules to this contract, which shall be an integral part hereof.

Section 2
Security of tenure

2.1 The Contractor shall have security of tenure and this contract shall not be suspended, terminated or revised except in accordance with sections 20, 21 and 24 hereof.

2.2 The Contractor shall have the exclusive right to explore for polymetallic sulphides in the exploration area in accordance with the terms and conditions of this contract. The Authority shall ensure that no other entity operates in the exploration area for a different category of resources in a manner that might unreasonably interfere with the operations of the Contractor.

2.3 The Contractor, by notice to the Authority, shall have the right at any time to renounce without penalty the whole or part of its rights in the exploration area, provided that the Contractor shall remain liable for all obligations accrued prior to the date of such renunciation in respect of the area renounced.

2.4 Nothing in this contract shall be deemed to confer any right on the Contractor other than those rights expressly granted herein. The Authority reserves the right to enter into contracts with respect to resources other than polymetallic sulphides with third parties in the area covered by this contract.

Section 3
Contract term

3.1 This contract shall enter into force on signature by both parties and shall remain in force for a period of fifteen years thereafter unless:

(a) The Contractor obtains a contract for exploitation in the exploration area which enters into force before the expiration of such period of fifteen years; or

(b) The contract is sooner terminated,

provided that the term of the contract may be extended in accordance with sections 3.2 and 17.2 hereof.

3.2 Upon application by the Contractor, not later than six months before the expiration of this contract, this contract may be extended for periods of not more than five years each on such terms and conditions as the Authority and the Contractor may then agree in accordance with the Regulations. Such extensions shall be approved if the Contractor has made efforts in good faith to comply with the requirements of this contract but for reasons beyond the Contractor's control has been unable to complete the necessary preparatory work for proceeding to the exploitation stage or if the prevailing economic circumstances do not justify proceeding to the exploitation stage.

3.3 Notwithstanding the expiration of this contract in accordance with section 3.1 hereof, if the Contractor has, at least 90 days prior to the date of expiration, applied for a contract for exploitation, the Contractor's rights and obligations under this contract shall continue until such time as the application has been considered and a contract for exploitation has been issued or refused.

Section 4
Exploration

4.1 The Contractor shall commence exploration in accordance with the time schedule stipulated in the programme of activities set out in schedule 2 hereto and shall adhere to such time periods or any modification thereto as provided for by this contract.

4.2 The Contractor shall carry out the programme of activities set out in schedule 2 hereto. In carrying out such activities the Contractor shall spend in each contract year not less than the amount specified in such programme, or any agreed review thereof, in actual and direct exploration expenditures.

4.3 The Contractor, with the consent of the Authority, which consent shall not be unreasonably withheld, may from time to time make such changes in the programme of activities and the expenditures specified therein as may be necessary and prudent in accordance with good mining industry practice, and taking into account the market conditions for the metals contained in polymetallic sulphides and other relevant global economic conditions.

4.4 Not later than 90 days prior to the expiration of each five-year period from the date on which this contract enters into force in accordance with section 3 hereof, the Contractor and the Secretary-General shall jointly undertake a review of the implementation of the plan of work for exploration under this contract. The Secretary-General may require the Contractor to submit such additional data and information as may be necessary for the purposes of the review. In the light of the review, the Contractor shall make such adjustments to its plan of work as are necessary and shall indicate its programme of activities for the following five-year period, including a revised schedule of anticipated yearly expenditures. Schedule 2 hereto shall be adjusted accordingly.

Section 5
Environmental monitoring

5.1 The Contractor shall take necessary measures to prevent, reduce and control pollution and other hazards to the marine environment arising from its activities in the Area as far as reasonably possible applying a precautionary approach and best environmental practices.

5.2 Prior to the commencement of exploration activities, the Contractor shall submit to the Authority:

(a) An impact assessment of the potential effects on the marine environment of the proposed activities;

(b) A proposal for a monitoring programme to determine the potential effect on the marine environment of the proposed activities; and

(c) Data that could be used to establish an environmental baseline against which to assess the effect of the proposed activities.

5.3 The Contractor shall, in accordance with the Regulations, gather environmental baseline data as exploration activities progress and develop and shall establish environmental baselines against which to assess the likely effects of the Contractor's activities on the marine environment.

5.4 The Contractor shall, in accordance with the Regulations, establish and carry out a programme to monitor and report on such effects on the marine environment. The Contractor shall cooperate with the Authority in the implementation of such monitoring.

5.5 The Contractor shall, within 90 days of the end of each calendar year, report to the Secretary-General on the implementation and results of the monitoring programme referred to in section 5.4 hereof and shall submit data and information in accordance with the Regulations.

Section 6
Contingency plans and emergencies

6.1 The Contractor shall, prior to the commencement of its programme of activities under this contract, submit to the Secretary-General a contingency plan to respond effectively to incidents that are likely to cause serious harm or a threat of serious harm to the marine environment arising from the Contractor's activities at sea in the exploration area. Such contingency plan shall establish special procedures and provide for adequate and appropriate equipment to deal with such incidents and, in particular, shall include arrangements for:

(a) The immediate raising of a general alarm in the area of the exploration activities;

(b) Immediate notification to the Secretary-General;

(c) The warning of ships which might be about to enter the immediate vicinity;

(d) A continuing flow of full information to the Secretary-General relating to particulars of the contingency measures already taken and further actions required;

(e) The removal, as appropriate, of polluting substances;

(f) The reduction and, so far as reasonably possible, prevention of serious harm to the marine environment, as well as mitigation of such effects;

(g) As appropriate, cooperation with other contractors with the Authority to respond to an emergency; and

(h) Periodic emergency response exercises.

6.2 The Contractor shall promptly report to the Secretary-General any incident arising from its activities that has caused, is causing or poses a threat of serious harm to the marine environment. Each such report shall contain the details of such incident, including, inter alia:

(a) The coordinates of the area affected or which can reasonably be anticipated to be affected;

(b) The description of the action being taken by the Contractor to prevent, contain, minimize and repair the serious harm or threat of serious harm to the marine environment;

(c) A description of the action being taken by the Contractor to monitor the effects of the incident on the marine environment; and

(d) Such supplementary information as may reasonably be required by the Secretary-General.

6.3 The Contractor shall comply with emergency orders issued by the Council and immediate measures of a temporary nature issued by the Secretary-General in accordance with the Regulations, to prevent, contain, minimize or repair serious harm or the threat of serious harm to the marine environment, which may include orders to the Contractor to immediately suspend or adjust any activities in the exploration area.

6.4 If the Contractor does not promptly comply with such emergency orders or immediate measures of a temporary nature, the Council may take such reasonable measures as are necessary to prevent, contain, minimize or repair any such serious harm or the threat of serious harm to the marine environment at the Contractor's expense. The Contractor shall promptly reimburse the Authority the amount of such expenses. Such expenses shall be in addition to any monetary penalties which may be imposed on the Contractor pursuant to the terms of this contract or the Regulations.

Section 7
Human remains and objects and sites of an archaeological or historical nature

The Contractor shall immediately notify the Secretary-General in writing of any finding in the exploration area of any human remains of an archaeological or historical nature, or any object or site of a similar nature and its location, including the preservation and protection measures taken. The Secretary-General shall transmit such information to the Director-General of the United Nations Educational, Scientific and Cultural Organization and any other competent international organization. Following the finding of any such human remains, object or site in the exploration area, and in order to avoid disturbing such human remains, object or site, no further prospecting or exploration shall take place, within a reasonable radius, until such time as the Council decides otherwise after taking account of the views of the Director-General of the United Nations Educational, Scientific and Cultural Organization or any other competent international organization.

Section 8
Training

8.1 In accordance with the Regulations, the Contractor shall, prior to the commencement of exploration under this contract, submit to the Authority for approval proposed training programmes for the training of personnel of the Authority and developing States, including the participation of such personnel in all of the Contractor's activities under this contract.

8.2 The scope and financing of the training programme shall be subject to negotiation between the Contractor, the Authority and the sponsoring State or States.

8.3 The Contractor shall conduct training programmes in accordance with the specific programme for the training of personnel referred to in section 8.1 hereof approved by the Authority in accordance with the Regulations, which programme, as revised and developed from time to time, shall become a part of this contract as schedule 3.

Section 9
Books and records

The Contractor shall keep a complete and proper set of books, accounts and financial records, consistent with internationally accepted accounting principles. Such books, accounts and financial records shall include information which will fully disclose the actual and direct expenditures for exploration and such other information as will facilitate an effective audit of such expenditures.

Section 10
Annual reports

10.1 The Contractor shall, within 90 days of the end of each calendar year, submit a report to the Secretary-General in such format as may be recommended from time to time by the Legal and Technical Commission covering its programme of activities in the exploration area and containing, as applicable, information in sufficient detail on:

(a) The exploration work carried out during the calendar year, including maps, charts and graphs illustrating the work that has been done and the results obtained;

(b) The equipment used to carry out the exploration work, including the results of tests conducted of proposed mining technologies, but not equipment design data; and

(c) The implementation of training programmes, including any proposed revisions to or developments of such programmes.

10.2 Such reports shall also contain:

(a) The results obtained from environmental monitoring programmes, including observations, measurements, evaluations and analyses of environmental parameters;

(b) A statement of the quantity of polymetallic sulphides recovered as samples or for the purpose of testing;

(c) A statement, in conformity with internationally accepted accounting principles and certified by a duly qualified firm of public accountants, or, where the Contractor is a State or a State enterprise, by the sponsoring State, of the actual and direct exploration expenditures of the Contractor in carrying out the programme of activities during the Contractor's accounting year. Such expenditures may be claimed by the contractor as part of the contractor's development costs incurred prior to the commencement of commercial production; and

(d) Details of any proposed adjustments to the programme of activities and the reasons for such adjustments.

10.3 The Contractor shall also submit such additional information to supplement the reports referred to in section 10.1 and 10.2 hereof as the Secretary-General may from time to time reasonably require in order to carry out the Authority's functions under the Convention, the Regulations and this contract.

10.4 The Contractor shall keep, in good condition, a representative portion of samples and cores of the polymetallic sulphides obtained in the course of exploration until the expiration of this contract. The Authority may request the Contractor in writing to deliver to it for analysis a portion of any such sample and cores obtained during the course of exploration.

Section 11
Data and information to be submitted on expiration of the contract

11.1 The Contractor shall transfer to the Authority all data and information that are both necessary for and relevant to the effective exercise of the powers and functions of the Authority in respect of the exploration area in accordance with the provisions of this section.

11.2 Upon expiration or termination of this contract the Contractor, if it has not already done so, shall submit the following data and information to the Secretary-General:

(a) Copies of geological, environmental, geochemical and geophysical data acquired by the Contractor in the course of carrying out the programme of activities that are necessary for and relevant to the effective exercise of the powers and functions of the Authority in respect of the exploration area;

(b) The estimation of mineable deposits, when such deposits have been identified, which shall include details of the grade and quantity of the proven, probable and possible polymetallic sulphide reserves and the anticipated mining conditions;

(c) Copies of geological, technical, financial and economic reports made by or for the Contractor that are necessary for and relevant to the effective exercise of the powers and functions of the Authority in respect of the exploration area;

(d) Information in sufficient detail on the equipment used to carry out the exploration work, including the results of tests conducted of proposed mining technologies, but not equipment design data;

(e) A statement of the quantity of polymetallic sulphides recovered as samples or for the purpose of testing; and

(f) A statement on how and where samples of cores are archived and their availability to the Authority.

11.3 The data and information referred to in section 11.2 hereof shall also be submitted to the Secretary-General if, prior to the expiration of this contract, the Contractor applies for approval of a plan of work for exploitation or if the Contractor renounces its rights in the exploration area to the extent that such data and information relates to the renounced area.

Section 12
Confidentiality

Data and information transferred to the Authority in accordance with this contract shall be treated as confidential in accordance with the provisions of the Regulations.

Section 13
Undertakings

13.1 The Contractor shall carry out exploration in accordance with the terms and conditions of this contract, the Regulations, Part XI of the Convention, the Agreement and other rules of international law not incompatible with the Convention.

13.2 The Contractor undertakes:

(a) To accept as enforceable and comply with the terms of this contract;

(b) To comply with the applicable obligations created by the provisions of the Convention, the rules, regulations and procedures of the Authority and the decisions of the relevant organs of the Authority;

(c) To accept control by the Authority of activities in the Area as authorized by the Convention;

(d) To fulfil its obligations under this contract in good faith; and

(e) To observe, as far as reasonably practicable, any recommendations which may be issued from time to time by the Legal and Technical Commission.

13.3 The Contractor shall actively carry out the programme of activities:

(a) With due diligence, efficiency and economy;

(b) With due regard to the impact of its activities on the marine environment; and

(c) With reasonable regard for other activities in the marine environment.

13.4 The Authority undertakes to fulfil in good faith its powers and functions under the Convention and the Agreement in accordance with article 157 of the Convention.

Section 14
Inspection

14.1 The Contractor shall permit the Authority to send its inspectors on board vessels and installations used by the Contractor to carry out activities in the exploration area to:

(a) Monitor the Contractor's compliance with the terms and conditions of this contract and the Regulations; and

(b) Monitor the effects of such activities on the marine environment.

14.2 The Secretary-General shall give reasonable notice to the Contractor of the projected time and duration of inspections, the name of the inspectors and any activities the inspectors are to perform that are likely to require the availability of special equipment or special assistance from personnel of the Contractor.

14.3 Such inspectors shall have the authority to inspect any vessel or installation, including its log, equipment, records, facilities, all other recorded data and any relevant documents which are necessary to monitor the Contractor's compliance.

14.4 The Contractor, its agents and employees shall assist the inspectors in the performance of their duties and shall:

(a) Accept and facilitate prompt and safe boarding of vessels and installations by inspectors;

(b) Cooperate with and assist in the inspection of any vessel or installation conducted pursuant to these procedures;

(c) Provide access to all relevant equipment, facilities and personnel on vessels and installations at all reasonable times;

(d) Not obstruct, intimidate or interfere with inspectors in the performance of their duties;

(e) Provide reasonable facilities, including, where appropriate, food and accommodation, to inspectors; and

(f) Facilitate safe disembarkation by inspectors.

14.5 Inspectors shall avoid interference with the safe and normal operations on board vessels and installations used by the Contractor to carry out activities in the area visited and shall act in accordance with the Regulations and the measures adopted to protect confidentiality of data and information.

14.6 The Secretary-General and any duly authorized representatives of the Secretary-General, shall have access, for purposes of audit and examination, to any books, documents, papers and records of the Contractor which are necessary and directly pertinent to verify the expenditures referred to in section 10.2 (c).

14.7 The Secretary-General shall provide relevant information contained in the reports of inspectors to the Contractor and its sponsoring State or States where action is necessary.

14.8 If for any reason the Contractor does not pursue exploration and does not request a contract for exploitation, it shall, before withdrawing from the exploration area, notify the Secretary-General in writing in order to permit the Authority, if it so decides, to carry out an inspection pursuant to this section.

Section 15
Safety, labour and health standards

15.1 The Contractor shall comply with the generally accepted international rules and standards established by competent international organizations or general diplomatic conferences concerning the safety of life at sea, and the prevention of collisions and such rules, regulations and procedures as may be adopted by the Authority relating to safety at sea. Each vessel used for carrying out activities in the Area shall possess current valid certificates required by and issued pursuant to such international rules and standards.

15.2 The Contractor shall, in carrying out exploration under this contract, observe and comply with such rules, regulations and procedures as may be adopted by the Authority relating to protection against discrimination in employment, occupational safety and health, labour relations, social security, employment security and living conditions at the work site. Such rules, regulations and procedures shall take into account conventions and recommendations of the International Labour Organization and other competent international organizations.

Section 16
Responsibility and liability

16.1 The Contractor shall be liable for the actual amount of any damage, including damage to the marine environment, arising out of its wrongful acts or omissions, and those of its employees, subcontractors, agents and all persons engaged in working or acting for them in the conduct of its operations under this contract, including the costs of reasonable measures to prevent or limit damage to the marine environment, account being taken of any contributory acts or omissions by the Authority.

16.2 The Contractor shall indemnify the Authority, its employees, subcontractors and agents against all claims and liabilities of any third party arising out of any wrongful acts or omissions of the Contractor and its employees, agents and subcontractors, and all persons engaged in working or acting for them in the conduct of its operations under this contract.

16.3 The Authority shall be liable for the actual amount of any damage to the Contractor arising out of its wrongful acts in the exercise of its powers and functions, including violations under article 168, paragraph 2, of the Convention, account being taken of contributory acts or omissions by the Contractor, its employees, agents and subcontractors, and all persons engaged in working or acting for them in the conduct of its operations under this contract.

16.4 The Authority shall indemnify the Contractor, its employees, subcontractors, agents and all persons engaged in working or acting for them in the conduct of its operations under this contract, against all claims and liabilities of any third party arising out of any wrongful acts or omissions in the exercise of its powers and functions hereunder, including violations under article 168, paragraph 2, of the Convention.

16.5 The Contractor shall maintain appropriate insurance policies with internationally recognized carriers, in accordance with generally accepted international maritime practice.

Section 17
Force majeure

17.1 The Contractor shall not be liable for an unavoidable delay or failure to perform any of its obligations under this contract due to force majeure. For the purposes of this contract, force majeure shall mean an event or condition that the Contractor could not reasonably be expected to prevent or control; provided that the event or condition was not caused by negligence or by a failure to observe good mining industry practice.

17.2 The Contractor shall, upon request, be granted a time extension equal to the period by which performance was delayed hereunder by force majeure and the term of this contract shall be extended accordingly.

17.3 In the event of force majeure, the Contractor shall take all reasonable measures to remove its inability to perform and comply with the terms and conditions of this contract with a minimum of delay.

17.4 The Contractor shall give notice to the Authority of the occurrence of an event of force majeure as soon as reasonably possible, and similarly give notice to the Authority of the restoration of normal conditions.

Section 18
Disclaimer

Neither the Contractor nor any affiliated company or subcontractor shall in any manner claim or suggest, whether expressly or by implication, that the Authority or any official thereof has, or has expressed, any opinion with respect to polymetallic sulphides in the exploration area and a statement to that effect shall not be included in or endorsed on any prospectus, notice, circular, advertisement, press release or similar document issued by the Contractor, any affiliated company or any subcontractor that refers directly or indirectly to this contract. For the purposes of this section, an "affiliated company" means any person, firm or company or State-owned entity controlling, controlled by, or under common control with, the Contractor.

Section 19
Renunciation of rights

The Contractor, by notice to the Authority, shall have the right to renounce its rights and terminate this contract without penalty, provided that the Contractor shall remain liable for all obligations accrued prior to the date of such renunciation and those obligations required to be fulfilled after termination in accordance with the Regulations.

Section 20
Termination of sponsorship

20.1 If the nationality or control of the Contractor changes or the Contractor's sponsoring State, as defined in the Regulations, terminates its sponsorship, the Contractor shall promptly notify the Authority forthwith.

20.2 In either such event, if the Contractor does not obtain another sponsor meeting the requirements prescribed in the Regulations which submits to the Authority a certificate of sponsorship for the Contractor in the prescribed form within the time specified in the Regulations, this contract shall terminate forthwith.

Section 21
Suspension and termination of contract and penalties

21.1 The Council may suspend or terminate this contract, without prejudice to any other rights that the Authority may have, if any of the following events should occur:

(a) If, in spite of written warnings by the Authority, the Contractor has conducted its activities in such a way as to result in serious persistent and wilful violations of the fundamental terms of this contract, Part XI of the Convention, the Agreement and the rules, regulations and procedures of the Authority; or

(b) If the Contractor has failed to comply with a final binding decision of the dispute settlement body applicable to it; or

(c) If the Contractor becomes insolvent or commits an act of bankruptcy or enters into any agreement for composition with its creditors or goes into liquidation or receivership, whether compulsory or voluntary, or petitions or applies to any tribunal for the appointment of a receiver or a trustee or receiver for itself or commences any proceedings relating to itself under any bankruptcy, insolvency or readjustment of debt law, whether now or hereafter in effect, other than for the purpose of reconstruction.

21.2 The Council may, without prejudice to Section 17, after consultation with the contractor, suspend or terminate this contract, without prejudice to any other rights that the Authority may have, if the Contractor is prevented from performing its obligations under this contract by reason of an event or condition of force majeure, as described in Section 17.1, which has persisted for a continuous period exceeding two years, despite the Contractor having taken all reasonable measures to remove its inability to perform and comply with the terms and conditions of this contract with a minimum of delay.

21.3 Any suspension or termination shall be by notice, through the Secretary-General, which shall include a statement of the reasons for taking such action. The suspension or termination shall be effective 60 days after such notice, unless the Contractor within such period disputes the Authority's right to suspend or terminate this contract in accordance with Part XI, section 5, of the Convention.

21.4 If the Contractor takes such action, this contract shall only be suspended or terminated in accordance with a final binding decision in accordance with Part XI, section 5, of the Convention.

21.5 If the Council has suspended this contract, the Council may by notice require the Contractor to resume its operations and comply with the terms and conditions of this contract, not later than 60 days after such notice.

21.6 In the case of any violation of this contract not covered by section 21.1 (a) hereof, or in lieu of suspension or termination under section 21.1 hereof, the Council may impose upon the Contractor monetary penalties proportionate to the seriousness of the violation.

21.7 The Council may not execute a decision involving monetary penalties until the Contractor has been accorded a reasonable opportunity to exhaust the judicial remedies available to it pursuant to Part XI, section 5, of the Convention.

21.8 In the event of termination or expiration of this contract, the Contractor shall comply with the Regulations and shall remove all installations, plant, equipment and materials in the exploration area and shall make the area safe so as not to constitute a danger to persons, shipping or to the marine environment.

Section 22
Transfer of rights and obligations

22.1 The rights and obligations of the Contractor under this contract may be transferred in whole or in part only with the consent of the Authority and in accordance with the Regulations.

22.2 The Authority shall not unreasonably withhold consent to the transfer if the proposed transferee is in all respects a qualified applicant in accordance with the Regulations and assumes all of the obligations of the Contractor and if the transfer does not confer to the transferee a plan of work, the approval of which would be forbidden by Annex III, article 6, paragraph 3 (c), of the Convention.

22.3 The terms, undertakings and conditions of this contract shall inure to the benefit of and be binding upon the parties hereto and their respective successors and assigns.

Section 23
No waiver

No waiver by either party of any rights pursuant to a breach of the terms and conditions of this contract to be performed by the other party shall be construed as a waiver by the party of any succeeding breach of the same or any other term or condition to be performed by the other party.

Section 24
Revision

24.1 When circumstances have arisen or are likely to arise which, in the opinion of the Authority or the Contractor, would render this contract inequitable or make it impracticable or impossible to achieve the objectives set out in this contract or in Part XI of the Convention or the Agreement, the parties shall enter into negotiations to revise it accordingly.

24.2 This contract may also be revised by agreement between the Contractor and the Authority to facilitate the application of any rules, regulations and procedures adopted by the Authority subsequent to the entry into force of this contract.

24.3 This contract may be revised, amended or otherwise modified only with the consent of the Contractor and the Authority by an appropriate instrument signed by the authorized representatives of the parties.

Section 25
Disputes

25.1 Any dispute between the parties concerning the interpretation or application of this contract shall be settled in accordance with Part XI, section 5, of the Convention.

25.2 In accordance with article 21, paragraph 2, of Annex III to the Convention, any final decision rendered by a court or tribunal having jurisdiction under the Convention relating to the rights and obligations of the Authority and of the Contractor shall be enforceable in the territory of any State Party to the Convention affected thereby.

Section 26
Notice

26.1 Any application, request, notice, report, consent, approval, waiver, direction or instruction hereunder shall be made by the Secretary-General or by the designated representative of the Contractor, as the case may be, in writing. Service shall be by hand, or by telex, facsimile, registered airmail or electronic mail containing an authorized signature to the Secretary-General at the headquarters of the Authority or to the designated representative. The requirement to provide any information in writing under these Regulations is satisfied by the provision of the information in an electronic document containing a digital signature.

26.2 Either party shall be entitled to change any such address to any other address by not less than ten days' notice to the other party.

26.3 Delivery by hand shall be effective when made. Delivery by telex shall be deemed to be effective on the business day following the day when the "answer back" appears on the sender's telex machine. Delivery by facsimile shall be effective when the "transmit confirmation report" confirming the transmission to the recipient's published facsimile number is received by the transmitter. Delivery by registered airmail shall be deemed to be effective 21 days after posting. An electronic document is presumed to have been received by the addressee when it enters an information system designated or used by the addressee for the purpose of receiving documents of the type sent and it is capable of being retrieved and processed by the addressee.

26.4 Notice to the designated representative of the Contractor shall constitute effective notice to the Contractor for all purposes under this contract, and the designated representative shall be the Contractor's agent for the service of process or notification in any proceeding of any court or tribunal having jurisdiction.

26.5 Notice to the Secretary-General shall constitute effective notice to the Authority for all purposes under this contract, and the Secretary-General shall be the Authority's agent for the service of process or notification in any proceeding of any court or tribunal having jurisdiction.

Section 27
Applicable law

27.1 This contract shall be governed by the terms of this contract, the rules, regulations and procedures of the Authority, Part XI of the Convention, the Agreement and other rules of international law not incompatible with the Convention.

27.2 The Contractor, its employees, subcontractors, agents and all persons engaged in working or acting for them in the conduct of its operations under this contract shall observe the applicable law referred to in section 27.1 hereof and shall not engage in any transaction, directly or indirectly, prohibited by the applicable law.

27.3 Nothing contained in this contract shall be deemed an exemption from the necessity of applying for and obtaining any permit or authority that may be required for any activities under this contract.

Section 28
Interpretation

The division of this contract into sections and subsections and the insertion of headings are for convenience of reference only and shall not affect the construction or interpretation hereof.

Section 29
Additional documents

Each party hereto agrees to execute and deliver all such further instruments, and to do and perform all such further acts and things as may be necessary or expedient to give effect to the provisions of this contract.

— — — — —

ISBA/17/C/CRP.1
1 February 2011
English only

Regulations on prospecting and exploration for cobalt-rich ferromanganese crusts in the Area

Draft Regulations as proposed by the Legal and Technical Commission in document ISBA/16/C/WP.2 showing the additional revisions that would be necessary to align the draft regulations with the Regulations on Prospecting and Exploration for Polymetallic Sulphides in the Area as approved by the Assembly during the sixteenth session and published as ISBA/16/A/12/Rev.1 (except for provisions specific to cobalt-crusts, i.e. definitions, provisions dealing with the size of areas for exploration and relinquishment: regulations 12 and 28; and descriptions of data requirements: Annex 2, Section II, paragraph 1)

Provisions requiring alignment marked in bold text: Regulations 21(4) and (5); 23(1) and (7); 45(3); Annex 4, Section 17.3, Section 21.2, Section 25.2.

Preamble

In accordance with the United Nations Convention on the Law of the Sea ("the Convention"), the seabed and ocean floor and the subsoil thereof beyond the limits of national jurisdiction, as well as its resources, are the common heritage of mankind, the exploration and exploitation of which shall be carried out for the benefit of mankind as a whole, on whose behalf the International Seabed Authority acts. The objective of this set of Regulations is to provide for prospecting and exploration for cobalt-rich ferromanganese crusts.

Part I
Introduction

Regulation 1
Use of terms and scope

1. Terms used in the Convention shall have the same meaning in these Regulations.

2. In accordance with the Agreement relating to the Implementation of Part XI of the United Nations Convention on the Law of the Sea of 10 December 1982 ("the Agreement"), the provisions of the Agreement and Part XI of the United Nations Convention on the Law of the Sea of 10 December 1982 shall be interpreted and applied together as a single instrument. These Regulations and references in these Regulations to the Convention are to be interpreted and applied accordingly.

3. For the purposes of these Regulations:

(a) "cobalt crusts" means hydroxide/oxide deposits of cobalt-rich iron/manganese (ferromanganese) crust formed from direct precipitation of minerals from seawater onto hard substrates containing minor but significant concentrations of cobalt, titanium, nickel, platinum, molybdenum, tellurium, cerium, other metallic and rare earth elements;

(b) "exploitation" means the recovery for commercial purposes of cobalt crusts in the Area and the extraction of minerals therefrom, including the construction and operation of mining, processing and transportation systems, for the production and marketing of metals;

(c) "exploration" means searching for deposits of cobalt crusts in the Area with exclusive rights, the analysis of such deposits, the use and testing of recovery systems and equipment, processing facilities and transportation systems, and the carrying out of studies of the environmental, technical, economic, commercial and other appropriate factors that must be taken into account in exploitation;

(d) "marine environment" includes the physical, chemical, geological and biological components, conditions and factors which interact and determine the productivity, state, condition and quality of the marine ecosystem, the waters of the seas and oceans and the airspace above those waters, as well as the seabed and ocean floor and subsoil thereof;

(e) "prospecting" means the search for deposits of cobalt crusts in the Area, including estimation of the composition, sizes and distributions of deposits of cobalt crusts and their economic values, without any exclusive rights;

(f) "serious harm to the marine environment" means any effect from activities in the Area on the marine environment which represents a significant adverse change in the marine environment determined according to the rules, regulations and procedures adopted by the Authority on the basis of internationally recognized standards and practices.

4. These Regulations shall not in any way affect the freedom of scientific research, pursuant to article 87 of the Convention, or the right to conduct marine scientific research in the Area pursuant to articles 143 and 256 of the Convention. Nothing in these Regulations shall be construed in such a way as to restrict the exercise by States of the freedom of the high seas as reflected in article 87 of the Convention.

5. These Regulations may be supplemented by further rules, regulations and procedures, in particular on the protection and preservation of the marine environment. These Regulations shall be subject to the provisions of the Convention and the Agreement and other rules of international law not incompatible with the Convention.

Part II
Prospecting

Regulation 2
Prospecting

1. Prospecting shall be conducted in accordance with the Convention and these Regulations and may commence only after the prospector has been informed by the Secretary-General that its notification has been recorded pursuant to regulation 4, paragraph 2.

2. Prospectors and the Secretary-General shall apply a precautionary approach, as reflected in Principle 15 of the Rio Declaration.[1] Prospecting shall not be undertaken if substantial evidence indicates the risk of serious harm to the marine environment.

3. Prospecting shall not be undertaken in an area covered by an approved plan of work for exploration for cobalt crusts or in a reserved area; nor may there be prospecting in an area which the Council has disapproved for exploitation because of the risk of serious harm to the marine environment.

4. Prospecting shall not confer on the prospector any rights with respect to resources. A prospector may, however, recover a reasonable quantity of minerals, being the quantity necessary for testing, and not for commercial use.

5. There shall be no time limit on prospecting except that prospecting in a particular area shall cease upon written notification to the prospector by the Secretary-General that a plan of work for exploration has been approved with regard to that area.

6. Prospecting may be conducted simultaneously by more than one prospector in the same area or areas.

Regulation 3
Notification of prospecting

1. A proposed prospector shall notify the Authority of its intention to engage in prospecting.

2. Each notification of prospecting shall be in the form prescribed in annex 1 to these Regulations, addressed to the Secretary-General, and shall conform to the requirements of these Regulations.

---

[1] Report of the United Nations Conference on Environment and Development, Rio de Janeiro, 3 14 June 1991 (United Nations publication, Sales No. E.91.1.8 and corrigenda), vol. 1: Resolutions adopted by the Conference, resolution 1, annex 1.

3. Each notification shall be submitted:

(a) in the case of a State, by the authority designated for that purpose by it;

(b) in the case of an entity, by its designated representative;

(c) in the case of the Enterprise, by its competent authority.

4. Each notification shall be in one of the languages of the Authority and shall contain:

(a) the name, nationality and address of the proposed prospector and its designated representative;

(b) the coordinates of the broad area or areas within which prospecting is to be conducted, in accordance with the most recent generally accepted international standard used by the Authority;

(c) a general description of the prospecting programme, including the proposed date of commencement and its approximate duration;

(d) a satisfactory written undertaking that the proposed prospector will:

(i) comply with the Convention and the relevant rules, regulations and procedures of the Authority concerning:
  a. cooperation in the training programmes in connection with marine scientific research and transfer of technology referred to in articles 143 and 144 of the Convention; and
  b. protection and preservation of the marine environment;

(ii) accept verification by the Authority of compliance therewith; and

(iii) make available to the Authority, as far as practicable, such data as may be relevant to the protection and preservation of the marine environment.

Regulation 4
Consideration of notifications

1. The Secretary-General shall acknowledge in writing receipt of each notification submitted under regulation 3, specifying the date of receipt.

2. The Secretary-General shall review and act on the notification within 45 days of its receipt. If the notification conforms with the requirements of the Convention and these Regulations, the Secretary-General shall record the particulars of the notification in a register maintained for that purpose and shall inform the prospector in writing that the notification has been so recorded.

3. The Secretary-General shall, within 45 days of receipt of the notification, inform the proposed prospector in writing if the notification includes

any part of an area included in an approved plan of work for exploration or exploitation of any category of resources, or any part of a reserved area, or any part of an area which has been disapproved by the Council for exploitation because of the risk of serious harm to the marine environment, or if the written undertaking is not satisfactory, and shall provide the proposed prospector with a written statement of reasons. In such cases, the proposed prospector may, within 90 days, submit an amended notification. The Secretary-General shall, within 45 days, review and act upon such amended notification.

4. A prospector shall inform the Secretary-General in writing of any change in the information contained in the notification.

5. The Secretary-General shall not release any particulars contained in the notification except with the written consent of the prospector. The Secretary-General shall, however, from time to time inform all members of the Authority of the identity of prospectors and the general areas in which prospecting is being conducted.

Regulation 5
Protection and preservation of the marine environment during prospecting

1. Each prospector shall take necessary measures to prevent, reduce and control pollution and other hazards to the marine environment arising from prospecting as far as reasonably possible, applying a precautionary approach and best environmental practices. In particular, each prospector shall minimize or eliminate:

(a) adverse environmental impacts from prospecting; and

(b) actual or potential conflicts or interference with existing or planned marine scientific research activities, in accordance with the relevant future guidelines in this regard.

2. Prospectors shall cooperate with the Authority in the establishment and implementation of programmes for monitoring and evaluating the potential impacts of the exploration for and exploitation of cobalt crusts on the marine environment.

3. A prospector shall immediately notify the Secretary-General in writing, using the most effective means, of any incident arising from prospecting which has caused, is causing or poses a threat of serious harm to the marine environment. Upon receipt of such notification the Secretary-General shall act in a manner consistent with regulation 35.

Regulation 6
Annual report

1. A prospector shall, within 90 days of the end of each calendar year, submit a report to the Authority on the status of prospecting. Such reports

shall be submitted by the Secretary-General to the Legal and Technical Commission. Each such report shall contain:

(a) a general description of the status of prospecting and of the results obtained;

(b) information on compliance with the undertakings referred to in regulation 3, paragraph (4) (d); and

(c) information on adherence to the relevant guidelines in this regard.

2. If the prospector intends to claim expenditures for prospecting as part of the development costs incurred prior to the commencement of commercial production, the prospector shall submit an annual statement, in conformity with internationally accepted accounting principles and certified by a duly qualified firm of public accountants, of the actual and direct expenditures incurred by the prospector in carrying out prospecting.

Regulation 7
Confidentiality of data and information from prospecting contained in the annual report

1. The Secretary-General shall ensure the confidentiality of all data and information contained in the reports submitted under regulation 6 applying *mutatis mutandis* the provisions of regulations 38 and 39, provided that data and information relating to the protection and preservation of the marine environment, in particular those from environmental monitoring programmes, shall not be considered confidential. The prospector may request that such data not be disclosed for up to three years following the date of their submission.

2. The Secretary-General may, at any time, with the consent of the prospector concerned, release data and information relating to prospecting in an area in respect of which a notification has been submitted. If, after having made reasonable efforts for at least two years, the Secretary-General determines that the prospector no longer exists or cannot be located, the Secretary-General may release such data and information.

Regulation 8
Objects of an archaeological or historical nature

A prospector shall immediately notify the Secretary-General in writing of any finding in the Area of an object of actual or potential archaeological or historical nature and its location. The Secretary-General shall transmit such information to the Director-General of the United Nations Educational, Scientific and Cultural Organization.

Part III
Applications for approval of plans of work for exploration in the form of contracts

Section 1
General provisions

Regulation 9
General

Subject to the provisions of the Convention, the following may apply to the Authority for approval of plans of work for exploration:

(a) the Enterprise, on its own behalf or in a joint arrangement;

(b) States Parties, state enterprises or natural or juridical persons which possess the nationality of States or are effectively controlled by them or their nationals, when sponsored by such States, or any group of the foregoing which meets the requirements of these Regulations.

Section 2
Content of applications

Regulation 10
Form of applications

1. Each application for approval of a plan of work for exploration shall be in the form prescribed in annex 2 to these Regulations, shall be addressed to the Secretary-General, and shall conform to the requirements of these Regulations.

2. Each application shall be submitted:

(a) in the case of a State, by the authority designated for that purpose by it;

(b) in the case of an entity, by its designated representative or the authority designated for that purpose by the sponsoring State or States; and

(c) in the case of the Enterprise, by its competent authority.

3. Each application by a state enterprise or one of the entities referred to in subparagraph (b) of regulation 9 shall also contain:

(a) sufficient information to determine the nationality of the applicant or the identity of the State or States by which, or by whose nationals, the applicant is effectively controlled; and

(b) the principal place of business or domicile and, if applicable, place of registration of the applicant.

4. Each application submitted by a partnership or consortium of entities shall contain the required information in respect of each member of the partnership or consortium.

Regulation 11
Certificate of sponsorship

1. Each application by a state enterprise or one of the entities referred to in subparagraph (b) of regulation 9 shall be accompanied by a certificate of sponsorship issued by the State of which it is a national or by which or by whose nationals it is effectively controlled. If the applicant has more than one nationality, as in the case of a partnership or consortium of entities from more than one State, each State involved shall issue a certificate of sponsorship.

2. Where the applicant has the nationality of one State but is effectively controlled by another State or its nationals, each State involved shall issue a certificate of sponsorship.

3. Each certificate of sponsorship shall be duly signed on behalf of the State by which it is submitted, and shall contain:

(a) the name of the applicant;

(b) the name of the sponsoring State;

(c) a statement that the applicant is:

(i) a national of the sponsoring State; or

(ii) subject to the effective control of the sponsoring State or its nationals;

(d) a statement by the sponsoring State that it sponsors the applicant;

(e) the date of deposit by the sponsoring State of its instrument of ratification of, or accession or succession to, the Convention;

(f) a declaration that the sponsoring State assumes responsibility in accordance with article 139, article 153, paragraph 4, and annex III, article 4, paragraph 4, of the Convention.

4. States or entities in a joint arrangement with the Enterprise shall also comply with this regulation.

Regulation 12
Total area covered by the application

1. For the purposes of these Regulations, a "cobalt crust block" is one or more cells of a grid as provided by the Authority, which may be square or rectangular in shape, no greater than 20 square kilometres.

2. The area covered by each application for approval of a plan of work for exploration for cobalt crusts shall be comprised of not more than 100 cobalt crust blocks which shall be arranged by the applicant in clusters, as set out in paragraph 3 below.

3. Five contiguous cobalt crust blocks form a cluster of cobalt crust blocks. Two such blocks that touch at any point shall be considered to be contiguous. Clusters of cobalt crust blocks need not be contiguous but shall be proximate and located entirely within a geographical area measuring not more than 550 kilometres by 550 kilometres.

4. Notwithstanding the provisions in paragraph 2 above, where an applicant has elected to contribute a reserved area to carry out activities pursuant to article 9 of annex III to the Convention, in accordance with regulation 17, the total area covered by an application shall not exceed 200 cobalt crust blocks. Such blocks shall be arranged in two groups of equal estimated commercial value and each such group of cobalt crust blocks shall be arranged by the applicant in clusters, as set out in paragraph 3 above.

Regulation 13
Financial and technical capabilities

1. Each application for approval of a plan of work for exploration shall contain specific and sufficient information to enable the Council to determine whether the applicant is financially and technically capable of carrying out the proposed plan of work for exploration and of fulfilling its financial obligations to the Authority.

2. An application for approval of a plan of work for exploration by the Enterprise shall include a statement by its competent authority certifying that the Enterprise has the necessary financial resources to meet the estimated costs of the proposed plan of work for exploration.

3. An application for approval of a plan of work for exploration by a State or a state enterprise shall include a statement by the State or the sponsoring State certifying that the applicant has the necessary financial resources to meet the estimated costs of the proposed plan of work for exploration.

4. An application for approval of a plan of work for exploration by an entity shall include copies of its audited financial statements, including balance sheets and profit-and-loss statements, for the most recent three years, in conformity with internationally accepted accounting principles and certified by a duly qualified firm of public accountants; and

(a) if the applicant is a newly organized entity and a certified balance sheet is not available, a pro forma balance sheet certified by an appropriate official of the applicant;

(b) if the applicant is a subsidiary of another entity, copies of such financial statements of that entity and a statement from that entity, in conformity with internationally accepted accounting principles and certified by a duly qualified firm of public accountants, that the applicant will have the financial resources to carry out the plan of work for exploration;

(c) if the applicant is controlled by a State or a state enterprise, a statement from the State or state enterprise certifying that the applicant will have the financial resources to carry out the plan of work for exploration.

5. Where an applicant referred to in paragraph 4 intends to finance the proposed plan of work for exploration by borrowings, its application shall include the amount of such borrowings, the repayment period and the interest rate.

6. Each application shall include:

(a) a general description of the applicant's previous experience, knowledge, skills, technical qualifications and expertise relevant to the proposed plan of work for exploration;

(b) a general description of the equipment and methods expected to be used in carrying out the proposed plan of work for exploration and other relevant non-proprietary information about the characteristics of such technology;

(c) a general description of the applicant's financial and technical capability to respond to any incident or activity which causes serious harm to the marine environment.

7. Where the applicant is a partnership or consortium of entities in a joint arrangement, each member of the partnership or consortium shall provide the information required by this regulation.

Regulation 14
Previous contracts with the Authority

Where the applicant or, in the case of an application by a partnership or consortium of entities in a joint arrangement, any member of the partnership or consortium, has previously been awarded any contract with the Authority, the application shall include:

(a) the date of the previous contract or contracts;

(b) the dates, reference numbers and titles of each report submitted to the Authority in connection with the contract or contracts; and

(c) the date of termination of the contract or contracts, if applicable.

Regulation 15
Undertakings

Each applicant, including the Enterprise, shall, as part of its application for approval of a plan of work for exploration, provide a written undertaking to the Authority that it will:

(a) accept as enforceable and comply with the applicable obligations created by the provisions of the Convention and the rules, regulations and procedures of the Authority, the decisions of the organs of the Authority and the terms of its contracts with the Authority;

(b) accept control by the Authority of activities in the Area, as authorized by the Convention; and

(c) provide the Authority with a written assurance that its obligations under the contract will be fulfilled in good faith.

Regulation 16
Applicant's election of a reserved area contribution or equity interest in a joint venture arrangement

Each applicant shall, in the application, elect either to:

(a) contribute a reserved area to carry out activities pursuant to Annex III, article 9, of the Convention, in accordance with regulation 17; or

(b) offer an equity interest in a joint venture arrangement in accordance with regulation 19.

Regulation 17
Data and information to be submitted before the designation of a reserved area

1. Where the applicant elects to contribute a reserved area to carry out activities pursuant to article 9 of annex III to the Convention, the area covered by the application shall be sufficiently large and of sufficient estimated commercial value to allow two mining operations and shall be configured by the applicant in accordance with regulation 12, paragraph 4.

2. Each such application shall contain sufficient data and information, as prescribed in section II of annex 2 to these Regulations, with respect to the area under application to enable the Council, on the recommendation of the Legal and Technical Commission, to designate a reserved area based on the estimated commercial value of each part. Such data and information shall consist of data available to the applicant with respect to both parts of the area under application, including the data used to determine their commercial value.

3. The Council, on the basis of the data and information submitted by the applicant pursuant to section II of annex 2 to these Regulations, if found satisfactory, and taking into account the recommendation of the Legal and Technical Commission, shall designate the part of the area under application which is to be a reserved area. The area so designated shall become a reserved area as soon as the plan of work for exploration for the non-reserved area is approved and the contract is signed. If the Council determines that additional information, consistent with these Regulations and annex 2, is needed to designate the reserved area, it shall refer the matter back to the Commission for further consideration, specifying the additional information required.

4. Once the plan of work for exploration is approved and a contract has been issued, the data and information transferred to the Authority by the applicant in respect of the reserved area may be disclosed by the Authority in accordance with article 14, paragraph 3, of annex III to the Convention.

Regulation 18
Applications for approval of plans of work with respect to a reserved area

1. Any State which is a developing State or any natural or juridical person sponsored by it and effectively controlled by it or by any other developing State, or any group of the foregoing, may notify the Authority that it wishes to submit a plan of work for exploration with respect to a reserved area. The Secretary-General shall forward such notification to the Enterprise, which shall inform the Secretary-General in writing within six months whether or not it intends to carry out activities in that area. If the Enterprise intends to carry out activities in that area, it shall, pursuant to paragraph 4, also inform in writing the contractor whose application for approval of a plan of work for exploration originally included that area.

2. An application for approval of a plan of work for exploration in respect of a reserved area may be submitted at any time after such an area becomes available following a decision by the Enterprise that it does not intend to carry out activities in that area or where the Enterprise has not, within six months of the notification by the Secretary-General, either taken a decision on whether it intends to carry out activities in that area or notified the Secretary-General in writing that it is engaged in discussions regarding a potential joint venture. In the latter instance, the Enterprise shall have one year from the date of such notification in which to decide whether to conduct activities in that area.

3. If the Enterprise or a developing State or one of the entities referred to in paragraph 1 does not submit an application for approval of a plan of work for exploration for activities in a reserved area within 15 years of the commencement by the Enterprise of its functions independent of the Secretariat of the Authority or within 15 years of the date on which that area is reserved for the Authority, whichever is the later, the contractor whose application for approval of a plan of work for exploration originally included that area shall be entitled to apply for a plan of work for exploration for that area provided it offers in good faith to include the Enterprise as a joint-venture partner.

4. A contractor has the right of first refusal to enter into a joint venture arrangement with the Enterprise for exploration of the area which was included in its application for approval of a plan of work for exploration and which was designated by the Council as a reserved area.

Regulation 19
Equity interest in a joint venture arrangement

1. Where the applicant elects to offer an equity interest in a joint venture arrangement, it shall submit data and information in accordance with regulation 20. The area to be allocated to the applicant shall be subject to the provisions of regulation 27.

2. The joint venture arrangement, which shall take effect at the time the applicant enters into a contract for exploitation, shall include the following:

(a) The Enterprise shall obtain a minimum of 20 percent of the equity participation in the joint venture arrangement on the following basis:

(i) Half of such equity participation shall be obtained without payment, directly or indirectly, to the applicant and shall be treated *pari passu* for all purposes with the equity participation of the applicant;

(ii) The remainder of such equity participation shall be treated *pari passu* for all purposes with the equity participation of the applicant except that the Enterprise shall not receive any profit distribution with respect to such participation until the applicant has recovered its total equity participation in the joint venture arrangement;

(b) Notwithstanding subparagraph (a), the applicant shall nevertheless offer the Enterprise the opportunity to purchase a further thirty percent of the equity participation in the joint venture arrangement, or such lesser percentage as the Enterprise may elect to purchase, on the basis of *pari passu* treatment with the applicant for all purposes;[2]

(c) Except as specifically provided in the agreement between the applicant and the Enterprise, the Enterprise shall not by reason of its equity participation be otherwise obligated to provide funds or credits or issue guarantees or otherwise accept any financial liability whatsoever for or on behalf of the joint venture arrangement, nor shall the Enterprise be required to subscribe for additional equity participation so as to maintain its proportionate participation in the joint venture arrangement.

Regulation 20
Data and information to be submitted for approval of the plan of work for exploration

1. Each applicant shall submit, with a view to receiving approval of the plan of work for exploration in the form of a contract, the following information:

(a) a general description and a schedule of the proposed exploration programme, including the programme of activities for the immediate five-year period, such as studies to be undertaken in respect of the environmental,

---

[2] The terms and conditions upon which such equity participation may be obtained would need to be further elaborated.

technical, economic and other appropriate factors that must be taken into account in exploration;

(b) a description of the programme for oceanographic and environmental baseline studies in accordance with these Regulations and any environmental rules, regulations and procedures established by the Authority that would enable an assessment of the potential environmental impact including, but not restricted to, the impact on biodiversity, of the proposed exploration activities, taking into account any recommendations issued by the Legal and Technical Commission;

(c) a preliminary assessment of the possible impact of the proposed exploration activities on the marine environment;

(d) a description of proposed measures for the prevention, reduction and control of pollution and other hazards, as well as possible impacts, to the marine environment;

(e) data necessary for the Council to make the determination it is required to make in accordance with regulation 13, paragraph 1; and

(f) a schedule of anticipated yearly expenditures in respect of the programme of activities for the immediate five-year period.

2. Where the applicant elects to contribute a reserved area, the data and information relating to such area shall be transferred by the applicant to the Authority after the Council has designated the reserved area in accordance with regulation 17, paragraph 3.

3. Where the applicant elects to offer an equity interest in a joint venture arrangement the data and information relating to such area shall be transferred by the applicant to the Authority at the time of the election.

Section 3
Fees

Regulation 21
Fee for applications

1. The fee for processing a plan of work for exploration for cobalt crusts shall consist of an initial fixed fee of 50,000 United States dollars or its equivalent in a freely convertible currency, payable by the applicant at the time of submitting an application, and an annual fee calculated as set out in paragraph 2.

2. The annual fee shall be calculated as follows:

(i) 25 United States dollars multiplied by the area factor from the date of the first anniversary of the contract;

(ii) 50 United States dollars multiplied by the area factor from the date of the first relinquishment in accordance with regulation 27(2); and

(iii) 100 United States dollars multiplied by the area factor from the date of the second relinquishment in accordance with regulation 27(3).[3]

3. The "Area Factor" means the number of square kilometres comprised in the exploration area at the date upon which the periodic payment in question becomes due.

4. Upon notification by the Secretary-General that the amount of the fee has been insufficient to cover the administrative costs incurred by the Authority in processing an application, the fee set out in paragraph (a) of this regulation shall be reviewed by the Council.

5. If the administrative costs incurred by the Authority in processing an application are less than the fixed amount, the Authority shall refund the difference to the applicant.

Section 4
Processing of applications

Regulation 22
Receipt, acknowledgement and safe custody of applications

The Secretary-General shall:

(a) acknowledge in writing within 30 days receipt of every application for approval of a plan of work for exploration submitted under this Part, specifying the date of receipt;

(b) place the application together with the attachments and annexes thereto in safe custody and ensure the confidentiality of all confidential data and information contained in the application; and

(c) notify the members of the Authority of the receipt of such application and circulate to them information of a general nature which is not confidential regarding the application.

Regulation 23
Consideration by the Legal and Technical Commission

1. Upon receipt of an application for approval of a plan of work for exploration, the Secretary-General shall notify the members of the Legal and Technical Commission and place consideration of the application as an item on the agenda for the next meeting of the Commission. **The Commission shall only consider applications in respect of which notification and information has been circulated by the Secretary-General in accordance with regulation 22 (c) at least 30 days prior to the commencement of the meeting of the Commission at which they are to be considered.**

---

[3] The 2006 workshop recommended that the fee per block retained should double again in the event of an extension of the contract for exploration beyond 15 years pursuant to regulation 29.

2. The Commission shall examine applications in the order in which they are received.

3. The Commission shall determine if the applicant:

(a) has complied with the provisions of these Regulations;

(b) has given the undertakings and assurances specified in regulation 15;

(c) possesses the financial and technical capability to carry out the proposed plan of work for exploration and has provided details as to its ability to comply promptly with emergency orders; and

(d) has satisfactorily discharged its obligations in relation to any previous contract with the Authority.

4. The Commission shall, in accordance with the requirements set forth in these Regulations and its procedures, determine whether the proposed plan of work for exploration will:

(a) provide for effective protection of human health and safety;

(b) provide for effective protection and preservation of the marine environment including, but not restricted to, the impact on biodiversity;

(c) ensure that installations are not established where interference may be caused to the use of recognized sea lanes essential to international navigation or in areas of intense fishing activity.

5. If the Commission makes the determinations specified in paragraph 3 and determines that the proposed plan of work for exploration meets the requirements of paragraph 4, the Commission shall recommend approval of the plan of work for exploration to the Council.

6. The Commission shall not recommend approval of the plan of work for exploration if part or all of the area covered by the proposed plan of work for exploration is included in:

(a) a plan of work for exploration approved by the Council for cobalt crusts; or

(b) a plan of work approved by the Council for exploration for or exploitation of other resources if the proposed plan of work for exploration for cobalt crusts might cause undue interference with activities under such approved plan of work for other resources; or

(c) an area disapproved for exploitation by the Council in cases where substantial evidence indicates the risk of serious harm to the marine environment.

7. The Legal and Technical Commission may recommend approval of a plan of work if it determines that such approval would not permit a State Party or entities sponsored by it to monopolize the conduct of

activities in the Area with regard to polymetallic sulphides or to preclude other States Parties from activities in the Area with regard to polymetallic sulphides.

8. Except in the case of applications by the Enterprise, on its own behalf or in a joint venture, and applications under regulation 18, the Commission shall not recommend approval of the plan of work for exploration if part or all of the area covered by the proposed plan of work for exploration is included in a reserved area or an area designated by the Council to be a reserved area.

9. If the Commission finds that an application does not comply with these Regulations, it shall notify the applicant in writing, through the Secretary-General, indicating the reasons. The applicant may, within 45 days of such notification, amend its application. If the Commission after further consideration is of the view that it should not recommend approval of the plan of work for exploration, it shall so inform the applicant and provide the applicant with a further opportunity to make representations within 30 days of such information. The Commission shall consider any such representations made by the applicant in preparing its report and recommendation to the Council.

10. In considering a proposed plan of work for exploration, the Commission shall have regard to the principles, policies and objectives relating to activities in the Area as provided for in part XI and annex III of the Convention and the Agreement.

11. The Commission shall consider applications expeditiously and shall submit its report and recommendations to the Council on the designation of the areas and on the plan of work for exploration at the first possible opportunity, taking into account the schedule of meetings of the Authority.

12. In discharging its duties, the Commission shall apply these Regulations and the rules, regulations and procedures of the Authority in a uniform and non-discriminatory manner.

Regulation 24
Consideration and approval of plans of work for exploration by the Council

The Council shall consider the reports and recommendations of the Commission relating to approval of plans of work for exploration in accordance with paragraphs 11 and 12 of section 3 of the annex to the Agreement.

Part IV
Contracts for exploration

Regulation 25
The contract

1. After a plan of work for exploration has been approved by the Council, it shall be prepared in the form of a contract between the Authority and the

applicant as prescribed in annex 3 to these Regulations. Each contract shall incorporate the standard clauses set out in annex 4 in effect at the date of entry into force of the contract.

2. The contract shall be signed by the Secretary-General on behalf of the Authority and by the applicant. The Secretary-General shall notify all members of the Authority in writing of the conclusion of each contract.

Regulation 26
Rights of the contractor

1. The contractor shall have the exclusive right to explore an area covered by a plan of work for exploration in respect of cobalt crusts. The Authority shall ensure that no other entity operates in the same area for other resources in a manner that might interfere with the operations of the contractor.

2. A contractor who has an approved plan of work for exploration only shall have a preference and a priority among applicants submitting plans of work for exploitation of the same area and resources. Such preference or priority may be withdrawn by the Council if the contractor has failed to comply with the requirements of its approved plan of work for exploration within the time period specified in a written notice or notices from the Council to the contractor indicating which requirements have not been complied with by the contractor. The time period specified in any such notice shall not be unreasonable. The contractor shall be accorded a reasonable opportunity to be heard before the withdrawal of such preference or priority becomes final. The Council shall provide the reasons for its proposed withdrawal of preference or priority and shall consider any contractor's response. The decision of the Council shall take account of that response and shall be based on substantial evidence.

3. A withdrawal of preference or priority shall not become effective until the contractor has been accorded a reasonable opportunity to exhaust the judicial remedies available to it pursuant to part XI, section 5, of the Convention.

Regulation 27
Size of area and relinquishment

1. The contractor shall relinquish the area allocated to it in accordance with paragraphs 2, 3 and 4 of this regulation. Areas to be relinquished need not be contiguous and shall be defined by the contractor in the form of sub-blocks comprising one or more cells of a grid as provided by the Authority.

2. By the end of the fifth year from the date of the contract, the contractor shall have relinquished at least 50 per cent of the original area allocated to it;

3. By the end of the tenth year from the date of the contract, the contractor shall have relinquished at least 75 per cent of the original area allocated to it; or

4. At the end of the fifteenth year from the date of the contract, or when the contractor applies for exploitation rights, whichever is the earlier, the contractor shall nominate an area from the remaining area allocated to it to be retained for exploitation.

5. The contractor may at any time relinquish parts of the area allocated to it in advance of the schedule set out in paragraphs 2, 3 and 4.

6. Relinquished areas shall revert to the Area.

7. The Council may, at the request of the contractor, and on the recommendation of the Commission, in exceptional circumstances, defer the schedule of relinquishment. Such exceptional circumstances shall be determined by the Council and shall include, inter alia, consideration of prevailing economic circumstances or other unforeseen exceptional circumstances arising in connection with the operational activities of the contractor.

Regulation 28
Duration of contracts

1. A plan of work for exploration shall be approved for a period of 15 years. Upon expiration of a plan of work for exploration, the contractor shall apply for a plan of work for exploitation unless the contractor has already done so, has obtained an extension for the plan of work for exploration or decides to renounce its rights in the area covered by the plan of work for exploration.

2. Not later than six months before the expiration of a plan of work for exploration, a contractor may apply for extensions for the plan of work for exploration for periods of not more than five years each. Such extensions shall be approved by the Council, on the recommendation of the Commission, if the contractor has made efforts in good faith to comply with the requirements of the plan of work but for reasons beyond the contractor's control has been unable to complete the necessary preparatory work for proceeding to the exploitation stage or if the prevailing economic circumstances do not justify proceeding to the exploitation stage.

Regulation 29
Training

Pursuant to article 15 of annex III to the Convention, each contract shall include as a schedule a practical programme for the training of personnel of the Authority and developing States and drawn up by the contractor in cooperation with the Authority and the sponsoring State or States. Training programmes shall focus on training in the conduct of exploration, and shall provide for full participation by such personnel in all activities covered by the contract. Such training programmes may be revised and developed from time to time as necessary by mutual agreement.

Regulation 30
Periodic review of the implementation of the plan of work for exploration

1. The contractor and the Secretary-General shall jointly undertake a periodic review of the implementation of the plan of work for exploration at intervals of five years. The Secretary-General may request the contractor to submit such additional data and information as may be necessary for the purposes of the review.

2. In the light of the review, the contractor shall indicate its programme of activities for the following five-year period, making such adjustments to its previous programme of activities as are necessary.

3. The Secretary-General shall report on the review to the Commission and to the Council. The Secretary-General shall indicate in the report whether any observations transmitted to him by States Parties to the Convention concerning the manner in which the contractor has discharged its obligations under these Regulations relating to the protection and preservation of the marine environment were taken into account in the review.

Regulation 31
Termination of sponsorship

1. Each contractor shall have the required sponsorship throughout the period of the contract.

2. If a State terminates its sponsorship it shall promptly notify the Secretary-General in writing. The sponsoring State should also inform the Secretary-General of the reasons for terminating its sponsorship. Termination of sponsorship shall take effect six months after the date of receipt of the notification by the Secretary-General, unless the notification specifies a later date.

3. In the event of termination of sponsorship the contractor shall, within the period referred to in paragraph 2, obtain another sponsor. Such sponsor shall submit a certificate of sponsorship in accordance with regulation 11. Failure to obtain a sponsor within the required period shall result in the termination of the contract.

4. A sponsoring State shall not be discharged by reason of the termination of its sponsorship from any obligations accrued while it was a sponsoring State, nor shall such termination affect any legal rights and obligations created during such sponsorship.

5. The Secretary-General shall notify the members of the Authority of the termination or change of sponsorship.

Regulation 32
Responsibility and liability

Responsibility and liability of the contractor and of the Authority shall be in accordance with the Convention. The contractor shall continue to have responsibility for any damage arising out of wrongful acts in the conduct of its operations, in particular damage to the marine environment, after the completion of the exploration phase.

Part V
Protection and preservation of the marine environment

Regulation 33
Protection and preservation of the marine environment

1. The Authority shall, in accordance with the Convention and the Agreement, establish and keep under periodic review environmental rules, regulations and procedures to ensure effective protection for the marine environment from harmful effects which may arise from activities in the Area.

2. In order to ensure effective protection for the marine environment from harmful effects which may arise from activities in the Area, the Authority and sponsoring States shall apply a precautionary approach, as reflected in principle 15 of the Rio Declaration, and best environmental practices.

3. The Legal and Technical Commission shall make recommendations to the Council on the implementation of paragraphs 1 and 2 above.

4. The Commission shall develop and implement procedures for determining, on the basis of the best available scientific and technical information, including information provided pursuant to regulation 20, whether proposed exploration activities in the Area would have serious harmful effects on vulnerable marine ecosystems, in particular hydrothermal vents, and ensure that, if it is determined that certain proposed exploration activities would have serious harmful effects on vulnerable marine ecosystems, those activities are managed to prevent such effects or not authorized to proceed.

5. Pursuant to article 145 of the Convention and paragraph 2 of this regulation, each contractor shall take necessary measures to prevent, reduce and control pollution and other hazards to the marine environment arising from its activities in the Area as far as reasonably possible, applying a precautionary approach and best environmental practices.

6. Contractors, sponsoring States and other interested States or entities shall cooperate with the Authority in the establishment and implementation of programmes for monitoring and evaluating the impacts of deep seabed mining on the marine environment. When required by the Council, such programmes shall include proposals for areas to be set aside and used exclusively as impact reference zones and preservation reference zones. "Impact

reference zones" means areas to be used for assessing the effect of activities in the Area on the marine environment and which are representative of the environmental characteristics of the Area. "Preservation reference zones" means areas in which no mining shall occur to ensure representative and stable biota of the seabed in order to assess any changes in the biodiversity of the marine environment.

Regulation 34
Environmental baselines and monitoring

1. Each contract shall require the contractor to gather environmental baseline data and to establish environmental baselines, taking into account any recommendations issued by the Legal and Technical Commission pursuant to regulation 41, against which to assess the likely effects of its programme of activities under the plan of work for exploration on the marine environment and a programme to monitor and report on such effects. The recommendations issued by the Commission may, inter alia, list those exploration activities which may be considered to have no potential for causing harmful effects on the marine environment. The contractor shall cooperate with the Authority and the sponsoring State or States in the establishment and implementation of such monitoring programme.

2. The contractor shall report annually in writing to the Secretary-General on the implementation and results of the monitoring programme referred to in paragraph 1 and shall submit data and information, taking into account any recommendations issued by the Commission pursuant to regulation 41. The Secretary-General shall transmit such reports to the Commission for its consideration pursuant to article 165 of the Convention.

Regulation 35
Emergency orders

1. A contractor shall promptly report to the Secretary-General in writing, using the most effective means, any incident arising from activities which have caused, are causing, or pose a threat of, serious harm to the marine environment.

2. When the Secretary-General has been notified by a contractor or otherwise becomes aware of an incident resulting from or caused by a contractor's activities in the Area that has caused, is causing or poses a threat of, serious harm to the marine environment, the Secretary-General shall cause a general notification of the incident to be issued, shall notify in writing the contractor and the sponsoring State or States, and shall report immediately to the Legal and Technical Commission, to the Council and to all other members of the Authority. A copy of the report shall be circulated to competent international organizations and to concerned subregional, regional and global organizations and bodies. The Secretary-General shall monitor developments with respect to all such incidents and shall report on them as

appropriate to the Commission, the Council and all other members of the Authority.

3. Pending any action by the Council, the Secretary-General shall take such immediate measures of a temporary nature as are practical and reasonable in the circumstances to prevent, contain and minimize serious harm or the threat of serious harm to the marine environment. Such temporary measures shall remain in effect for no longer than 90 days, or until the Council decides at its next regular session or a special session, what measures, if any, to take pursuant to paragraph 6 of this regulation.

4. After having received the report of the Secretary-General, the Commission shall determine, based on the evidence provided to it and taking into account the measures already taken by the contractor, which measures are necessary to respond effectively to the incident in order to prevent, contain and minimize serious harm or the threat of serious harm to the marine environment, and shall make its recommendations to the Council.

5. The Council shall consider the recommendations of the Commission.

6. The Council, taking into account the recommendations of the Commission, the report of the Secretary-General, any information provided by the Contractor and any other relevant information, may issue emergency orders, which may include orders for the suspension or adjustment of operations, as may be reasonably necessary to prevent, contain and minimize serious harm or the threat of serious harm to the marine environment arising out of activities in the Area.

7. If a contractor does not promptly comply with an emergency order to prevent, contain and minimize serious harm or the threat of serious harm to the marine environment arising out of its activities in the Area, the Council shall take by itself or through arrangements with others on its behalf, such practical measures as are necessary to prevent, contain and minimize any such serious harm or threat of serious harm to the marine environment.

8. In order to enable the Council, when necessary, to take immediately the practical measures to prevent, contain and minimize the serious harm or threat of serious harm to the marine environment referred to in paragraph 7, the contractor, prior to the commencement of testing of collecting systems and processing operations, will provide the Council with a guarantee of its financial and technical capability to comply promptly with emergency orders or to assure that the Council can take such emergency measures. If the contractor does not provide the Council with such a guarantee, the sponsoring State or States shall, in response to a request by the Secretary-General and pursuant to articles 139 and 235 of the Convention, take necessary measures to ensure that the contractor provides such a guarantee or shall take measures to ensure that assistance is provided to the Authority in the discharge of its responsibilities under paragraph 7.

Regulation 36
Rights of coastal States

1. Nothing in these Regulations shall affect the rights of coastal States in accordance with article 142 and other relevant provisions of the Convention.

2. Any coastal State which has grounds for believing that any activity in the Area by a contractor is likely to cause serious harm or a threat of serious harm to the marine environment under its jurisdiction or sovereignty may notify the Secretary-General in writing of the grounds upon which such belief is based. The Secretary-General shall provide the Contractor and its sponsoring State or States with a reasonable opportunity to examine the evidence, if any, provided by the coastal State as the basis for its belief. The contractor and its sponsoring State or States may submit their observations thereon to the Secretary-General within a reasonable time.

3. If there are clear grounds for believing that serious harm to the marine environment is likely to occur, the Secretary-General shall act in accordance with regulation 35 and, if necessary, shall take immediate measures of a temporary nature as provided for in paragraph 3 of regulation 35.

4. Contractors shall take all measures necessary to ensure that their activities are conducted so as not to cause serious harm to the marine environment, including, but not restricted to, pollution, under the jurisdiction or sovereignty of coastal States, and that such serious harm or pollution arising from incidents or activities in its exploration area does not spread beyond such area.

Regulation 37
Human remains and objects and sites of an archaeological or historical nature

The contractor shall immediately notify the Secretary-General in writing of any finding in the exploration area of any human remains of an archaeological or historical nature, or any object or site of a similar nature and its location, including the preservation and protection measures taken. The Secretary-General shall transmit such information to the Director-General of the United Nations Educational, Scientific and Cultural Organization and any other competent international organization. Following the finding of any such human remains, object or site in the exploration area, and in order to avoid disturbing such human remains, object or site, no further prospecting or exploration shall take place, within a reasonable radius, until such time as the Council decides otherwise after taking account of the views of the Director-General of the United Nations Educational, Scientific and Cultural Organization or any other competent international organization.

Part VI
Confidentiality

Regulation 38
Confidentiality of data and information

1. Data and information submitted or transferred to the Authority or to any person participating in any activity or programme of the Authority pursuant to these Regulations or a contract issued under these Regulations, and designated by the contractor, in consultation with the Secretary-General, as being of a confidential nature, shall be considered confidential unless it is data and information which:

(a) is generally known or publicly available from other sources;

(b) has been previously made available by the owner to others without an obligation concerning its confidentiality; or

(c) is already in the possession of the Authority with no obligation concerning its confidentiality.

Data and information that is necessary for the formulation by the Authority of rules, regulations and procedures concerning protection and preservation of the marine environment and safety, other than proprietary equipment design data, shall not be deemed confidential.

2. Confidential data and information may only be used by the Secretary-General and staff of the Secretariat, as authorized by the Secretary-General, and by the members of the Legal and Technical Commission as necessary for and relevant to the effective exercise of their powers and functions. The Secretary-General shall authorize access to such data and information only for limited use in connection with the functions and duties of the staff of the Secretariat and the functions and duties of the Legal and Technical Commission.

3. Ten years after the date of submission of confidential data and information to the Authority or the expiration of the contract for exploration, whichever is the later, and every five years thereafter, the Secretary-General and the contractor shall review such data and information to determine whether they should remain confidential. Such data and information shall remain confidential if the contractor establishes that there would be a substantial risk of serious and unfair economic prejudice if the data and information were to be released. No such data and information shall be released until the contractor has been accorded a reasonable opportunity to exhaust the judicial remedies available to it pursuant to Part XI, section 5, of the Convention.

4. If, at any time following the expiration of the contract for exploration, the contractor enters into a contract for exploitation in respect of any part of the exploration area, confidential data and information relating to that

part of the area shall remain confidential in accordance with the contract for exploitation.

5. The contractor may at any time waive confidentiality of data and information.

Regulation 39
Procedures to ensure confidentiality

1. The Secretary-General shall be responsible for maintaining the confidentiality of all confidential data and information and shall not, except with the prior written consent of the contractor, release such data and information to any person external to the Authority. To ensure the confidentiality of such data and information, the Secretary-General shall establish procedures, consistent with the provisions of the Convention, governing the handling of confidential information by members of the Secretariat, members of the Legal and Technical Commission and any other person participating in any activity or programme of the Authority. Such procedures shall include:

(a) maintenance of confidential data and information in secure facilities and development of security procedures to prevent unauthorized access to or removal of such data and information;

(b) development and maintenance of a classification, log and inventory system of all written data and information received, including its type and source and routing from the time of receipt until final disposition.

2. A person who is authorized pursuant to these Regulations to have access to confidential data and information shall not disclose such data and information except as permitted under the Convention and these Regulations. The Secretary-General shall require any person who is authorized to have access to confidential data and information to make a written declaration witnessed by the Secretary-General or his or her authorized representative to the effect that the person so authorized:

(a) acknowledges his or her legal obligation under the Convention and these Regulations with respect to the non-disclosure of confidential data and information;

(b) agrees to comply with the applicable regulations and procedures established to ensure the confidentiality of such data and information.

3. The Legal and Technical Commission shall protect the confidentiality of confidential data and information submitted to it pursuant to these Regulations or a contract issued under these Regulations. In accordance with the provisions of article 163, paragraph 8, of the Convention, members of the Commission shall not disclose, even after the termination of their functions, any industrial secret, proprietary data which are transferred to the Authority in accordance with Annex III, article 14, of the Convention, or any other confidential information coming to their knowledge by reason of their duties for the Authority.

4. The Secretary-General and staff of the Authority shall not disclose, even after the termination of their functions with the Authority, any industrial secret, proprietary data which are transferred to the Authority in accordance with Annex III, article 14, of the Convention, or any other confidential information coming to their knowledge by reason of their employment with the Authority.

5. Taking into account the responsibility and liability of the Authority pursuant to Annex III, article 22, of the Convention, the Authority may take such action as may be appropriate against any person who, by reason of his or her duties for the Authority, has access to any confidential data and information and who is in breach of the obligations relating to confidentiality contained in the Convention and these Regulations.

Part VII
General Procedures

Regulation 40
Notice and general procedures

1. Any application, request, notice, report, consent, approval, waiver, direction or instruction hereunder shall be made by the Secretary-General or by the designated representative of the prospector, applicant or contractor, as the case may be, in writing. Service shall be by hand, or by telex, facsimile, registered airmail or electronic mail containing an authorized electronic signature to the Secretary-General at the headquarters of the Authority or to the designated representative.

2. Delivery by hand shall be effective when made. Delivery by telex shall be deemed to be effective on the business day following the day when the "answer back" appears on the sender's telex machine. Delivery by facsimile shall be effective when the "transmit confirmation report" confirming the transmission to the recipient's published facsimile number is received by the transmitter. Delivery by registered airmail shall be deemed to be effective 21 days after posting. An electronic document is presumed to be received by the addressee when it enters an information system designated or used by the addressee for the purpose of receiving documents of the type sent and is capable of being retrieved and processed by the addressee.

3. Notice to the designated representative of the prospector, applicant or contractor shall constitute effective notice to the prospector, applicant or contractor for all purposes under these Regulations, and the designated representative shall be the agent of the prospector, applicant or contractor for the service of process or notification in any proceeding of any court or tribunal having jurisdiction.

4. Notice to the Secretary-General shall constitute effective notice to the Authority for all purposes under these Regulations, and the Secretary-General shall be the Authority's agent for the service of process or notification in any proceeding of any court or tribunal having jurisdiction.

Regulation 41
Recommendations for the guidance of contractors

1. The Legal and Technical Commission may from time to time issue recommendations of a technical or administrative nature for the guidance of contractors to assist them in the implementation of the rules, regulations and procedures of the Authority.

2. The full text of such recommendations shall be reported to the Council. Should the Council find that a recommendation is inconsistent with the intent and purpose of these Regulations, it may request that the recommendation be modified or withdrawn.

Part VIII
Settlement of disputes

Regulation 42
Disputes

1. Disputes concerning the interpretation or application of these Regulations shall be settled in accordance with Part XI, section 5, of the Convention.

2. Any final decision rendered by a court or tribunal having jurisdiction under the Convention relating to the rights and obligations of the Authority and of the Contractor shall be enforceable in the territory of each State Party to the Convention.

Part IX
Resources other than cobalt crusts

Regulation 43
Resources other than cobalt crusts

If a prospector or contractor finds resources in the Area other than cobalt crusts, the prospecting and exploration for and exploitation of such resources shall be subject to the rules, regulations and procedures of the Authority relating to such resources in accordance with the Convention and the Agreement. The prospector or contractor shall notify the Authority of its find.

Part X
Review

Regulation 44
Review

1. Five years following the approval of these Regulations by the Assembly, or at any time thereafter, the Council shall undertake a review of the manner in which the Regulations have operated in practice.

2. If, in the light of improved knowledge or technology, it becomes apparent that the Regulations are not adequate, any State Party, the Legal and Technical Commission, or any contractor through its sponsoring State may at any

time request the Council to consider, at its next ordinary session, revisions to these Regulations.

3. In the light of the review, the Council may adopt and apply provisionally, pending approval by the Assembly, amendments to the provisions of these Regulations, taking into account the recommendations of the Legal and Technical Commission or other subordinate organs concerned. Any such amendments shall be without prejudice to the rights conferred on any Contractor with the Authority under the provisions of a contract entered into pursuant to these Regulations in force at the time of any such amendment.

4. In the event that any provisions of these Regulations are amended, the Contractor and the Authority may revise the contract in accordance with section 24 of annex 4.

Annex 1
Notification of intention to engage in prospecting

1. Name of prospector:
2. Street address of prospector:
3. Postal address (if different from above):
4. Telephone number:
5. Facsimile number:
6. Electronic mail address:
7. Nationality of prospector:
8. If prospector is a juridical person, identify prospector's
   (a) place of registration; and
   (b) principal place of business/domicile.

and attach a copy of the prospector's certificate of registration.

9. Name of prospector's designated representative:
10. Street address of prospector's designated representative (if different from above):
11. Postal address (if different from above):
12. Telephone number:
13. Facsimile number:
14. Electronic mail address:
15. Attach the coordinates of the broad area or areas in which prospecting is to be conducted (in accordance with the World Geodetic System WGS 84).
16. Attach a general description of the prospecting programme, including the date of commencement and the approximate duration of the programme.
17. Attach a written undertaking that the prospector will:

(a) comply with the Convention and the relevant rules, regulations and procedures of the Authority concerning:

(i) cooperation in the training programmes in connection with marine scientific research and transfer of technology referred to in articles 143 and 144 of the Convention; and

(ii) protection and preservation of the marine environment; and

(b) accept verification by the Authority of compliance therewith.

18. List hereunder all the attachments and annexes to this notification (all data and information should be submitted in hard copy and in a digital format specified by the Authority):

Date:________________ ____________________________

Signature of prospector's designated representative

ATTESTATION:

____
Signature of person attesting

____
Name of person attesting

____
Title of person attesting

Annex 2
Application for approval of a plan of work for exploration to obtain a contract

Section I
Information concerning the applicant

1. Name of applicant:
2. Street address of applicant:
3. Postal address (if different from above):
4. Telephone number:
5. Facsimile number:
6. Electronic mail address:
7. Name of applicant's designated representative:
8. Street address of applicant's designated representative (if different from above):
9. Postal address (if different from above):
10. Telephone number:
11. Facsimile number:
12. Electronic mail address:
13. If the applicant is a juridical person, identify applicant's
    (a) place of registration; and
    (b) principal place of business/domicile.

and attach a copy of the applicant's certificate of registration.

14. Identify the sponsoring State or States.
15. In respect of each sponsoring State, provide the date of deposit of its instrument of ratification of, or accession or succession to, the 1982 United Nations Convention on the Law of the Sea and the date of its consent to be bound by the Agreement relating to the Implementation of Part XI of the United Nations Convention on the Law of the Sea of 10 December 1982.
16. A certificate of sponsorship issued by the sponsoring State must be attached with this application. If the applicant has more than one nationality, as in the case of a partnership or consortium of entities from more than one State, certificates of sponsorship issued by each of the States involved must be attached.

Section II
Information relating to the area under application

17. Define the boundaries of the blocks under application by attaching a chart (on a scale and projection specified by the Authority) and a list of geographical coordinates (in accordance with the World Geodetic System WGS 84).
18. Indicate whether the applicant elects to contribute a reserved area in accordance with regulation 17 or offer an equity interest in a joint venture arrangement in accordance with regulation 19.

19. If the applicant elects to contribute a reserved area:

(a) Attach a chart (on a scale and projection specified by the Authority) and a list of the coordinates dividing the total area into two parts of equal estimated commercial value; and

(b) Include in an attachment sufficient information to enable the Council to designate a reserved area based on the estimated commercial value of each part of the area under application. Such attachment must include the data available to the applicant with respect to both parts of the area under application, including:

(i) Data on the location, survey and evaluation of the cobalt crusts in the areas, including:

a. A description of the technology related to the recovery and processing of cobalt crusts that is necessary for making the designation of a reserved area;
b. A map of the physical and geological characteristics, such as seabed topography, bathymetry and bottom currents and information on the reliability of such data;
c. A map showing the remotely sensed data (such as electromagnetic surveys) and other survey data used to determine the lateral extent of each cobalt crust deposit;
d. Data showing the average tonnage (in metric tonnes) of each cobalt crust body that will comprise the mine site and an associated tonnage map showing the location of sampling sites;
e. Combined maps of tonnage and grade of cobalt crusts;
f. A calculation based on standard procedures, including statistical analysis, using the data submitted and assumptions made in the calculations that the two areas could be expected to contain cobalt crusts of equal estimated commercial value expressed as recoverable metals in mineable areas;
g. A description of the techniques used by the applicant;

(ii) Information concerning environmental parameters (seasonal and during test period) including, inter alia, wind speed and direction, water salinity, temperature and biological communities.

20. If the area under application includes any part of a reserved area, attach a list of coordinates of the area which forms part of the reserved area and indicate the applicant's qualifications in accordance with regulation 18 of the Regulations.

Section III
Financial and technical information

21. Attach sufficient information to enable the Council to determine whether the applicant is financially capable of carrying out the proposed plan of work for exploration and of fulfilling its financial obligations to the Authority:

(a) If the application is made by the Enterprise, attach certification by its competent authority that the Enterprise has the necessary financial resources to meet the estimated costs of the proposed plan of work for exploration;

(b) If the application is made by a State or a state enterprise, attach a statement by the State or the sponsoring State certifying that the applicant has the necessary financial resources to meet the estimated costs of the proposed plan of work for exploration;

(c) If the application is made by an entity, attach copies of the applicant's audited financial statements, including balance sheets and profit-and-loss statements, for the most recent three years in conformity with internationally accepted accounting principles and certified by a duly qualified firm of public accountants; and

- (i) if the applicant is a newly organized entity and a certified balance sheet is not available, a pro forma balance sheet certified by an appropriate official of the applicant;
- (ii) if the applicant is a subsidiary of another entity, copies of such financial statements of that entity and a statement from that entity in conformity with internationally accepted accounting practices and certified by a duly qualified firm of public accountants that the applicant will have the financial resources to carry out the plan of work for exploration;
- (iii) if the applicant is controlled by a State or a state enterprise, a statement from the State or state enterprise certifying that the applicant will have the financial resources to carry out the plan of work for exploration.

22. If it is intended to finance the proposed plan of work for exploration by borrowings, attach a statement of the amount of such borrowings, the repayment period and the interest rate.

23. Attach sufficient information to enable the Council to determine whether the applicant is technically capable of carrying out the proposed plan of work for exploration, including:

(a) a general description of the applicant's previous experience, knowledge, skills, technical qualifications and expertise relevant to the proposed plan of work for exploration;

(b) a general description of the equipment and methods expected to be used in carrying out the proposed plan of work for exploration and other relevant non-proprietary information about the characteristics of such technology;

(c) a general description of the applicant's financial and technical capability to respond to any incident or activity which causes serious harm to the marine environment.

Section IV
The plan of work for exploration

24. Attach the following information relating to the plan of work for exploration:

(a) a general description and a schedule of the proposed exploration programme, including the programme of activities for the immediate five-year period, such as studies to be undertaken in respect of the environmental, technical, economic and other appropriate factors which must be taken into account in exploration;

(b) a description of a programme for oceanographic and environmental baseline studies in accordance with the Regulations and any environmental rules, regulations and procedures established by the Authority that would enable an assessment of the potential environmental impact including, but not restricted to, the impact on biodiversity, of the proposed exploration activities, taking into account any recommendations issued by the Legal and Technical Commission;

(c) a preliminary assessment of the possible impact of the proposed exploration activities on the marine environment;

(d) a description of proposed measures for the prevention, reduction and control of pollution of other hazards, as well as possible impacts, to the marine environment;

(e) a schedule of anticipated yearly expenditures in respect of the programme of activities for the immediate five-year period.

Section V
Undertakings

25. Attach a written undertaking that the applicant will:

(a) accept as enforceable and comply with the applicable obligations created by the provisions of the Convention and the rules, regulations and procedures of the Authority, the decisions of the relevant organs of the Authority and the terms of its contracts with the Authority;

(b) accept control by the Authority of activities in the Area as authorized by the Convention;

(c) provide the Authority with a written assurance that its obligations under the contract will be fulfilled in good faith.

Section VI
Previous contracts

26. Has the applicant or, in the case of an application by a partnership or consortium of entities in a joint arrangement, any member of the partnership or consortium previously been awarded any contract with the Authority?

27. If the answer to 26 is "yes", the application must include:

(a) the date of the previous contract or contracts;

(b) the dates, reference numbers and titles of each report submitted to the Authority in connection with the contact or contracts; and

(c) the date of termination of the contract or contracts, if applicable.

Section VII
Attachments

28. List all the attachments and annexes to this application (all data and information should be submitted in hard copy and in a digital format specified by the Authority):

Date:______________ ________________________________

Signature of applicant's designated representative

ATTESTATION:

____
Signature of person attesting

____
Name of person attesting

____
Title of person attesting

Annex 3
Contract for exploration

THIS CONTRACT made the ... day of ... between the **INTERNATIONAL SEABED AUTHORITY** represented by its **SECRETARY-GENERAL** (hereinafter referred to as "the Authority") and ... represented by ... (hereinafter referred to as "the Contractor") **WITNESSETH** as follows:

Incorporation of clauses

A. The standard clauses set out in annex 4 to the Regulations on Prospecting and Exploration for Cobalt-rich Ferromanganese Crusts in the Area shall be incorporated herein and shall have effect as if herein set out at length.

Exploration area

B. For the purposes of this contract, the "exploration area" means that part of the Area allocated to the Contractor for exploration, defined by the coordinates listed in schedule 1 hereto, as reduced from time to time in accordance with the standard clauses and the Regulations.

Grant of rights

C. In consideration of:

(1) Their mutual interest in the conduct of exploration activities in the exploration area pursuant to the Convention and the Agreement;

(2) The responsibility of the Authority to organize and control activities in the Area, particularly with a view to administering the resources of the Area, in accordance with the legal regime established in Part XI of the Convention and the Agreement and Part XII of the Convention respectively; and

(3) The interest and financial commitment of the Contractor in conducting activities in the exploration area and the mutual covenants made herein;

the Authority hereby grants to the Contractor the exclusive right to explore for cobalt crusts in the exploration area in accordance with the terms and conditions of this contract.

Entry into force and contract term

D. This contract shall enter into force on signature by both parties and, subject to the standard clauses, shall remain in force for a period of fifteen years thereafter unless:

(1) The Contractor obtains a contract for exploitation in the exploration area which enters into force before the expiration of such period of fifteen years; or

(2) The contract is sooner terminated provided that the term of the contract may be extended in accordance with standard clauses 3.2 and 17.2.

Schedules

E. The schedules referred to in the standard clauses, namely section 4 and section 8, are for the purposes of this contract schedules 2 and 3 respectively.

Entire agreement

F. This contract expresses the entire agreement between the parties, and no oral understanding or prior writing shall modify the terms hereof.

IN WITNESS WHEREOF the undersigned, being duly authorized thereto by the respective parties, have signed this contract at …, this … day of …

Schedule 1

[Coordinates and illustrative chart of the exploration area]

Schedule 2

[The current five-year programme of activities as revised from time to time]

Schedule 3

[The training programme shall become a schedule to the contract when approved by the Authority in accordance with section 8 of the standard clauses.]

Annex 4
Standard clauses for exploration contract

Section 1
Definitions

1.1 In the following clauses:

(a) "exploration area" means that part of the Area allocated to the Contractor for exploration, described in schedule 1 hereto, as the same may be reduced from time to time in accordance with this contract and the Regulations;

(b) "programme of activities" means the programme of activities which is set out in schedule 2 hereto as the same may be adjusted from time to time in accordance with sections 4.3 and 4.4 hereof;

(c) "regulations" means the Regulations on Prospecting and Exploration for Cobalt-rich Ferromanganese Crusts in the Area, adopted by the Authority.

1.2 Terms and phrases defined in the Regulations shall have the same meaning in these standard clauses.

1.3 In accordance with the Agreement relating to the Implementation of Part XI of the United Nations Convention on the Law of the Sea of 10 December 1982, its provisions and Part XI of the Convention are to be interpreted and applied together as a single instrument; this contract and references in this contract to the Convention are to be interpreted and applied accordingly.

1.4 This contract includes the schedules to this contract, which shall be an integral part hereof.

Section 2
Security of tenure

2.1 The Contractor shall have security of tenure and this contract shall not be suspended, terminated or revised except in accordance with sections 20, 21 and 24 hereof.

2.2 The Contractor shall have the exclusive right to explore for cobalt crusts in the exploration area in accordance with the terms and conditions of this contract. The Authority shall ensure that no other entity operates in the exploration area for a different category of resources in a manner that might unreasonably interfere with the operations of the Contractor.

2.3 The Contractor, by notice to the Authority, shall have the right at any time to renounce without penalty the whole or part of its rights in the exploration area, provided that the Contractor shall remain liable for all obligations accrued prior to the date of such renunciation in respect of the area renounced.

2.4 Nothing in this contract shall be deemed to confer any right on the Contractor other than those rights expressly granted herein. The Authority reserves the right to enter into contracts with respect to resources other than cobalt crusts with third parties in the area covered by this contract.

Section 3
Contract term

3.1 This contract shall enter into force on signature by both parties and shall remain in force for a period of fifteen years thereafter unless:

(a) the Contractor obtains a contract for exploitation in the exploration area which enters into force before the expiration of such period of fifteen years; or

(b) the contract is sooner terminated,

provided that the term of the contract may be extended in accordance with sections 3.2 and 17.2 hereof.

3.2 Upon application by the Contractor, not later than six months before the expiration of this contract, this contract may be extended for periods of not more than five years each on such terms and conditions as the Authority and the Contractor may then agree in accordance with the Regulations. Such extensions shall be approved if the Contractor has made efforts in good faith to comply with the requirements of this contract but for reasons beyond the Contractor's control has been unable to complete the necessary preparatory work for proceeding to the exploitation stage or if the prevailing economic circumstances do not justify proceeding to the exploitation stage.

3.3 Notwithstanding the expiration of this contract in accordance with section 3.1 hereof, if the Contractor has, at least 90 days prior to the date of expiration, applied for a contract for exploitation, the Contractor's rights and obligations under this contract shall continue until such time as the application has been considered and a contract for exploitation has been issued or refused.

Section 4
Exploration

4.1 The Contractor shall commence exploration in accordance with the time schedule stipulated in the programme of activities set out in schedule 2 hereto and shall adhere to such time periods or any modification thereto as provided for by this contract.

4.2 The Contractor shall carry out the programme of activities set out in schedule 2 hereto. In carrying out such activities the Contractor shall spend in each contract year not less than the amount specified in such programme, or any agreed review thereof, in actual and direct exploration expenditures.

4.3 The Contractor, with the consent of the Authority, which consent shall not be unreasonably withheld, may from time to time make such changes in the programme of activities and the expenditures specified therein as may be necessary and prudent in accordance with good mining industry practice, and taking into account the market conditions for the metals contained in cobalt crusts and other relevant global economic conditions.

4.4 Not later than 90 days prior to the expiration of each five-year period from the date on which this contract enters into force in accordance with section 3 hereof, the Contractor and the Secretary-General shall jointly undertake a review of the implementation of the plan of work for exploration under this contract. The Secretary-General may require the Contractor to submit such additional data and information as may be necessary for the purposes of the review. In the light of the review, the Contractor shall make such adjustments to its plan of work as are necessary and shall indicate its programme of activities for the following five-year period, including a revised schedule of anticipated yearly expenditures. Schedule 2 hereto shall be adjusted accordingly.

Section 5
Environmental monitoring

5.1 The Contractor shall take necessary measures to prevent, reduce and control pollution and other hazards to the marine environment arising from its activities in the Area as far as reasonably possible applying a precautionary approach and best environmental practices.

5.2 Prior to the commencement of exploration activities, the Contractor shall submit to the Authority:

(a) an impact assessment of the potential effects on the marine environment of the proposed activities;

(b) a proposal for a monitoring programme to determine the potential effect on the marine environment of the proposed activities; and

(c) data that could be used to establish an environmental baseline against which to assess the effect of the proposed activities.

5.3 The Contractor shall, in accordance with the Regulations, gather environmental baseline data as exploration activities progress and develop and shall establish environmental baselines against which to assess the likely effects of the Contractor's activities on the marine environment.

5.4 The Contractor shall, in accordance with the Regulations, establish and carry out a programme to monitor and report on such effects on the marine environment. The Contractor shall cooperate with the Authority in the implementation of such monitoring.

5.5 The Contractor shall, within 90 days of the end of each calendar year, report to the Secretary-General on the implementation and results of the monitoring programme referred to in section 5.4 hereof and shall submit data and information in accordance with the Regulations.

Section 6
Contingency plans and emergencies

6.1 The Contractor shall, prior to the commencement of its programme of activities under this contract, submit to the Secretary-General a contingency plan to respond effectively to incidents that are likely to cause serious harm or a threat of serious harm to the marine environment arising from the Contractor's activities at sea in the exploration area. Such contingency plan shall establish special procedures and provide for adequate and appropriate equipment to deal with such incidents and, in particular, shall include arrangements for:

(a) the immediate raising of a general alarm in the area of the exploration activities;

(b) immediate notification to the Secretary-General;

(c) the warning of ships which might be about to enter the immediate vicinity;

(d) a continuing flow of full information to the Secretary-General relating to particulars of the contingency measures already taken and further actions required;

(e) the removal, as appropriate, of polluting substances;

(f) the reduction and, so far as reasonably possible, prevention of serious harm to the marine environment, as well as mitigation of such effects;

(g) as appropriate, cooperation with other contractors with the Authority to respond to an emergency; and

(h) periodic emergency response exercises.

6.2 The Contractor shall promptly report to the Secretary-General any incident arising from its activities that has caused, is causing or poses a threat of serious harm to the marine environment. Each such report shall contain the details of such incident, including, inter alia:

(a) the coordinates of the area affected or which can reasonably be anticipated to be affected;

(b) the description of the action being taken by the Contractor to prevent, contain, minimize and repair the serious harm or threat of serious harm to the marine environment;

(c) a description of the action being taken by the Contractor to monitor the effects of the incident on the marine environment; and

(d) such supplementary information as may reasonably be required by the Secretary-General.

6.3 The Contractor shall comply with emergency orders issued by the Council and immediate measures of a temporary nature issued by the Secretary-General in accordance with the Regulations, to prevent, contain, minimize or repair serious harm or the threat of serious harm to the marine environment, which may include orders to the Contractor to immediately suspend or adjust any activities in the exploration area.

6.4 If the Contractor does not promptly comply with such emergency orders or immediate measures of a temporary nature, the Council may take such reasonable measures as are necessary to prevent, contain, minimize or repair any such serious harm or the threat of serious harm to the marine environment at the Contractor's expense. The Contractor shall promptly reimburse the Authority the amount of such expenses. Such expenses shall be in addition to any monetary penalties which may be imposed on the Contractor pursuant to the terms of this contract or the Regulations.

Section 7
Human remains and objects and sites of an archaeological or historical nature

The Contractor shall immediately notify the Secretary-General in writing of any finding in the exploration area of any human remains of an archaeological or historical nature, or any object or site of a similar nature and its location, including the preservation and protection measures taken. The Secretary-General shall transmit such information to the Director-General of the United Nations Educational, Scientific and Cultural Organization and any other competent international organization. Following the finding of any such human remains, object or site in the exploration area, and in order to avoid disturbing such human remains, object or site, no further prospecting or exploration shall take place, within a reasonable radius, until such time as the Council decides otherwise after taking account of the views of the Director-General of the United Nations Educational, Scientific and Cultural Organization or any other competent international organization.

Section 8
Training

8.1 In accordance with the Regulations, the Contractor shall, prior to the commencement of exploration under this contract, submit to the Authority for approval proposed training programmes for the training of personnel of the Authority and developing States, including the participation of such personnel in all of the Contractor's activities under this contract.

8.2 The scope and financing of the training programme shall be subject to negotiation between the Contractor, the Authority and the sponsoring State or States.

8.3 The Contractor shall conduct training programmes in accordance with the specific programme for the training of personnel referred to in section 8.1 hereof approved by the Authority in accordance with the Regulations, which programme, as revised and developed from time to time, shall become a part of this contract as schedule 3.

Section 9
Books and records

The Contractor shall keep a complete and proper set of books, accounts and financial records, consistent with internationally accepted accounting principles. Such books, accounts and financial records shall include information which will fully disclose the actual and direct expenditures for exploration and such other information as will facilitate an effective audit of such expenditures.

Section 10
Annual reports

10.1 The Contractor shall, within 90 days of the end of each calendar year, submit a report to the Secretary-General in such format as may be recommended from time to time by the Legal and Technical Commission covering its programme of activities in the exploration area and containing, as applicable, information in sufficient detail on:

(a) the exploration work carried out during the calendar year, including maps, charts and graphs illustrating the work that has been done and the results obtained;

(b) the equipment used to carry out the exploration work, including the results of tests conducted of proposed mining technologies, but not equipment design data; and

(c) the implementation of training programmes, including any proposed revisions to or developments of such programmes.

10.2 Such reports shall also contain:

(a) the results obtained from environmental monitoring programmes, including observations, measurements, evaluations and analyses of environmental parameters;

(b) a statement of the quantity of cobalt crusts recovered as samples or for the purpose of testing;

(c) a statement, in conformity with internationally accepted accounting principles and certified by a duly qualified firm of public accountants, or, where the Contractor is a State or a state enterprise, by the sponsoring State, of the actual and direct exploration expenditures of the Contractor in carrying out the programme of activities during the Contractor's accounting year. Such expenditures may be claimed by the contractor as part of the contractor's development costs incurred prior to the commencement of commercial production; and

(d) details of any proposed adjustments to the programme of activities and the reasons for such adjustments.

10.3 The Contractor shall also submit such additional information to supplement the reports referred to in sections 10.1 and 10.2 hereof as the Secretary-General may from time to time reasonably require in order to carry out the Authority's functions under the Convention, the Regulations and this contract.

10.4 The Contractor shall keep, in good condition, a representative portion of samples and cores of the cobalt crusts obtained in the course of exploration until the expiration of this contract. The Authority may request the Contractor in writing to deliver to it for analysis a portion of any such sample and cores obtained during the course of exploration.

Section 11
Data and information to be submitted on expiration of the contract

11.1 The Contractor shall transfer to the Authority all data and information that are both necessary for and relevant to the effective exercise of the powers and functions of the Authority in respect of the exploration area in accordance with the provisions of this section.

11.2 Upon expiration or termination of this contract the Contractor, if it has not already done so, shall submit the following data and information to the Secretary-General:

(a) copies of geological, environmental, geochemical and geophysical data acquired by the Contractor in the course of carrying out the programme of activities that are necessary for and relevant to the effective exercise of the powers and functions of the Authority in respect of the exploration area;

(b) the estimation of mineable deposits, when such deposits have been identified, which shall include details of the grade and quantity of the proven, probable and possible cobalt crust reserves and the anticipated mining conditions;

(c) copies of geological, technical, financial and economic reports made by or for the Contractor that are necessary for and relevant to the effective exercise of the powers and functions of the Authority in respect of the exploration area;

(d) information in sufficient detail on the equipment used to carry out the exploration work, including the results of tests conducted of proposed mining technologies, but not equipment design data;

(e) a statement of the quantity of cobalt crusts recovered as samples or for the purpose of testing; and

(f) a statement on how and where samples of cores are archived and their availability to the Authority.

11.3 The data and information referred to in section 11.2 hereof shall also be submitted to the Secretary-General if, prior to the expiration of this contract, the Contractor applies for approval of a plan of work for exploitation or if the

Contractor renounces its rights in the exploration area to the extent that such data and information relates to the renounced area.

Section 12
Confidentiality

Data and information transferred to the Authority in accordance with this contract shall be treated as confidential in accordance with the provisions of the Regulations.

Section 13
Undertakings

13.1 The Contractor shall carry out exploration in accordance with the terms and conditions of this contract, the Regulations, Part XI of the Convention, the Agreement and other rules of international law not incompatible with the Convention.

13.2 The Contractor undertakes:

(a) to accept as enforceable and comply with the terms of this contract;

(b) to comply with the applicable obligations created by the provisions of the Convention, the rules, regulations and procedures of the Authority and the decisions of the relevant organs of the Authority;

(c) to accept control by the Authority of activities in the Area as authorized by the Convention;

(d) to fulfil its obligations under this contract in good faith; and

(e) to observe, as far as reasonably practicable, any recommendations which may be issued from time to time by the Legal and Technical Commission.

13.3 The Contractor shall actively carry out the programme of activities:

(a) with due diligence, efficiency and economy;

(b) with due regard to the impact of its activities on the marine environment; and

(c) with reasonable regard for other activities in the marine environment.

13.4 The Authority undertakes to fulfil in good faith its powers and functions under the Convention and the Agreement in accordance with article 157 of the Convention.

Section 14
Inspection

14.1 The Contractor shall permit the Authority to send its inspectors on board vessels and installations used by the Contractor to carry out activities in the exploration area to:

(a) monitor the Contractor's compliance with the terms and conditions of this contract and the Regulations; and

(b) monitor the effects of such activities on the marine environment.

14.2 The Secretary-General shall give reasonable notice to the Contractor of the projected time and duration of inspections, the name of the inspectors and any activities the inspectors are to perform that are likely to require the availability of special equipment or special assistance from personnel of the Contractor.

14.3 Such inspectors shall have the authority to inspect any vessel or installation, including its log, equipment, records, facilities, all other recorded data and any relevant documents which are necessary to monitor the Contractor's compliance.

14.4 The Contractor, its agents and employees shall assist the inspectors in the performance of their duties and shall:

(a) accept and facilitate prompt and safe boarding of vessels and installations by inspectors;

(b) cooperate with and assist in the inspection of any vessel or installation conducted pursuant to these procedures;

(c) provide access to all relevant equipment, facilities and personnel on vessels and installations at all reasonable times;

(d) not obstruct, intimidate or interfere with inspectors in the performance of their duties;

(e) provide reasonable facilities, including, where appropriate, food and accommodation, to inspectors; and

(f) facilitate safe disembarkation by inspectors.

14.5 Inspectors shall avoid interference with the safe and normal operations on board vessels and installations used by the Contractor to carry out activities in the area visited and shall act in accordance with the Regulations and the measures adopted to protect confidentiality of data and information.

14.6 The Secretary-General and any duly authorized representatives of the Secretary-General, shall have access, for purposes of audit and examination, to any books, documents, papers and records of the Contractor which are necessary and directly pertinent to verify the expenditures referred to in section 10.2 (c).

14.7 The Secretary-General shall provide relevant information contained in the reports of inspectors to the Contractor and its sponsoring State or States where action is necessary.

14.8 If for any reason the Contractor does not pursue exploration and does not request a contract for exploitation, it shall, before withdrawing from the exploration area, notify the Secretary-General in writing in order to permit the Authority, if it so decides, to carry out an inspection pursuant to this section.

Section 15
Safety, labour and health standards

15.1 The Contractor shall comply with the generally accepted international rules and standards established by competent international organizations or general diplomatic conferences concerning the safety of life at sea, and the prevention of collisions and such rules, regulations and procedures as may be adopted by the Authority relating to safety at sea. Each vessel used for carrying out activities in the Area shall possess current valid certificates required by and issued pursuant to such international rules and standards.

15.2 The Contractor shall, in carrying out exploration under this contract, observe and comply with such rules, regulations and procedures as may be adopted by the Authority relating to protection against discrimination in employment, occupational safety and health, labour relations, social security, employment security and living conditions at the work site. Such rules, regulations and procedures shall take into account conventions and recommendations of the International Labour Organization and other competent international organizations.

Section 16
Responsibility and liability

16.1 The Contractor shall be liable for the actual amount of any damage, including damage to the marine environment, arising out of its wrongful acts or omissions, and those of its employees, subcontractors, agents and all persons engaged in working or acting for them in the conduct of its operations under this contract, including the costs of reasonable measures to prevent or limit damage to the marine environment, account being taken of any contributory acts or omissions by the Authority.

16.2 The Contractor shall indemnify the Authority, its employees, subcontractors and agents against all claims and liabilities of any third party arising out of any wrongful acts or omissions of the Contractor and its employees, agents and subcontractors, and all persons engaged in working or acting for them in the conduct of its operations under this contract.

16.3 The Authority shall be liable for the actual amount of any damage to the Contractor arising out of its wrongful acts in the exercise of its powers and functions, including violations under article 168, paragraph 2, of the Convention, account being taken of contributory acts or omissions by the Contractor, its employees, agents and subcontractors, and all persons engaged in working or acting for them in the conduct of its operations under this contract.

16.4 The Authority shall indemnify the Contractor, its employees, subcontractors, agents and all persons engaged in working or acting for them in the conduct of its operations under this contract, against all claims and liabilities of any third party arising out of any wrongful acts or omissions in the exercise of its powers and functions hereunder, including violations under article 168, paragraph 2, of the Convention.

16.5 The Contractor shall maintain appropriate insurance policies with internationally recognized carriers, in accordance with generally accepted international maritime practice.

Section 17
Force majeure

17.1 The Contractor shall not be liable for an unavoidable delay or failure to perform any of its obligations under this contract due to force majeure. For the purposes of this contract, force majeure shall mean an event or condition that the Contractor could not reasonably be expected to prevent or control; provided that the event or condition was not caused by negligence or by a failure to observe good mining industry practice.

17.2 The Contractor shall, upon request, be granted a time extension equal to the period by which performance was delayed hereunder by force majeure and the term of this contract shall be extended accordingly.

17.3 In the event of force majeure, the Contractor shall take all reasonable measures to remove its inability to perform and comply with the terms and conditions of this contract with a minimum of delay.

17.4 The Contractor shall give notice to the Authority of the occurrence of an event of force majeure as soon as reasonably possible, and similarly give notice to the Authority of the restoration of normal conditions.

Section 18
Disclaimer

Neither the Contractor nor any affiliated company or subcontractor shall in any manner claim or suggest, whether expressly or by implication, that the Authority or any official thereof has, or has expressed, any opinion with respect to cobalt crusts in the exploration area and a statement to that effect shall not be included in or endorsed on any prospectus, notice, circular, advertisement, press release or similar document issued by the Contractor, any affiliated company or any subcontractor that refers directly or indirectly to this contract. For the purposes of this section, an "affiliated company" means any person, firm or company or State-owned entity controlling, controlled by, or under common control with, the Contractor.

Section 19
Renunciation of rights

The Contractor, by notice to the Authority, shall have the right to renounce its rights and terminate this contract without penalty, provided that the Contractor shall remain liable for all obligations accrued prior to the date of such renunciation and those obligations required to be fulfilled after termination in accordance with the Regulations.

Section 20
Termination of sponsorship

20.1 If the nationality or control of the Contractor changes or the Contractor's sponsoring State, as defined in the Regulations, terminates its sponsorship, the Contractor shall promptly notify the Authority forthwith.

20.2 In either such event, if the Contractor does not obtain another sponsor meeting the requirements prescribed in the Regulations which submits to the Authority a certificate of sponsorship for the Contractor in the prescribed form within the time specified in the Regulations, this contract shall terminate forthwith.

Section 21
Suspension and termination of contract and penalties

21.1 The Council may suspend or terminate this contract, without prejudice to any other rights that the Authority may have, if any of the following events should occur:

(a) if, in spite of written warnings by the Authority, the Contractor has conducted its activities in such a way as to result in serious persistent and wilful violations of the fundamental terms of this contract, Part XI of the Convention, the Agreement and the rules, regulations and procedures of the Authority; or

(b) if the Contractor has failed to comply with a final binding decision of the dispute settlement body applicable to it; or

(c) if the Contractor becomes insolvent or commits an act of bankruptcy or enters into any agreement for composition with its creditors or goes into liquidation or receivership, whether compulsory or voluntary, or petitions or applies to any tribunal for the appointment of a receiver or a trustee or receiver for itself or commences any proceedings relating to itself under any bankruptcy, insolvency or readjustment of debt law, whether now or hereafter in effect, other than for the purpose of reconstruction.

21.2 The Council may, without prejudice to Section 17, after consultation with the Contractor, suspend or terminate this contract, without prejudice to any other rights that the Authority may have, if the Contractor is prevented from performing its obligations under this contract by reason of an event or condition of force majeure, as described in Section 17.1, which has persisted for a continuous period exceeding two years, despite the Contractor having taken all reasonable measures to remove its inability to perform and comply with the terms and conditions of this contract with a minimum of delay.

21.3 Any suspension or termination shall be by notice, through the Secretary-General, which shall include a statement of the reasons for taking such action. The suspension or termination shall be effective 60 days after such notice, unless the Contractor within such period disputes the Authority's right to suspend or terminate this contract in accordance with Part XI, section 5, of the Convention.

21.4 If the Contractor takes such action, this contract shall only be suspended or terminated in accordance with a final binding decision in accordance with Part XI, section 5, of the Convention.

21.5 If the Council has suspended this contract, the Council may by notice require the Contractor to resume its operations and comply with the terms and conditions of this contract, not later than 60 days after such notice.

21.6 In the case of any violation of this contract not covered by section 21.1 (a) hereof, or in lieu of suspension or termination under section 21.1 hereof, the Council may impose upon the Contractor monetary penalties proportionate to the seriousness of the violation.

21.7 The Council may not execute a decision involving monetary penalties until the Contractor has been accorded a reasonable opportunity to exhaust the judicial remedies available to it pursuant to Part XI, section 5, of the Convention.

21.8 In the event of termination or expiration of this contract, the Contractor shall comply with the Regulations and shall remove all installations, plant, equipment and materials in the exploration area and shall make the area safe so as not to constitute a danger to persons, shipping or to the marine environment.

Section 22
Transfer of rights and obligations

22.1 The rights and obligations of the Contractor under this contract may be transferred in whole or in part only with the consent of the Authority and in accordance with the Regulations.

22.2 The Authority shall not unreasonably withhold consent to the transfer if the proposed transferee is in all respects a qualified applicant in accordance with the Regulations and assumes all of the obligations of the Contractor and if the transfer does not confer to the transferee a plan of work, the approval of which would be forbidden by Annex III, article 6, paragraph 3 (c), of the Convention.

22.3 The terms, undertakings and conditions of this contract shall inure to the benefit of and be binding upon the parties hereto and their respective successors and assigns.

Section 23
No waiver

No waiver by either party of any rights pursuant to a breach of the terms and conditions of this contract to be performed by the other party shall be construed as a waiver by the party of any succeeding breach of the same or any other term or condition to be performed by the other party.

Section 24
Revision

24.1 When circumstances have arisen or are likely to arise which, in the opinion of the Authority or the Contractor, would render this contract inequitable or make it impracticable or impossible to achieve the objectives set out in this contract or in Part XI of the Convention or the Agreement, the parties shall enter into negotiations to revise it accordingly.

24.2 This contract may also be revised by agreement between the Contractor and the Authority to facilitate the application of any rules, regulations and procedures adopted by the Authority subsequent to the entry into force of this contract.

24.3 This contract may be revised, amended or otherwise modified only with the consent of the Contractor and the Authority by an appropriate instrument signed by the authorized representatives of the parties.

Section 25
Disputes

25.1 Any dispute between the parties concerning the interpretation or application of this contract shall be settled in accordance with Part XI, section 5, of the Convention.

25.2 **In accordance with article 21, paragraph 2, of Annex III to the Convention, any** final decision rendered by a court or tribunal having jurisdiction under the Convention relating to the rights and obligations of the Authority and of the Contractor shall be enforceable in the territory of **any State Party to the Convention affected thereby.**

Section 26
Notice

26.1 Any application, request, notice, report, consent, approval, waiver, direction or instruction hereunder shall be made by the Secretary-General or by the designated representative of the Contractor, as the case may be, in writing. Service shall be by hand, or by telex, facsimile, registered airmail or electronic mail containing an authorized signature to the Secretary-General at the headquarters of the Authority or to the designated representative. The requirement to provide any information in writing under these Regulations is satisfied by the provision of the information in an electronic document containing a digital signature.

26.2 Either party shall be entitled to change any such address to any other address by not less than ten days' notice to the other party.

26.3 Delivery by hand shall be effective when made. Delivery by telex shall be deemed to be effective on the business day following the day when the "answer back" appears on the sender's telex machine. Delivery by facsimile shall be effective when the "transmit confirmation report" confirming the transmission to the recipient's published facsimile number is received by the transmitter. Delivery by registered airmail shall be deemed to be effective 21 days after posting. An electronic document is presumed to have been received by the addressee when it enters an information system designated or used by the addressee for the purpose of receiving documents of the type sent and it is capable of being retrieved and processed by the addressee.

26.4 Notice to the designated representative of the Contractor shall constitute effective notice to the Contractor for all purposes under this contract, and the designated representative shall be the Contractor's agent for the service of process or notification in any proceeding of any court or tribunal having jurisdiction.

26.5 Notice to the Secretary-General shall constitute effective notice to the Authority for all purposes under this contract, and the Secretary-General shall be the Authority's agent for the service of process or notification in any proceeding of any court or tribunal having jurisdiction.

Section 27
Applicable law

27.1 This contract shall be governed by the terms of this contract, the rules, regulations and procedures of the Authority, Part XI of the Convention, the Agreement and other rules of international law not incompatible with the Convention.

27.2 The Contractor, its employees, subcontractors, agents and all persons engaged in working or acting for them in the conduct of its operations under this contract shall observe the applicable law referred to in section 27.1 hereof and shall not engage in any transaction, directly or indirectly, prohibited by the applicable law.

27.3 Nothing contained in this contract shall be deemed an exemption from the necessity of applying for and obtaining any permit or authority that may be required for any activities under this contract.

Section 28
Interpretation

The division of this contract into sections and subsections and the insertion of headings are for convenience of reference only and shall not affect the construction or interpretation hereof.

Section 29
Additional documents

Each party hereto agrees to execute and deliver all such further instruments, and to do and perform all such further acts and things as may be necessary or expedient to give effect to the provisions of this contract.

PART II

THE INTERNATIONAL TRIBUNAL FOR THE LAW OF THE SEA

STATUTE OF THE INTERNATIONAL TRIBUNAL FOR THE LAW OF THE SEA

Article 1
General provisions

1. The International Tribunal for the Law of the Sea is constituted and shall function in accordance with the provisions of this Convention and this Statute.

2. The seat of the Tribunal shall be in the Free and Hanseatic City of Hamburg in the Federal Republic of Germany.

3. The Tribunal may sit and exercise its functions elsewhere whenever it considers this desirable.

4. A reference of a dispute to the Tribunal shall be governed by the provisions of Parts XI and XV.

SECTION 1. ORGANIZATION OF THE TRIBUNAL

Article 2
Composition

1. The Tribunal shall be composed of a body of 21 independent members, elected from among persons enjoying the highest reputation for fairness and integrity and of recognized competence in the field of the law of the sea.

2. In the Tribunal as a whole the representation of the principal legal systems of the world and equitable geographical distribution shall be assured.

Article 3
Membership

1. No two members of the Tribunal may be nationals of the same State. A person who for the purposes of membership in the Tribunal could be regarded as a national of more than one State shall be deemed to be a national of the one in which he ordinarily exercises civil and political rights.

2. There shall be no fewer than three members from each geographical group as established by the General Assembly of the United Nations.

Article 4
Nominations and elections

1. Each State Party may nominate not more than two persons having the qualifications prescribed in article 2 of this Annex. The members of the Tribunal shall be elected from the list of persons thus nominated.

2. At least three months before the date of the election, the Secretary-General of the United Nations in the case of the first election and the Registrar of the Tribunal in the case of subsequent elections shall address a written invitation to the States Parties to submit their nominations for members of the

Tribunal within two months. He shall prepare a list in alphabetical order of all the persons thus nominated, with an indication of the States Parties which have nominated them, and shall submit it to the States Parties before the seventh day of the last month before the date of each election.

3. The first election shall be held within six months of the date of entry into force of this Convention.

4. The members of the Tribunal shall be elected by secret ballot. Elections shall be held at a meeting of the States Parties convened by the Secretary-General of the United Nations in the case of the first election and by a procedure agreed to by the States Parties in the case of subsequent elections. Two thirds of the States Parties shall constitute a quorum at that meeting. The persons elected to the Tribunal shall be those nominees who obtain the largest number of votes and a two-thirds majority of the States Parties present and voting, provided that such majority includes a majority of the States Parties.

Article 5
Term of office

1. The members of the Tribunal shall be elected for nine years and may be re-elected; provided, however, that of the members elected at the first election, the terms of seven members shall expire at the end of three years and the terms of seven more members shall expire at the end of six years.

2. The members of the Tribunal whose terms are to expire at the end of the above-mentioned initial periods of three and six years shall be chosen by lot to be drawn by the Secretary-General of the United Nations immediately after the first election.

3. The members of the Tribunal shall continue to discharge their duties until their places have been filled. Though replaced, they shall finish any proceedings which they may have begun before the date of their replacement.

4. In the case of the resignation of a member of the Tribunal, the letter of resignation shall be addressed to the President of the Tribunal. The place becomes vacant on the receipt of that letter.

Article 6
Vacancies

1. Vacancies shall be filled by the same method as that laid down for the first election, subject to the following provision: the Registrar shall, within one month of the occurrence of the vacancy, proceed to issue the invitations provided for in article 4 of this Annex, and the date of the election shall be fixed by the President of the Tribunal after consultation with the States Parties.

2. A member of the Tribunal elected to replace a member whose term of office has not expired shall hold office for the remainder of his predecessor's term.

Article 7
Incompatible activities

1. No member of the Tribunal may exercise any political or administrative function, or associate actively with or be financially interested in any of the operations of any enterprise concerned with the exploration for or exploitation of the resources of the sea or the seabed or other commercial use of the sea or the seabed.

2. No member of the Tribunal may act as agent, counsel or advocate in any case.

3. Any doubt on these points shall be resolved by decision of the majority of the other members of the Tribunal present.

Article 8
Conditions relating to participation of members in a particular case

1. No member of the Tribunal may participate in the decision of any case in which he has previously taken part as agent, counsel or advocate for one of the parties, or as a member of a national or international court or tribunal, or in any other capacity.

2. If, for some special reason, a member of the Tribunal considers that he should not take part in the decision of a particular case, he shall so inform the President of the Tribunal.

3. If the President considers that for some special reason one of the members of the Tribunal should not sit in a particular case, he shall give him notice accordingly.

4. Any doubt on these points shall be resolved by decision of the majority of the other members of the Tribunal present.

Article 9
Consequence of ceasing to fulfil required conditions

If, in the unanimous opinion of the other members of the Tribunal, a member has ceased to fulfil the required conditions, the President of the Tribunal shall declare the seat vacant.

Article 10
Privileges and immunities

The members of the Tribunal, when engaged on the business of the Tribunal, shall enjoy diplomatic privileges and immunities.

Article 11
Solemn declaration by members

Every member of the Tribunal shall, before taking up his duties, make a solemn declaration in open session that he will exercise his powers impartially and conscientiously.

Article 12
President, Vice-President and Registrar

1. The Tribunal shall elect its President and Vice-President for three years; they may be re-elected.

2. The Tribunal shall appoint its Registrar and may provide for the appointment of such other officers as may be necessary.

3. The President and the Registrar shall reside at the seat of the Tribunal.

Article 13
Quorum

1. All available members of the Tribunal shall sit; a quorum of 11 elected members shall be required to constitute the Tribunal.

2. Subject to article 17 of this Annex, the Tribunal shall determine which members are available to constitute the Tribunal for the consideration of a particular dispute, having regard to the effective functioning of the chambers as provided for in articles 14 and 15 of this Annex.

3. All disputes and applications submitted to the Tribunal shall be heard and determined by the Tribunal, unless article 14 of this Annex applies, or the parties request that it shall be dealt with in accordance with article 15 of this Annex.

Article 14
Seabed Disputes Chamber

A Seabed Disputes Chamber shall be established in accordance with the provisions of section 4 of this Annex. Its jurisdiction, powers and functions shall be as provided for in Part XI, section 5.

Article 15
Special chambers

1. The Tribunal may form such chambers, composed of three or more of its elected members, as it considers necessary for dealing with particular categories of disputes.

2. The Tribunal shall form a chamber for dealing with a particular dispute submitted to it if the parties so request. The composition of such a chamber shall be determined by the Tribunal with the approval of the parties.

3. With a view to the speedy dispatch of business, the Tribunal shall form annually a chamber composed of five of its elected members which may hear and determine disputes by summary procedure. Two alternative members shall be selected for the purpose of replacing members who are unable to participate in a particular proceeding.

4. Disputes shall be heard and determined by the chambers provided for in this article if the parties so request.

5. A judgment given by any of the chambers provided for in this article and in article 14 of this Annex shall be considered as rendered by the Tribunal.

Article 16
Rules of the Tribunal

The Tribunal shall frame rules for carrying out its functions. In particular it shall lay down rules of procedure.

Article 17
Nationality of members

1. Members of the Tribunal of the nationality of any of the parties to a dispute shall retain their right to participate as members of the Tribunal.

2. If the Tribunal, when hearing a dispute, includes upon the bench a member of the nationality of one of the parties, any other party may choose a person to participate as a member of the Tribunal.

3. If the Tribunal, when hearing a dispute, does not include upon the bench a member of the nationality of the parties, each of those parties may choose a person to participate as a member of the Tribunal.

4. This article applies to the chambers referred to in articles 14 and 15 of this Annex. In such cases, the President, in consultation with the parties, shall request specified members of the Tribunal forming the chamber, as many as necessary, to give place to the members of the Tribunal of the nationality of the parties concerned, and, failing such, or if they are unable to be present, to the members specially chosen by the parties.

5. Should there be several parties in the same interest, they shall, for the purpose of the preceding provisions, be considered as one party only. Any doubt on this point shall be settled by the decision of the Tribunal.

6. Members chosen in accordance with paragraphs 2, 3 and 4 shall fulfil the conditions required by articles 2, 8 and 11 of this Annex. They shall participate in the decision on terms of complete equality with their colleagues.

Article 18
Remuneration of members

1. Each elected member of the Tribunal shall receive an annual allowance and, for each day on which he exercises his functions, a special allowance, provided that in any year the total sum payable to any member as special allowance shall not exceed the amount of the annual allowance.

2. The President shall receive a special annual allowance.

3. The Vice-President shall receive a special allowance for each day on which he acts as President.

4. The members chosen under article 17 of this Annex, other than elected members of the Tribunal, shall receive compensation for each day on which they exercise their functions.

5. The salaries, allowances and compensation shall be determined from time to time at meetings of the States Parties, taking into account the work-load of the Tribunal. They may not be decreased during the term of office.

6. The salary of the Registrar shall be determined at meetings of the States Parties, on the proposal of the Tribunal.

7. Regulations adopted at meetings of the States Parties shall determine the conditions under which retirement pensions may be given to members of the Tribunal and to the Registrar, and the conditions under which members of the Tribunal and Registrar shall have their travelling expenses refunded.

8. The salaries, allowances, and compensation shall be free of all taxation.

Article 19
Expenses of the Tribunal

1. The expenses of the Tribunal shall be borne by the States Parties and by the Authority on such terms and in such a manner as shall be decided at meetings of the States Parties.

2. When an entity other than a State Party or the Authority is a party to a case submitted to it, the Tribunal shall fix the amount which that party is to contribute towards the expenses of the Tribunal.

SECTION 2. COMPETENCE

Article 20
Access to the Tribunal

1. The Tribunal shall be open to States Parties.

2. The Tribunal shall be open to entities other than States Parties in any case expressly provided for in Part XI or in any case submitted pursuant to any other agreement conferring jurisdiction on the Tribunal which is accepted by all the parties to that case.

Article 21
Jurisdiction

The jurisdiction of the Tribunal comprises all disputes and all applications submitted to it in accordance with this Convention and all matters specifically provided for in any other agreement which confers jurisdiction on the Tribunal.

Article 22
Reference of disputes subject to other agreements

If all the parties to a treaty or convention already in force and concerning the subject-matter covered by this Convention so agree, any disputes concerning the interpretation or application of such treaty or convention may, in accordance with such agreement, be submitted to the Tribunal.

Article 23
Applicable law

The Tribunal shall decide all disputes and applications in accordance with article 293.

SECTION 3. PROCEDURE

Article 24
Institution of proceedings

1. Disputes are submitted to the Tribunal, as the case may be, either by notification of a special agreement or by written application, addressed to the Registrar. In either case, the subject of the dispute and the parties shall be indicated.

2. The Registrar shall forthwith notify the special agreement or the application to all concerned.

3. The Registrar shall also notify all States Parties.

Article 25
Provisional measures

1. In accordance with article 290, the Tribunal and its Seabed Disputes Chamber shall have the power to prescribe provisional measures.

2. If the Tribunal is not in session or a sufficient number of members is not available to constitute a quorum, the provisional measures shall be prescribed by the chamber of summary procedure formed under article 15, paragraph 3, of this Annex. Notwithstanding article 15, paragraph 4, of this Annex, such provisional measures may be adopted at the request of any party to the dispute. They shall be subject to review and revision by the Tribunal.

Article 26
Hearing

1. The hearing shall be under the control of the President or, if he is unable to preside, of the Vice-President. If neither is able to preside, the senior judge present of the Tribunal shall preside.

2. The hearing shall be public, unless the Tribunal decides otherwise or unless the parties demand that the public be not admitted.

Article 27
Conduct of case

The Tribunal shall make orders for the conduct of the case, decide the form and time in which each party must conclude its arguments, and make all arrangements connected with the taking of evidence.

Article 28
Default

When one of the parties does not appear before the Tribunal or fails to defend its case, the other party may request the Tribunal to continue the proceedings and make its decision. Absence of a party or failure of a party to defend its case shall not constitute a bar to the proceedings. Before making its decision, the Tribunal must satisfy itself not only that it has jurisdiction over the dispute, but also that the claim is well founded in fact and law.

Article 29
Majority for decision

1. All questions shall be decided by a majority of the members of the Tribunal who are present.

2. In the event of an equality of votes, the President or the member of the Tribunal who acts in his place shall have a casting vote.

Article 30
Judgment

1. The judgment shall state the reasons on which it is based.

2. It shall contain the names of the members of the Tribunal who have taken part in the decision.

3. If the judgment does not represent in whole or in part the unanimous opinion of the members of the Tribunal, any member shall be entitled to deliver a separate opinion.

4. The judgment shall be signed by the President and by the Registrar. It shall be read in open court, due notice having been given to the parties to the dispute.

Article 31
Request to intervene

1. Should a State Party consider that it has an interest of a legal nature which may be affected by the decision in any dispute, it may submit a request to the Tribunal to be permitted to intervene.

2. It shall be for the Tribunal to decide upon this request.

3. If a request to intervene is granted, the decision of the Tribunal in respect of the dispute shall be binding upon the intervening State Party in so far as it relates to matters in respect of which that State Party intervened.

Article 32
Right to intervene in cases of interpretation or application

1. Whenever the interpretation or application of this Convention is in question, the Registrar shall notify all States Parties forthwith.

2. Whenever pursuant to article 21 or 22 of this Annex the interpretation or application of an international agreement is in question, the Registrar shall notify all the parties to the agreement.

3. Every party referred to in paragraphs 1 and 2 has the right to intervene in the proceedings; if it uses this right, the interpretation given by the judgment will be equally binding upon it.

Article 33
Finality and binding force of decisions

1. The decision of the Tribunal is final and shall be complied with by all the parties to the dispute.

2. The decision shall have no binding force except between the parties in respect of that particular dispute.

3. In the event of dispute as to the meaning or scope of the decision, the Tribunal shall construe it upon the request of any party.

Article 34
Costs

Unless otherwise decided by the Tribunal, each party shall bear its own costs.

SECTION 4. SEABED DISPUTES CHAMBER

Article 35
Composition

1. The Seabed Disputes Chamber referred to in article 14 of this Annex shall be composed of 11 members, selected by a majority of the elected members of the Tribunal from among them.

2. In the selection of the members of the Chamber, the representation of the principal legal systems of the world and equitable geographical distribution shall be assured. The Assembly of the Authority may adopt recommendations of a general nature relating to such representation and distribution.

3. The members of the Chamber shall be selected every three years and may be selected for a second term.

4. The Chamber shall elect its President from among its members, who shall serve for the term for which the Chamber has been selected.

5. If any proceedings are still pending at the end of any three-year period for which the Chamber has been selected, the Chamber shall complete the proceedings in its original composition.

6. If a vacancy occurs in the Chamber, the Tribunal shall select a successor from among its elected members, who shall hold office for the remainder of his predecessor's term.

7. A quorum of seven of the members selected by the Tribunal shall be required to constitute the Chamber.

Article 36
Ad hoc chambers

1. The Seabed Disputes Chamber shall form an *ad hoc* chamber, composed of three of its members, for dealing with a particular dispute submitted to it in accordance with article 188, paragraph 1(b). The composition of such a chamber shall be determined by the Seabed Disputes Chamber with the approval of the parties.

2. If the parties do not agree on the composition of an *ad hoc* chamber, each party to the dispute shall appoint one member, and the third member shall be appointed by them in agreement. If they disagree, or if any party fails

to make an appointment, the President of the Seabed Disputes Chamber shall promptly make the appointment or appointments from among its members, after consultation with the parties.

3. Members of the *ad hoc* chamber must not be in the service of, or nationals of, any of the parties to the dispute.

Article 37
Access

The Chamber shall be open to the States Parties, the Authority and the other entities referred to in Part XI, section 5.

Article 38
Applicable law

In addition to the provisions of article 293, the Chamber shall apply:

(a) the rules, regulations and procedures of the Authority adopted in accordance with this Convention; and

(b) the terms of contracts concerning activities in the Area in matters relating to those contracts.

Article 39
Enforcement of decisions of the Chamber

The decisions of the Chamber shall be enforceable in the territories of the States Parties in the same manner as judgments or orders of the highest court of the State Party in whose territory the enforcement is sought.

Article 40
Applicability of other sections of this Annex

1. The other sections of this Annex which are not incompatible with this section apply to the Chamber.

2. In the exercise of its functions relating to advisory opinions, the Chamber shall be guided by the provisions of this Annex relating to procedure before the Tribunal to the extent to which it recognizes them to be applicable.

SECTION 5. AMENDMENTS

Article 4l
Amendments

1. Amendments to this Annex, other than amendments to section 4, may be adopted only in accordance with article 313 or by consensus at a conference convened in accordance with this Convention.

2. Amendments to section 4 may be adopted only in accordance with article 314.

3. The Tribunal may propose such amendments to this Statute as it may consider necessary, by written communications to the States Parties for their consideration in conformity with paragraphs 1 and 2.

AGREEMENT

BETWEEN

THE INTERNATIONAL TRIBUNAL FOR THE LAW OF THE SEA

AND

THE FEDERAL REPUBLIC OF GERMANY

REGARDING THE HEADQUARTERS OF THE TRIBUNAL

CONTENTS

AGREEMENT BETWEEN THE INTERNATIONAL TRIBUNAL FOR THE LAW OF THE SEA AND THE FEDERAL REPUBLIC OF GERMANY REGARDING THE HEADQUARTERS OF THE TRIBUNAL

THE INTERNATIONAL TRIBUNAL FOR THE LAW OF THE SEA AND THE FEDERAL REPUBLIC OF GERMANY,

HAVING REGARD to Annex VI to the United Nations Convention on the Law of the Sea which provides that the seat of the International Tribunal for the Law of the Sea shall be in the Free and Hanseatic City of Hamburg in the Federal Republic of Germany,

HAVING REGARD to the legal personality of the Tribunal and to the provisions of the Agreement on the Privileges and Immunities of the International Tribunal for the Law of the Sea, adopted by the Meeting of States Parties to the United Nations Convention on the Law of the Sea on 23 May 1997,

RECOGNIZING that the Tribunal should enjoy such legal capacity, privileges and immunities as are necessary for the exercise of its functions,

RECALLING that the Statute of the Tribunal provides, in article 10, that the Members of the Tribunal, when engaged on the business of the Tribunal, shall enjoy diplomatic privileges and immunities,

HAVE AGREED AS FOLLOWS:

Article 1

Use of terms

For the purposes of this Agreement:

(a) "Convention" means the United Nations Convention on the Law of the Sea, concluded at Montego Bay, Jamaica on 10 December 1982 and the Agreement relating to the implementation of Part XI of the United Nations Convention on the Law of the Sea, done at New York on 28 July 1994;

(b) "Statute" means the Statute of the International Tribunal for the Law of the Sea, Annex VI to the Convention;

(c) "Rules" means the Rules of the International Tribunal for the Law of the Sea;

(d) "General Agreement" means the Agreement on the Privileges and Immunities of the International Tribunal for the Law of the Sea adopted by the Meeting of States Parties to the Convention on 23 May 1997;

(e) "States Parties" shall have the same meaning as that given in article 1 of the Convention;

(f) "Tribunal" means the International Tribunal for the Law of the Sea;

(g) "host country" means the Federal Republic of Germany;

(h) "Government" means the Government of the Federal Republic of Germany;

(i) "competent authorities" means such federal (Bund), Land (state), or local authorities in the Federal Republic of Germany as may be appropriate in the context and in accordance with the laws, regulations and customs of the Federal Republic of Germany, including the laws, regulations and customs of the Land (state) and local authorities involved;

(j) "Member" means an elected member of the Tribunal, as referred to in article 2 of the Statute, or a person chosen under article 17 of the Statute for the purposes of a particular case, while such person is exercising his or her functions;

(k) "officials of the Tribunal" means the members of the staff of the Registry of the Tribunal;

(l) "expert" means a person called at the instance of a party to a dispute or at the instance of the Tribunal to present testimony in the form of expert opinions, based on special knowledge, skills, experience or training;

(m) "expert appointed under article 289 of the Convention" means a person appointed in accordance with that article to sit with the Tribunal;

(n) "Headquarters district" means the area defined in article 3 of this Agreement;

(o) "international organization" means an intergovernmental organization.

Article 2

Juridical personality of the Tribunal

In accordance with its juridical personality the Tribunal has, in particular, the capacity:

(a) to contract;

(b) to acquire and dispose of movable and immovable property;

(c) to institute legal proceedings.

Article 3

The Headquarters district

1. The seat of the Tribunal shall be the Headquarters district, which shall comprise:

(a) the area with the buildings upon it of the permanent premises of the Tribunal on the site located on the street "Am Internationalen

Seegerichtshof" in the Free and Hanseatic City of Hamburg as defined in the Agreement between the International Tribunal for the Law of the Sea and the Government of the Federal Republic of Germany on the Occupancy and Use of the Premises of the International Tribunal for the Law of the Sea in the Free and Hanseatic City of Hamburg (hereinafter "Additional Agreement"); and

(b) any other lands, buildings or part of buildings which may from time to time be included therein by supplementary agreement between the Tribunal and the Government.

2. The area with the buildings referred to in paragraph 1 (a), together with the installations, equipment, fittings and all other facilities therein which are required for the effective functioning of the Tribunal, shall be made available to it in accordance with the Additional Agreement.

Article 4

Law and authority in the Headquarters district

1. The Headquarters district shall be under the control and authority of the Tribunal, in accordance with this Agreement.

2. The Tribunal shall have the power to make regulations operative throughout the Headquarters district for the purpose of establishing therein the conditions in all respects necessary for the full execution of its functions. The Tribunal shall promptly inform the competent authorities of regulations thus enacted in accordance with this paragraph. No law or regulation of the host country which is inconsistent with a regulation of the Tribunal authorized by this paragraph shall, to the extent of such inconsistency, be applicable within the Headquarters district.

3. Any dispute between the Tribunal and the host country as to whether a regulation of the Tribunal is authorized by paragraph 2, or as to whether a law or regulation of the host country is inconsistent with any regulation of the Tribunal authorized by paragraph 2, shall be promptly settled by the procedure set out in article 33. Pending such settlement, the regulation of the Tribunal shall apply and the law or regulation of the host country shall not apply in the Headquarters district to the extent that the Tribunal claims it to be inconsistent with the regulation of the Tribunal.

4. Except as otherwise provided in this Agreement or in the General Agreement, and subject to the provisions of paragraph 2, the laws and regulations of the host country shall apply in the Headquarters district.

5. Except as otherwise provided in this Agreement or in the General Agreement, the courts or other competent authorities of the host country shall have jurisdiction, as provided in applicable laws, over acts done and transactions taking place in the Headquarters district.

6. The courts or other competent authorities, when dealing with cases arising out of or relating to acts done or transactions taking place in the Headquarters

district, shall take into account the regulations enacted by the Tribunal under this article.

Article 5

Inviolability of the Headquarters district

1. The Headquarters district shall be inviolable. No officer or official of the host country or other person exercising any public authority within the host country shall enter the Headquarters district to discharge any official duty except upon the express consent of or at the request of the Registrar of the Tribunal and in accordance with conditions approved by the President of the Tribunal.

2. Judicial actions and the service or execution of legal process, including the seizure of private property, cannot be enforced in the Headquarters district except with the consent of and in accordance with conditions approved by the President of the Tribunal.

3. In case of fire or other emergency requiring prompt protective action, or in the event that the competent authorities have reasonable cause to believe that such an emergency has occurred or is about to occur in the Headquarters district, the consent of the Registrar of the Tribunal to any necessary entry of the Headquarters district shall be presumed if the Registrar cannot be reached in time.

4. Subject to paragraphs 1 and 3, the competent authorities shall take the necessary action to protect the premises of the Tribunal against fire or other emergency.

5. Without prejudice to the Convention, this Agreement and the General Agreement, the Tribunal shall not allow the Headquarters district to become a refuge from justice for persons against whom a penal judgment had been made or who are pursued flagrante delicto, or against whom a warrant of arrest or an order of extradition, expulsion or deportation has been issued by the competent authorities.

6. Subject to paragraphs 1 and 2, nothing in this article shall preclude the official delivery by the postal service to the Headquarters district of letters and documents.

7. The Tribunal may expel or exclude persons from the Headquarters district either for violation of its regulations adopted under article 4 or for any other reason.

Article 6

Vicinity of the Headquarters district

1. The competent authorities shall take all reasonable measures to ensure that the amenities of the Headquarters district are not impaired and that the use for which the Headquarters district is intended is not obstructed by

the use made of the land and buildings in the vicinity of the Headquarters district.

2. The Tribunal shall ensure that the Headquarters district is not used for purposes other than those for which it is intended and shall take all reasonable measures to ensure that the land and buildings in its vicinity are not unreasonably obstructed.

Article 7

Protection of the Headquarters district

1. The competent authorities shall take whatever measures may be necessary to ensure that the Tribunal shall not be dispossessed of all or any part of the Headquarters district without the express consent of the Tribunal.

2. The Government shall protect the premises of the Tribunal against unauthorized entry or damage of any kind and take appropriate measures to prevent any disturbance of the peace or impairment of the dignity and proper functioning of the Tribunal due to disturbances of public security or order in the Headquarters district or the immediate vicinity thereof.

3. The competent authorities shall provide the police or security forces necessary for the preservation of law and order in the Headquarters district and the removal therefrom of persons, if so requested by the Registrar of the Tribunal.

Article 8

Immunity of the Tribunal, its property, assets and funds

1. The Tribunal shall enjoy immunity from legal process, except insofar as in any particular case it has expressly waived its immunity. It is, however, understood that no waiver of immunity shall extend to any measure of execution.

2. The property, assets and funds of the Tribunal, wherever located and by whomsoever held, shall be immune from search, requisition, confiscation, seizure, expropriation or any other form of interference, whether by executive, administrative, judicial or legislative enforcement action.

3. The property and assets of the Tribunal shall be exempt from restrictions, regulations, controls and moratoria of any nature.

4. The Tribunal shall have insurance coverage against third-party risks in respect of vehicles owned or operated by it, pursuant to the laws and regulations of the host country.

Article 9

Archives

The archives of the Tribunal, and all documents belonging to it or held by it, shall be inviolable at all times and wherever they may be located in the host country. The location of the archives and any documents shall be made known to the competent authorities if it is at a place other than in the Headquarters district.

Article 10

Public services in the Headquarters district

1. At the request of a duly authorized official of the Tribunal, the competent authorities shall do their utmost to ensure or assist, as appropriate, the provision on equitable terms of the public services needed by the Tribunal such as postal, telephone, telegraph, fax communications and on-line services, electricity, water, gas, sewerage, waste collection, fire protection, local transportation and cleaning of public streets.

2. In the event of interruption or threatened interruption of any such services, the competent authorities shall consider the needs of the Tribunal as being of equal importance with the needs of the essential agencies and organs of the Government and of the constitutional organs of the Free and Hanseatic City of Hamburg and will take steps accordingly to ensure that the work of the Tribunal is not impaired.

3. Upon request of the competent authorities, the Registrar of the Tribunal shall make suitable arrangements to enable duly authorized representatives of the appropriate public services to inspect, repair, maintain, reconstruct and relocate utilities, conduits, mains and sewers within the Headquarters district under conditions which shall not unreasonably disturb the carrying out of the functions of the Tribunal. Underground constructions may be undertaken by the competent authorities within the Headquarters district only after consultation with the Registrar of the Tribunal and under conditions which shall not disturb the carrying out of the functions of the Tribunal.

4. In cases where gas, electricity or water are supplied by the competent authorities or where the prices thereof are under their control, the Tribunal shall be supplied at rates which shall not exceed the lowest comparable rates accorded to the federal or local governmental or administrative authorities.

Article 11

Communications

1. The Tribunal shall enjoy, as far as compatible with the international treaties, regulations and arrangements to which the host country is a party, for its official communications treatment not less favourable than that accorded by the host country to federal and local authorities or to international organizations and diplomatic missions, in the matter of priorities and rates for mail, cables, telegrams, radiograms, telex, facsimile, telephotos, television, telephone and other forms of communications as well as rates for information to press and radio.

2. The competent authorities shall ensure the inviolability of all communications and correspondence directed to the Tribunal, its Members or officials in

the Headquarters district, as well as all outgoing communications and correspondence of the Tribunal and its Members or officials, by whatever means or in whatever form transmitted. Such inviolability shall extend, without limitation by reason of this enumeration, to publications, still and moving pictures, films and sound or videotape recordings.

3. The Tribunal shall have the right to use codes and cipher and to dispatch and receive correspondence and other materials or communications by courier or in sealed bags, which shall have the same privileges and immunities as diplomatic couriers and bags.

4. If so requested by a duly authorized official of the Tribunal, the competent authorities shall provide for the official purposes of the Tribunal appropriate radio and other telecommunications facilities. These facilities may be specified by supplementary agreement between the Tribunal and the competent authorities.

5. Subject to the necessary authorization by the Meeting of States Parties and with the agreement of the Government as may be included in a supplementary agreement, the Tribunal may also establish and operate at the Headquarters district:

(a) its own short-wave sending and receiving radio broadcasting facilities (including emergency link equipment) which may be used on the same frequencies (within the tolerance prescribed for the broadcasting service by applicable regulations of the host country) for radiograph, radiotelephone and similar services;

(b) such other radio facilities as may be specified by supplementary agreement between the Tribunal and the competent authorities.

6. The Tribunal shall have the right to publish and broadcast freely and without restriction within the host country for purposes in conformity with the Convention and the Statute.

Article 12

Flag and emblem

The Tribunal shall be entitled to display its flag and emblem in the Headquarters district and on vehicles used for official purposes.

Article 13

Social security

1. Due to the fact that officials of the Tribunal are subject to regulations consistent with the United Nations Staff Regulations and Rules, including Article VI thereof, which establishes a comprehensive social security scheme, the Tribunal, the Registrar and other officials of the Tribunal, irrespective of nationality, shall be exempt from the laws of the host country on mandatory

coverage by and compulsory contributions to the social security schemes of the host country during their employment with the Tribunal. This shall also apply insofar as another system of social security operated by the Tribunal or a system joined by the Tribunal provides for corresponding benefits.

2. The provisions of paragraph 1 shall not preclude voluntary participation by the Members and officials of the Tribunal in any social security scheme in the host country to the extent that such voluntary participation is permitted by the laws of the host country.

Article 14

Work permits for family members

Work permits for taking up gainful employment are granted to family members of Members, who have their residence or are normally staying in the host country, and of officials of the Tribunal. Family members within the meaning of the first sentence include the spouse as well as the children forming part of the household who are under 21 years of age or economically dependent.

Article 15

Exemption from taxes, customs duties and import or export restrictions

1. The Tribunal, its assets, income and other property, and its operations and transactions shall be exempt from all direct taxes in the host country. It is understood, however, that the Tribunal shall not claim exemption from taxes which are no more than charges for public utility services. The motor vehicles belonging to or operated by the Tribunal shall, upon notification, be exempted from motor vehicle tax.

2. The Tribunal shall be exempt from all customs duties, import turnover taxes, prohibitions and restrictions on imports and exports in respect of articles imported or exported by the Tribunal for its official use. Goods imported or purchased under such an exemption shall not be sold or otherwise disposed of in the territory of the host country, except under conditions agreed with the competent authorities. The Tribunal shall also be exempt from all customs duties, import turnover taxes, prohibitions and restrictions on imports and exports in respect of its publications.

3. The Tribunal shall be exempt from all indirect taxes including insurance tax as well as value added tax/turnover tax (Umsatzsteuer) and excise duties which form part of the price of important purchases intended for the official use of the Tribunal. However, exemption from mineral oil tax included in the price of petrol, diesel and heating oil and value added tax/turnover tax (Umsatzsteuer) shall take the form of a refund of these taxes to the Tribunal under the conditions to be agreed upon between the Tribunal and the Government. It is understood, however, that the Tribunal shall not claim exemption from taxes and duties which are no more than charges for public utility

services. Goods purchased under an exemption or reimbursement shall not be sold or otherwise disposed of, except in accordance with the conditions agreed upon between the Tribunal and the Government.

Article 16

Funds and freedom from currency restrictions

1. Without being restricted by financial controls, regulations or moratoria of any kind, whilst carrying out its activities:

(a) the Tribunal may receive and hold funds, gold, securities or currency of any kind and operate accounts in any currency;

(b) the Tribunal shall be free to transfer its funds, gold, securities or currency from one country to another or within any country and to convert any currency held by it into any other currency;

(c) the Tribunal may receive, hold, negotiate, transfer, convert or otherwise deal with bonds and other financial securities.

2. In exercising its rights under paragraph 1, the Tribunal shall pay due regard to any representations made by the competent authorities insofar as it is considered that effect can be given to such representations without detriment to the interests of the Tribunal.

Article 17

Privileges, immunities, facilities and prerogatives

The privileges, immunities, facilities and prerogatives of the individuals referred to in articles 18 to 22 are granted in the interests of the administration of justice by the Tribunal in order to safeguard the independent performance of their official functions and not for the personal benefit of the individuals themselves.

Article 18

Privileges and immunities for the Members and officials of the Tribunal

1. Subject to the provisions of this Agreement and without prejudice to the provisions of article 19, the privileges and immunities to be accorded to the Members and officials of the Tribunal within the territory of the host country shall be consistent with those accorded to diplomatic agents in accordance with the Vienna Convention on Diplomatic Relations of 18 April 1961 and shall in particular be as follows:

(a) the Members and the Registrar of the Tribunal, or any official acting as Registrar during his or her absence from duty, shall enjoy the same privileges, immunities, facilities and prerogatives as are accorded by the host country to the heads of diplomatic missions accredited to the host country;

(b) the officials of the Tribunal of P-5 level and above shall enjoy the same privileges, immunities, facilities and prerogatives as are accorded by the host country to members of comparable rank of the diplomatic staff of missions established in the host country;

(c) the other officials of the Tribunal shall enjoy the same privileges, immunities and facilities as are accorded by the host country to members of comparable rank of diplomatic missions established in the host country;

(d) the spouses and dependent relatives forming part of the household of the Members, the Registrar of the Tribunal and the other officials of the Tribunal shall receive the same treatment as is accorded by the host country to spouses and dependent relatives forming part of the household of members of comparable rank of diplomatic missions established in the host country.

2. The Members shall enjoy the treatment provided for in this article even after expiry of their terms of office, if they continue to exercise their functions.

3. In order to secure complete freedom of speech and complete independence in the discharge of their duties, the Members and officials of the Tribunal shall continue to enjoy immunity from legal process in respect of words spoken and written and all acts done by them in the discharge of their duties even when they are no longer engaged in the business of the Tribunal.

4. Members and officials of the Tribunal shall be given, together with their spouses and dependent relatives forming part of their household, the same repatriation facilities in time of international crises as diplomatic agents are given under the Vienna Convention on Diplomatic Relations of 18 April 1961 and international law.

5. The Members and officials of the Tribunal shall have insurance coverage against third-party risks in respect of vehicles owned or operated by them pursuant to the laws and regulations of the host country.

6. The Government undertakes to issue visas and residence permits, where required, to household employees of Members, of the Registrar or other officials of the Tribunal as speedily as possible; no work permit will be required in such cases.

7. The Members and officials of the Tribunal, together with their spouses and dependent relatives forming part of their households, shall be exempt from national service obligations and alien registration.

8. The officials of the Tribunal shall be accorded the same privileges in respect of exchange facilities as are accorded to the officials of comparable rank forming part of diplomatic missions established in the host country.

9. The names of the Members, the Registrar and the Deputy Registrar of the Tribunal shall be included in the Diplomatic list.

10. The provisions of this article shall be applicable irrespective of the relations existing between the Government of the country of which such an individual is a national and the host country.

Article 19

Privileges and exemptions with regard to taxes and duties for the Members and officials of the Tribunal

The Members and officials of the Tribunal shall enjoy the following privileges and exemptions with regard to taxes, duties and customs duties within the territory of the host country:

(a) the Members and the Registrar of the Tribunal, or any official acting as Registrar during his or her absence from duty, shall enjoy the same privileges and exemptions as are accorded by the host country to the heads of diplomatic missions accredited to the host country;

(b) the officials of the Tribunal of P-5 level and above shall enjoy the same privileges and exemptions as are accorded by the host country to members of comparable rank of the diplomatic staff of missions established in the host country;

(c) the Members and the officials of the Tribunal, irrespective of their ranking, shall enjoy exemption from taxation on the salaries and emoluments paid to them by the Tribunal;

(d) the spouses and dependent relatives forming part of the household of a Member or the Registrar of the Tribunal or of officials of the Tribunal of P-5 level and above, shall enjoy the same privileges and exemptions as are accorded to spouses and dependent relatives forming part of the household of diplomatic agents of comparable rank of diplomatic missions established in the host country;

(e) the officials of the Tribunal shall have the right to import free of duty their furniture and effects at the time of first taking up their post in the host country.

Article 20

Experts appointed under article 289 of the Convention

The privileges, immunities, facilities and prerogatives accorded to Members, their spouses and dependent relatives forming part of their household and domestic staff, in accordance with articles 18 and 19, shall apply mutatis mutandis to experts appointed under article 289 of the Convention in the discharge of their duties and to their spouses and dependent relatives forming part of their household and domestic staff while such experts are exercising their functions. The provisions of article 18, paragraph 3, shall apply mutatis mutandis to experts appointed under article 289 of the Convention even when they are no longer engaged in the business of the Tribunal.

Article 21

Agents representing parties, counsel and advocates designated to appear before the Tribunal

1. Agents representing parties to proceedings before the Tribunal as well as counsel and advocates appearing before it shall, without prejudice to paragraph 2, be accorded the privileges, immunities and facilities necessary for the independent exercise of their duties during their journey to and from the Headquarters district, and while exercising their functions. They shall be accorded:

(a) immunity from any form of personal arrest, search or detention and from seizure of their personal baggage;

(b) exemption from inspection of personal baggage, unless there are serious grounds for believing that the baggage contains articles not for personal use or articles the import or export of which is prohibited by the law or controlled by the quarantine regulations of the host country. An inspection in such a case shall be conducted in the presence of the agent, counsel or advocate concerned;

(c) immunity from legal process of every kind in respect of words spoken and written and all acts done by them while discharging their duties as representatives of parties before the Tribunal, which immunity shall continue even after they have ceased to exercise their functions;

(d) inviolability of documents and papers;

(e) the right to receive papers or correspondence by courier or in sealed bags;

(f) exemption in respect of themselves and their spouses from immigration restrictions or alien registration;

(g) the same facilities in respect of their personal baggage and in respect of currency or exchange restrictions as are accorded to representatives of foreign Governments on temporary official missions;

(h) the same repatriation facilities in time of international crises as are accorded to diplomatic agents under the Vienna Convention on Diplomatic Relations of 18 April 1961 and international law.

2. The representatives of States and States Parties who may be agents, counsel or advocates appearing before the Tribunal shall, notwithstanding anything to the contrary in paragraph 1, enjoy the privileges, immunities, facilities and prerogatives which, in accordance with the Vienna Convention on Diplomatic Relations of 18 April 1961 and international law, are accorded to diplomatic agents.

3. For the purposes of paragraph 1, parties to proceedings before the Tribunal shall include States other than States Parties, entities other than States, the

International Seabed Authority, natural and juridical persons and sponsoring States or entities representing parties to proceedings in accordance with article 190 of the Convention.

4. The provisions of paragraphs 1 and 2 shall be applicable irrespective of the relations existing between the Government of which such an individual is a national and the host country.

5. Upon receipt of notification from parties to proceedings before the Tribunal as to the appointment of an agent, counsel or advocate, a certification of the status of such representative shall be provided under the signature of the Registrar of the Tribunal and limited to a period reasonably required for the proceedings.

6. The Registrar of the Tribunal shall notify the competent authorities of the appointment of agents, counsel or advocates of parties, indicating the prospective period for which their presence in and travel within the host country will be required.

7. The competent authorities shall accord the privileges, immunities, facilities and prerogatives to agents, counsel and advocates provided in this article upon production of the certification referred to in paragraph 5.

Article 22

Witnesses, experts and persons performing missions

1. Witnesses, experts and persons performing missions by order of the Tribunal shall be accorded the privileges, immunities and facilities necessary for the independent exercise of their functions, while on mission and during their journey to and from the Headquarters district. In particular, they shall be accorded the privileges, immunities and facilities accorded to agents, counsel and advocates under article 21, paragraph 1, subparagraphs (a) to (h), provided that a witness, expert or person performing missions who is a diplomatic agent of a State or a State Party shall be accorded the same treatment accorded to agents, counsel or advocates who are diplomatic agents under article 21, paragraph 2.

2. The federal (Bund), Land (state) or local authorities of the host country shall not impose any impediment to the transit to and from the Headquarters district of persons invited to the Headquarters district by the Tribunal on official business. The competent authorities shall afford any necessary protection to such persons while in transit to or from the Headquarters district. Such persons shall mutatis mutandis enjoy the privileges, immunities and facilities accorded to persons performing official missions for the Tribunal in accordance with this article.

3. The provisions of this article shall be applicable irrespective of the relations existing between the Government of which such an individual is a national and the host country.

Article 23

Nationals and permanent residents of the host country

Persons referred to in articles 18 to 22 shall not enjoy the privileges and immunities provided therein if they are German nationals or have their permanent residence in Germany, with the exception of:

(a) the exemption from social security provisions provided that they are subject to the social security law of their home State or they participate in a voluntary insurance scheme with adequate benefits;

(b) the exemption from taxation on the salaries and emoluments paid to them by the Tribunal; and

(c) the immunity from legal process in respect of words spoken or written and all acts done by them in discharging their duties, which immunity shall continue even after the persons have ceased to exercise their functions.

Article 24

Waiver

1. A State which is a party to proceedings before the Tribunal not only has the right but is under a duty to waive the immunity of agents, counsel and advocates representing or designated by it and of witnesses, experts and persons performing missions referred to in article 22 who are diplomatic agents of the State concerned, in any case where in the opinion of the State concerned the immunity would impede the course of justice and can be waived without prejudice to the administration of justice by the Tribunal and the purpose for which the immunity is accorded.

2. The right and the duty to waive the immunity of agents, counsel and advocates, representing or designated by an entity other than a State shall lie with the Tribunal, after hearing the individual concerned, where, in its opinion, the immunity is not directly related to or incidental to the performance of official functions and would impede the course of justice and it can be waived without prejudice to the administration of justice by the Tribunal and the purpose for which the immunity is accorded.

3. The right and the duty to waive the immunity of witnesses, experts and persons performing missions referred to in article 22, who are not diplomatic agents, shall lie with the Tribunal, after hearing the individual concerned, where, in its opinion, the immunity is not directly related to or incidental to the performance of official functions and would impede the course of justice and it can be waived without prejudice to the administration of justice by the Tribunal and the purpose for which the immunity is accorded.

4. The right and the duty to waive the immunity of the Registrar, or the Deputy Registrar or any other official of the Tribunal, when acting as Registrar,

or experts appointed under article 289 of the Convention, and members of their households shall lie with the Tribunal, after hearing the individual concerned, where, in its opinion, the immunity is not directly related to or incidental to the performance of official functions and would impede the course of justice and it can be waived without prejudice to the administration of justice by the Tribunal and the purpose for which the immunity is accorded.

5. The right and the duty to waive the immunity of other officials of the Tribunal and members of their households shall lie with the Registrar of the Tribunal, with the approval of the President of the Tribunal, and after hearing the individual concerned, where, in the Registrar's opinion, the immunity is not directly related to or incidental to the performance of official functions and would impede the course of justice and it can be waived without prejudice to the administration of justice by the Tribunal and the purpose for which the immunity is accorded.

Article 25

Laissez-passer, identity cards and notification

1. The Government shall recognise and accept the United Nations laissez-passer issued to Members, officials of the Tribunal and experts appointed under article 289 of the Convention as a valid travel document.

2. Persons referred to in articles 18 to 22 who do not present a United Nations laissez-passer shall be immune from immigration restrictions provided that they produce either a valid travel document with an entry visa and evidence of their official capacity or a valid travel document and the competent authorities are notified of their arrival by the Tribunal.

3. The Registrar of the Tribunal shall, on behalf of the Tribunal, furnish persons referred to in articles 20 to 22 with an identity card stating the name, date and place of birth and the number of passport or number of national identity card and bearing a photograph and signature of the person concerned. This identity card shall serve to identify the holder and his official capacity in relation to the Tribunal, to the competent authorities. In the case of a stateless person, the travel documents issued by a State will for the purpose of this paragraph be treated as a passport or a national identity card.

4. The Registrar of the Tribunal shall notify the competent authorities when any person mentioned in article 18 takes up or relinquishes duties, and shall periodically send the competent authorities a list of all such persons with information as to the name, date and place of birth, nationality, home address, functions with the Tribunal and the anticipated duration of service.

5. The Registrar of the Tribunal shall notify the competent authorities of the nomination of agents, counsel and advocates referred to in article 21. When attendance before the Tribunal by a person referred to in article 21 or article 22 is required, the Registrar of the Tribunal shall notify the competent authorities immediately. This information shall state the name, date and place of

birth and home address of the person concerned as well as the functions of the person before the Tribunal and the anticipated duration of the functions.

Article 26

Entry, transit and sojourn in the host country

1. The competent authorities shall take all necessary measures to facilitate the entry into and sojourn in the host country, and shall place no impediment in the way of departure from the host country, of the persons referred to in articles 18 to 22 and also ensure them the necessary protection. The competent authorities shall ensure that no impediment is placed in the way of their transit to or from the Headquarters seat and shall afford them the necessary protection.

2. Paragraph 1 shall not apply in the case of general interruptions of transportation, and shall not impair the effectiveness of generally applicable laws relating to the operation of means of transportation.

3. Visas which may be required by persons referred to in articles 18 to 22 shall be granted without charge and as promptly as possible.

4. Applications for visas (where required) from the Members and the Registrar of the Tribunal should be dealt with as speedily as possible. All other holders of United Nations laissez-passer should receive the same facilities when their applications for visas are accompanied by a certificate stating that they are travelling on the business of the Tribunal. In addition, all holders of United Nations laissez-passer should be granted facilities for speedy travel.

5. Similar facilities to those specified in paragraph 4 should be accorded to witnesses, experts and other persons who, though not the holders of United Nations laissez-passer, have a certificate stating that they are travelling on the business of the Tribunal.

6. No activity performed by any person referred to in articles 18 to 22 in an official capacity with respect to the Tribunal shall constitute a reason for preventing the entry into or departure from the territory of the host country of the person or for requiring the person to leave the territory of the host country.

7. It is understood that the persons referred to in articles 18 to 22 are not exempt from any reasonable application of the internationally accepted rules governing quarantine and public health.

Article 27

Maintenance of security and public order

1. Nothing in this Agreement shall affect the right of the host country to take, with the approval of the President of the Tribunal, the precautions necessary for its security or for the maintenance of public order.

2. If the host country considers it necessary to apply paragraph 1, it shall approach the Tribunal as rapidly as circumstances allow in order to determine by mutual agreement the measures necessary to protect the Tribunal.

Article 28

Responsibility, liability and insurance

1. The host country shall not incur, by reason of the location of the seat of the Tribunal within its territory, any international responsibility for acts or omissions of the Tribunal or of its officials acting or abstaining from acting within the scope of their functions other than the international responsibility which the host country would incur as a State Party.

2. Without prejudice to its immunities under this Agreement or the General Agreement, the Tribunal shall carry insurance to cover liability for any injury or damage arising from the activities of the Tribunal in the host country or from its use of the Headquarters district or buildings erected thereon or vehicles owned or operated by it that may be suffered by persons other than officials of the Tribunal, or by the Government. To this end, the competent authorities shall secure for the Tribunal, at reasonable rates, insurance coverage permitting claims to be submitted directly to the insurer by parties suffering injury or damage. Such claims and liability shall, without prejudice to the privileges and immunities of the Tribunal, be governed by the laws of the host country.

Article 29

Cooperation with the competent authorities

1. The Tribunal shall cooperate at all times with the competent authorities to facilitate to the extent possible the proper administration of justice, secure the observance of police regulations and prevent any abuse of the privileges, immunities and facilities accorded to officials of the Tribunal referred to in article 18, paragraph 1, subparagraphs (c) and (d), and the persons referred to in articles 19 to 22.

2. If the Government considers that there has been an abuse of privilege or immunity conferred by this Agreement, consultations will be held between the competent authorities and the President of the Tribunal to determine whether any such abuse has occurred and, if so, to attempt to ensure that no repetition occurs. If such consultations fail to achieve a result satisfactory to the Government and to the Tribunal, either party may submit the question as to whether such an abuse has occurred for resolution in accordance with the provisions on settlement of disputes under article 33.

3. The Government may only require persons referred to in articles 18 to 22, other than Members, the Registrar or the Deputy Registrar or any other official of the Tribunal when acting as Registrar or representatives of States Parties, to leave the country on account of any activities performed by them

which are an abuse of the right of residence in the host country and are not directly related to, or incidental to the performance of, official functions, with the approval of the Minister for Foreign Affairs of the Federal Republic of Germany, after consultation with the Registrar in the case of officials of the Tribunal, and the President of the Tribunal in the case of the other persons herein referred to. Representatives of States Parties other than agents, representing such States Parties in proceedings before the Tribunal may only be required to leave the country in accordance with the diplomatic procedure applicable to diplomatic agents accredited to the host country.

Article 30

Exchange of Notes

The Exchange of Notes of 14th December 2004 between the Tribunal and the Government with regard to this Agreement forms an integral part thereof.

Article 31

Supplementary agreements

The Tribunal and the Government may conclude supplementary agreements to this Agreement insofar as this is deemed desirable.

Article 32

Relationship with the General Agreement

The provisions of this Agreement shall be complementary to the provisions of the General Agreement. Insofar as any provision of this Agreement and any provision of the General Agreement relate to the same subject-matter, the two provisions shall, wherever possible, be treated as complementary, so that both provisions shall be applicable and neither shall limit the effect of the other; but in case of conflict, the provisions of this Agreement shall prevail.

Article 33

Settlement of disputes

1. The Tribunal shall make suitable provision for the satisfactory settlement of:

(a) disputes arising out of contracts and other disputes of a private law character to which the Tribunal is a party;

(b) disputes involving any person within the scope of article 29, paragraph 3, who by reason of his or her official position enjoys immunity, if immunity has not been waived in accordance with article 24.

2. Any dispute between the Tribunal and the Government arising out of or concerning the interpretation or application of this Agreement or of any supplementary agreement, or any question affecting the Headquarters district or

the relationship between the Tribunal and the Government which is not settled by consultation, negotiation or other agreed mode of settlement, shall be referred, at the request of either party to the dispute, for a final and binding decision to a panel of three arbitrators, one to be chosen by the Tribunal, one to be chosen by the Government, and the third, who shall be the Chairman of the panel, to be chosen by the first two arbitrators. Should the first two arbitrators fail to agree upon the appointment of the third member within three months following the appointment of the first two arbitrators, the Chairman shall be chosen by the Secretary-General of the United Nations within one month of the making of a request by the Tribunal or the Government. If either party to this Agreement has failed to make its appointment of an arbitrator within two months of the appointment of an arbitrator by the other party, the Secretary-General of the United Nations shall, at the request of either party, make such appointment within one month of such a request.

Article 34

Amendments

The provisions of this Agreement may only be amended by agreement between the International Tribunal for the Law of the Sea and the Federal Republic of Germany.

Article 35

Entry into force

This Agreement shall enter into force on the first day of the month following the date of receipt of the last of the notifications by which the Tribunal and the Federal Republic of Germany have informed each other of the completion of their respective formal requirements for the entry into force of this Agreement.

Article 36

Registration

Registration of this Agreement with the Secretariat of the United Nations, in accordance with Article 102 of the Charter of the United Nations, shall be initiated by the Government immediately following its entry into force. The Tribunal shall be informed of registration, and of the United Nations registration number, as soon as this has been confirmed by the Secretariat.

DONE at Berlin on14th December 2004 in duplicate in the English, German and French languages, all language texts being equally authentic.

For the International Tribunal for the Law of the Sea	For the Federal Republic of Germany

INTERNATIONAL TRIBUNAL FOR THE LAW OF THE SEA

TRIBUNAL INTERNATIONAL DU DROIT DE LA MER

Dolliver Nelson

The President

14 December 2004

Excellency,

I have the honour to acknowledge receipt of your Note of 14 December 2004 in which you confirm the understandings concerning the interpretation of certain provisions of the Agreement between the International Tribunal for the Law of the Sea and the Federal Republic of Germany regarding the Headquarters of the Tribunal which reads as follows:

"I have the honour to refer, on the occasion of the signing of the Agreement between the Federal Republic of Germany and the International Tribunal for the Law of the Sea regarding the Headquarters of the Tribunal (hereinafter referred to as "the Agreement"), to the discussions held between the representatives of the Government of the Federal Republic of Germany and the representatives of the International Tribunal for the Law of the Sea concerning the interpretation of certain provisions of the Agreement and to confirm the following understandings:

1. It is the understanding of the Parties that the regulations to be issued by the Tribunal under article 4, paragraph 2, of the Agreement will be those necessary for the conduct of its operations and activities in the execution of its mandate and to establish conditions necessary for the exercise of its functions and fulfilment of its purposes.

2. It is the understanding of the Parties that officials of the Tribunal whose membership in the German statutory health insurance scheme ended on account of employment with the Tribunal may join the German statutory health insurance scheme by analogous application of article 9, paragraph 1, number 5 of the Social Code, Book V, if they take up employment in the Federal Republic of Germany within two months of their employment with the Tribunal coming to an end. The health insurance fund is to be notified accordingly by the person concerned within three months of such employment being taken up.

3. It is the understanding of the Parties that the privileges and exemptions with regard to value added tax/turnover tax (Umsatzsteuer) in the Federal Republic of Germany granted to the Members and to the officials of the Tribunal in accordance with article 19, subparagraphs (a) and (b), of the Agreement shall be accorded on the basis of the most favourable treatment under the currently applicable ordinance concerning the reimbursement of value added tax/turnover tax (Umsatzsteuer) to permanent diplomatic missions and career consular posts as well as to their non-German members.

It is the understanding of the Parties that the Federal Finance Office shall, on request, reimburse the Tribunal for the amount of value added tax/turnover tax (Umsatzsteuer) paid in respect of supplies and services purchased from a taxable person for the official use of the Tribunal provided that the tax due exceeds €25 per invoice in the aggregate and the tax has been separately identified in the invoice. If the reimbursed value added tax/turnover tax (Umsatzsteuer) is subsequently reduced as a result of a review of the price originally paid for the supplies and services in question, the Tribunal shall inform the Federal Finance Office of such a reduction in price and shall subsequently return the balance of the tax previously reimbursed.

Likewise the Federal Finance Office shall, on request, also reimburse the Tribunal for the mineral oil tax for petrol, diesel and heating oil included in the price of purchases intended for the official use of the Tribunal provided that the tax exceeds €25 per invoice in the aggregate.

If goods purchased in the European Union or imported from outside the European Union by the Tribunal for its official use, for which the Tribunal was granted exemption from value added tax/turnover tax (Umsatzsteuer) or import turnover tax (Einfuhrumsatzsteuer), are sold, given away or otherwise disposed of to taxable persons who have the full right of deduction, international organizations entitled to tax exemption, or to other entities entitled to tax exempt status, no value added tax/turnover tax (Umsatzsteuer) shall be paid. If goods referred to above are sold, given away or otherwise disposed of to persons and entities other than those referred to above, the part of the value added tax/turnover tax (Umsatzsteuer) which corresponds to the sales price or the current market value of such goods, as appropriate, shall be payable to the Federal Finance Office. The amount of the tax due shall be determined on the basis of the tax rate applicable on the actual date of the transaction in question. The goods imported exempt from customs duties shall not be sold or otherwise disposed of in the Federal Republic of Germany except with the consent of the Government and subject to the payment of the applicable customs duties.

4. It is the understanding of the Parties that in well-founded individual cases, the Federal Republic of Germany shall, on request, grant to officials of P-4 level whose functions justify it the same privileges, immunities and facilities as are accorded to officials of P-5 level and above in accordance with article 18, paragraph 1 (b) and article 19, subparagraph (b) of the Agreement. Requests on the matter shall be submitted by the Registrar of the Tribunal to the Federal Foreign Office.

5. It is the understanding of the Parties that the Members shall be exempt from German law on mandatory coverage in the field of Social Security by virtue of their diplomatic status under article 10 of the Statute of the Tribunal as well as article 18 of the Agreement. With regard to Members who are German nationals or have their permanent residence in Germany this shall only apply insofar as the conditions of article 23, subparagraph (a), of the Agreement are fulfilled.

6. With reference to article 19 of the Agreement, it is the understanding of the Parties that:

(a) for the purposes of German taxation law, the tax exemption referred to in article 19, subparagraph (c), shall not be granted for pensions and annuities paid by the Tribunal to former Members or officials of the Tribunal. In this respect, the same treatment shall be granted as is accorded to the United Nations institutions established in the host country. This shall be without prejudice to any Agreement for the avoidance of double taxation between the host country and the country of nationality or residence of the persons referred to;

(b) the Tribunal shall notify the Government of the names and addresses of residence in the host country of the officials of the Tribunal who are not accorded the privileges and exemptions of diplomatic agents;

(c) where the incidence of any form of taxation depends upon residence, periods during which Members or officials of the Tribunal are present in the host country for the discharge of their functions shall not be considered as periods of residence if such Members or officials are accorded diplomatic privileges, immunities and facilities.

7. It is the understanding of the Parties that following retirement from active service with the Tribunal, after a number of years of service in Hamburg, officials of the Tribunal and members of their families forming part of their households (spouses, unmarried children under the age of 21 and other relatives dependent on them) shall, upon application, be issued with a residence permit, insofar as they are in a position to support themselves, including payment of health insurance and long term care insurance (Kranken- und Pflegeversicherung) contributions, in accordance with applicable German legislation.

8. It is the understanding of the Parties that pursuant to article 25, paragraph 2, of the Agreement:

(a) the Government shall inform the Tribunal of the competent authorities referred to therein;

(b) on presentation of a valid travel document, the persons referred to in article 25, paragraph 2, will receive a visa at the border, if required, and travel to the seat of the Tribunal will be facilitated. The Tribunal will only make use of this procedure in case of urgency or unforeseen circumstances and will provide information on these circumstances.

9. It is the understanding of the Parties that restrictions regarding entry into, sojourn in, or departure from the territory of the host country shall not apply to persons referred to in articles 18 to 22 of the Agreement who enjoy diplomatic immunity or similar legal status. Restrictions regarding entry into, sojourn in, or departure from the territory of the host country may apply to persons referred to in articles 21 and 22 of the Agreement who do not enjoy diplomatic immunity or similar legal status if the person in question has been

convicted of or is charged with a serious criminal offence as referred to in the law of the host country relating to aliens. The name of any such person to whom such restrictions are intended to be applied shall be communicated to the Tribunal and such person shall be provided safe conduct at the request of the Tribunal.

10. It is the understanding of the Parties that if the Government enters into any agreement with an international organization containing terms and conditions more favourable than those extended to the Tribunal under the Agreement, either Party may ask for consultations as to whether such terms and conditions could be extended to the Tribunal.

11. This Exchange of Notes is concluded in the English, French and German languages, all language texts being equally authentic. Should the International Tribunal for the Law of the Sea agree to the understandings contained in paragraphs 1 to 11 above, Your Excellency is requested to confirm the acceptance of these 5 understandings by the Tribunal. This Exchange of Notes shall form then an integral part of the Agreement in accordance with article 30 thereof."

I confirm that the understandings set out in your Note correspond to those of the International Tribunal for the Law of the Sea. I agree that this Exchange of Notes shall form an integral part of the Agreement in accordance with article 30 thereof.

Please accept, Excellency, the assurances of my highest consideration.

Mr Jürgen Chrobog

State Secretary

Foreign Office

Berlin

Postal address: Am Internationalen Seegerichtshof 1, 22609 Hamburg, Germany

Tel +49 40 3560 7184 Fax +49 40 3560 7287 E-mail: nelson@itlos.org

Agreement on the Privileges and Immunities of the International Tribunal for the Law of the Sea

Adopted on 23 May 1997

The States Parties to the present Agreement,

Considering that the United Nations Convention on the Law of the Sea establishes the International Tribunal for the Law of the Sea,

Recognizing that the Tribunal should enjoy such legal capacity, privileges and immunities as are necessary for the exercise of its functions,

Recalling that the Statute of the Tribunal provides, in article 10, that the Members of the Tribunal, when engaged on the business of the Tribunal, shall enjoy diplomatic privileges and immunities,

Recognizing that persons participating in proceedings and officials of the Tribunal should enjoy such privileges and immunities as are necessary for the independent exercise of their functions in connection with the Tribunal,

Have agreed as follows:

Article 1
Use of terms

For the purposes of this Agreement:

(a) "Convention" means the United Nations Convention on the Law of the Sea of 10 December 1982;

(b) "Statute" means the Statute of the International Tribunal for the Law of the Sea in Annex VI to the Convention;

(c) "States Parties" means States Parties to this Agreement;

(d) "Tribunal" means the International Tribunal for the Law of the Sea;

(e) "Member of the Tribunal" means an elected member of the Tribunal or a person chosen under article 17 of the Statute for the purpose of a particular case;

(f) "Registrar" means the Registrar of the Tribunal and includes any official of the Tribunal acting as Registrar;

(g) "officials of the Tribunal" means the Registrar and other members of the staff of the Registry;

(h) "Vienna Convention" means the Vienna Convention on Diplomatic Relations of 18 April 1961.

Article 2
Juridical personality of the Tribunal

The Tribunal shall possess juridical personality. It shall have the capacity:

(a) to contract;

(b) to acquire and dispose of immovable and movable property;

(c) to institute legal proceedings.

Article 3
Inviolability of the premises of the Tribunal

The premises of the Tribunal shall be inviolable, subject to such conditions as may be agreed with the State Party concerned.

Article 4
Flag and emblem

The Tribunal shall be entitled to display its flag and emblem at its premises and on vehicles used for official purposes.

Article 5
Immunity of the Tribunal, its property, assets and funds

1. The Tribunal shall enjoy immunity from legal process, except insofar as in any particular case it has expressly waived its immunity. It is, however, understood that no waiver of immunity shall extend to any measure of execution.

2. The property, assets and funds of the Tribunal, wherever located and by whomsoever held, shall be immune from search, requisition, confiscation, seizure, expropriation or any other form of interference, whether by executive, administrative, judicial or legislative action.

3. To the extent necessary to carry out its functions, the property, assets and funds of the Tribunal shall be exempt from restrictions, regulations, controls and moratoria of any nature.

4. The Tribunal shall have insurance coverage against third-party risks in respect of vehicles owned or operated by it, as required by the laws and regulations of the State in which the vehicle is operated.

Article 6
Archives

The archives of the Tribunal, and all documents belonging to it or held by it, shall be inviolable at all times and wherever they may be located. The State Party where the archives are located shall be informed of the location of such archives and documents.

Article 7
Exercise of the functions of the Tribunal outside the Headquarters

In the event that the Tribunal considers it desirable to sit or otherwise exercise its functions elsewhere than at its Headquarters, it may conclude with the State concerned an arrangement concerning the provision of the appropriate facilities for the exercise of its functions.

Article 8
Communications

1. For the purposes of its official communications and correspondence, the Tribunal shall enjoy in the territory of each State Party, insofar as

is compatible with the international obligations of the State concerned, treatment not less favourable than that which the State Party accords to any intergovernmental organization or diplomatic mission in the matter of priorities, rates and taxes applicable to mail and the various forms of communication and correspondence.

2. The Tribunal may use all appropriate means of communication and make use of codes or cipher for its official communications or correspondence. The official communications and correspondence of the Tribunal shall be inviolable.

3. The Tribunal shall have the right to dispatch and receive correspondence and other materials or communications by courier or in sealed bags, which shall have the same privileges, immunities and facilities as diplomatic couriers and bags.

Article 9

Exemption from taxes, customs duties and import or export restrictions

1. The Tribunal, its assets, income and other property, and its operations and transactions shall be exempt from all direct taxes; it is understood, however, that the Tribunal shall not claim exemption from taxes which are no more than charges for public utility services.

2. The Tribunal shall be exempt from all customs duties, import turnover taxes and prohibitions and restrictions on imports and exports in respect of articles imported or exported by the Tribunal for its official use.

3. Goods imported or purchased under such an exemption shall not be sold or otherwise disposed of in the territory of a State Party, except under conditions agreed with the Government of that State Party. The Tribunal shall also be exempt from all customs duties, import turnover taxes, prohibitions and restrictions on imports and exports in respect of its publications.

Article 10

Reimbursement of duties and/or taxes

1. The Tribunal shall not, as a general rule, claim exemption from duties and taxes which are included in the price of movable and immovable property and taxes paid for services rendered. Nevertheless, when the Tribunal for its official use makes major purchases of property and goods or services on which duties and taxes are charged or are chargeable, States Parties shall make appropriate administrative arrangements for the exemption of such charges or reimbursement of the amount of duty and/or tax paid.

2. Goods purchased under such an exemption or reimbursement shall not be sold or otherwise disposed of, except in accordance with the conditions laid down by the State Party which granted the exemption or reimbursement. No exemption or reimbursement shall be accorded in respect of charges for public utility services provided to the Tribunal.

Article 11
Taxation

1. The salaries, emoluments and allowances paid to Members and officials of the Tribunal shall be exempt from taxation.

2. Where the incidence of any form of taxation depends upon residence, periods during which such Members or officials are present in a State for the discharge of their functions shall not be considered as periods of residence if such Members or officials are accorded diplomatic privileges, immunities and facilities.

3. States Parties shall not be obliged to exempt from income tax pensions or annuities paid to former Members and former officials of the Tribunal.

Article 12
Funds and freedom from currency restrictions

1. Without being restricted by financial controls, regulations or financial moratoriums of any kind, while carrying out its activities:

(a) the Tribunal may hold funds, currency of any kind or gold and operate accounts in any currency;

(b) the Tribunal shall be free to transfer its funds, gold or its currency from one country to another or within any country and to convert any currency held by it into any other currency;

(c) the Tribunal may receive, hold, negotiate, transfer, convert or otherwise deal with bonds and other financial securities.

2. In exercising its rights under paragraph 1, the Tribunal shall pay due regard to any representations made by any State Party insofar as it is considered that effect can be given to such representations without detriment to the interests of the Tribunal.

Article 13
Members of the Tribunal

1. Members of the Tribunal shall, when engaged on the business of the Tribunal, enjoy the privileges, immunities, facilities and prerogatives accorded to heads of diplomatic missions in accordance with the Vienna Convention.

2. Members of the Tribunal and members of their families forming part of their households shall be accorded every facility for leaving the country where they may happen to be and for entering and leaving the country where the Tribunal is sitting. On journeys in connection with the exercise of their functions, they shall in all countries through which they may have to pass enjoy all the privileges, immunities and facilities granted by these countries to diplomatic agents in similar circumstances.

3. If Members of the Tribunal, for the purpose of holding themselves at the disposal of the Tribunal, reside in any country other than that of which they are nationals or permanent residents, they shall, together with

the members of their families forming part of their households, be accorded diplomatic privileges, immunities and facilities during the period of their residence there.

4. Members of the Tribunal shall be accorded, together with members of their families forming part of their households, the same repatriation facilities in time of international crises as are accorded to diplomatic agents under the Vienna Convention.

5. Members of the Tribunal shall have insurance coverage against third-party risks in respect of vehicles owned or operated by them, as required by the laws and regulations of the State in which the vehicle is operated.

6. Paragraphs 1 to 5 of this article shall apply to Members of the Tribunal even after they have been replaced if they continue to exercise their functions in accordance with article 5, paragraph 3, of the Statute.

7. In order to secure, for Members of the Tribunal, complete freedom of speech and independence in the discharge of their functions, the immunity from legal process in respect of words spoken or written and all acts done by them in discharging their functions shall continue to be accorded, notwithstanding that the persons concerned are no longer Members of the Tribunal or performing those functions.

Article 14
Officials

1. The Registrar shall, when engaged on the business of the Tribunal, be accorded diplomatic privileges, immunities and facilities.

2. Other officials of the Tribunal shall enjoy in any country where they may be on the business of the Tribunal, or in any country through which they may pass on such business, such privileges, immunities and facilities as are necessary for the independent exercise of their functions. In particular, they shall be accorded:

(a) immunity from personal arrest or detention and from seizure of their personal baggage;

(b) the right to import free of duty their furniture and effects at the time of first taking up their post in the country in question and to re-export the same free of duty to their country of permanent residence;

(c) exemption from inspection of personal baggage, unless there are serious grounds for believing that the baggage contains articles not for personal use or articles the import or export of which is prohibited by the law or controlled by the quarantine regulations of the State Party concerned; an inspection in such a case shall be conducted in the presence of the official concerned;

(d) immunity from legal process in respect of words spoken or written and all acts done by them in discharging their functions, which immunity shall continue even after they have ceased to exercise their functions;

(e) immunity from national service obligations;

(f) together with members of their families forming part of their household, exemption from immigration restrictions or alien registration;

(g) the same privileges in respect of currency and exchange facilities as are accorded to the officials of comparable rank forming part of diplomatic missions to the Government concerned;

(h) together with members of their families forming part of their household, the same repatriation facilities in time of international crises as are accorded to diplomatic agents under the Vienna Convention.

3. The officials of the Tribunal shall be required to have insurance coverage against third-party risks in respect of vehicles owned or operated by them, as required by the laws and regulations of the State in which the vehicle is operated.

4. The Tribunal shall communicate to all States Parties the categories of officials to which the provisions of this article shall apply. The names of the officials included in these categories shall from time to time be communicated to all States Parties.

Article 15
Experts appointed under article 289 of the Convention

Experts appointed under article 289 of the Convention shall be accorded, during the period of their missions, including the time spent on journeys in connection with their missions, such privileges, immunities and facilities as are necessary for the independent exercise of their functions. In particular, they shall be accorded:

(a) immunity from personal arrest or detention and from seizure of their personal baggage;

(b) exemption from inspection of personal baggage, unless there are serious grounds for believing that the baggage contains articles not for personal use or articles the import or export of which is prohibited by law or controlled by the quarantine regulations of the State Party concerned; an inspection in such a case shall be conducted in the presence of the expert concerned;

(c) immunity from legal process in respect of words spoken or written and acts done by them in discharging their functions, which immunity shall continue even after they have ceased to exercise their functions;

(d) inviolability of documents and papers;

(e) exemption from immigration restrictions or alien registration;

(f) the same facilities in respect of currency and exchange restrictions as are accorded to representatives of foreign Governments on temporary official missions;

(g) such experts shall be accorded the same repatriation facilities in time of international crises as are accorded to diplomatic agents under the Vienna Convention.

Article 16
Agents, counsel and advocates

1. Agents, counsel and advocates before the Tribunal shall be accorded, during the period of their missions, including the time spent on journeys in

connection with their missions, the privileges, immunities and facilities necessary for the independent exercise of their functions. In particular, they shall be accorded:

(a) immunity from personal arrest or detention and from seizure of their personal baggage;

(b) exemption from inspection of personal baggage, unless there are serious grounds for believing that the baggage contains articles not for personal use or articles the import or export of which is prohibited by law or controlled by the quarantine regulations of the State Party concerned; an inspection in such a case shall be conducted in the presence of the agent, counsel or advocate concerned;

(c) immunity from legal process in respect of words spoken or written and all acts done by them in discharging their functions, which immunity shall continue even after they have ceased to exercise their functions;

(d) inviolability of documents and papers;

(e) the right to receive papers or correspondence by courier or in sealed bags;

(f) exemption from immigration restrictions or alien registration;

(g) the same facilities in respect of their personal baggage and in respect of currency or exchange restrictions as are accorded to representatives of foreign Governments on temporary official missions;

(h) the same repatriation facilities in time of international crises as are accorded to diplomatic agents under the Vienna Convention.

2. Upon receipt of notification from parties to proceedings before the Tribunal as to the appointment of an agent, counsel or advocate, a certification of the status of such representative shall be provided under the signature of the Registrar and limited to a period reasonably required for the proceedings.

3. The competent authorities of the State concerned shall accord the privileges, immunities and facilities provided for in this article upon production of the certification referred to in paragraph 2.

4. Where the incidence of any form of taxation depends upon residence, periods during which such agents, counsel or advocates are present in a State for the discharge of their functions shall not be considered as periods of residence.

Article 17

Witnesses, experts and persons performing missions

1. Witnesses, experts and persons performing missions by order of the Tribunal shall be accorded, during the period of their missions, including the time spent on journeys in connection with their missions, the privileges, immunities and facilities provided for in article 15, subparagraphs (a) to (f).

2. Witnesses, experts and such persons shall be accorded repatriation facilities in time of international crises.

Article 18
Nationals and permanent residents

Except insofar as additional privileges and immunities may be granted by the State Party concerned, and without prejudice to article 11, a person enjoying immunities and privileges under this Agreement shall, in the territory of the State Party of which he or she is a national or permanent resident, enjoy only immunity from legal process and inviolability in respect of words spoken or written and all acts done by that person in the discharge of his or her duties, which immunity shall continue even after the person has ceased to exercise his or her functions in connection with the Tribunal.

Article 19
Respect for laws and regulations

1. Privileges, immunities, facilities and prerogatives as provided for in articles 13 to 17 of this Agreement are granted not for the personal benefit of the individuals themselves but in order to safeguard the independent exercise of their functions in connection with the Tribunal.

2. Without prejudice to their privileges and immunities, it is the duty of all persons referred to in articles 13 to 17 to respect the laws and regulations of the State Party in whose territory they may be on the business of the Tribunal or through whose territory they may pass on such business. They also have a duty not to interfere in the internal affairs of that State.

Article 20
Waiver

1. Inasmuch as the privileges and immunities provided for in this Agreement are granted in the interests of the good administration of justice and not for the personal benefit of the individuals themselves, the competent authority has the right and the duty to waive the immunity in any case where, in its opinion, the immunity would impede the course of justice and can be waived without prejudice to the administration of justice.

2. For this purpose, the competent authority in the case of agents, counsel and advocates representing or designated by a State which is a party to proceedings before the Tribunal will be the State concerned. In the case of other agents, counsel and advocates, the Registrar, experts appointed under article 289 of the Convention and witnesses, experts and persons performing missions, the competent authority will be the Tribunal. In the case of other officials of the Tribunal, the competent authority will be the Registrar, acting with the approval of the President of the Tribunal.

Article 21
Laissez-passer and visas

1. The States Parties shall recognize and accept the United Nations laissez-passer issued to Members and officials of the Tribunal or experts appointed under article 289 of the Convention as a valid travel document.

2. Applications for visas (where required) from the Members of the Tribunal and the Registrar shall be dealt with as speedily as possible.

Applications for visas from all other persons holding or entitled to hold laissez-passer referred to in paragraph 1 of this Article and from persons referred to in articles 16 and 17, when accompanied by a certificate that they are travelling on the business of the Tribunal, shall be dealt with as speedily as possible.

Article 22
Freedom of movement

No administrative or other restrictions shall be imposed on the free movement of Members of the Tribunal, as well as other persons mentioned in articles 13 to 17, to and from the Headquarters of the Tribunal or the place where the Tribunal is sitting or otherwise exercising its functions.

Article 23
Maintenance of security and public order

1. If the State Party concerned considers it necessary to take, without prejudice to the independent and proper working of the Tribunal, measures necessary for the security or for the maintenance of public order of the State Party in accordance with international law, it shall approach the Tribunal as rapidly as circumstances allow in order to determine by mutual agreement the measures necessary to protect the Tribunal.

2. The Tribunal shall cooperate with the Government of such State Party to avoid any prejudice to the security or public order of the State Party resulting from its activities.

Article 24
Cooperation with the authorities of States Parties

The Tribunal shall cooperate at all times with the appropriate authorities of States Parties to facilitate the execution of their laws and to prevent any abuse in connection with the privileges, immunities, facilities and prerogatives referred to in this Agreement.

Article 25
Relationship with special agreements

Insofar as the provisions of this Agreement and the provisions of any special agreement between the Tribunal and a State Party relate to the same subject matter, the two provisions shall, whenever possible, be treated as complementary, so that both provisions shall be applicable and neither provision shall narrow the effect of the other; but in case of conflict the provision of the special agreement shall prevail.

Article 26
Settlement of disputes

1. The Tribunal shall make suitable provisions for the settlement of:

(a) disputes arising out of contracts and other disputes of a private law character to which the Tribunal is a party;

(b) disputes involving any person referred to in this Agreement who by reason of his official position enjoys immunity, if such immunity has not been waived.

2. All disputes arising out of the interpretation or application of this Agreement shall be referred to an arbitral tribunal unless the parties have agreed to another mode of settlement. If a dispute arises between the Tribunal and a State Party which is not settled by consultation, negotiation or other agreed mode of settlement within three months following a request by one of the parties to the dispute, it shall at the request of either party be referred for final decision to a panel of three arbitrators: one to be chosen by the Tribunal, one to be chosen by the State Party and the third, who shall be Chairman of the panel, to be chosen by the first two arbitrators. If either party has failed to make its appointment of an arbitrator within two months of the appointment of an arbitrator by the other party, the Secretary-General of the United Nations shall make such appointment. Should the first two arbitrators fail to agree upon the appointment of the third arbitrator within three months following the appointment of the first two arbitrators the third arbitrator shall be chosen by the Secretary-General of the United Nations upon the request of the Tribunal or the State Party.

Article 27
Signature

This Agreement shall be open for signature by all States and shall remain open for signature at United Nations Headquarters for twenty-four months from 1 July 1997.

Article 28
Ratification

This Agreement is subject to ratification. The instruments of ratification shall be deposited with the Secretary-General of the United Nations.

Article 29
Accession

This Agreement shall remain open for accession by all States. The instruments of accession shall be deposited with the Secretary-General of the United Nations.

Article 30
Entry into force

1. This Agreement shall enter into force 30 days after the date of deposit of the tenth instrument of ratification or accession.

2. For each State which ratifies this Agreement or accedes thereto after the deposit of the tenth instrument of ratification or accession, this Agreement shall enter into force on the thirtieth day following the deposit of its instrument of ratification or accession.

Article 31
Provisional application

A State which intends to ratify or accede to this Agreement may at any time notify the depositary that it will apply this Agreement provisionally for a period not exceeding two years.

Article 32
Ad hoc application

Where a dispute has been submitted to the Tribunal in accordance with the Statute, any State not a party to this Agreement which is a party to the dispute may, ad hoc for the purposes and duration of the case relating thereto, become a party to this Agreement by the deposit of an instrument of acceptance. Instruments of acceptance shall be deposited with the Secretary-General of the United Nations and shall become effective on the date of deposit.

Article 33
Denunciation

1. A State Party may, by written notification addressed to the Secretary-General of the United Nations, denounce this Agreement. The denunciation shall take effect one year after the date of receipt of the notification, unless the notification specifies a later date.

2. The denunciation shall not in any way affect the duty of any State Party to fulfil any obligation embodied in this Agreement to which it would be subject under international law independently of this Agreement.

Article 34
Depositary

The Secretary-General of the United Nations shall be the depositary of this Agreement.

Article 35
Authentic texts

The Arabic, Chinese, English, French, Russian and Spanish texts of this Agreement are equally authentic.

IN WITNESS WHEREOF, the undersigned Plenipotentiaries, being duly authorized thereto, have signed this Agreement.

OPENED FOR SIGNATURE at New York, this first day of July, one thousand nine hundred and ninety-seven, in a single original, in the Arabic, Chinese, English, French, Russian and Spanish languages.

AGREEMENT ON COOPERATION AND RELATIONSHIP BETWEEN THE UNITED NATIONS AND THE INTERNATIONAL TRIBUNAL FOR THE LAW OF THE SEA

The United Nations and the International Tribunal for the Law of the Sea,

Bearing in mind that, in accordance with the Charter of the United Nations, the United Nations is the principal organization dealing with matters relating to the maintenance of international peace and security and that one of the main purposes of the Organization is to bring about by peaceful means the settlement of international disputes or situations that might lead to a breach of the peace,

Acknowledging the key role played by the United Nations under the Charter in the peaceful settlement of international disputes,

Bearing in mind that the General Assembly of the United Nations in its resolution 3067 (XXVIII) of 16 November 1973 decided to convene the Third United Nations Conference on the Law of the Sea for the adoption of a convention dealing with all matters relating to the law of the sea and that the Conference adopted the United Nations Convention on the Law of the Sea 3/ (hereinafter referred to as “the Convention”),

Bearing in mind also that the International Tribunal for the Law of the Sea (hereinafter referred to as “the International Tribunal”) has been established in accordance with article 287, paragraph 1 (a), and annex VI to the Convention as an autonomous international judicial body,

Noting the role of the International Tribunal in the peaceful settlement of disputes in relation to the uses of the seas and the oceans and their resources,

Noting also that the functions of the International Tribunal are consistent with Article 2, paragraph 3, of the Charter of the United Nations, which provides that international disputes shall be settled by peaceful means,

Noting further the responsibilities entrusted to the Secretary-General of the United Nations under article 319 and other provisions of the Convention,

Recalling General Assembly resolution 51/204 of 17 December 1996 inviting the International Tribunal to participate in the sessions and the work of the General Assembly in the capacity of observer,

Taking note of General Assembly resolution 51/34 of 9 December 1996 and the decision of the first session of the International Tribunal calling for the conclusion of a relationship agreement between the United Nations and the International Tribunal,

Have agreed as follows:

Article 1
General

1. The United Nations recognizes the International Tribunal for the Law of the Sea as an autonomous international judicial body with jurisdiction as provided for in the relevant provisions of the Convention and the statute of the International Tribunal annexed thereto.

2. The International Tribunal recognizes the responsibilities of the United Nations under the Charter, in particular in the fields of international peace and security, economic, social, cultural and humanitarian development and the peaceful settlement of international disputes.

3. The United Nations and the International Tribunal each undertake to respect the status and mandate of the other and to establish cooperative working relations pursuant to the provisions of the present Agreement.

Article 2
Cooperation and coordination

The United Nations and the International Tribunal, with a view to facilitating the effective attainment of their objectives and the coordination of their activities, shall:

(a) Consult and cooperate, whenever appropriate, on matters of mutual concern; and

(b) Pursue, whenever appropriate, initiatives to coordinate their activities.

Article 3
Reciprocal representation

1. Without prejudice to the decision of the General Assembly in its resolution 51/204 granting observer status to the International Tribunal, and subject to such decisions as may be taken concerning the attendance of meetings by observers, the United Nations shall, subject to the rules and practices of the bodies concerned, invite the International Tribunal to attend meetings and conferences convened under the auspices of the United Nations, where observers are allowed, and whenever matters of interest to the International Tribunal are under discussion.

2. Subject to the applicable provisions of the rules of the International Tribunal, the Secretary-General of the United Nations or representatives of the Secretary-General may attend public meetings of the International Tribunal or its Seabed Disputes Chamber, including oral hearings.

3. Subject to the rules of the International Tribunal, written statements submitted by the United Nations to the International Tribunal for distribution shall be distributed by the Registry to the members of the International Tribunal. Written statements presented by the International Tribunal to the United

Nations for distribution shall be distributed by the Secretariat of the United Nations to all members of the appropriate organs of the United Nations in accordance with the relevant rules of procedure. Such written statements shall be circulated in the quantities and languages in which they were made available to the Registry or the Secretariat.

Article 4
Exchange of information and documents

1. The United Nations and the International Tribunal shall, to the fullest extent possible and practicable, and subject to paragraphs 2 and 3 of the present article, arrange for the regular exchange of information and documents of mutual interest. In particular:

(a) The Secretary-General of the United Nations shall:

(i) Periodically transmit to the International Tribunal information on developments relating to the Convention that are relevant to the work of the International Tribunal, including copies of communications received by the Secretary-General in the capacity of depositary of the Convention or depositary of any other agreement which confers jurisdiction on the International Tribunal;

(ii) Transmit to the International Tribunal copies of any documents notified to the Secretary-General or otherwise communicated to the United Nations by the International Court of Justice pursuant to its Statute and Rules of Court;

(iii) Subject to the applicable rules and regulations and the obligations of the United Nations under the relevant agreements, furnish to the International Tribunal information requested by it as relevant to a case before it.

(b) The Registrar of the International Tribunal shall:

(i) Periodically transmit to the United Nations information concerning developments under the Convention that are related to the activities of the International Tribunal;

(ii) Transmit to the United Nations information and documentation relating to the work of the International Tribunal, including documentation relating to pleadings, oral proceedings, orders, judgements and other communications and documentation, including those relating to applications submitted to the International Tribunal in accordance with articles 290 and 292 of the Convention;

(iii) Furnish to the United Nations, with the concurrence of the International Tribunal and subject to its statute and rules, any information relating to the work of the International Tribunal requested by the International Court of Justice.

2. Nothing in the present Agreement shall be construed to require either the United Nations or the International Tribunal to furnish any information, the provision of which would, in its judgement, constitute a violation of the confidentiality of such information or of rights in proprietary materials.

3. The United Nations and the International Tribunal shall make every effort to achieve maximum cooperation with a view to avoiding undesirable duplication in the collection, analysis, publication and dissemination of information related to matters of mutual interest. They shall strive to combine their efforts, where appropriate, to secure the greatest possible usefulness and utilization of such information and to minimize the burdens placed upon national Governments and other organizations from which such information may be collected.

Article 5
Reports to the United Nations

The International Tribunal shall keep the United Nations informed of its activities that may require the attention of the United Nations. For this purpose, the International Tribunal may, when it deems it appropriate:

(a) Submit reports to the United Nations through the Secretary-General of the United Nations; and

(b) Notify the Secretary-General of the United Nations whenever, in its opinion, a question within the competence of the Security Council, in particular relating to the application of article 298, paragraph 1 (c), of the Convention, arises in connection with the work of the International Tribunal.

Article 6
Personnel arrangements

1. The United Nations and the International Tribunal agree to apply, as far as practicable, common personnel standards, methods and arrangements designed to avoid serious discrepancies in terms and conditions of employment, to avoid competition in recruitment of personnel and to facilitate any mutually desirable interchange of personnel in order to obtain the maximum benefit from their services.

2. The United Nations and the International Tribunal agree to cooperate to the fullest extent possible in achieving these ends and in particular they agree to:

(a) Consult periodically on matters of mutual interest relating to the employment of their officers and staff, including conditions of service, duration of appointments, classification, salary scale and allowances, retirement and pension rights and staff regulations and rules, with a view to securing as much uniformity in these matters as shall be found feasible;

(b) Cooperate in the interchange of personnel, when desirable, on a temporary or permanent basis, making due provision for the retention of seniority and pension rights;

(c) Strive for maximum cooperation in order to achieve the most efficient use of specialized personnel, systems and services;

(d) Cooperate in seeking an arrangement that will allow the extension of the competence of the United Nations Administrative Tribunal to the staff of the Registry of the International Tribunal.

Article 7
Conference services

1. Upon the request of the International Tribunal, the United Nations may, subject to availability, provide to the International Tribunal, on a reimbursable basis, such facilities and services as may be required for the sessions of the International Tribunal, including translation and interpretation services, documentation and conference services.

2. The terms and conditions under which any facilities or services of the United Nations in connection with the matters referred to in the present article may be extended to the International Tribunal shall, where necessary, be the subject of supplementary arrangements concluded for this purpose.

Article 8
Administrative cooperation

The United Nations and the International Tribunal recognize the desirability of cooperation in administrative matters of mutual interest. They shall consult from time to time concerning the most efficient use of facilities, staff and services with a view to avoiding the establishment and operation of overlapping facilities and services. They shall also consult to explore the possibility of continuing or establishing common facilities or services in specific areas.

Article 9
Laissez-passer

Members of the International Tribunal, the Registrar and other officials of the Registry shall be entitled, in accordance with such special arrangements as may be concluded between the Secretary-General of the United Nations and the International Tribunal, to use the laissez-passer of the United Nations as a valid travel document where such use is recognized by States parties to the Agreement on the Privileges and Immunities of the International Tribunal for the Law of the Sea or other agreements defining the privileges and immunities of the International Tribunal, its members and officials. The above is without prejudice to the right of the International Tribunal to issue its own travel documents.

Article 10
Budgetary and financial matters

1. The International Tribunal recognizes the desirability of establishing close budgetary and financial relationships with the United Nations so that the maximum measure of coordination and uniformity with respect to administrative operations may be secured.

2. The United Nations and the International Tribunal agree to cooperate to the fullest extent possible in achieving these ends.

3. The International Tribunal agrees to conform, as far as may be practicable and appropriate, to standard practices and forms recommended by the United Nations.

4. The Registrar of the International Tribunal may consult with the Secretary-General of the United Nations with a view to achieving consistency in the presentation of the budget of the International Tribunal with that of the United Nations.

5. The United Nations may, upon request of the International Tribunal, provide advice on financial and fiscal questions of interest to the International Tribunal with a view to achieving coordination and securing uniformity in such matters.

Article 11
Financing of services

The costs and expenses resulting from the cooperation or the provision of services pursuant to the present Agreement shall be subject to separate arrangements between the United Nations and the International Tribunal. To that end, the United Nations and the International Tribunal shall consult each other with a view to determining the most equitable manner in which such costs and expenses shall be borne.

Article 12
Implementation of the Agreement

The Secretary-General of the United Nations and the Registrar of the International Tribunal may enter into such supplementary arrangements for the implementation of the present Agreement as may be found desirable in the light of the operating experience of the United Nations and the International Tribunal.

Article 13
Amendments

The present Agreement may be amended by agreement between the United Nations and the International Tribunal. Any such amendment agreed upon shall enter into force on its approval by the General Assembly of the United Nations and by the International Tribunal.

Article 14
Entry into force

1. The present Agreement shall come into force on its approval by the General Assembly of the United Nations and by the International Tribunal.

2. Pending such approval the present Agreement shall be applied provisionally from the date of its signature by the Secretary-General of the United Nations and the President of the International Tribunal.

IN WITNESS WHEREOF, the undersigned have signed the present Agreement.

SIGNED this 18th day of December 1997 at United Nations Headquarters in New York in two originals in the English language.

For the United Nations :

Secretary-General
(Signed) Kofi A. Annan

For the International Tribunal for the Law of the Sea

President
(Signed) Thomas A. Mensah

ITLOS/8
17 March 2009

INTERNATIONAL TRIBUNAL FOR THE LAW OF THE SEA

RULES OF THE TRIBUNAL

CONTENTS

PART III. PROCEDURE

RULES OF THE TRIBUNAL

Adopted on 28 October 1997
(amended on 15 March and 21 September 2001 and on 17 March 2009)

PREAMBLE

The Tribunal,

Acting pursuant to article 16 of the Statute of the International Tribunal for the Law of the Sea, Annex VI to the United Nations Convention on the Law of the Sea,

Adopts the following Rules of the Tribunal.

PART I

USE OF TERMS

Article 1

For the purposes of these Rules:

(a) "Convention" means the United Nations Convention on the Law of the Sea of 10 December 1982, together with the Agreement of 28 July 1994 relating to the implementation of Part XI of the Convention;

(b) "Statute" means the Statute of the International Tribunal for the Law of the Sea, Annex VI to the Convention;

(c) "States Parties" has the meaning set out in article 1, paragraph 2, of the Convention and includes, for the purposes of Part XI of the Convention, States and entities which are members of the Authority on a provisional basis in accordance with section 1, paragraph 12, of the Annex to the Agreement relating to the implementation of Part XI;

(d) "international organization" has the meaning set out in Annex IX, article 1, to the Convention, unless otherwise specified;

(e) "Member" means an elected judge;

(f) "judge" means a Member as well as a judge *ad hoc;*

(g) "judge *ad hoc*" means a person chosen under article 17 of the Statute for the purposes of a particular case;

(h) "Authority" means the International Seabed Authority;

(i) "certified copy" means a copy of a document bearing an attestation by or on behalf of the custodian of the original or the party submitting it that it is a true and accurate copy thereof.

PART II

ORGANIZATION

Section A. The Tribunal

Subsection 1. The Members

Article 2

1. The term of office of Members elected at a triennial election shall begin to run from 1 October following the date of the election.

2. The term of office of a Member elected to replace a Member whose term of office has not expired shall run from the date of the election for the remainder of that term.

Article 3

The Members, in the exercise of their functions, are of equal status, irrespective of age, priority of election or length of service.

Article 4

1. The Members shall, except as provided in paragraphs 3 and 4, take precedence according to the date on which their respective terms of office began.

2. Members whose terms of office began on the same date shall take precedence in relation to one another according to seniority of age.

3. A Member who is re-elected to a new term of office which is continuous with his previous term shall retain his precedence.

4. The President and the Vice-President of the Tribunal, while holding these offices, shall take precedence over the other Members.

5. The Member who, in accordance with the foregoing paragraphs, takes precedence next after the President and the Vice-President of the Tribunal is in these Rules designated the "Senior Member". If that Member is unable to act, the Member who is next after him in precedence and able to act is considered as Senior Member.

Article 5

1. The solemn declaration to be made by every Member in accordance with article 11 of the Statute shall be as follows:

> "I solemnly declare that I will perform my duties and exercise my powers as judge honourably, faithfully, impartially and conscientiously".

2. This declaration shall be made at the first public sitting at which the Member is present. Such sitting shall be held as soon as practicable after his term of office begins and, if necessary, a special sitting shall be held for the purpose.

3. A Member who is re-elected shall make a new declaration only if his new term is not continuous with his previous one.

Article 6

1. In the case of the resignation of a Member, the letter of resignation shall be addressed to the President of the Tribunal. The place becomes vacant on the receipt of the letter.

2. In the case of the resignation of the President of the Tribunal, the letter of resignation shall be addressed to the Vice-President of the Tribunal or, failing him, the Senior Member. The place becomes vacant on the receipt of the letter.

Article 7

In any case in which the application of article 9 of the Statute is under consideration, the Member concerned shall be so informed by the President of the Tribunal or, if the circumstances so require, by the Vice-President of the Tribunal, in a written statement which shall include the grounds therefor and any relevant evidence. He shall subsequently, at a private meeting of the Tribunal specially convened for the purpose, be afforded an opportunity of making a statement, of furnishing any information or explanations he wishes to give and of supplying answers, orally or in writing, to any questions put to him. The Member concerned may be assisted or represented by counsel or any other person of his choice. At a further private meeting, at which the Member concerned shall not be present, the matter shall be discussed; each Member shall state his opinion, and if requested a vote shall be taken.

Subsection 2. Judges *ad hoc*

Article 8

1. Judges *ad hoc* shall participate in the case in which they sit on terms of complete equality with the other judges.

2. Judges *ad hoc* shall take precedence after the Members and in order of seniority of age.

3. In the case of the resignation of a judge *ad hoc*, the letter of resignation shall be addressed to the President of the Tribunal. The place becomes vacant on the receipt of the letter.

Article 9

1. The solemn declaration to be made by every judge *ad hoc* in accordance with articles 11 and 17, paragraph 6, of the Statute shall be as set out in article 5, paragraph 1, of these Rules.

2. This declaration shall be made at a public sitting in the case in which the judge *ad hoc* is participating.

3. Judges *ad hoc* shall make the declaration in relation to each case in which they are participating.

Subsection 3. President and Vice-President

Article 10

1. The term of office of the President and that of the Vice-President of the Tribunal shall begin to run from the date on which the term of office of the Members elected at a triennial election begins.

2. The elections of the President and the Vice-President of the Tribunal shall be held on that date or shortly thereafter. The former President, if still a

Member, shall continue to exercise the functions of President of the Tribunal until the election to this position has taken place.

Article 11

1. If, on the date of the election to the presidency, the former President of the Tribunal is still a Member, he shall conduct the election. If he has ceased to be a Member, or is unable to act, the election shall be conducted by the Member exercising the functions of the presidency.

2. The election shall take place by secret ballot, after the presiding Member has declared the number of affirmative votes necessary for election; there shall be no nominations. The Member obtaining the votes of the majority of the Members composing the Tribunal at the time of the election shall be declared elected and shall enter forthwith upon his functions.

3. The new President of the Tribunal shall conduct the election of the Vice-President of the Tribunal either at the same or at the following meeting. Paragraph 2 applies to this election.

Article 12

1. The President of the Tribunal shall preside at all meetings of the Tribunal. He shall direct the work and supervise the administration of the Tribunal.

2. He shall represent the Tribunal in its relations with States and other entities.

Article 13

1. In the event of a vacancy in the presidency or of the inability of the President of the Tribunal to exercise the functions of the presidency, these shall be exercised by the Vice-President of the Tribunal or, failing him, by the Senior Member.

2. When the President of the Tribunal is precluded by a provision of the Statute or of these Rules either from sitting or from presiding in a particular case, he shall continue to exercise the functions of the presidency for all purposes save in respect of that case.

3. The President of the Tribunal shall take the measures necessary in order to ensure the continuous exercise of the functions of the presidency at the seat of the Tribunal. In the event of his absence, he may, so far as is compatible with the Statute and these Rules, arrange for these functions to be exercised by the Vice-President of the Tribunal or, failing him, by the Senior Member.

4. If the President of the Tribunal decides to resign the presidency, he shall communicate his decision in writing to the Tribunal through the Vice-President of the Tribunal or, failing him, the Senior Member. If the Vice-President of the Tribunal decides to resign the vice-presidency, he shall communicate his decision in writing to the President of the Tribunal.

Article 14

If a vacancy in the presidency or the vice-presidency occurs before the date when the current term is due to expire, the Tribunal shall decide whether or not the vacancy shall be filled during the remainder of the term.

Subsection 4. Experts appointed under article 289 of the Convention

Article 15

1. A request by a party for the selection by the Tribunal of scientific or technical experts under article 289 of the Convention shall, as a general rule, be made not later than the closure of the written proceedings. The Tribunal may consider a later request made prior to the closure of the oral proceedings, if appropriate in the circumstances of the case.

2. When the Tribunal decides to select experts, at the request of a party or *proprio motu*, it shall select such experts upon the proposal of the President of the Tribunal, who shall consult the parties before making such a proposal.

3. Experts shall be independent and enjoy the highest reputation for fairness, competence and integrity. An expert in a field mentioned in Annex VIII, article 2, to the Convention shall be chosen preferably from the relevant list prepared in accordance with that annex.

4. This article applies *mutatis mutandis* to any chamber and its President.

5. Before entering upon their duties, such experts shall make the following solemn declaration at a public sitting:

> "I solemnly declare that I will perform my duties as an expert honourably, impartially and conscientiously and that I will faithfully observe all the provisions of the Statute and of the Rules of the Tribunal".

Subsection 5. The composition of the Tribunal for particular cases

Article 16

1. No Member who is a national of a party in a case, a national of a State member of an international organization which is a party in a case or a national of a sponsoring State of an entity other than a State which is a party in a case, shall exercise the functions of the presidency in respect of the case.

2. The Member who is presiding in a case on the date on which the Tribunal meets in accordance with article 68 shall continue to preside in that case until completion of the current phase of the case, notwithstanding the election in the meantime of a new President or Vice-President of the Tribunal. If he should become unable to act, the presidency for the case shall be determined in accordance with article 13 and on the basis of the composition of the Tribunal on the date on which it met in accordance with article 68.

Article 17

Members who have been replaced following the expiration of their terms of office shall continue to sit in a case until the completion of any phase in respect of which the Tribunal has met in accordance with article 68.

Article 18

1. Whenever doubt arises on any point in article 8 of the Statute, the President of the Tribunal shall inform the other Members. The Member concerned shall be afforded an opportunity of furnishing any information or explanations.

2. If a party desires to bring to the attention of the Tribunal facts which it considers to be of possible relevance to the application of article 8 of the Statute, but which it believes may not be known to the Tribunal, that party shall communicate confidentially such facts to the President of the Tribunal in writing.

Article 19

1. If a party intends to choose a judge *ad hoc* in a case, it shall notify the Tribunal of its intention as soon as possible. It shall inform the Tribunal of the name, nationality and brief biographical details of the person chosen, preferably at the same time but in any event not later than two months before the time-limit fixed for the filing of the counter-memorial. The judge *ad hoc* may be of a nationality other than that of the party which chooses him.

2. If a party proposes to abstain from choosing a judge *ad hoc*, on condition of a like abstention by the other party, it shall so notify the Tribunal, which shall inform the other party. If the other party thereafter gives notice of its intention to choose, or chooses, a judge *ad hoc*, the time-limit for the party which had previously abstained from choosing a judge may be extended up to 30 days by the President of the Tribunal.

3. A copy of any notification relating to the choice of a judge *ad hoc* shall be communicated by the Registrar to the other party, which shall be requested to furnish, within a time-limit not exceeding 30 days to be fixed by the President of the Tribunal, such observations as it may wish to make. If within the said time-limit no objection is raised by the other party, and if none appears to the Tribunal itself, the parties shall be so informed. In the event of any objection or doubt, the matter shall be decided by the Tribunal, if necessary after hearing the parties.

4. A judge *ad hoc* who becomes unable to sit may be replaced.

5. If the Tribunal finds that the reasons for the participation of a judge *ad hoc* no longer exist, that judge shall cease to sit on the bench.

Article 20

1. If the Tribunal finds that two or more parties are in the same interest and are therefore to be considered as one party only, and that there is no Member of the nationality of any one of these parties upon the bench, the Tribunal shall fix a time-limit within which they may jointly choose a judge *ad hoc*.

2. Should any party among those found by the Tribunal to be in the same interest allege the existence of a separate interest of its own or put forward any other objection, the matter shall be decided by the Tribunal, if necessary after hearing the parties.

Article 21

1. If a Member having the nationality of one of the parties is or becomes unable to sit in any phase of a case, that party is entitled to choose a judge *ad hoc* within a time-limit to be fixed by the Tribunal, or by the President of the Tribunal if the Tribunal is not sitting.

2. Parties in the same interest shall be deemed not to have a Member of one of their nationalities upon the bench if every Member having one of their nationalities is or becomes unable to sit in any phase of the case.

3. If a Member having the nationality of one of the parties becomes able to sit not later than the closure of the written proceedings in that phase of the case, that Member shall resume the seat on the bench in the case.

Article 22

1. An entity other than a State may choose a judge *ad hoc* only if:

(a) one of the other parties is a State Party and there is upon the bench a judge of its nationality or, where such party is an international organization, there is upon the bench a judge of the nationality of one of its member States or the State Party has itself chosen a judge *ad hoc*; or

(b) there is upon the bench a judge of the nationality of the sponsoring State of one of the other parties.

2. However, an international organization or a natural or juridical person or state enterprise is not entitled to choose a judge *ad hoc* if there is upon the bench a judge of the nationality of one of the member States of the international organization or a judge of the nationality of the sponsoring State of such natural or juridical person or state enterprise.

3. Where an international organization is a party to a case and there is upon the bench a judge of the nationality of a member State of the organization, the other party may choose a judge *ad hoc*.

4. Where two or more judges on the bench are nationals of member States of the international organization concerned or of the sponsoring States of a

party, the President may, after consulting the parties, request one or more of such judges to withdraw from the bench.

Section B. The Seabed Disputes Chamber

Subsection 1. The members and judges *ad hoc*

Article 23

The members of the Seabed Disputes Chamber shall be selected following each triennial election to the Tribunal as soon as possible after the term of office of Members elected at such election begins. The term of office of members of the Chamber shall begin to run from the date of their selection. The term of office of members selected at the first selection shall expire on 30 September 1999; the terms of office of members selected at subsequent triennial selections shall expire on 30 September every three years thereafter. Members of the Chamber who remain on the Tribunal after the expiry of their term of office shall continue to serve on the Chamber until the next selection.

Article 24

The President of the Chamber, while holding that office, takes precedence over the other members of the Chamber. The other members take precedence according to their precedence in the Tribunal in the case where the President and Vice-President of the Tribunal are not exercising the functions of those offices.

Article 25

Articles 8 and 9 apply *mutatis mutandis* to the judges *ad hoc* of the Chamber.

Subsection 2. The presidency

Article 26

1. The Chamber shall elect its President by secret ballot and by a majority vote of its members.

2. The President shall preside at all meetings of the Chamber.

3. In the event of a vacancy in the presidency or of the inability of the President of the Chamber to exercise the functions of the presidency, these shall be exercised by the member of the Chamber who is senior in precedence and able to act.

4. In other respects, articles 10 to 14 apply *mutatis mutandis*.

Subsection 3. *Ad hoc* chambers of the Seabed Disputes Chamber

Article 27

1. Any request for the formation of an *ad hoc* chamber of the Seabed Disputes Chamber in accordance with article 188, paragraph 1 (b), of the Convention shall be made within three months from the date of the institution of proceedings.

2. If, within a time-limit fixed by the President of the Seabed Disputes Chamber, the parties do not agree on the composition of the chamber, the President shall establish time-limits for the parties to make the necessary appointments.

Section C. Special chambers

Article 28

1. The Chamber of Summary Procedure shall be composed of the President and Vice-President of the Tribunal, acting ex officio, and three other Members. In addition, two Members shall be selected to act as alternates.

2. The members and alternates of the Chamber shall be selected by the Tribunal upon the proposal of the President of the Tribunal.

3. The selection of members and alternates of the Chamber shall be made as soon as possible after 1 October in each year. The members of the Chamber and the alternates shall enter upon their functions on their selection and serve until 30 September of the following year. Members of the Chamber and alternates who remain on the Tribunal after that date shall continue to serve on the Chamber until the next selection.

4. If a member of the Chamber is unable, for whatever reason, to sit in a given case, that member shall be replaced for the purposes of that case by the senior in precedence of the two alternates.

5. If a member of the Chamber resigns or otherwise ceases to be a member, the place of that member shall be taken by the senior in precedence of the two alternates, who shall thereupon become a full member of the Chamber and be replaced by the selection of another alternate.

6. The quorum for meetings of the Chamber is three members.

Article 29

1. Whenever the Tribunal decides to form a standing special chamber provided for in article 15, paragraph 1, of the Statute, it shall determine the particular category of disputes for which it is formed, the number of its members, the period for which they will serve, the date when they will enter upon their duties and the quorum for meetings.

2. The members of such chamber shall be selected by the Tribunal upon the proposal of the President of the Tribunal from among the Members, having regard to any special knowledge, expertise or previous experience which any of the Members may have in relation to the category of disputes the chamber deals with.

3. The Tribunal may decide to dissolve a standing special chamber. The chamber shall finish any cases pending before it.

Article 30

1. A request for the formation of a special chamber to deal with a particular dispute, as provided for in article 15, paragraph 2, of the Statute, shall be made within two months from the date of the institution of proceedings. Upon receipt of a request made by one party, the President of the Tribunal shall ascertain whether the other party assents.

2. When the parties have agreed, the President of the Tribunal shall ascertain their views regarding the composition of the chamber and shall report to the Tribunal accordingly.

3. The Tribunal shall determine, with the approval of the parties, the Members who are to constitute the chamber. The same procedure shall be followed in filling any vacancy. The Tribunal shall also determine the quorum for meetings of the chamber.

4. Members of a chamber formed under this article who have been replaced, in accordance with article 5 of the Statute, following the expiration of their terms of office, shall continue to sit in all phases of the case, whatever the stage it has then reached.

Article 31

1. If a chamber when formed includes the President of the Tribunal, the President shall preside over the chamber. If it does not include the President but includes the Vice-President, the Vice-President shall preside. In any other event, the chamber shall elect its own President by secret ballot and by a majority of votes of its members. The member who, under this paragraph, presides over the chamber at the time of its formation shall continue to preside so long as he remains a member of that chamber.

2. Subject to paragraph 3, the President of a chamber shall exercise, in relation to cases being dealt with by that chamber and from the time it begins dealing with the case, the functions of the President of the Tribunal in relation to cases before the Tribunal.

3. The President of the Tribunal shall take such steps as may be necessary to give effect to article 17, paragraph 4, of the Statute.

4. If the President of a chamber is prevented from sitting or acting as President of the chamber, the functions of the presidency of the chamber shall

be assumed by the member of the chamber who is the senior in precedence and able to act.

Section D. The Registry

Article 32

1. The Tribunal shall elect its Registrar by secret ballot from among candidates nominated by Members. The Registrar shall be elected for a term of five years and may be re-elected.

2. The President of the Tribunal shall give notice of a vacancy or impending vacancy to Members, either forthwith upon the vacancy arising or, where the vacancy will arise on the expiration of the term of office of the Registrar, not less than three months prior thereto. The President of the Tribunal shall fix a date for the closure of the list of candidates so as to enable nominations and information concerning the candidates to be received in sufficient time.

3. Nominations shall be accompanied by the relevant information concerning the candidates, in particular information as to age, nationality, present occupation, academic and other qualifications, knowledge of languages and any previous experience in law, especially the law of the sea, diplomacy or the work of international organizations.

4. The candidate obtaining the votes of the majority of the Members composing the Tribunal at the time of the election shall be declared elected.

Article 33

The Tribunal shall elect a Deputy Registrar; it may also elect an Assistant Registrar. Article 32 applies to their election and terms of office.

Article 34

Before taking up their duties, the Registrar, the Deputy Registrar and the Assistant Registrar shall make the following solemn declaration at a meeting of the Tribunal:

> "I solemnly declare that I will perform my duties as Registrar (Deputy Registrar or Assistant Registrar as the case may be) of the International Tribunal for the Law of the Sea in all loyalty, discretion and good conscience and that I will faithfully observe all the provisions of the Statute and of the Rules of the Tribunal".

Article 35

1. The staff of the Registry, other than the Registrar, the Deputy Registrar and the Assistant Registrar, shall be appointed by the Tribunal on proposals submitted by the Registrar. Appointments to such posts as the Tribunal shall

determine may, however, be made by the Registrar with the approval of the President of the Tribunal.

2. The paramount consideration in the recruitment and employment of the staff and in the determination of the conditions of service shall be the necessity of securing the highest standards of efficiency, competence and integrity. Due regard shall be paid to the importance of recruiting the staff on as wide a geographical basis as possible.

3. Before taking up their duties, the staff shall make the following solemn declaration before the President of the Tribunal, the Registrar being present:

> "I solemnly declare that I will perform my duties as an official of the International Tribunal for the Law of the Sea in all loyalty, discretion and good conscience and that I will faithfully observe all the provisions of the Statute and of the Rules of the Tribunal".

Article 36

1. The Registrar, in the discharge of his functions, shall:

(a) be the regular channel of communications to and from the Tribunal and in particular shall effect all communications, notifications and transmission of documents required by the Convention, the Statute, these Rules or any other relevant international agreement and ensure that the date of dispatch and receipt thereof may be readily verified;

(b) keep, under the supervision of the President of the Tribunal, and in such form as may be laid down by the Tribunal, a List of cases, entered and numbered in the order in which the documents instituting proceedings or requesting an advisory opinion are received in the Registry;

(c) keep copies of declarations and notices of revocation or withdrawal thereof deposited with the Secretary-General of the United Nations under articles 287 and 298 of the Convention or Annex IX, article 7, to the Convention;

(d) keep copies of agreements conferring jurisdiction on the Tribunal;

(e) keep notifications received under article 110, paragraph 2;

(f) transmit to the parties certified copies of pleadings and annexes upon receipt thereof in the Registry;

(g) communicate to the Government of the State in which the Tribunal or a chamber is sitting, or is to sit, and any other Governments which may be concerned, the necessary information as to the persons from time to time entitled, under the Statute and the relevant agreements, to privileges, immunities or facilities;

(h) be present in person or represented by the Deputy Registrar, the Assistant Registrar or in their absence by a senior official of the Registry designated by him, at meetings of the Tribunal, and of the chambers, and be responsible for preparing records of such meetings;

(i) make arrangements for such provision or verification of translations and interpretations into the Tribunal's official languages as the Tribunal may require;

(j) sign all judgments, advisory opinions and orders of the Tribunal and the records referred to in subparagraph (h);

(k) be responsible for the reproduction, printing and publication of the Tribunal's judgments, advisory opinions and orders, the pleadings and statements and the minutes of public sittings in cases and of such other documents as the Tribunal may direct to be published;

(l) be responsible for all administrative work and in particular for the accounts and financial administration in accordance with the financial procedures of the Tribunal;

(m) deal with inquiries concerning the Tribunal and its work;

(n) assist in maintaining relations between the Tribunal and the Authority, the International Court of Justice and the other organs of the United Nations, its related agencies, the arbitral and special arbitral tribunals referred to in article 287 of the Convention and international bodies and conferences concerned with the codification and progressive development of international law, in particular the law of the sea;

(o) ensure that information concerning the Tribunal and its activities is accessible to Governments, the highest national courts of justice, professional and learned societies, legal faculties and schools of law and public information media;

(p) have custody of the seals and stamps of the Tribunal, of the archives of the Tribunal and of such other archives as may be entrusted to the Tribunal.

2. The Tribunal may at any time entrust additional functions to the Registrar.

3. In the discharge of his functions the Registrar shall be responsible to the Tribunal.

Article 37

1. The Deputy Registrar shall assist the Registrar, act as Registrar in the latter's absence and, in the event of the office becoming vacant, exercise the functions of Registrar until the office has been filled.

2. If the Registrar, the Deputy Registrar and the Assistant Registrar are unable to carry out the duties of Registrar, the President of the Tribunal shall appoint an official of the Registry to discharge those duties for such time as may be necessary. If the three offices are vacant at the same time,

the President, after consulting the Members, shall appoint an official of the Registry to discharge the duties of Registrar pending an election to that office.

Article 38

1. The Registry consists of the Registrar, the Deputy Registrar, the Assistant Registrar and such other staff as required for the efficient discharge of its functions.

2. The Tribunal shall determine the organization of the Registry and shall for this purpose request the Registrar to make proposals.

3. Instructions for the Registry shall be drawn up by the Registrar and approved by the Tribunal.

4. The staff of the Registry shall be subject to Staff Regulations drawn up by the Registrar and approved by the Tribunal.

Article 39

1. The Registrar may resign from office with two months' notice tendered in writing to the President of the Tribunal. The Deputy Registrar and the Assistant Registrar may resign from office with one month's notice tendered in writing to the President of the Tribunal through the Registrar.

2. The Registrar may be removed from office only if, in the opinion of two thirds of the Members, he has either committed a serious breach of his duties or become permanently incapacitated from exercising his functions. Before a decision to remove him is taken under this paragraph, he shall be informed by the President of the Tribunal of the action contemplated, in a written statement which shall include the grounds therefor and any relevant evidence. When the action contemplated concerns permanent incapacity, relevant medical information shall be included. The Registrar shall subsequently, at a private meeting of the Tribunal, be afforded an opportunity of making a statement, of furnishing any information or explanations he wishes to give and of supplying answers, orally or in writing, to any questions put to him. He may be assisted or represented at such meeting by counsel or any other person of his choice.

3. The Deputy Registrar and the Assistant Registrar may be removed from office only on the same grounds and by the same procedure as specified in paragraph 2.

Section E. Internal functioning of the Tribunal

Article 40

The internal judicial practice of the Tribunal shall, subject to the Convention, the Statute and these Rules, be governed by any resolutions on the subject adopted by the Tribunal.

Article 41

1. The quorum specified by article 13, paragraph 1, of the Statute applies to all meetings of the Tribunal. The quorum specified in article 35, paragraph 7, of the Statute applies to all meetings of the Seabed Disputes Chamber. The quorum specified for a special chamber applies to all meetings of that chamber.

2. Members shall hold themselves permanently available to exercise their functions and shall attend all such meetings, unless they are absent on leave as provided for in paragraph 4 or prevented from attending by illness or for other serious reasons duly explained to the President of the Tribunal, who shall inform the Tribunal.

3. Judges *ad hoc* are likewise bound to hold themselves at the disposal of the Tribunal and to attend all meetings held in the case in which they are participating unless they are prevented from attending by illness or for other serious reasons duly explained to the President of the Tribunal, who shall inform the Tribunal. They shall not be taken into account for the calculation of the quorum.

4. The Tribunal shall fix the dates and duration of the judicial vacations and the periods and conditions of leave to be accorded to individual Members, having regard in both cases to the state of the List of cases and to the requirements of its current work.

5. Subject to the same considerations, the Tribunal shall observe the public holidays customary at the place where the Tribunal is sitting.

6. In case of urgency the President of the Tribunal may convene the Tribunal at any time.

Article 42

1. The deliberations of the Tribunal shall take place in private and remain secret. The Tribunal may, however, at any time decide in respect of its deliberations on other than judicial matters to publish or allow publication of any part of them.

2. Only judges and any experts appointed in accordance with article 289 of the Convention take part in the Tribunal's judicial deliberations. The Registrar, or his Deputy, and other members of the staff of the Registry as may be required shall be present. No other person shall be present except by permission of the Tribunal.

3. The records of the Tribunal's judicial deliberations shall contain only the title or nature of the subjects or matters discussed and the results of any vote taken. They shall not contain any details of the discussions nor the views expressed, provided however that any judge is entitled to require that a statement made by him be inserted in the records.

Section F. Official languages

Article 43

The official languages of the Tribunal are English and French.

PART III

PROCEDURE

Section A. General provisions

Article 44

1. The proceedings consist of two parts: written and oral.

2. The written proceedings shall consist of the communication to the Tribunal and to the parties of memorials, counter-memorials and, if the Tribunal so authorizes, replies and rejoinders, as well as all documents in support.

3. The oral proceedings shall consist of the hearing by the Tribunal of agents, counsel, advocates, witnesses and experts.

Article 45

In every case submitted to the Tribunal, the President shall ascertain the views of the parties with regard to questions of procedure. For this purpose, he may summon the agents of the parties to meet him as soon as possible after their appointment and whenever necessary thereafter, or use other appropriate means of communication.

Article 46

Time-limits for the completion of steps in the proceedings may be fixed by assigning a specified period but shall always indicate definite dates. Such time-limits shall be as short as the character of the case permits.

Article 47

The Tribunal may at any time direct that the proceedings in two or more cases be joined. It may also direct that the written or oral proceedings, including the calling of witnesses, be in common; or the Tribunal may, without effecting any formal joinder, direct common action in any of these respects.

Article 48

The parties may jointly propose particular modifications or additions to the Rules contained in this Part, which may be applied by the Tribunal or by a chamber if the Tribunal or the chamber considers them appropriate in the circumstances of the case.

Article 49

The proceedings before the Tribunal shall be conducted without unnecessary delay or expense.

Article 50

The Tribunal may issue guidelines consistent with these Rules concerning any aspect of its proceedings, including the length, format and presentation of written and oral pleadings and the use of electronic means of communication.

Article 51

All communications to the Tribunal under these Rules shall be addressed to the Registrar unless otherwise stated. Any request made by a party shall likewise be addressed to the Registrar unless made in open court in the course of the oral proceedings.

Article 52

1. All communications to the parties shall be sent to their agents.

2. The communications to a party before it has appointed an agent and to an entity other than a party shall be sent as follows:

(a) in the case of a State, the Tribunal shall direct all communications to its Government;

(b) in the case of the International Seabed Authority or the Enterprise, any international organization and any other intergovernmental organization, the Tribunal shall direct all communications to the competent body or executive head of such organization at its headquarters location;

(c) in the case of state enterprises or natural or juridical persons referred to in article 153, paragraph 2 (b), of the Convention, the Tribunal shall direct all communications through the Government of the sponsoring or certifying State, as the case may be;

(d) in the case of a group of States, state enterprises or natural or juridical persons referred to in article 153, paragraph 2 (b), of the Convention, the Tribunal shall direct all communications to each member of the group according to subparagraphs (a) and (c) above;

(e) in the case of other natural or juridical persons, the Tribunal shall direct all communications through the Government of the State in whose territory the communication has to be received.

3. The same provisions apply whenever steps are to be taken to procure evidence on the spot.

Article 53

1. The parties shall be represented by agents.

2. The parties may have the assistance of counsel or advocates before the Tribunal.

Section B. Proceedings before the Tribunal

Subsection 1. Institution of proceedings

Article 54

1. When proceedings before the Tribunal are instituted by means of an application, the application shall indicate the party making it, the party against which the claim is brought and the subject of the dispute.

2. The application shall specify as far as possible the legal grounds upon which the jurisdiction of the Tribunal is said to be based; it shall also specify the precise nature of the claim, together with a succinct statement of the facts and grounds on which the claim is based.

3. The original of the application shall be signed by the agent of the party submitting it or by the diplomatic representative of that party in the country in which the Tribunal has its seat or by some other duly authorized person. If the application bears the signature of someone other than such diplomatic representative, the signature must be authenticated by the latter or by the competent governmental authority.

4. The Registrar shall forthwith transmit to the respondent a certified copy of the application.

5. When the applicant proposes to found the jurisdiction of the Tribunal upon a consent thereto yet to be given or manifested by the party against which the application is made, the application shall be transmitted to that party. It shall not however be entered in the List of cases, nor any action be taken in the proceedings, unless and until the party against which such application is made consents to the jurisdiction of the Tribunal for the purposes of the case.

Article 55

1. When proceedings are brought before the Tribunal by the notification of a special agreement, the notification may be effected by the parties jointly or by any one or more of them. If the notification is not a joint one, a certified copy of it shall forthwith be communicated by the Registrar to any other party.

2. In each case the notification shall be accompanied by an original or certified copy of the special agreement. The notification shall also, insofar as this is not already apparent from the agreement, indicate the precise subject of the dispute and identify the parties to it.

Article 56

1. Except in the circumstances contemplated by article 54, paragraph 5, all steps on behalf of the parties after proceedings have been instituted shall be taken by agents. Agents shall have an address for service at the seat of the Tribunal or in the capital of the country where the seat is located, to which all communications concerning the case are to be sent.

2. When proceedings are instituted by means of an application, the name of the agent for the applicant shall be stated. The respondent, upon receipt of the certified copy of the application, or as soon as possible thereafter, shall inform the Tribunal of the name of its agent.

3. When proceedings are brought by notification of a special agreement, the party or parties making the notification shall state the name of its agent or the names of their agents, as the case may be. Any other party to the special agreement, upon receiving from the Registrar a certified copy of such notification, or as soon as possible thereafter, shall inform the Tribunal of the name of its agent if it has not already done so.

Article 57

1. Whenever proceedings are instituted on the basis of an agreement other than the Convention, the application or the notification shall be accompanied by a certified copy of the agreement in question.

2. In a dispute to which an international organization is a party, the Tribunal may, at the request of any other party or *proprio motu*, request the international organization to provide, within a reasonable time, information as to which, as between the organization and its member States, has competence in respect of any specific question which has arisen. If the Tribunal considers it necessary, it may suspend the proceedings until it receives such information.

Article 58

In the event of a dispute as to whether the Tribunal has jurisdiction, the matter shall be decided by the Tribunal.

Subsection 2. The written proceedings

Article 59

1. In the light of the views of the parties ascertained by the President of the Tribunal, the Tribunal shall make the necessary orders to determine, *inter alia*, the number and the order of filing of the pleadings and the time-limits

within which they must be filed. The time-limits for each pleading shall not exceed six months.

2. The Tribunal may at the request of a party extend any time-limit or decide that any step taken after the expiration of the time-limit fixed therefor shall be considered as valid. It may not do so, however, unless it is satisfied that there is adequate justification for the request. In either case the other party shall be given an opportunity to state its views within a time-limit to be fixed by the Tribunal.

3. If the Tribunal is not sitting, its powers under this article may be exercised by the President of the Tribunal, but without prejudice to any subsequent decision of the Tribunal.

Article 60

1. The pleadings in a case begun by means of an application shall consist, in the following order, of: a memorial by the applicant and a counter-memorial by the respondent.

2. The Tribunal may authorize or direct that there shall be a reply by the applicant and a rejoinder by the respondent if the parties are so agreed or if the Tribunal decides, at the request of a party or *proprio motu*, that these pleadings are necessary.

Article 61

1. In a case begun by the notification of a special agreement, the number and order of the pleadings shall be governed by the provisions of the agreement, unless the Tribunal, after ascertaining the views of the parties, decides otherwise.

2. If the special agreement contains no such provision, and if the parties have not subsequently agreed on the number and order of pleadings, they shall each file a memorial and counter-memorial, within the same time-limits.

3. The Tribunal shall not authorize the presentation of replies and rejoinders unless it finds them to be necessary.

Article 62

1. A memorial shall contain: a statement of the relevant facts, a statement of law and the submissions.

2. A counter-memorial shall contain: an admission or denial of the facts stated in the memorial; any additional facts, if necessary; observations concerning the statement of law in the memorial; a statement of law in answer thereto; and the submissions.

3. A reply and rejoinder shall not merely repeat the parties' contentions, but shall be directed to bringing out the issues that still divide them.

4. Every pleading shall set out the party's submissions at the relevant stage of the case, distinctly from the arguments presented, or shall confirm the submissions previously made.

Article 63

1. There shall be annexed to the original of every pleading certified copies of any relevant documents adduced in support of the contentions contained in the pleading. Parties need not annex or certify copies of documents which have been published and are readily available to the Tribunal and the other party.

2. If only parts of a document are relevant, only such extracts as are necessary for the purpose of the pleading in question or for identifying the document need be annexed. A copy of the whole document shall be filed in the Registry, unless it has been published and is readily available to the Tribunal and the other party.

3. A list of all documents annexed to a pleading shall be furnished at the time the pleading is filed.

Article 64

1. The parties shall submit any pleading or any part of a pleading in one or both of the official languages.

2. A party may use a language other than one of the official languages for its pleadings. A translation into one of the official languages, certified as accurate by the party submitting it, shall be submitted together with the original of each pleading.

3. When a document annexed to a pleading is not in one of the official languages, it shall be accompanied by a translation into one of these languages certified as accurate by the party submitting it. The translation may be confined to part of an annex, or to extracts therefrom, but in this case it must be accompanied by an explanatory note indicating what passages are translated. The Tribunal may, however, require a more extensive or a complete translation to be furnished.

4. When a language other than one of the official languages is chosen by the parties and that language is an official language of the United Nations, the decision of the Tribunal shall, at the request of any party, be translated into that official language of the United Nations at no cost for the parties.

Article 65

1. The original of every pleading shall be signed by the agent and filed in the Registry. It shall be accompanied by a certified copy of the pleading, any document annexed thereto and any translations, for communication to the other party. It shall also be accompanied by the number of additional copies

required by the Registry; further copies may be required should the need arise later.

2. All pleadings shall be dated. When a pleading has to be filed by a certain date, it is the date of receipt of the pleading in the Registry which will be regarded by the Tribunal as the material date.

3. If the Registrar arranges for the reproduction of a pleading at the request of a party, the text must be supplied in sufficient time to enable the pleading to be filed in the Registry before expiration of any time-limit which may apply to it. The reproduction is done under the responsibility of the party in question.

4. The correction of a slip or error in any document which has been filed may be made at any time with the consent of the other party or by leave of the President of the Tribunal. Any correction so effected shall be notified to the other party in the same manner as the pleading to which it relates.

Article 66

A certified copy of every pleading and any document annexed thereto produced by one party shall be communicated by the Registrar to the other party upon receipt.

Article 67

1. Copies of the pleadings and documents annexed thereto shall, as soon as possible after their filing, be made available by the Tribunal to a State or other entity entitled to appear before the Tribunal and which has asked to be furnished with such copies. However, if the party submitting the memorial so requests, the Tribunal shall make the memorial available at the same time as the counter-memorial.

2. Copies of the pleadings and documents annexed thereto shall be made accessible to the public on the opening of the oral proceedings, or earlier if the Tribunal or the President if the Tribunal is not sitting so decides after ascertaining the views of the parties.

3. However, the Tribunal, or the President if the Tribunal is not sitting, may, at the request of a party, and after ascertaining the views of the other party, decide otherwise than as set out in this article.

Subsection 3. Initial deliberations

Article 68

After the closure of the written proceedings and prior to the opening of the oral proceedings, the Tribunal shall meet in private to enable judges to exchange views concerning the written pleadings and the conduct of the case.

Subsection 4. Oral proceedings

Article 69

1. Upon the closure of the written proceedings, the date for the opening of the oral proceedings shall be fixed by the Tribunal. Such date shall fall within a period of six months from the closure of the written proceedings unless the Tribunal is satisfied that there is adequate justification for deciding otherwise. The Tribunal may also decide, when necessary, that the opening or the continuance of the oral proceedings be postponed.

2. When fixing the date for the opening of the oral proceedings or postponing the opening or continuance of such proceedings, the Tribunal shall have regard to:

(a) the need to hold the hearing without unnecessary delay;

(b) the priority required by articles 90 and 112;

(c) any special circumstances, including the urgency of the case or other cases on the List of cases; and

(d) the views expressed by the parties.

3. When the Tribunal is not sitting, its powers under this article shall be exercised by the President.

Article 70

The Tribunal may, if it considers it desirable, decide pursuant to article 1, paragraph 3, of the Statute that all or part of the further proceedings in a case shall be held at a place other than the seat of the Tribunal. Before so deciding, it shall ascertain the views of the parties.

Article 71

1. After the closure of the written proceedings, no further documents may be submitted to the Tribunal by either party except with the consent of the other party or as provided in paragraph 2. The other party shall be held to have given its consent if it does not lodge an objection to the production of the document within 15 days of receiving it.

2. In the event of objection, the Tribunal, after hearing the parties, may authorize production of the document if it considers production necessary.

3. The party desiring to produce a new document shall file the original or a certified copy thereof, together with the number of copies required by the Registry, which shall be responsible for communicating it to the other party and shall inform the Tribunal.

4. If a new document is produced under paragraph 1 or 2, the other party shall have an opportunity of commenting upon it and of submitting documents in support of its comments.

5. No reference may be made during the oral proceedings to the contents of any document which has not been produced as part of the written proceedings or in accordance with this article, unless the document is part of a publication readily available to the Tribunal and the other party.

6. The application of this article shall not in itself constitute a ground for delaying the opening or the course of the oral proceedings.

Article 72

Without prejudice to the provisions of these Rules concerning the production of documents, each party shall communicate to the Registrar, in sufficient time before the opening of the oral proceedings, information regarding any evidence which it intends to produce or which it intends to request the Tribunal to obtain. This communication shall contain a list of the surnames, first names, nationalities, descriptions and places of residence of the witnesses and experts whom the party intends to call, with indications of the point or points to which their evidence will be directed. A certified copy of the communication shall also be furnished for transmission to the other party.

Article 73

1. The Tribunal shall determine whether the parties should present their arguments before or after the production of the evidence; the parties shall, however, retain the right to comment on the evidence given.

2. The Tribunal, after ascertaining the views of the parties, shall determine the order in which the parties will be heard, the method of handling the evidence and examining any witnesses and experts and the number of counsel and advocates to be heard on behalf of each party.

Article 74

The hearing shall, in accordance with article 26, paragraph 2, of the Statute, be public, unless the Tribunal decides otherwise or unless the parties request that the public be not admitted. Such a decision or request may concern either the whole or part of the hearing, and may be made at any time.

Article 75

1. The oral statements made on behalf of each party shall be as succinct as possible within the limits of what is requisite for the adequate presentation of that party's contentions at the hearing. Accordingly, they shall be directed to the issues that still divide the parties, and shall not go over the whole ground covered by the pleadings or merely repeat the facts and arguments these contain.

2. At the conclusion of the last statement made by a party at the hearing, its agent, without recapitulation of the arguments, shall read that party's final

submissions. A copy of the written text of these, signed by the agent, shall be communicated to the Tribunal and transmitted to the other party.

Article 76

1. The Tribunal may at any time prior to or during the hearing indicate any points or issues which it would like the parties specially to address, or on which it considers that there has been sufficient argument.

2. The Tribunal may, during the hearing, put questions to the agents, counsel and advocates, and may ask them for explanations.

3. Each judge has a similar right to put questions, but before exercising it he should make his intention known to the President of the Tribunal.

4. The agents, counsel and advocates may answer either immediately or within a time-limit fixed by the President of the Tribunal.

Article 77

1. The Tribunal may at any time call upon the parties to produce such evidence or to give such explanations as the Tribunal may consider to be necessary for the elucidation of any aspect of the matters in issue, or may itself seek other information for this purpose.

2. The Tribunal may, if necessary, arrange for the attendance of a witness or expert to give evidence in the proceedings.

Article 78

1. The parties may call any witnesses or experts appearing on the list communicated to the Tribunal pursuant to article 72. If at any time during the hearing a party wishes to call a witness or expert whose name was not included in that list, it shall make a request therefor to the Tribunal and inform the other party, and shall supply the information required by article 72. The witness or expert may be called either if the other party raises no objection or, in the event of objection, if the Tribunal so authorizes after hearing the other party.

2. The Tribunal may, at the request of a party or *proprio motu*, decide that a witness or expert be examined otherwise than before the Tribunal itself. The President of the Tribunal shall take the necessary steps to implement such a decision.

Article 79

Unless on account of special circumstances the Tribunal decides on a different form of words,

(a) every witness shall make the following solemn declaration before giving any evidence:

> "I solemnly declare upon my honour and conscience that I will speak the truth, the whole truth and nothing but the truth";

(b) every expert shall make the following solemn declaration before making any statement:

> "I solemnly declare upon my honour and conscience that I will speak the truth, the whole truth and nothing but the truth, and that my statement will be in accordance with my sincere belief".

Article 80

Witnesses and experts shall, under the control of the President of the Tribunal, be examined by the agents, counsel or advocates of the parties starting with the party calling the witness or expert. Questions may be put to them by the President of the Tribunal and by the judges. Before testifying, witnesses and experts other than those appointed under article 289 of the Convention shall remain out of court.

Article 81

The Tribunal may at any time decide, at the request of a party or *proprio motu*, to exercise its functions with regard to the obtaining of evidence at a place or locality to which the case relates, subject to such conditions as the Tribunal may decide upon after ascertaining the views of the parties. The necessary arrangements shall be made in accordance with article 52.

Article 82

1. If the Tribunal considers it necessary to arrange for an inquiry or an expert opinion, it shall, after hearing the parties, issue an order to this effect, defining the subject of the inquiry or expert opinion, stating the number and mode of appointment of the persons to hold the inquiry or of the experts and laying down the procedure to be followed. Where appropriate, the Tribunal shall require persons appointed to carry out an inquiry, or to give an expert opinion, to make a solemn declaration.

2. Every report or record of an inquiry and every expert opinion shall be communicated to the parties, which shall be given the opportunity of commenting upon it.

Article 83

Witnesses and experts who appear at the instance of the Tribunal under article 77, paragraph 2, and persons appointed by the Tribunal under article 82, paragraph 1, to carry out an inquiry or to give an expert opinion, shall, where appropriate, be paid out of the funds of the Tribunal.

Article 84

1. The Tribunal may, at any time prior to the closure of the oral proceedings, at the request of a party or *proprio motu*, request an appropriate intergovernmental organization to furnish information relevant to a case before it. The Tribunal, after consulting the chief administrative officer of the organization concerned, shall decide whether such information shall be presented to it orally or in writing and fix the time-limits for its presentation.

2. When such an intergovernmental organization sees fit to furnish, on its own initiative, information relevant to a case before the Tribunal, it shall do so in the form of a memorial to be filed in the Registry before the closure of the written proceedings. The Tribunal may require such information to be supplemented, either orally or in writing, in the form of answers to any questions which it may see fit to formulate, and also authorize the parties to comment, either orally or in writing, on the information thus furnished.

3. Whenever the construction of the constituent instrument of such an intergovernmental organization or of an international convention adopted thereunder is in question in a case before the Tribunal, the Registrar shall, on the instructions of the Tribunal, or of the President if the Tribunal is not sitting, so notify the intergovernmental organization concerned and shall communicate to it copies of all the written proceedings. The Tribunal, or the President if the Tribunal is not sitting, may, as from the date on which the Registrar has communicated copies of the written proceedings and after consulting the chief administrative officer of the intergovernmental organization concerned, fix a time-limit within which the organization may submit to the Tribunal its observations in writing. These observations shall be communicated to the parties and may be discussed by them and by the representative of the said organization during the oral proceedings.

4. In the foregoing paragraphs, "intergovernmental organization" means an intergovernmental organization other than any organization which is a party or intervenes in the case concerned.

Article 85

1. Unless the Tribunal decides otherwise, all speeches and statements made and evidence given at the hearing in one of the official languages of the Tribunal shall be interpreted into the other official language. If they are made or given in any other language, they shall be interpreted into the two official languages of the Tribunal.

2. Whenever a language other than an official language is used, the necessary arrangements for interpretation into one of the official languages shall be made by the party concerned. The Registrar shall make arrangements for the verification of the interpretation provided by a party at the expense of that party. In the case of witnesses or experts who appear at the instance of the Tribunal, arrangements for interpretation shall be made by the Registrar.

3. A party on behalf of which speeches or statements are to be made, or evidence is to be given, in a language which is not one of the official languages of the Tribunal shall so notify the Registrar in sufficient time for the necessary arrangements to be made, including verification.

4. Before entering upon their duties in the case, interpreters provided by a party shall make the following solemn declaration:

> "I solemnly declare upon my honour and conscience that my interpretation will be faithful and complete".

Article 86

1. Minutes shall be made of each hearing. For this purpose, a verbatim record shall be made by the Registrar of every hearing, in the official language or languages of the Tribunal used during the hearing. When another language is used, the verbatim record shall be prepared in one of the official languages of the Tribunal.

2. In order to prepare such a verbatim record, the party on behalf of which speeches or statements are made in a language which is not one of the official languages shall supply to the Registry in advance a text thereof in one of the official languages.

3. The transcript of the verbatim record shall be preceded by the names of the judges present, and those of the agents, counsel and advocates of the parties.

4. Copies of the transcript shall be circulated to the judges sitting in the case and to the parties. The latter may, under the supervision of the Tribunal, correct the transcripts of speeches and statements made on their behalf, but in no case may such corrections affect the meaning and scope thereof. The judges may likewise make corrections in the transcript of anything they have said.

5. Witnesses and experts shall be shown that part of the transcript which relates to the evidence given or the statements made by them, and may correct it in like manner as the parties.

6. One certified copy of the corrected transcript, signed by the President of the Tribunal and the Registrar, shall constitute the authentic minutes of the hearing. The minutes of public hearings shall be printed and published by the Tribunal.

Article 87

Any written reply by a party to a question put under article 76 or any evidence or explanation supplied by a party under article 77 received by the

Tribunal after the closure of the oral proceedings shall be communicated to the other party, which shall be given the opportunity of commenting upon it. The oral proceedings may be reopened for that purpose, if necessary.

Article 88

1. When, subject to the control of the Tribunal, the agents, counsel and advocates have completed their presentation of the case, the President of the Tribunal shall declare the oral proceedings closed. The agents shall remain at the disposal of the Tribunal.

2. The Tribunal shall withdraw to consider the judgment.

Section C. Incidental proceedings

Subsection 1. Provisional measures

Article 89

1. A party may submit a request for the prescription of provisional measures under article 290, paragraph 1, of the Convention at any time during the course of the proceedings in a dispute submitted to the Tribunal.

2. Pending the constitution of an arbitral tribunal to which a dispute is being submitted, a party may submit a request for the prescription of provisional measures under article 290, paragraph 5, of the Convention:

(a) at any time if the parties have so agreed;

(b) at any time after two weeks from the notification to the other party of a request for provisional measures if the parties have not agreed that such measures may be prescribed by another court or tribunal.

3. The request shall be in writing and specify the measures requested, the reasons therefor and the possible consequences, if it is not granted, for the preservation of the respective rights of the parties or for the prevention of serious harm to the marine environment.

4. A request for the prescription of provisional measures under article 290, paragraph 5, of the Convention shall also indicate the legal grounds upon which the arbitral tribunal which is to be constituted would have jurisdiction and the urgency of the situation. A certified copy of the notification or of any other document instituting the proceedings before the arbitral tribunal shall be annexed to the request.

5. When a request for provisional measures has been made, the Tribunal may prescribe measures different in whole or in part from those requested and indicate the parties which are to take or to comply with each measure.

Article 90

1. Subject to article 112, paragraph 1, a request for the prescription of provisional measures has priority over all other proceedings before the Tribunal.

2. The Tribunal, or the President if the Tribunal is not sitting, shall fix the earliest possible date for a hearing.

3. The Tribunal shall take into account any observations that may be presented to it by a party before the closure of the hearing.

4. Pending the meeting of the Tribunal, the President of the Tribunal may call upon the parties to act in such a way as will enable any order the Tribunal may make on the request for provisional measures to have its appropriate effects.

Article 91

1. If the President of the Tribunal ascertains that at the date fixed for the hearing referred to in article 90, paragraph 2, a sufficient number of Members will not be available to constitute a quorum, the Chamber of Summary Procedure shall be convened to carry out the functions of the Tribunal with respect to the prescription of provisional measures.

2. The Tribunal shall review or revise provisional measures prescribed by the Chamber of Summary Procedure at the written request of a party within 15 days of the prescription of the measures. The Tribunal may also at any time decide *proprio motu* to review or revise the measures.

Article 92

The rejection of a request for the prescription of provisional measures shall not prevent the party which made it from making a fresh request in the same case based on new facts.

Article 93

A party may request the modification or revocation of provisional measures. The request shall be submitted in writing and shall specify the change in, or disappearance of, the circumstances considered to be relevant. Before taking any decision on the request, the Tribunal shall afford the parties an opportunity of presenting their observations on the subject.

Article 94

Any provisional measures prescribed by the Tribunal or any modification or revocation thereof shall forthwith be notified to the parties and to such other States Parties as the Tribunal considers appropriate in each case.

Article 95

1. Each party shall inform the Tribunal as soon as possible as to its compliance with any provisional measures the Tribunal has prescribed. In particular, each party shall submit an initial report upon the steps it has taken or proposes to take in order to ensure prompt compliance with the measures prescribed.

2. The Tribunal may request further information from the parties on any matter connected with the implementation of any provisional measures it has prescribed.

Subsection 2. Preliminary proceedings

Article 96

1. When an application is made in respect of a dispute referred to in article 297 of the Convention, the Tribunal shall determine at the request of the respondent or may determine *proprio motu*, in accordance with article 294 of the Convention, whether the claim constitutes an abuse of legal process or whether *prima facie* it is well founded.

2. The Registrar, when transmitting an application to the respondent under article 54, paragraph 4, shall notify the respondent of the time-limit fixed by the President of the Tribunal for requesting a determination under article 294 of the Convention.

3. The Tribunal may also decide, within two months from the date of an application, to exercise *proprio motu* its power under article 294, paragraph 1, of the Convention.

4. The request by the respondent for a determination under article 294 of the Convention shall be in writing and shall indicate the grounds for a determination by the Tribunal that:

(a) the application is made in respect of a dispute referred to in article 297 of the Convention; and

(b) the claim constitutes an abuse of legal process or is *prima facie* unfounded.

5. Upon receipt of such a request or *proprio motu*, the Tribunal, or the President if the Tribunal is not sitting, shall fix a time-limit not exceeding 60 days within which the parties may present their written observations and submissions. The proceedings on the merits shall be suspended.

6. Unless the Tribunal decides otherwise, the further proceedings shall be oral.

7. The written observations and submissions referred to in paragraph 5, and the statements and evidence presented at the hearings contemplated by

paragraph 6, shall be confined to those matters which are relevant to the determination of whether the claim constitutes an abuse of legal process or is *prima facie* unfounded, and of whether the application is made in respect of a dispute referred to in article 297 of the Convention. The Tribunal may, however, request the parties to argue all questions of law and fact, and to adduce all evidence, bearing on the issue.

8. The Tribunal shall make its determination in the form of a judgment.

Subsection 3. Preliminary objections

Article 97

1. Any objection to the jurisdiction of the Tribunal or to the admissibility of the application, or other objection the decision upon which is requested before any further proceedings on the merits, shall be made in writing within 90 days from the institution of proceedings.

2. The preliminary objection shall set out the facts and the law on which the objection is based, as well as the submissions.

3. Upon receipt by the Registry of a preliminary objection, the proceedings on the merits shall be suspended and the Tribunal, or the President if the Tribunal is not sitting, shall fix a time-limit not exceeding 60 days within which the other party may present its written observations and submissions. It shall fix a further time-limit not exceeding 60 days from the receipt of such observations and submissions within which the objecting party may present its written observations and submissions in reply. Copies of documents in support shall be annexed to such statements and evidence which it is proposed to produce shall be mentioned.

4. Unless the Tribunal decides otherwise, the further proceedings shall be oral.

5. The written observations and submissions referred to in paragraph 3, and the statements and evidence presented at the hearings contemplated by paragraph 4, shall be confined to those matters which are relevant to the objection. Whenever necessary, however, the Tribunal may request the parties to argue all questions of law and fact and to adduce all evidence bearing on the issue.

6. The Tribunal shall give its decision in the form of a judgment, by which it shall uphold the objection or reject it or declare that the objection does not possess, in the circumstances of the case, an exclusively preliminary character. If the Tribunal rejects the objection or declares that it does not possess an exclusively preliminary character, it shall fix time-limits for the further proceedings.

7. The Tribunal shall give effect to any agreement between the parties that an objection submitted under paragraph 1 be heard and determined within the framework of the merits.

Subsection 4. Counter-claims

Article 98

1. A party may present a counter-claim provided that it is directly connected with the subject-matter of the claim of the other party and that it comes within the jurisdiction of the Tribunal.

2. A counter-claim shall be made in the counter-memorial of the party presenting it and shall appear as part of the submissions of that party.

3. In the event of doubt as to the connection between the question presented by way of counter-claim and the subject-matter of the claim of the other party the Tribunal shall, after hearing the parties, decide whether or not the question thus presented shall be joined to the original proceedings.

Subsection 5. Intervention

Article 99

1. An application for permission to intervene under the terms of article 31 of the Statute shall be filed not later than 30 days after the counter-memorial becomes available under article 67, paragraph 1, of these Rules. In exceptional circumstances, an application submitted at a later stage may however be admitted.

2. The application shall be signed in the manner provided for in article 54, paragraph 3, and state the name and address of an agent. It shall specify the case to which it relates and shall set out:

(a) the interest of a legal nature which the State Party applying to intervene considers may be affected by the decision in that case;

(b) the precise object of the intervention.

3. Permission to intervene under the terms of article 31 of the Statute may be granted irrespective of the choice made by the applicant under article 287 of the Convention.

4. The application shall contain a list of the documents in support, copies of which documents shall be annexed.

Article 100

1. A State Party or an entity other than a State Party referred to in article 32, paragraphs 1 and 2, of the Statute which desires to avail itself of the right of intervention conferred upon it by article 32, paragraph 3, of the Statute shall file a declaration to that effect. The declaration shall be filed not later than 30 days after the counter-memorial becomes available under article 67, paragraph 1, of these Rules. In exceptional circumstances, a declaration submitted at a later stage may, however, be admitted.

2. The declaration shall be signed in the manner provided for in article 54, paragraph 3, and state the name and address of an agent. It shall specify the case to which it relates and shall:

(a) identify the particular provisions of the Convention or of the international agreement the interpretation or application of which the declaring party considers to be in question;

(b) set out the interpretation or application of those provisions for which it contends;

(c) list the documents in support, copies of which documents shall be annexed.

Article 101

1. Certified copies of the application for permission to intervene under article 31 of the Statute, or of the declaration of intervention under article 32 of the Statute, shall be communicated forthwith to the parties to the case, which shall be invited to furnish their written observations within a time-limit to be fixed by the Tribunal or by the President if the Tribunal is not sitting.

2. The Registrar shall also transmit copies to: (a) States Parties; (b) any other parties which have to be notified under article 32, paragraph 2, of the Statute; (c) the Secretary-General of the United Nations; (d) the Secretary-General of the Authority when the proceedings are before the Seabed Disputes Chamber.

Article 102

1. The Tribunal shall decide whether an application for permission to intervene under article 31 of the Statute should be granted or whether an intervention under article 32 of the Statute is admissible as a matter of priority unless in view of the circumstances of the case the Tribunal determines otherwise.

2. If, within the time-limit fixed under article 101, an objection is filed to an application for permission to intervene, or to the admissibility of a declaration of intervention, the Tribunal shall hear the State Party or entity other than a State Party seeking to intervene and the parties before deciding.

Article 103

1. If an application for permission to intervene under article 31 of the Statute is granted, the intervening State Party shall be supplied with copies of the pleadings and documents annexed and shall be entitled to submit a written statement within a time-limit to be fixed by the Tribunal. A further time-limit shall be fixed within which the parties may, if they so

desire, furnish their written observations on that statement prior to the oral proceedings. If the Tribunal is not sitting, these time-limits shall be fixed by the President.

2. The time-limits fixed according to paragraph 1 shall, so far as possible, coincide with those already fixed for the pleadings in the case.

3. The intervening State Party shall be entitled, in the course of the oral proceedings, to submit its observations with respect to the subject-matter of the intervention.

4. The intervening State Party shall not be entitled to choose a judge *ad hoc* or to object to an agreement to discontinue the proceedings under article 105, paragraph 1.

Article 104

1. If an intervention under article 32 of the Statute is admitted, the intervenor shall be supplied with copies of the pleadings and documents annexed and shall be entitled, within a time-limit to be fixed by the Tribunal, or the President if the Tribunal is not sitting, to submit its written observations on the subject-matter of the intervention.

2. These observations shall be communicated to the parties and to any other State Party or entity other than a State Party admitted to intervene. The intervenor shall be entitled, in the course of the oral proceedings, to submit its observations with respect to the subject-matter of the intervention.

3. The intervenor shall not be entitled to choose a judge *ad hoc* or to object to an agreement to discontinue the proceedings under article 105, paragraph 1.

Subsection 6. Discontinuance

Article 105

1. If at any time before the final judgment on the merits has been delivered the parties, either jointly or separately, notify the Tribunal in writing that they have agreed to discontinue the proceedings, the Tribunal shall make an order recording the discontinuance and directing the Registrar to remove the case from the List of cases.

2. If the parties have agreed to discontinue the proceedings in consequence of having reached a settlement of the dispute and if they so desire, the Tribunal shall record this fact in the order for the removal of the case from the List, or indicate in, or annex to, the order the terms of the settlement.

3. If the Tribunal is not sitting, any order under this article may be made by the President.

Article 106

1. If, in the course of proceedings instituted by means of an application, the applicant informs the Tribunal in writing that it is not going on with the proceedings, and if, at the date on which this communication is received by the Registry, the respondent has not yet taken any step in the proceedings, the Tribunal shall make an order officially recording the discontinuance of the proceedings and directing the removal of the case from the List of cases. A copy of this order shall be sent by the Registrar to the respondent.

2. If, at the time when the notice of discontinuance is received, the respondent has already taken some step in the proceedings, the Tribunal shall fix a time-limit within which the respondent may state whether it opposes the discontinuance of the proceedings. If no objection is made to the discontinuance before the expiration of the time-limit, acquiescence will be presumed and the Tribunal shall make an order recording the discontinuance of the proceedings and directing the Registrar to remove the case from the List of cases. If objection is made, the proceedings shall continue.

3. If the Tribunal is not sitting, its powers under this article may be exercised by the President.

Section D. Proceedings before special chambers

Article 107

Proceedings before the special chambers mentioned in article 15 of the Statute shall, subject to the provisions of the Convention, the Statute and these Rules relating specifically to the special chambers, be governed by the Rules applicable in contentious cases before the Tribunal.

Article 108

1. When it is desired that a case should be dealt with by one of the chambers which has been formed in accordance with article 15, paragraph 1 or 3, of the Statute, a request to this effect shall either be made in the document instituting the proceedings or accompany it. Effect shall be given to the request if the parties are in agreement.

2. Upon receipt by the Registry of this request, the President of the Tribunal shall communicate it to the members of the chamber concerned.

3. Effect shall be given to a request that a case be brought before a chamber to be formed in accordance with article 15, paragraph 2, of the Statute as soon as the chamber has been formed in accordance with article 30 of these Rules.

4. The President of the Tribunal shall convene the chamber at the earliest date compatible with the requirements of the procedure.

Article 109

1. Written proceedings in a case before a chamber shall consist of a single pleading by each party. The time-limits concerning the filing of written pleadings shall be fixed by the chamber, or its President if the chamber is not sitting.

2. The chamber may authorize or direct the filing of further pleadings if the parties are so agreed, or if the chamber decides, *proprio motu* or at the request of one of the parties, that such pleadings are necessary.

3. Oral proceedings shall take place unless the parties agree to dispense with them and the chamber consents. Even when no oral proceedings take place, the chamber may call upon the parties to supply information or furnish explanations orally.

Section E. Prompt release of vessels and crews

Article 110

1. An application for the release of a vessel or its crew from detention may be made in accordance with article 292 of the Convention by or on behalf of the flag State of the vessel.

2. A State Party may at any time notify the Tribunal of:

(a) the State authorities competent to authorize persons to make applications on its behalf under article 292 of the Convention;

(b) the name and address of any person who is authorized to make an application on its behalf;

(c) the office designated to receive notice of an application for the release of a vessel or its crew and the most expeditious means for delivery of documents to that office;

(d) any clarification, modification or withdrawal of such notification.

3. An application on behalf of a flag State shall be accompanied by an authorization under paragraph 2, if such authorization has not been previously submitted to the Tribunal, as well as by documents stating that the person submitting the application is the person named in the authorization. It shall also contain a certification that a copy of the application and all supporting documentation has been delivered to the flag State.

Article 111

1. The application shall contain a succinct statement of the facts and legal grounds upon which the application is based.

2. The statement of facts shall:

(a) specify the time and place of detention of the vessel and the present location of the vessel and crew, if known;

(b) contain relevant information concerning the vessel and crew including, where appropriate, the name, flag and the port or place of registration of the vessel and its tonnage, cargo capacity and data relevant to the determination of its value, the name and address of the vessel owner and operator and particulars regarding its crew;

(c) specify the amount, nature and terms of the bond or other financial security that may have been imposed by the detaining State and the extent to which such requirements have been complied with;

(d) contain any further information the applicant considers relevant to the determination of the amount of a reasonable bond or other financial security and to any other issue in the proceedings.

3. Supporting documents shall be annexed to the application.

4. A certified copy of the application shall forthwith be transmitted by the Registrar to the detaining State, which may submit a statement in response with supporting documents annexed, to be filed as soon as possible but not later than 96 hours before the hearing referred to in article 112, paragraph 3.

5. The Tribunal may, at any time, require further information to be provided in a supplementary statement.

6. The further proceedings relating to the application shall be oral.

Article 112

1. The Tribunal shall give priority to applications for release of vessels or crews over all other proceedings before the Tribunal. However, if the Tribunal is seized of an application for release of a vessel or its crew and of a request for the prescription of provisional measures, it shall take the necessary measures to ensure that both the application and the request are dealt with without delay.

2. If the applicant has so requested in the application, the application shall be dealt with by the Chamber of Summary Procedure, provided that, within five days of the receipt of notice of the application, the detaining State notifies the Tribunal that it concurs with the request.

3. The Tribunal, or the President if the Tribunal is not sitting, shall fix the earliest possible date, within a period of 15 days commencing with the first working day following the date on which the application is received, for a hearing at which each of the parties shall be accorded, unless otherwise decided, one day to present its evidence and arguments.

4. The decision of the Tribunal shall be in the form of a judgment. The judgment shall be adopted as soon as possible and shall be read at a public

sitting of the Tribunal to be held not later than 14 days after the closure of the hearing. The parties shall be notified of the date of the sitting.

Article 113

1. The Tribunal shall in its judgment determine in each case in accordance with article 292 of the Convention whether or not the allegation made by the applicant that the detaining State has not complied with a provision of the Convention for the prompt release of the vessel or the crew upon the posting of a reasonable bond or other financial security is well-founded.

2. If the Tribunal decides that the allegation is well-founded, it shall determine the amount, nature and form of the bond or financial security to be posted for the release of the vessel or the crew.

3. Unless the parties agree otherwise, the Tribunal shall determine whether the bond or other financial security shall be posted with the Registrar or with the detaining State.

Article 114

1. If the bond or other financial security has been posted with the Registrar, the detaining State shall be promptly notified thereof.

2. The Registrar shall endorse or transmit the bond or other financial security to the detaining State to the extent that it is required to satisfy the final judgment, award or decision of the competent authority of the detaining State.

3. The bond or other financial security shall be endorsed or transmitted, to the extent that it is not required to satisfy the final judgment, award or decision, to the party at whose request the bond or other financial security is issued.

Section F. Proceedings in contentious cases before the Seabed Disputes Chamber

Article 115

Proceedings in contentious cases before the Seabed Disputes Chamber and its *ad hoc* chambers shall, subject to the provisions of the Convention, the Statute and these Rules relating specifically to the Seabed Disputes Chamber and its *ad hoc* chambers, be governed by the Rules applicable in contentious cases before the Tribunal.

Article 116

Articles 117 to 121 apply to proceedings in all disputes before the Chamber with the exception of disputes exclusively between States Parties and between States Parties and the Authority.

Article 117

When proceedings before the Chamber are instituted by means of an application, the application shall indicate:

(a) the name of the applicant and, where the applicant is a natural or juridical person, the permanent residence or address or registered office address thereof;

(b) the name of the respondent and, where the respondent is a natural or juridical person, the permanent residence or address or registered office address thereof;

(c) the sponsoring State, in any case where the applicant is a natural or juridical person or a state enterprise;

(d) the sponsoring State of the respondent, in any case where the party against which the claim is brought is a natural or juridical person or state enterprise;

(e) an address for service at the seat of the Tribunal;

(f) the subject of the dispute and the legal grounds on which jurisdiction is said to be based; the precise nature of the claim, together with a statement of the facts and legal grounds on which the claim is based;

(g) the decision or measure sought by the applicant;

(h) the evidence on which the application is founded.

Article 118

1. The application shall be served on the respondent. The application shall also be served on the sponsoring State in any case where the applicant or respondent is a natural or juridical person or a state enterprise.

2. Within two months after service of the application, the respondent shall lodge a defence, stating:

(a) the name of the respondent and, where the respondent is a natural or juridical person, the permanent residence or address or registered office address thereof;

(b) an address for service at the seat of the Tribunal;

(c) the matters in issue between the parties and the facts and legal grounds on which the defence is based;

(d) the decision or measure sought by the respondent;

(e) the evidence on which the defence is founded.

3. At the request of the respondent, the President of the Chamber may extend the time-limit referred to in paragraph 2, if satisfied that there is adequate justification for the request.

Article 119

1. Within two months after service of the application in accordance with article 118, paragraph 1, where the respondent is a State Party in a case brought by a natural or juridical person sponsored by another State Party in a dispute referred to in article 187, subparagraph (c), of the Convention, the respondent State may make an application in accordance with article 190, paragraph 2, of the Convention for the sponsoring State of the applicant to appear in the proceedings on behalf of the applicant.

2. Notice of an application under paragraph 1 shall be communicated to the applicant and its sponsoring State. If, within a time-limit fixed by the President of the Chamber, the sponsoring State does not indicate it will appear in the proceedings on behalf of the applicant, the respondent State may designate a juridical person of its nationality to represent it.

3. Within two months after service of the application in accordance with article 118, paragraph 1, on the sponsoring State of a party, such State may give written notice of its intention to submit written or oral statements in accordance with article 190, paragraph 1, of the Convention.

4. Upon receipt of such a notice, the President of the Chamber shall fix the time-limit within which the sponsoring State may submit its written statements. The sponsoring State shall be notified of such time-limit. It shall also be notified of the date of the hearing. The written statements shall be communicated to the parties and to any other sponsoring State of a party.

5. At the request of the respondent or a sponsoring State, the President of the Chamber may extend a time-limit referred to in this article, if satisfied that there is adequate justification for the request.

Article 120

1. When proceedings are brought before the Chamber by the notification of a special agreement, the notification shall indicate:

(a) the parties to the case and any sponsoring States of the parties;

(b) the subject of the dispute and the precise nature of the claims of the parties, together with a statement of the facts and legal grounds on which the claims are based;

(c) the decisions or measures sought by the parties;

(d) the evidence on which the claims are founded.

2. The notification shall also provide information regarding participation and appearance in the proceedings by sponsoring States Parties in accordance with article 190 of the Convention.

Article 121

1. The Chamber may authorize or direct the filing of further pleadings if the parties are so agreed or the Chamber decides, *proprio motu* or at the request of a party, that these pleadings are necessary.

2. The President of the Chamber shall fix the time-limits within which these pleadings are to be filed.

Article 122

Proceedings by the Council on behalf of the Authority under article 185, paragraph 2, of the Convention shall be instituted by means of an application in accordance with article 162, paragraph 2 (u), of the Convention. The application shall be accompanied by a certified copy of the decision or resolution of the Council upon which it is based and the full records of all discussions within the Authority on the matter.

Article 123

1. When a commercial arbitral tribunal, pursuant to article 188, paragraph 2, of the Convention, refers to the Chamber a question of interpretation of Part XI of the Convention and the annexes relating thereto upon which its decision depends, the document submitting the question to the Chamber shall contain a precise statement of the question and be accompanied by all relevant information and documents.

2. Upon receipt of the document, the President of the Chamber shall fix a time-limit not exceeding three months within which the parties to the proceedings before the arbitral tribunal and the States Parties may submit their written observations on the question. The parties to the proceedings and the States Parties shall be notified of the time-limit. The States Parties shall be informed of the contents of the submission.

3. The President of the Chamber shall fix a date for a hearing if, within one month from the expiration of the time-limit for submitting written observations, a party to the proceedings before the arbitral tribunal or a State Party gives written notice of its intention to submit oral observations.

4. The Chamber shall give its ruling in the form of a judgment.

Section G. Judgments, interpretation and revision

Subsection 1. Judgments

Article 124

1. When the Tribunal has completed its deliberations and adopted its judgment, the parties shall be notified of the date on which it will be read.

2. The judgment shall be read at a public sitting of the Tribunal and shall become binding on the parties on the day of the reading.

Article 125

1. The judgment, which shall state whether it is given by the Tribunal or by a chamber, shall contain:

(a) the date on which it is read;

(b) the names of the judges participating in it;

(c) the names of the parties;

(d) the names of the agents, counsel and advocates of the parties;

(e) the names of the experts, if any, appointed under article 289 of the Convention;

(f) a summary of the proceedings;

(g) the submissions of the parties;

(h) a statement of the facts;

(i) the reasons of law on which it is based;

(j) the operative provisions of the judgment;

(k) the decision, if any, in regard to costs;

(l) the number and names of the judges constituting the majority and those constituting the minority, on each operative provision;

(m) a statement as to the text of the judgment which is authoritative.

2. Any judge may attach a separate or dissenting opinion to the judgment; a judge may record concurrence or dissent without stating reasons in the form of a declaration. The same applies to orders.

3. One copy of the judgment, signed by the President and by the Registrar and sealed, shall be placed in the archives of the Tribunal and other copies shall be transmitted to each party. Copies shall be sent to: (a) States Parties; (b) the Secretary-General of the United Nations; (c) the Secretary-General of the Authority; (d) in a case submitted under an agreement other than the Convention, the parties to such agreement.

Subsection 2. Requests for the interpretation or revision of a judgment

Article 126

1. In the event of dispute as to the meaning or scope of a judgment, any party may make a request for its interpretation.

2. A request for the interpretation of a judgment may be made either by an application or by the notification of a special agreement to that effect between the parties; the precise point or points in dispute as to the meaning or scope of the judgment shall be indicated.

3. If the request for interpretation is made by an application, the requesting party's contentions shall be set out therein, and the other party shall be entitled to file written observations thereon within a time-limit fixed by the Tribunal or by the President if the Tribunal is not sitting.

4. Whether the request is made by an application or by notification of a special agreement, the Tribunal may, if necessary, afford the parties the opportunity of furnishing further written or oral explanations.

Article 127

1. A request for revision of a judgment may be made only when it is based upon the discovery of some fact of such a nature as to be a decisive factor, which fact was, when the judgment was given, unknown to the Tribunal and also to the party requesting revision, always provided that such ignorance was not due to negligence. Such request must be made at the latest within six months of the discovery of the new fact and before the lapse of ten years from the date of the judgment.

2. The proceedings for revision shall be opened by a decision of the Tribunal in the form of a judgment expressly recording the existence of the new fact, recognizing that it has such a character as to lay the case open to revision, and declaring the application admissible on this ground.

Article 128

1. A request for the revision of a judgment shall be made by an application containing the particulars necessary to show that the conditions specified in article 127, paragraph 1, are fulfilled. Any document in support of the application shall be annexed to it.

2. The other party shall be entitled to file written observations on the admissibility of the application within a time-limit fixed by the Tribunal or by the President if the Tribunal is not sitting. These observations shall be communicated to the party making the application.

3. The Tribunal, before giving its judgment on the admissibility of the application, may afford the parties a further opportunity of presenting their views thereon.

4. If the Tribunal decides to make the admission of the proceedings in revision conditional on previous compliance with the judgment, it shall make an order accordingly.

5. If the Tribunal finds that the application is admissible it shall fix time-limits for such further proceedings on the merits of the application as, after ascertaining the views of the parties, it considers necessary.

Article 129

1. If the judgment to be revised or to be interpreted was given by the Tribunal, the request for its revision or interpretation shall be dealt with by the Tribunal.

2. If the judgment was given by a chamber, the request for its revision or interpretation shall, if possible, be dealt with by that chamber. If that is not possible, the request shall be dealt with by a chamber composed in conformity with the relevant provisions of the Statute and these Rules. If, according to the Statute and these Rules, the composition of the chamber requires the approval of the parties which cannot be obtained within time-limits fixed by the Tribunal, the request shall be dealt with by the Tribunal.

3. The decision on a request for interpretation or revision of a judgment shall be given in the form of a judgment.

Section H. Advisory proceedings

Article 130

1. In the exercise of its functions relating to advisory opinions, the Seabed Disputes Chamber shall apply this section and be guided, to the extent to which it recognizes them to be applicable, by the provisions of the Statute and of these Rules applicable in contentious cases.

2. The Chamber shall consider whether the request for an advisory opinion relates to a legal question pending between two or more parties. When the Chamber so determines, article 17 of the Statute applies, as well as the provisions of these Rules concerning the application of that article.

Article 131

1. A request for an advisory opinion on a legal question arising within the scope of the activities of the Assembly or the Council of the Authority shall contain a precise statement of the question. It shall be accompanied by all documents likely to throw light upon the question.

2. The documents shall be transmitted to the Chamber at the same time as the request or as soon as possible thereafter in the number of copies required by the Registry.

Article 132

If the request for an advisory opinion states that the question necessitates an urgent answer the Chamber shall take all appropriate steps to accelerate the procedure.

Article 133

1. The Registrar shall forthwith give notice of the request for an advisory opinion to all States Parties.

2. The Chamber, or its President if the Chamber is not sitting, shall identify the intergovernmental organizations which are likely to be able to furnish information on the question. The Registrar shall give notice of the request to such organizations.

3. States Parties and the organizations referred to in paragraph 2 shall be invited to present written statements on the question within a time-limit fixed by the Chamber or its President if the Chamber is not sitting. Such statements shall be communicated to States Parties and organizations which have made written statements. The Chamber, or its President if the Chamber is not sitting, may fix a further time-limit within which such States Parties and organizations may present written statements on the statements made.

4. The Chamber, or its President if the Chamber is not sitting, shall decide whether oral proceedings shall be held and, if so, fix the date for the opening of such proceedings. States Parties and the organizations referred to in paragraph 2 shall be invited to make oral statements at the proceedings.

Article 134

The written statements and documents annexed shall be made accessible to the public as soon as possible after they have been presented to the Chamber.

Article 135

1. When the Chamber has completed its deliberations and adopted its advisory opinion, the opinion shall be read at a public sitting of the Chamber.

2. The advisory opinion shall contain:

(a) the date on which it is delivered;

(b) the names of the judges participating in it;

(c) the question or questions on which the advisory opinion of the Chamber is requested;

(d) a summary of the proceedings;

(e) a statement of the facts;

(f) the reasons of law on which it is based;

(g) the reply to the question or questions put to the Chamber;

(h) the number and names of the judges constituting the majority and those constituting the minority, on each question put to the Chamber;

(i) a statement as to the text of the opinion which is authoritative.

3. Any judge may attach a separate or dissenting opinion to the advisory opinion of the Chamber; a judge may record concurrence or dissent without stating reasons in the form of a declaration.

Article 136

The Registrar shall inform the Secretary-General of the Authority as to the date and the time fixed for the public sitting to be held for the reading of the opinion. He shall also inform the States Parties and the intergovernmental organizations immediately concerned.

Article 137

One copy of the advisory opinion, signed by the President and by the Registrar and sealed, shall be placed in the archives of the Tribunal, others shall be sent to the Secretary-General of the Authority and to the Secretary-General of the United Nations. Copies shall be sent to the States Parties and the intergovernmental organizations immediately concerned.

Article 138

1. The Tribunal may give an advisory opinion on a legal question if an international agreement related to the purposes of the Convention specifically provides for the submission to the Tribunal of a request for such an opinion.

2. A request for an advisory opinion shall be transmitted to the Tribunal by whatever body is authorized by or in accordance with the agreement to make the request to the Tribunal.

3. The Tribunal shall apply *mutatis mutandis* articles 130 to 137.

(*Signed*)
THOMAS A. MENSAH,
President

(*Signed*)
GRITAKUMAR E. CHITTY,
Registrar

ITLOS/9
14 November 2006

INTERNATIONAL TRIBUNAL FOR THE LAW OF THE SEA

GUIDELINES CONCERNING THE PREPARATION AND PRESENTATION OF CASES BEFORE THE TRIBUNAL

GUIDELINES CONCERNING THE PREPARATION AND PRESENTATION OF CASES BEFORE THE TRIBUNAL

(ISSUED BY THE INTERNATIONAL TRIBUNAL FOR THE LAW OF THE SEA ON 28 OCTOBER 1997)

The Tribunal,

Acting pursuant to article 50 of the Rules of the Tribunal,

Issues the following Guidelines.

WRITTEN PROCEEDINGS

1. Every pleading and its supporting documents should be printed or typewritten or prepared electronically in the format 19 × 26 cm (7 1/2″ × 10 1/4″). In addition, parties should present the text of their pleadings in electronic form. The parties should consult the Registry's *Rules for the Preparation of Typed and Printed Texts*.

2. A pleading should be as short as possible.

3. Every pleading should contain a table of contents with a list of documents, including material in electronic or digital form. The table and list should be placed at the beginning of the pleading but before the commencement of Part I.

4. Every pleading and its supporting documents should be arranged, where practicable, in two parts, viz., Part I – memorial or counter-memorial or reply or rejoinder, as the case may be, and Part II – documents in support. The documents should be arranged in the same order as in the table of contents. Each document should be given a heading, which should be repeated at the top of each page over which the document extends.

5. If the reproduction in large numbers of a particular annex (e.g., a large map) presents technical problems, the matter should be raised with the Registrar at the earliest opportunity, so that appropriate arrangements can be made.

6. Every pleading should be divided into paragraphs, numbered consecutively, each paragraph being confined to a distinct portion of the subject. It should contain at the end of Part I a short summary of the arguments together with the page and paragraph numbers within which such arguments may be found. The name of the other party and the name and address of the agent should be clearly and properly stated.

7. Whenever the contents of any document are to be referred to in a pleading, it will be sufficient if the pleading states the effect thereof as briefly as possible, without setting out the whole document or any part thereof, unless the precise words of such a document or any part thereof are material.

8. A party should in its pleading deal specifically with each allegation of fact in the pleading of the other party of which it does not admit the truth; it will not be sufficient for it to deny generally the facts alleged by the other party.

9. Unless otherwise specified by the Registrar, each party should furnish to the Registry 125 additional copies of its pleading with supporting documents.

10. Upon receipt of a pleading, the Registrar will endorse on it the date of its receipt in the Registry. All pleadings, documents and other communications may be submitted to the Tribunal directly in person or through courier or regular mail. They may also be submitted through facsimile or electronic means in clear form. In determining whether a party has submitted its pleadings, documents or other communications within the time-limits fixed by or under the Rules, the date on which the Tribunal receives them through facsimile or electronically will be regarded as the material date provided they are followed without unreasonable delay by the paper originals thereof.

11. Where a pleading or an application or a declaration does not satisfy the formal requirements of the Rules of the Tribunal, the Registrar will return the same to the party seeking to file it for rectification. Where necessary, the Registrar will consult the President. In determining whether a party has submitted a pleading, etc., within the time-limit fixed by or under the Rules, the time taken by the Registrar to examine whether the pleading satisfies the requirements of the Rules will be excluded.

12. The time-limits fixed in each case for the filing of the pleadings are not to be understood by the parties as authorizations to hold back a pleading until the last possible moment.

13. It is not a strict requirement that the parties print their pleadings, though this remains an option. If independently printed pleadings are submitted, it is requested that all diskettes and films used for that production be made available to the Registry on request in due course, particularly those which have been used to produce maps in colour.

ORAL PROCEEDINGS

14. Each party should submit to the Tribunal, prior to the opening of the oral proceedings, (a) a brief note on the points which in its opinion constitute the issues that still divide the parties; (b) a brief outline of the arguments that it wishes to make in its oral statement; and (c) a list of authorities, including, where appropriate, relevant extracts from such authorities, proposed to be relied upon in its oral statement. None of these materials will be treated as documents or parts of the pleadings.

15. The oral statements should be as succinct as possible and should not repeat the facts and arguments contained in the written pleadings.

16. The parties should keep within the time allotted for the presentation of their oral statements.

17. Unless otherwise decided, the Tribunal sits between 09.00 and 13.00 on all days on which the Tribunal holds oral proceedings.

18. Visual demonstration facilities for display of maps, charts, diagrams, illustrations of texts, etc., which a party intends to exhibit to the Tribunal will at the request of that party be provided by the Registrar upon payment of fees, if any, fixed for that purpose.

ADVISORY PROCEEDINGS

19. These Guidelines apply, *mutatis mutandis*, to advisory proceedings as they apply to contentious proceedings.

(*signed*)
Thomas A. MENSAH,
President

(*signed*)
Gritakumar E. CHITTY,
Registrar

ITLOS/10
27 April 2005

INTERNATIONAL TRIBUNAL FOR THE LAW OF THE SEA

RESOLUTION ON THE INTERNAL JUDICIAL PRACTICE OF THE TRIBUNAL

RESOLUTION ON THE INTERNAL JUDICIAL PRACTICE OF THE TRIBUNAL

adopted on 31 October 1997

The Tribunal,

Acting in accordance with article 40 of the Rules,

Adopts this Resolution.

Article 1
Use of terms

In this Resolution:

(a) "President" means the person presiding over the Tribunal in a particular case;

(b) "Rules" means the Rules of the Tribunal;

(c) references to the "Tribunal" include any chamber of the Tribunal.

Article 2
Preparatory documentation

1. After the closure of the written proceedings, each judge may within five weeks prepare a brief written note identifying without further elaboration:

(a) the principal issues for decision as they emerge from the written pleadings; and

(b) points, if any, which should be clarified during the oral proceedings.

2. Notes received by the Registry are circulated to the other judges.

3. On the basis of the written pleadings and the judges' notes, the President draws up a working paper containing:

(a) a summary of the facts and the principal contentions of the parties advanced in their written pleadings; and

(b) proposals concerning:

(i) indications to be given, or questions to be put, to the parties in accordance with article 76 of the Rules;

(ii) evidence or explanations to be requested from the parties in accordance with article 77 of the Rules; and

(iii) issues which, in the opinion of the President, should be discussed and decided by the Tribunal.

4. The Registrar shall send the working paper to the judges as soon as possible and normally within eight weeks after the closure of the written proceedings.

Article 3
Deliberations before the oral proceedings

After the circulation of the working paper and before the date fixed for the opening of the oral proceedings, the Tribunal deliberates in private, as provided for in article 68 of the Rules, in order to allow the judges an opportunity to:

(a) exchange views concerning the written pleadings and the conduct of the case;

(b) consider whether to give any indications, or put any questions, to the parties in accordance with article 76 of the Rules;

(c) consider whether to call upon the parties to produce any evidence or to give any explanations in accordance with article 77 of the Rules; and

(d) consider the nature, scope and terms of the questions and issues which will have to be decided by the Tribunal.

Article 4
Deliberations during oral proceedings

During the course of the oral proceedings, the President may convene brief meetings in order to permit the judges to exchange views concerning the case and to inform each other of possible questions which judges may wish to put to the parties in accordance with article 76 of the Rules.

Article 5
Initial deliberations after oral proceedings

1. Unless the Tribunal decides otherwise, the judges have four working days after the closure of the oral proceedings in order to study the arguments presented to the Tribunal in the case. During this time, judges may also summarize their tentative opinions in writing in the form of speaking notes.

2. If the President considers it appropriate in the light of the oral proceedings, a revised list of issues for examination is circulated.

3. During its initial deliberations after the closure of the oral proceedings, the Tribunal reaches conclusions on what are the issues which need to be decided and then hears the tentative opinions of the judges on those issues, as well as on the correct disposal of the case.

4. The Tribunal next deliberates on each issue in turn, addressing also the question of the disposal of the case and the main reasons for the decision to be given.

5. During these deliberations, judges will be called upon by the President in the order in which they signify their wish to speak.

6. The President may seek to establish a majority opinion as it appears then to exist on each issue and on the reasons to be given.

7. Instead of establishing majority opinions at that stage, the Tribunal may decide that every judge should prepare a brief written note, expressing the judge's tentative opinion on the issues and the correct disposal of the case, for circulation to the other judges before a specified date. The Tribunal resumes its deliberations as soon as possible on the basis of the written notes.

Article 6
Establishment of a Drafting Committee

1. As soon as possible during the deliberations, the Tribunal sets up a Drafting Committee for the case, composed of five judges belonging to the majority as it appears then to exist. Subject to paragraph 2, the members of the Committee are selected on the proposal of the President by an absolute majority of the judges present, taking into account the need to select judges who, from their statements, clearly support the opinion of the majority as it appears then to exist.

2. The President is a member ex officio of the Committee unless the President does not share the opinion of the majority as it appears then to exist, in which case the Vice-President acts instead. If the Vice-President is ineligible for the same reason, all the members of the Committee are selected by the Tribunal.

3. Unless the Tribunal or the members of the Committee decide otherwise, the judge who is senior in precedence among the members of the Committee acts as its chairman.

Article 7
Work of the Drafting Committee

1. The Drafting Committee meets immediately after its establishment in order to prepare a first draft of the judgment, for completion normally within three weeks. To this end, any member of the Committee may send written proposals for its consideration and inclusion in the draft.

2. The Drafting Committee should prepare a draft judgment which not only states the opinion of the majority as it appears then to exist but which may also attract wider support within the Tribunal.

3. The first draft of the judgment shall be distributed to all the judges in the case. Any judge who wishes to offer amendments or comments submits them in writing to the Committee within three weeks from the date of circulation.

4. After the members of the Committee have received the comments, they will normally meet in order to revise the draft, unless they decide a meeting is not required.

5. When the members of the Committee have completed the second draft of the judgment, the Registrar shall circulate copies to all judges.

6. If the President is not a member of the Committee, its chairman keeps the President informed of work on the draft judgment, as well as its terms.

Article 8
Deliberations on the draft judgment

1. Deliberations on the draft judgment are held as soon as possible after its circulation and in principle not later than three months after the closure of the oral proceedings.

2. The chairman of the Drafting Committee introduces the draft.

3. The draft is examined by the Tribunal in first reading. A judge wishing to modify the draft proposes amendments in writing.

4. At this stage, a judge who, after taking cognizance of the draft judgment, wishes to deliver a separate or dissenting opinion so informs the other judges and puts forward at least an outline of the opinion, making the text available within a time-limit fixed by the Tribunal before the second reading. Such a judge continues to participate in the examination of the draft judgment and cognizance is taken by the Tribunal of such opinions.

5. The Drafting Committee circulates a revised draft judgment for consideration at a second reading, during the course of which the President asks if the judges wish to propose new amendments.

6. Separate or dissenting opinions, which may be individual or collective, should be submitted within a time-limit fixed by the Tribunal. They should take account of any changes made to the draft judgment pursuant to paragraphs 4 and 5 and should concentrate on the remaining points of difference with the judgment.

Article 9
Voting

1. After the Tribunal has completed its second reading of the draft judgment, the President takes the vote in accordance with article 29 of the

Statute in order to adopt the judgment. A separate vote is normally taken on each operative provision in the judgment. Any judge may request a separate vote on issues which are separable. Each judge votes by means solely of an affirmative or a negative vote, cast in person and in inverse order of seniority, provided that in exceptional circumstances accepted by the Tribunal an absent judge may vote by appropriate means of communications.

2. A judge who has been absent, because of illness or other reason duly explained to the President, from any part of the hearing or the deliberations may vote provided the Tribunal accepts that the judge has taken a sufficient part in the hearing and the deliberations to be able to reach a judicial determination of all issues of fact and law material to the decision to be given in the case.

Article 10
Experts appointed under article 289 of the Convention

Experts appointed under article 289 of the Convention for a particular case before the Tribunal shall be sent copies of the written pleadings and other documents in the case in good time before the beginning of the deliberations. They sit with the judges during the oral proceedings and take part in the deliberations in accordance with article 42 of the Rules. They receive the written notes and other documents. They may be consulted by the Drafting Committee, as appropriate.

Article 11
Procedures in particular instances

1. The Tribunal may decide to vary the procedures and arrangements set out above in a particular case for reasons of urgency or if circumstances so justify.

2. Deliberations concerning applications for provisional measures and applications for the prompt release of a vessel or crew are conducted in accordance with the principles and procedures set out in this Resolution, taking account of the nature and urgency of the case.

3. The Chamber for Summary Procedure deliberates in accordance with the principles and procedures set out in this Resolution, taking account of the summary nature of the proceedings and the urgency of the case.

Article 12
Application

The foregoing provisions apply whether the proceedings before the Tribunal are contentious or advisory.

Article 13
Review

This Resolution may be reviewed in the light of experience and revised whenever considered appropriate.

(*Signed*)
Thomas A. MENSAH,
President

(*Signed*)
Gritakumar E. CHITTY,
Registrar

17 March 2009

INTERNATIONAL TRIBUNAL FOR THE LAW OF THE SEA

GUIDELINES CONCERNING THE POSTING OF A BOND OR OTHER FINANCIAL SECURITY WITH THE REGISTRAR

GUIDELINES CONCERNING THE POSTING OF A BOND OR OTHER FINANCIAL SECURITY WITH THE REGISTRAR

Issued by the International Tribunal for the Law of the Sea
on 17 March 2009

The Tribunal,

Acting pursuant to article 50 of the Rules of the Tribunal,

Issues the following Guidelines:

I. Scope of application

1. These Guidelines apply to the posting of a bond or other financial security with the Registrar in accordance with articles 113, paragraph 3, and 114 of the Rules of the Tribunal.

II. Use of terms

2. For the purposes of these Guidelines:

(a) "account party" means the party at whose request the bond or other financial security is issued, including, *inter alia*, the owner or the operator of the vessel;

(b) "beneficiary" means the party in whose favour the bond or other financial security is issued, namely, the competent authority of the detaining State;

(c) "guarantor" means the banking institution or Protection and Indemnity Club (P&I Club) issuing the bond or other financial security;

(d) "posting party" means the competent authority of the flag State or any person or institution authorized in writing to act on behalf of the flag State;

(e) "representative of the detaining State" means the competent authority of the detaining State or any person authorized in writing to act on its behalf.

III. General provisions

Form of the bond or other financial security

3. Subject to the judgment of the Tribunal, a bond or other financial security may be posted with the Registrar in one of the following forms:

(a) bank transfer;
(b) bank guarantee;
(c) P&I Club Letter of Undertaking.

Posting of bond or other financial security

4. A bond or other financial security should be posted with the Registrar by the posting party.

Communications and official languages

5. All communications from the Registrar will be sent to the posting party and the representative of the detaining State.

6. When a communication or document annexed thereto is not in one of the official languages of the Tribunal, it should be accompanied by a translation into one of these languages certified as accurate by the party submitting it.

7. If the bond or other financial security is not in one of the official languages of the Tribunal, it should be accompanied by a translation into one of the official languages certified as accurate by the posting party.

Terms and conditions

8. The posting party should ensure that the bond or other financial security is in conformity with the requirements contained in the judgment of the Tribunal and that its terms and conditions indicate:

(a) the name of the vessel;

(b) the port or place of registration;

(c) the name and address of the account party;

(d) the name and address of the beneficiary;

(e) the name and address of the guarantor and the name and address of its representative;

(f) a statement to the effect that the bond or other financial security is issued in consideration of the detaining State releasing from detention the vessel and its crew in accordance with the judgment delivered by the Tribunal in relation to the incident that occurred with respect to the vessel and its crew;

(g) the maximum amount payable according to the judgment of the Tribunal;

(h) the need for the production of a final judgment, award or decision of the competent authority of the detaining State as a condition for demanding payment.

9. Where the bond or other financial security does not satisfy the requirements or the terms and conditions specified in paragraph 8, the Registrar will return it to the posting party for rectification.

10. The Registrar will give effect to any agreement between the parties concluded after the judgment of the Tribunal as to the terms and conditions of

the bond or other financial security, provided that such terms and conditions are in conformity with the requirements contained in the judgment. The parties should either jointly or severally notify the Registrar of the agreement. If the notification is not a joint one, the Registrar will forthwith transmit a certified copy thereof to the other party. In each case the notification should be accompanied by a certified copy of the agreement.

Notification

11. In order to post the bond or other financial security pursuant to the judgment of the Tribunal, the posting party should transmit a communication to that effect to the Registrar. Upon receipt of the bond or other financial security, the Registrar will forthwith notify the representative of the detaining State thereof.

Reimbursement of costs

12. In the communication referred to in paragraph 11, the posting party should undertake to reimburse the Tribunal for any financial costs the Tribunal may incur in relation to the posting of the bond or other financial security.

13. The posting party should bear all costs relating to the transmittal of the bond or other financial security to the detaining State. The Registrar, after fixing the amount payable, will request the posting party to reimburse the Tribunal for such amount as a condition for the transmittal of the bond or other financial security to the detaining State.

IV. Specific provisions for a bank transfer

14. A bond or other financial security posted in the form of a bank transfer should be deposited by the posting party in a special, interest-bearing bank account of the Tribunal with a reputable bank designated by the Registrar.

15. While making the bank transfer, the posting party should transmit to the Registrar a document on compliance with the terms and conditions indicated in paragraphs 8 and 12.

16. Upon receipt of the bank transfer, the Registrar will furnish a receipt to the posting party.

17. Upon receipt of a written demand signed by the representative of the detaining State, the Registrar will promptly transmit the bond or other financial security to the detaining State to the extent that it is required to satisfy the final judgment, award or decision of the competent authority of the detaining State. The written demand should be accompanied by a certified copy of the final judgment, award or decision. The Registrar will forthwith transmit a copy of the written demand to the posting party.

18. The Registrar will transmit the bond or other financial security to the detaining State in accordance with these Guidelines and rule 108.5 of the Financial Rules of the Tribunal. Where appropriate, all costs and charges

relating to the transmittal of the bond or other financial security will be paid from the accrued interest of the special account referred to in paragraph 14.

19. The Registrar will transmit any cash surplus, to the extent that it is not required to satisfy the final judgment, award or decision, to the account party. If the account party is not an authority of the flag State, the Registrar will notify the flag State and the posting party of the refund of such surplus.

V. Specific provisions for a bank guarantee or P&I Club Letter of Undertaking

20. A bond or other financial security in the form of a bank guarantee or a P&I Club Letter of Undertaking should be posted with the Registrar.

21. Upon receipt of the bank guarantee or P&I Club Letter of Undertaking, the Registrar will furnish a receipt to the posting party. The bank guarantee or P&I Club Letter of Undertaking will be kept by the Registrar.

22. Upon receipt of a written demand signed by the representative of the detaining State, the Registrar will promptly transmit the bank guarantee or P&I Club Letter of Undertaking to the representative of the detaining State together with a statement indicating the amount required to satisfy the final judgment, award or decision of the competent authority of the detaining State. The Registrar will forthwith transmit a copy of the written demand and the statement to the posting party and the guarantor.

23. The written demand should be accompanied by a certified copy of the final judgment, award or decision. The demand should also indicate the amount required to satisfy the final judgment, award or decision of the competent authority of the detaining State.

24. The Registrar will transmit the bank guarantee or P&I Club Letter of Undertaking to the representative of detaining State, who will be requested to acknowledge receipt thereof.

VI. Final provision

25. In the absence of specific provisions in these Guidelines, the Registrar will apply, *mutatis mutandis*, the provisions of the Rules of the Tribunal.

(*signed*)
José Luís JESUS,
President

(*signed*)
Philippe GAUTIER,
Registrar

PART III

COMMISSION ON THE LIMITS OF THE CONTINENTAL SHELF

United Nations Convention on the Law of the Sea CLCS/40

Commission on the Limits of the Continental Shelf

Distr.: General
2 July 2004

Original: English

Thirteenth session
New York, 26–30 April 2004

Rules of Procedure of the Commission on the Limits of the Continental Shelf[1]

Contents *Page*

[1] The Rules of Procedure were submitted for translation later than originally scheduled owing to the need for additional consultations with the members of the Commission.

Foreword

This document contains the latest version of the Rules of Procedure of the Commission on the Limits of the Continental Shelf, embodying amendments and additions adopted by the Commission as at 30 April 2004. Annexes I and II of the present Rules were adopted by the Commission at its fourth session, held from 31 August to 4 September 1998. Annex III was adopted by the Commission at its thirteenth session, held from 26 to 30 April 2004, and replaced the Modus Operandi of the Commission (CLCS/L.3 — 12 September 1997) and the Internal procedure of the subcommission of the Commission on the Limits of the Continental Shelf (CLCS/L.12 — 25 May 2002).

Consequently, the present Rules and their annexes supersede and replace documents CLCS/L.3 (12 September 1997) and CLCS/L.12 (25 May 2002) as well as all previously issued documents containing the Rules of Procedure of the Commission and their revisions or corrections (documents CLCS/3 (12 September 1997), CLCS/3/Corr.1 (27 April 1998), CLCS/3/Rev.1 (14 May 1998), CLCS/3/Rev.2 (4 September 1998), CLCS/3/Rev.2/Corr.1 (28 March 2000), CLCS/3/Rev.3 (6 February 2001), CLCS/3/Rev.3/Corr.1 (22 May 2001)).

Rules of Procedure of the Commission on the Limits of the Continental Shelf

I. Introduction

Rule 1
Use of terms

For the purposes of these Rules:

"Convention" means the 1982 United Nations Convention on the Law of the Sea;

"Statement of Understanding" means the Statement of Understanding adopted on 29 August 1980 by the Third United Nations Conference on the Law of the Sea and contained in Annex II to its Final Act;

"Guidelines" means the Scientific and Technical Guidelines of the Commission on the Limits of the Continental Shelf, unless otherwise specified;

"Commission" means the Commission on the Limits of the Continental Shelf, established in accordance with article 76, paragraph 8, and Annex II to the Convention;

"Secretary-General" means the Secretary-General of the United Nations, unless otherwise specified;

"Secretariat" means the Secretariat of the United Nations;

"States Parties" means States Parties to the Convention;

"Meeting of States Parties" means a meeting of States Parties to the Convention convened in accordance with the relevant provisions of the Convention.

II. Sessions and meetings

Rule 2
Sessions and meetings

1. The Commission shall hold sessions at least once a year and as often as is required for the effective performance of its functions under the Convention, in particular, to consider submissions by coastal States and to make recommendations thereon. A session may include several meetings of the Commission and its subcommissions.

2. Taking into account financial considerations that may influence the frequency of its sessions, the Commission shall be convened:

(a) At the request of the Chairperson of the Commission;

(b) At the request of a majority of the members of the Commission;

(c) At the request of the Secretary-General; or

(d) By a decision of the Commission.

Rule 3
Notification of opening date of session

The Secretary-General shall notify the members of the Commission of the date, place and duration of a session as soon as possible, but no later than sixty days in advance of its opening date. Any coastal State whose submission is to be considered at the session shall also be notified.

Rule 4
Venue

1. Sessions of the Commission and its subcommissions shall normally be held at United Nations Headquarters in New York.

2. Another venue for an entire session, or any part thereof, may be designated by the Commission in consultation with any coastal State which made a submission to be considered at that session and with the Secretary-General, subject to the requirements established by the United Nations that no additional costs are directly or indirectly incurred by the United Nations.

Rule 5
Agenda

1. The provisional agenda of each session shall be prepared by the Secretary-General in consultation with the Chairperson of the Commission.[2]

2. The Secretary-General shall transmit the provisional agenda to the members of the Commission together with the notification referred to in rule 3 and with the names of any members of the Commission who have provided any coastal State concerned with scientific and technical advice.

3. The Commission may include in its agenda any other item relevant to the effective performance of its functions.

---

[2] For the preparation of the provisional agenda in case of coastal State submissions, see rule 51, paragraph 1, as well as paragraph 2 of Annex III to the Rules of Procedure.

4. The Commission shall adopt the agenda at the beginning of the session.

5. During a session, the Commission may revise the agenda.

III. Members of the Commission

Rule 6
Members

The Commission shall consist of the members elected pursuant to article 2 of Annex II to the Convention.

Rule 7
Term of office

1. In accordance with article 2, paragraph 4, of Annex II to the Convention, the members of the Commission shall be elected for a term of five years and they shall be eligible for re-election.

2. The members of the Commission elected at the first election shall begin their term of office on the date of the first meeting of the Commission.

3. The term of office of the members of the Commission elected at subsequent elections shall begin on the day after the date of expiry of the term of office of the members of the Commission whom they replace.

Rule 8
By-elections

If a member of the Commission dies or resigns or for any other cause can no longer perform his or her duties, the Meeting of States Parties shall elect a member for the remainder of the predecessor's term. Such by-elections shall be carried out in accordance with article 76 and Annex II to the Convention.

Rule 9
Expenses of members

In accordance with article 2, paragraph 5, of Annex II to the Convention:

(a) The State Party which submitted the nomination of a member of the Commission shall defray the expenses of that member while in performance of Commission duties;

(b) The coastal States requesting the scientific and technical advice referred to in article 3, paragraph 1 (b), of Annex II to the Convention shall defray the expenses incurred in respect of this advice.

Rule 10
Solemn declaration

Before assuming his or her duties, each member of the Commission shall make the following solemn declaration in the Commission:

> "I solemnly declare that I will perform my duties as a member of the Commission on the Limits of the Continental Shelf honourably, faithfully, impartially and conscientiously."

Rule 11
Duty to act independently

In the performance of their duties, members of the Commission shall not seek or receive instructions from any Government or from any other authority external to the Commission. They shall refrain from any action which might reflect negatively on their position as members of the Commission.

IV. Officers

Rule 12
Elections

The Commission shall elect from among its members a Chairperson and four Vice-Chairpersons.

Rule 13
Term of office

The officers of the Commission shall be elected for a term of two and a half years. They shall be eligible for re-election.

Rule 14
Acting Chairperson

1. If the Chairperson is absent from a session, or any part thereof, the Commission shall designate one of the Vice-Chairpersons to act in his or her place.

2. A Vice-Chairperson acting as Chairperson shall have the same powers and duties as the Chairperson.

Rule 15
Replacement of officers

If any of the officers of the Commission ceases to be, or declares his or her inability to continue serving as, a member of the Commission, or for any reason is no longer able to act as an officer, a new officer shall be elected for the unexpired term of his or her predecessor.

V. Secretariat

Rule 16
Duties of the Secretary-General

1. The Secretary-General shall act in that capacity in all sessions of the Commission and meetings of its subcommissions and any subsidiary bodies which it may establish. The Secretary-General may designate a member of the Secretariat to participate on his or her behalf.

2. The Secretary-General shall be responsible for making the arrangements related to the sessions of the Commission and meetings of its subcommissions and any subsidiary bodies which it may establish and shall provide and direct the staff required for such sessions and meetings.

3. The Secretariat shall perform all work that the Commission may require for the effective performance of its functions.

Rule 17
Statements by the Secretary-General and members of the Secretariat

The Secretary-General or any member of the Secretariat designated by him or her may make oral or written statements at any meeting of the Commission and of its subcommissions.

Rule 18
Financial implications of proposals

Before any proposal that involves expenditures is approved by the Commission, the Secretary-General shall prepare and circulate to the members of the Commission, as early as possible, an estimate of the cost involved in the proposal. The Chairperson shall draw the attention of members to this estimate and invite discussion on it when the proposal is considered by the Commission or any subsidiary body.

VI. Languages

Rule 19
Official and working languages

1. The official and working languages of the Commission shall be Arabic, Chinese, English, French, Russian and Spanish.

2. In the absence of objections by any member, the Commission may decide not to use some of its official and working languages for any particular meeting, taking into account the language preferences

of the members of the Commission participating at that meeting and of any coastal State whose submission is under consideration.[3]

Rule 20
Interpretation

Subject to rule 19, paragraph 2, speeches made in any of the languages of the Commission shall be interpreted into the other languages.

Rule 21
Interpretation from a language other than the languages of the Commission

Oral statements may be made in a language other than the languages of the Commission, provided the person making the statement arranges for interpretation into one of the languages of the Commission. Interpretation into the other languages of the Commission may be based on the interpretation given in the first such language.

Rule 22
Languages of documents of the Commission

Documents of the Commission shall be issued in the languages of the Commission, unless otherwise decided by the Commission. The languages of the recommendations of the Commission shall be in accordance with rule 53, paragraph 3.

VII. Public and private meetings

Rule 23
Public and private meetings

The meetings of the Commission, its subcommissions and subsidiary bodies shall be held in private, unless the Commission decides otherwise.

VIII. Conduct of business

Rule 24
Quorum

Two thirds of the members of the Commission, subcommission or subsidiary body shall constitute a quorum.

---

[3] For the working language of the subcommissions see paragraph 4 of Annex III.

Rule 25
Powers of the Chairperson

1. In addition to exercising the powers conferred upon him or her elsewhere by these Rules, the Chairperson shall declare the opening and closing of each session and meeting of the Commission, direct the discussion, ensure observance of these Rules, accord the right to speak, put questions to the vote and announce decisions. The Chairperson shall rule on points of order and, subject to these Rules, shall have complete control over the proceedings and over the maintenance of order thereat. He or she may propose to the Commission the limitation of time to be allowed to speakers, the limitation of the number of times each representative may speak on any question, the closure of the list of speakers, the adjournment or closure of the debate and the suspension or adjournment of a meeting.

2. The Chairperson, in the exercise of his or her functions, remains under the authority of the Commission.

Rule 26
Points of order

During the discussion of any matter, a member may at any time raise a point of order, which shall be immediately decided by the Chairperson in accordance with the present Rules. Any appeal against the ruling of the Chairperson shall be immediately put to the vote, and the ruling of the Chairperson shall stand unless overruled by a majority of the members present and voting. A member may not, in raising a point of order, speak on the substance of the matter under discussion.

Rule 27
Time limits on speakers

The Commission may limit the time allowed to each speaker on any question. When debate is limited and a speaker exceeds the allotted time, the Chairperson shall call the speaker to order without delay.

Rule 28
Closure of debate

During the discussion of any matter, a member may move the closure of the debate on the item under discussion, whether or not any other member has signified a wish to speak. Permission to speak on the closure of the debate shall be accorded only to the member who proposed the motion, and to one member who opposes it and one member who favours it, after which the motion shall be immediately put to the vote.

Rule 29
Adjournment of debate

During the discussion of any matter, a member may move the adjournment of the debate on the item under discussion. Permission to speak on the adjournment of the debate shall be accorded only to the member who proposed the motion, and to one member who opposes it and one member who favours it, after which the motion shall be immediately put to the vote.

Rule 30
Suspension or adjournment of the meeting

During the discussion of any matter, a member may move the suspension or adjournment of the meeting. No discussion on such motions shall be permitted, and they shall be immediately put to the vote.

Rule 31
Order of motions

The motions indicated below shall have precedence in the following order over all proposals or other motions before the meeting:

(a) To suspend the meeting;

(b) To adjourn the meeting;

(c) To adjourn the debate on the question under discussion; and

(d) To close the debate on the question under discussion.

Rule 32
Submission of proposals by members of the Commission

Proposals by members of the Commission shall be submitted in writing to the Chairperson of the Commission and copies thereof shall be circulated to all members of the Commission by the Secretariat.

Rule 33
Decisions on competence

Any motion calling for a decision on the competence of the Commission to adopt a proposal submitted to it shall be put to the vote before a decision is taken on the proposal in question.

Rule 34
Reconsideration of proposals by members of the Commission

When a proposal has been adopted or rejected, it may not be reconsidered unless the Commission, by a two-thirds majority of the members present and voting, so decides. Permission to speak on a motion to reconsider shall be accorded only to two speakers opposing reconsideration, after which the motion shall be immediately put to the vote.

IX. Voting

Rule 35
General agreement

1. The Commission, its subcommissions and subsidiary bodies shall make their best endeavours to ensure that their work is accomplished by general agreement.

2. Accordingly, the Commission, its subcommissions and subsidiary bodies shall make every effort to reach agreement on substantive matters by way of consensus and there shall be no voting on such matters until all efforts to achieve consensus have been exhausted.

Rule 36
Voting rights

Each member of the Commission shall have one vote.

Rule 37
Majority required

1. Subject to rule 35, decisions of the Commission, subcommission or subsidiary body on all matters of substance shall be taken by a two-thirds majority of the members present and voting. For the Commission, this shall include the establishment of subcommissions, the approval of the recommendations prepared by a subcommission, requests for advice by specialists, cooperation with competent international organizations, as well as the amendment of the existing and the adoption of new Rules and other regulations, guidelines and annexes to these Rules.

2. Except as otherwise provided in these Rules, decisions of the Commission on all matters of procedure shall be taken by a majority of the members present and voting.

3. If the question arises whether a matter is one of procedure or of substance, the Chairperson of the Commission shall rule on the question. Any appeal against this ruling shall be put to the vote immediately, and the Chairperson's ruling shall stand unless overruled by a majority of the members present and voting.

4. If a vote is equally divided on a matter other than the election of officers, which is regulated by rule 40, paragraph 4, the proposal or motion shall be regarded as rejected.

5. For the purpose of these Rules, the phrase "members present and voting" means members casting an affirmative or negative vote. Members who abstain from voting shall be regarded as not voting.

Rule 38
Method of voting

The Commission shall normally vote by a show of hands, except as provided for in rule 40.

Rule 39
Conduct during voting

After the Chairperson has announced the commencement of voting, no member shall interrupt the voting except on a point of order raised in connection with the process of voting.

Rule 40
Election of officers

1. All elections shall be held by secret ballot unless, in the absence of any objection, the Commission decides to proceed without taking a ballot when there is an agreed candidate or slate.

2. A single ballot shall be taken in respect of all places to be filled at one time under the same conditions. Those candidates, in a number not exceeding the number of places to be filled, obtaining a majority of the votes cast and the largest number of votes, shall be elected.

3. If the number of candidates obtaining such a majority is less than the number of places to be filled, additional ballots shall be held to fill the remaining places, the voting being restricted to the candidates obtaining the greatest number of votes in the previous ballot to a number not more than twice the places remaining to be filled.

4. If a tie vote between two or more candidates persists for two successive ballots, a decision, by lot drawn by the Chairperson, shall be taken as to which candidate shall be chosen.

Rule 41
Announcement of the outcome of a voting and of the election of the officers

The Chairperson shall announce the outcome of any voting and, in the case of elections pursuant to rule 40, the names of the officers who have been elected.

X. Subcommissions and other subsidiary bodies

Rule 42
Subcommissions

1. If, in accordance with article 5 of Annex II to the Convention, the Commission decides to establish a subcommission for the consideration of a submission, it shall:

(a) Identify any members of the Commission who are defined as ineligible, in accordance with article 5 of Annex II to the Convention, i.e. nationals of the coastal State making the submission and members who have assisted the coastal State by providing scientific and technical advice with respect to the delineation;

(b) Identify any members of the Commission who may, for other reasons, be perceived to have a conflict of interest regarding the submission, e.g., members who are nationals of a State which may have a dispute or unresolved border with the submitting State;

(c) Through informal consultations among the members of the Commission, nominate candidates for the subcommission other than those identified in subparagraph (a), taking into account the factors regarding the members identified in paragraph (b), and the specific elements of the submission as well as, to the extent possible, the need to ensure a scientific and geographical balance; and

(d) Appoint from among the nominated candidates seven members of the subcommission.

2. The term of a subcommission shall extend from the time of its appointment to the time that the submitting coastal State deposits, in accordance with article 76, paragraph 9, of the Convention, the charts and relevant information, including geodetic data, regarding the outer limits for that part of the continental shelf for which the submission was originally made.

3. A member of the Commission can be appointed to be a member of more than one subcommission. Members of the Commission identified under subparagraph 1 (a) have the right to participate as members in the proceedings of the Commission concerning the said submission. Such members, by prior consultation and agreement within the subcommission, may be invited to participate in the proceedings of the subcommission on specific issues concerning the said submission without the right to vote.

Rule 43
Other subsidiary bodies

The Commission may establish such other subsidiary bodies composed of its members as may be required for the effective performance of its functions.

Rule 44
Conduct of business

1. Each subcommission or other subsidiary body established by the Commission shall elect its own Chairperson and two Vice-Chairpersons, and report the results of the election to the Commission.

2. The present Rules apply mutatis mutandis to the conduct of business of the subcommissions and other subsidiary bodies.

XI. Submission by a coastal State

Rule 45
Submission by a coastal State

In accordance with article 4 of Annex II to the Convention:

(a) Where a coastal State intends to establish the outer limits of its continental shelf beyond 200 nautical miles from the baselines from which the breadth of the territorial sea is measured, it shall submit particulars of such limits to the Commission along with supporting scientific and technical data as soon as possible, but in any case within ten years of the entry into force of the Convention for that State. In the case of a State Party for which the Convention entered into force before 13 May 1999, it is understood, in accordance with the "Decision regarding the date of commencement of the ten-year period for making submissions to the Commission on the Limits of the Continental Shelf set out in article 4 of Annex II to the United Nations Convention on the Law of the Sea" (SPLOS/72 of 29 May 2001), that the ten-year time period referred to in article 4 of Annex II to the Convention shall be taken to have commenced on 13 May 1999.[4]

---

[4] The election of the members of the Commission was postponed until March 1997 by a decision of the Third Meeting of States Parties to the Convention, held from 27 November to 1 December 1995. Since the Convention entered into force on 16 November 1994 for the 60 States whose ratifications made that entry into force possible and the commencement of the ten-year period began for them on that date, the Meeting agreed that should any one of those States be affected adversely in respect of its obligations under the Convention as a consequence of the change in the date of the election, States Parties, at the request of such a State, would review the situation with a view to ameliorating the difficulty in respect of that obligation (SPLOS/5, paragraph 20). The Eleventh Meeting of States Parties to the Convention, held from 14 to 18 May 2001, noted that it was only after the adoption of the Scientific and Technical Guidelines by the Commission on 13 May 1999 that States had before them the basic documents concerning submissions in accordance with article 76, paragraph 8, of the Convention. Considering the problems encountered by States Parties, in particular developing countries, including small island developing States, in complying with the time limit set out in article 4 of Annex II to the Convention, the Meeting of States Parties decided that (a) in the case of a State Party for which the Convention entered into force before 13 May 1999, it is understood that the ten-year time period referred to in article 4 of Annex II to the Convention shall be taken to have commenced on 13 May 1999; and that (b) the general issue of the ability of States, particularly developing States, to fulfil the requirements of article 4 of Annex II to the Convention be kept under review (SPLOS/72).

(b) The submitting State shall at the same time give the names of any Commission members who have provided it with scientific and technical advice.

Rule 46
Submissions in case of a dispute between States with opposite or adjacent coasts or in other cases of unresolved land or maritime disputes

1. In case there is a dispute in the delimitation of the continental shelf between opposite or adjacent States or in other cases of unresolved land or maritime disputes, submissions may be made and shall be considered in accordance with Annex I to these Rules.

2. The actions of the Commission shall not prejudice matters relating to the delimitation of boundaries between States.

Rule 47
Form and language of submission

1. A submission shall conform to the requirements established by the Commission.[5]

2. A submission, as well as its annexes, attachments and other supporting material, shall be made in one of the official languages of the Commission. If made in an official language other than English, it shall be translated by the Secretariat into English. In order to enable the Secretary-General to make public the proposed outer limits pursuant to the submission, as envisaged in rule 50, the executive summary of the submission shall be translated expeditiously, given the time frame required for such translation by the rules of the Secretariat. Taking into account the volume and complexity of the main body and supporting scientific and technical data of the submission, a reasonable time should be allowed for the completion of the translation of the full submission, including its annexes and charts, and the conversion of the data, if necessary, before the Commission shall meet for consideration of the submission.

Rule 48
Recording of the submission

1. Each submission shall be recorded by the Secretary-General upon receipt.

2. The record shall contain the date of receipt of the submission, a list of attachments and annexes thereto and the date of entry into force of the Convention for the coastal State which made the submission.

---

[5] For the format of the submission, *see* paragraph 1 of Annex III.

Rule 49
Acknowledgement of the receipt of the submission

The Secretary-General shall promptly acknowledge by letter to the submitting State the receipt of its submission and attachments and annexes thereto, specifying the date of receipt.

Rule 50
Notification of the receipt of a submission and publication of the proposed outer limits of the continental shelf related to the submission

The Secretary-General shall, through the appropriate channels, promptly notify the Commission and all States Members of the United Nations, including States Parties to the Convention, of the receipt of the submission, and make public the executive summary including all charts and coordinates referred to in paragraph 9.1.4 of the Guidelines and contained in that summary, upon completion of the translation of the executive summary referred to in rule 47, paragraph 3.

Rule 51
Consideration of the submission[6]

1. Upon receipt of a submission by the Secretary-General, the consideration of that submission shall be included in the provisional agenda of the next ordinary session of the Commission prepared in accordance with rule 5 and paragraph 2 of Annex III, provided that that session, as convened in accordance with rule 2, is held not earlier than three months after the date of the publication by the Secretary-General of the executive summary including all charts and coordinates referred to in rule 50.

2. If the next ordinary session of the Commission is not scheduled within a reasonable time, the Chairperson of the Commission may, upon the notification by the Secretary-General of the receipt of the submission in accordance with rule 50, request an additional session to be convened in accordance with rule 2, within a suitable time for the purpose of considering the submission.

3. The submission shall be considered in accordance with the rules on confidentiality contained in Annex II to these Rules.

4. Unless it decides otherwise, the Commission shall establish a subcommission in accordance with rule 42 for the consideration of each submission.

---

[6] For the Modus Operandi for the consideration of a submission made to the Commission see Annex III.

5. The recommendations prepared by the subcommission[7] shall be submitted in writing to the Chairperson of the Commission.

Rule 52
Attendance by the coastal State at the consideration of its submission

The Commission shall, through the Secretary-General, notify the coastal State which has made a submission, no later than sixty days prior to the opening date of the session, of the date and place at which its submission will be first considered. The coastal State shall, in accordance with article 5 of Annex II to the Convention, be invited to send its representatives to participate, without the right to vote, in the proceedings deemed relevant by the Commission pursuant to section VII of Annex III to these Rules.

Rule 53
Recommendations of the Commission

1. The Commission shall consider and approve or amend the recommendations prepared by the subcommission following their submission by the subcommission, ensuring that sufficient time is allowed in each case.

2. The recommendations of the Commission based on the recommendations prepared by the subcommission shall be approved in accordance with rule 35 and rule 37, paragraph 1.

3. The recommendations of the Commission on matters related to the establishment of the outer limits of the continental shelf shall be submitted in writing to the coastal State which made the submission and to the Secretary-General, in accordance with article 6, paragraph 3, of Annex II to the Convention. For this purpose the Chairperson of the Commission shall transmit to the Secretariat two copies of the recommendations, one to be submitted to the coastal State, and one to remain in the custody of the Secretary-General. If the submission was not originally made in English, the recommendations shall be translated by the Secretariat into the official language in which the submission was originally made. The translation shall be transmitted to the coastal State together with the original English text of the recommendations.

4. In the case of disagreement by the coastal State with the recommendations of the Commission, the coastal State shall, in accordance with article 8 of Annex II to the Convention, make a revised or new submission to the Commission within a reasonable time.

---

[7] For the provisions regulating the preparation of recommendations by a subcommission see section V of Annex III.

5. The outer limits of the continental shelf established by a coastal State on the basis of the recommendations of the Commission shall be final and binding, in accordance with article 76, paragraph 8, of the Convention.

Rule 54
Deposit and publicity of the limits of the continental shelf

1. The coastal State shall, in accordance with article 76, paragraph 9, and article 84 of the Convention, deposit with the Secretary-General of the United Nations and the Secretary-General of the International Seabed Authority charts and relevant information, including geodetic data permanently describing the outer limits of its continental shelf.

2. Pursuant to article 84 of the Convention, in the case of delimitation of the continental shelf between States with opposite or adjacent coasts, charts and/or coordinates describing the lines of delimitation drawn in accordance with article 83 of the Convention shall be deposited with the Secretary-General of the United Nations.

3. Upon giving due publicity to the charts and relevant information, including geodetic data, permanently describing the outer limits of the continental shelf deposited by the coastal State in accordance with article 76, paragraph 9, of the Convention, the Secretary-General shall give due publicity also to the recommendations of the Commission which in the view of the Commission are related to those limits.

XII. Advice to a coastal State

Rule 55
Advice to a coastal State

1. A coastal State may request scientific and technical advice from the Commission, in accordance with article 3, paragraph 1 (b), of Annex II to the Convention.

2. The Commission shall elect a standing subsidiary body composed of five of its members, which will prepare with respect to each request a list of proposed members who may provide advice taking into consideration the technical and scientific nature of each request. The list shall contain a copy of the scientific curriculum vitae of each proposed member. The preparation of this list may take into consideration an explicit request made by a coastal State for the advice of any member of the Commission.

3. The maximum number of members of the Commission who may provide advice to a coastal State in support of a submission shall not exceed three.

4. The dates and terms of advice shall be determined by agreement between the selected members of the Commission and the coastal State.

5. The members selected to provide technical and scientific advice to the coastal State shall submit to the Commission a report outlining their activities.

XIII. Cooperation with competent international organizations

Rule 56
Cooperation with competent international organizations

The procedure for cooperation referred to in article 3, paragraph 2, of Annex II to the Convention shall be decided by the Commission on a case-by-case basis.

XIV. Advice by specialists

Rule 57
Advice by specialists

1. The Commission may, to the extent considered necessary and useful, consult specialists in any field relevant to the work of the Commission.

2. The Commission shall decide in each case the way in which such consultations may be conducted.

XV. Adoption of other regulations, guidelines and annexes to the Rules of Procedure

Rule 58
Adoption of other regulations, guidelines and annexes to the Rules of Procedure

1. Subject to rules 35 and 37, the Commission may adopt such regulations, guidelines and annexes to the present Rules as are required for the effective performance of its functions.

2. The annexes form an integral part of these Rules, and a reference to the Rules or any part thereof includes a reference to the annexes relating thereto.

XVI. Amendments to the Rules of Procedure

Rule 59
Amendments to the Rules of Procedure

Subject to rules 35 and 37, the Commission may amend the present Rules and its annexes as well as other regulations and guidelines.

Annex I

Submissions in case of a dispute between States with opposite or adjacent coasts or in other cases of unresolved land or maritime disputes

1. The Commission recognizes that the competence with respect to matters regarding disputes which may arise in connection with the establishment of the outer limits of the continental shelf rests with States.

2. In case there is a dispute in the delimitation of the continental shelf between opposite or adjacent States, or in other cases of unresolved land or maritime disputes, related to the submission, the Commission shall be:

(a) Informed of such disputes by the coastal States making the submission; and

(b) Assured by the coastal States making the submission to the extent possible that the submission will not prejudice matters relating to the delimitation of boundaries between States.

3. A submission may be made by a coastal State for a portion of its continental shelf in order not to prejudice questions relating to the delimitation of boundaries between States in any other portion or portions of the continental shelf for which a submission may be made later, notwithstanding the provisions regarding the ten-year period established by article 4 of Annex II to the Convention.

4. Joint or separate submissions to the Commission requesting the Commission to make recommendations with respect to delineation may be made by two or more coastal States by agreement:

(a) Without regard to the delimitation of boundaries between those States; or

(b) Having indicated by means of geodetic coordinates the extent to which a submission is without prejudice to the matters relating to the delimitation of boundaries with another or other States Parties to this Agreement.

5. (a) In cases where a land or maritime dispute exists, the Commission shall not consider and qualify a submission made by any of the States concerned in the dispute. However, the Commission may consider one or more submissions in the areas under dispute with prior consent given by all States that are parties to such a dispute.

(b) The submissions made before the Commission and the recommendations approved by the Commission thereon shall not prejudice the position of States which are parties to a land or maritime dispute.

6. The Commission may request a State making a submission to cooperate with it in order not to prejudice matters relating to the delimitation of boundaries between opposite or adjacent States.

Annex II

Confidentiality

1. Safe custody of the submission

The Secretary-General shall ensure the safe custody of the submission and the attachments and annexes thereto at United Nations Headquarters in New York until such time as they are required by the Commission.

2. Classification as confidential of data and information by the coastal State

1. The coastal State making a submission may classify as confidential any data and other material, not otherwise publicly available, that it submits in accordance with rule 45. In dealing with such classified material and in the exercise of all their other functions, the members of the Commission shall enjoy the privileges and immunities as experts on mission for the United Nations in accordance with article VI of the Convention on the Privileges and Immunities of the United Nations.[a]

2. Confidential material so classified by the coastal State shall be submitted in accordance with rule 47, paragraph 2, to the Chairperson of the Commission in a separate sealed package, with a list of the material included therein.

3. Confidential material so classified by the coastal State shall remain confidential after the consideration of the submission is concluded unless decided otherwise by the Commission with the written consent of the coastal State concerned.

3. Access to confidential data and information

1. Save with the consent of the coastal State making the submission, access to confidential material shall be in accordance with the procedures set out in this rule and shall be confined to:

(a) The members of the Commission; and

(b) The Secretary-General and other members of the Secretariat designated for that purpose.

---

[a] The legal opinion on the applicability of the Convention on the Privileges and Immunities of the United Nations to the members of the Commission was provided in a letter dated 11 March 1998 from the Legal Counsel, Under-Secretary-General of the United Nations for Legal Affairs, addressed to the Commission on the Limits of the Continental Shelf (CLCS/5).

2. Access to confidential material shall only be given by the Secretary-General at the request of the Chairperson of the Commission and of the chairpersons of the relevant subcommissions.

3. Access to confidential material submitted by the coastal State or States shall be given by the Secretary-General through the chairpersons to the members of the Commission or the relevant subcommissions that have been established to consider the submission.

4. All confidential material forwarded with the submission shall be consulted in the room designated for that purpose and only in the presence of the Secretary-General or one of his or her staff members designated for that purpose.

5. Whenever confidential material is consulted, the name of the person who has authorized access and the time and date of such consultation shall be recorded in the register maintained for that purpose by the Secretary-General or one of his or her designated staff members. The member consulting the confidential material and the staff member present during the consultation shall print their names clearly and sign the entry.

6. Confidential material shall not be copied, duplicated or reproduced in any manner without the written authorization of the coastal State that submitted it.

4. Duty to preserve confidentiality

1. The deliberations of the Commission and subcommissions on all submissions made in accordance with article 76, paragraph 8, of the Convention shall take place in private and remain confidential.

2. Only members of the subcommission and, if necessary, specialists appointed in accordance with rule 57 shall take part in the subcommission deliberations on submissions. The Secretary and other members of the staff of the Secretariat as may be required shall be present. No other person shall be present except by permission of the subcommission.

3. Any records of the Commission and subcommission deliberations on all submissions shall contain only the title or nature of the subjects or matters discussed and the results of any vote taken. They shall not contain any details of the discussions or the views expressed, provided, however, that any member is entitled to require that a statement made by him be inserted in the records.

4. The members of the Commission shall not disclose, also after they cease to be members, any confidential information

coming to their knowledge by reason of their duties in relation to the Commission.

5. The duty of the members of the Commission not to disclose confidential information constitutes an obligation in respect of the individual's membership in the Commission.

5. Enforcement of rules on confidentiality

1. The Commission shall elect a standing Committee on Confidentiality composed of five of its members to deal with issues of confidentiality. In case of an alleged breach of confidentiality by a member of the Commission, the Commission may institute appropriate proceedings. In such cases, the Committee on Confidentiality shall establish an investigating body consisting of three or five of its members. The work of the investigating body shall be conducted in strict confidentiality and shall follow established procedures with regard to due process. Having completed its examination of the case, the investigating body shall prepare a report on its findings. The report shall contain the following:

(a) The allegations of a breach of confidentiality;

(b) The statement of the member of the Commission concerned;

(c) A synopsis of the evidence and the evaluation of it by the investigating body;

(d) The findings, indicating which of the allegations, if any, appear to be supported by the evidence;

(e) The conclusions reached by the investigating body; and

(f) Dissenting or separate opinions, if any.

2. The report shall be presented by the Chairperson of the Committee on Confidentiality to the Commission. The Commission shall inform the Meeting of States Parties of the allegations and the results of the investigation, together with its recommendations.

3. The Secretary-General shall provide the Commission with all necessary assistance in enforcing the rules concerning confidentiality.

6. Cessation of confidentiality

The charts and relevant information, including geodetic data, describing the outer limits of the continental shelf, which are deposited by the coastal State with the Secretary-General and which are to be given due publicity by the Secretary-General in accordance with article 76, paragraph 9, of the Convention, shall cease to be classified as confidential, if they had been so classified earlier, upon their receipt by the Secretary-General.

7. Return of confidential data and information to the coastal State

Any and all confidential material submitted by the coastal State, other than materials subject to the provisions of paragraph 6 of this Annex, shall be returned to the coastal State upon its request at any time, and in any event after receipt by the Secretary-General of the charts and relevant information, including geodetic data, referred to in paragraph 6 of this Annex.

Annex III

Modus operandi for the consideration of a submission made to the Commission on the Limits of the Continental Shelf

I. Submission by a coastal State

1. Format and number of copies of the submission

1. In accordance with paragraphs 9.1.3, 9.1.4, 9.1.5 and 9.1.6 of the Guidelines, the submission shall contain three separate parts: an executive summary, a main analytical and descriptive part (main body), and a part containing all data referred to in the analytical and descriptive part (supporting scientific and technical data).

2. If the submission is made in hard copy only, it shall be made in accordance with paragraph 9.1.3 of the Guidelines, i.e. the submission shall consist of the following number of copies: 22 copies of the executive summary, 8 copies of the main analytical and descriptive part, and 2 copies of the part containing all data referred to in the analytical and descriptive part. Should a coastal State choose to make a submission in electronic form as well, it is required to be in a secure unalterable format, and to be certified to contain a true and complete copy of the hard copy of the submission. In the case of discrepancies between the electronic and hard copy of the submission, the latter will be deemed the primary source.

II. Organization of the work of the Commission

2. Agenda items related to the submission

Upon notification that a submission has been received and made public in accordance with rule 50, and after a period of at least three months following the date of publication, in accordance with rule 51, paragraph 1, the Commission shall convene its session with the following items on the provisional agenda prepared in accordance with rule 5 and rule 51, paragraph 1:

(a) Presentation of the submission by coastal State representatives, to include the following subjects:

(i) Charts indicating the proposed limits;

(ii) The criteria of article 76 of the Convention which were applied;

(iii) Names of members of the Commission who have assisted the coastal State by providing scientific and technical advice with respect to the delineation;

(iv) Information regarding any disputes related to the submission; and

(v) Comments on any note verbale from other States regarding the data reflected in the executive summary including all charts and coordinates as made public by the Secretary-General in accordance with rule 50.

(b) Consideration of any information regarding any disputes related to the submission, and decisions in accordance with rule 46 and Annex I to these Rules as to whether to proceed with the consideration of the submission, or part thereof, or not. The Commission may defer these decisions to a subcommission in accordance with paragraph 7.

(c) Consideration of how to proceed with the further work of the Commission, inter alia, by way of a subcommission, in accordance with article 5 of Annex II to the Convention.

III. Initial examination of the submission

3. Format and completeness of the submission

The subcommission shall examine whether the format of the submission is in compliance with the requirements set out in paragraph 1, and shall ensure that all necessary information has been included in the submission. If it is deemed necessary, the subcommission may request the coastal State to correct the format and/or to provide any necessary additional information, in a timely manner.

4. Working language of the subcommissions

In recognition of the size and complexity of the submission, the resources and the time-constraints involved in the translation, and the timely consideration of the submission by the Commission, the working language of the subcommission shall be English.

5. Preliminary analysis of the submission

The subcommission shall undertake a preliminary analysis of the submission in accordance with article 76 of the Convention and the Guidelines in order to determine:

(a) If the test of appurtenance is satisfied by the coastal State;

(b) Which portions of the outer limits of the continental shelf are determined by each of the formulae and constraint lines provided for in article 76 of the Convention and the Statement of Understanding;

(c) If the construction of the outer limits contains straight lines not longer than 60 M;

(d) If the subcommission intends to recommend that the advice of specialists, in accordance with rule 57, or that the cooperation of relevant international organizations, in accordance with rule 56, be sought; and

(e) The estimated time required by the subcommission to review all the data and prepare its recommendations for the Commission.

6. Clarifications

1. The subcommission shall determine whether there are any matters to be clarified by the coastal State.

2. If necessary, the Chairperson of the subcommission shall, through the Secretariat, request clarification from the representatives of the coastal State on those matters. Clarifications should be sought in the form of written questions and answers and translated by the Secretariat, if necessary, into the language in which the submission was made. If the delegation of experts from the submitting State is available at United Nations Headquarters in New York, the written communication should be combined with consultations between the national experts and members of the subcommission at meetings arranged by the Secretariat.

7. Disputes related to a submission

The subcommission shall examine all information regarding any disputes related to the submission, in accordance with rule 46. If necessary, the subcommission shall take action based on the procedures in Annex I to these Rules.

8. Notification to the Commission

1. The initial examination shall be completed within a period of not more than one week, after which the subcommission shall notify the Commission of the estimated time and possible advice it might need in order to complete the review of the submission and prepare recommendations thereon for the Commission.

2. The Commission or the subcommission, through the Secretariat, shall notify the coastal State of the preliminary timetable for the examination of the submission by the subcommission.

IV. Main scientific and technical examination of the submission

9. Examination of the submission

1. The subcommission shall conduct an examination of the submission based on the Guidelines in order to evaluate the following, where applicable:

(a) The data and methodology employed by the State to determine the location of the foot of the continental slope;

(b) The methodology used to determine the formula line at a distance of 60 M from the foot of the continental slope;

(c) The data and methodology used to determine the formula line delineated by reference to the outermost fixed points at each of which the thickness of sedimentary rocks is at least 1 per cent of the shortest distance from such point to the foot of the continental slope, or not less than 1 kilometre in the cases in which the Statement of Understanding applies;

(d) The data and methodology employed in the determination of the 2,500-metre isobath;

(e) The methodology used to determine the constraint line at a distance of 100 M from the 2,500-metre isobath;

(f) The data and methodology used to determine the constraint line at a distance of 350 M from the baselines from which the breadth of the territorial sea is measured;

(g) The construction of the formulae line as the outer envelope of the two formulae;

(h) The construction of the constraint line as the outer envelope of the two constraints;

(i) The construction of the inner envelope of the formulae and constraint lines;

(j) The delineation of the outer limit of the continental shelf by means of straight lines not longer than 60 M with a view to ensuring that only the portion of the seabed that satisfies all the provisions of article 76 of the Convention and the Statement of Understanding is enclosed;

(k) The estimates of the uncertainties in the methods applied, with a view to identifying the main source(s) of such uncertainties and their effect on the submission; and, in all cases,

(l) That the data submitted are sufficient in terms of quantity and quality to justify the proposed limits.

2. The subcommission shall operate through working sessions of suitable duration in the designated facilities at United Nations Headquarters in New York. In addition, the subcommission may decide to assign further work to its members on specific parts of the submission in intersessional periods.

10. Additional data, information or advice

1. At any stage of the examination, should the subcommission arrive at the conclusion that there is a need for additional data, information or clarifications, its Chairperson shall request the coastal State to provide such data or information or to make clarifications. Such a request, articulated in precise technical terms, shall be transmitted through the Secretariat. If necessary, the Secretariat will translate the request and questions. The data, information or clarifications requested shall be provided within a time period agreed upon between the coastal State and the subcommission.

2. If necessary, the subcommission may request the advice of other members of the Commission and/or, on behalf of the Commission, request the advice of a specialist in accordance with rule 57, and/or the cooperation of relevant international organizations, in accordance with rule 56.

V. Recommendations prepared by the subcommission

11. Formulation of the recommendations

1. The recommendations prepared by the subcommission shall be in accordance with article 76 of the Convention, the Statement of Understanding, these Rules and the Guidelines.

2. The recommendations prepared by the subcommission shall focus on the data and other material submitted by the coastal States in support of the establishment of the outer limits of their continental shelf.

3. The recommendations prepared by the subcommission shall include a summary thereof, and such summary shall not contain information which might be of a confidential nature and/or which might violate the proprietary rights of the coastal State over the data and information provided in the submission. The Secretary-General shall make public the summary of the recommendations upon their approval by the Commission.

12. Drafting of the recommendations

1. The subcommission may appoint one of its members to produce, after consultation with the other members, a first draft

of the recommendations. Each member shall produce notes to be considered for the preparation of the draft.

2. The subcommission may prepare an "Outline of the recommendations prepared by the subcommission" containing the agreed format, contents and main conclusions at an appropriate time. Based on this outline and under the coordination and supervision of an appointed member, each member of the subcommission may be assigned the task of drafting various parts of the recommendations during intersessional periods.

3. At the next session of the subcommission, the combined draft, consolidated by an appointed member, shall be examined by the subcommission at a first reading. Any member who wishes to modify the draft may propose amendments in writing.

4. If the submission contains sufficient data and other material upon which the outer limits of the continental shelf are based, the recommendations shall include the rationale on which such recommendations are based.

5. If the submission contains sufficient data and other material supporting outer limits of the continental shelf which would be different from those proposed in the submission, the recommendations shall contain the rationale on which the recommended outer limits are based.

6. If the submission does not contain sufficient data and other material upon which the outer limits of the continental shelf could be based, the recommendations shall include provisions regarding the additional data and other material that may be needed to support the preparation of a revised or new submission in accordance with the Guidelines.

13. Adoption of the recommendations by the subcommission

1. Pursuant to rule 35, the subcommission shall make its best endeavours to ensure that its work is accomplished by general agreement. Accordingly, the subcommission shall make every effort to reach agreement on recommendations by way of consensus. There shall be no voting on such matters until all efforts to achieve consensus have been exhausted.

2. Should it prove impossible to achieve consensus, the subcommission shall proceed to vote according to rules 36 to 39.

14. Submission of the recommendations prepared by the subcommission to the Commission

The recommendations prepared by the subcommission shall be submitted in writing to the Chairperson of the

Commission in accordance with rule 51, paragraph 45, through the Secretariat.

VI. Participation by coastal State representatives in the proceedings

15. Definition of relevant proceedings

1. Representatives of the submitting coastal State can participate in the relevant proceedings of the Commission, in accordance with rule 52. For this purpose, the Commission, taking into consideration the particulars of each submission, will identify the proceedings deemed relevant for the participation of the representatives of the submitting coastal State. The Commission understands that there are two proceedings deemed relevant for all submissions:

(a) The presentation of the submission by coastal State representatives at the first meeting of the Commission concerning the submission in accordance with paragraph 2 (a) of section II; and

(b) Meetings at which the subcommission invites the representatives of the coastal State for consultation.

2. The proceedings at which the Commission considers the recommendations submitted by the subcommission shall be deemed not relevant for the participation of the representatives of the submitting coastal State.

VII. Summary flow chart of the procedures concerning a submission made to the Commission

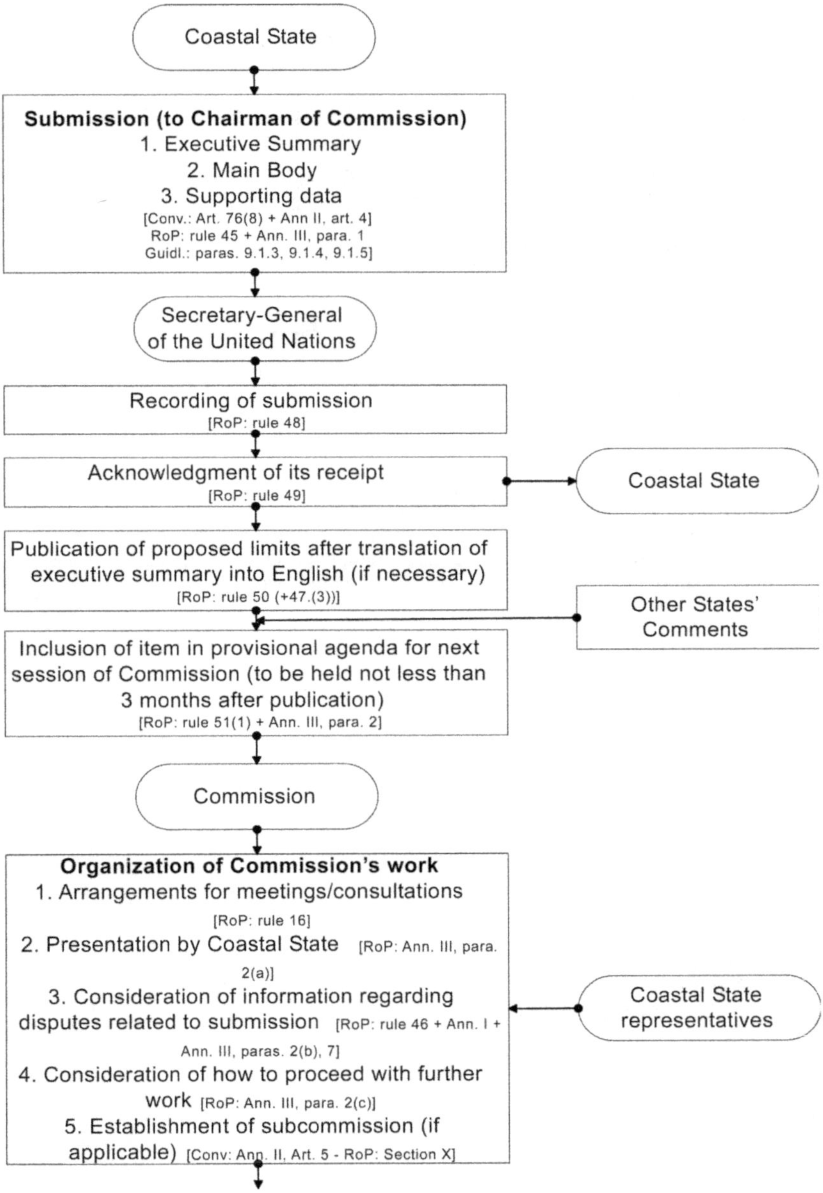

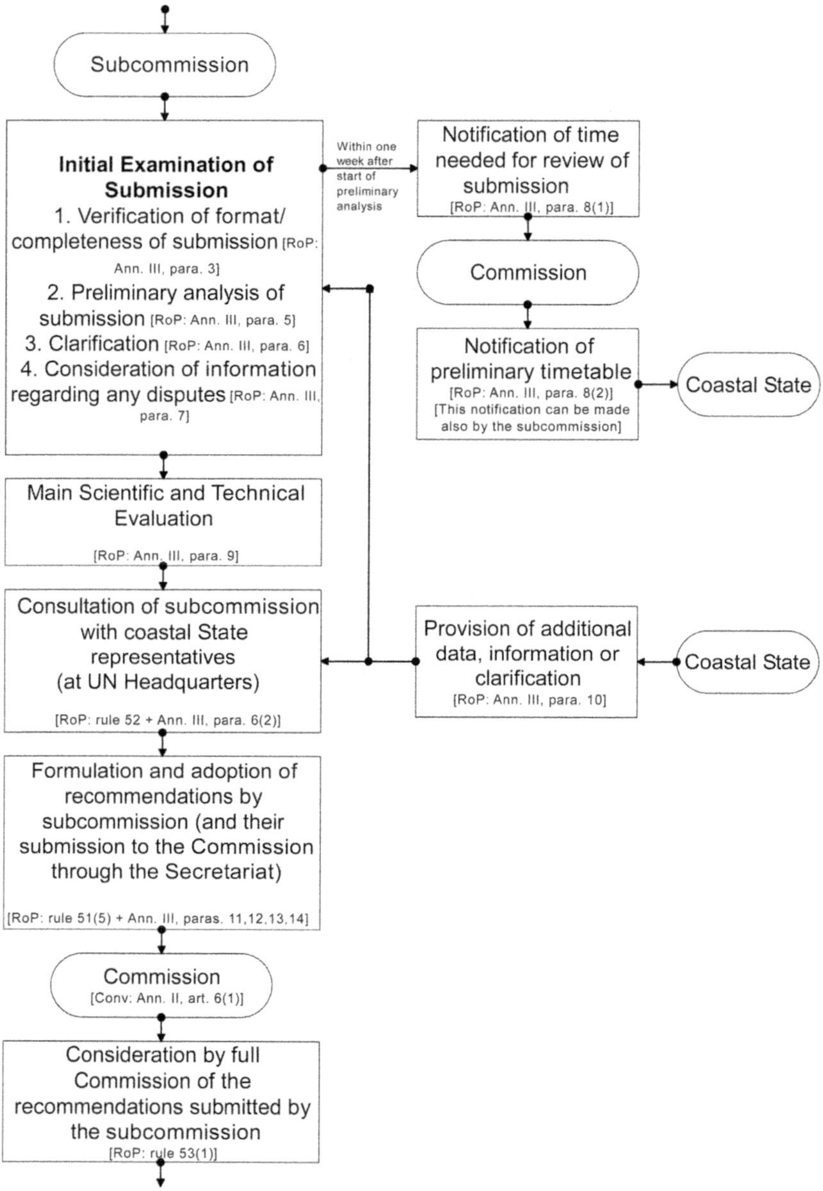
Subcommission
Initial Examination of Submission
1. Verification of format/ completeness of submission [RoP: Ann. III, para. 3]
2. Preliminary analysis of submission [RoP: Ann. III, para. 5]
3. Clarification [RoP: Ann. III, para. 6]
4. Consideration of information regarding any disputes [RoP: Ann. III, para. 7]
Within one week after start of preliminary analysis
Notification of time needed for review of submission [RoP: Ann. III, para. 8(1)]
Commission
Notification of preliminary timetable [RoP: Ann. III, para. 8(2)] [This notification can be made also by the subcommission]
Coastal State
Main Scientific and Technical Evaluation [RoP: Ann. III, para. 9]
Consultation of subcommission with coastal State representatives (at UN Headquarters) [RoP: rule 52 + Ann. III, para. 6(2)]
Provision of additional data, information or clarification [RoP: Ann. III, para. 10]
Coastal State
Formulation and adoption of recommendations by subcommission (and their submission to the Commission through the Secretariat) [RoP: rule 51(5) + Ann. III, paras. 11,12,13,14]
Commission [Conv: Ann. II, art. 6(1)]
Consideration by full Commission of the recommendations submitted by the subcommission [RoP: rule 53(1)]

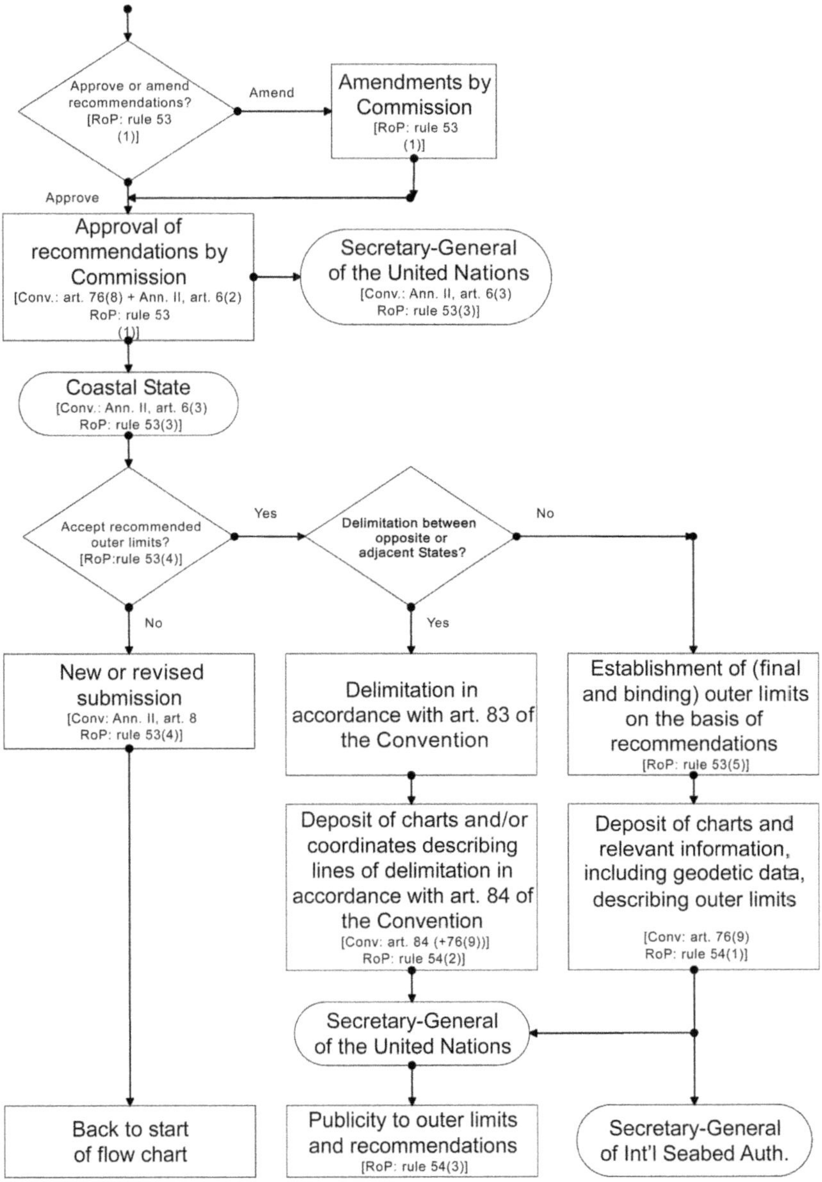
Approve or amend recommendations? [RoP: rule 53 (1)]
Amend
Amendments by Commission [RoP: rule 53 (1)]
Approve
Approval of recommendations by Commission [Conv.: art. 76(8) + Ann. II, art. 6(2) RoP: rule 53 (1)]
Secretary-General of the United Nations [Conv.: Ann. II, art. 6(3) RoP: rule 53(3)]
Coastal State [Conv.: Ann. II, art. 6(3) RoP: rule 53(3)]
Accept recommended outer limits? [RoP:rule 53(4)]
Yes
Delimitation between opposite or adjacent States?
No
No
Yes
New or revised submission [Conv: Ann. II, art. 8 RoP: rule 53(4)]
Delimitation in accordance with art. 83 of the Convention
Establishment of (final and binding) outer limits on the basis of recommendations [RoP: rule 53(5)]
Deposit of charts and/or coordinates describing lines of delimitation in accordance with art. 84 of the Convention [Conv: art. 84 (+76(9))] RoP: rule 54(2)]
Deposit of charts and relevant information, including geodetic data, describing outer limits [Conv: art. 76(9) RoP: rule 54(1)]
Secretary-General of the United Nations
Back to start of flow chart
Publicity to outer limits and recommendations [RoP: rule 54(3)]
Secretary-General of Int'l Seabed Auth.

United Nations Convention on the Law of the Sea CLCS/47

Commission on the Limits of the Continental Shelf

Distr.: General
8 September 2005

Original: English

Sixteenth session
New York, 29 August-16 September 2005

Internal code of conduct for members of the Commission on the Limits of the Continental Shelf

1. Introduction

The members of the Commission on the Limits of the Continental Shelf ("the Commission") have been elected to undertake important and specific responsibilities pursuant to the United Nations Convention on the Law of the Sea ("the Convention"). A high standard of conduct is expected of them in discharging their duties in conformity with the Rules of Procedure of the Commission and their solemn declaration:

> "I solemnly declare that I will perform my duties as a member of the Commission on the Limits of the Continental Shelf honourably, faithfully, impartially and conscientiously."

The present guidelines set ethical standards expected of the members of the Commission. They do not modify or otherwise affect the rights, duties and obligations of the members of the Commission under the Convention.

2. Duty to preserve integrity, independence and impartiality

While the personal views and convictions of the members of the Commission, including their political and religious convictions, remain inviolable, they shall ensure that those views and convictions do not adversely affect their official duties. Members of the Commission shall conduct themselves at all times in a manner befitting their status. They shall not engage in any activity that is incompatible with the proper discharge of their duties. They shall avoid any action and, in particular, any kind of public pronouncement that may adversely reflect on their status, or on the integrity, independence and impartiality that are required by that status.

3. Confidentiality

In accordance with the Rules of Procedure of the Commission and their annex II, each Member shall at all times maintain the confidentiality of the deliberations and proceedings of the Commission together with any information identified as confidential. No member shall at any time use such information acquired during such deliberations and proceedings to gain personal advantage or advantage for others.

4. Duty to avoid conflict of interest

Members of the Commission shall not use their knowledge or official functions for private gain, financial or otherwise, or for the gain of any third party, including family, friends and those they favour. Nor shall they use their office for personal reasons to prejudice the positions of those they do not favour.

5. Duty to act independently

In accordance with rule 11 of the Rules of Procedure, members of the Commission shall not seek or receive instructions from any Government or from any other authority external to the Commission. They shall exercise the utmost discretion in regard to all matters of official business. They shall not communicate to any Government, entity, person or any other source any information known to them by reason of their official position that they know or ought to have known has not been made public, except as appropriate in the normal course of their duties or by the authorization of the Commission. These obligations do not cease upon the cessation of their official functions.

6. Disclaimer

Publication of material on issues related to the work of the Commission and the continental shelf shall require the following disclaimer:

> "The views expressed herein are solely those of the author(s) and do not necessarily reflect the views of the Commission on the Limits of the Continental Shelf."

United Nations Convention on the Law of the Sea CLCS/46

Commission on the Limits of the Continental Shelf

Distr.: General
7 September 2005

Original: English

Sixteenth session
New York, 29 August–16 September 2005

Letter dated 25 August 2005 from the Legal Counsel, Under-Secretary-General of the United Nations for Legal Affairs, addressed to the Chairman of the Commission on the Limits of the Continental Shelf

Legal opinion on whether it is permissible, under the United Nations Convention on the Law of the Sea and the rules of procedure of the Commission, for a coastal State, which has made a submission to the Commission in accordance with article 76 of the Convention, to provide to the Commission in the course of the examination by it of the submission, additional material and information relating to the limits of its continental shelf or substantial part thereof, which constitute a significant departure from the original limits and formulae lines that were given due publicity by the Secretary-General of the United Nations in accordance with rule 50 of the rules of procedure of the Commission

I am writing in response to your letter of 27 May 2005. By that letter you informed me that, at its fifteenth session, held in New York from 4 to 22 April 2005, the Commission on the Limits of the Continental Shelf decided, following the report of the Chairman of the subcommission established to examine the submission of Brazil, to seek a legal opinion from the Legal Counsel of the United Nations on the following question:

> "Is it permissible, under the United Nations Convention on the Law of the Sea and the rules of procedure of the Commission, for a coastal State, which has made a submission to the Commission in accordance with article 76 of the Convention, to provide to the Commission in the course of the examination by it of the submission, additional material and information relating to the limits of its continental shelf or substantial part thereof, which constitute a significant departure from the original limits and formulae lines that were given due publicity by the Secretary-General of the United Nations in accordance with rule 50 of the rules of procedure of the Commission?"

In the letter you indicated that the Commission would like to receive the legal opinion before the next session of the Commission, which will be held from 29 August to 16 September 2005. You also provided me with a copy of your statement on the progress of work in the Commission at its fifteenth session (CLCS/44), paragraphs 12 to 16 of which reflect the discussions and the decision of the Commission on the matter.

I would like to inform you that in connection with the request by the Commission for a legal opinion, I received, on 15 June 2005, a note verbale from the Permanent Mission of Brazil to the United Nations, dated 13 June 2005, asking for a meeting with me for the purpose of clarifying specific aspects of the information on the Brazilian submission contained in your statement on the progress of work of the Commission at the fifteenth session.

At a subsequent meeting, held on 20 June 2005, the Acting Permanent Representative of Brazil to the United Nations handed to me a paper entitled "Clarifications to the Legal Counsel regarding the CLCS consultation contained in CLCS/44". It is my understanding that Brazil has also provided a copy of the paper to the Commission.

It is worthy of note for the purpose of the present legal opinion that the paper states in its introduction that the need to consult the Legal Counsel of the United Nations:

> "was perceived during the consideration of item 4 of the agenda of the fifteenth session of the CLCS, regarding the 'consideration of the submission by Brazil to the Commission pursuant to article 76, paragraph 8, of the 1982 United Nations Convention on the Law of the Sea'. However, the formulation of the above question by the CLCS could lead to the assumption that the referred 'additional material and information relating to the limits of its continental shelf or substantial part thereof' has no relation to the process of examination of the submission conducted by the subcommission. Such an assumption would be mistaken in the case of the Brazilian submission, given that the additional material and information submitted does not constitute a new or revised submission."

My response to the request by the Commission for a legal opinion on the question at issue is contained in a paper attached to this letter (see annex).

(*Signed*) Nicolas **Michel**
Under-Secretary-General for Legal Affairs
The Legal Counsel

Annex to the letter dated 25 August 2005 from the Legal Counsel, Under-Secretary-General of the United Nations for Legal Affairs, addressed to the Chairman of the Commission on the Limits of the Continental Shelf

Contents

Introduction

The question with regard to which the Commission on the Limits of the Continental Shelf (CLCS) decided to seek a legal opinion reads as follows:

> "Is it permissible, under the United Nations Convention on the Law of the Sea and the rules of procedure of the Commission, for a coastal State, which has made a submission to the Commission in accordance with article 76 of the Convention, to provide to the Commission in the course of the examination by it of the submission, additional material and information relating to the limits of its continental shelf or substantial part thereof, which constitute a significant departure from the original limits and formulae lines that were given due publicity by the Secretary-General of the United Nations in accordance with rule 50 of the rules of procedure of the Commission?"

A description of the context within which this legal opinion was sought can be found in the Statement by the Chairman of the Commission on the Limits of the Continental Shelf on the progress of work in the Commission at its fifteenth session (CLCS/44, paras. 12–16).

Part I
United Nations Convention on the Law of the Sea

(a) General observations

The United Nations Convention on the Law of the Sea is a multilateral treaty the provisions of which are therefore binding on the Commission and States parties to the Convention submitting particulars regarding the outer limit of their continental shelf along with supporting scientific and technical data to the Commission. Therefore, it is important initially to identify the provisions of the Convention which are pertinent to the question on which a legal opinion is being sought by the Commission.

(b) Pertinent provisions of the Convention

It appears that the following provisions of the Convention are relevant to the question at issue.

> *"Article 76*
>
> *"Definition of the continental shelf*
>
> "1. The continental shelf of a coastal State comprises the seabed and subsoil of the maritime areas that

extend beyond its territorial sea throughout the natural prolongation of its territory to the outer edge of the continental margin, or to a distance of 200 nautical miles from the baselines from which the breadth of the territorial sea is measured where the outer edge of the continental margin does not extend up to that distance.

"2. The continental shelf of a coastal State shall not extend beyond the limits provided for in paragraphs 4 to 6.

. . .

"7. The coastal State shall delineate the outer limits of its continental shelf, where that shelf extends beyond 200 nautical miles from the baselines from which the breadth of the territorial sea is measured, by straight lines not exceeding 60 nautical miles in length, connecting fixed points, defined by coordinates of latitude and longitude.

"8. Information on the limits of the continental shelf beyond 200 nautical miles from the baselines from which the breadth of the territorial sea is measured shall be submitted by the coastal State to the Commission on the Limits of the Continental Shelf set up under Annex II on the basis of equitable geographical representation. The Commission shall make recommendations to coastal States on matters related to the establishment of the outer limits of their continental shelf. The limits of the shelf established by a coastal State on the basis of these recommendations shall be final and binding.

. . .

"ANNEX II. COMMISSION ON THE LIMITS OF THE CONTINENTAL SHELF

"Article 1

"In accordance with the provisions of article 76, a Commission on the Limits of the Continental Shelf beyond 200 nautical miles shall be established in conformity with the following articles.

. . .

"Article 3

"1. The functions of the Commission shall be:

"(a) to consider the data and other material submitted by coastal States concerning the outer limits of the continental shelf in areas where those limits extend beyond 200 nautical miles, and to make recommendations in accordance with article 76 and the Statement of Understanding adopted on 29 August 1980 by the Third United Nations Conference on the Law of the Sea;

...

"Article 4

"Where a coastal State intends to establish, in accordance with article 76, the outer limits of its continental shelf beyond 200 nautical miles, it shall submit particulars of such limits to the Commission along with supporting scientific and technical data as soon as possible but in any case within 10 years of the entry into force of this Convention for that State. The coastal State shall at the same time give the names of any Commission members who have provided it with scientific and technical advice.

"Article 5

"Unless the Commission decides otherwise, the Commission shall function by way of sub-commissions composed of seven members, appointed in a balanced manner ..."

(c) Analysis of the pertinent provisions of the Convention

It follows from the above provisions of the Convention that a coastal State, which is entitled pursuant to the provisions of article 76 of the Convention to the continental shelf extending beyond 200 nautical miles, is required to submit to the Commission for its consideration information on the limits of its continental shelf beyond 200 nautical miles. The Convention further provides that such information should include particulars of such limits accompanied by supporting scientific and technical data. Thus, under the Convention, scientific and technical data are provided by a coastal State for the purpose of supporting particulars of the limits of the continental shelf submitted by that coastal State to the Commission.

In its request for the legal opinion, the Commission enquires as to whether it is permissible, under the Convention, for a coastal State to provide to the Commission, in the course of the examination by it of the submission of that State, additional material and information relating to the limits of its continental shelf or substantial part thereof, which constitute a significant departure from the original limits and formulae lines that were submitted to the Commission and which were given due publicity by the Secretary-General of the United Nations in accordance with rule 50 of the rules of procedure of the Commission.

It may be assumed that since additional data is presented by a coastal State in support of the particulars of the limits of the continental shelf submitted by it to the Commission, it should not contradict them. In other words, it is expected that the additional material and information should not amount to a revision of the original submission.

It appears, however, that there is nothing in the Convention that could preclude a coastal State from informing the Commission in the course of its examination of the submission of that State that further analysis of the scientific and technical data originally presented to the Commission in support of particulars of the limits of its continental shelf or substantial part thereof has brought this State to a conclusion that some of these particulars were not correct and therefore the outer limits of the continental shelf need to be adjusted.

Likewise, it appears that there is nothing in the Convention that prevents a coastal State from submitting to the Commission, in the course of the examination by the Commission of its original information, new particulars of the limits of its continental shelf or substantial part thereof if in the view of the coastal State concerned it is justified by additional scientific and technical data obtained by it.

The coastal State concerned will be expected in both cases to explain to the Commission why it believes that some of the limits of the continental shelf originally presented by it to the Commission need to be adjusted or modified and to provide the necessary scientific and technical data supporting this conclusion. It will, of course, then be for the Commission to examine, in the light of its mandate as defined by the Convention, the original submission together with the proposed new limits of part of the continental shelf of the coastal State concerned and to determine whether they meet the requirements of article 76 of the Convention. The findings of the Commission will be reflected in its recommendations on the submission.

Coastal States are expected to act in good faith and exercise caution so that the work of the Commission and the establishment of the outer limits of the continental shelf of these States are not unreasonably prolonged or delayed.

The analysis of the legislative history of the Convention indirectly supports the above conclusions. The travaux preparatoires of the Convention [Official Records of the Third United

Nations Conference on the Law of the Sea, Vols. I-XVII][1] show that delegations did not discuss the modalities through which a coastal State would provide the Commission with the particulars of the limits of its continental shelf and the supporting scientific and technical data. Consequently, the fact that the Convention does not expressly permit the coastal State to submit new particulars during the course of the examination of the original submission by the Commission cannot be interpreted to imply that States cannot do so.

Part II
Rules of procedure and other documents of the Commission

(a) General observations

The Commission is a treaty body which is established by the Convention to perform functions defined in article 3, paragraph 1, of annex II to the Convention. In accordance with subparagraph 1 (a) of that article, the Commission, as noted above, is entrusted with the responsibility to consider the data and other material submitted by a coastal State concerning the outer limits of the continental shelf in areas where those limits extend beyond 200 nautical miles, and to make recommendations in accordance with article 76 and the statement of understanding adopted by the Conference.

In addition to the explicit authority conferred upon it by the Convention, it is recognized that as a treaty body the Commission has certain implied powers that are essential for the fulfilment of its responsibilities under the Convention.

This is the case of the power to adopt rules of procedure and other relevant documents with a view to facilitating the discharge of the functions of the Commission in an orderly and effective manner. Due to the nature of the functions of the Commission, its rules of procedure and other relevant documents are not merely organizational, or internal, in nature. On the contrary, they also offer guidance to States which make a submission to the Commission. Unlike the case of the International Seabed Authority (see article 149, para. 4), the Convention does not contain any article providing the Commission with the power to adopt its own rules or procedure. The Commission, therefore, can do so only by exercising a power which is conferred upon it

[1] United Nations publications, Sales Nos. E.75.V.3, E.75.V.4, E.75.V.5, E.75.V.10, E.76.V.8, E.77.V.2, E.78.V.3, E.78.V.4, E.79.V.3, E.79.V.4, E.80.V.6, E.80.V.12, E.81.V.5, E.82.V.2, E.83.V.4, E.84.V.2 and E.84.V.3.

by necessary implication as being essential to the performance of its duties. The same applies to other relevant documents. This is consistent with the 1949 advisory opinion by the International Court of Justice on *Reparations for injuries suffered in the service of the United Nations*. The Court found in that opinion, inter alia, that "under international law, the Organization must be deemed to have those powers, which, though not expressly provided in the Charter, are conferred upon it by necessary implication as being essential to the performance of its duties" (*I.C.J. Reports, 1949*, p. 182). The same considerations can be applied to the Commission with regard to powers which are essential to the performance of its duties, even though not expressly provided in the Convention.

It should be underlined, however, that rules of procedure and other relevant documents adopted by the Commission should be in strict conformity with the pertinent provisions of the Convention, which is the main instrument guiding the work of the Commission. In the case of any conflict between the provisions of these documents, which are supplementary by their nature, and those of the Convention, the latter shall prevail.

In this regard, it must be recalled that the Commission has adopted two documents: the rules of procedure of the Commission (CLCS/40) and the Scientific and Technical Guidelines of the Commission (CLCS/11 and Add.1).

Although the rules of procedure and the Guidelines are two separate documents, they are interrelated. The reference to the Guidelines is contained in various articles of the rules of procedure, which, inter alia, provide that "the Commission may adopt such regulations, guidelines and annexes to the present rules as are required for the effective performance of its functions" (rule 58, para. 1).

The rules of procedure of the Commission currently have three annexes, which — as provided for by rule 58, paragraph 2 — form an integral part of the rules of procedure. Of particular relevance to the present legal opinion is annex III, entitled "Modus operandi for the consideration of a submission made to the Commission on the Limits of the Continental Shelf".

It should be observed that the States parties to the Convention acknowledged in one of their decisions the right of the Commission to adopt documents necessary for the proper discharge of its responsibilities under the Convention. In the decision regarding the date of commencement of the 10-year period for making submissions to the Commission set out in article 4 of annex II to the Convention (SPLOS/72), adopted at their Eleventh Meeting, held from 14 to 18 May 2001, the States parties noted "that it was only after the adoption by the Commission of its Scientific and Technical Guidelines on 13 May 1999 that States had before them the basic documents concerning submissions in accordance with article 76, paragraph 8, of the Convention". By that decision, the States parties thus recognized the role played by the Guidelines and highlighted the particular importance they attached to them in the context of implementation of article 76, paragraph 8, of the Convention.

(b) Pertinent provisions of the rules of procedure

It appears that the following provisions of the rules of procedure of the Commission are relevant to the question at issue.

"Rule 45

"Submission by a coastal State

"In accordance with article 4 of Annex II to the Convention:

"Where a coastal State intends to establish the outer limits of its continental shelf beyond 200 nautical miles from the baselines from which the breadth of the territorial sea is measured, it shall submit particulars of such limits to the Commission along with supporting scientific and technical data as soon as possible, but in any case within ten years of the entry into force of the Convention for that State.

. . .

"Rule 47

"Form and language of submission

"1. A submission shall conform to the requirements established by the Commission.

. . .

"Rule 48

"Recording of the submission

"1. Each submission shall be recorded by the Secretary-General upon receipt.

. . .

"Rule 50

"Notification of the receipt of a submission and publication of the proposed outer limits of the continental shelf related to the submission

"The Secretary-General shall, through the appropriate channels, promptly notify the Commission and all States Members of the United Nations, including States Parties to the Convention, of the receipt of the submission, and make public the executive summary including all charts and coordinates referred to in paragraph 9.1.4 of the Guidelines and contained in that summary, upon completion of the translation of the executive summary referred to in rule 47, paragraph 3.

...

"Annex III

"Modus operandi for the consideration of a submission made to the Commission on the Limits of the Continental Shelf

"I. Submission by a coastal State

"1. Format and number of copies of the submission

"1. In accordance with paragraphs 9.1.3, 9.1.4, 9.1.5 and 9.1.6 of the Guidelines, the submission shall contain three separate parts: an executive summary, a main analytical and descriptive part (main body), and a part containing all data referred to in the analytical and descriptive part (supporting scientific and technical data).

...

"III. Initial examination of the submission

"3. Format and completeness of the submission

"The subcommission shall examine whether the format of the submission is in compliance with the requirements set out in paragraph 1, and shall ensure that all necessary information has been included in the submission. If it is deemed necessary, the subcommission may request the coastal State to correct the format and/or to provide any necessary additional information, in a timely manner.

...

"6. Clarifications

"1. The subcommission shall determine whether there are any matters to be clarified by the coastal State.

"2. If necessary, the Chairperson of the subcommission shall, through the Secretariat, request clarification from the representatives of the coastal State on those matters. Clarifications should be sought in the form of written questions and answers and translated by the Secretariat, if necessary, into the language in which the submission was made.

. . .

"IV. Main scientific and technical examination of the submission

"10. Additional data, information or advice

"1. At any stage of the examination, should the subcommission arrive at the conclusion that there is a need for additional data, information or clarifications, its Chairperson shall request the coastal State to provide such data or information or to make clarifications. Such a request, articulated in precise technical terms, shall be transmitted through the Secretariat. If necessary, the Secretariat will translate the request and questions. The data, information or clarifications requested shall be provided within a time period agreed upon between the coastal State and the subcommission."

(c) Pertinent provisions of the Guidelines

"1.2. The Commission prepared these Guidelines for the purpose of providing direction to coastal States which intend to submit data and other material concerning the outer limits of the continental shelf in areas where those limits extend beyond 200 nautical miles from the baselines from which the breadth of the territorial sea is measured. The Guidelines aim to clarify the scope and depth of admissible scientific and technical evidence to be examined by the Commission during its consideration of each submission for the purpose of making recommendations.

. . .

"9.1.3. The submission will be divided in three separate parts in accordance with the Modus Operandi of the Commission (CLCS/L.3). The requested format contains an executive summary (22 copies), a main body (8 copies) and all supporting scientific and technical data (2 copies).

"9.1.4. The executive summary will contain the following information:

"(a) Charts at an appropriate scale and coordinates indicating the outer limits of the continental shelf and the relevant territorial sea baselines;

"(b) Which provisions of article 76 are invoked to support the submission;

"(c) The names of any Commission members who gave advice in the preparation of the submission; and

"(d) Any disputes as referred to in rule 44 and annex I to the Rules of Procedure of the Commission."

(d) Analysis of the relevant provisions of the rules of procedure and Guidelines

In analysing the provisions of the rules of procedure of the Commission and of the Scientific and Technical Guidelines it must be taken into account that, as noted above, these documents need to be read, understood and interpreted in the light of the Convention, the provisions of which prevail.

It follows from the rules of procedure and the Guidelines that particulars of the limits of the continental shelf and supporting scientific and technical data should be presented to the Commission by a coastal State in the form of a submission. The latter should consist of three separate parts (executive summary, main body and supporting scientific and technical data). It also follows from paragraphs 3, 6 and 10 of annex III to the rules of procedure that the subcommission established by the Commission to consider a submission may, in the course of the initial as well as at any stage of the main examination of that submission, request the coastal State concerned to provide additional data, information or clarifications regarding that submission.

As noted in the section concerning the analysis of the pertinent provisions of the Convention, it is expected that additional data, information and clarifications provided by the coastal State to the Commission in response to such requests should support, integrate and clarify the particulars of the limits of the continental shelf contained in the submission, and that they should not amount to a new or revised submission.

However, as pointed out in the same section, it is quite possible that, in preparing a response to requests for additional information, a coastal State, while reassessing the data originally submitted to the Commission, could reach the conclusion that some of the particulars of the outer limits of its continental shelf contained in its original submission to the Commission need to be adjusted. A situation may also arise in which a coastal State reaches that conclusion not in response to a request by the subcommission but on its own. This may occur, for instance, in the light of additional scientific and technical data obtained by the

State concerned, or if errors or miscalculations in the submission are discovered that need to be rectified. The State concerned could then bring these to the attention of the subcommission and the Commission.

The rules of procedure and the Guidelines do not directly address these contingencies. The question, however, arises of how they should be treated in the light of the rules of procedure and the Guidelines. It may be recalled in this regard that the rules of procedure contain certain procedural requirements concerning the handling of submissions. After recording a submission (rule 48), acknowledging its receipt to the submitting coastal State (rule 49) and notifying the Commission and all States Members of the United Nations, including States parties to the Convention, of the receipt of the submission (rule 50), the Secretary-General of the United Nations is required to make public the executive summary of the submission, including all charts and coordinates indicating the outer limits of the continental shelf (paragraph 9.1.4 of the Guidelines).

In the event that a coastal State submits new particulars related to the proposed outer limits of its continental shelf, either in response to requests by the Commission for additional data and information or clarifications or on its own, an issue may arise with regard to the due publicity given to the original submission. If the new particulars lead to a significant departure from the original limits contained in the executive summary that was given due publicity by the Secretary-General of the United Nations, it appears that the newly proposed particulars of the outer limits of the continental shelf should be given similar publicity. All States have an interest in being notified about the limits proposed in a submission. The outer limits of the continental shelf of a State also define the Area (the seabed and ocean floor and subsoil thereof, beyond the limits of national jurisdiction), which is, together with its resources, the common heritage of mankind (article 136 of the Convention). According to the preamble of the Convention, the exploration and exploitation of the Area and its resources "shall be carried out for the benefit of mankind as a whole, irrespective of the geographical location of States". The Commission therefore should consider whether it would be advisable to address the issue of due publicity with regard to new particulars submitted to the Commission in the course of the examination of the original submission in one of its documents.

The question of whether there is a significant discrepancy between the originally submitted and the newly proposed particulars can be properly addressed only by the body with the required scientific and technical competence, namely the Commission. If the Commission concludes that such a discrepancy is significant, it may consider requesting the coastal State concerned to provide the Secretary-General of the United Nations with an addendum to its executive summary so that due publicity is given to this new information through its circulation to all States Members of the United Nations, including States parties to the Convention. The coastal State, of course, could make such a determination itself and directly provide an addendum to the Secretary-General for the purposes of due publicity. However, the Secretary-General should be guided in this regard by the Commission.

It should be observed that the analysis of State practice which has developed following the circulation of the executive summary of the first submission shows that sometimes other States find it necessary to provide comments on particular aspects of the executive summary by sending notes verbales to the Secretary-General with a request that those comments be brought to the attention of the Commission and be circulated to all States Members of the United Nations. The Commission may wish to consider whether this emerging practice should be taken into account and a time frame be established giving States an opportunity to provide comments on the addendum to the executive summary containing the new particulars of the limits of the continental shelf or substantial part thereof of the coastal State concerned.

Conclusions

Additional material and information relating to the limits of the continental shelf or substantial part thereof, provided by a coastal State to the Commission in response to its requests for additional data, information or clarification in the course of the examination by the Commission of the submission of that coastal State, is expected to support, integrate and clarify the particulars of the limits of the continental shelf contained in the submission.

However, there is nothing in the Convention that precludes a coastal State from submitting to the Commission, in the course of the examination by it of the submission of that State, revised particulars of the limits of its continental shelf if the State concerned reaches a conclusion, while reassessing in good faith the data contained in its submission, that some of the particulars of the limits of the continental shelf in the original submission should be adjusted, or if it discovers errors or miscalculations in the submission that need to be rectified.

Likewise, the Convention does not prevent a coastal State from submitting to the Commission, in the course of the examination by it of the submission of that State, new particulars of the limits of its continental shelf, or substantial part thereof, if in the view of the coastal State concerned, acting in good faith, this is justified by additional scientific and technical data obtained by it.

Consequently, in the cases described above it is permissible for a coastal State which has made a submission to the Commission in accordance with article 76 of the Convention to provide to the Commission, in the course of the examination by it of the submission, additional material and information relating to the limits of its continental shelf or substantial part thereof, which constitute a significant departure from the original limits and formulae lines that were given due publicity by the Secretary-General of the United Nations in accordance with rule 50 of the rules of procedure of the Commission.

As the rules of procedure and the Guidelines do not address the contingencies described above and at the same time require that the executive summary of the submission by a coastal State be given due publicity by the Secretary-General of the United Nations, the Commission may wish to consider whether it would be advisable to address this issue in one of its documents and to provide the necessary guidance to the Secretary-General of the United Nations in this regard.

In concluding, it should be emphasized that it is ultimately up to the Commission in the light of its mandate defined by the Convention to determine, after examining and evaluating data and information provided to it by a coastal State, what particulars of the limits of the continental shelf of the coastal State concerned meet the requirements of article 76 of the Convention.

UNITED NATIONS CONVENTION ON THE LAW OF THE SEA

CLCS

COMMISSION ON THE LIMITS OF THE CONTINENTAL SHELF

Distr.: General

CLCS/11
13 May 1999

Original: English

Fifth session
New York, 3–14 May 1999

SCIENTIFIC AND TECHNICAL GUIDELINES OF THE COMMISSION ON THE LIMITS OF THE CONTINENTAL SHELF

Adopted by the Commission on 13 May 1999 at its fifth session

CONTENTS

CONTENTS (continued)

CONTENTS (continued)

Preface

The preparation of the Scientific and Technical Guidelines of the Commission on the Limits of the Continental Shelf was conducted in two stages. The first stage consisted of background research conducted along disciplinary and interdisciplinary lines. The Commission organized six research groups for this purpose, established at its second session in September 1997:

(a) Hydrography (Srinivasan, Chairman; Albuquerque, Astiz, Awosika, Carrera, Francis and Lamont, with Rio as an alternate);

(b) Geodesy (Carrera, Chairman; Albuquerque, Astiz, Brekke, Francis, Hamuro, Jaafar, Mdala and Srinivasan, with Rio as an alternate);

(c) Geology (Park, Chairman; Betah, Brekke, Hamuro, Jura_i_, Kazmin, Lu, Mdala and Srinivasan, with Carrera as an alternate);

(d) Geophysics (Croker, Chairman; Awosika, Carrera, Hinz, Lu, Mdala and Park, with Francis as an alternate);

(e) Foot of the continental slope (Rio, Chairman; Carrera, Francis, Hamuro, Kazmin, Lamont and Srinivasan);

(f) Outer edge of the continental margin (Brekke, Chairman; Albuquerque, Astiz, Betah, Carrera, Croker, Hamuro, Jura_i_, Kazmin, Lu, Mdala and Park).

The second stage consisted of the preparation of draft Guidelines, which began at the third session of the Commission, held at United Nations Headquarters in New York from 4 to 15 May 1998. An Editorial Committee was established at the session and Galo Carrera was elected as its Chairman. The Editorial Committee considered and adopted the document structure for the Guidelines proposed by its Chairman.

The Editorial Committee was organized into 13 working groups, whose Chairmen reported to the Chairman of the Editorial Committee, as follows:

(1) Introduction (Carrera, Chairman; Editorial Committee);

(2) Entitlement to and delineation of the outer limits of the continental shelf (Carrera, Chairman; Albuquerque, Brekke, Hamuro, Hinz, Lamont and Rio);

(3) Geodetic methodologies and the outer limits of the continental shelf (Carrera, Chairman; Albuquerque, Astiz, Francis, Hamuro, Jaafar, Mdala, Rio and Srinivasan);

(4) The 2,500 metre isobath (Lamont, Chairman; Albuquerque, Astiz, Awosika, Carrera, Francis, Hinz, Kazmin, Rio and Srinivasan);

(5) Foot of the continental slope determined as the point of maximum change in the gradient at its base (Rio, Chairman; Albuquerque, Astiz, Carrera, Croker, Francis, Hamuro, Kazmin and Lamont);

(6) Foot of the continental slope determined by means of evidence to the contrary (Hinz, Chairman; Betah, Brekke, Carrera, Jaafar, Jura_i_, Kazmin and Park);

(7) Ridges (Hamuro, Chairman; Brekke, Hinz, Jura_i_, Kazmin, Lu and Park);

(8) Delineation of the outer limits of the continental shelf based on sediment thickness (Brekke, Chairman; Awosika, Croker, Jura_i_ and Park);

(9) Information on the outer limits of the extended continental shelf (Albuquerque, Chairman; Brekke, Carrera, Hamuro, Hinz, Lamont and Rio);

(10) References and bibliography (Carrera, Chairman; Editorial Committee);

(11) List of international organizations (Carrera, Chairman; Editorial Committee);

(12) Flowcharts, tables and illustrations summarizing the procedure for establishing the outer limits of the continental shelf (Jaafar, Chairman; Carrera, Chan Chim Yuk, Jura_i_, Lamont, Rio);

(13) Oversight (Awosika, Chairman; Astiz, Beltagy, Betah, Chan Chim Yuk and Hamuro).

The Editorial Committee assigned to the first 12 working groups the task of preparing 10 chapters and 2 annexes. The Oversight Working Group was entrusted with two assignments: it was first asked to identify the totality of issues raised in the studies prepared by the Division for Ocean Affairs and the Law of the Sea on the basis of discussions held during two meetings of groups of experts in 1993 and 1995. Secondly, it was requested to determine whether those issues were addressed in the Guidelines. The 12 drafting groups produced a preliminary outline draft of the Guidelines, which was discussed during the last plenary meeting of the Editorial Committee held during the third session of the Commission.

All working groups conducted their main drafting efforts during the inter-session period of 1998. On 20 July 1998, the revised version of the draft Guidelines was submitted to the Chairman of the Editorial Committee, who proceeded to edit them for consistency in content and style.

The Editorial Committee reconvened at the fourth session of the Commission, held at United Nations Headquarters from 31 August to 4 September 1998. The draft of the Guidelines edited by the Chairman of the Editorial Committee was discussed at various plenary meetings of the Editorial Committee, where amendments and clarifications were introduced in an iterative revision process. The oversight group then proceeded to prepare and submit an interim report based on the final draft produced by the Editorial Committee at that session.

The Chairman of the Editorial Committee submitted the final draft Guidelines to the Commission at large for consideration during the last meeting of its fourth session. The Commission, in turn, considered them and agreed to adopt them provisionally. The Commission also agreed to make them available to States on 4 September 1998 as a document in the "L" (limited distribution) series.

The Commission worked during the inter-session period 1998–1999 with a view to considering the recommendations made in the interim report prepared by the Oversight Working Group at its 4th meeting. The members of the Commission also considered other issues on which consensus was not reached, which were left open for further discussion at its 5th meeting. Editorial comments on the English text of the Guidelines were produced during this inter-session period by Albuquerque, Astiz, Brekke, Carrera, Chan Chim Yuk, Croker, Lamont, Lu and Srinivasan.

The following members revised the translation of the Guidelines from English into other official languages of the United Nations: Arabic translation (Beltagy); Chinese translation (Lu); French translation (Albuquerque, Betah, Chan Chim Yuk and Rio); Russian translation (Kazmin); and Spanish translation (Albuquerque, Astiz and Carrera).

The Guidelines were discussed and amended at the fifth session of the Commission and adopted on 13 May 1999.

The drafting of the Scientific and Technical Guidelines of the Commission on the Limits of the Continental Shelf during a relatively short period of time represents an important achievement towards the implementation of article 76 of the United Nations Convention on the Law of the Sea.

The Guidelines, which the Commission adopted by consensus, serve multiple purposes: they are primarily intended to assist coastal States in preparing their submissions. They are also designed to provide an important scientific and technical reference for the consideration of these submissions and the preparation of the Commission's own recommendations. And last but not least, they form the basis on which the Commission shall provide advice, if requested by coastal States during the preparation of their necessary data.

The members of the Commission have an obligation to perform their duties honourably, faithfully, impartially and conscientiously. These principles, which form the essence of their solemn declaration, have guided them in the preparation of their Scientific and Technical Guidelines.

The Commission expresses its gratitude to the Division for Ocean Affairs and the Law of the Sea under the leadership of Mr. Ismat Steiner, Director. Special thanks goes to the Secretary of the Commission, Mr. Alexei Zinchenko, and to Lynette Cunningham, Vladimir Jares, Cynthia Hardeman and Josefa Velasco, who ably assisted in the preparation of the Guidelines and in their expedient publication.

1. Introduction

1.1. The Commission on the Limits of the Continental Shelf recognizes the integral character of the United Nations Convention on the Law of the Sea (the Convention). These Scientific and Technical Guidelines form the basis for the Commission to make its recommendations with respect to submissions prepared by States according to article 76 and Annex II to the Convention in a manner that is consistent with the Convention and international law.

1.2. The Commission prepared these Guidelines for the purpose of providing direction to coastal States which intend to submit data and other material concerning the outer limits of the continental shelf in areas where those limits extend beyond 200 nautical miles from the baselines from which the breadth of the territorial sea is measured. The Guidelines aim to clarify the scope and depth of admissible scientific and technical evidence to be examined by the Commission during its consideration of each submission for the purpose of making recommendations.

1.3. With these Guidelines, the Commission aims also to clarify its interpretation of scientific, technical and legal terms contained in the Convention. Clarification is required in particular because the Convention makes use of scientific terms in a legal context which at times departs significantly from accepted scientific definitions and terminology. In other cases, clarification is required because various terms in the Convention might be left open to several possible and equally acceptable interpretations. It is also possible that it may not have been felt necessary at the time of the Third United Nations Conference on the Law of the Sea to determine the precise definition of various scientific and technical terms. In still other cases, the need for clarification arises as a result of the complexity of several provisions and the potential scientific and technical difficulties which might be encountered by States in making a single and unequivocal interpretation of each of them.

1.4. The Commission designed these Guidelines with a view to ensuring a uniform and extended State practice during the preparation of scientific and technical evidence submitted by coastal States. The Commission is aware that there might be other scientific and technical methodologies used by States to implement the provisions of article 76 to prepare a submission which may not be covered in this document. These Guidelines are not intended to exhaust the full range of possible methodologies contemplated by States. Whereas several scientific and technical avenues are available to develop an admissible body of evidence which may conform equally to all the relevant provisions contained in the Convention, the Commission has endeavoured to emphasize those which might minimize costs and result in the optimization of existing information and resources.

1.5. The scientific nature and the order of the paragraphs in article 76 define the structure of the Guidelines. Each chapter starts with a formulation of the problem posed by each of its provisions, followed by an in-depth discussion of its implementation. Chapter 2 presents an overview of questions relating to the entitlement to an extended continental shelf and the delineation of its outer limits. Chapter 3 reviews units of length and describes the geodetic methodology used to determine outer limits based on metrics. Chapter 4 describes the hydrographic methodology used to determine the 2,500 metre isobath and other geomorphologic features. Chapter 5 discusses the determination of the location of the foot of the continental slope as the point of maximum change in gradient at its base. Chapter 6 examines the case in which evidence to the contrary might be presented as an alternative to the methodology described in chapter 5 to determine the location of the foot of the continental slope. Chapter 7 discusses the classification and treatment of oceanic and submarine ridges, and other submarine elevations. Chapter 8 discusses the geophysical methodology applied for the determination of sediment thickness and its error estimates. Chapter 9 describes the data and other material to be included in a submission regarding the outer limits of the continental shelf.

1.6. The Commission recognizes that the Convention poses in-depth requirements in several scientific disciplines and also poses the need for interdisciplinary scientific and technical cooperation for the preparation of data and materials in each submission. These Guidelines are not aimed at describing in detail the scientific theories or precise technical methodologies involved in each discipline. For that purpose, experts assigned to the preparation of submissions are advised to consult the contributions made by many scientific and technical, governmental and non-governmental organizations and disseminated through journals, conference proceedings and other publications.

1.7. The annex provides a non-exhaustive list of international scientific and technical organizations whose data and information might be of interest to States which intend to prepare a submission. Whereas those international organizations have the primary responsibility to promote the development of knowledge and research in their respective disciplines, the Commission has the sole responsibility to make recommendations and to provide scientific and technical advice in relation to submissions on the limits of extended continental shelves made by coastal States according to article 76 and Annex II to the United Nations Convention on the Law of the Sea.

2. Entitlement to an extended continental shelf and the delineation of its outer limits

2.1. Formulation of the problem: article 76

2.2. Test of appurtenance

2.3. Delineation of the outer limits of the continental shelf

2.1. Formulation of the problem: article 76

2.1.1. Article 76, paragraph 1, establishes the right of coastal States to determine the outer limits of the continental shelf by means of two criteria based on either natural prolongation or distance:

> "The continental shelf of a coastal State comprises the sea-bed and subsoil of the submarine areas that extend beyond its territorial sea throughout the natural prolongation of its land territory to the outer edge of the continental margin, or to a distance of 200 nautical miles from the baselines from which the breadth of the territorial sea is measured where the outer edge of the continental margin does not extend up to that distance."

2.1.2. Paragraph 4 (a) suggests the formulation of a test of appurtenance in order to entitle a coastal State to extend the outer limits of the continental shelf beyond the limit set by the 200-nautical-mile distance criterion. This test consists in the demonstration of the fact that the natural prolongation of its land territory to the outer edge of the continental margin extends beyond a line delineated at a distance of 200 nautical miles from the baselines from which the breadth of the territorial sea is measured:

> "For the purposes of this Convention, the coastal State shall establish the outer edge of the continental margin wherever the margin extends beyond 200 nautical miles from the baselines from which the breadth of the territorial sea is measured ..."

2.1.3. The Convention offers two complementary provisions designed to provide the definition of the continental margin and the breadth of its outer limit. The first provision, contained in paragraph 3, provides its definition:

> "The continental margin comprises the submerged prolongation of the land mass of the coastal State, and consists of the sea-bed and subsoil of the shelf, the slope and the rise. It does not include the deep ocean floor with its oceanic ridges or the subsoil thereof."

2.1.4. The second provision, contained in paragraph 4 (a) (i) and (ii), subject to paragraphs 5 and 6, determines the position of the outer limit of the continental margin by means of a complex formula based on four rules. Two of these rules are affirmative and the remaining two are negative. The two positive rules, herein referred to as formulae, are connected through an inclusive disjunction:

> "(i) a line delineated in accordance with paragraph 7 by reference to the outermost fixed points at each of which the thickness of sedimentary rocks is at least 1 per cent of the shortest distance from such point to the foot of the continental slope; or
>
> "(ii) a line delineated in accordance with paragraph 7 by reference to fixed points not more than 60 nautical miles from the foot of the slope."

2.1.5. The use of an inclusive disjunction as a connective between the two formulae implies that the compound is true so long as at least one of the components is true. Thus, the limit of the continental shelf can be extended up to a 1 per cent sediment thickness line delineated by reference to fixed points, or to a line delineated by reference to fixed points at a distance of 60 nautical miles from the foot of the continental slope, or both.

2.1.6. When both formulae lines are used, their outer envelope determines the maximum potential extent of entitlement over the continental shelf by a coastal State. This envelope forms the basis of a claim but it is still subject to spatial constraints in order to produce the delineation of the outer limits of the continental shelf.

2.1.7. The extent of the outer envelope formed by the lines derived from the two formulae is restricted by a line derived from the two negative rules, herein referred to as constraints, which are connected by another inclusive disjunction. According to paragraph 5, the simultaneous application of these two constraints defines the outer limit beyond which an extended claim cannot be made:

> "The fixed points comprising the line of the outer limits of the continental shelf on the sea-bed, drawn in accordance with paragraph 4 (a) (i) and (ii), either shall not exceed 350 nautical miles from the baselines from which the breadth of the territorial sea is measured or shall not exceed 100 nautical miles from the 2,500 metre isobath, which is a line connecting the depth of 2,500 metres."

2.1.8. The application of a negation over each of the two components connected by an inclusive disjunction implies that the compound is true so long as at least one of the constraints is satisfied. Thus, the outer limits of the continental shelf can extend either beyond a line delineated by reference to fixed points at a distance of 350 nautical miles from baselines from which the breadth of the territorial sea is measured, or beyond a line delineated by reference to fixed points at a distance of 100 nautical miles from the 2,500 metre isobath, but not both.

2.1.9. In practice, the use of an inclusive disjunction means that the outer envelope of the constraint lines identifies the breadth beyond which the outer limits of the continental shelf of a coastal State cannot extend. This outer envelope of the constraints does not provide per se the basis for entitlement to an extended continental shelf. It is solely a constraint placed over the envelope line produced by the formulae in order to delineate the outer limits of the continental shelf.

2.1.10. Submarine ridges constitute a special case which is subject to the rules of entitlement given by paragraph 4 (a) (i) and (ii), but it is also subject to the more stringent constraint provided by paragraph 6:

> "Notwithstanding the provisions of paragraph 5, on submarine ridges, the outer limit of the continental shelf shall not exceed 350 nautical miles from the baselines from which the breadth of the territorial sea is measured. This paragraph does not apply to submarine elevations that are natural components of the continental margin, such as its plateaux, rises, caps, banks and spurs."

2.1.11. Submarine elevations are exempted from the provisions applied to submarine ridges. They are subject instead to the constraints provided in paragraph 5.

2.1.12. Pursuant to the above provisions, paragraph 4 (b) provides a dual regime for the identification of the foot of the slope based on either geomorphological and bathymetric evidence or an additional source of evidence:

> "In the absence of evidence to the contrary, the foot of the continental slope shall be determined as the point of maximum change in the gradient at its base."

2.1.13. Whereas the point of maximum change in the gradient at its base identifies the position of the foot of the continental slope as a general rule, the Commission is bound by this provision to examine all additional evidence provided by a coastal State for the identification of alternative points to locate the foot of the continental slope.

2.1.14. As a summary, where the natural prolongation of a coastal State to the outer edge of the continental margin extends beyond 200 nautical miles from the baselines from which the breadth of the territorial sea is measured, the outer limits of the continental shelf can be extended up to a 1 per cent sediment thickness line, or to a line delineated at a distance of 60 nautical miles from the foot of the slope, <u>and</u> no further than a line delineated at a distance of 350 nautical miles from baselines from which the breadth of the territorial sea is measured, or no further than a line delineated at a distance of 100 nautical miles from the 2,500 metre isobath.

2.1.15. The use of a conjunction as a connective between the two components formed, in turn, by a formula compound and a constraint compound, implies that the full compound is true only so long as both components are true. Thus, at least one of the formulae and one of the constraints must be satisfied at all times.

2.1.16. In practice, the use of a conjunction means that the outer limit of the continental shelf is delineated by the inner envelope of two lines: the outer envelope of the formulae, and the outer envelope of the constraints. Section 2.3 illustrates the methodology used to combine these envelopes.

2.2. Test of appurtenance

2.2.1. Both the basis for entitlement to delineate the outer limits of an extended continental shelf and the methods to be applied in this delineation are embedded in article 76. However, it is clear that the positive proof of the former precedes the implementation of the latter, as stated in article 76, paragraph 4 (a):

> "For the purposes of this Convention, the coastal State shall establish the outer edge of the continental margin wherever the margin extends beyond 200 nautical miles from the baselines from which the breadth of the territorial sea is measured …"

2.2.2. The Commission defines the term "test of appurtenance" as the process by means of which the above provision is examined. The test of appurtenance is designed to determine the legal entitlement of a coastal State to delineate the outer limits of the continental shelf throughout the natural prolongation of its land territory to the outer edge of the continental margin, or to a distance of 200 nautical miles from the baselines from which the breadth of the territorial sea is measured where the outer edge of the continental margin does not extend up to that distance.

2.2.3. If a State is able to demonstrate to the Commission that the natural prolongation of its submerged land territory to the outer edge of its continental margin extends beyond the 200-nautical-mile distance criterion, the outer limit of its continental shelf can be delineated by means of the application of the complex set of rules described in paragraphs 4 to 10.

2.2.4. If, on the other hand, a State does not demonstrate to the Commission that the natural prolongation of its submerged land territory to the outer edge of its continental margin extends beyond the 200-nautical-mile distance criterion, the outer limit of its continental shelf is automatically delineated up to that distance as prescribed in paragraph 1. In this case, coastal States do not have an obligation to submit information on the limits of the continental shelf to the Commission, nor is the Commission entitled by the Convention to make recommendations on those limits.

2.2.5. The Commission finds that the proof of entitlement over the continental shelf and the method of delineation of the outer limits of the continental shelf are two distinct but complementary questions. The basis for delineation cannot be other than pertinent to that of entitlement itself.

2.2.6. The Commission shall use at all times: the provisions contained in paragraph 4 (a) (i) and (ii), defined as the formulae lines, and paragraph 4 (b), to determine whether a coastal State is entitled to delineate the outer limits of the continental shelf beyond 200 nautical miles. The Commission shall accept that a State is entitled to use all the other provisions contained in paragraphs 4 to 10 provided that the application of either of the two formulae produces a line beyond 200 nautical miles.

2.2.7. The Commission finds multiple justifications for the application of the formulae rules in the test of appurtenance:

- The geological and geomorphological provisions contained in paragraph 3 are satisfied;
- The application of any other criteria would be inconsistent with the provisions contained in the Convention for the delineation of the outer limits of the continental shelf;
- The application of other rules would have set a legal precedent not contained in the Convention, and perhaps also created unnecessary uncertainties and the burden of additional time and expense on States; and
- The Commission is not precluded by the Convention from applying these rules.

2.2.8. The formulation of the test of appurtenance can be described as follows:

If either the line delineated at a distance of 60 nautical miles from the foot of the continental slope, or the line delineated at a distance where the thickness of sedimentary rocks is at least 1 per cent of the shortest distance from such point to the foot of the slope, or both, extend beyond 200 nautical miles from the baselines from which the breadth of the territorial sea is measured, then a coastal State is entitled to delineate the outer limits of the continental shelf as prescribed by the provisions contained in article 76, paragraphs 4 to 10.

2.2.9. If the test of appurtenance is positively satisfied, a coastal State has an obligation to submit to the Commission information on the limits of the continental shelf beyond 200 nautical miles, according to paragraph 8:

"Information on the limits of the continental shelf beyond 200 nautical miles from the baselines from which the breadth of the territorial sea is measured shall be submitted by the coastal State to the Commission on the Limits of the Continental Shelf set up under Annex II on the basis of equitable geographical representation. The Commission shall make recommendations to coastal States on matters related to the establishment of the outer limits of their continental shelf. The limits of the shelf established by a coastal State on the basis of these recommendations shall be final and binding."

2.3. Delineation of the outer limits of the continental shelf

2.3.1. Article 76 contains a complex combination of four rules, two formulae and two constraints, based on concepts of geodesy, geology, geophysics and hydrography:

Formulae

- A line delineated in accordance with paragraph 7 by reference to the outermost fixed points at each of which the thickness of sedimentary rocks is at least 1 per cent of the shortest distance from such point to the foot of the continental slope (figure 2.1); or
- A line delineated in accordance with paragraph 7 by reference to fixed points not more than 60 nautical miles from the foot of the continental slope (figure 2.2).

Constraints

- A line delineated by reference to fixed points at a distance of 350 nautical miles from the baselines from which the breadth of the territorial sea is measured (figure 2.3); or
- A line delineated by reference to fixed points at a distance of 100 nautical miles from the 2,500 metre isobath (figure 2.4).

2.3.2. Whereas the application of at least one of the two formulae to determine a line beyond 200 nautical miles suffices to provide the basis for entitlement to delineate the outer limits of an extended continental shelf, the application of all four rules may be necessary in order to actually delineate the outer limits of the continental shelf.

2.3.3. Once the outer limits defined by each of the four rules included in article 76 are determined, the delineation of the outer limit of the extended continental shelf can be summarized as a three-step process:

(i) The two limits computed by the application of each of the affirmative rules are used to create their outer envelope or formulae line (figure 2.5);

(ii) The two limits computed by the application of each of the negative rules are used to create their outer envelope or constraint line (figure 2.6); and

(iii) The inner envelope of the formulae and constraint lines described above determines the outer limit of the extended continental shelf (figure 2.7).

2.3.4. In the special case of submarine ridges, the constraint line created in step (ii) above is formed only by the 350-nautical-miles limit.

2.3.5. Article 76, paragraph 7, describes the geometric character of the outer limit of the continental shelf:

> "The coastal State shall delineate the outer limits of its continental shelf, where that shelf extends beyond 200 nautical miles from the baselines from which the breadth of the territorial sea is measured, by straight lines not exceeding 60 nautical miles in length, connecting fixed points, defined by coordinates of latitude and longitude."

2.3.6. This provision does not specify explicitly the geometric definition of these straight lines. Several line definitions could be conceivably adopted. These could be, among others, loxodromes, normal sections from either end point of a segment, or great circles. The Commission acknowledges that this provision implements a new norm of international law and that there is no precedent or State practice which might suggest the existence of a uniform and extended application of a particular geodetic methodology for this particular purpose.

2.3.7. In view of the rigorous geometric definition of a straight line as the line of shortest distance between two points, the Commission will employ geodesics on the surface of the official geodetic reference ellipsoid used by a State in each submission to define the path and distances of these specific straight lines. This decision is adopted without prejudice to, and is independent from, the interpretation made by the Commission with respect to straight lines as prescribed under the provisions of article 7 and as discussed in section 3.3 of these Guidelines.

2.3.8. The length of straight lines used to connect fixed points, which define the outer limit of the continental shelf, shall not exceed 60 nautical miles. These straight lines can connect fixed points located on one of, or any combination formed by, the four outer limits produced by each of the two formulae and the two constraints contained in article 76.

2.3.9. In the case of straight lines connecting fixed points at each of which the thickness of sedimentary rocks is at least 1 per cent of the shortest distance from such points to the foot of the continental slope, only points located not more than 60 nautical miles apart along the same continental margin will be connected. These straight lines should not be used to connect fixed points located on opposite and separate continental margins. This provision is implemented by the Commission with a view to ensuring that only the portion of the seabed that meets all the provisions of article 76 is enclosed by these straight lines. Any portion of the seabed allocated to a continental shelf by the construction of these lines must fully meet the requirements of the provisions of article 76. Figure 2.8 illustrates a practical example of this provision.

2.3.10. The outer limit of the continental shelf is also determined by means of straight lines, which may connect fixed points located along arcs. These arcs may be located at 100 nautical miles from the 2,500 metre isobath, not more than 60 nautical miles from the foot of the slope, or 350 nautical miles from the baselines from which the breadth of the territorial sea is measured. In these cases, straight lines should be constructed with a view to ensuring that only the portion of the seabed that meets all the provisions of article 76 is enclosed.

2.3.11. The Commission acknowledges that the character of the limits established by a coastal State based on its recommendations, according to paragraph 8, is final and binding and that, according to paragraph 2, coastal States shall not extend the outer limits of their continental shelf beyond these limits:

> "The continental shelf of a coastal State shall not extend beyond the limits provided for in paragraphs 4 to 6."

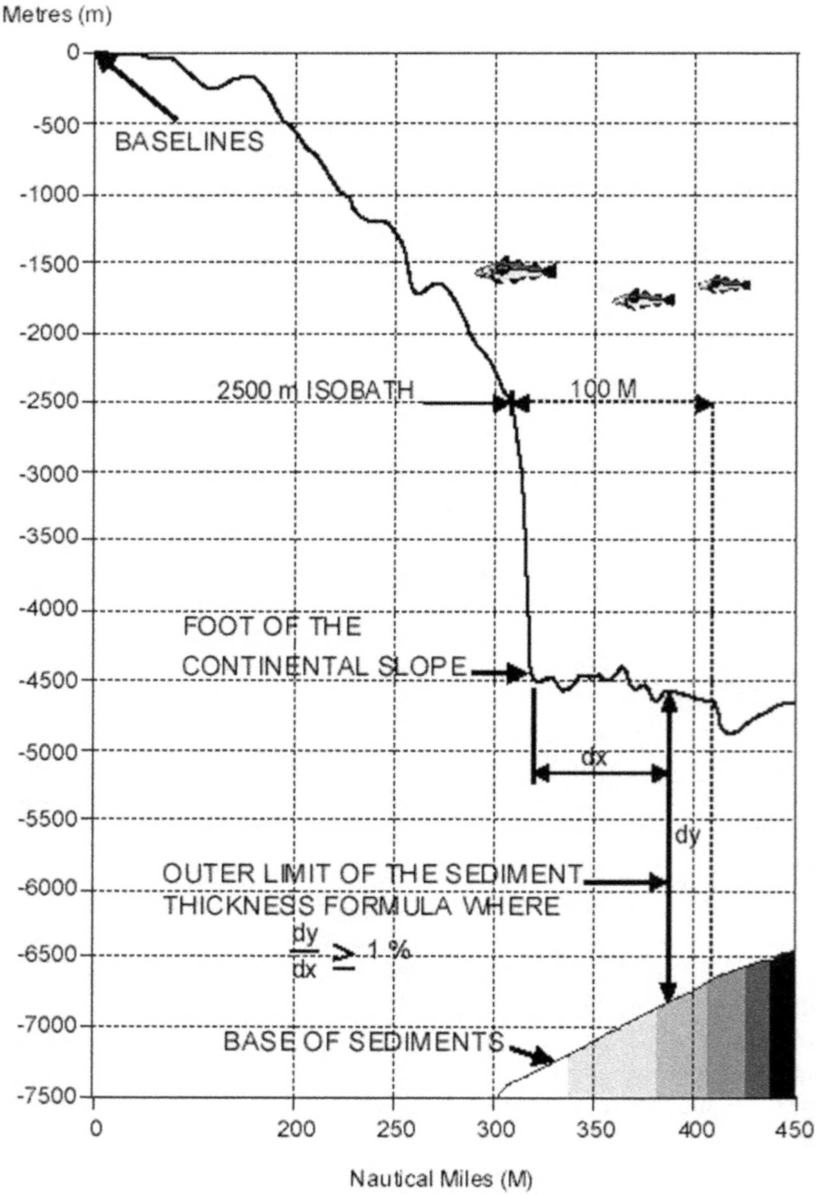

Figure 2.1. One per cent sediment thickness formula.

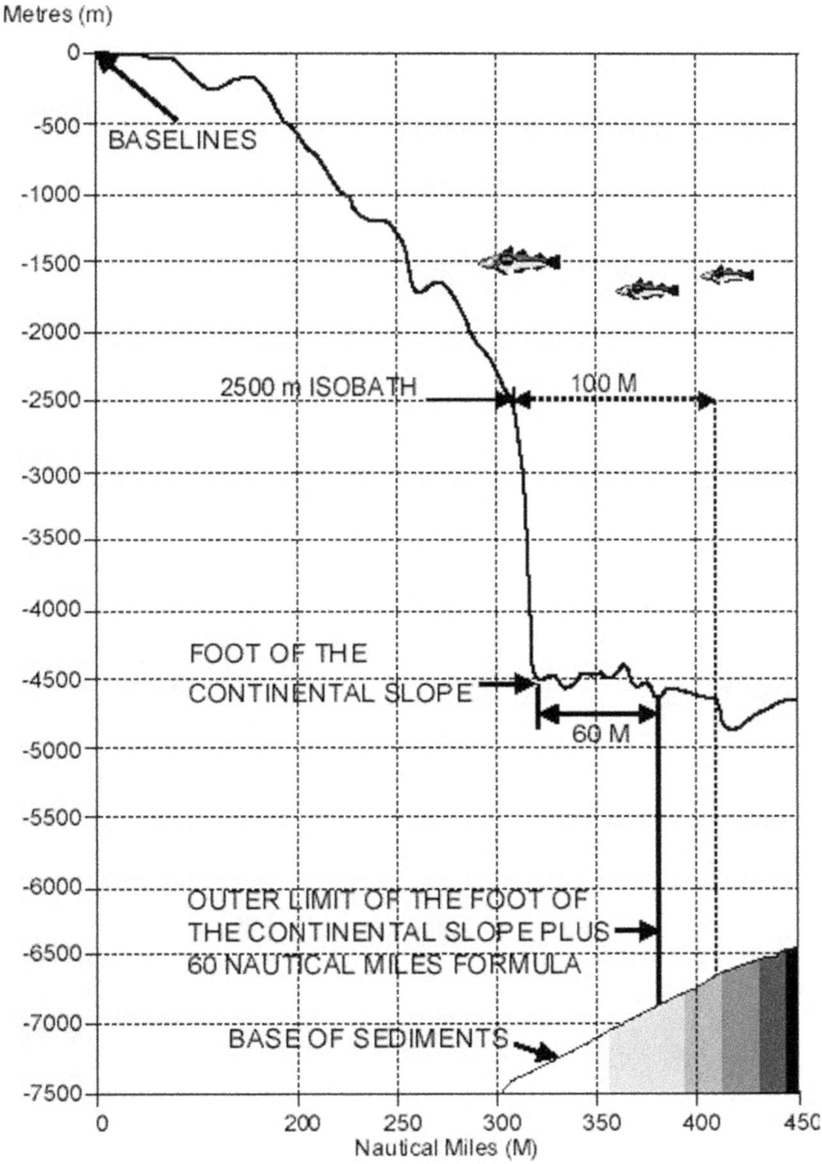

Figure 2.2. Foot of the continental slope plus 60 M formula.

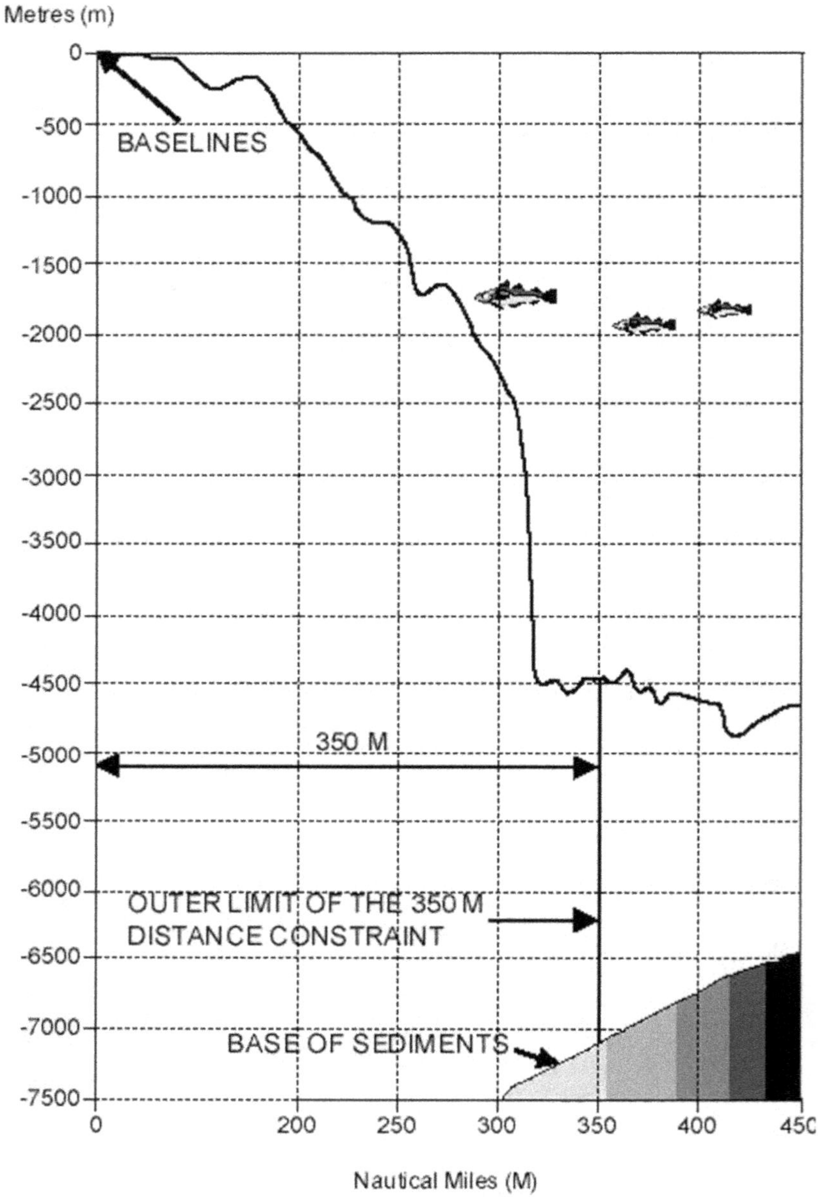

Figure 2.3. 350 M distance constraint.

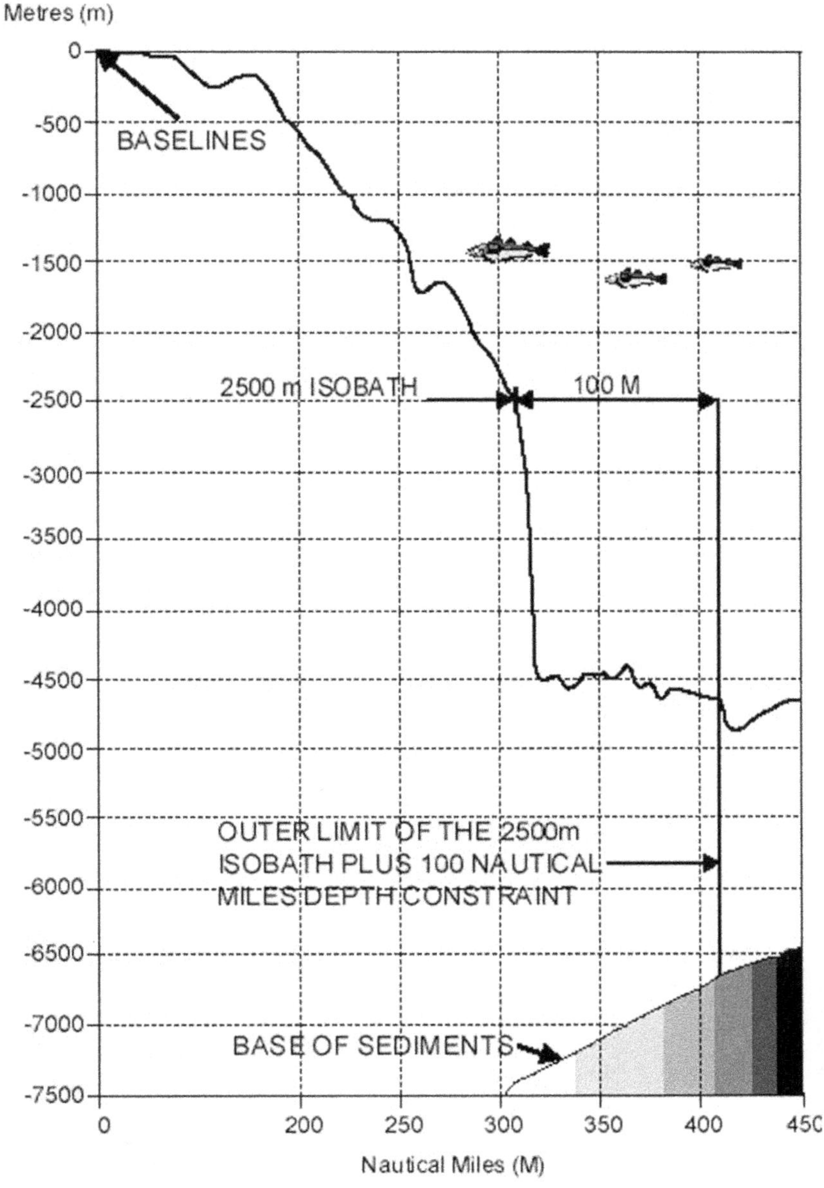

Figure 2.4. 2,500 m isobath plus 100 M depth constraint.

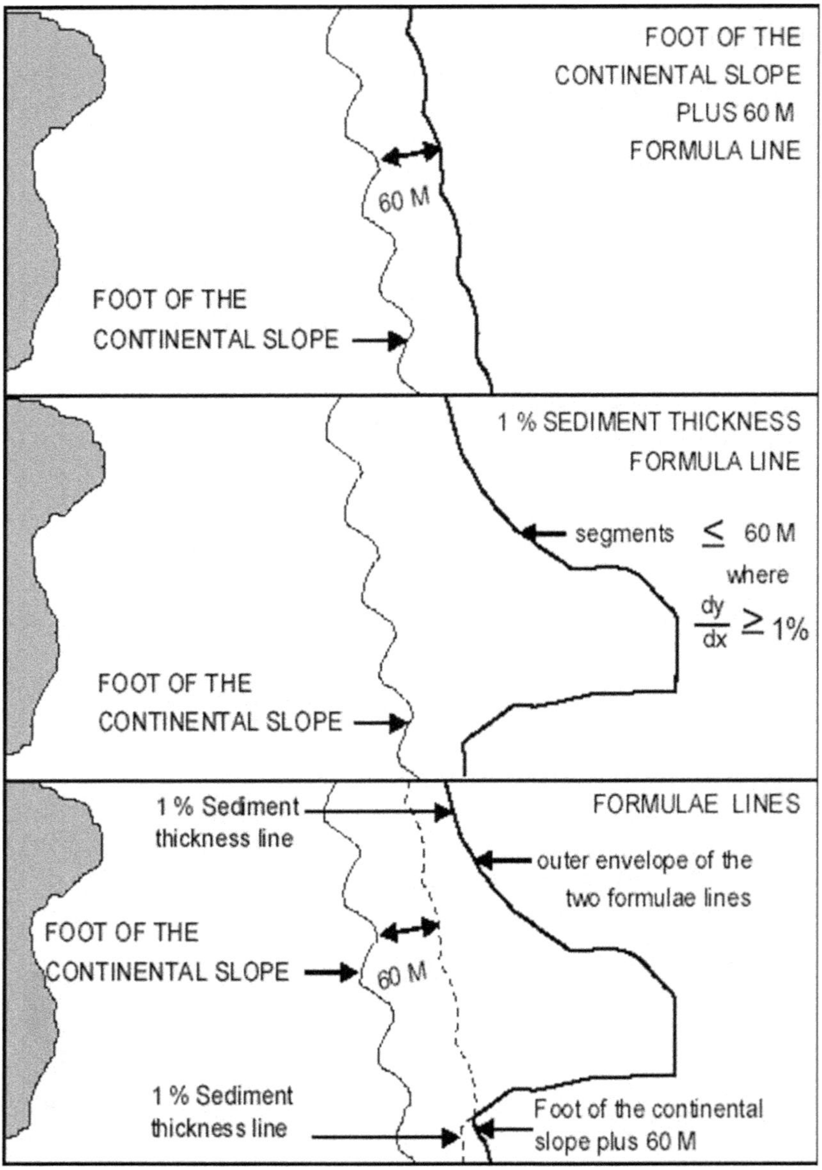

Figure 2.5. Delineation of the formulae line.

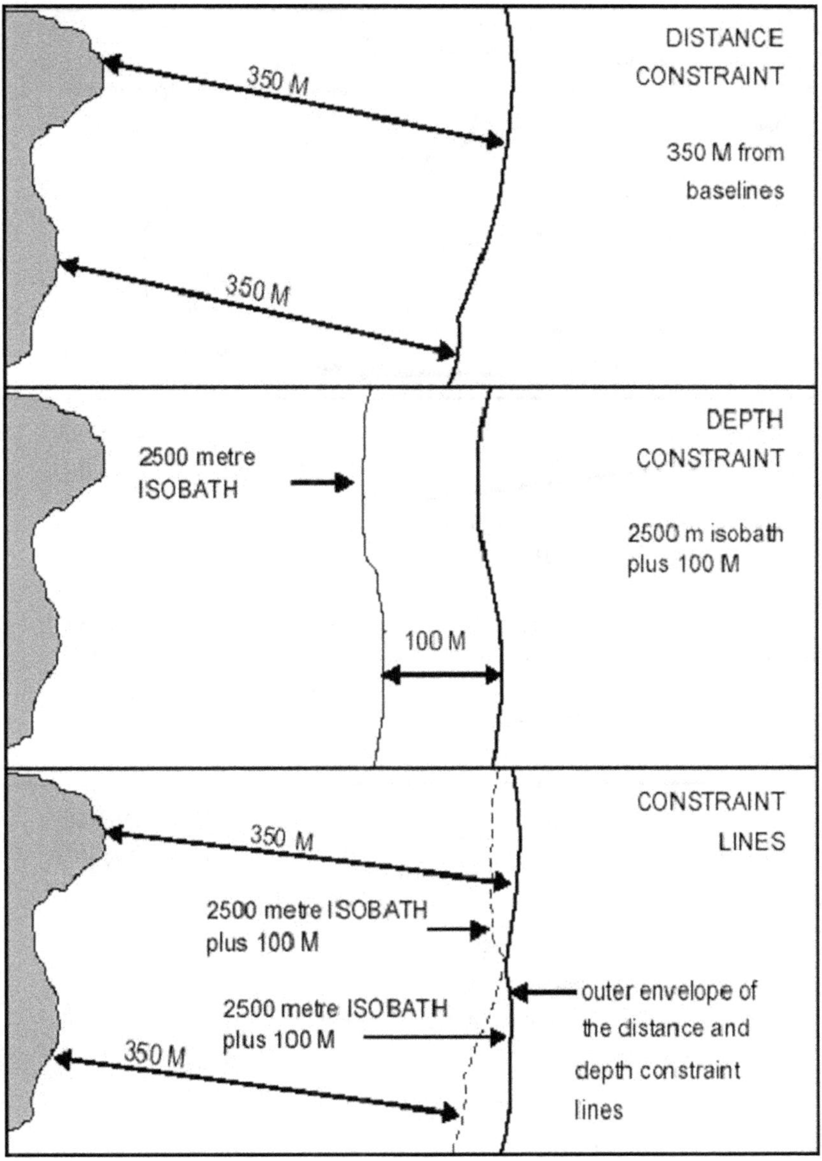

Figure 2.6. Delineation of the constraint line.

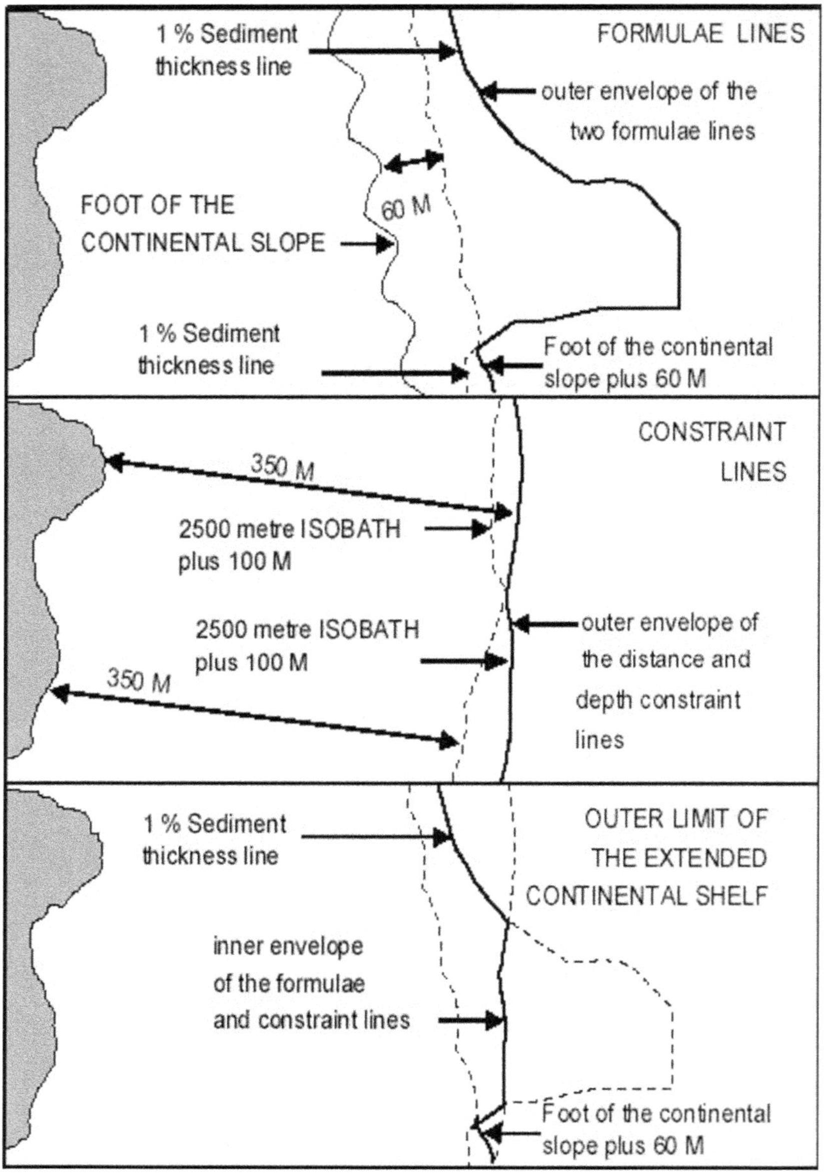

Figure 2.7. Delineation of the outer limits of the extended continental shelf.

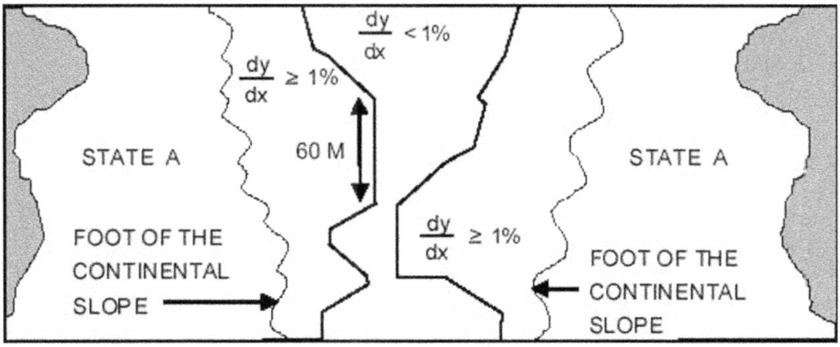

Figure 2.8. Sediment thickness lines not exceeding 60 M whose end-points satisfy the condition dy/dx ≥ 1% from opposite and separate margins of the same coastal State.

3. Geodetic methodologies and the outer limits of the continental shelf

3.1. Formulation of the problem: paragraphs 1, 4, 5 and 7

3.2. Units, geodetic reference systems and coordinate transformations

3.3. Geodetic definition of baselines

3.4. Outer limits and their confidence zones

3.1. Formulation of the problem: paragraphs 1, 4, 5 and 7

3.1.1. The Commission on the Limits of the Continental Shelf recognizes that the Convention poses specific scientific requirements in the field of geodesy. States are requested to delineate the outer limits of the extended continental shelf based on different distance criteria. These criteria are applied from baselines from which the breadth of the territorial sea is measured, the foot of the continental slope and the 2,500 metre isobath.

3.1.2. Article 76, paragraph 1, establishes the right of coastal States to determine the outer limits of the continental shelf by means of a 200-nautical-mile distance criterion from baselines:

> "The continental shelf of a coastal State comprises the sea-bed and subsoil of the submarine areas that extend beyond its territorial sea throughout the natural prolongation of its land territory to the outer edge of the continental margin, or to a distance of 200 nautical miles from the baselines from which the breadth of the territorial sea is measured where the outer edge of the continental margin does not extend up to that distance."

3.1.3. Paragraph 4 (a) also places the same requirement as part of the appurtenance test:

> "For the purposes of this Convention, the coastal State shall establish the outer edge of the continental margin wherever the margin extends beyond 200 nautical miles from the baselines from which the breadth of the territorial sea is measured, by either: …"

3.1.4. Paragraph 4 (a) (i) establishes the need to measure the distance between the foot of the continental slope and a point at which the sediment thickness produces a ratio between them of 1 per cent:

> "(i) a line delineated in accordance with paragraph 7 by reference to the outermost fixed points at each of which the thickness of sedimentary rocks is at least 1 per cent of the shortest distance from such point to the foot of the continental slope; or"

3.1.5. Paragraph 4 (a) (ii) establishes the need to delineate a limit up to a distance of 60 nautical miles from the foot of the continental slope:

> "(ii) a line delineated in accordance with paragraph 7 by reference to fixed points not more than 60 nautical miles from the foot of the continental slope."

3.1.6. Paragraph 5 poses requirements to delineate limits at distances of 350 nautical miles from baselines, and/or 100 nautical miles from the 2,500 metre isobath:

> "The fixed points comprising the line of the outer limits of the continental shelf on the sea-bed, drawn in accordance with paragraph 4 (a) (i) and (ii), either shall not exceed 350 nautical miles from the baselines from which the breadth of the territorial sea is measured or shall not exceed 100 nautical miles from the 2,500 metre isobath, which is a line connecting the depth of 2,500 metres."

3.1.7. Paragraph 6 requires, in the case of submarine ridges, that the limit should be delineated at a distance of no more than 350 nautical miles from the baselines. Thus, implicitly, it imposes the requirement to delineate a limit of 350 nautical miles from the baselines:

> "Notwithstanding the provisions of paragraph 5, on submarine ridges, the outer limit of the continental shelf shall not exceed 350 nautical miles from the baselines from which the breadth of the territorial sea is measured. This paragraph does not apply to submarine elevations that are natural components of the continental margin, such as its plateaux, rises, caps, banks and spurs."

3.1.8. Article 76, paragraph 7, poses a requirement to ensure that the straight lines which form the outer limit of the continental shelf do not extend beyond 60 nautical miles:

> "The coastal State shall delineate the outer limits of its continental shelf, where the shelf extends beyond 200 nautical miles from the baselines from which the breadth of the territorial sea is measured, by straight lines not exceeding 60 nautical miles in length, connecting fixed points, defined by coordinates of latitude and longitude."

3.2. <u>Units, geodetic reference systems and coordinate transformations</u>

3.2.1. The Convention makes use of two units of length: the metre (m) and the nautical mile (M). Both units are part of the Système International d'Unités (SI) (Bureau International des Poids et Mesures, 1991). The current international definition of the metre was adopted by the Conference Générale des Poids et Mesures (CGPM) in 1983. Following the proposal adopted by the International Hydrographic Bureau (IHB) in 1929, the international nautical mile is a unit of length defined by the identity:

$$1\,\text{M} = 1{,}852\,\text{m}.$$

3.2.2. The Commission discourages the use of any approximation to the above exact definition. The approximation to the nautical mile based on the length of an arc of 1 minute of latitude should be avoided in particular. Figure 3.1 illustrates the continuous variable length of an arc of 1 minute of latitude as a function of latitude from the equator to either of the poles on the ellipsoid shared by the Geodetic Reference System 1980 (GRS80) and the World Geodetic System 1984 (WGS84).

3.2.3. The Commission feels compelled to emphasize that the abbreviation adopted by the International Hydrographic Organization (IHO) for a nautical mile is M and that this abbreviation applies equally in all languages (International Hydrographic Organization, 1990, p. 22).

3.2.4. The Convention does not identify explicitly the surface over which all distances prescribed to delineate the outer limits of maritime spaces under national jurisdiction should be measured. Several surface options could conceivably be available to measure them. These could be mean sea level, the geoid or the seabed, among others. Alternatively, the chord segment joining the two end points of a line could also be proposed as an option to measure distances. The Commission feels that the use of any of these options might result in the uneven application of distance criteria in the analysis of each submission.

3.2.5. The surface of a geodetic reference ellipsoid associated with the reference system adopted by a coastal State in each submission shall be accepted by the Commission to determine all distances in order to ensure the application of a uniform metric at all times. This choice ensures consistency from a geodetic perspective and appears to be also justified under international customary law. The Commission recognizes that there is an established uniform State practice which demonstrates the use of this surface for the determination of the outer limits of the territorial sea, the contiguous zone, the exclusive economic zone and, most importantly, the continental shelf when it is defined by means of a distance criterion up to 200 M.

3.2.6. The Commission acknowledges the requirements stated in article 76, paragraphs 7 and 9, and article 84, paragraphs 1 and 2, for the specification of the geodetic coordinates of the outer limit of the continental shelf. Article 84, paragraph 1, highlights in particular the requirement to specify the geodetic datum used, to which the coordinates of the outer limit are referred.

3.2.7. The Commission is aware of the sovereign right of each State to make submissions in fulfilment of the above requirements, selecting for this purpose either the geodetic reference system officially used for its national geodetic control or nautical charting activities, or any other international reference system adopted by the State. The Commission shall use the geodetic reference system used by each State in the preparation of its submission as the basis for all geodetic computations, analyses and recommendations.

3.2.8. In the interest of ensuring that the international dissemination of all relevant geodetic information relating to the outer limit of the continental shelf is conducted in a manner readily recognizable by third States, the submitting State may be required by the Commission to provide:

- Coordinates of the outer limit of the continental shelf in an International Terrestrial Reference System (ITRS) adopted by the Commission;

- Transformation parameters between the reference system used in the submission and an ITRS adopted by the Commission; and
- Full information relating to the scientific methodology employed to determine these transformation parameters.

3.2.9. The Commission acknowledges the convergence of two separate realizations of an ITRS into a single international standard. One of these realizations is recommended by the International Union of Geodesy and Geophysics (IUGG) and the other by the International Hydrographic Organization.

3.2.10. IUGG recommends the use of the International Terrestrial Reference System according to Resolution No. 2 adopted at its 20th General Assembly held at Vienna in 1991. ITRS is monitored by the International Earth Rotation Service (IERS). Practical realizations of ITRS are produced periodically under the name of International Terrestrial Reference Frames (ITRF) (e.g., Boucher et al., 1996, 1998), which are defined by means of coordinates and their velocities for a number of IERS sites distributed worldwide (McCarthy, 1996).

3.2.11. Whenever geodetic coordinates (φ, λ, h) are computed from ITRF-yy positions, the ellipsoid associated with GRS80 adopted by the IUGG in Resolution No. 7 at its 17th General Assembly held at Canberra in 1979 will be used (Moritz, 1984).

3.2.12. IHO, on the other hand, recommends the use of WGS84 as an international hydrographic positioning standard, according to its Technical Resolution B1.1 and Special Publications Nos. 44 and 52 (International Hydrographic Organization, 1988, 1993). WGS84 has been preceded by three previous reference systems: WGS60, WGS66 and WGS72.

3.2.13. The Commission notes that for all practical purposes involved in the determination of positions relating to a submission, ITRF94, recommended by IUGG, and WGS84 (G873), recommended by IHO, can be regarded as equivalent realizations of an ITRS. Geodetic coordinates referred to one system will be regarded by the Commission as equivalent in the other.

3.2.14. The Commission highlights the value of the geodetic products made freely available to States by the International GPS Service (Neilan et al., 1997). The availability of clock corrections and precise ephemerides is extremely useful in producing geodetic positions in ITRF-yy free from systematic errors induced deliberately in the GPS satellite signal through Selective Availability (SA).

3.2.15. The Commission acknowledges that SA remains the single most important source of error in the determination of WGS84 positions from GPS satellite broadcast ephemerides. The use of products from the International GPS Service is the most inexpensive, accessible and accurate avenue to determine WGS84 (G873) point positions through ITRF94.

3.2.16. The Commission acknowledges that the transformation of coordinates from one reference system to another can be a very complex problem (Vanícek, 1990, 1992). Sometimes the estimation of transformation parameters has been carried out among different realizations of the same ITRS by an international scientific organization. Transformation parameters valid at given epochs among the various ITRF-yy, for example, are produced by IERS (McCarthy, 1996). The Commission regards the transformation parameters estimated by IERS and their mathematical formulation as admissible geodetic methodologies in a submission that involves transformations between and among all ITRF-yy realizations.

3.2.17. However, the estimation of coordinate transformation parameters between a national reference system and a particular realization of an ITRS is a far more complex problem. This coordinate transformation involves deformations in addition to a seven-parameter transformation composed of three rigid rotations, three rigid translations and a scale change. Commission X of the International Association of Geodesy (IAG) is currently developing transformation methodologies between different reference systems. The Commission acknowledges the existence of several methodologies designed in the past to address this problem (e.g., Applebaum, 1982) and that attempts have been made to implement them in practice, for example, between WGS84 and many local reference systems (Defense Mapping Agency, 1984). The Commission feels that the ultimate responsibility for the preparation of all the scientific and technical evidence, including coordinate transformations, which supports a submission lies with the coastal State.

3.2.18. The Commission will pay special attention to the determination of transformation parameters and their mathematical formulation when a national reference system different from ITRF94 or WGS84 (G873) is used in a submission made by a coastal State. The Commission's role is limited to making a potential request for information about the geodetic position and definition of the baselines used in a submission made by a coastal State.

3.3. Geodetic definition of baselines

3.3.1. The Commission is not entitled by the Convention to issue any recommendations with respect to the delineation of baselines from which the breadth of the territorial sea is measured. Its role is limited to a potential request for information about the geodetic position and definition of the baselines used in a submission made by a coastal State.

3.3.2. There are only two instances in which the Commission might request geodetic information about baselines. First, it must be satisfied that the test of appurtenance has been positively met. Secondly, if the 350 M limit is employed as a constraint in a submission, the Commission might also find it useful to make recommendations in relation to the methodology employed in the delineation of this limit.

3.3.3. The Commission acknowledges that it is not entitled by the Convention to make recommendations vis-à-vis the delineation of the outer limits of the continental shelf up to a distance of 200 M. A submitting coastal State will not be requested to provide any information about the baselines that generate the portion of the limits of the continental shelf delineated at that distance.

3.3.4. Article 5 prescribes the use of the low water line as the basis for defining normal baselines. However, the Convention does not provide guidance in relation to the exact meaning of this term. The Commission acknowledges that many different definitions are used in State practice and that some define a lower tidal datum than others. Some States use simultaneously two or more definitions of the low water line in separate geographic regions in view of the challenges posed to navigation by specific regional tidal regimes. Different low water lines are used routinely to display the profile of the coastline on official nautical charts.

3.3.5. The Commission feels that there is a uniform and extended State practice which justifies the acceptance of multiple interpretations of the low water line. All of them are regarded as equally valid in a submission.

3.3.6. The Commission is aware that there are different chart datum transfer techniques designed to provide the location of the low water line at sites along the coastline other than at tide gauge sites. The Commission may require background technical information in relation to the methodology used by coastal States for this purpose in each submission.

3.3.7. Articles 7, 9, 10 and 47 entitle States to delineate straight, closing and archipelagic baselines. The Convention does not specify the geodetic definition of these baselines. In the case of straight baselines delineated in accordance with the provisions of article 7, at least two definitions, loxodromes and ellipsoidal geodesics, have been adopted in State practice (United Nations, 1989).

3.3.8. In accordance with established State practice, the Commission shall accept the definition of straight, closing and archipelagic baselines as either geodesics or loxodromes. However, only one line definition can be consistently selected by a submitting State for all of its baselines. In the case of loxodromes, the Commission shall use the definition of a line of a constant azimuth on the surface of a geodetic reference ellipsoid (Bowring, 1985). The Commission strongly discourages the use of apparent straight lines as literally drawn on various paper nautical charts employing a variety of map projections.

3.3.9. The Commission remains open to consider all forms and combinations of methods used to determine the position of baselines by a State in a submission. The Commission may request during the consideration of a submission the following geodetic information about baselines:

- Source of the data;
- Positioning survey technique;
- Time and date of the survey;

- Corrections applied to the data;
- A priori or a posteriori estimates of random and systematic errors;
- Geodetic reference system; and
- Geometric definition of straight, archipelagic and closing lines.

3.4. Outer limits and their confidence zones

3.4.1. The delineation of the outer limits of the extended continental shelf according to article 76 requires the determination of up to four outer limits delineated:

- By reference to the outermost fixed points at each of which the thickness of sedimentary rocks is at least 1 per cent of the shortest distance from such point to the foot of the continental slope;
- At a distance of 60 M from the foot of the slope;
- At a distance of 350 M from baselines from which the breadth of the territorial sea is measured; and
- At a distance of 100 M from the 2,500 m isobath.

3.4.2. Boggs (1930) originally defined the technique used to determine the outer limits of the territorial sea from a selection of points along baselines as the method of envelopes of arcs. It was first introduced as a proposal for codification in international law by the United States delegation at the Hague Codification Conference in 1930. This method provides an outer limit every point of which is located at a prescribed distance from the nearest point on the coast. Shalowitz (1962, p. 171) has advanced a more refined definition of this method, where the outer limit:

"is the locus of the centre of a circle the circumference of which is always in contact with the coastline, that is, with the low water line or the seaward limits of inland waters."

3.4.3. The application of the method of envelopes of arcs is independent of the actual breadth of the limit. Thus, although the method was originally designed as a tool to determine the outer limit of the territorial sea, its mathematical application remains equally valid to determine the outer limit of other maritime spaces based on metric criteria.

3.4.4. The Commission regards the application of the method of envelopes of arcs on the surface of the geodetic reference ellipsoid in a submission as an admissible methodology to determine outer limits based on distances from the nearest points located on baselines, the 2,500 m isobath and the foot of the continental slope. The actual implementation of this method is carried out by solving iteratively a system of linearized distance equations in a resection mathematical model. An exhaustive combinatorial search algorithm is recommended in order to ensure that all possible combinations of pairs of points are analysed and that the nearest points are the ones which generate the outer limit.

3.4.5. The distance resection model described above relies on the solution of the direct and inverse positioning problems formulated in geodesy. A large number of solutions to these classic problems have been developed over the last two centuries. They can be broadly classified into three groups, based upon: the integration of differential equations; transferring an ellipsoid polar triangle to a concentric sphere; and using a conformal projection from the ellipsoid to the sphere (Schnadelbach, 1974). The Commission does not have a preference for the use of a particular solution and it is aware that the correct application of several of them must produce identical results.

3.4.6. The Commission acknowledges the existence of the method of tracés parallèles to determine the outer limits of maritime spaces from straight baselines as prescribed by the International Court of Justice in the Anglo-Norwegian Fisheries case of 1951. This method is a generalization of the method of envelopes of arcs for the cases of continuous straight, closing and archipelagic baselines.

3.4.7. The Commission regards the application of the method of tracés parallèles on the surface of the geodetic reference ellipsoid used in each submission as an admissible methodology to determine outer limits at distances of 200 M and 350 M from the nearest points located on straight, closing and archipelagic baselines from which the breadth of the territorial sea is measured.

3.4.8. The mathematical model for the determination of outer limits from straight baselines on the surface of a geodetic reference ellipsoid is computationally more intensive than the method of envelopes of arcs. It involves the successive application of the direct and inverse problems described above over a large series of discrete points along straight, closing and archipelagic baselines.

3.4.9. For the sake of simplicity, the two formulations described above have not made any reference to the introduction of a priori statistical information about the position of the baselines. In practice, this information must be incorporated in order to derive the confidence region associated with the limit (Sjoberg, 1996). It is clear, however, that the derived offshore limit will never surpass the accuracy of the positions of the baselines themselves, and therefore those States aiming to achieve the highest standards of accuracy in the determination of their outer limits should focus first on the accuracy of their baselines.

3.4.10. The Commission strongly discourages the application of the methods of envelopes of arcs and tracés parallèles through the use of manual graphical procedures on the surface of paper nautical charts. The distortions produced by inherent scale factors in map projections and the inapplicability

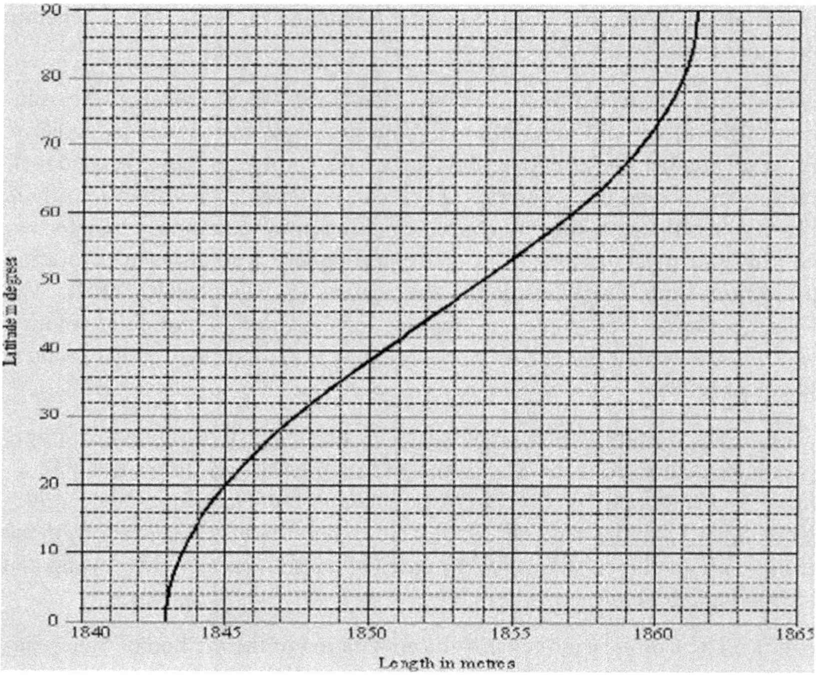

Figure 3.1. Length of an arc of 1 minute of latitude as a function of the latitude of its midpoint from the equator to either of the poles on GRS80 and WGS84.

of Euclidean geometry principles on the surface of a geodetic ellipsoid rule out the admissibility of this manual methodology.

3.4.11. The Commission highlights three observations made by Gidel (1932, p. 510) more than half a century ago: first, that there is no parallelism between the coast and the limit; secondly, that the outer limit is simpler than the normal baseline; and, most importantly, that only a few points contribute to the delineation of the outer limit. There may be no need to submit the data on the full extent of the coastline, a full 2,500 m isobath or the continuous foot of the slope. Only the most seaward points which effectively contribute to the delineation of the outer limit need to be supported.

4. The 2,500 metre isobath

4.1. Formulation of the problem: paragraph 5

4.2. Sources of data and hydrographic measurements

4.3. Bathymetric model

4.4. Selection of points for the delineation of the 100 M limit

4.1. Formulation of the problem: paragraph 5

4.1.1. The Commission recognizes that the 2,500 m isobath is an essential feature for the implementation of article 76. It serves as the basis for the application of one of the constraint rules to the formulae lines in order to produce the outer limits of the continental shelf. According to paragraph 5, it is the reference baseline from which the 100 M line is measured:

> "The fixed points comprising the line of the outer limits of the continental shelf on the sea-bed, drawn in accordance with paragraph 4 (a) (i) and (ii), either shall not exceed 350 nautical miles from the baselines from which the breadth of the territorial sea is measured or shall not exceed 100 nautical miles from the 2,500 metre isobath, which is a line connecting the depth of 2,500 metres."

4.1.2. A line determined at a distance of 100 M from the 2,500 metre isobath may not be used in the delineation of the outer limits of the extended continental shelf in the special case of submarine ridges. Paragraph 6 makes an exception of submarine elevations where it is required:

> "Notwithstanding the provisions of paragraph 5, on submarine ridges, the outer limit of the continental shelf shall not exceed 350 nautical miles from the baselines from which the breadth of the territorial sea is measured. This paragraph does not apply to submarine elevations that are natural components of the continental margin, such as its plateaux, rises, caps, banks and spurs."

4.2. Sources of data and hydrographic measurements

4.2.1. The complete bathymetric database used in the delineation of the 2,500 m isobath in a submission may only include a combination of the following data:

- Single-beam echo sounding measurements;
- Multi-beam echo sounding measurements;
- Bathymetric side-scan sonar measurements;
- Interferometric side-scan sonar measurements; and
- Seismic reflection-derived bathymetric measurements.

4.2.2. The Commission will consider single- and multi-beam echo sounding measurements as the primary source of evidence for the delineation of the

2,500 m isobath. All other admissible evidence provided by bathymetric and interferometric side-scan sonar measurements and seismic reflection-derived bathymetric measurements will be regarded as complementary information in general.

4.2.3. However, bathymetric information derived from seismic reflection and interferometric side-scan sonar measurements may be considered as the primary source in a submission for the purpose of delineating the 2,500 m isobath in special cases such as in ice-covered areas. The Commission may pay particular attention to the calibration and corrections applied to these data.

4.2.4. Bathymetric side-scan sonars are hybrid measuring systems, which collect both estimates of sea-floor slope and bathymetry. Whereas their sea-floor slope information might be relevant in other parts of a submission, potentially for the delineation of the foot of the slope, only their bathymetric component will be considered for the purpose of delineating the 2,500 m isobath.

4.2.5. The bathymetric data produced by light-detection-and-ranging (LIDAR) airborne systems may be particularly valuable to provide bathymetric information for the shallow regions of the seabed included in a submission. However, laser (light amplification by stimulated emission of radiation) profiling is clearly inapplicable to the delineation of the 2,500 m isobath, or the seabed region associated with the base of the continental slope.

4.2.6. Other sources of evidence, such as satellite altimetry-derived bathymetric data or imaging side-scan sonar information, will not be regarded as admissible for the purpose of delineating the 2,500 m isobath. This information, however, might be useful as additional qualitative information in support of other parts of a submission but will not be considered during the determination of this or any other isobaths. However, this data will be considered admissible as supporting information in a submission.

4.2.7. A full technical description of the bathymetric database used in the delineation of the 2,500 metre isobath will include the following information:

- Source of the data;
- Sounding survey techniques and classification;
- Geodetic reference system, navigational positioning methods and their errors;
- Time and date of the survey;
- Corrections applied to the data, such as ray path sound velocity, calibration, tides and other; and
- A priori or a posteriori estimates of random and systematic errors.

4.2.8. A priori depth error estimates, *s*, may be computed by means of the following internationally accepted formulae:

$$s = (a^2 + (b\, d)^2)^{1/2}$$

where:

a constant depth error, i.e., the sum of all constant errors

bd depth-dependent error, i.e., the sum of all depth-dependent errors

b factor of depth-dependent error; and

d depth

with a 95 per cent confidence interval (IHO, 1998).

4.2.9. A posteriori errors may be obtained from the estimated covariance matrix of the estimated depth parameters, which results from an adjustment of an overdetermined system of linear equations formed by cross-over analysis of sounding lines (cf. Vanícek and Krakiwsky, 1982, p. 213).

4.2.10. Coastal States may use the a posteriori error estimation method where there is redundant information in order to assess the quality of historical bathymetric data whose positioning, survey technique and technical description are not available.

4.3. Bathymetric model

4.3.1. The submission will include the necessary cartographic products derived from the compiled bathymetric database to portray the 2,500 metre isobath. These cartographic products may include the following analytic or digital forms:

- Two-dimensional bathymetric profiles;
- Three-dimensional bathymetric models;
- Nautical charts and maps with contours.

4.3.2. Each cartographic product, including nautical charts officially recognized by the State, will be accompanied by a detailed description of the mathematical methodology and data used to produce it. The Commission will pay particular attention to the transit from numerical soundings to analytical functions.

4.3.3. The coastal State will be required to document the following information:

- Interpolation or approximation method;
- Density of measured bathymetric data;
- Perceptual elements such as map projections, vertical and horizontal scales, contour intervals, units, colours and symbols.

4.3.4. Wherever the bathymetric information presented to the Commission may be a filtered or smoothed subset of the original data, a full description of the methodology employed to produce it will be reported by the coastal State.

4.3.5. Full bathymetric models in three dimensions may be required in order to gain a spatial understanding of natural prolongation and may be essential in selecting the full extent of the 2,500 m isobath relevant to the determination of the 100 M outer limit.

4.3.6. The Commission is aware that the seabed can exhibit fractal properties in two and three dimensions (Mandlebrot, 1977). It is also aware that the generation of an analytical model, be it that described by means of contours on a chart or a mathematical expression, results in the generalization of line and surface features at various scales (Fox and Hayes, 1985). The Commission may require geostatistical, fractal, wavelet or other tests and analyses, as it feels appropriate, in order to determine the degree of uncertainty underlying a particular bathymetric model.

4.3.7. The Commission is aware that issues relating to scale, colour, type and others fall within the realm of perception. These issues will be taken into account in order to assess correctly the perception of important technical details.

4.4. Selection of points for the delineation of the 100 M limit

4.4.1. The line determined at a distance of 100 M from the 2,500 metre isobath becomes effective as a constraint over the outer limits of the continental shelf wherever this isobath is located at a distance of 250 M or greater from the baselines from which the territorial sea is measured.

4.4.2. The selection of the most salient points along the 2,500 m isobath for the purpose of delineating the 100 M limit may be straightforward when isobaths are simple. However, when isobaths are complex or repeated in multiples, the selection of points along the 2,500 m isobath becomes difficult. Such situations arise as a result of geological and tectonic processes shaping the present continental margins. They can create multiple repetitions of the 2,500 m isobath, for example, by faulting, folding and thrusting along continental margins. Unless there is evidence to the contrary, the Commission may recommend the use of the first 2,500 m isobath from the baselines from which the breadth of the territorial sea is measured that conforms to the general configuration of the continental margin.

5. Foot of the continental slope determined as the point of maximum change in the gradient at its base

5.1. Formulation of the problem: paragraph 4

5.2. Sources of data

5.3. Filtering and smoothing

5.4. Delineation of the foot of the continental slope

5.1. <u>Formulation of the problem: paragraph 4</u>

5.1.1. The Commission recognizes that the foot of the continental slope is an essential feature that serves as the basis for entitlement to the extended continental shelf and the delineation of its outer limits. According to paragraph 4 (a) (i) and (ii), it is the reference baseline from which the breadths of the limits specified by formulae rules are measured:

> "(i) a line delineated in accordance with paragraph 7 by reference to the outermost fixed points at each of which the thickness of sedimentary rocks is at least 1 per cent of the shortest distance from such point to the foot of the continental slope; or
>
> "(ii) a line delineated in accordance with paragraph 7 by reference to fixed points not more than 60 nautical miles from the foot of the continental slope."

5.1.2. Paragraph 4 (b) provides a dual regime for the determination of the foot of the continental slope:

> "In the absence of evidence to the contrary, the foot of the continental slope shall be determined as the point of maximum change in the gradient at its base."

5.1.3. The Commission interprets the determination of the foot of the continental slope by means of the point of maximum change in gradient at its base, as a provision with the character of a general rule. The fundamental requirements posed by this provision are:

- The identification of the region defined as the base of the continental slope; and

- The determination of the location of the point of maximum change in the gradient at the base of the continental slope.

5.1.4. Its implementation will be guided by bathymetric, geomorphologic, geologic and geophysical sources of evidence.

5.2. <u>Sources of data</u>

5.2.1. Bathymetric and geological data provide the evidence to be used in the geomorphological analysis conducted to identify the region defined as the base of the continental slope. Only bathymetric information will be used to determine the location of the point of maximum change in the gradient at the base of the continental slope.

5.2.2. The bathymetric database used in the delineation of the foot of the slope in a submission may include only one, or a combination of the following data:

- Single-beam echo sounding measurements;
- Multi-beam echo sounding measurements;
- Hybrid side-scan sonar measurements;
- Interferometric side-scan sonar measurements; and
- Seismic reflection-derived bathymetric measurements.

5.2.3. The Commission will require a full technical description of the bathymetric database used in the implementation of this provision. It will also determine the relative value from each of these sources of data in a manner that is consistent with that applied to the determination of the 2,500 metre isobath (refer to section 4.2).

5.2.4. The Commission will also consider as admissible evidence synthetic bathymetric data produced in the form of grids and profiles derived from cartographic and analog sources officially recognized by the coastal State. These cartographic and analog sources may only be based, in turn, on a combination of the bathymetric measurements listed above. Synthetic bathymetric data will be accompanied by a detailed and complete technical description of the method applied and the bathymetric measurements used to produce the cartographic and analog sources from which it stems.

5.2.5. The coastal State will be required to document the following information about cartographic and analog sources:

- Interpolation or approximation methods;
- Spatial density and position of measured bathymetric data;
- Information on perceptual elements such as map projections, vertical and horizontal scales, contour intervals, units, colours and symbols.

5.2.6. The geological and geophysical database used in the identification of the region defined as the base of the foot of the continental slope in a submission may include a combination of the following sources of data:

- In situ samples and measurements;
- Geochemical and radiometric data;
- Geophysical measurements; and
- Side-scan imagery.

5.2.7. Evidence collected as in situ core samples will be accompanied by a complete technical description and their catalogue information will also be enclosed. In situ measurements may include any borehole or ocean-bottom geophysical measurements and their technical description.

5.2.8. Evidence collected in the form of geochemical and radiometric data will also be accompanied by a full technical description and their catalogue information will be enclosed.

5.2.9. Evidence collected in the form of geophysical measurements includes the full range of geophysical methods, including, but not limited to, seismic, gravity, magnetic, palaeomagnetic and side-scan sonar imagery data.

5.3. Filtering and smoothing

5.3.1. The Commission recognizes that filtering and smoothing of bathymetric data might be required in order to facilitate the identification of the location of the foot of the continental slope at the point of maximum change in the gradient at its base. This procedure might be required in some instances because the use of second derivatives of the bathymetric surface produces an enhancement of all features which may obscure the exact location of the foot of the slope.

5.3.2. Filtering in signal theory presupposes a clear differentiation between signal and noise, that is, what is to be regarded as wanted and unwanted information. In the context of the application of paragraph 4 (b), the shelf, the slope and the rise are signal. Any other information that obstructs the location of these features is regarded as noise.

5.3.3. The Commission is aware that the application of some filtering procedures presupposes the use of regularly spaced data. Bathymetric data are seldom collected in the field at equally spaced intervals. In these instances, a coastal State might produce a regularly spaced data set from irregularly spaced data. The Commission is aware that there are many approaches to performing this operation. It will pay close attention to the methodology employed to produce a regularly spaced data set, and it might request the original irregularly spaced data, details about the mathematical technique employed and the output comprised of regularly spaced data.

5.3.4. The Commission is aware that filter design is a wide field and that the frequency response functions of various filters can be very different even if they are designed to cut off information at specific thresholds. The Commission will pay special attention to the admittance function of the filters used in the wavelength or wave number domain which might be applied to two-dimensional bathymetric profiles and three-dimensional bathymetric surfaces.

5.3.5. The Commission shall not accept the artificial amplification or enhancement of any information at wavelengths at which the bathymetric information can be decomposed. Only the removal of unwanted noise at wavelengths shorter than those relevant to the description of the shelf, the slope and the rise will be regarded as admissible. The Commission might request full disclosure of the original unfiltered information, the mathematical details of the filter and the filtered data produced when filtering is applied.

5.3.6. Smoothing is an empirical procedure which also might have an important role to play in facilitating the identification of the main features of the continental margin. It might have a particularly useful application when other bathymetric features might have similar wavelengths to those which define the location of the foot of the continental slope.

5.3.7. The Commission is aware that the full array of empirical data smoothing techniques is vast. It remains open to considering the application of any smoothing technique, but it will examine closely the proper application of each one in this context. The Commission might request full disclosure of the original data, the mathematical details of the smoothing algorithm and the output data.

5.4. <u>Delineation of the foot of the continental slope</u>

5.4.1. The methodology used to determine the foot of the continental slope by means of the point of maximum change in gradient at its base can be regarded also as a two- or three-dimensional problem. This mathematical methodology has some similarities to the second derivative technique employed in the enhancement of potential field maps produced routinely in gravity and magnetic geophysical prospecting. The Commission recognizes the usefulness and complementarity of the use of both two- and three-dimensional approaches.

5.4.2. The Commission is aware of the large number of techniques and methods available for sea-floor classification and roughness analyses (e.g., Fox and Hayes, 1985; Stewart et al. 1992; and Herzfeld, 1993). Many methods based on, for example, fractal and geostatistical analysis have been developed.

5.4.3. The Commission will not prescribe the use of a single mathematical methodology based on bathymetric data for the identification of the region defined as base of the continental slope. It will make recommendations based on the mathematical methodology applied on a case-by-case basis, and in view of all other geological and geophysical evidence presented by the coastal State.

5.4.4. For the purpose of identifying the region defined as the base, the Commission defines the continental slope as the outer portion of the continental margin that extends from the shelf edge to the upper part of the rise or to the deep ocean floor where a rise is not developed. The rise, in turn, is the wedge-shaped sedimentary body having a smaller gradient than the continental slope. Many continental margins, however, depart from this ideal picture (see chap. 6, sect. 6.2, and figs. 6.1A-6.1F), and in such cases geological and geophysical data may be used to assist in identifying the region referred to here as the base of the continental slope.

5.4.5. The Commission defines the base of the continental slope as a region where the lower part of the slope merges into the top of the continental rise, or into the top of the deep ocean floor where a continental rise does not exist. The Commission recommends that the search for the base of the continental slope be carried out by means of a two-step approach. First, the search for its seaward edge should start from the rise, or from the deep ocean floor where a rise is not developed, in a direction towards the continental slope. Secondly, the search for its landward edge should start from the lower part of the slope in the direction of the continental rise, or the deep ocean floor where a rise is not developed.

5.4.6. As a general rule, whenever the base of the continental slope can be clearly determined on the basis of morphological and bathymetric evidence, the Commission recommends the application of that evidence. Geological and geophysical data can also be submitted by coastal States to supplement proof that the base of the continental slope is found at that location.

5.4.7. The determination of the location of the point of maximum change in the gradient at the base of the continental slope will be conducted by means of the mathematical analyses of two-dimensional profiles, three-dimensional bathymetric models and preferably both. Methods based on a purely visual perception of bathymetric data will not be accepted by the Commission.

5.4.8. The determination of the location of the point of maximum change in the gradient was envisaged originally by its proponent as a two-dimensional problem based on the mathematical analyses of two-dimensional bathymetric profiles (Hedberg, 1976). This methodology is acceptable to the Commission with the provision that their three-dimensional location on a bathymetric map or nautical chart is provided at all times. The Commission recommends that the orientation of this profile be such that it runs in a perpendicular direction to the isobaths located at the point of maximum change in the gradient at the base of the continental slope.

5.4.9. The Commission is aware that several three-dimensional techniques have been designed in the past to produce a continuous trace of the foot of the continental slope. These techniques are based on the determination of the total curvature surface (Vanícek and Ou, 1996), the second derivative surface in the direction of the gradient (Bennet, 1996) and other second derivative-based analyses.

5.4.10. The Commission is also aware that the application of different two-dimensional and three-dimensional methodologies might yield different results in a given submission using the same data set, but it is ready to consider the application of one or several of them. In these cases, the Commission might perform comparative analyses of the results obtained by the application of two-dimensional methods, three-dimensional methods or both.

5.4.11. The Commission will request a complete technical description of the original three-dimensional bathymetric model, the details of the mathematical methodology and the output surface and the point or line defining the foot of the continental slope.

5.4.12. Where more than a single change in the gradient is located at the base of the continental slope, the Commission recognizes as a general rule the selection of the point of maximum change in the gradient as the method to identify the location of the foot of the continental slope. The selection of any other local change in the gradient at its base, i.e., any change other than the maximum, will be regarded by the Commission as an exception. The justification for the application of this exception will require the presentation of evidence to the contrary to the general rule, as described in the following chapter.

6. Foot of the continental slope determined by means of evidence to the contrary to the general rule

6.1. Formulation of the problem: paragraph 4 (b)

6.1.1. The Commission recognizes that the determination of the foot of the continental slope is achieved as a general rule by means of the point of maximum change in the gradient at its base. However, article 76, paragraph 4 (b), also incorporates a possible exception when evidence to the contrary of this general rule might be submitted by a coastal State:

> "In the absence of evidence to the contrary, the foot of the continental slope shall be determined as the point of maximum change in the gradient at its base."

6.1.2. The Commission interprets the determination of the foot of the continental slope when evidence to the contrary to the general rule is invoked, as a provision with the character of an exception to the rule. This provision not only does not oppose, but in fact complements, the general rule established by the determination of the foot of the continental slope as the point of maximum change in the gradient at its base. Both approaches aim to find the foot of the continental slope at its base.

6.1.3. The complementary character of this provision is emphasized by the fact that in addition to bathymetric and geomorphological evidence, all other necessary and sufficient geological and geophysical evidence must also be included as part of a submission by a coastal State.

6.1.4. The Commission feels it important to outline the breadth and scope of the necessary and sufficient evidence which will be required from States that might deem it appropriate to invoke this provision. The clarification of relevant scientific terms precedes the description of this evidence below.

6.1.5. The Commission acknowledges that article 76 makes use of scientific terms in a legal context, which at times departs significantly from accepted scientific definitions and terminology. The trend for the creation of separate interpretations of terms can be traced back to the work carried out for the first United Nations Conference on the Law of the Sea by the International Law Commission (Oxman, 1969). Article 76, paragraph 1, which defines the legal concept of the continental shelf by means of a reference to the outer edge of the continental margin, provides a measure of the current gap between the juridical and the scientific use of terms.

6.1.6. The definition of the continental margin in the earth sciences had a geomorphologic inception at the time of its adoption by various scientific organizations (Wiseman and Ovey, 1953). Current scientific knowledge about the nature and extent of the continental margin has evolved greatly from its original definition. It incorporates many additional geological and geophysical concepts within the framework provided by plate tectonics (COSOD II, 1987; ODP/JOIDES, 1996).

6.1.7. Although article 76 refers to the continental shelf as a juridical term, it defines its outer limit with a reference to the outer edge of the continental margin with its natural components such as the shelf, the slope and the rise as geological and geomorphological features. According to article 76, paragraph 1:

> "The continental shelf of a coastal State comprises the sea-bed and subsoil of the submarine areas that extend beyond its territorial sea throughout the natural prolongation of its land territory to the outer edge of the continental margin, or to a distance of 200 nautical miles from the baselines from which the breadth of the territorial sea is measured where the outer edge of the continental margin does not extend up to that distance."

6.1.8. Article 76, paragraph 3, provides further guidance to the Commission:

> "The continental margin comprises the submerged prolongation of the land mass of the coastal State, and consists of the sea-bed and subsoil of the shelf, the slope and the rise. It does not include the deep ocean floor with its oceanic ridges or the subsoil thereof."

6.1.9. These paragraphs are valuable to the Commission on several grounds. They help clarify concepts such as natural prolongation of the land territory to the outer edge of the continental margin in the geological sense of these terms, which require the consideration of tectonics, sedimentology and other aspects of geology. But also, they provide guidance to the Commission in interpreting the meaning of the term "evidence to the contrary" to the general rule if this provision, with the character of an exception, is invoked by a coastal State in a submission to determine the foot of the continental slope.

6.1.10. The Convention does not prescribe the application of a specific scientific methodology to define the location of the foot of the continental slope when evidence to the contrary to the general rule is invoked. The Commission interprets this provision as an opportunity for coastal States to use the best geological and geophysical evidence available to them to locate the foot of the continental slope at its base when the geomorphological evidence given by the maximum change in the gradient as a general rule does not or can not locate reliably the foot of the continental slope.

6.2. Geological and geophysical evidence

6.2.1. Some continental margins consist of three elements - the shelf, the slope and the rise - whereas others show no rise. The continental slope forms a portion of the continental margin and extends from the shelf edge to the top of the rise, or to the top of the deep ocean floor where no rise exists. The rise is normally a wedge-shaped sedimentary body having a smaller gradient than the continental slope. The rise developed predominantly in a rifted margin realm with sufficient supply of sediments from the continent after breakup and commencement of sea-floor spreading.

6.2.2. From a geomorphological perspective, the shelf in ideal cases is the part of the seabed adjacent to the continent, which forms a large submerged terrace that dips gently seaward. The breadth of the shelf depends on the geological evolution of the adjacent continent. The continental shelf extends seaward to the continental slope, which is characterized by a marked increase in gradient. The base of the slope is a zone where the lower part of the slope merges into the top of the continental rise or into the top of the deep ocean floor, in the case where no rise exists.

6.2.3. The shelf and the continental slope have characteristics typical of continental crust, often including thick layers of sediments. The foot and the base of the continental slope are inseparable, and commonly lie close to the outer edge of the continent, that is, near the place where the crust changes from continental to oceanic.

6.2.4. The Commission is aware of the difficulties arising from the determination of the foot of the continental slope and the edge of the continental margin from a geological perspective. Continental crust is compositionally distinct from oceanic crust, but the boundary between these two crustal types may not be clearly defined. Simple subdivision of margins into shelf, slope and rise may not always exist owing to the variety of geological and geomorphological continental margin types resulting from different tectonic and geological settings.

6.2.5. It is difficult to generalize the geological and geomorphological parameters that a coastal State may consider to establish the foot of the continental slope at its base by means of evidence to the contrary to the general rule. However, some examples and definitions are presented here based on evidence provided by plate tectonics. The Commission is well aware that these considerations may not exhaust all possible geological and geomorphologic types of continental margins as examples.

Types of continental margins

6.2.6. Over the last 20 years, geoscientific studies and activities such as the International Deep Sea Drilling Project/Ocean Drilling Programme (DSDP/ODP) have demonstrated the presence of a variety of continental margins (e.g. COSOD II, 1987), which can be grouped into three major categories:

(a) Convergent (active) continental margins are formed along plate boundaries linked to active and inactive subduction zones often, but not always, associated with a trench (e.g. ODP/JOIDES, 1996; Bally, 1988;

Taylor and Natland, 1995). The convergent continental margins comprise three different types:

(i) The accretionary convergent continental margin consists of a wide wedge of accreted sediments which were scraped off from the downgoing (lower) plate (fig. 6.1A);

(ii) The poor- or non-accretionary convergent continental margin is characterized by a poorly developed accretionary wedge. Most of the incoming sediments are underplated beneath the upper plate or are removed by the downgoing (subducting) plate (fig. 6.1B);

(iii) The destructive convergent continental margin shows no accretion. Material from the upper plate is eroded ("tectonic erosion") at the foot and from the base of the upper plate by the subducting lower plate (fig. 6.1C);

(b) Rifted (extensional, passive) continental margins were formed along incipient plate boundaries during continental breakup and subsequent initial production of oceanic crust by sea-floor spreading (e.g. Bally, 1988; Edwards and Santogrossi, 1990; von Rad et al., 1982; Coffin and Eldholm, 1991). The category of rifted continental margins can be subdivided into two types:

(i) The wide, thin-crusted continental margin type (rifted non-volcanic margin) with widths of several hundreds of kilometres is characterized by a complex system of horsts and intervening grabens and half-grabens formed during the rifting and early drifting phases, and by a thinned continental crust (fig. 6.1D);

(ii) The narrow, thick-crusted continental margin type (rifted volcanic margin) is characterized by a thick lower-crustal lens with seismic velocities in the range of 7.2–7.6 km/s, and by a huge volcanic construction in the upper crustal level displayed in seismic sections by an average 100 km wide and several thousands of metres thick wedge of seaward-dipping reflectors (fig. 6.1E). Results of DSDP/ODP drilling have confirmed previous interpretations (e.g. Hinz, 1981) that the wedge of seaward-dipping reflections consists predominantly of basaltic lavas extruded in a shallow marine or subaerial environment. This voluminous volcanic body extending often continuously over distances of several thousands of kilometres along rifted continental margins was formed within a relatively short episode of transient volcanism during initial continental breakup. Recent studies have shown that approximately 70 per cent of the rifted Atlantic continental margins are volcanic continental margins;

(c) Sheared continental margins were created along zones of translational continental rupturing during continental breakup and subsequent sea-floor spreading (fig. 6.1F).

6.3. Determination of the foot of the continental slope

6.3.1. Evidence to the contrary to the general rule in article 76, paragraph 4 (b), is interpreted by the Commission as a provision designed to allow coastal States to use the best geological and geophysical evidence available to them to locate the foot of the continental slope at its base when the geomorphological evidence given by the maximum change in the gradient does not or can not locate reliably the foot of the continental slope.

6.3.2. The inability of the general rule to locate the foot of the slope by means of the maximum change in the gradient at its base can be found in a number of scenarios. One of these scenarios can be envisaged, for example, when the curvature of the seabed along the base of the continental slope is constant. In this case, the maximum change in the gradient encompasses not only a point, but also a region.

6.3.3. Another scenario where the maximum change in the gradient may not clearly render the location of the foot of the continental slope at its base was already identified at the end of the previous chapter. In a scenario where irregular seabed topography reveals a number of local maxima in the change of the gradient at the base of the continental slope, it is possible that its maximum maximorum may not be indicative of the location of its foot.

6.3.4. In these exceptional cases, geological and geophysical evidence may be introduced as an alternative for determining the location of the foot of the continental slope at its base.

6.3.5. Article 76, paragraph 1, defines the breadth of the continental shelf with a reference to the edge of the geological continental margin. The Commission finds guidance in this paragraph to determine that any point identified on the basis of geological or geophysical evidence as the foot of the continental slope shall be located inside the geological continental margin.

(a) Convergent (active) continental margins

6.3.6. From a geoscientific perspective, the seaward extent of convergent continental margins is defined either by the seaward edge of the accretionary wedge (figs. 6.1A and 6.1B), or in the case of the destructive convergent margin type by the foot of the upper plate and by the foot of the inner trench wall, respectively (fig. 6.1C).

6.3.7. This distinct seaward limit or plate boundary can be determined with acceptable accuracy by modern multi-channel seismic techniques and modern bathymetric techniques (see chap. 8).

(b) Rifted (non-volcanic) and sheared continental margins

6.3.8. From a geoscientific perspective, the seaward limit of both the rifted non-volcanic continental margin and the sheared continental margin is defined as the transition between continental crust and oceanic crust created by sea-floor spreading and related volcanic/magmatic processes. Although continental crust has a different composition from that of oceanic crust, the boundary between the two crustal types may not be clearly defined; sometimes gradational or oceanic crust may even intrude into extended and downthrown continental crust.

6.3.9. Modern multi-channel and deep-penetrating seismic reflection studies and wide-angle reflection/refraction studies in parallel with magnetic and gravity measurements (see chap. 8) are needed to determine the location of the transitional zone of the rifted non-volcanic continental margins and of the sheared continental margins, especially in areas where magnetic sea-floor spreading anomalies are not well developed.

6.3.10. Apart from drilling, sampling and coring of crustal outcrops, including seamounts in the transitional area between continental and oceanic crust, can provide evidence of rock type or lithology and supply material for a variety of studies, for example, radiometric age dating, palaeontological age correlation, geochemical-isotope chemical analyses and palaeomagnetic studies. These results can be of use in determining the ocean-continent boundary along rifted non-volcanic and sheared continental margins. If the foot of the continental slope is very difficult to define on the basis of bathymetric data, the Commission might consider the continental-oceanic transitional (COT) zone (figs. 6.1D and 6.1F) as the place to determine the outer edge of the continental margin. Since the transitional zone can extend over several tens of kilometres, the Commission may consider the landward limit of the transitional zone as an equivalent of the foot of the continental slope in the context of paragraph 4, provided that the submitted geophysical and geological data conclusively demonstrate that the submerged land mass of the coastal State extends to this point.

(c) Rifted volcanic continental margins

6.3.11. Rifted volcanic continental margins are characterized by a thick low-crustal lens with high seismic velocities in the range of 7.0–7.6 km/s and a thick sequence of seaward-dipping reflectors (SDRS) beneath the basement surface. The SDRS merge seaward without a sharp boundary into oceanic crust created at a pre-existing oceanic ridge. Since the feather edge of the SDRS overlies rifted continental crust, a major part of the rifted volcanic continental margin can be considered as "the natural prolongation of the land territory" (article 76, paras. 1 and 3). The seaward extent of rifted volcanic continental margins can be defined as an area in which the SDRS terminate seaward and where the thickness of the igneous continental crust decreases to values typical of oceanic crust, i.e. less than 15 kilometres. Wide-angle reflection/refraction data and magnetic and multi-channel seismic reflection measurements are needed for determining the landward limit of the transitional zone (COT in fig. 6.1E) of the rifted volcanic continental margins, which might be considered by the Commission as an equivalent of the foot of the continental slope in the context of paragraph 4.

6.3.12. Although geological (plate tectonic) considerations are very important for coastal States in the determination of the foot of the continental slope, geomorphological aspects must also be considered. Among geological considerations, in addition to plate tectonics, it is recommended to consider also the sedimentary history of the margin resulting in the depositional build-up and geomorphological shaping of the margin.

6.3.13. The Commission understands that some coastal States may have difficulties in obtaining the necessary data to define the oceanic-continental crust boundary, which in some cases is not clear.

6.4. Considerations to be given with respect to evidence to the contrary

6.4.1. If a State has given evidence to the contrary to the general rule against using the foot of the continental slope (article 76 (4) (b)) in its submission, the Commission will deal with, inter alia, the following questions:

(i) Is that evidence acceptable to the Commission?

(ii) Does that evidence pertain to the identification of the foot of the continental slope? Is that evidence purely bathymetric and/or morphological?

(iii) Does that evidence include subsurface information aimed at establishing that the limit obtained by the rule of maximum change in gradient would not, for example, equate to the limit of the geological continental margin?

(iv) If such evidence to the contrary is presented as part of a submission, the Commission will request that it be also accompanied by the results of applying the rule of maximum change in gradient.

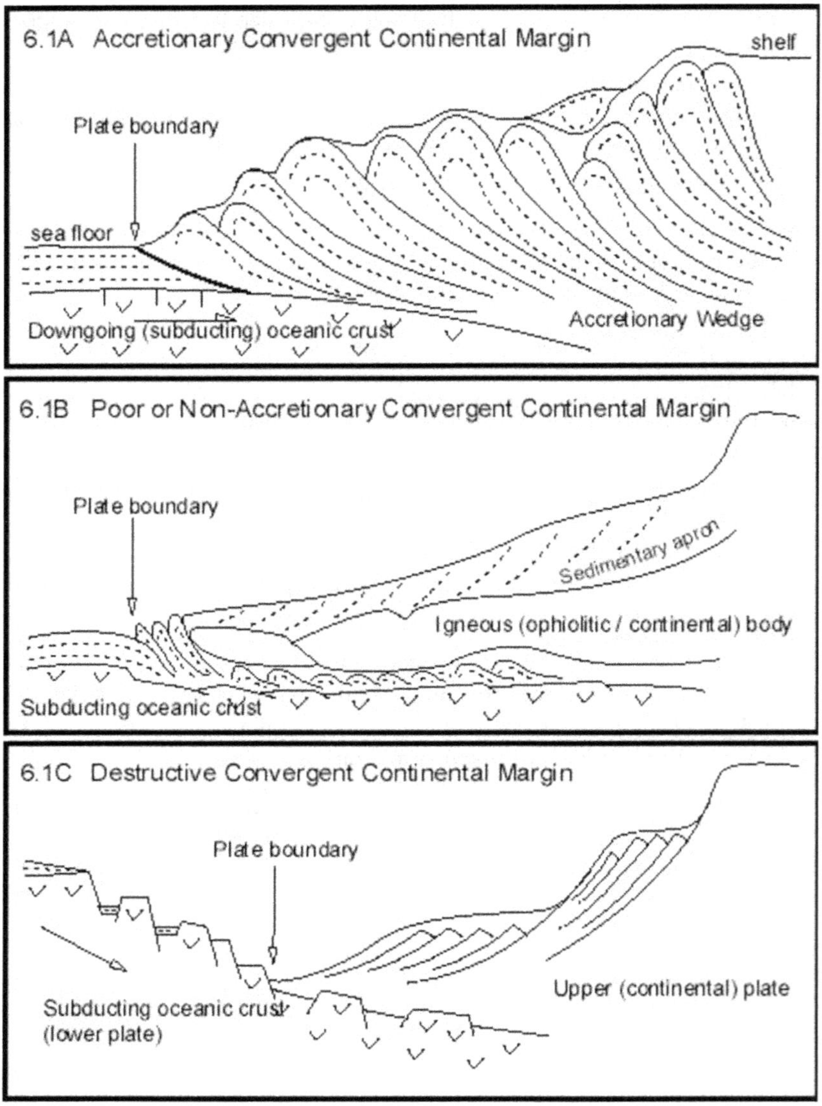

Figure 6.1. Schematic illustrations of different continental margin types.

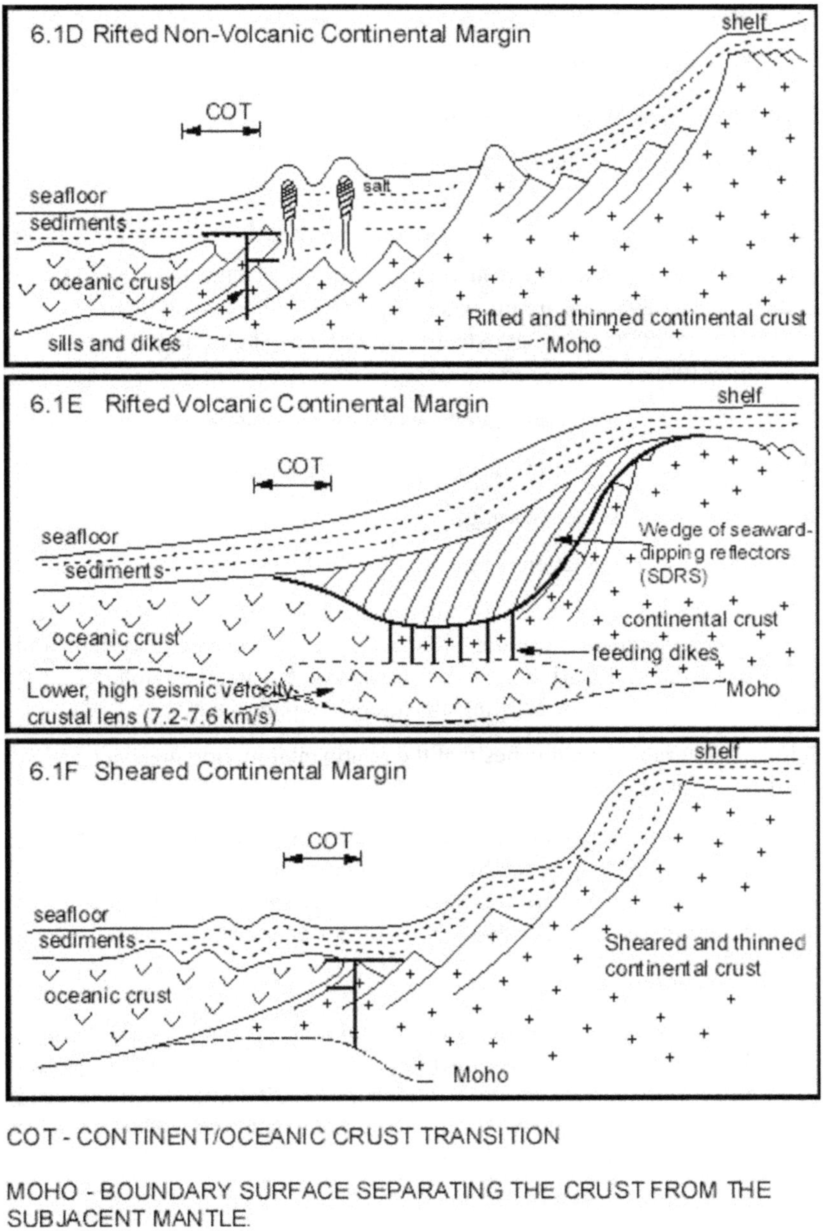
6.1D Rifted Non-Volcanic Continental Margin
shelf
COT
seafloor
sediments
salt
oceanic crust
Rifted and thinned continental crust
sills and dikes
Moho
6.1E Rifted Volcanic Continental Margin
shelf
COT
seafloor
sediments
Wedge of seaward-dipping reflectors (SDRS)
oceanic crust
continental crust
feeding dikes
Lower, high seismic velocity crustal lens (7.2-7.6 km/s)
Moho
6.1F Sheared Continental Margin
shelf
COT
seafloor
sediments
oceanic crust
Sheared and thinned continental crust
Moho
COT - CONTINENT/OCEANIC CRUST TRANSITION
MOHO - BOUNDARY SURFACE SEPARATING THE CRUST FROM THE SUBJACENT MANTLE.

Figure 6.1.

7. Ridges

7.1. Formulation of the problem: paragraphs 3 and 6

7.1.1. The Commission is aware that oceanic and submarine ridges as well as submarine elevations are given special attention in article 76 with respect to issues of entitlement to an extended continental shelf and the delineation of its outer limits.

7.1.2. Article 76 mentions three types of sea floor highs:

- Oceanic ridges of the deep ocean floor (para. 3);
- Submarine ridges (para. 6);
- Submarine elevations (para. 6).

7.1.3. None of these terms is precisely defined. It seems that the term "ridge" is used on purpose, but the link between the "oceanic ridges" of paragraph 3 and the "submarine ridges" of paragraph 6 is unclear. Both terms are distinct from the term "submarine elevations" of paragraph 6.

7.1.4. Paragraph 3 establishes that the continental margin does not include the deep ocean floor with its oceanic ridges:

> "The continental margin comprises the submerged prolongation of the land mass of the coastal State, and consists of the sea-bed and subsoil of the shelf, the slope and the rise. It does not include the deep ocean floor with its oceanic ridges or the subsoil thereof."

7.1.5. According to paragraph 6:

> "Notwithstanding the provisions of paragraph 5, on submarine ridges, the outer limit of the continental shelf shall not exceed 350 nautical miles from the baselines from which the breadth of the territorial sea is measured. This paragraph does not apply to submarine elevations that are natural components of the continental margin, such as its plateaux, rises, caps, banks and spurs."

7.1.6. This seems to imply that "submarine ridges" and "submarine elevations" are also distinct legal categories, as they are subject to separate provisions regarding the maximum outer limit.

7.1.7. The constraints contained in paragraph 6 for submarine ridges do not apply to submarine elevations that are natural components of the continental margin, such as "plateaux, rises, caps, banks and spurs".

7.1.8. The distinction between the "submarine elevations" and "submarine ridges" or "oceanic ridges" shall not be based on their geographical denominations and names used so far in the preparation of the published maps and charts and other relevant literature. Such a distinction for the purpose of article 76 shall be made on the basis of scientific evidence taking into account the appropriate provisions of these Guidelines.

7.2. Oceanic ridges and submarine ridges

7.2.1. Ridges under the sea may be formed in a variety of geological processes, including:

- Ridges formed by the sea-floor spreading and associated volcanic-magmatic processes;
- Ridges formed along transform faults and created as an inherent part of the sea-floor spreading process;
- Ridges formed by later tectonic activity resulting in uplift of oceanic crust;
- Ridges formed by volcanic activity related to the movement of crust over a hot spot. These ridges are commonly composed of coalescing volcanic features or seamounts and generally occur on oceanic crust;
- Ridges formed by interaction of oceanic crustal plates;
- Ridges formed by regional excessive volcanism related to plumes of anomalously hot mantle;
- Ridges associated with active plate boundaries and the formation of island arc systems. They could occur as active and inactive (remnant) volcanic arcs, and forearc and back-arc ridges. Such ridges commonly reflect different stages in the progressive development of island arc systems and may result from variations in factors such as the rate and direction of convergence, and from the nature of the plate being subducted;
- Ridges formed by rifting (extension and thinning) of continental crust. This process commonly forms broader features, such as marginal plateaux and rises, but sometimes creates elongated slivers of continental crust separated by oceanic or highly extended continental crust.

7.2.2. This categorization of ridges is not exhaustive and complete owing to the variety of the tectonic settings of the sea floor.

7.2.3. In scientific literature the term "oceanic ridges" is not used in an entirely strict sense. In some cases it clearly refers to oceanic spreading ridges only, while in others it seems to apply to all ridges composed of oceanic basaltic rocks (i.e. the first five categories in the list above). Transform ridges, in cases where they develop through time from a continental crustal environment into an oceanic crustal environment, may be difficult to classify as only one or the other along their full length. The other ridge types, except perhaps for some back-arc ridges, have no relationship to oceanic crust.

7.2.4. Some ridges located within the continental margins have been present since the early evolution of the margin and have influenced it since then. Because of their presence, sediment dispersal and thickness and the morphology of the sea floor may have acquired a unique configuration and individualization within the regional context.

7.2.5. It should be noted that paragraph 6 makes reference to both the category of submarine ridges, and that of submarine elevations that are natural components of the continental margin. At the same time, the Convention recognizes that the provision of paragraph 6 concerning the maximum limit of 350 M applies to submarine ridges.

7.2.6. The Commission feels that the provisions of paragraphs 3 and 6 may create some difficulties in defining ridges for which the criterion of 350 M in paragraph 6 may apply on the basis of the origin of the ridges and their composition.

7.2.7. For example, if the oceanic ridges include the first five types of ridges mentioned above (composed of oceanic basaltic rocks), one may find some examples where the ridges formed along transform faults or by later tectonic activity infringe the continental margin of continents.

7.2.8. Some ridges (including active spreading ridges) may have islands on them. In such cases it would be difficult to consider that those parts of the ridge belong to the deep ocean floor.

7.2.9. Article 76 makes no systematic reference to the different types of the earth's crust. Instead it only makes reference to the two terms: "the natural prolongation of … land territory" and "the submerged prolongation of the land mass" of coastal States as opposed to oceanic ridges of the deep ocean floor. The terms "land mass" and "land territory" are both neutral terms with regard to crustal types in the geological sense. Therefore, the Commission feels that geological crust types cannot be the sole qualifier in the classification of ridges and elevations of the sea floor into the legal categories of paragraph 6 of article 76, even in the case of island States.

7.2.10. Therefore the Commission feels that in cases of ridges its view shall be based on such scientific and legal considerations as natural prolongation of land territory and land mass, morphology of ridges and their relation to the continental margin as defined in paragraph 4, and continuity of ridges.

7.2.11. As it is difficult to define the details concerning various conditions, the Commission feels it appropriate that the issue of ridges be examined on a case-by-case basis.

7.3. <u>Submarine elevations</u>

7.3.1. The term "submarine elevations" in paragraph 6 includes a selection of highs: "such as plateaux, rises, caps, banks and spurs". The phrase "such as" implies that the list is not complete. Common to all of these elevations is that they are natural components of the continental margin. This makes it relevant to consider the processes that form the continental margins and how continents grow. The growth of the present continents is and/or was primarily caused by geological processes along the continental margins (e.g., Rudnick, 1995). Consequently, the Commission will base its views on "submarine elevations" mainly on the following considerations:

(a) In the active margins, a natural process by which a continent grows is the accretion of sediments and crustal material of oceanic, island arc or continental origin onto the continental margin. Therefore, any crustal fragment or sedimentary wedge that is accreted to the continental margin should be regarded as a natural component of that continental margin;

(b) In the passive margins, the natural process by which a continent breaks up prior to the separation by seafloor spreading involves thinning, extension and rifting of the continental crust and extensive intrusion of magma into and extensive extrusion of magma through that crust. This process adds to the growth of the continents. Therefore, seafloor highs that are formed by this breakup process should be regarded as natural components of the continental margin where such highs constitute an integral part of the prolongation of the land mass.

8. Delineation of the outer limits of the continental shelf based on sediment thickness

8.1. Formulation of the problem: paragraph 4 (a) (i)

8.1.1. The Commission recognizes that the sediment thickness rule is one of two equally valid formulae for entitlement to the extended continental shelf and the delineation of its outer limits subject to the constraints contained in paragraphs 5 and 6. Paragraph 4 (a) (i) describes this formula as follows:

> "(i) a line delineated in accordance with paragraph 7 by reference to the outermost fixed points at each of which the thickness of sedimentary rocks is at least 1 per cent of the shortest distance from such point to the foot of the continental slope; or ..."

8.1.2. The sediment thickness formula opens an avenue for the admission of geophysical evidence in a submission of an extended continental shelf by a coastal State. It has the advantage of accounting for variations in continental rises throughout the world.

8.1.3. This formula is based on a model in which the sediments of the rise thin gradually in a seaward direction. This model links the outer limit of the rise to the thickness of the sediments beneath it (Gardiner, 1978).

8.1.4. A coastal State that intends to apply this provision will have to document the position of the foot of the continental slope and the thickness of sediments in a seaward direction from it. Geoscientists have long recognized that a series of technical issues arises during its implementation. These relate to the identification of the sediment/basement interface, the calculation of sediment thickness and the variability of sediment distribution.

8.1.5. In the ideal morphological model of a passive continental margin, these sediments belong to the continental rise. The geology and morphology of active and sheared continental margins are more complex and usually lack the classical rise but may still comprise considerable volumes of sediments beyond the foot of the slope (see chap. 6).

8.1.6. The sediments of the classical rise and other sediment wedges adjacent to the foot of the continental slope may consist of material eroded from the adjacent continent and deposited by turbidity and contour currents. These sediments are mixed with pelagic and hemipelagic material and/or pyroclastics, such as ash and lava. The sedimentary facies and morphology of the slope and rise are often severely modified by the slumping and redeposition of sediments.

8.1.7. The rise on a passive continental margin is ideally a wedge-shaped apron formed by sediments lying on oceanic and partly continental basements. The sediment thickness is expected to decrease gradually from the foot of the continental slope towards the abyssal plains of the deep ocean. The basement at the base of the sediments may have very variable dips, but in many cases has a gentle general dip towards the continent. However, for the purpose of implementing paragraph 4 (a) (i), the Commission understands the term "sediment thickness" in accordance with the following definition:

8.1.8. The sediment thickness at any location on the continental margin is the vertical distance from the sea floor to the top of the basement at the base of the sediments, regardless of the slope of the sea floor or the slope of the top basement surface.

8.1.9. The thickness of sediments can be determined by means of direct sampling and indirect methods. Direct sampling is conducted by means of drilling. This is a very costly process, particularly in deep water, and only gives spot values. Indirect methods include acoustic and potential field measurements. These are less expensive, more expeditious and give a better understanding of sediment distribution. However, they require additional information. The method of seismic profiling, for example, needs velocity calibration.

8.1.10. Paragraph 4 (a) (i) implies the determination of the sediment thickness by a measurement of the depth of the top of the basement from the seabed. This determination requires the application of methods to establish the position and shape of the seabed relative to the top of the basement. The most relevant combined data sets for these purposes are those derived from bathymetric and seismic reflection and refraction measurements. The calculation of the vertical distance between the basement and seabed surfaces (i.e. the sediment thickness) involves a conversion of the two-way travel times of the seismic wavelet into depth in metres.

8.1.11. In some cases, especially where seismic reflection data are of poor quality, gravimetric and magnetic data may also be relevant for mapping the top of the basement.

8.1.12. The Commission acknowledges that, for the coastal States located in the southern part of the Bay of Bengal, an exception to the provisions of paragraph 4 is provided for by the Statement of Understanding in Annex II of the Final Act of the Third United Nations Conference on the Law of the Sea. A State that is entitled to implement this provision, and opts to do so, is expected by the Commission to submit data at fixed points not more than 60 M apart along the submitted boundary line of the continental shelf to document that the thickness of sedimentary rock is not less than 1 kilometre at each of these fixed points.

8.2. Relevant geophysical techniques and data

8.2.1. The Commission will regard the data provided by seismic reflection and seismic refraction surveys as the primary source of evidence for mapping and determining the sediment thickness. Gravimetric and magnetic data may be provided at all times as complementary sources of evidence. These complementary forms of evidence are particularly relevant in instances where only a non-comprehensive seismic database may be available.

Seismic reflection data

8.2.2. A typical area of continental margin will generally have four different types of seismic reflection data derived from:

(a) Regional government/academic/industry multi-channel seismic surveys for reconnaissance of the continental margin;

(b) Localized and detailed 2D and 3D surveys acquired predominantly on the shelf by the hydrocarbon industry;

(c) Localized 2D multi-channel surveys acquired by research institutions for the preparation of scientific drilling of the International Ocean Drilling Programme (ODP) on continental margins; and

(d) Widely spaced and scattered academic/oceanographic institution surveys, often only recorded by means of a single-channel technique.

8.2.3. Multi-channel reflection data form a much more comprehensive source of evidence than data collected by means of single-channel techniques. The overall greater quality and penetration of these multi-channel data offer many advantages for the delineation of the outer edge of the continental margin. Single-channel data are generally of poorer quality, shallower and without velocity information. They are less valuable and often are very randomly distributed.

8.2.4. The Commission will regard multi-channel reflection data as the most authoritative source of evidence for the determination of sediment thickness. Single-channel reflection data may also be provided at all times by coastal States as a supplementary source of evidence.

8.2.5. The Commission is aware that single-channel data might be the only source of seismic reflection data available in some submissions. In these instances, the coastal State will be expected to have analysed all acoustic and potential field geophysical measurements available by means of inverse theory techniques to help render the thickness of sediments in the outer parts of the continental margin.

Seismic refraction data

8.2.6. Seismic refraction methods, including wide-angle reflection methods, give information on the transmission velocities and the nature of the subsurface rock layers. The two main features of the wide-angle method are that:

(a) It employs rather low frequency sources;

(b) The seismic rays are projected obliquely through the geological structures.

8.2.7. The low frequencies allow good penetration. The oblique angles allow the detection and measurement of velocity gradient zones as well as the more abrupt changes, which show up well on reflection profiles. In typical marine wide-angle reflection surveys on continental margins, the recording stations (ocean bottom seismographs) are placed typically 5 km to 10 km apart, providing a corresponding moderate accuracy of the ray trace modelling solutions, velocity and depth estimates. Full details of the source of the data and the processing methods utilized are required in order to determine the validity of the interpretation presented.

Gravity

8.2.8. Geodetic measurements of the Earth's gravity field may provide evidence in support of a submission. Gravity data can be obtained from sea-floor gravity measurements (Beyer et al., 1966; Zumberge et al., 1994), surface marine gravity surveys (Torge, 1989) and airborne gravity surveys (LaCoste, 1967; Valliant et al., 1985). They can also be derived on a global basis from a combination of multi-satellite altimetry measurements and dynamic orbital analyses (Seeber, 1993). The combination of terrestrial and extraterrestrial gravity estimates, via inverse theory techniques, can provide important insights into the composition and structure of the continental margin, including the delineation of sedimentary basins, and the modelling of sediment thickness and deep crustal structures. Free air anomalies, in particular, may be used as a diagnosis element in order to outline the potential outer edge of the continental margin.

Magnetics

8.2.9. Magnetic data are particularly useful for distinguishing oceanic from continental crust since the magnetic stripes of the oceanic crust are unmistakable. These features led to the scientific breakthrough of the sea-floor spreading hypothesis. Similarly to satellite-derived gravity data, satellite-derived magnetic data can only produce intermediate- to long-wavelength anomaly maps. These satellite-derived magnetic data can be useful in regional compilations of marine magnetic data (Arkani-Hamed et al., 1995).

8.2.10. Again, individual marine magnetic profiles can be modelled to gain greater insight into the nature and depth of the oceanic and continental basements beneath the sediments.

Mapping the top of the sediments

8.2.11. Mapping the top of the sedimentary wedge of the rise is equivalent to mapping the seabed. Modern single-beam and multi-beam swath bathymetric technologies provide the most accurate depth measurements of the seabed (see chap. 4). However, this information is also collected as a by-product of seismic reflection surveys. This by-product information may be used to gain an understanding about the bathymetry and morphology of the sea floor wherever hydrographic measurements are not available.

8.2.12. Seismic reflection-derived bathymetric information should be interpolated and calibrated with that provided by hydrographic surveys wherever possible. This correction is necessary in order to remove errors that arise owing to the lower resolution achieved as a result of the use of lower frequencies in seismic surveys.

8.2.13. The Commission will regard the data provided by hydrographic bathymetric surveys as the primary source of evidence for mapping the sea floor. Bathymetric-derived information from seismic reflection surveys may be provided at all times by coastal States as a complementary source of evidence in a submission. This complementary evidence is particularly relevant in instances where only a non-comprehensive bathymetric database may be available.

8.2.14. However, seismic reflection data have the advantage that the entire sedimentary wedge, from the top to the basement, may be interpreted in the same data set for the purpose of determining its thickness. And for this purpose the errors inherent to seismic-derived bathymetry are not significant.

Mapping the top of the basement

8.2.15. The basement of the sediment wedge can be oceanic, continental or a combination of both. In the simplest cases, the sediments of the rise rest on oceanic basement all the way from the foot of the continental slope. The oceanic basement generally forms at an oceanic spreading ridge and consists of a peridotitic and gabbroic root complex, an intermediate zone of basaltic dyke intrusions and a thick series of submarine basalt lavas on top. Normally, the formation of the oceanic crust at the spreading ridge is in the range of a few centimetres per year in an environment of moderate sediment input. This means that it is possible to regard the top of the uppermost lava flow as the top of the basement.

8.2.16. In more complex cases, there may be a zone of stretched and thinned continental basement at the base of the sediments proximal to the foot of the slope. The sediments may comprise a pre-rift and a syn-rift sequence overlaid by a post-rift sediment wedge (fig. 8.1). If syn-rift or pre-rift sediments are preserved below the post-rift unconformity, these may be included in the sediment thickness estimation.

8.2.17. The top of the oceanic and continental basements represents a sharp increase in seismic velocities and gives high acoustic impedance contrast relative to the overlying sediments. Much of the energy will be reflected from this surface, and the penetration of energy into the underlying basement is significantly reduced. This results in a very low signal-to-noise ratio of the energy reflected from within the basement, and the internal signature of the basement will be that of random noise. Hence, on a seismic reflection profile, the top of the basement will stand out as a prominent reflector between the well-defined reflectors of an overlying bedded sedimentary sequence and an underlying, high-velocity "noisy" section of the basement. In most cases this will be true where the top of the basement is not too deeply buried (less than ca. 5–6 km). However, in those areas where paragraph 4 (a) (i) applies, the total sediment thickness will usually be of the order of only 1 km to 2 km at the critical location of the outer limit line. In this way, seismic reflection data in most cases will be the best method of identifying the top of the basement in the most critical areas.

8.2.18. In areas of very large sediment thickness or where seismic signals from the top of the basement are masked by interbedded lava, one may resort to seismic refraction methods to define the depth-to-top of the true basement. The identification of the top of the basement is then based on an interpretation of the velocity structure of the whole crust. An estimation of the depth-to-basement within an acceptable range of error requires a data set of good quality and reasonable resolution as well as some degree of calibration by reflection data and gravity modelling. Good quality seismic refraction data may be acquired by modern ocean bottom seismograph (OBS) techniques. The 10 km spacing generally used between the sonobuoys may, however, prove to be too large to provide an acceptable range of error. Experiments show that a closer OBS spacing combined with seismic reflection data improves the resolution considerably (Mjelde et al., 1997).

8.2.19. Modelling based on a combination of gravity and magnetic data may also give an estimated depth-to-top of the basement in areas with thick sediment piles and no interbedded lava or intrusions. The range of error from this method is very large relative to the seismic methods. The error in the determination of the depth-to-top of the basement depends upon the quality of the magnetic data, the densities and susceptibilities used in the calculations and the relative position of the Moho. However, in areas with ice cover or very deep basements, modelling of a combination of a heterogeneous gravity and a magnetic data set may be a valuable supplement to a sparse seismic database used in the mapping of the top of the basement.

Minimum data coverage

8.2.20. Article 76, paragraph 7, states that "the coastal State shall delineate the outer limits of its continental shelf … by straight lines not exceeding 60 nautical miles in length, connecting fixed points …" This requirement must be combined with the requirement of paragraph 4 (a) (i) that the sediment thickness at each of the fixed points shall be at least 1 per cent of the shortest distance to the foot of the slope.

8.2.21. The above requirement means that the minimum requirement is a data coverage that documents the required sediment thickness at fixed points at a spacing of maximum 60 M. In principle, the survey must be designed to prove the continuity of the sediments from each selected fixed point to the foot of the slope (see sect. 8.5). One way to achieve the implied minimum standard is to select a series of well documented geophysical profiles from the foot of the slope to their intersection with the claimed delineation line at a spacing of less than 60 M. The seismic lines therefore need to be a maximum of 60 M apart when planning a seismic survey for the purpose of delineating the outer limit of the continental shelf. However, this does not allow for any deviations in the straight-line segments. Thus, a closer line spacing may be considered in order to give more flexibility. The allowed deviation increases with a closer line spacing according to the approximate formula:

Line spacing in nautical miles = Cosine max. angle of deviation from orthogonal * 60 M (see fig. 8.2).

8.2.22. The 60 M maximum spacing requirement allows coastal States to bridge natural indentations in the sediment thickness rather than following the sometimes meandering path of the precisely measured feature. This may also permit a less detailed sampling over the margin, with a possible reduction of the costs involved in the collection and interpretation of the data. However, it is evident that such a formal minimum data coverage could miss some important details of the morphology of the outer limit of the continental margin, and the resulting 1 per cent line could only be a rough approximation of the true geological limit. Coastal States that suspect that such an approximation will be to their disadvantage will benefit from executing more comprehensive and detailed surveys. In general, the data coverage should reflect the complexity of the outer margin.

8.3. Depth conversion and thickness determination

8.3.1. The estimation of sediment thickness requires the depth conversion of the interpreted profiles and maps. This depth conversion of the interpreted geophysical data should be documented by the relevant database and the description of the method applied.

Seismic velocity

8.3.2. Determination of sediment thickness from seismic profiles requires knowledge of the propagation velocity of the seismic signal through the sedimentary section. This velocity can be calculated during the processing of multi-channel seismic data, but owing to uncertainties involved in the procedure, inaccuracies in the calculated interval velocity, and therefore sediment thickness, could typically be 10 per cent.

8.3.3. The velocity of transmission of the acoustic wave through the subseabed layers is required not only to determine their thickness, but also to give an indication of the nature of the material. Lower velocities are generally associated with sedimentary material, whereas higher velocities are often associated with metamorphic, igneous or "basement" material. A distinct change in velocities may assist in identifying the base of the sedimentary section.

8.3.4. Velocities of the offshore sedimentary sequence can be obtained by the following methods:

(a) In situ velocity surveys carried out in boreholes;

(b) Measurement of velocity in cores drilled in the sedimentary section;

(c) Analyses of multi-channel seismic reflection data;

(d) Seismic refraction and wide-angle reflection data analysis.

In situ and core measurements are accurate, but rare, and are only locally significant.

8.3.5. In the case of seismic reflection data, the interval velocities are derived from seismic stacking velocities using the Dix equation.[1] Such results are extensive but inherently somewhat inaccurate and only valid to a depth that is related to the length of the receiver array, and are generally more accurate at shallower depths. The accuracy is also related to the geometry and altitude of the reflecting interfaces.

8.3.6. Analysis of seismic refraction and wide-angle reflection data can be used to obtain the velocities of the various major layers, but the derived velocities are averaged over the length of the refraction spread.

8.3.7. The sparsity of samples collected by the Deep Sea Drilling Project/ Ocean Drilling Programme throughout the continental margins of the world and the lack of full seismic refraction data coverage point to the seismic velocity data as the most relevant source of information to be collected in order to develop velocity models in most cases.

8.3.8. The Commission regards the combined use of refraction and reflection seismic data as the primary source of evidence to estimate propagation velocities throughout the sedimentary wedge. Other forms of velocity estimation may also be provided at all times by coastal States as a complementary source of evidence.

Depth conversion of seismic data

8.3.9. Depth conversion of seismic data requires velocity data to build a velocity model for the sediment wedge. Such velocity models describe the

---

[1] The Dix equation states that, for reflections from a sequence of flat, parallel layers, the velocity in the nth layer V_n (interval velocity) is given by:

$$V_n = [\,(W_n^{2} * t_n - W_{n-1}^{2} * t_{n-1}) / (t_n - t_{n-1})\,]^{½}$$

where W_{n-1} and W_n are the average velocities from the datum to reflectors above and below the layer and tn-1 and tn are reflection arrival times.

vertical and/or the lateral variation in seismic propagation velocities within the sedimentary sequences.

8.3.10. All of the available velocity data need to be combined to generate the most comprehensive velocity model for the sedimentary sequence on the continental margin. This would generally be in the form of an interval velocity map/profile or a series of interval velocity maps/profiles, together with a listing of the seismic velocity data, including a brief description of how they were derived, where they apply and an estimate of their accuracy. Where the sedimentary sequence is thick and/or is well known, it may be appropriate to build a more complex multi-layer velocity model that deals separately with distinct sedimentary intervals.

8.3.11. The Commission recommends that the relative range of error inherent in the velocity analysis/velocity picks be presented by coastal States in areas where there are no borehole data for calibration of the Dix interval velocities with respect to real propagation velocities. This may be done by presenting the standard deviation (in Dix interval velocities) for each interval velocity applied in the velocity model.

8.3.12. The normal approach for depth conversion would be to multiply the previously derived time isopach map (or two-way time profile) for the total sediment thickness from the seabed to the top of the basement with the velocity model to arrive at the total sediment thickness. Different outputs might be obtained in general as a result of this operation if the calculations are based on the product of point measurements, or instead the calculations are based on the product of the two contoured surfaces. The former method would seem preferable to the latter.

8.3.13. At the current stage of software development, new techniques (e.g., iterative ray-tracing simulation, pre-stack migration processing) may be a real alternative for some States in the depth conversion of seismic data (both seismic reflection and seismic refraction data). The application of these methods may have real advantages in areas with complex structures and significant velocity anomalies. However, the Commission will consider any depth conversion method the coastal State opts to apply to their data.

8.3.14. The Commission will have to determine the weight it gives to the different types of evidence on a case-by-case basis. It will have to check whether errors have occurred in calculating the sedimentary thicknesses and, if so, whether they were attributable solely to the available velocity control or some other source. The Commission will also have to verify whether the sedimentary extrapolation has been applied correctly from the location of the foot of the continental slope.

Gravity and magnetic data

8.3.15. The inversion of gravity and magnetic data is not as straightforward as that of seismic data. The existence, uniqueness and optimization of the solution must be analysed. The final output of this inversion is a physical model of the sedimentary wedge that fits all the observations in an optimal way. When the uncertainties in the resulting model are unacceptable, additional data are incorporated in an iterative process.

8.3.16. Whereas bathymetry plays an important role in the three-dimensional modelling of gravity data, the inversion of magnetic data into an analytical signal is essential to define the position of the magnetic source. The final output physical model from an inversion is often very sensitive to inaccuracies in the measured data. The quality of the data is of prime importance in order to ensure the reliability of depth conversion in potential field methods.

8.3.17. The depth data obtained from both gravimetric and magnetic methods should be documented with all the modelling parameters used and a description of the inverse methods applied as well as an assessment of the quality of the data involved in the determinations.

8.4. Sources and magnitudes of error

8.4.1. The two most important variables in the determination of sediment thickness are the depth estimates of the top of the basement and the velocity model used for the depth conversion of seismic data.

Depth estimate of the top of the basement

8.4.2. In many areas the top of the oceanic or continental basement is readily identified by a clear reflector on seismic surveys, owing to its large impedance contrast, in areas where sediment cover is moderate (< 3–4 km). The possibility of selecting the wrong reflector in such areas is low. Thus, the uncertainty in the definition of the top of the basement is also low.

8.4.3. In areas of intercalated lava flows and intrusive magmatic rocks that mask the seismic reflection from the basement surface, the definition of the top of the basement may not be satisfactorily achieved by seismic reflection alone. The application of additional geophysical techniques is necessary. The best supplementary and/or alternative method is probably provided by seismic refraction methods, and ocean bottom seismograph (OBS) methods in particular. In addition, interpretations of the velocity structure of the subsurface based on refraction seismic data are often constrained by gravity modelling of the density structure. The uncertainty in the definition of the top of the basement by refraction data is equal to the uncertainty in the depth conversion based on those data. The range of error in depth to the basement based on a modern OBS data set is typically of the order of 10 per cent to 20 per cent (Mjelde et al., 1997).

Depth conversion of seismic data

8.4.4. The magnitude of errors in the converted depth of an interpreted seismic section is directly proportional to the magnitude of errors in the velocity model applied in the conversion. The magnitude of errors in velocity models based on stacking velocities of seismic reflection data is typically 5 per cent to 15 per cent, depending on the depth and dip of the reflectors interpreted, the quality of the velocity analysis and, to an extent, on the data processing. In general, the combination of shallow depths and good quality velocity analysis results in small errors in depth estimates.

8.4.5. In an iterative ray-tracing process, the magnitude of error in depth estimates is a function of how close it is possible to fit the calculated to the observed travel times.

8.4.6. The Commission will require documentation of the expected ranges of error to be submitted by a coastal State along with a description of the conversion methods applied.

Propagation of thickness errors to position errors

8.4.7. The expected error in the estimated thickness propagates into errors in the position of the 1 per cent sediment line, regardless of the depth conversion method applied.

8.4.8. The 1993 study entitled Definition of the Continental Shelf (United Nations, 1993) briefly mentions the calculation of the magnitude of error in horizontal distance owing to error in the calculation of sediment thickness. The Commission proposes a more sophisticated method by applying the following formula, which also takes into account the slope of the seabed and the dip of the top surface of the basement:

$$\Delta X = \Delta Y / \tan (0.57° + \theta) + \tan \alpha$$

where ΔX is the error in distance, ΔY is the error in thickness, θ is the angle of dip of the top of the basement, α is the slope of the sea floor and 0.57° is the angle between the top of the basement and the 1 per cent line (i.e., the line showing the thickness increasing by 1 per cent of the distance from the starting point). For the normal range in gradient of the rise (between 0.07° and 1.15°) and with a 0.2° dip of the top of the basement towards the continent, an error of ±100 m in thickness translates to between ±7 km and ±3 km error in distance. From figure 8.3 it can be seen that the error in distance decreases as the dip of the base of the sediments towards the foot of the continental slope increases (θ increases). The same effects appear when keeping the top of the basement fixed and imagining varying degrees of slopes of the ocean floor: steepening of the ocean floor leads to smaller ranges of error in distance (α increases).

8.5. Selection of outermost fixed points of 1 per cent sediment thickness

8.5.1. Paragraph 4 (a) (i) establishes the requirement of a line delineated in accordance with paragraph 7 by reference to the outermost fixed points at each of which the thickness of sedimentary rocks is at least 1 per cent of the shortest distance from such point to the foot of the continental slope.

This implies that the sediment thickness at each fixed point must be documented by data acquired at that location by either borehole, seismic or other geophysical data. Locating the fixed points on the basis of an isopach map is not an acceptable procedure to the Commission since the interpolation inherent in the contouring introduces a new source of uncertainty and it is not strictly covered by paragraph 4 (a) (i).

8.5.2. A jagged sea-floor and/or basement surface may cause large local variations in sediment thickness. This is a typical feature of oceanic and rifted continental basements. In these cases, the sediments in the area of the outer limit of the continental margin may, over a relatively short distance, repeatedly vary from the required thickness to less than the required thickness. This bathymetric and geological scenario may then produce several locations where the requirement for a 1 per cent or greater sediment thickness is satisfied along the same profile.

8.5.3. The Commission is guided here by paragraph 4 (a) (i), which states that the line shall be delineated by reference to "the outermost fixed points at each of which the thickness of sedimentary rocks is at least 1 per cent . . ." The Commission invokes a principle of continuity in the implementation of this provision to state that:

(a) To establish fixed points a coastal State may choose the outermost location where the 1 per cent or greater sediment thickness occurs within and below the same continuous sedimentary apron; and that

(b) For each of the fixed points chosen the Commission expects documentation of the continuity between the sediments at those points and the sediments at the foot of the continental slope.

8.5.4. Locating the fixed points based on a calculated distributed average sediment thickness is not regarded as an acceptable solution to the problem of a jagged topography.

8.5.5. Another aspect of paragraph 4 (a) (i) is the measurement of distance: "the outermost fixed points at each of which the thickness of sedimentary rocks is at least 1 per cent of the shortest distance from such point to the foot of the continental slope". By "the shortest distance" the Commission understands: the shortest distance measured along a geodesic on the surface of the ellipsoid associated to the geodetic reference system used by the coastal State in the submission.

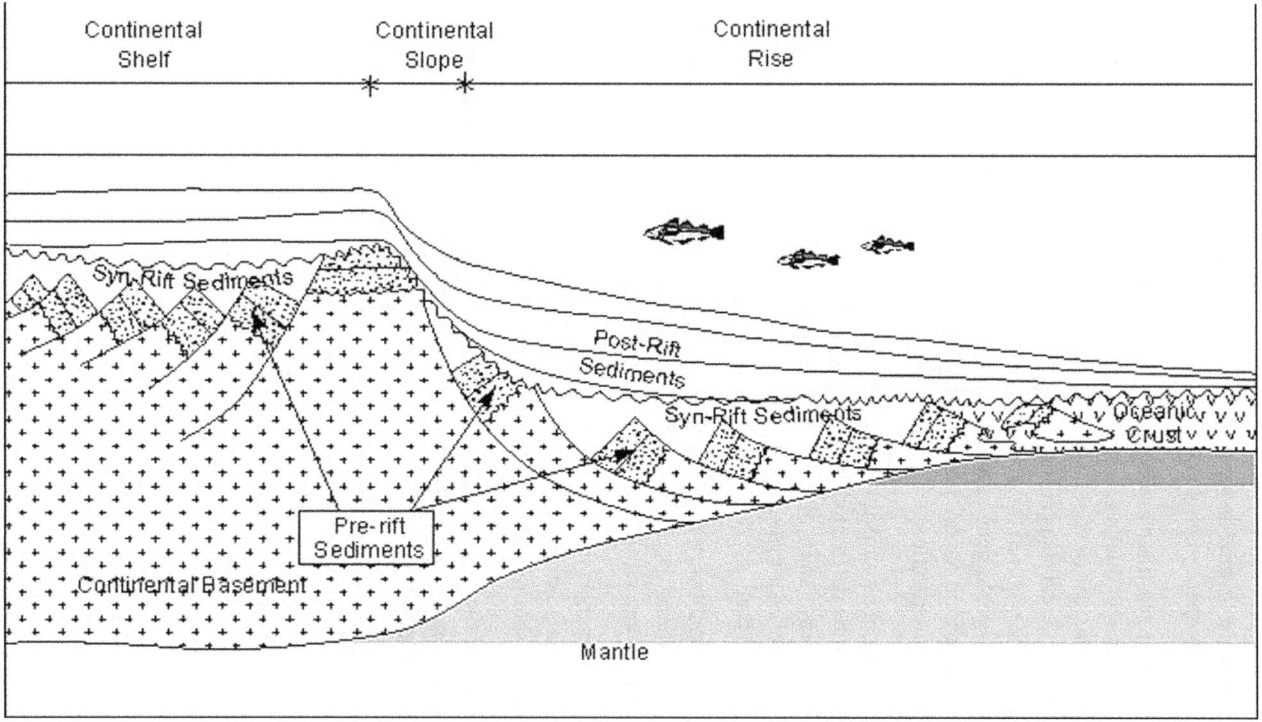

Figure 8.1. Idealised section through a rifted non-volcanic continental margin, showing the relatonship between the sediments deposited prior to, during, and after the rifting process leading to the rupturing of the continent.

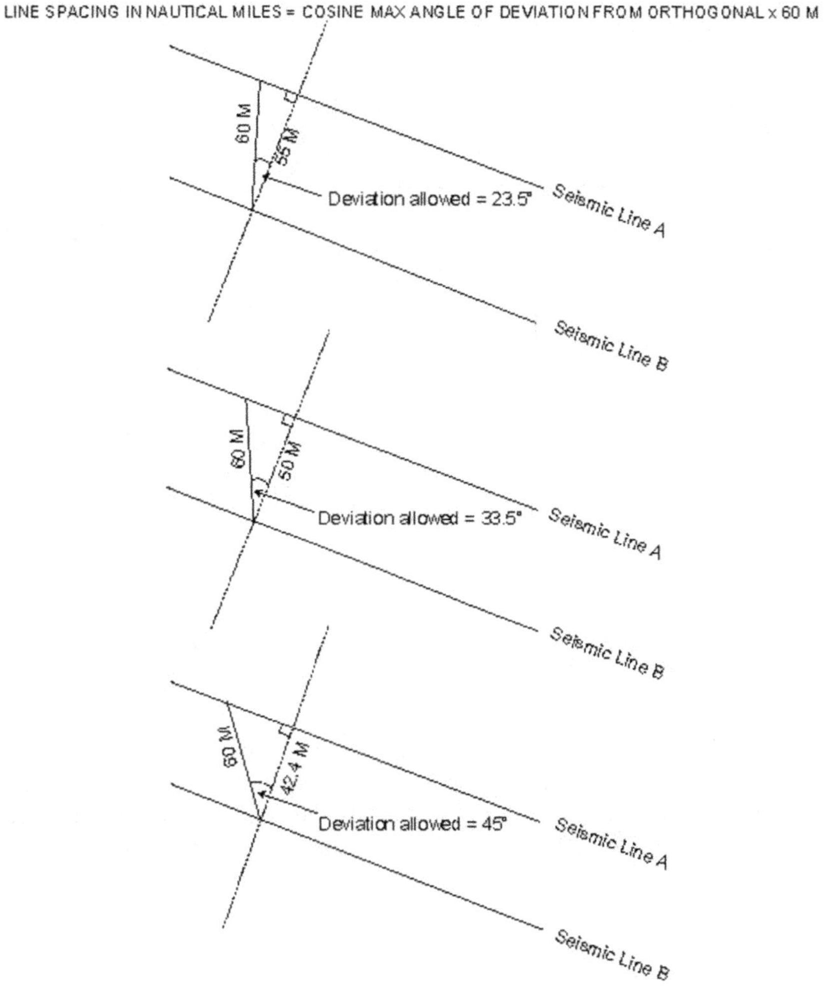

Figure 8.2. Different spacing of seismic lines and allowed deviations from the orthogonal.

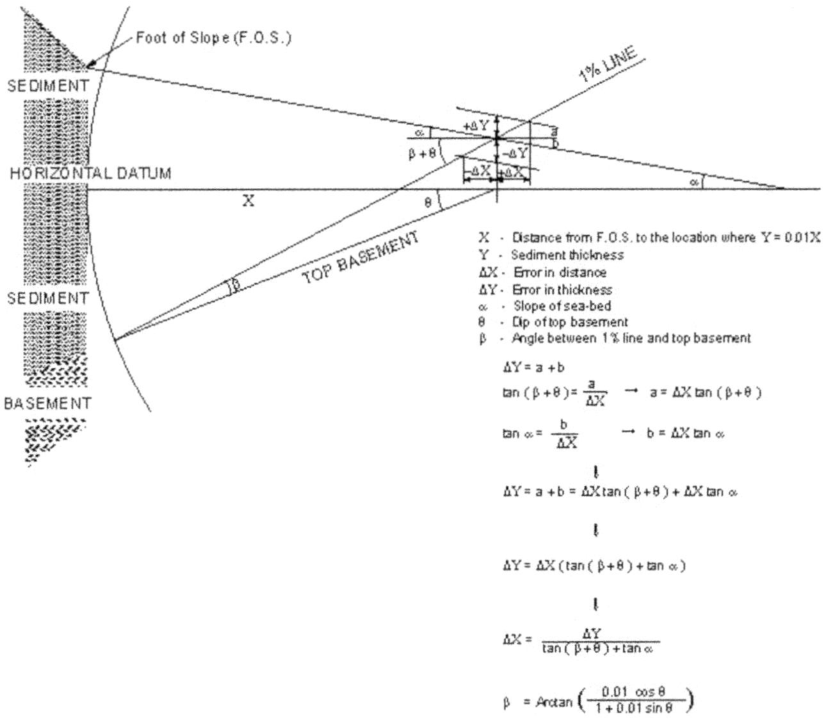

Figure 8.3. The relationship between error in thickness and distance, the slope of the seabed and the dip of surface of the top of the basement, on applying the limit criteria of the 1 % thickness line (i.e., the line showing the thickness increasing by 1 % of the distance from the starting point).

9. Information on the limits of the extended continental shelf

9.1. Formulation of the problem: paragraph 8 and Annex II

9.2. Bathymetric and geodetic data

9.3. Geophysical and geological data

9.4. Digital and non-digital data

9.5. Checklist of relevant supporting information and data

9.1. Formulation of the problem: paragraph 8 and Annex II

9.1.1. The Commission acknowledges that coastal States have an obligation to submit information on the limits of the extended continental shelf for the purpose of making recommendations. Paragraph 8 describes this obligation as follows:

> "Information on the limits of the continental shelf beyond 200 nautical miles from the baselines from which the breadth of the territorial sea is measured shall be submitted by the coastal State to the Commission on the Limits of the Continental Shelf set up under Annex II on the basis of geographical representation. The Commission shall make recommendations to coastal States on matters related to the establishment of the outer limits of their continental shelf. The limits of the shelf established by a coastal State on the basis of these recommendations shall be final and binding."

9.1.2. The Commission recognizes that one of its two functions prescribed in Annex II is to consider the data and material submitted by coastal States and to make recommendations in accordance with article 76 and the Statement of Understanding of 1980. Annex II, article 3 (1) (a), describes this function as follows:

> "1. The functions of the Commission shall be:
>
> (a) to consider the data and other material submitted by coastal States concerning the outer limits of the continental shelf in areas where those limits extend beyond 200 nautical miles, and to make recommendations in accordance with article 76 and the Statement of Understanding adopted on 29 August 1980 by the Third United Nations Conference on the Law of the Sea".

9.1.3. The submission will be divided in three separate parts in accordance with the Modus Operandi of the Commission (CLCS/L.3). The requested format contains an executive summary (22 copies), a main body (8 copies) and all supporting scientific and technical data (2 copies).

9.1.4. The executive summary will contain the following information:

(a) Charts at an appropriate scale and coordinates indicating the outer limits of the continental shelf and the relevant territorial sea baselines;

(b) Which provisions of article 76 are invoked to support the submission;

(c) The names of any Commission members who gave advice in the preparation of the submission; and

(d) Any disputes as referred to in rule 44 and annex I to the Rules of Procedure of the Commission.

9.1.5. The main body will contain a detailed description of the data set, maps, technical procedures and scientific methodologies applied in the implementation of article 76. References to the basic data will be documented at each relevant step.

9.1.6. The third part will contain a copy of all data referred to in the main body, which will be arranged in separate annexes. All data submitted by the coastal State in support of its submission will be considered by the Commission.

9.2. <u>Bathymetric and geodetic data</u>

<u>Bathymetric data</u>

9.2.1. The complete bathymetric data set used in the preparation of a submission may include any of the following measurements, or a combination thereof:

(a) Single-beam echo sounding measurements;

(b) Multi-beam echo sounding measurements;

(c) Bathymetric side-scan sonar measurements;

(d) Interferometric side-scan sonar measurements;

(e) Seismic reflection-derived bathymetric measurements;

(f) Light detection and ranging (LIDAR) measurements.

9.2.2. This information will be included in the second and third parts of the submission. Whereas only a part of it may be needed in the <u>main body</u>, the full bathymetric database will be regarded as an essential component of the <u>supporting scientific and technical data</u>.

9.2.3. The complete bathymetric data set used in the submission will be included by the coastal State in its third part as an annex. This information can be made available to the Commission in an analytical form as compilation charts depicting soundings or, whenever possible, in digital form in a Hydrographic Information System (HIS) database by means of coordinates of latitude, longitude and depth.

9.2.4. Bathymetric data should be processed as much as possible to represent the correct depth. Spurious depth measurements should have been edited out.

9.2.5. A full technical description of the bathymetric database will include the following information:

- Source of the data;
- Sounding survey techniques and their technical specifications;
- Geodetic positioning methods and reference system;
- Time and date of the survey;
- Corrections applied to the data for speed of sound in water, calibration and other;
- A priori or a posteriori estimates of random and systematic errors;
- Geodetic reference system;
- Geometric definition of straight, archipelagic and closing baselines.

9.2.6. The main body of the submission will include all the necessary cartographic products derived from the compiled bathymetric database. These cartographic products may include the following analytic or digital forms:

- Two-dimensional depth profiles;
- Three-dimensional bathymetric models;
- Charts and maps with contours.

9.2.7. Each cartographic product will be accompanied by a detailed description of the mathematical methodology and bathymetric data used to produce it. The Commission will pay particular attention to the transit from numeric soundings to analytic functions. The coastal State may be requested by the Commission to document the following information:

- Interpolation or approximation method;
- Density of measured bathymetric data;
- Perceptual elements such as map projections, vertical and horizontal scales, contour intervals, units, colours and symbols.

9.2.8. Wherever the bathymetric information presented to the Commission may be a filtered or smoothed subset of the original data, a full description of the methodology employed to produce it will be reported by the coastal State.

Geodetic data

9.2.9. Coastal States will be requested to provide information about the geodetic reference system used in the submission. Coordinate transformation parameters from this system to ITRF94 or WGS84 (G873) will be requested whenever one of these systems is not used in a submission.

9.2.10. Geodetic information may need to be included about some baselines from which the breadth of the territorial sea is measured. This will be the case only for those baselines which define a line at a distance of 350 M, if this constraint is applied at all to define the outer limits of the continental shelf. The following information may be requested by the Commission:

- Source of the data;
- Geodetic positioning technique and reference system;
- Corrections applied to the data;
- Geodetic definition in the case of straight or archipelagic baselines;
- A priori or a posteriori estimates of random and systematic errors;
- Geodetic reference system;
- Geometric definition of straight, archipelagic and closing baselines.

9.3. Geophysical and geological data

Seismic data

9.3.1. Seismic data may include both seismic reflection and seismic wide–angle reflection/refraction data.

9.3.2. The submission ought to include a list of all seismic surveys used in relation to the submission. This should be supplemented with one or several maps showing the line coverage of each survey. Several surveys may be combined in one map provided that the distinction between them is indicated.

9.3.3. Navigation and data records should be annotated in the same units. Multi-channel seismic reflection lines are usually annotated in shot points, common depth points (CDPs) or both. These are not interchangeable, and should accordingly be labelled clearly.

9.3.4. Seismic lines must be tied to a navigation plot and annotated in the same units as the seismic line (shot points, CDPs).

9.3.5. Multi-channel seismic data should be processed to at least the necessary level of quality to justify the particular approach used. A description of the acquisition parameters and the processing sequence should either appear on the individual seismic line or be included separately for each survey in the submission. This should also include information on the cruise or ship on which the data were collected and the dates of collection and of processing of the data. In addition, seismic lines should have a vertical scale in seconds, an indication of direction and an indication of horizontal scale.

9.3.6. Unmarked copies of the seismic lines are needed, together with the interpretation of the same lines, in order for the Commission to observe the details of the interpretation.

9.3.7. The format of analogue records is essentially the same as for digital seismic records. The records are often annotated with time-of-day, and navigation data with this annotation need to be provided. Vertical and horizontal scales should be noted, as well as an indication of the direction of the profile.

9.3.8. Seismic velocity data used for depth conversion should be submitted together with a description of how they were derived, where they apply and an estimate of their accuracy. This applies to both stacking velocities from multi-channel reflection seismic and interval velocities derived from wide-angle reflection/refraction seismic data. For the specific seismic lines that document the sediment thickness at the outermost fixed points of the outer limit line, the actual velocity analysis from the processing job should be submitted at least for a part of the line where it crosses the fixed points.

Gravity data

9.3.9. The complete gravity database used in the preparation of a submission may include a combination of:

- Marine, aerial and sea-bottom gravimeter measurements; and
- Gravity values derived from satellite altimetry and orbital analyses.

9.3.10. This information will be included in the second and third parts of the submission. Whereas only a part of it may be needed in the main body, the full gravity database will be regarded as an essential component of the supporting scientific and technical data.

9.3.11. The complete gravity database used in the submission will be included by the coastal State in its third part as an annex. This information can be made available to the Commission in an analytical form as compilation maps depicting observed values or, whenever possible, in digital form in a Geographic Information System (GIS) database by means of coordinates of latitude, longitude and gravity or gravity anomaly. The coastal State will be required to document the following information:

- Source of the data;
- Gravity meters and their technical specifications;
- Geodetic positioning methods;
- Time and date of the survey;
- Corrections applied to the data: tides, Eötvös and other;
- A priori or a posteriori estimates of random and systematic errors;
- Geodetic reference system; and
- Geometric definition of straight, archipelagic and closing baselines.

9.3.12. The data should be accompanied by a description of the acquisition parameters (including track direction, elevation and position control), correction procedures and a contoured anomaly map which also displays the actual data coverage.

9.3.13. Maps and profiles should be clearly marked with geodetic coordinates and a reference to original data on which they are based (survey names).

Magnetic data

9.3.14. The complete magnetic database used in the preparation of a submission may include a combination of:

- Marine and aerial fluxgate and proton-precession magnetometer measurements; and
- Magnetic values derived from satellite observation campaigns.

9.3.15. Magnetic data may include data of varying vintages and acquisition methods (ship or airborne). A list of all magnetic surveys and their year of acquisition should be provided together with a map showing the outline of each separate survey.

9.3.16. The data should be accompanied by a description of the acquisition parameters (including track direction, elevation and position control), correction procedures and a contoured anomaly map which also displays the actual data coverage.

Geological data

9.3.17. In the case of evidence to the contrary, it is recommended, in addition to the information described in the checklist in section 9.5, to include the following data obtained from sampling and coring of crustal subcrops at the continental margin with information about the source of the data:

- Lithology;
- Radiometric/palaeontological/palaeomagnetic age dating;
- Geochemical-isotope geochemical results.

9.4. Digital and non-digital data

Profiles and cross-sections

9.4.1. All the previous types of data may be presented as geological/geomorphologic profiles and cross-sections. Such profiles and cross-sections should be clearly marked with references to the specific data (seismic, gravity, magnetic or bathymetry) on which they are based (e.g., on a geological cross-section based on a seismic interpretation, the shot-point positions and the identification of the seismic line may be included along the base of the cross-section; if a cross-section consists of a combination of several segments of different seismic lines, each of the original segments should be labelled and the tie points between them indicated).

9.4.2. The geodetic positions of all profiles must be given, preferably on maps. Geological/geomorphologic features shall be shown on those maps. Vertical and horizontal scales should be noted, as well as an indication of the direction of the profile or cross-section. Vertical axis may be in time (milliseconds) or depth (metres).

9.4.3. In the case of depth sections based on seismic data, a description of the velocity data and the conversion method is requested.

9.4.4. In the case of crustal structure cross-sections based on gravity data, information on the densities and the calculation methods and software applied must be included.

Maps and charts

9.4.5. It is recommended that the geophysical and bathymetric data and their interpretation documenting the sediment thickness and the foot of the continental slope be presented as a series of charts, maps, profiles and other graphics.

9.4.6. The final graphics may vary greatly depending on the chosen vertical and horizontal scales, and the methods of interpolation, extrapolation, contouring and various types of digital processing. The Commission therefore requires due references to the original data and a description of the methods involved in order to verify the quality and reliability of a graphic presentation.

9.4.7. An important part of any submission should be a series of maps which ties all the data submitted into a common geodetic frame of reference. It is reasonable to suggest that the scale and projection for all submitted maps or groups of maps (ships' tracks, bathymetry, sediment isopach maps, depth of basement, as well as other possible maps, such as magnetic anomaly maps, gravity maps or wide-angle reflection/refraction lines) should be the same. Every map should be supported by the database, preferably in digital form, from which it was derived.

9.4.8. Latitude and longitude should be clearly marked on maps. It should be clear whether the units are degrees/minutes or decimal degrees. Maps should be large enough so that details of the cruise tracks are visible and track annotations are legible.

9.4.9. In support of the executive summary to be submitted, it will be necessary to prepare a map of the outer limits of the continental shelf, indicating the criteria on which the submission is based. Such a map should be on a scale suitable to fit A4 size paper and should cover the full extent of the continental shelf, up to its outer limit.

9.4.10. The coastal State can use the colour schemes, symbology and type of projection deemed adequate to the cartographic representation.

9.4.11. Maps, charts and databases submitted to the Commission must bear the authentication from the national agency of the respective coastal State which is legally authorized to certify its quality and reliability.

Digital data

9.4.12. The coastal State may use data collected with a range of techniques from a wide variety of sources in establishing the outer limits of the continental shelf. In recent years, however, most bathymetric and geophysical data have been captured, processed and stored in digital form. Therefore, the coastal State may find it convenient to submit much of its material in digital form.

9.4.13. The coastal State can submit digital data in any internationally recognized format.

9.5. Checklist of relevant supporting information and data

9.5.1. The submission in support of the outer limit of the continental shelf of a coastal State may include one of five possible cases at any point along the limiting line:

1:A line delineated at a distance of 60 M seaward from the foot of the continental slope (in accordance with article 76 (4) (a) (ii)); or

2:A line along which the sediment thickness is 1 per cent of the shortest distance from the foot of the slope (in accordance with article 76 (4) (a) (i));

and not further than

3:A line delineated at a distance of 350 M from the baselines; or

4:A line delineated at a distance of 100 M from the 2,500-metre isobath; or

5:A limit agreed to by States with opposite or adjacent coasts (in accordance with article 83).

9.5.2. For each of these cases, the Commission may request that it be provided with the information indicated under the corresponding case code in the table below:

"Y" indicates that provision of this information is necessary for the Commission and the subcommission to discharge their responsibilities;

"R" indicates that provision of this information is recommended to assist the Commission and the subcommission in discharging their responsibilities.

Type of information to be submitted	Cases for which this information is to be submitted				
	1	2	3	4	5
Limit of overall continental shelf for coastal State (map)	Y	Y	Y	Y	Y
Limit of continental shelf for different parts of the margin (larger-scale maps)	Y	Y	Y	Y	Y
Criteria by which the limit is defined, each of the five criteria being indicated by a coded line (map)	Y	Y	Y	Y	Y
Baselines used in defining the limit if not shown on the limit maps (map)	–	–	Y	–	R
Baselines used for different parts of the margin (large-scale maps)	–	–	Y	–	R
200 M limit (map)	Y	Y	Y	Y	Y
350 M limit (map)	Y	Y	Y	Y	Y
Location of the foot of the continental slope (FOS), specifying how it was determined (map)	Y	Y	Y	Y	Y
Lines used to determine FOS (map), showing line identifier, navigation, shot points, etc., including the 60 M extension line	Y	Y	Y	Y	–
Lines used to define the 2,500-metre isobath (map), showing line identifier, navigation, shot points, etc., including the 100 M extension line	Y	Y	Y	Y	R
Bathymetric contour (map):					
–Where it identifies the 2,500-metre isobath	Y	Y	Y	Y	–
–Where not used as the basis for FOS	R	R	R	R	–
–Where used as the basis for FOS	Y	Y	Y	Y	–
–FOS base points used for 60 M extrapolation (map)	Y	–	Y	Y	–
All bathymetric profiles (sections) annotated with locations of the determined FOS:					
–Where used as the basis for FOS	Y	Y	Y	Y	–
–Where not used	R	R	R	R	–

Type of information to be submitted	Cases for which this information is to be submitted				
	1	2	3	4	5
Bathymetric profiles annotated with the location of the determined FOS to indicate the character of the margin	R	R	R	R	–
Bathymetric survey parameters (table) keyed by cruise or line identifier showing reliability of FOS and 2,500-metre isobath, including sound velocity used and accuracy of location and velocity/depth profiles	Y	Y	Y	Y	–
Digital multi-channel seismic tracks (map) used in the determination of sediment thickness, including shot-point numbers and navigation	–	Y	–	–	–
Analog single-channel seismic tracks (map) used in determination of sediment thickness, including shot points and navigation	–	Y	–	–	–
FOS points used to derive the 1 per cent sediment thickness line (map)	–	Y	–	–	–
Seismic profiles (travel-time sections) used to determine sediment thickness (two copies: one original, one interpreted)	–	Y	–	–	–
Representative seismic profiles (travel-time sections) used to determine sediment thickness (two copies: one original, one interpreted) to indicate character of the margin	–	R	–	–	–
Travel-time difference between sea floor and the basement (map)					
–If 1 per cent points based on profiles	–	R	–	–	–
Sediment thickness (map) showing depth-converted versions of travel time difference maps					
–If 1 per cent points based on profiles	–	R	–	–	–
Survey parameters keyed to seismic profiles (table), including the acquisition method, time/depth conversion table/plot and accuracy indicators for location and velocity	–	Y	–	–	–

	Cases for which this information is to be submitted				
Type of information to be submitted	1	2	3	4	5
Velocity analysis (table) on which time/depth conversion was based	–	Y	–	–	–
Location of all data used as basis for velocity analysis (map), indicating whether refraction, ocean bottom seismometer, sonobuoy, borehole, wide-angle reflection or other method was used	–	Y	–	–	–
All depth-converted profiles (sections or horizontal plots) annotated to show sea floor, basement surface, FOS and 1 per cent points:					
–If 1 per cent points based on profiles	–	Y	–	–	–
Representative depth-converted profiles (sections or horizon plots) annotated to show sea floor, basement surface, FOS and 1 per cent points to indicate the character of the margin	–	R	–	–	–

10. References and bibliography

Alexander, L. M. (1990). Alternative Interpretations of Geographic Articles in the 1982 LOS Convention. Center for Ocean Management Studies, Kingston, University of Rhode Island.

Allaby, A. and M. Allaby (1991), The Concise Oxford Dictionary of Earth Sciences, Oxford, Oxford University Press.

American Geological Institute (1976), Dictionary of Geological Terms. Garden City, New York, Anchor Press/Doubleday.

Appelbaum, L. T. (1982). Geodetic Datum Transformation by Multiple Regression Equations. Proceedings of the Third International Geodetic Symposium on Satellite Doppler Positioning, New Mexico State University, Las Cruces, New Mexico, 8–12 February, p. 207–223.

Arkani-Hamed, J.; J. Verhoef; W. Roest; R. Macnab (1995). The intermediate-wavelength magnetic anomaly maps of the North Atlantic Ocean derived from satellite and shipborne data. Geophysical Journal International 123, 727–743.

Bally, A. W. (ed.) (1988) Atlas of Seismic Stratigraphy. AAPG Studies in Geology No. 27, vol. 1–3, American Association of Petroleum Geologists.

Bell, T. H. (1979). Mesoscale sea floor roughness. Deep-Sea Research 26 (1A): 65–76.

Bennet, J. O. (1996). Mapping the Foot of the Continental Slope with Spline Smoothed Data using the Second Derivative in the Gradient Direction. Proceedings of the Second International Conference on Geodetic Aspects of the Law of the Sea, Bali, Indonesia, 1–4 July, p. 303–335.

Beyer, L. A., R. E. von Huene, T. H. McCullogh and J. R. Lovett (1966). Measuring gravity on the sea floor in deep water. Journal of Geophysical Research 71: 2091–2100.

Boggs, S. W. (1930). Delimitation of the Territorial Sea: the Method of Delimitation Proposed by the Delegation of the United States at the Hague Conference for the Codification of International Law. American Journal of International Law 24 (3): 541–555.

Boucher, C., Z. Altamimi, M. Feissel and P. Sillard (1996). Results and Analysis of the ITRF94. International Earth Rotation Service. IERS Technical Note 20, Paris, Observatoire de Paris.

Boucher, C., Z. Altamimi and P. Sillard (1998). Results and Analysis of the ITRF94. International Earth Rotation Service. IERS Technical Note 24, Paris, Observatoire de Paris.

Bowring, B. R. (1985). The Geometry of the Loxodrome. Canadian Surveyor 39 (3): 223–230.

Bureau international des poids et mesures (1991). Le Système international d'unités. Sèvres.

Carrera, G. (1992). An Iterative Method for the Investigation of Archipelagic Status. Proceedings of the First International Conference on Geodetic Aspects of the Law of the Sea, Bali, Indonesia, 8–11 June, p. 80–84.

Carrera, G. (1992). The Electronic Chart Display and Information System (ECDIS) and International Maritime Boundaries. Proceedings of the First International Conference on Geodetic Aspects of the Law of the Sea, Bali, Indonesia, 8–11 June.

Carrera, G. and R. Macnab (1996). Maritime Spaces in the Arctic Ocean: some hypothetical and not-so-hypothetical scenarios. Presentation at the Boundaries and Energy: Problems and Prospects Conference. International Boundaries Research Unit, Durham, United Kingdom, 18 July 1996. Also in the Proceedings of the Second International Conference on Geodetic Aspects of the Law of the Sea, Bali, Indonesia, 1–4 July 1996, p. 169–182.

Coffin, M. F. and O. Eldholm (eds.) (1991). Large Igneous Provinces: JOI/ USSAC Workshop Report. University of Texas at Austin for Geophysics, Technical Report No. 4.

COSOD II (1987): Report of Second Conference of Scientific Ocean Drilling <COSOD II>. France, European Science Foundation (ESF).

Couper, A. D. (1989). The Times Atlas and Encyclopaedia of the Sea. London, Times Books Limited.

Cunningham, J. and V. L. Curtis (1996). WGS84 Coordinate Validation and Improvement for the NIMA and Air Force GPS Tracking Stations. Dahlgren Division, Naval Surface Warfare Center, NSWCDD/ TR-96/201, November 1996.

Defense Mapping Agency (1984). Department of Defense World Geodetic System 1984: Its Definition and relationships with Local Geodetic Systems. DMA Technical Report TR 8350.2, 2nd ed. (1991).

Edwards, J. D. and P. A. Sangrossi (eds.) (1990). Divergent/Passive Margin Basins. AAPG Memoir 48, American Association of Petroleum Geologists.

Fox, C. G. and D. E. Hayes (1985). Quantitative methods for analyzing the roughness of the seafloor. Reviews of Geophysics 23 (1): 1–48.

Gardiner, P. R. (1978). Reasons and methods for fixing the outer limit of the legal continental shelf beyond 200 nautical miles. Revue iranienne des relations internationales (Tehran), Nos. 11–12, 145–170.

Gidel, G. C. (1932). Le droit international de la mer, vol. 3, p. 510.

Harsson, B. G. (1992). Baseline determination: Experiences in Norway. Proceedings of the First International Conference on Geodetic Aspects of the Law of the Sea, Bali, Indonesia, 8–11 June 1992, p. 31–33.

Hedberg, H. D. (1976). Relation of Political Boundaries on the Ocean Floor to the Continental Margin. Virginia Journal of International Law 17 (1): 57–75.

Herzfeld, U. C. (1993). A Method for Seafloor Classification Using Directional Variograms, Demonstrated for Data from the Western Flank of the Mid-Atlantic Ridge. Mathematical Geology 25 (7): 901–924.

Hinz, K. (1981). An Hypothesis on Terrestrial Catastrophes: Wedges of very thick oceanward dipping layers beneath passive continental margins. Geol. Jahrbuch, Reihe E, H.22: 3–23.

International Hydrographic Organization (1993). Specifications for Chart content and display aspects of ECDIS, 3rd ed. International Hydrographic Bureau, Special Publication No. 52, Monaco.

International Hydrographic Organization (1998). IHO Standards for Hydrographic Surveys, 4th ed. Special Publication No. 44, Monaco.

Kumar, M. (1992). Use of World Geodetic System 1984 as a Global Reference. Proceedings of the First International Conference on Geodetic Aspects of the Law of the Sea, Bali, Indonesia, 8–11 June 1992, p. 106–115.

LaCoste, L. J. B. (1967). Measurement of gravity at sea and in the air. Reviews of Geophysics 5, 477–526.

Lapidus, D. F. (1990). Collins Dictionary of Geology. London, Harper Collins.

Malys, S. and J. A. Slater (1994). Maintenance and Enhancement of the World Geodetic System 1980. Proceedings of ION GPS-94, 7th International Technical Meeting of the Satellite Division of the Institute of Navigation, Salt Lake City, Utah, p. 17–24.

Malys, S., J. A. Slater, R. W. Smith, L. E. Kunz and S. C. Kenyon (1997). Refinements to the World Geodetic System 1984. Proceedings of ION GPS-97, 10th International Technical Meeting of the Satellite Division of the Institute of Navigation, Kansas City, Missouri, p. 841–850.

Mandelbrot, B. (1977). Fractals: Form, Chance and Dimension. San Francisco, W. H. Freeman.

McCarthy, D. D. (ed.) (1996). IERS Conventions (1996). International Earth Rotation Service. IERS Technical Note 21, Paris, Observatoire de Paris.

Macnab, R., M. Sorokin, R. Jackson and Y. Kazmin (1996). Submerged Prolongations of the Continental Margin beyond 200 Nautical Miles in the Arctic Ocean: Implications for Article 76 Implementations. Proceedings of the Second International Conference on Geodetic Aspects of the Law of the Sea, Bali, Indonesia, 1–4 July 1996, p. 365–376.

Mjelde, R., S. Kodaira, P. Digranes, H. Shimamura, T. Kanazawa, H. Shiobara, E. W. Berg and O. Riise (1997). Comparison between a Regional and Semi-regional Crustal OBS Model in the Vøring Basin, Mid-Norway Margin. Pure and Applied Geophysics 149: 641–665.

Monahan, D. and M. J. Casey (1985). Contours and contouring in hydrography. Part I - The Fundamental Issues. The International Hydrographic Review, July, vol. LXII, No. 2, pp. 105–120.

Moritz, H. (1984). Geodetic Reference System 1980. Bulletin géodésique, vol. 58, No. 3: 388–398.

Neilan, R. E., J. F. Zumberge, G. Beutler, and J. Kouba (1997). The International GPS Service: A Global Resource for GPS Applications and Research. Proceedings of ION GPS-97, 10th International Technical Meeting of the Satellite Division of the Institute of Navigation, Kansas City, Missouri, p. 883–889.

Nordquist, M. H. (Editor-in-Chief) (1985–1993). United Nations Convention on the Law of the Sea 1982: A Commentary. Volume I: Text of

Convention and Introductory Material. Nordquist, M. H. (ed.); Volume II: Second Committee: Articles 1 to 85. Annexes I and II, and Final Act, Annex II. Nandan, S. N., S. Rosenne and N. R. Grandy (eds.); Volume III: Second Committee: Articles 86 to 132, and supplementary documents. Nandan, S. N., S. Rosenne and N. R. Grandy (eds.); Volume IV: Third Committee: Articles 192 to 278, and Final Act, Annex VI. Rosenne, S. and A. Yankov (eds.); Volume V: Settlement of Disputes, General and Final Provisions: Articles 279 to 320, Annexes V, VI, VII, VIII and IX, and Final Act, Annex I, Resolutions I, III and IV. Rosenne, S. and L. B. Sohn (eds.). Dordrecht, Martinus Nijhoff.

Ocean Drilling Program (ODP)/JOIDES (1996). Understanding our dynamic earth through ocean drilling. Ocean Drilling Program Long Range Plan. Washington, D.C., Joint Oceanographic Institutions, Inc.

Ou, Z. and P. Vanícek (1996). Automatic Tracing of the Foot of the Continental Slope. Marine Geodesy 19 (2): 181–195.

Ou, Z. and P. Vanícek (1996). The Effect of Data Density on the Accuracy of Foot-line Determination through Maximum Curvature Surface by Automatic Ridge-tracing Algorithm. International Hydrographic Review LXXIII (2): 27–38.

Oxman, B. H. (1969). The preparation of article 1 of the Convention on the Continental Shelf. Prepared for Commission on Marine Science, Engineering and Resources. Springfield, Virginia, National Technical Information Service.

Price, W. F. (1986). The New Definition of the Metre. Survey Review 28 (219): 276–279.

Quine, W. V. (1966). Methods of Logic., rev. ed. New York: Holt, Rinehart and Winston.

Rudnick, R. F. (1995). Making continental crust. Nature, vol. 378: 571–578.

Schnadelbach, K. (1974). Entwicklungstendenzen in Rechenverfahren der mathematischen Geodäsie. Zeitschrift für Vermessungswesen 99: 421–430.

Seeber, G. (1993). Satellite Geodesy. New York, Walter de Gruyter.

Shalowitz, A. L. (1962). Shore and Sea Boundaries: with Special Reference to the Interpretation and Use of Coast and Geodetic Survey Data. Volume 1, Boundary Problems Associated with the Submerged Lands Cases and the Submerged Lands Acts. Washington, D.C., U.S. Department of Commerce, Coast and Geodetic Survey.

Sjoberg, L. (1996). Error propagation in maritime delimitation. Proceedings of the Second International Conference on Geodetic Aspects of the Law of the Sea, Bali, Indonesia, 1–4 July 1996, p. 153–168.

Stewart, W. K., Marra, M. and M. Jiang (1992). A Hierarchical Approach to Seafloor Classification Using Neural Networks. Proceedings of the IEEE Oceans 92 Conference, Honolulu, Hawaii, p. 109–113.

Swift, E. R. (1994). Improved WGS84 Coordinates for the DMA and Air Force GPS Tracking Sites. Proceedings of ION GPS-94, 7th International Technical Meeting of the Satellite Division of the Institute of Navigation, Salt Lake City, Utah, p. 285–292.

Taylor, B. and Natland, J. H. (eds.) (1995). Active Margins and Marginal Basins of the Western Pacific. Geophys. Monograph, vol. 88.

Torge, W. (1989). Gravimetry. New York, Walter de Gruyter.

United Nations (1983). Office for Ocean Affairs and the Law of the Sea. The Law of the Sea. United Nations Convention on the Law of the Sea with Index and Final Act of the Third United Nations Conference on the Law of the Sea. (A/CONF.62/122). Sales No. E.83.V5.

United Nations (1989). Office for Ocean Affairs and the Law of the Sea. The Law of the Sea. Baselines: National Legislation with Illustrative Maps. Sales No. E.89.V.10.

United Nations (1993). Office of Legal Affairs: Division for Ocean Affairs and the Law of the Sea. The Law of the Sea. Definition of the Continental Shelf. Sales No. E.93.V.16.

United Nations (1997). Office of Legal Affairs: Division for Ocean Affairs and the Law of the Sea. Commission on the Limits of the Continental Shelf: its functions and scientific and technical needs in assessing the submission of a coastal State. 10 June 1996 (SPLOS/CLCS/INF/1).

United Nations (1997). Office of Legal Affairs: Division for Ocean Affairs and the Law of the Sea. The Law of the Sea. Official Texts of the United Nations Convention on the Law of the Sea of 10 December 1982 and of the Agreement relating to the Implementation of Part XI of the United Nations Convention on the Law of the Sea of 10 December 1982 with Index and excerpts from the Final Act of the Third United Nations Conference on the Law of the Sea. Sales No. E.97.V.10.

United Nations (1998). Commission on the Limits of the Continental Shelf. Rules of Procedure of the Commission on the Limits of the Continental Shelf. 4 September 1998 (CLCS/3/Rev.2).

Valliant, H. D., Halpenny, J., and Coopper, R. V. (1985). A microprocessor-based controller and data acquisition system for LaCoste and Romberg air-sea meters. Geophysics 50: 840–845.

Vanícek, P. (ed.) (1990). Geodetic Commentary to TALOS Manual. Appendix to Special Publication No. 51. Monaco, International Hydrographic Bureau.

Vanícek, P. (1992). The problem of a maritime boundary involving two horizontal geodetic datums. Proceedings of the First International Conference on Geodetic Aspects of the Law of the Sea, Bali, Indonesia, 8–11 June 1992, p. 97–105.

Vanícek, P. and E. Krakiwsky (1982). Geodesy: The Concepts, 2nd ed., Amsterdam, Elsevier, 1992.

Vanícek, P. and Z. Ou (1996). Automatic tracing of continental slope footline from real bathymetric data. Proceedings of the Second International Conference on Geodetic Aspects of the Law of the Sea, Bali, Indonesia, 1–4 July 1996, p. 267–302.

von Rad, U., K. Hinz, M. Sarntheim and G. Seibold (eds.) (1982). Geology of the Northwest African Continental Margin. Berlin, Heidelberg, New York, SpringerVerlag.

Wiseman, J. D. H. and C. D. Ovey (1953). Definitions of Features on the Deep Sea Floor. Deep-Sea Research 1 (1): 11–16.

Zumberge, M. A., E. L. Canuteson and J. A. Hildebrand (1994). The utility of absolute gravity measurements on the sea floor, Proceedings of the International Symposium on Marine Positioning, INSMAP 94, University of Hanover, Hanover, Germany, 19–23 September, p. 87–94.

Annex

LIST OF INTERNATIONAL ORGANIZATIONS

The list provided below is a non-exhaustive compilation of the names and Web sites of international organizations which might have access to data and information of potential interest to coastal States during the preparation of submissions in respect of the outer limits of their continental shelf beyond 200 nautical miles. The Commission includes the names of these organizations in an attempt to foster international scientific cooperation. The list is not intended to identify the names of international organizations with which the Commission may cooperate with a view to exchanging scientific and technical information which might be of assistance in discharging its responsibilities according to annex II, article 3, paragraph 2.

The list is arranged under five main sections. The first contains specialized agencies of the United Nations system. The second names other scientific bodies of the United Nations. The third section includes the names of relevant international members, scientific associates and other bodies of the International Council of Scientific Unions (ICSU), a Formal Associate of the United Nations Educational, Scientific and Cultural Organization (UNESCO) since 1995. The fourth section contains the names of ongoing international scientific programmes conducted by a number of organizations whose data and research might prove valuable to coastal States. The last section includes the names of regional organizations and programmes.

Whereas the following international organizations have the responsibility of promoting the development of knowledge and research in their respective disciplines, according to Annex II, the Commission has the sole responsibility of making recommendations and providing scientific and technical advice in relation to submissions of limits of the extended continental shelf made by coastal States.

1. Specialized agencies of the United Nations system

1.1 International Maritime Organization (IMO)
http://www.imo.org/imo/

1.2 United Nations Educational, Scientific and Cultural Organization (UNESCO)
http://www.unesco.org/

1.2.1 Intergovernmental Oceanographic Commission (IOC)
http://ioc.unesco.org/iocweb/

Committee on International Oceanographic Data and Information Exchange (IODE)
http://ioc.unesco.org/iode/

Consultative Group on Ocean Mapping (COM)
http://ioc.unesco.org/iocweb/activities/ocean_sciences/ocemap.htm

Global Ocean Observing System (GOOS)
http://ioc.unesco.org/goos/

Joint IOC-IHO Guiding Committee for the General Bathymetric Chart of the Oceans (GEBCO)
http://www.nbi.ac.uk/bodc/gebco.html

2. Other United Nations bodies

2.1 Coordinating Committee for Coastal and Offshore Geoscience Programmes in East and South-East Asia (CCOP)
ccopts@ccop.or.th

2.2 Inter-secretariat Committee on Scientific Programmes relating to Oceanography (ICSPRO)
http://www.un.org/Depts/los/loscord.htm#ICSPRO

3. International Council of Scientific Unions (ICSU)
http://www.icsu.org/

Members:

3.1 International Geographical Union (IGU)
http://www.helsinki.fi/science/igu/

Commission on Marine Geography
http://www.helsinki.fi/science/igu/html/commissions_list_13.html

3.2 International Union of Geodesy and Geophysics (IUGG)
http://www.omp.obs-mip.fr/uggi/

3.2.1 International Association of Geodesy (IAG)
http://www.gfy.ku.dk/Điag/

Committee on Geodetic Aspects of the Law of the Sea (GALOS)
http://www.unb.ca/GGE/GALOS/GALOS.HTM

3.2.2 International Association of Physical Sciences of the Oceans (IAPSO)
http://www.olympus.net/IAPSO/

3.3 International Union of Geological Sciences (IUGS)
http://www.iugs.org/

Working Group on Marine Geology
http://www.iugs.org/iugs/science/sci-wmg.htm

Scientific associates:

3.4 Fédération International des Géometres (FIG)
http://www.ddl.org/figtree/

Commission 4 Hydrography http://biachss.bur.dfo.ca/fig4/

3.5 International Cartographic Association (ICA)
http://www.msu.edu/Ðolsonj/ica/

Working Group on Marine Cartography
http://www.msu.edu/Ðolsonj/ica/

Working Group on Map Generalization
http://loo.geo.unizh.ch/ICA-bin/index.html

3.6 International Hydrographic Organization (IHO)
http://iho.shom.fr/

International Data Center for Digital Bathymetry (IHO DCDB)
http://www.ngdc.noaa.gov/mgg/bathymetry/iho.html

Advisory Board on Hydrographic and Geodetic Aspects of the Law of the Sea (ABLOS) with the International Association of Geodesy (IAG)
http://www.gmat.unsw.edu.au/ablos/

3.7 International Society for Photogrammetry and Remote Sensing (ISPRS) http://www.geod.ethz.ch/isprs/

Interdisciplinary bodies:

3.8 International Arctic Science Committee (IASC)
http://www.iasc.no/

3.9 Scientific Committee on Antarctic Research (SCAR)
http://www.icsu.org/Structure/scar.html

3.10 Scientific Council on Oceanic Research (SCOR)
http://www.jhu.edu/Ðscor/

Permanent services and panels:

3.11 Federation of Astronomical and Geophysical Data Analysis Services (FAGS)
http://www.wdc.rl.ac.uk/wdcmain/appendix/gdappena2.html

3.11.1 Bureau Gravimétrique International (BGI)
http://www-projet.cnes.fr:8110/

3.11.2 International GPS Service
http://igscb.jpl.nasa.gov/

3.12 Panel on World Data Centres (WDC)
http://www.ngdc.noaa.gov/wdc/wdcmain.html#wdc

3.12.1 WDC-A for Solid Earth Geophysics
http://www.ngdc.noaa.gov/seg/wdca/

3.12.2 WDC-A Oceanography
http://www.nodc.noaa.gov/NODC-wdca.html

3.12.3 WDC-B Marine Geology and Geophysics
http://www.sea.ru/cmgd/wdc.html

3.12.4 WDC-B Oceanography
http://www.wdcb.rssi.ru/WDCB/wdcb_oce.html

Inter-Union Commissions:

3.13 Inter-Union Commission on the Lithosphere (ICSU-IUGG-IUGS)
http://www.iugs.org/iugs/links.htm

4. International scientific programmes

4.1 International Geological Correlation Programmes
http://www.unesco.org/science/programme/environ/igcp/index.html

4.2 International Lithosphere Programme
http://www.gfz-potsdam.de/pb4/ilp/

4.3 Ocean Drilling Program (ODP)
http://www-odp.tamu.edu/

5. Regional organizations and programmes

5.1 South Pacific Applied Geoscience Commission
http://www.sopac.org.fj/

CLCS

UNITED NATIONS CONVENTION

ON THE LAW OF THE SEA

COMMISSION ON THE LIMITS
OF THE CONTINENTAL SHELF

Distr.
GENERAL

CLCS/11/Add.1
3 September 1999

ORIGINAL: ENGLISH

Sixth session

New York, 30 August-3 September 1999

SCIENTIFIC AND TECHNICAL GUIDELINES OF THE COMMISSION ON THE LIMITS OF THE CONTINENTAL SHELF

Annexes II–IV* to the Guidelines adopted by the Commission on 3 September 1999 at its sixth session

CONTENTS

* The first annex was adopted together with the Guidelines on 13 May 1999 at the fifth session of the Commission and is contained in document CLCS/11.

CONTENTS (continued)

ANNEX II

FLOWCHARTS AND ILLUSTRATIONS SUMMARIZING THE PROCEDURE FOR ESTABLISHING THE OUTER LIMITS OF THE CONTINENTAL SHELF

1. The purpose of Annex II is to provide a simplified outline of the Scientific and Technical Guidelines of the Commission, and to illustrate the procedures involved. It is not intended to introduce any new information or interpretation of the detailed descriptions contained in chapters 1 to 9 of the Guidelines. If the need for clarification arises, the reader is encouraged to consult the relevant parts of the chapters. Should any apparent contradiction between this Annex and the Guidelines occur as a result of this simplification process, then the Guidelines shall prevail.

2. The entire process for a coastal State to establish the outer limits of its continental shelf under article 76 of the Convention is presented in the Master Flowchart (fig. II.1) and five sub-flowcharts (figs. II.2 – II.6). These sub-flowcharts outline in greater detail the following five procedures shown in bold in the Master Flowchart:

I. Establishment of the 200 M limit from the baselines (article 76 (1));

II. Determination of the foot of the continental slope:

(a) Maximum change in the gradient at the foot of the continental slope (article 76 (4));

(b) Evidence to the contrary to the general rule (article 76 (4) (b));

III. Application of the formulae:

(a) Sediment thickness (article 76 (4) (a) (i));

(b) 60 M from the foot of the continental slope (article 76 (4) (a) (ii);

IV. Determination of the limits in the case of submarine elevations and/or ridges (article 76 (3) and (6));

V. Application of the constraints:

(a) 350 M from the baselines (article 76 (5), first provision);

(b) 2500 metre isobath plus 100 M (article 76 (5), second provision).

3. For the application of the distance criteria of 200 or 350 nautical miles from the baselines from which the breadth of the territorial sea is measured, a coastal State may refer to the methodologies described in chapter 3 of the Guidelines.

4. The application of the formulae and constraints for establishing the outer limits of the continental shelf, defined by the criteria contained in article 76, is illustrated in figure II.7.

List of figures

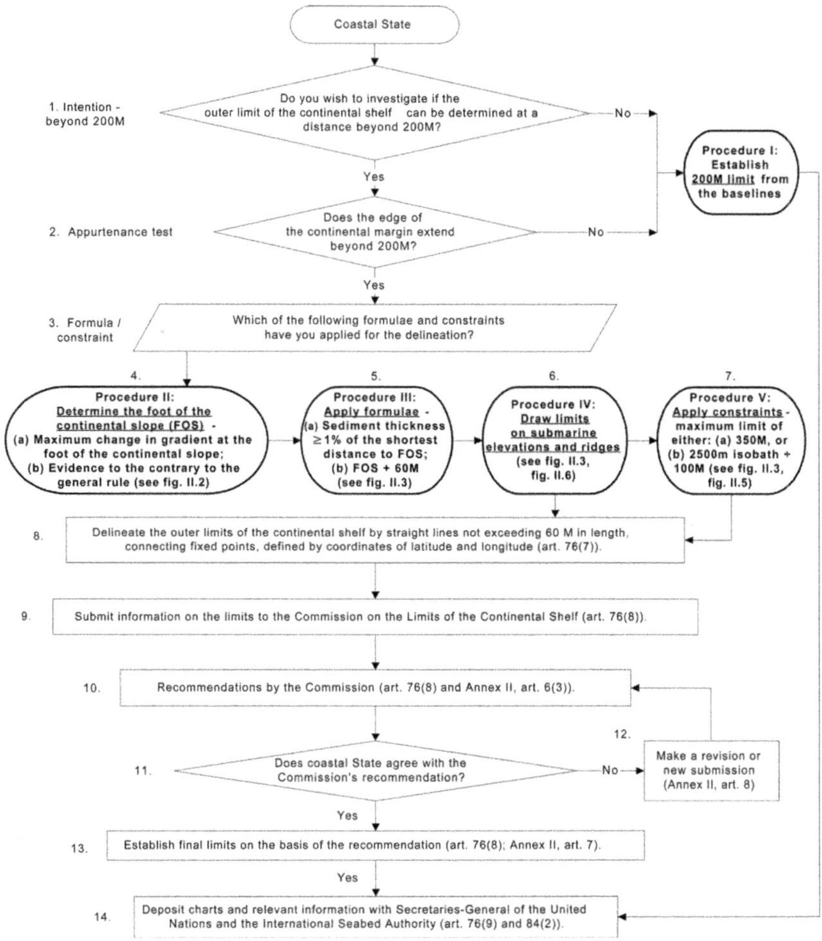

Figure II.1. Master Flowchart for the establishment of the outer limits of the continental shelf.

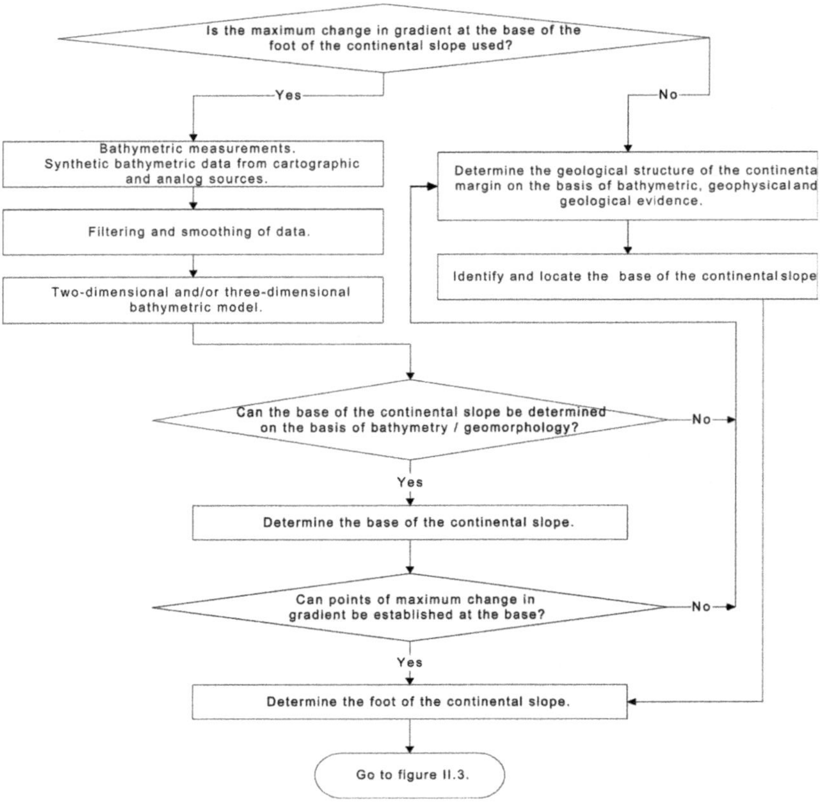

Figure II.2. Sub-flowchart showing the determination of the foot of the continental slope – indicated on Master Flowchart (fig. II.1) as procedure II.

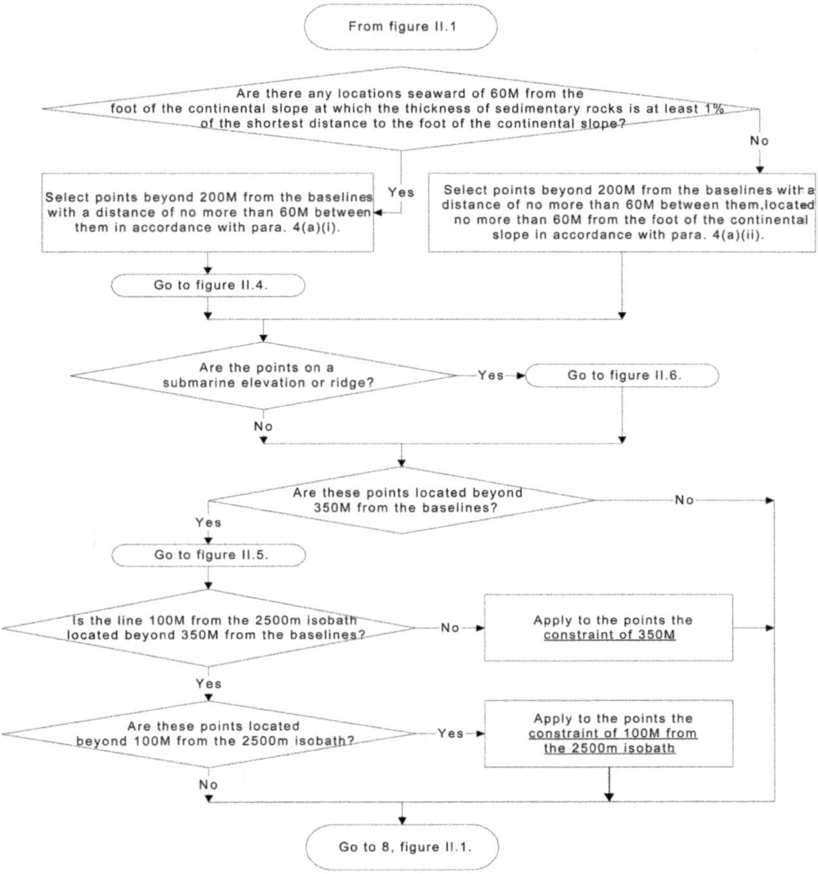

Figure II.3. Sub-flowchart showing the application of the distance formulae and constraints – indicated in Master Flowchart (fig. II.1) as procedures III and V.

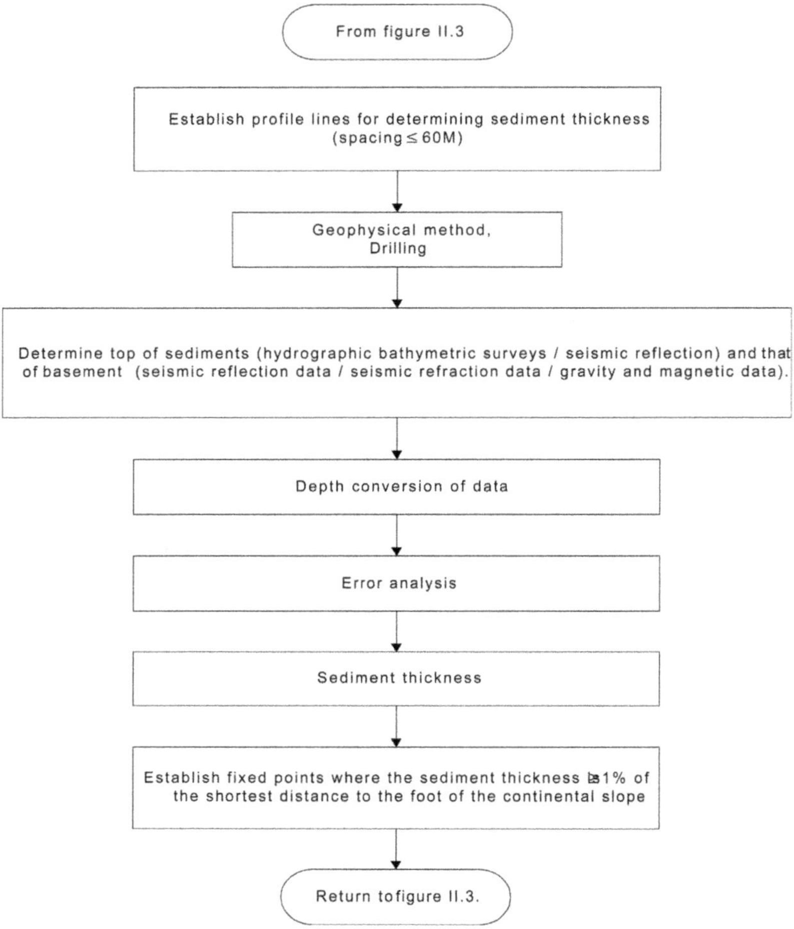

Figure II.4. Sub-flowchart showing the establishment of fixed points where the sediment thickness is ≥ 1% of the shortest distance to the foot of the continental slope – indicated on Master Flowchart (fig. II.1) as procedure III – application of formulae.

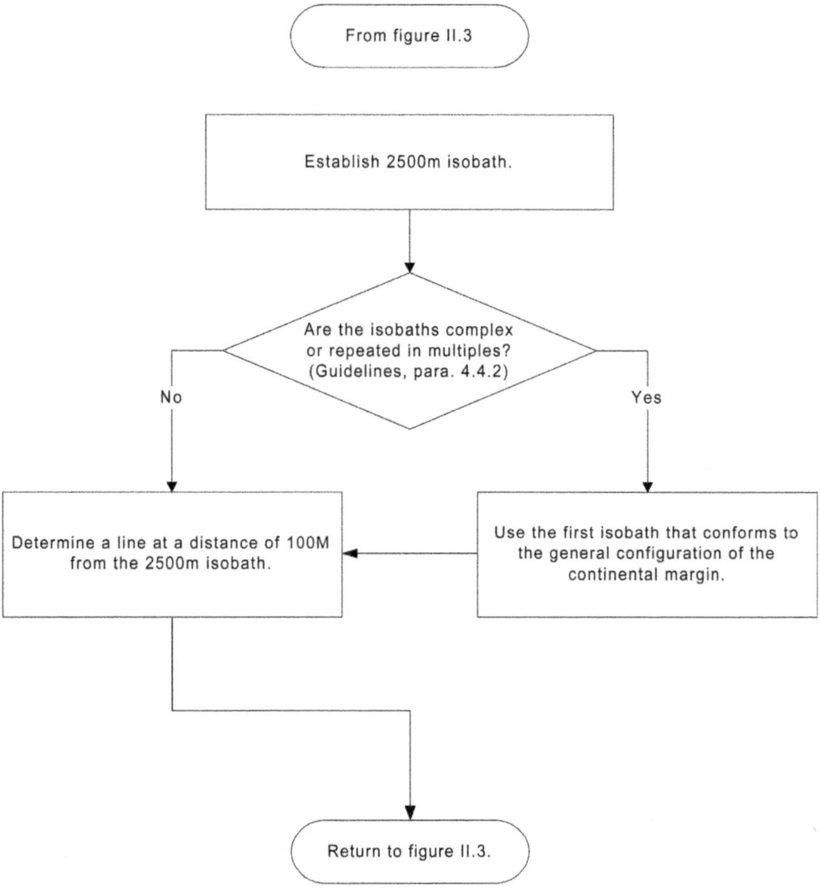

Figure II.5. Sub-flowchart showing the establishment of the 2500m isobath and determination of the 100M line from that isobath – indicated on Master Flowchart (fig. II.1) as procedure V – application of constraints.

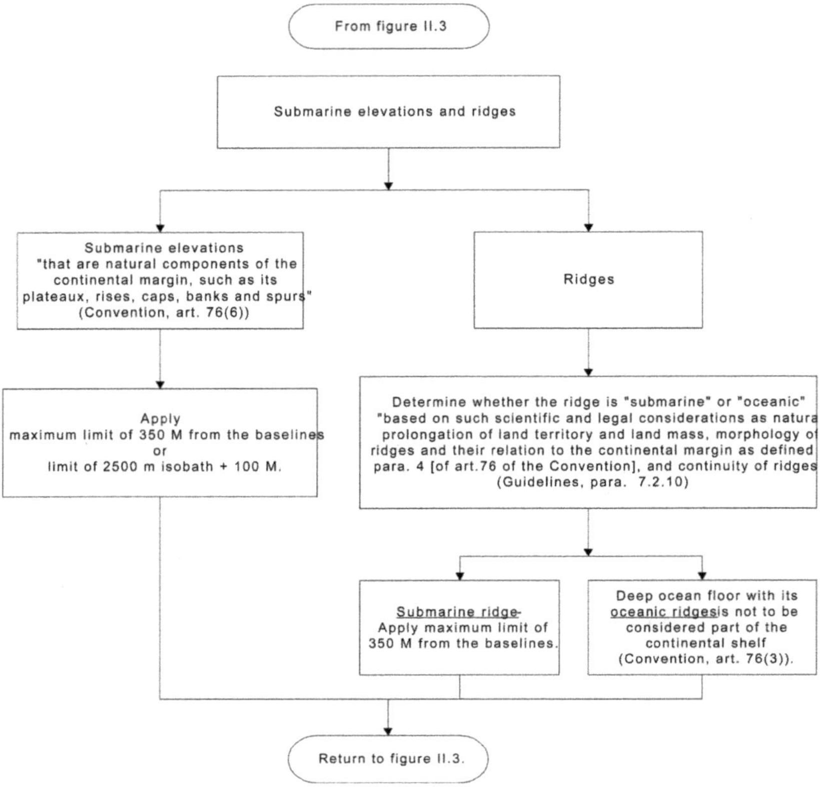

Figure II.6. Sub-flowchart showing the formulation of the solution to the problem arising from article 76 (3) and (6) and relating to sea floor highs, whether submarine elevations or ridges, indicated on Master Flowchart (fig. II.1) as procedure IV – determination of the limits in the case of submarine elevations and/or ridges.

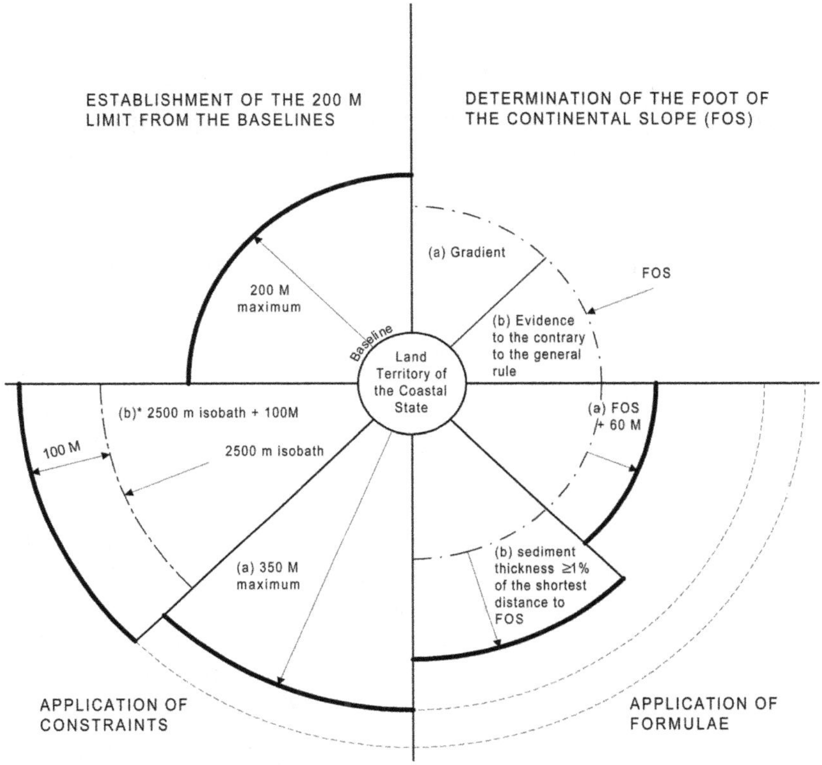

Note:
* This criterion applies in the case of submarine elevations but does not apply in the case of submarine ridges (see fig. II.6).

Figure II.7. Illustration of the application of various formulae and constraints for establishing the outer limits of the continental shelf.

ANNEX III

EXCERPTS FROM THE UNITED NATIONS CONVENTION ON THE LAW OF THE SEA AND THE FINAL ACT OF THE THIRD UNITED NATIONS CONFERENCE ON THE LAW OF THE SEA OF DIRECT RELEVANCE TO THE ISSUE OF THE CONTINENTAL SHELF

1. UNITED NATIONS CONVENTION ON THE LAW OF THE SEA

PART VI

CONTINENTAL SHELF

Article 76

Definition of the continental shelf

1. The continental shelf of a coastal State comprises the seabed and subsoil of the submarine areas that extend beyond its territorial sea throughout the natural prolongation of its land territory to the outer edge of the continental margin, or to a distance of 200 nautical miles from the baselines from which the breadth of the territorial sea is measured where the outer edge of the continental margin does not extend up to that distance.

2. The continental shelf of a coastal State shall not extend beyond the limits provided for in paragraphs 4 to 6.

3. The continental margin comprises the submerged prolongation of the land mass of the coastal State, and consists of the seabed and subsoil of the shelf, the slope and the rise. It does not include the deep ocean floor with its oceanic ridges or the subsoil thereof.

4. (a) For the purposes of this Convention, the coastal State shall establish the outer edge of the continental margin wherever the margin extends beyond 200 nautical miles from the baselines from which the breadth of the territorial sea is measured, by either:

(i) a line delineated in accordance with paragraph 7 by reference to the outermost fixed points at each of which the thickness of sedimentary rocks is at least 1 per cent of the shortest distance from such point to the foot of the continental slope; or

(ii) a line delineated in accordance with paragraph 7 by reference to fixed points not more than 60 nautical miles from the foot of the continental slope.

(b) In the absence of evidence to the contrary, the foot of the continental slope shall be determined as the point of maximum change in the gradient at its base.

5. The fixed points comprising the line of the outer limits of the continental shelf on the seabed, drawn in accordance with paragraph 4 (a) (i) and (ii), either shall not exceed 350 nautical miles from the baselines from which the breadth of the territorial sea is measured or shall not exceed 100 nautical miles from the 2,500 metre isobath, which is a line connecting the depth of 2,500 metres.

6. Notwithstanding the provisions of paragraph 5, on submarine ridges, the outer limit of the continental shelf shall not exceed 350 nautical miles from the baselines from which the breadth of the territorial sea is measured. This paragraph does not apply to submarine elevations that are natural components of the continental margin, such as its plateaux, rises, caps, banks and spurs.

7. The coastal State shall delineate the outer limits of its continental shelf, where that shelf extends beyond 200 nautical miles from the baselines from which the breadth of the territorial sea is measured, by straight lines not exceeding 60 nautical miles in length, connecting fixed points, defined by coordinates of latitude and longitude.

8. Information on the limits of the continental shelf beyond 200 nautical miles from the baselines from which the breadth of the territorial sea is measured shall be submitted by the coastal State to the Commission on the Limits of the Continental Shelf set up under Annex II on the basis of equitable geographical representation. The Commission shall make recommendations to coastal States on matters related to the establishment of the outer limits of their continental shelf. The limits of the shelf established by a coastal State on the basis of these recommendations shall be final and binding.

9. The coastal State shall deposit with the Secretary-General of the United Nations charts and relevant information, including geodetic data, permanently describing the outer limits of its continental shelf. The Secretary-General shall give due publicity thereto.

10. The provisions of this article are without prejudice to the question of delimitation of the continental shelf between States with opposite or adjacent coasts.

Article 77

Rights of the coastal State over the continental shelf

1. The coastal State exercises over the continental shelf sovereign rights for the purpose of exploring it and exploiting its natural resources.

2. The rights referred to in paragraph 1 are exclusive in the sense that if the coastal State does not explore the continental shelf or exploit its natural resources, no one may undertake these activities without the express consent of the coastal State.

3. The rights of the coastal State over the continental shelf do not depend on occupation, effective or notional, or on any express proclamation.

4. The natural resources referred to in this Part consist of the mineral and other non-living resources of the seabed and subsoil together with living organisms belonging to sedentary species, that is to say, organisms which, at the harvestable stage, either are immobile on or under the seabed or are unable to move except in constant physical contact with the seabed or the subsoil.

Article 78

Legal status of the superjacent waters and airspace and the rights and freedoms of other States

1. The rights of the coastal State over the continental shelf do not affect the legal status of the superjacent waters or of the airspace above those waters.

2. The exercise of the rights of the coastal State over the continental shelf must not infringe or result in any unjustifiable interference with navigation and other rights and freedoms of other States as provided for in this Convention.

Article 79

Submarine cables and pipelines on the continental shelf

1. All States are entitled to lay submarine cables and pipelines on the continental shelf, in accordance with the provisions of this article.

2. Subject to its right to take reasonable measures for the exploration of the continental shelf, the exploitation of its natural resources and the prevention, reduction and control of pollution from pipelines, the coastal State may not impede the laying or maintenance of such cables or pipelines.

3. The delineation of the course for the laying of such pipelines on the continental shelf is subject to the consent of the coastal State.

4. Nothing in this Part affects the right of the coastal State to establish conditions for cables or pipelines entering its territory or territorial sea, or its jurisdiction over cables and pipelines constructed or used in connection with the exploration of its continental shelf or exploitation of its resources or the operations of artificial islands, installations and structures under its jurisdiction.

5. When laying submarine cables or pipelines, States shall have due regard to cables or pipelines already in position. In particular, possibilities of repairing existing cables or pipelines shall not be prejudiced.

Article 80

Artificial islands, installations and structures on the continental shelf

Article 60 applies mutatis mutandis to artificial islands, installations and structures on the continental shelf.

Article 81

Drilling on the continental shelf

The coastal State shall have the exclusive right to authorize and regulate drilling on the continental shelf for all purposes.

Article 82

Payments and contributions with respect to the exploitation of the continental shelf beyond 200 nautical miles

1. The coastal State shall make payments or contributions in kind in respect of the exploitation of the non-living resources of the continental shelf beyond 200 nautical miles from the baselines from which the breadth of the territorial sea is measured.

2. The payments and contributions shall be made annually with respect to all production at a site after the first five years of production at that site. For the sixth year, the rate of payment or contribution shall be 1 per cent of the value or volume of production at the site. The rate shall increase by 1 per cent for each subsequent year until the twelfth year and shall remain at 7 per cent thereafter. Production does not include resources used in connection with exploitation.

3. A developing State which is a net importer of a mineral resource produced from its continental shelf is exempt from making such payments or contributions in respect of that mineral resource.

4. The payments or contributions shall be made through the Authority, which shall distribute them to States Parties to this Convention, on the basis of equitable sharing criteria, taking into account the interests and needs of developing States, particularly the least developed and the land-locked among them.

Article 83

Delimitation of the continental shelf between States with opposite or adjacent coasts

1. The delimitation of the continental shelf between States with opposite or adjacent coasts shall be effected by agreement on the basis of international law, as referred to in Article 38 of the Statute of the International Court of Justice, in order to achieve an equitable solution.

2. If no agreement can be reached within a reasonable period of time, the States concerned shall resort to the procedures provided for in Part XV.

3. Pending agreement as provided for in paragraph 1, the States concerned, in a spirit of understanding and cooperation, shall make every effort to enter into provisional arrangements of a practical nature and, during this transitional period, not to jeopardize or hamper the reaching of the final

agreement. Such arrangements shall be without prejudice to the final delimitation.

4. Where there is an agreement in force between the States concerned, questions relating to the delimitation of the continental shelf shall be determined in accordance with the provisions of that agreement.

Article 84

Charts and lists of geographical coordinates

1. Subject to this Part, the outer limit lines of the continental shelf and the lines of delimitation drawn in accordance with article 83 shall be shown on charts of a scale or scales adequate for ascertaining their position. Where appropriate, lists of geographical coordinates of points, specifying the geodetic datum, may be substituted for such outer limit lines or lines of delimitation.

2. The coastal State shall give due publicity to such charts or lists of geographical coordinates and shall deposit a copy of each such chart or list with the Secretary-General of the United Nations and, in the case of those showing the outer limit lines of the continental shelf, with the Secretary-General of the Authority.

Article 85

Tunnelling

This Part does not prejudice the right of the coastal State to exploit the subsoil by means of tunnelling, irrespective of the depth of water above the subsoil.

2. UNITED NATIONS CONVENTION ON THE LAW OF THE SEA

ANNEX II. COMMISSION ON THE LIMITS OF THE CONTINENTAL SHELF

Article 1

In accordance with the provisions of article 76, a Commission on the Limits of the Continental Shelf beyond 200 nautical miles shall be established in conformity with the following articles.

Article 2

1. The Commission shall consist of 21 members who shall be experts in the field of geology, geophysics or hydrography, elected by States Parties to this Convention from among their nationals, having due regard to the need to ensure equitable geographical representation, who shall serve in their personal capacities.

2. The initial election shall be held as soon as possible but in any case within 18 months after the date of entry into force of this Convention. At least three months before the date of each election, the Secretary-General of the United Nations shall address a letter to the States Parties, inviting the submission of nominations, after appropriate regional consultations, within three months. The Secretary-General shall prepare a list in alphabetical order of all persons thus nominated and shall submit it to all the States Parties.

3. Elections of the members of the Commission shall be held at a meeting of States Parties convened by the Secretary-General at United Nations Headquarters. At that meeting, for which two thirds of the States Parties shall constitute a quorum, the persons elected to the Commission shall be those nominees who obtain a two-thirds majority of the votes of the representatives of States Parties present and voting. Not less than three members shall be elected from each geographical region.

4. The members of the Commission shall be elected for a term of five years. They shall be eligible for re-election.

5. The State Party which submitted the nomination of a member of the Commission shall defray the expenses of that member while in performance of Commission duties. The coastal State concerned shall defray the expenses incurred in respect of the advice referred to in article 3, paragraph 1 (b), of this Annex. The secretariat of the Commission shall be provided by the Secretary-General of the United Nations.

Article 3

1. The functions of the Commission shall be:

   (a) to consider the data and other material submitted by coastal States concerning the outer limits of the continental shelf in areas where those limits extend beyond 200 nautical miles, and to make recommendations in accordance with article 76 and the Statement of Understanding adopted on 29 August 1980 by the Third United Nations Conference on the Law of the Sea;

(b) to provide scientific and technical advice, if requested by the coastal State concerned during the preparation of the data referred to in subparagraph (a).

2. The Commission may cooperate, to the extent considered necessary and useful, with the Intergovernmental Oceanographic Commission of UNESCO, the International Hydrographic Organization and other competent international organizations with a view to exchanging scientific and technical information which might be of assistance in discharging the Commission's responsibilities.

Article 4

Where a coastal State intends to establish, in accordance with article 76, the outer limits of its continental shelf beyond 200 nautical miles, it shall submit particulars of such limits to the Commission along with supporting scientific and technical data as soon as possible but in any case within 10 years of the entry into force of this Convention for that State. The coastal State shall at the same time give the names of any Commission members who have provided it with scientific and technical advice.

Article 5

Unless the Commission decides otherwise, the Commission shall function by way of subcommissions composed of seven members, appointed in a balanced manner taking into account the specific elements of each submission by a coastal State. Nationals of the coastal State making the submission who are members of the Commission and any Commission member who has assisted a coastal State by providing scientific and technical advice with respect to the delineation shall not be a member of the subcommission dealing with that submission but has the right to participate as a member in the proceedings of the Commission concerning the said submission. The coastal State which has made a submission to the Commission may send its representatives to participate in the relevant proceedings without the right to vote.

Article 6

1. The subcommission shall submit its recommendations to the Commission.

2. Approval by the Commission of the recommendations of the subcommission shall be by a majority of two thirds of Commission members present and voting.

3. The recommendations of the Commission shall be submitted in writing to the coastal State which made the submission and to the Secretary-General of the United Nations.

Article 7

Coastal States shall establish the outer limits of the continental shelf in conformity with the provisions of article 76, paragraph 8, and in accordance with the appropriate national procedures.

Article 8

In the case of disagreement by the coastal State with the recommendations of the Commission, the coastal State shall, within a reasonable time, make a revised or new submission to the Commission.

Article 9

The actions of the Commission shall not prejudice matters relating to delimitation of boundaries between States with opposite or adjacent coasts.

3. FINAL ACT OF THE THIRD UNITED NATIONS CONFERENCE ON THE LAW OF THE SEA

ANNEX II. STATEMENT OF UNDERSTANDING CONCERNING A SPECIFIC METHOD TO BE USED IN ESTABLISHING THE OUTER EDGE OF THE CONTINENTAL MARGIN

The Third United Nations Conference on the Law of the Sea,

Considering the special characteristics of a State's continental margin where: (1) the average distance at which the 200 metre isobath occurs is not more than 20 nautical miles; (2) the greater proportion of the sedimentary rock of the continental margin lies beneath the rise; and

Taking into account the inequity that would result to that State from the application to its continental margin of article 76 of the Convention, in that, the mathematical average of the thickness of sedimentary rock along a line established at the maximum distance permissible in accordance with the provisions of paragraph 4 (a) (i) and (ii) of that article as representing the entire outer edge of the continental margin would not be less than 3.5 kilometres; and that more than half of the margin would be excluded thereby;

Recognizes that such State may, notwithstanding the provisions of article 76, establish the outer edge of its continental margin by straight lines not exceeding 60 nautical miles in length connecting fixed points, defined by latitude and longitude, at each of which the thickness of sedimentary rock is not less than 1 kilometre,

Where a State establishes the outer edge of its continental margin by applying the method set forth in the preceding paragraph of this statement, this method may also be utilized by a neighbouring State for delineating the outer edge of its continental margin on a common geological feature, where its outer edge would lie on such feature on a line established at the maximum distance permissible in accordance with article 76, paragraph 4 (a) (i) and (ii), along which the mathematical average of the thickness of sedimentary rock is not less than 3.5 kilometres,

The Conference requests the Commission on the Limits of the Continental Shelf set up pursuant to Annex II of the Convention, to be governed by the terms of this Statement when making its recommendations on matters related to the establishment of the outer edge of the continental margins of these States in the southern part of the Bay of Bengal.

ANNEX IV

MEMBERS OF THE COMMISSION ON THE LIMITS OF THE CONTINENTAL SHELF (1997–2002)

Comandante Alexandre Tagore Medeiros de **ALBUQUERQUE**
Diretoria de Hidrografia e Navegagao (DHN)
Rua Barao de Jaceguay s/n
24048-900 Niterói
Rio de Janeiro
BRAZIL

Captain Osvaldo Pedro **ASTIZ**
Dirección de Límites y Fronteras
Ministerio de Relaciones Exteriores,
Comercio Internacional y Culto
Esmeralda 1212
1007 Buenos Aires
ARGENTINA

Mr. Lawrence Folajimi **AWOSIKA**
Nigerian Institute for Oceanography and Marine Research
P.M.B. 12729, Bar Beach
Victoria Island
Lagos
NIGERIA

Mr. Ali Ibrahim **BELTAGY**
Chairman, Shore Processes Laboratory
National Institute of Oceanography and Fisheries
Kayet Bey, Anfoushi
Alexandria
EGYPT

Mr. Samuel Sona **BETAH**
Director of Geology
Ministry of Mines, Water and Energy
Yaoundé
CAMEROON

Mr. Harald **BREKKE**
Senior Geologist
Norwegian Petroleum Directorate (NPD)
P.O. Box 600
N-4001 Stavanger
NORWAY

Dr. Galo **CARRERA HURTADO**
Consulate of **Mexico** in Nova Scotia

53 Hawthorne Street
Darthmouth
Nova Scotia, B2Y 2Y7
CANADA

Mr. André C.W. **CHAN CHIM YUK**
Associate Professor and Dean
Faculty of Engineering
University of Mauritius
Réduit
MAURITIUS

Mr. Peter F. **CROKER**
Geophysicist
Petroleum Affairs Division
Department of Marine and Natural Resources
Beggars Bush
Haddington Road
Dublin 4
IRELAND

Mr. Noel Newton St. Claver **FRANCIS**
Deputy Director of Surveys
Survey Department
23½ Charles Street
Kingston
JAMAICA

Dr. Kazuchika **HAMURO**
Counsellor
Embassy of **Japan** in Jamaica
Mutual Life Centre, North Tower, 6th Floor
2 Oxford Road
Kingston
JAMAICA

Dr. Karl H. F. **HINZ**
Head of the Geological and Geophysical Research Division
Bundesanstalt für Geowissenschaften
und Rohstoffe
(Federal Institute for Geosciences and Natural Resources)
P.O. Box 51-01-53
D-30631 Hanover
GERMANY

Dato' Dr. A. Bakar **JAAFAR**
Managing Director
Alam Sekitar Malaysia Sdn. Bhd. (ASMA)
No.19, Jalan Astaka (U8/84)

Bukit Jelutong Business & Technology Centre
40150 Shah Alam, Selangor
MALAYSIA

Dr. Mladen **JURAČIĆ**
Professor of Marine Geology
Department of Geology
Faculty of Science
University of Zagreb
Kralja Zvonimira 8
10 000 Zagreb
CROATIA

Dr. Yuri Borisovitch **KAZMIN**
Counsellor
Russian Ministry of Natural Resources
4/6 Bolshaya Gruzinskaya Street
Moscow, 123812
RUSSIAN FEDERATION

Mr. Iain C. **LAMONT**
Manager Nautical Information Services
Hydrographic Office
Royal New Zealand Navy
19 Byron Avenue
P.O. Box 33341
Takapuna
Auckland 9
NEW ZEALAND

Mr. Wenzheng **LU**
Second Institute of Oceanography (SIO)
State Oceanic Administration (SOA)
Wener Road
Hangzhou
PEOPLE'S REPUBLIC OF CHINA, P.C. 310012

Dr. Chisengu Leo **MDALA**
Geology Department
School of Mines
University of Zambia
Box 32379
Lusaka
ZAMBIA

Dr. Yong Ahn **PARK**
Professor of Marine Geology
Department of Oceanography
Seoul National University

Seoul 151–742
REPUBLIC OF KOREA

Mr. Daniel **RIO**
Ingénieur du service hydrographique et oceanographique
de la Marine
Ministère de la Défense
SHOM-BP426
29275 Brest CEDEX
FRANCE

Rear Admiral Krishna-swamy Ramachandran **SRINIVASAN,** AVSM
Chief Hydrographer to the Government of India
50, “A” Block Hutments
Naval Headquarters
New Delhi – 110011
INDIA

*** * ***

UNITED NATIONS CONVENTION ON THE LAW OF THE SEA **CLCS**

COMMISSION ON THE LIMITS OF THE CONTINENTAL SHELF

Distr.
General

CLCS/11/Add.1/Corr.1
19 November 1999

ENGLISH ONLY

Sixth session
New York, 30 August–3 September 1999

SCIENTIFIC AND TECHNICAL GUIDELINES OF THE COMMISSION ON THE LIMITS OF THE CONTINENTAL SHELF

Annexes II–IV to the Guidelines adopted by the Commission on 3 September 1999 at its sixth session

Corrigendum

Annex II

1. Page 3, para. 2, II. Determination of the foot of the continental slope:

Subparagraph (a) should read

(a) Maximum change in the gradient at the base of the continental slope (article 76 (4));

2. Page 5, figure II.1

Page 6, figure II.2

Replace the figures with the attached.

Note: Figures II.1 and II.2 could not be obtained for reprinting in this volume. Please visit the Official Document System of the United Nations to view the PDF version of this document which contains the two figures: http://documents.un.org/default.asp

–Supplementary Documents Editors

United Nations Convention on the Law of the Sea **CLCS/11/Corr.1**

COMMISSION ON THE LIMITS OF THE CONTINENTAL SHELF

Distr. General
24 February 2000

Original: English

Sixth session
New York, 30 August-3 September 1999

SCIENTIFIC AND TECHNICAL GUIDELINES OF THE COMMISSION ON THE LIMITS OF THE CONTINENTAL SHELF

Adopted by the Commission on 13 May 1999 at its fifth session

Corrigendum

8. Delineation of the outer limits of the continental shelf based on sediment thickness

8.4. Sources and magnitudes of error

Propagation of thickness errors to position errors

1. **Page 66, paragraph 8.4.8**

The second sentence *should read*:

The Commission proposes a more sophisticated method by applying the following formula, which also takes into account the slope of the seabed and the dip of the top surface of the basement:

$$)X =)Y/(\tan(\beta + \theta) + \tan\alpha)$$

where)X is the error in distance,)Y is the error in thickness, θ is the angle of dip of the top of the basement, α is the slope of the sea floor and β is the angle between the top of the basement and the 1 per cent line (i.e., the line showing the thickness increasing by 1 per cent of the distance from the starting point).

2. **Page 70, figure 8.3**

Replace the existing figure with the attached.

NOTE: This updated figure 8.3 has already been inserted in the CLCS/11 document reprinted in this volume. –Supplementary Documents Editors

PART IV

INTERNATIONAL FISHERIES AGREEMENTS ASSOCIATED WITH THE 1982 CONVENTION

AGREEMENT TO PROMOTE COMPLIANCE WITH INTERNATIONAL CONSERVATION AND MANAGEMENT MEASURES BY FISHING VESSELS ON THE HIGH SEAS

PREAMBLE

The Parties to this Agreement,

Recognizing that all States have the right for their nationals to engage in fishing on the high seas, subject to the relevant rules of international law, as reflected in the United Nations Convention on the Law of the Sea,

Further recognizing that, under international law as reflected in the United Nations Convention on the Law of the Sea, all States have the duty to take, or to cooperate with other States in taking, such measures for their respective nationals as may be necessary for the conservation of the living resources of the high seas,

Acknowledging the right and interest of all States to develop their fishing sectors in accordance with their national policies, and the need to promote cooperation with developing countries to enhance their capabilities to fulfil their obligations under this Agreement,

Recalling that Agenda 21, adopted by the United Nations Conference on Environment and Development, calls upon States to take effective action, consistent with international law, to deter reflagging of vessels by their nationals as a means of avoiding compliance with applicable conservation and management rules for fishing activities on the high seas,

Further recalling that the Declaration of Cancun, adopted by the International Conference on Responsible Fishing, also calls on States to take action in this respect,

Bearing in mind that under Agenda 21, States commit themselves to the conservation and sustainable use of marine living resources on the high seas,

Calling upon States which do not participate in global, regional or subregional fisheries organizations or arrangements to join or, as appropriate, to enter into understandings with such organizations or with parties to such organizations or arrangements with a view to achieving compliance with international conservation and management measures,

Conscious of the duties of every State to exercise effectively its jurisdiction and control over vessels flying its flag, including fishing vessels and vessels engaged in the transhipment of fish,

Mindful that the practice of flagging or reflagging fishing vessels as a means of avoiding compliance with international conservation and management measures for living marine resources, and the failure of flag States to fulfil their responsibilities with respect to fishing vessels entitled to fly their flag, are among the factors that seriously undermine the effectiveness of such measures,

Realizing that the objective of this Agreement can be achieved through specifying flag States' responsibility in respect of fishing vessels entitled to fly their flags and operating on the high seas, including the authorization by the flag State of such operations, as well as through strengthened international cooperation and increased transparency through the exchange of information on high seas fishing,

Noting that this Agreement will form an integral part of the International Code of Conduct for Responsible Fishing called for in the Declaration of Cancun,

Desiring to conclude an international agreement within the framework of the Food and Agriculture Organization of the United Nations, hereinafter referred to as FAO, under Article XIV of the FAO Constitution,

Have agreed as follows:

ARTICLE I

Definitions

For the purposes of this Agreement:

(a) "fishing vessel" means any vessel used or intended for use for the purposes of the commercial exploitation of living marine resources, including mother ships and any other vessels directly engaged in such fishing operations;
(b) "international conservation and management measures" means measures to conserve or manage one or more species of living marine resources that are adopted and applied in accordance with the relevant rules of international law as reflected in the 1982 United Nations Convention on the Law of the Sea. Such measures may be adopted either by global, regional or subregional fisheries organizations, subject to the rights and obligations of their members, or by treaties or other international agreements;
(c) "length" means

(i) for any fishing vessel built after 18 July 1982, 96 percent of the total length on a waterline at 85 percent of the least moulded depth measured from the top of the keel, or the length from the foreside of the stem to the axis of the rudder stock on that waterline, if that be greater. In ships designed with a rake of keel the waterline on which this length is measured shall be parallel to the designed waterline;
(ii) for any fishing vessel built before 18 July 1982, registered length as entered on the national register or other record of vessels;

(d) "record of fishing vessels" means a record of fishing vessels in which are recorded pertinent details of the fishing vessel. It may constitute a separate record for fishing vessels or form part of a general record of vessels;
(e) "regional economic integration organization" means a regional economic integration organization to which its Member States have transferred

competence over matters covered by this Agreement, including the authority to make decisions binding on its Member States in respect of those matters;
(f) "vessels entitled to fly its flag" and "vessels entitled to fly the flag of a State", includes vessels entitled to fly the flag of a Member State of a regional economic integration organization.

ARTICLE II

Application

1. Subject to the following paragraphs of this Article, this Agreement shall apply to all fishing vessels that are used or intended for fishing on the high seas.
2. A Party may exempt fishing vessels of less than 24 metres in length entitled to fly its flag from the application of this Agreement unless the Party determines that such an exemption would undermine the object and purpose of this Agreement, provided that such exemptions:

(a) shall not be granted in respect of fishing vessels operating in fishing regions referred to in paragraph 3 below, other than fishing vessels that are entitled to fly the flag of a coastal State of that fishing region; and

(b) shall not apply to the obligations undertaken by a Party under paragraph 1 of Article III, or paragraph 7 of Article VI of this Agreement.

3. Without prejudice to the provisions of paragraph 2 above, in any fishing region where bordering coastal States have not yet declared exclusive economic zones, or equivalent zones of national jurisdiction over fisheries, such coastal States as are Parties to this Agreement may agree, either directly or through appropriate regional fisheries organizations, to establish a minimum length of fishing vessels below which this Agreement shall not apply in respect of fishing vessels flying the flag of any such coastal State and operating exclusively in such fishing region.

ARTICLE III

Flag State Responsibility

1.

(a) Each Party shall take such measures as may be necessary to ensure that fishing vessels entitled to fly its flag do not engage in any activity that undermines the effectiveness of international conservation and management measures.

(b) In the event that a Party has, pursuant to paragraph 2 of Article II, granted an exemption for fishing vessels of less than 24 metres in length entitled to fly its flag from the application of other provisions of this Agreement, such Party shall nevertheless take effective measures in respect of any such fishing vessel that undermines the effectiveness of international conservation and management measures. These measures shall be such as to ensure that the fishing vessel ceases to engage in activities that undermine the effectiveness of the international conservation and management measures.

2. In particular, no Party shall allow any fishing vessel entitled to fly its flag to be used for fishing on the high seas unless it has been authorized to be so used by the appropriate authority or authorities of that Party. A fishing vessel so authorized shall fish in accordance with the conditions of the authorization.

3. No Party shall authorize any fishing vessel entitled to fly its flag to be used for fishing on the high seas unless the Party is satisfied that it is able, taking into account the links that exist between it and the fishing vessel concerned, to exercise effectively its responsibilities under this Agreement in respect of that fishing vessel.

4. Where a fishing vessel that has been authorized to be used for fishing on the high seas by a Party ceases to be entitled to fly the flag of that Party, the authorization to fish on the high seas shall be deemed to have been cancelled.

5.

(a) No Party shall authorize any fishing vessel previously registered in the territory of another Party that has undermined the effectiveness of international conservation and management measures to be used for fishing on the high seas, unless it is satisfied that

(i) any period of suspension by another Party of an authorization for such fishing vessel to be used for fishing on the high seas has expired; and

(ii) no authorization for such fishing vessel to be used for fishing on the high seas has been withdrawn by another Party within the last three years.

(b) The provisions of subparagraph (a) above shall also apply in respect of fishing vessels previously registered in the territory of a State which is not a Party to this Agreement, provided that sufficient information is available to the Party concerned on the circumstances in which the authorization to fish was suspended or withdrawn.

(c) The provisions of subparagraphs (a) and (b) shall not apply where the ownership of the fishing vessel has subsequently changed, and the new owner has provided sufficient evidence demonstrating that the previous owner or operator has no further legal, beneficial or financial interest in, or control of, the fishing vessel.

(d) Notwithstanding the provisions of subparagraphs (a) and (b) above, a Party may authorize a fishing vessel, to which those subparagraphs would otherwise apply, to be used for fishing on the high seas, where the Party concerned, after having taken into account all relevant facts, including the circumstances in which the fishing authorization has been withdrawn by the other Party or State, has determined that to grant an authorization to use the vessel for fishing on the high seas would not undermine the object and purpose of this Agreement.

6. Each Party shall ensure that all fishing vessels entitled to fly its flag that it has entered in the record maintained under Article IV are marked in such a way that they can be readily identified in accordance with generally accepted standards, such as the FAO Standard Specifications for the Marking and Identification of Fishing Vessels.

7. Each Party shall ensure that each fishing vessel entitled to fly its flag shall provide it with such information on its operations as may be necessary to enable the Party to fulfil its obligations under this Agreement, including in particular information pertaining to the area of its fishing operations and to its catches and landings.

8. Each Party shall take enforcement measures in respect of fishing vessels entitled to fly its flag which act in contravention of the provisions of this Agreement, including, where appropriate, making the contravention of such provisions an offence under national legislation. Sanctions applicable in respect of such contraventions shall be of sufficient gravity as to be effective in securing compliance with the requirements of this Agreement and to deprive offenders of the benefits accruing from their illegal activities. Such sanctions shall, for serious offences, include refusal, suspension or withdrawal of the authorization to fish on the high seas.

ARTICLE IV

Records of Fishing Vessels

Each Party shall, for the purposes of this Agreement, maintain a record of fishing vessels entitled to fly its flag and authorized to be used for fishing on the high seas, and shall take such measures as may be necessary to ensure that all such fishing vessels are entered in that record.

ARTICLE V

International Cooperation

1. The Parties shall cooperate as appropriate in the implementation of this Agreement, and shall, in particular, exchange information, including evidentiary material, relating to activities of fishing vessels in order to assist the flag State in identifying those fishing vessels flying its flag reported to have engaged in activities undermining international conservation and management measures, so as to fulfil its obligations under Article III.

2. When a fishing vessel is voluntarily in the port of a Party other than its flag State, that Party, where it has reasonable grounds for believing that the fishing vessel has been used for an activity that undermines the effectiveness of international conservation and management measures, shall promptly notify the flag State accordingly. Parties may make arrangements regarding the undertaking by port States of such investigatory measures as may be considered

necessary to establish whether the fishing vessel has indeed been used contrary to the provisions of this Agreement.
3. The Parties shall, when and as appropriate, enter into cooperative agreements or arrangements of mutual assistance on a global, regional, subregional or bilateral basis so as to promote the achievement of the objectives of this Agreement.

ARTICLE VI

Exchange of Information

1. Each Party shall make readily available to FAO the following information with respect to each fishing vessel entered in the record required to be maintained under Article IV:

(a) name of fishing vessel, registration number, previous names (if known), and port of registry;
(b) previous flag (if any);
(c) International Radio Call Sign (if any);
(d) name and address of owner or owners;
(e) where and when built;
(f) type of vessel;
(g) length.

2. Each Party shall, to the extent practicable, make available to FAO the following additional information with respect to each fishing vessel entered in the record required to be maintained under Article IV:

(a) name and address of operator (manager) or operators (managers) (if any);
(b) type of fishing method or methods;
(c) moulded depth;
(d) beam;
(e) gross register tonnage;
(f) power of main engine or engines.

3. Each Party shall promptly notify to FAO any modifications to the information listed in paragraphs 1 and 2 of this Article.
4. FAO shall circulate periodically the information provided under paragraphs 1, 2, and 3 of this Article to all Parties, and, on request, individually to any Party. FAO shall also, subject to any restrictions imposed by the Party concerned regarding the distribution of information, provide such information on request individually to any global, regional or subregional fisheries organization.
5. Each Party shall also promptly inform FAO of -

(a) any additions to the record;
(b) any deletions from the record by reason of -
(i) the voluntary relinquishment or nonrenewal of the fishing authorization by the fishing vessel owner or operator;

(ii) the withdrawal of the fishing authorization issued in respect of the fishing vessel under paragraph 8 of Article III;

(iii) the fact that the fishing vessel concerned is no longer entitled to fly its flag;

(iv) the scrapping, decommissioning or loss of the fishing vessel concerned; or

(v) any other reason.

6. Where information is given to FAO under paragraph 5(b) above, the Party concerned shall specify which of the reasons listed in that paragraph is applicable.

7. Each Party shall inform FAO of

(a) any exemption it has granted under paragraph 2 of Article II, the number and type of fishing vessel involved and the geographical areas in which such fishing vessels operate; and

(b) any agreement reached under paragraph 3 of Article II.

8.

(a) Each Party shall report promptly to FAO all relevant information regarding any activities of fishing vessels flying its flag that undermine the effectiveness of international conservation and management measures, including the identity of the fishing vessel or vessels involved and measures imposed by the Party in respect of such activities. Reports on measures imposed by a Party may be subject to such limitations as may be required by national legislation with respect to confidentiality, including, in particular, confidentiality regarding measures that are not yet final.

(b) Each Party, where it has reasonable grounds to believe that a fishing vessel not entitled to fly its flag has engaged in any activity that undermines the effectiveness of international conservation and management measures, shall draw this to the attention of the flag State concerned and may, as appropriate, draw it to the attention of FAO. It shall provide the flag State with full supporting evidence and may provide FAO with a summary of such evidence. FAO shall not circulate such information until such time as the flag State has had an opportunity to comment on the allegation and evidence submitted, or to object as the case may be.

9. Each Party shall inform FAO of any cases where the Party, pursuant to paragraph 5(d) of Article III, has granted an authorization notwithstanding the provisions of paragraph 5(a) or 5(b) of Article III. The information shall include pertinent data permitting the identification of the fishing vessel and the owner or operator and, as appropriate, any other information relevant to the Party's decision.

10. FAO shall circulate promptly the information provided under paragraphs 5, 6, 7, 8 and 9 of this Article to all Parties, and, on request, individually to any Party. FAO shall also, subject to any restrictions imposed by the Party concerned regarding the distribution of information, provide such

information promptly on request individually to any global, regional or subregional fisheries organization.

11. The Parties shall exchange information relating to the implementation of this Agreement, including through FAO and other appropriate global, regional and subregional fisheries organizations.

ARTICLE VII

Cooperation with Developing Countries

The Parties shall cooperate, at a global, regional, subregional or bilateral level, and, as appropriate, with the support of FAO and other international or regional organizations, to provide assistance, including technical assistance, to Parties that are developing countries in order to assist them in fulfilling their obligations under this Agreement.

ARTICLE VIII

NonParties

1. The Parties shall encourage any State not party to this Agreement to accept this Agreement and shall encourage any nonParty to adopt laws and regulations consistent with the provisions of this Agreement.
2. The Parties shall cooperate in a manner consistent with this Agreement and with international law to the end that fishing vessels entitled to fly the flags of nonParties do not engage in activities that undermine the effectiveness of international conservation and management measures.
3. The Parties shall exchange information amongst themselves, either directly or through FAO, with respect to activities of fishing vessels flying the flags of nonParties that undermine the effectiveness of international conservation and management measures.

ARTICLE IX

Settlement of Disputes

1. Any Party may seek consultations with any other Party or Parties on any dispute with regard to the interpretation or application of the provisions of this Agreement with a view to reaching a mutually satisfactory solution as soon as possible.
2. In the event that the dispute is not resolved through these consultations within a reasonable period of time, the Parties in question shall consult among themselves as soon as possible with a view to having the dispute settled by negotiation, inquiry, mediation, conciliation, arbitration, judicial settlement or other peaceful means of their own choice.
3. Any dispute of this character not so resolved shall, with the consent of all Parties to the dispute, be referred for settlement to the International Court of Justice, to the International Tribunal for the Law of the Sea upon entry into force of the 1982 United Nations Convention on the Law of the Sea or to

arbitration. In the case of failure to reach agreement on referral to the International Court of Justice, to the International Tribunal for the Law of the Sea or to arbitration, the Parties shall continue to consult and cooperate with a view to reaching settlement of the dispute in accordance with the rules of international law relating to the conservation of living marine resources.

ARTICLE X

Acceptance

1. This Agreement shall be open to acceptance by any Member or Associate Member of FAO, and to any nonmember State that is a Member of the United Nations, or of any of the specialized agencies of the United Nations or of the International Atomic Energy Agency.
2. Acceptance of this Agreement shall be effected by the deposit of an instrument of acceptance with the Director General of FAO, hereinafter referred to as the Director-General.
3. The Director General shall inform all Parties, all Members and Associate Members of FAO and the Secretary General of the United Nations of all instruments of acceptance received.
4. When a regional economic integration organization becomes a Party to this Agreement, such regional economic integration organization shall, in accordance with the provisions of Article II.7 of the FAO Constitution, as appropriate, notify such modifications or clarifications to its declaration of competence submitted under Article II.5 of the FAO Constitution as may be necessary in light of its acceptance of this Agreement. Any Party to this Agreement may, at any time, request a regional economic integration organization that is a Party to this Agreement to provide information as to which, as between the regional economic integration organization and its Member States, is responsible for the implementation of any particular matter covered by this Agreement. The regional economic integration organization shall provide this information within a reasonable time.

ARTICLE XI

Entry into Force

1. This Agreement shall enter into force as from the date of receipt by the Director-General of the twenty fifth instrument of acceptance.
2. For the purpose of this Article, an instrument deposited by a regional economic integration organization shall not be counted as additional to those deposited by Member States of such an organization.

ARTICLE XII

Reservations

Acceptance of this Agreement may be made subject to reservations which shall become effective only upon unanimous acceptance by all Parties to this

Agreement. The Director General shall notify forthwith all Parties of any reservation. Parties not having replied within three months from the date of the notification shall be deemed to have accepted the reservation. Failing such acceptance, the State or regional economic integration organization making the reservation shall not become a Party to this Agreement.

ARTICLE XIII

Amendments

1. Any proposal by a Party for the amendment of this Agreement shall be communicated to the Director General.
2. Any proposed amendment of this Agreement received by the Director General from a Party shall be presented to a regular or special session of the Conference for approval and, if the amendment involves important technical changes or imposes additional obligations on the Parties, it shall be considered by an advisory committee of specialists convened by FAO prior to the Conference.
3. Notice of any proposed amendment of this Agreement shall be transmitted to the Parties by the Director General not later than the time when the agenda of the session of the Conference at which the matter is to be considered is dispatched.
4. Any such proposed amendment of this Agreement shall require the approval of the Conference and shall come into force as from the thirtieth day after acceptance by two thirds of the Parties. Amendments involving new obligations for Parties, however, shall come into force in respect of each Party only on acceptance by it and as from the thirtieth day after such acceptance. Any amendment shall be deemed to involve new obligations for Parties unless the Conference in approving the amendment, decides otherwise by consensus.
5. The instruments of acceptance of amendments involving new obligations shall be deposited with the Director General, who shall inform all Parties of the receipt of acceptance and the entry into force of amendments.
6. For the purpose of this Article, an instrument deposited by a regional economic integration organization shall not be counted as additional to those deposited by Member States of such an organization.

ARTICLE XIV

Withdrawal

Any Party may withdraw from this Agreement at any time after the expiry of two years from the date upon which the Agreement entered into force with respect to that Party, by giving written notice of such withdrawal to the Director General who shall immediately inform all the Parties and the Members and Associate Members of FAO of such withdrawal. Withdrawal shall become effective at the end of the calendar year following that in which the notice of withdrawal has been received by the Director General.

ARTICLE XV

Duties of the Depositary

The Director General shall be the Depositary of this Agreement. The Depositary shall:

(a) send certified copies of this Agreement to each Member and Associate Member of FAO and to such nonmember States as may become Party to this Agreement;

(b) arrange for the registration of this Agreement, upon its entry into force, with the Secretariat of the United Nations in accordance with Article 102 of the Charter of the United Nations;

(c) inform each Member and Associate Member of FAO and any nonmember States as may become Party to this Agreement of:

(i) instruments of acceptance deposited in accordance with Article X;

(ii) the date of entry into force of this Agreement in accordance with Article XI;

(iii) proposals for and the entry into force of amendments to this Agreement in accordance with Article XIII;

(iv) withdrawals from this Agreement pursuant to Article XIV.

ARTICLE XVI

Authentic Texts

The Arabic, Chinese, English, French, and Spanish texts of this Agreement are equally authentic.

Code of Conduct for Responsible Fisheries

PREFACE

From ancient times, fishing has been a major source of food for humanity and a provider of employment and economic benefits to those engaged in this activity. The wealth of aquatic resources was assumed to be an unlimited gift of nature. However, with increased knowledge and the dynamic development of fisheries after the second world war, this myth has faded in face of the realization that aquatic resources, although renewable, are not infinite and need to be properly managed, if their contribution to the nutritional, economic and social well-being of the growing world's population is to be sustained.

The widespread introduction in the mid-seventies of exclusive economic zones (EEZs) and the adoption in 1982, after long deliberations, of the United Nations Convention on the Law of the Sea provided a new framework for the better management of marine resources. The new legal regime of the ocean gave coastal States rights and responsibilities for the management and use of fishery resources within their EEZs which embrace some 90 percent of the world's marine fisheries. Such extended national jurisdiction was a necessary but insufficient step toward the efficient management and sustainable development of fisheries. Many coastal States continued to face serious challenges as, lacking experience and financial and physical resources, they sought to extract greater benefits from the fisheries within their EEZs.

In recent years, world fisheries have become a market-driven, dynamically developing sector of the food industry and coastal States have striven to take advantage of their new opportunities by investing in modern fishing fleets and processing factories in response to growing international demand for fish and fishery products. By the late 1980s it became clear, however, that fisheries resources could no longer sustain such rapid and often uncontrolled exploitation and development, and that new approaches to fisheries management embracing conservation and environmental considerations were urgently needed. The situation was aggravated by the realization that unregulated fisheries on the high seas, in some cases involving straddling and highly migratory fish species, which occur within and outside EEZs, were becoming a matter of increasing concern.

The Committee on Fisheries (COFI) at its Nineteenth Session in March 1991 called for the development of new concepts which would lead to responsible, sustained fisheries. Subsequently, the International Conference on Responsible Fishing, held in 1992 in Cancûn (Mexico) further requested FAO to prepare an international Code of Conduct to address these concerns. The outcome of this Conference, particularly the Declaration of Cancûn, was an important contribution to the 1992 United Nations Conference on Environment and Development (UNCED), in particular its Agenda 21. Subsequently, the United Nations Conference on Straddling Fish Stocks and Highly Migratory Fish Stocks was convened, to which FAO provided important technical back-up. In November 1993, the Agreement to Promote Compliance with International Conservation and Management Measures by Fishing Vessels on the High Seas was adopted at the Twenty-seventh Session of the FAO Conference (Annex 1).

Noting these and other important developments in world fisheries, the FAO Governing Bodies recommended the formulation of a global Code of Conduct for Responsible Fisheries which would be consistent with these instruments and, in a non-mandatory manner, establish principles and standards applicable to the conservation, management and development of all fisheries. The Code, which was unanimously adopted on 31 October 1995 by the FAO Conference, provides a necessary framework for national and international efforts to ensure sustainable exploitation of aquatic living resources in harmony with the environment (Annex 2).

FAO, in accordance with its mandate, is fully committed to assisting Member States, particularly developing countries, in the efficient implementation of the Code of Conduct for Responsible Fisheries and will report to the United Nations community on the progress achieved and further action required.

INTRODUCTION

Fisheries, including aquaculture, provide a vital source of food, employment, recreation, trade and economic well being for people throughout the world, both for present and future generations and should therefore be conducted in a responsible manner. This Code sets out principles and international standards of behaviour for responsible practices with a view to ensuring the effective conservation, management and development of living aquatic resources, with due respect for the ecosystem and biodiversity. The Code recognises the nutritional, economic, social, environmental and cultural importance of fisheries, and the interests of all those concerned with the fishery sector. The Code takes into account the biological characteristics of the resources and their environment and the interests of consumers and other users. States and all those involved in fisheries are encouraged to apply the Code and give effect to it.

---

1 - NATURE AND SCOPE OF THE CODE

1.1 This Code is voluntary. However, certain parts of it are based on relevant rules of international law, including those reflected in the United Nations Convention on the Law of the Sea of 10 December 1982.[1] The Code also contains provisions that may be or have already been given binding effect by means of other obligatory legal instruments amongst the Parties, such as the Agreement to Promote Compliance with International Conservation and Management Measures by Fishing Vessels on the High Seas, 1993, which, according to FAO Conference resolution 15/93, paragraph 3, forms an integral part of the Code.

1.2 The Code is global in scope, and is directed toward members and non-members of FAO, fishing entities, subregional, regional and global organizations, whether governmental or non-governmental, and all persons concerned with the conservation of fishery resources and management and development of fisheries, such as fishers, those engaged in processing and marketing of

---

[1] References in this Code to the United Nations Convention on the Law of the Sea, 1982, or to other international agreements do not prejudice the position of any State with respect to signature, ratification or accession to the Convention or with respect to such other agreements

fish and fishery products and other users of the aquatic environment in relation to fisheries.

1.3 The Code provides principles and standards applicable to the conservation, management and development of all fisheries. It also covers the capture, processing and trade of fish and fishery products, fishing operations, aquaculture, fisheries research and the integration of fisheries into coastal area management.

1.4 In this Code, the reference to States includes the European Community in matters within its competence, and the term fisheries applies equally to capture fisheries and aquaculture.

ARTICLE 2 - OBJECTIVES OF THE CODE

The objectives of the Code are to:

a. establish principles, in accordance with the relevant rules of international law, for responsible fishing and fisheries activities, taking into account all their relevant biological, technological, economic, social, environmental and commercial aspects;

b. establish principles and criteria for the elaboration and implementation of national policies for responsible conservation of fisheries resources and fisheries management and development;

c. serve as an instrument of reference to help States to establish or to improve the legal and institutional framework required for the exercise of responsible fisheries and in the formulation and implementation of appropriate measures;

d. provide guidance which may be used where appropriate in the formulation and implementation of international agreements and other legal instruments, both binding and voluntary;

e. facilitate and promote technical, financial and other cooperation in conservation of fisheries resources and fisheries management and development;

f. promote the contribution of fisheries to food security and food quality, giving priority to the nutritional needs of local communities;

g. promote protection of living aquatic resources and their environments and coastal areas;

h. promote the trade of fish and fishery products in conformity with relevant international rules and avoid the use of measures that constitute hidden barriers to such trade;

i. promote research on fisheries as well as on associated ecosystems and relevant environmental factors; and

j. provide standards of conduct for all persons involved in the fisheries sector.

---

3 - RELATIONSHIP WITH OTHER INTERNATIONAL INSTRUMENTS

3.1 The Code is to be interpreted and applied in conformity with the relevant rules of international law, as reflected in the United Nations Convention on the Law of the Sea, 1982. Nothing in this Code prejudices the rights, jurisdiction and duties of States under international law as reflected in the Convention.

3.2 The Code is also to be interpreted and applied:

a. in a manner consistent with the relevant provisions of the Agreement for the Implementation of the Provisions of the United Nations Convention on the Law of the Sea of 10 December 1982 Relating to the Conservation and Management of Straddling Fish Stocks and Highly Migratory Fish Stocks;

b. in accordance with other applicable rules of international law, including the respective obligations of States pursuant to international agreements to which they are party; and

c. in the light of the 1992 Declaration of Cancun, the 1992 Rio Declaration on Environment and Development, and Agenda 21 adopted by the United Nations Conference on Environment and Development (UNCED), in particular Chapter 17 of Agenda 21, and other relevant declarations and international instruments.

---

4 - IMPLEMENTATION, MONITORING AND UPDATING

4.1 All members and non-members of FAO, fishing entities and relevant subregional, regional and global organizations, whether governmental or non-governmental, and all persons concerned with the conservation, management and utilization of fisheries resources and trade in fish and fishery products should collaborate in the fulfilment and implementation of the objectives and principles contained in this Code.

4.2 FAO, in accordance with its role within the United Nations system, will monitor the application and implementation of the Code and its effects on fisheries and the Secretariat will report accordingly to the Committee on

Fisheries (COFI). All States, whether members or non-members of FAO, as well as relevant international organizations, whether governmental or non-governmental should actively cooperate with FAO in this work.

4.3 FAO, through its competent bodies, may revise the Code, taking into account developments in fisheries as well as reports to COFI on the implementation of the Code.

4.4 States and international organizations, whether governmental or non-governmental, should promote the understanding of the Code among those involved in fisheries, including, where practicable, by the introduction of schemes which would promote voluntary acceptance of the Code and its effective application.

---

5 - SPECIAL REQUIREMENTS OF DEVELOPING COUNTRIES

5.1 The capacity of developing countries to implement the recommendations of this Code should be duly taken into account.

5.2 In order to achieve the objectives of this Code and to support its effective implementation, countries, relevant international organizations, whether governmental or non-governmental, and financial institutions should give full recognition to the special circumstances and requirements of developing countries, including in particular the least-developed among them, and small island developing countries. States, relevant intergovernmental and non-governmental organizations and financial institutions should work for the adoption of measures to address the needs of developing countries, especially in the areas of financial and technical assistance, technology transfer, training and scientific cooperation and in enhancing their ability to develop their own fisheries as well as to participate in high seas fisheries, including access to such fisheries.

---

6 - GENERAL PRINCIPLES

6.1 States and users of living aquatic resources should conserve aquatic ecosystems. The right to fish carries with it the obligation to do so in a responsible manner so as to ensure effective conservation and management of the living aquatic resources.

6.2 Fisheries management should promote the maintenance of the quality, diversity and availability of fishery resources in sufficient quantities for present and future generations in the context of food security, poverty alleviation and sustainable development. Management measures should not only ensure the conservation of target species but also of species belonging to the same ecosystem or associated with or dependent upon the target species.

6.3 States should prevent overfishing and excess fishing capacity and should implement management measures to ensure that fishing effort is commensurate with the productive capacity of the fishery resources and their sustainable utilization. States should take measures to rehabilitate populations as far as possible and when appropriate.

6.4 Conservation and management decisions for fisheries should be based on the best scientific evidence available, also taking into account traditional knowledge of the resources and their habitat, as well as relevant environmental, economic and social factors. States should assign priority to undertake research and data collection in order to improve scientific and technical knowledge of fisheries including their interaction with the ecosystem. In recognizing the transboundary nature of many aquatic ecosystems, States should encourage bilateral and multilateral cooperation in research, as appropriate.

6.5 States and subregional and regional fisheries management organizations should apply a precautionary approach widely to conservation, management and exploitation of living aquatic resources in order to protect them and preserve the aquatic environment, taking account of the best scientific evidence available. The absence of adequate scientific information should not be used as a reason for postponing or failing to take measures to conserve target species, associated or dependent species and non-target species and their environment.

6.6 Selective and environmentally safe fishing gear and practices should be further developed and applied, to the extent practicable, in order to maintain biodiversity and to conserve the population structure and aquatic ecosystems and protect fish quality. Where proper selective and environmentally safe fishing gear and practices exist, they should be recognized and accorded a priority in establishing conservation and management measures for fisheries. States and users of aquatic ecosystems should minimize waste, catch of non-target species, both fish and non-fish species, and impacts on associated or dependent species.

6.7 The harvesting, handling, processing and distribution of fish and fishery products should be carried out in a manner which will maintain the nutritional value, quality and safety of the products, reduce waste and minimize negative impacts on the environment.

6.8 All critical fisheries habitats in marine and fresh water ecosystems, such as wetlands, mangroves, reefs, lagoons, nursery and spawning areas, should be protected and rehabilitated as far as possible and where necessary. Particular effort should be made to protect such habitats from destruction, degradation, pollution and other significant impacts resulting from human activities that threaten the health and viability of the fishery resources.

6.9 States should ensure that their fisheries interests, including the need for conservation of the resources, are taken into account in the multiple uses of the coastal zone and are integrated into coastal area management, planning and development.

6.10 Within their respective competences and in accordance with international law, including within the framework of subregional or regional fisheries conservation and management organizations or arrangements, States should ensure compliance with and enforcement of conservation and management measures and establish effective mechanisms, as appropriate, to monitor and control the activities of fishing vessels and fishing support vessels.

6.11 States authorizing fishing and fishing support vessels to fly their flags should exercise effective control over those vessels so as to ensure the proper application of this Code. They should ensure that the activities of such vessels do not undermine the effectiveness of conservation and management measures taken in accordance with international law and adopted at the national, subregional, regional or global levels. States should also ensure that vessels flying their flags fulfil their obligations concerning the collection and provision of data relating to their fishing activities.

6.12 States should, within their respective competences and in accordance with international law, cooperate at subregional, regional and global levels through fisheries management organizations, other international agreements or other arrangements to promote conservation and management, ensure responsible fishing and ensure effective conservation and protection of living aquatic resources throughout their range of distribution, taking into account the need for compatible measures in areas within and beyond national jurisdiction.

6.13 States should, to the extent permitted by national laws and regulations, ensure that decision making processes are transparent and achieve timely solutions to urgent matters. States, in accordance with appropriate procedures, should facilitate consultation and the effective participation of industry, fishworkers, environmental and other interested organizations in decision making with respect to the development of laws and policies related to fisheries management, development, international lending and aid.

6.14 International trade in fish and fishery products should be conducted in accordance with the principles, rights and obligations established in the World Trade Organization (WTO) Agreement and other relevant international agreements. States should ensure that their policies, programmes and practices related to trade in fish and fishery products do not result in obstacles to this trade, environmental degradation or negative social, including nutritional, impacts.

6.15 States should cooperate in order to prevent disputes. All disputes relating to fishing activities and practices should be resolved in a timely, peaceful and cooperative manner, in accordance with applicable international agreements or as may otherwise be agreed between the parties. Pending settlement of a dispute, the States concerned should make every effort to enter into provisional arrangements of a practical nature which should be without prejudice to the final outcome of any dispute settlement procedure.

6.16 States, recognising the paramount importance to fishers and fishfarmers of understanding the conservation and management of the fishery resources on which they depend, should promote awareness of responsible fisheries through education and training. They should ensure that fishers and fishfarmers are involved in the policy formulation and implementation process, also with a view to facilitating the implementation of the Code.

6.17 States should ensure that fishing facilities and equipment as well as all fisheries activities allow for safe, healthy and fair working and living conditions and meet internationally agreed standards adopted by relevant international organizations.

6.18 Recognizing the important contributions of artisanal and small- scale fisheries to employment, income and food security, States should appropriately protect the rights of fishers and fishworkers, particularly those engaged in subsistence, small-scale and artisanal fisheries, to a secure and just livelihood, as well as preferential access, where appropriate, to traditional fishing grounds and resources in the waters under their national jurisdiction.

6.19 States should consider aquaculture, including culture-based fisheries, as a means to promote diversification of income and diet. In so doing, States should ensure that resources are used responsibly and adverse impacts on the environment and on local communities are minimized.

---

7 - FISHERIES MANAGEMENT

7.1 General

7.1.1 States and all those engaged in fisheries management should, through an appropriate policy, legal and institutional framework, adopt measures for the long-term conservation and sustainable use of fisheries resources.

Conservation and management measures, whether at local, national, subregional or regional levels, should be based on the best scientific evidence available and be designed to ensure the long-term sustainability of fishery resources at levels which promote the objective of their optimum utilization and maintain their availability for present and future generations; short term considerations should not compromise these objectives.

7.1.2 Within areas under national jurisdiction, States should seek to identify relevant domestic parties having a legitimate interest in the use and management of fisheries resources and establish arrangements for consulting them to gain their collaboration in achieving responsible fisheries.

7.1.3 For transboundary fish stocks, straddling fish stocks, highly migratory fish stocks and high seas fish stocks, where these are exploited by two or more States, the States concerned, including the relevant coastal States in the case of straddling and highly migratory stocks, should cooperate to ensure effective conservation and management of the resources. This should be achieved, where appropriate, through the establishment of a bilateral, subregional or regional fisheries organization or arrangement.

7.1.4 A subregional or regional fisheries management organization or arrangement should include representatives of States in whose jurisdictions the resources occur, as well as representatives from States which have a real interest in the fisheries on the resources outside national jurisdictions. Where a subregional or regional fisheries management organization or arrangement exists and has the competence to establish conservation and management measures, those States should cooperate by becoming a member of such organization or a participant in such arrangement, and actively participate in its work.

7.1.5 A State which is not a member of a subregional or regional fisheries management organization or is not a participant in a subregional or regional fisheries management arrangement should nevertheless cooperate, in accordance with relevant international agreements and international law, in the conservation and management of the relevant fisheries resources by giving effect to any conservation and management measures adopted by such organization or arrangement.

7.1.6 Representatives from relevant organizations, both governmental and non-governmental, concerned with fisheries should be afforded the opportunity to take part in meetings of subregional and regional fisheries management organizations and arrangements as observers or otherwise, as appropriate, in accordance with the procedures of the organization or arrangement concerned. Such representatives should be given timely access to the records and reports of such meetings, subject to the procedural rules on access to them.

7.1.7 States should establish, within their respective competences and capacities, effective mechanisms for fisheries monitoring, surveillance, control and enforcement to ensure compliance with their conservation and management measures, as well as those adopted by subregional or regional organizations or arrangements.

7.1.8 States should take measures to prevent or eliminate excess fishing capacity and should ensure that levels of fishing effort are commensurate with the sustainable use of fishery resources as a means of ensuring the effectiveness of conservation and management measures.

7.1.9 States and subregional or regional fisheries management organizations and arrangements should ensure transparency in the mechanisms for fisheries management and in the related decision-making process.

7.1.10 States and subregional or regional fisheries management organizations and arrangements should give due publicity to conservation and management measures and ensure that laws, regulations and other legal rules governing their implementation are effectively disseminated. The bases and purposes of such measures should be explained to users of the resource in order to facilitate their application and thus gain increased support in the implementation of such measures.

7.2 Management objectives

7.2.1 Recognizing that long-term sustainable use of fisheries resources is the overriding objective of conservation and management, States and subregional or regional fisheries management organizations and arrangements should, inter alia, adopt appropriate measures, based on the best scientific evidence available, which are designed to maintain or restore stocks at levels capable of producing maximum sustainable yield, as qualified by relevant environmental and economic factors, including the special requirements of developing countries.

7.2.2 Such measures should provide inter alia that:

a. excess fishing capacity is avoided and exploitation of the stocks remains economically viable;

b. the economic conditions under which fishing industries operate promote responsible fisheries;

c. the interests of fishers, including those engaged in subsistence, small-scale and artisanal fisheries, are taken into account;

d. biodiversity of aquatic habitats and ecosystems is conserved and endangered species are protected;

e. depleted stocks are allowed to recover or, where appropriate, are actively restored;

f. adverse environmental impacts on the resources from human activities are assessed and, where appropriate, corrected; and

g. pollution, waste, discards, catch by lost or abandoned gear, catch of non-target species, both fish and non- fish species, and impacts on associated or dependent species are minimized, through measures including, to the extent practicable, the development and use of selective, environmentally safe and cost-effective fishing gear and techniques.

7.2.3 States should assess the impacts of environmental factors on target stocks and species belonging to the same ecosystem or associated with or dependent upon the target stocks, and assess the relationship among the populations in the ecosystem.

7.3 Management framework and procedures

7.3.1 To be effective, fisheries management should be concerned with the whole stock unit over its entire area of distribution and take into account previously agreed management measures established and applied in the same region, all removals and the biological unity and other biological characteristics of the stock. The best scientific evidence available should be used to determine, inter alia, the area of distribution of the resource and the area through which it migrates during its life cycle.

7.3.2 In order to conserve and manage transboundary fish stocks, straddling fish stocks, highly migratory fish stocks and high seas fish stocks throughout their range, conservation and management measures established for such stocks in accordance with the respective competences of relevant States or, where appropriate, through subregional and regional fisheries management organizations and arrangements, should be compatible. Compatibility should be achieved in a manner consistent with the rights, competences and interests of the States concerned.

7.3.3 Long-term management objectives should be translated into management actions, formulated as a fishery management plan or other management framework.

7.3.4 States and, where appropriate, subregional or regional fisheries management organizations and arrangements should foster and promote international cooperation and coordination in all matters related to fisheries, including information gathering and exchange, fisheries research, management and development.

7.3.5 States seeking to take any action through a non-fishery organization which may affect the conservation and management measures taken by a competent subregional or regional fisheries management organization or arrangement should consult with the latter, in advance to the extent practicable, and take its views into account.

7.4 Data gathering and management advice

7.4.1 When considering the adoption of conservation and management measures, the best scientific evidence available should be taken into account in order to evaluate the current state of the fishery resources and the possible impact of the proposed measures on the resources.

7.4.2 Research in support of fishery conservation and management should be promoted, including research on the resources and on the effects of climatic, environmental and socio-economic factors. The results of such research should be disseminated to interested parties.

7.4.3 Studies should be promoted which provide an understanding of the costs, benefits and effects of alternative management options designed to rationalize fishing, in particular, options relating to excess fishing capacity and excessive levels of fishing effort.

7.4.4 States should ensure that timely, complete and reliable statistics on catch and fishing effort are collected and maintained in accordance with applicable international standards and practices and in sufficient detail to allow sound statistical analysis. Such data should be updated regularly and verified through an appropriate system. States should compile and disseminate such data in a manner consistent with any applicable confidentiality requirements.

7.4.5 In order to ensure sustainable management of fisheries and to enable social and economic objectives to be achieved, sufficient knowledge of social, economic and institutional factors should be developed through data gathering, analysis and research.

7.4.6 States should compile fishery-related and other supporting scientific data relating to fish stocks covered by subregional or regional fisheries management organizations or arrangements in an internationally agreed format and provide them in a timely manner to the organization or arrangement. In cases of stocks which occur in the jurisdiction of more than one State and for which there is no such organization or arrangement, the States concerned should agree on a mechanism for cooperation to compile and exchange such data.

7.4.7 Subregional or regional fisheries management organizations or arrangements should compile data and make them available, in a manner consistent with any applicable confidentiality requirements, in a timely manner and in an agreed format to all members of these organizations and other interested parties in accordance with agreed procedures.

7.5 Precautionary approach

7.5.1 States should apply the precautionary approach widely to conservation, management and exploitation of living aquatic resources in order to protect them and preserve the aquatic environment. The absence of adequate scientific information should not be used as a reason for postponing or failing to take conservation and management measures.

7.5.2 In implementing the precautionary approach, States should take into account, inter alia, uncertainties relating to the size and productivity of the stocks, reference points, stock condition in relation to such reference points, levels and distribution of fishing mortality and the impact of fishing activities, including discards, on non-target and associated or dependent species, as well as environmental and socio-economic conditions.

7.5.3 States and subregional or regional fisheries management organizations and arrangements should, on the basis of the best scientific evidence available, inter alia, determine:

a. stock specific target reference points, and, at the same time, the action to be taken if they are exceeded; and

b. stock-specific limit reference points, and, at the same time, the action to be taken if they are exceeded; when a limit reference point is approached, measures should be taken to ensure that it will not be exceeded.

7.5.4 In the case of new or exploratory fisheries, States should adopt as soon as possible cautious conservation and management measures, including, inter alia, catch limits and effort limits. Such measures should remain in force until there are sufficient data to allow assessment of the impact of the fisheries on the long-term sustainability of the stocks, whereupon conservation and management measures based on that assessment should be implemented. The latter measures should, if appropriate, allow for the gradual development of the fisheries.

7.5.5 If a natural phenomenon has a significant adverse impact on the status of living aquatic resources, States should adopt conservation and management measures on an emergency basis to ensure that fishing activity does not exacerbate such adverse impact. States should also adopt such measures on an emergency basis where fishing activity presents a serious threat to the sustainability of such resources. Measures taken on an emergency basis should be temporary and should be based on the best scientific evidence available.

7.6 Management measures

7.6.1 States should ensure that the level of fishing permitted is commensurate with the state of fisheries resources.

7.6.2 States should adopt measures to ensure that no vessel be allowed to fish unless so authorized, in a manner consistent with international law for the high seas or in conformity with national legislation within areas of national jurisdiction.

7.6.3 Where excess fishing capacity exists, mechanisms should be established to reduce capacity to levels commensurate with the sustainable use of fisheries resources so as to ensure that fishers operate under economic conditions that promote responsible fisheries. Such mechanisms should include monitoring the capacity of fishing fleets.

7.6.4 The performance of all existing fishing gear, methods and practices should be examined and measures taken to ensure that fishing gear, methods and practices which are not consistent with responsible fishing are phased out and replaced with more acceptable alternatives. In this process, particular attention should be given to the impact of such measures on fishing communities, including their ability to exploit the resource.

7.6.5 States and fisheries management organizations and arrangements should regulate fishing in such a way as to avoid the risk of conflict among fishers using different vessels, gear and fishing methods.

7.6.6 When deciding on the use, conservation and management of fisheries resources, due recognition should be given, as appropriate, in accordance with national laws and regulations, to the traditional practices, needs and interests of indigenous people and local fishing communities which are highly dependent on fishery resources for their livelihood.

7.6.7 In the evaluation of alternative conservation and management measures, their cost-effectiveness and social impact should be considered.

7.6.8 The efficacy of conservation and management measures and their possible interactions should be kept under continuous review. Such measures should, as appropriate, be revised or abolished in the light of new information.

7.6.9 States should take appropriate measures to minimize waste, discards, catch by lost or abandoned gear, catch of non-target species, both fish and non-fish species, and negative impacts on associated or dependent species, in particular endangered species. Where appropriate, such measures may include technical measures related to fish size, mesh size or gear, discards, closed seasons and areas and zones reserved for selected fisheries, particularly artisanal fisheries. Such measures should be applied, where appropriate, to protect juveniles and spawners. States and subregional or regional fisheries management organizations and arrangements should promote, to the extent practicable, the development and use of selective, environmentally safe and cost effective gear and techniques.

7.6.10 States and subregional and regional fisheries management organizations and arrangements, in the framework of their respective competences, should introduce measures for depleted resources and those resources threatened with depletion that facilitate the sustained recovery of such stocks. They should make every effort to ensure that resources and habitats critical to the well-being of such resources which have been adversely affected by fishing or other human activities are restored.

7.7 Implementation

7.7.1 States should ensure that an effective legal and administrative framework at the local and national level, as appropriate, is established for fisheries resource conservation and fisheries management.

7.7.2 States should ensure that laws and regulations provide for sanctions applicable in respect of violations which are adequate in severity to be effective, including sanctions which allow for the refusal, withdrawal or suspension of authorizations to fish in the event of non-compliance with conservation and management measures in force.

7.7.3 States, in conformity with their national laws, should implement effective fisheries monitoring, control, surveillance and law enforcement measures including, where appropriate, observer programmes, inspection schemes and vessel monitoring systems. Such measures should be promoted and, where appropriate, implemented by subregional or regional fisheries management organizations and arrangements in accordance with procedures agreed by such organizations or arrangements.

7.7.4 States and subregional or regional fisheries management organizations and arrangements, as appropriate, should agree on the means by which the activities of such organizations and arrangements will be financed, bearing in mind, inter alia, the relative benefits derived from the fishery and the differing capacities of countries to provide financial and other contributions. Where appropriate, and when possible, such organizations and arrangements should aim to recover the costs of fisheries conservation, management and research.

7.7.5 States which are members of or participants in subregional or regional fisheries management organizations or arrangements should implement internationally agreed measures adopted in the framework of such organizations or arrangements and consistent with international law to deter the activities of vessels flying the flag of non-members or non-participants which engage in activities which undermine the effectiveness of conservation and management measures established by such organizations or arrangements.

7.8 Financial institutions

7.8.1 Without prejudice to relevant international agreements, States should encourage banks and financial institutions not to require, as a condition of a loan or mortgage, fishing vessels or fishing support vessels to be flagged in a jurisdiction other than that of the State of beneficial ownership where such a requirement would have the effect of increasing the likelihood of non-compliance with international conservation and management measures.

---

8 - FISHING OPERATIONS

8.1 Duties of all States

8.1.1 States should ensure that only fishing operations allowed by them are conducted within waters under their jurisdiction and that these operations are carried out in a responsible manner.

8.1.2 States should maintain a record, updated at regular intervals, on all authorizations to fish issued by them.

8.1.3 States should maintain, in accordance with recognized international standards and practices, statistical data, updated at regular intervals, on all fishing operations allowed by them.

8.1.4 States should, in accordance with international law, within the framework of subregional or regional fisheries management organizations or arrangements, cooperate to establish systems for monitoring, control, surveillance and enforcement of applicable measures with respect to fishing operations and related activities in waters outside their national jurisdiction.

8.1.5 States should ensure that health and safety standards are adopted for everyone employed in fishing operations. Such standards should be not less than the minimum requirements of relevant international agreements on conditions of work and service.

8.1.6 States should make arrangements individually, together with other States or with the appropriate international organization to integrate fishing operations into maritime search and rescue systems.

8.1.7 States should enhance through education and training programmes the education and skills of fishers and, where appropriate, their professional qualifications. Such programmes should take into account agreed international standards and guidelines.

8.1.8 States should, as appropriate, maintain records of fishers which should, whenever possible, contain information on their service and qualifications, including certificates of competency, in accordance with their national laws.

8.1.9 States should ensure that measures applicable in respect of masters and other officers charged with an offence relating to the operation of fishing vessels should include provisions which may permit, inter alia, refusal, withdrawal or suspension of authorizations to serve as masters or officers of a fishing vessel.

8.1.10 States, with the assistance of relevant international organizations, should endeavour to ensure through education and training that all those engaged in fishing operations be given information on the most important provisions of this Code, as well as provisions of relevant international conventions and applicable environmental and other standards that are essential to ensure responsible fishing operations.

8.2 Flag State duties

8.2.1 Flag States should maintain records of fishing vessels entitled to fly their flag and authorized to be used for fishing and should indicate in such records details of the vessels, their ownership and authorization to fish.

8.2.2 Flag States should ensure that no fishing vessels entitled to fly their flag fish on the high seas or in waters under the jurisdiction of other States unless such vessels have been issued with a Certificate of Registry and have been authorized to fish by the competent authorities. Such vessels should carry on board the Certificate of Registry and their authorization to fish.

8.2.3 Fishing vessels authorized to fish on the high seas or in waters under the jurisdiction of a State other than the flag State, should be marked in accordance with uniform and internationally recognizable vessel marking systems such as the FAO Standard Specifications and Guidelines for Marking and Identification of Fishing Vessels.

8.2.4 Fishing gear should be marked in accordance with national legislation in order that the owner of the gear can be identified. Gear marking requirements should take into account uniform and internationally recognizable gear marking systems.

8.2.5 Flag States should ensure compliance with appropriate safety requirements for fishing vessels and fishers in accordance with international conventions, internationally agreed codes of practice and voluntary guidelines. States should adopt appropriate safety requirements for all small vessels not covered by such international conventions, codes of practice or voluntary guidelines.

8.2.6 States not party to the Agreement to Promote Compliance with International Conservation and Management Measures by Vessels Fishing in the High Seas should be encouraged to accept the Agreement and to adopt laws and regulations consistent with the provisions of the Agreement.

8.2.7 Flag States should take enforcement measures in respect of fishing vessels entitled to fly their flag which have been found by them to have contravened applicable conservation and management measures, including, where appropriate, making the contravention of such measures an offence under national legislation. Sanctions applicable in respect of violations should be adequate in severity to be effective in securing compliance and to discourage violations wherever they occur and should deprive offenders of the benefits accruing from their illegal activities. Such sanctions may, for serious violations, include provisions for the refusal, withdrawal or suspension of the authorization to fish.

8.2.8 Flag States should promote access to insurance coverage by owners and charterers of fishing vessels. Owners or charterers of fishing vessels should carry sufficient insurance cover to protect the crew of such vessels and their interests, to indemnify third parties against loss or damage and to protect their own interests.

8.2.9 Flag States should ensure that crew members are entitled to repatriation, taking account of the principles laid down in the "Repatriation of Seafarers Convention (Revised), 1987, (No.166)".

8.2.10 In the event of an accident to a fishing vessel or persons on board a fishing vessel, the flag State of the fishing vessel concerned should provide details of the accident to the State of any foreign national on board the vessel involved in the accident. Such information should also, where practicable, be communicated to the International Maritime Organization.

8.3 Port State duties

8.3.1 Port States should take, through procedures established in their national legislation, in accordance with international law, including applicable international agreements or arrangements, such measures as are necessary to achieve and to assist other States in achieving the objectives of this Code, and should make known to other States details of regulations and measures they have established for this purpose. When taking such measures a port State should not discriminate in form or in fact against the vessels of any other State.

8.3.2 Port States should provide such assistance to flag States as is appropriate, in accordance with the national laws of the port State and international law, when a fishing vessel is voluntarily in a port or at an offshore terminal of the port State and the flag State of the vessel requests the port State for assistance in respect of non- compliance with subregional, regional or global conservation and management measures or with internationally agreed minimum standards for the prevention of pollution and for safety, health and conditions of work on board fishing vessels.

8.4 Fishing activities

8.4.1 States should ensure that fishing is conducted with due regard to the safety of human life and the International Maritime Organization International Regulations for Preventing Collisions at Sea, as well as International Maritime Organization requirements relating to the organization of marine traffic, protection of the marine environment and the prevention of damage to or loss of fishing gear.

8.4.2 States should prohibit dynamiting, poisoning and other comparable destructive fishing practices.

8.4.3 States should make every effort to ensure that documentation with regard to fishing operations, retained catch of fish and non-fish species and, as regards discards, the information required for stock assessment as decided by relevant management bodies, is collected and forwarded systematically to those bodies. States should, as far as possible, establish programmes, such as observer and inspection schemes, in order to promote compliance with applicable measures.

8.4.4 States should promote the adoption of appropriate technology, taking into account economic conditions, for the best use and care of the retained catch.

8.4.5 States, with relevant groups from industry, should encourage the development and implementation of technologies and operational methods that reduce discards. The use of fishing gear and practices that lead to the discarding of catch should be discouraged and the use of fishing gear and practices that increase survival rates of escaping fish should be promoted.

8.4.6 States should cooperate to develop and apply technologies, materials and operational methods that minimize the loss of fishing gear and the ghost fishing effects of lost or abandoned fishing gear.

8.4.7 States should ensure that assessments of the implications of habitat disturbance are carried out prior to the introduction on a commercial scale of new fishing gear, methods and operations to an area.

8.4.8 Research on the environmental and social impacts of fishing gear and, in particular, on the impact of such gear on biodiversity and coastal fishing communities should be promoted.

8.5 Fishing gear selectivity

8.5.1 States should require that fishing gear, methods and practices, to the extent practicable, are sufficiently selective so as to minimize waste, discards, catch of non-target species, both fish and non-fish species, and impacts on associated or dependent species and that the intent of related regulations is not circumvented by technical devices. In this regard, fishers should cooperate in the development of selective fishing gear and methods. States should ensure that information on new developments and requirements is made available to all fishers.

8.5.2 In order to improve selectivity, States should, when drawing up their laws and regulations, take into account the range of selective fishing gear, methods and strategies available to the industry.

8.5.3 States and relevant institutions should collaborate in developing standard methodologies for research into fishing gear selectivity, fishing methods and strategies.

8.5.4 International cooperation should be encouraged with respect to research programmes for fishing gear selectivity, and fishing methods and strategies, dissemination of the results of such research programmes and the transfer of technology.

8.6 Energy optimization

8.6.1 States should promote the development of appropriate standards and guidelines which would lead to the more efficient use of energy in harvesting and post-harvest activities within the fisheries sector.

8.6.2 States should promote the development and transfer of technology in relation to energy optimization within the fisheries sector and, in particular, encourage owners, charterers and managers of fishing vessels to fit energy optimization devices to their vessels.

8.7 Protection of the aquatic environment

8.7.1 States should introduce and enforce laws and regulations based on the International Convention for the Prevention of Pollution from Ships, 1973, as modified by the Protocol of 1978 relating thereto (MARPOL 73/78).

8.7.2 Owners, charterers and managers of fishing vessels should ensure that their vessels are fitted with appropriate equipment as required by MARPOL 73/78 and should consider fitting a shipboard compactor or incinerator to relevant classes of vessels in order to treat garbage and other shipboard wastes generated during the vessel's normal service.

8.7.3 Owners, charterers and managers of fishing vessels should minimize the taking aboard of potential garbage through proper provisioning practices.

8.7.4 The crew of fishing vessels should be conversant with proper shipboard procedures in order to ensure discharges do not exceed the levels set by MARPOL 73/78. Such procedures should, as a minimum, include the disposal of oily waste and the handling and storage of shipboard garbage.

8.8 Protection of the atmosphere

8.8.1 States should adopt relevant standards and guidelines which would include provisions for the reduction of dangerous substances in exhaust gas emissions.

8.8.2 Owners, charterers and managers of fishing vessels should ensure that their vessels are fitted with equipment to reduce emissions of ozone depleting substances. The responsible crew members of fishing vessels should be conversant with the proper running and maintenance of machinery on board.

8.8.3 Competent authorities should make provision for the phasing out of the use of chlorofluorocarbons (CFCs) and transitional substances such as hydrochlorofluorocarbons (HCFCs) in the refrigeration systems of fishing vessels and should ensure that the shipbuilding industry and those engaged in the fishing industry are informed of and comply with such provisions.

8.8.4 Owners or managers of fishing vessels should take appropriate action to refit existing vessels with alternative refrigerants to CFCs and HCFCs and alternatives to Halons in fire fighting installations. Such alternatives should be used in specifications for all new fishing vessels.

8.8.5 States and owners, charterers and managers of fishing vessels as well as fishers should follow international guidelines for the disposal of CFCs, HCFCs and Halons.

8.9 Harbours and landing places for fishing vessels

8.9.1 States should take into account, inter alia, the following in the design and construction of harbours and landing places:

a. safe havens for fishing vessels and adequate servicing facilities for vessels, vendors and buyers are provided;
b. adequate freshwater supplies and sanitation arrangements should be provided;
c. waste disposal systems should be introduced, including for the disposal of oil, oily water and fishing gear;
d. pollution from fisheries activities and external sources should be minimized; and
e. arrangements should be made to combat the effects of erosion and siltation.

8.9.2 States should establish an institutional framework for the selection or improvement of sites for harbours for fishing vessels which allows for consultation among the authorities responsible for coastal area management.

8.10 Abandonment of structures and other materials

8.10.1 States should ensure that the standards and guidelines for the removal of redundant offshore structures issued by the International Maritime

Organization are followed. States should also ensure that the competent fisheries authorities are consulted prior to decisions being made on the abandonment of structures and other materials by the relevant authorities.

8.11 Artificial reefs and fish aggregation devices

8.11.1 States, where appropriate, should develop policies for increasing stock populations and enhancing fishing opportunities through the use of artificial structures, placed with due regard to the safety of navigation, on or above the seabed or at the surface. Research into the use of such structures, including the impacts on living marine resources and the environment, should be promoted.

8.11.2 States should ensure that, when selecting the materials to be used in the creation of artificial reefs as well as when selecting the geographical location of such artificial reefs, the provisions of relevant international conventions concerning the environment and safety of navigation are observed.

8.11.3 States should, within the framework of coastal area management plans, establish management systems for artificial reefs and fish aggregation devices. Such management systems should require approval for the construction and deployment of such reefs and devices and should take into account the interests of fishers, including artisanal and subsistence fishers.

8.11.4 States should ensure that the authorities responsible for maintaining cartographic records and charts for the purpose of navigation, as well as relevant environmental authorities, are informed prior to the placement or removal of artificial reefs or fish aggregation devices.

---

9 - AQUACULTURE DEVELOPMENT

- Article 9.1 Resp. dev. of aquaculture under national jurisdiction
- Article 9.2 Resp. dev. within transboundary aquatic ecosystems
- Article 9.3 Use of aquatic genetic resources
- Article 9.4 Responsible aquaculture at the production level

---

9.1 Responsible development of aquaculture, including culture-based fisheries, in areas under national jurisdiction

9.1.1 States should establish, maintain and develop an appropriate legal and administrative framework which facilitates the development of responsible aquaculture.

9.1.2 States should promote responsible development and management of aquaculture, including an advance evaluation of the effects of aquaculture development on genetic diversity and ecosystem integrity, based on the best available scientific information.

9.1.3 States should produce and regularly update aquaculture development strategies and plans, as required, to ensure that aquaculture development is ecologically sustainable and to allow the rational use of resources shared by aquaculture and other activities.

9.1.4 States should ensure that the livelihoods of local communities, and their access to fishing grounds, are not negatively affected by aquaculture developments.

9.1.5 States should establish effective procedures specific to aquaculture to undertake appropriate environmental assessment and monitoring with the aim of minimizing adverse ecological changes and related economic and social consequences resulting from water extraction, land use, discharge of effluents, use of drugs and chemicals, and other aquaculture activities.

9.2 Responsible development of aquaculture including culture-based fisheries within transboundary aquatic ecosystems

9.2.1 States should protect transboundary aquatic ecosystems by supporting responsible aquaculture practices within their national jurisdiction and by cooperation in the promotion of sustainable aquaculture practices.

9.2.2 States should, with due respect to their neighbouring States, and in accordance with international law, ensure responsible choice of species, siting and management of aquaculture activities which could affect transboundary aquatic ecosystems.

9.2.3 States should consult with their neighbouring States, as appropriate, before introducing non-indigenous species into transboundary aquatic ecosystems.

9.2.4 States should establish appropriate mechanisms, such as databases and information networks to collect, share and disseminate data related to their aquaculture activities to facilitate cooperation on planning for aquaculture development at the national, subregional, regional and global level.

9.2.5 States should cooperate in the development of appropriate mechanisms, when required, to monitor the impacts of inputs used in aquaculture.

9.3 Use of aquatic genetic resources for the purposes of aquaculture including culture-based fisheries

9.3.1 States should conserve genetic diversity and maintain integrity of aquatic communities and ecosystems by appropriate management. In particular, efforts should be undertaken to minimize the harmful effects of introducing non-native species or genetically altered stocks used for aquaculture including culture-based fisheries into waters, especially where there is a significant potential for the spread of such non-native species or genetically altered stocks into waters under the jurisdiction of other States as well as waters under the jurisdiction of the State of origin. States should, whenever possible, promote steps to minimize adverse genetic, disease and other effects of escaped farmed fish on wild stocks.

9.3.2 States should cooperate in the elaboration, adoption and implementation of international codes of practice and procedures for introductions and transfers of aquatic organisms.

9.3.3 States should, in order to minimize risks of disease transfer and other adverse effects on wild and cultured stocks, encourage adoption of appropriate practices in the genetic improvement of broodstocks, the introduction of non-native species, and in the production, sale and transport of eggs, larvae or fry, broodstock or other live materials. States should facilitate the preparation and implementation of appropriate national codes of practice and procedures to this effect.

9.3.4 States should promote the use of appropriate procedures for the selection of broodstock and the production of eggs, larvae and fry.

9.3.5 States should, where appropriate, promote research and, when feasible, the development of culture techniques for endangered species to protect, rehabilitate and enhance their stocks, taking into account the critical need to conserve genetic diversity of endangered species.

9.4 Responsible aquaculture at the production level

9.4.1 States should promote responsible aquaculture practices in support of rural communities, producer organizations and fish farmers.

9.4.2 States should promote active participation of fishfarmers and their communities in the development of responsible aquaculture management practices.

9.4.3 States should promote efforts which improve selection and use of appropriate feeds, feed additives and fertilizers, including manures.

9.4.4 States should promote effective farm and fish health management practices favouring hygienic measures and vaccines. Safe, effective and minimal use of therapeutants, hormones and drugs, antibiotics and other disease control chemicals should be ensured.

9.4.5 States should regulate the use of chemical inputs in aquaculture which are hazardous to human health and the environment.

9.4.6 States should require that the disposal of wastes such as offal, sludge, dead or diseased fish, excess veterinary drugs and other hazardous chemical inputs does not constitute a hazard to human health and the environment.

9.4.7 States should ensure the food safety of aquaculture products and promote efforts which maintain product quality and improve their value through particular care before and during harvesting and on-site processing and in storage and transport of the products.

ARTICLE 10 - INTEGRATION OF FISHERIES INTO COASTAL AREA MANAGEMENT

- Article 10.1 Institutional framework
- Article 10.2 Policy measures
- Article 10.3 Regional cooperation
- Article 10.4 Implementation of Coastal Area Management

10.1 Institutional framework

10.1.1 States should ensure that an appropriate policy, legal and institutional framework is adopted to achieve the sustainable and integrated use of the resources, taking into account the fragility of coastal ecosystems and the finite nature of their natural resources and the needs of coastal communities.

10.1.2 In view of the multiple uses of the coastal area, States should ensure that representatives of the fisheries sector and fishing communities are consulted in the decision-making processes and involved in other activities related to coastal area management planning and development.

10.1.3 States should develop, as appropriate, institutional and legal frameworks in order to determine the possible uses of coastal resources and to govern access to them taking into account the rights of coastal fishing communities and their customary practices to the extent compatible with sustainable development.

10.1.4 States should facilitate the adoption of fisheries practices that avoid conflict among fisheries resources users and between them and other users of the coastal area.

10.1.5 States should promote the establishment of procedures and mechanisms at the appropriate administrative level to settle conflicts which arise within the fisheries sector and between fisheries resource users and other users of the coastal area.

10.2 Policy measures

10.2.1 States should promote the creation of public awareness of the need for the protection and management of coastal resources and the participation in the management process by those affected.

10.2.2 In order to assist decision-making on the allocation and use of coastal resources, States should promote the assessment of their respective value taking into account economic, social and cultural factors.

10.2.3 In setting policies for the management of coastal areas, States should take due account of the risks and uncertainties involved.

10.2.4 States, in accordance with their capacities, should establish or promote the establishment of systems to monitor the coastal environment as part of the coastal management process using physical, chemical, biological, economic and social parameters.

10.2.5 States should promote multi-disciplinary research in support of coastal area management, in particular on its environmental, biological, economic, social, legal and institutional aspects.

10.3 Regional cooperation

10.3.1 States with neighbouring coastal areas should cooperate with one another to facilitate the sustainable use of coastal resources and the conservation of the environment.

10.3.2 In the case of activities that may have an adverse transboundary environmental effect on coastal areas, States should:

a. provide timely information and, if possible, prior notification to potentially affected States; and
b. consult with those States as early as possible.

10.3.3 States should cooperate at the subregional and regional level in order to improve coastal area management.

10.4 Implementation

10.4.1 States should establish mechanisms for cooperation and coordination among national authorities involved in planning, development, conservation and management of coastal areas.

10.4.2 States should ensure that the authority or authorities representing the fisheries sector in the coastal management process have the appropriate technical capacities and financial resources.

---

11 - POST-HARVEST PRACTICES AND TRADE

- Article 11.1 Responsible fish utilization
- Article 11.2 Responsible international trade
- Article 11.3 Laws and regulations relating to fish trade

11.1 Responsible fish utilization

11.1.1 States should adopt appropriate measures to ensure the right of consumers to safe, wholesome and unadulterated fish and fishery products.

11.1.2 States should establish and maintain effective national safety and quality assurance systems to protect consumer health and prevent commercial fraud.

11.1.3 States should set minimum standards for safety and quality assurance and make sure that these standards are effectively applied throughout the industry. They should promote the implementation of quality standards agreed within the context of the FAO/WHO Codex Alimentarius Commission and other relevant organizations or arrangements.

11.1.4 States should cooperate to achieve harmonization, or mutual recognition, or both, of national sanitary measures and certification programmes as appropriate and explore possibilities for the establishment of mutually recognized control and certification agencies.

11.1.5 States should give due consideration to the economic and social role of the post-harvest fisheries sector when formulating national policies for the sustainable development and utilization of fishery resources.

11.1.6 States and relevant organizations should sponsor research in fish technology and quality assurance and support projects to improve post-harvest handling of fish, taking into account the economic, social, environmental and nutritional impact of such projects.

11.1.7 States, noting the existence of different production methods, should through cooperation and by facilitating the development and transfer of appropriate technologies, ensure that processing, transporting and storage methods are environmentally sound.

11.1.8 States should encourage those involved in fish processing, distribution and marketing to:

a. reduce post-harvest losses and waste;
b. improve the use of by-catch to the extent that this is consistent with responsible fisheries management practices; and
c. use the resources, especially water and energy, in particular wood, in an environmentally sound manner.

11.1.9 States should encourage the use of fish for human consumption and promote consumption of fish whenever appropriate.

11.1.10 States should cooperate in order to facilitate the production of value-added products by developing countries.

11.1.11 States should ensure that international and domestic trade in fish and fishery products accords with sound conservation and management practices through improving the identification of the origin of fish and fishery products traded.

11.1.12 States should ensure that environmental effects of post- harvest activities are considered in the development of related laws, regulations and policies without creating any market distortions.

11.2 Responsible international trade

11.2.1 The provisions of this Code should be interpreted and applied in accordance with the principles, rights and obligations established in the World Trade Organization (WTO) Agreement.

11.2.2 International trade in fish and fishery products should not compromise the sustainable development of fisheries and responsible utilization of living aquatic resources.

11.2.3 States should ensure that measures affecting international trade in fish and fishery products are transparent, based, when applicable, on scientific evidence, and are in accordance with internationally agreed rules.

11.2.4 Fish trade measures adopted by States to protect human or animal life or health, the interests of consumers or the environment, should not be discriminatory and should be in accordance with internationally agreed trade rules, in particular the principles, rights and obligations established in the Agreement on the Application of Sanitary and Phytosanitary Measures and the Agreement on Technical Barriers to Trade of the WTO.

11.2.5 States should further liberalize trade in fish and fishery products and eliminate barriers and distortions to trade such as duties, quotas and non-tariff barriers in accordance with the principles, rights and obligations of the WTO Agreement.

11.2.6 States should not directly or indirectly create unnecessary or hidden barriers to trade which limit the consumer's freedom of choice of supplier or that restrict market access.

11.2.7 States should not condition access to markets to access to resources. This principle does not preclude the possibility of fishing agreements between States which include provisions referring to access to resources, trade and access to markets, transfer of technology, scientific research, training and other relevant elements.

11.2.8 States should not link access to markets to the purchase of specific technology or sale of other products.

11.2.9 States should cooperate in complying with relevant international agreements regulating trade in endangered species.

11.2.10 States should develop international agreements for trade in live specimens where there is a risk of environmental damage in importing or exporting States.

11.2.11 States should cooperate to promote adherence to, and effective implementation of relevant international standards for trade in fish and fishery products and living aquatic resource conservation.

11.2.12 States should not undermine conservation measures for living aquatic resources in order to gain trade or investment benefits.

11.2.13 States should cooperate to develop internationally acceptable rules or standards for trade in fish and fishery products in accordance with the principles, rights, and obligations established in the WTO Agreement.

11.2.14 States should cooperate with each other and actively participate in relevant regional and multilateral fora, such as the WTO, in order to ensure equitable, non-discriminatory trade in fish and fishery products as well as wide adherence to multilaterally agreed fishery conservation measures.

11.2.15 States, aid agencies, multilateral development banks and other relevant international organizations should ensure that their policies and practices related to the promotion of international fish trade and export production do not result in environmental degradation or adversely impact the nutritional rights and needs of people for whom fish is critical to their health and well being and for whom other comparable sources of food are not readily available or affordable.

11.3 Laws and regulations relating to fish trade

11.3.1 Laws, regulations and administrative procedures applicable to international trade in fish and fishery products should be transparent, as simple as possible, comprehensible and, when appropriate, based on scientific evidence.

11.3.2 States, in accordance with their national laws, should facilitate appropriate consultation with and participation of industry as well as environmental and consumer groups in the development and implementation of laws and regulations related to trade in fish and fishery products.

11.3.3 States should simplify their laws, regulations and administrative procedures applicable to trade in fish and fishery products without jeopardizing their effectiveness.

11.3.4 When a State introduces changes to its legal requirements affecting trade in fish and fishery products with other States, sufficient information and time should be given to allow the States and producers affected to introduce, as appropriate, the changes needed in their processes and procedures. In this connection, consultation with affected States on the time frame for implementation of the changes would be desirable. Due consideration should be given to requests from developing countries for temporary derogations from obligations.

11.3.5 States should periodically review laws and regulations applicable to international trade in fish and fishery products in order to determine whether the conditions which gave rise to their introduction continue to exist.

11.3.6 States should harmonize as far as possible the standards applicable to international trade in fish and fishery products in accordance with relevant internationally recognized provisions.

11.3.7 States should collect, disseminate and exchange timely, accurate and pertinent statistical information on international trade in fish and fishery products through relevant national institutions and international organizations.

11.3.8 States should promptly notify interested States, WTO and other appropriate international organizations on the development of and changes to laws, regulations and administrative procedures applicable to international trade in fish and fishery products.

---

12 - FISHERIES RESEARCH

12.1 States should recognize that responsible fisheries requires the availability of a sound scientific basis to assist fisheries managers and other interested parties in making decisions. Therefore, States should ensure that appropriate research is conducted into all aspects of fisheries including biology, ecology, technology, environmental science, economics, social science, aquaculture and nutritional science. States should ensure the availability of research facilities and provide appropriate training, staffing and institution building to conduct the research, taking into account the special needs of developing countries.

12.2 States should establish an appropriate institutional framework to determine the applied research which is required and its proper use.

12.3 States should ensure that data generated by research are analyzed, that the results of such analyses are published, respecting confidentiality where appropriate, and distributed in a timely and readily understood fashion, in order that the best scientific evidence is made available as a contribution to fisheries conservation, management and development. In the absence of adequate scientific information, appropriate research should be initiated as soon as possible.

12.4 States should collect reliable and accurate data which are required to assess the status of fisheries and ecosystems, including data on bycatch, discards and waste. Where appropriate, this data should be provided, at an appropriate time and level of aggregation, to relevant States and subregional, regional and global fisheries organizations.

12.5 States should be able to monitor and assess the state of the stocks under their jurisdiction, including the impacts of ecosystem changes resulting from fishing pressure, pollution or habitat alteration. They should also establish the research capacity necessary to assess the effects of climate or environment change on fish stocks and aquatic ecosystems.

12.6 States should support and strengthen national research capabilities to meet acknowledged scientific standards.

12.7 States, as appropriate in cooperation with relevant international organizations, should encourage research to ensure optimum utilization of fishery resources and stimulate the research required to support national policies related to fish as food.

12.8 States should conduct research into, and monitor, human food supplies from aquatic sources and the environment from which they are taken and ensure that there is no adverse health impact on consumers. The results of such research should be made publicly available.

12.9 States should ensure that the economic, social, marketing and institutional aspects of fisheries are adequately researched and that comparable data are generated for ongoing monitoring, analysis and policy formulation.

12.10 States should carry out studies on the selectivity of fishing gear, the environmental impact of fishing gear on target species and on the behaviour of target and non-target species in relation to such fishing gear as an aid for management decisions and with a view to minimizing non-utilized catches as well as safeguarding the biodiversity of ecosystems and the aquatic habitat.

12.11 States should ensure that before the commercial introduction of new types of gear, a scientific evaluation of their impact on the fisheries and ecosystems where they will be used should be undertaken. The effects of such gear introductions should be monitored.

12.12 States should investigate and document traditional fisheries knowledge and technologies, in particular those applied to small-scale fisheries, in order to assess their application to sustainable fisheries conservation, management and development.

12.13 States should promote the use of research results as a basis for the setting of management objectives, reference points and performance criteria, as well as for ensuring adequate linkages between applied research and fisheries management.

12.14 States conducting scientific research activities in waters under the jurisdiction of another State should ensure that their vessels comply with the laws and regulations of that State and international law.

12.15 States should promote the adoption of uniform guidelines governing fisheries research conducted on the high seas.

12.16 States should, where appropriate, support the establishment of mechanisms, including, inter alia, the adoption of uniform guidelines, to facilitate research at the subregional or regional level and should encourage the sharing of the results of such research with other regions.

12.17 States, either directly or with the support of relevant international organizations, should develop collaborative technical and research programmes to improve understanding of the biology, environment and status of transboundary aquatic stocks.

12.18 States and relevant international organizations should promote and enhance the research capacities of developing countries, inter alia, in the areas of data collection and analysis, information, science and technology, human resource development and provision of research facilities, in order for them to participate effectively in the conservation, management and sustainable use of living aquatic resources.

12.19 Competent international organizations should, where appropriate, render technical and financial support to States upon request and when engaged in research investigations aimed at evaluating stocks which have been previously unfished or very lightly fished.

12.20 Relevant technical and financial international organizations should, upon request, support States in their research efforts, devoting special attention to developing countries, in particular the least-developed among them and small island developing countries.

Annex 1

BACKGROUND TO THE ORIGIN AND ELABORATION OF THE CODE

1. This annex describes the process of elaboration and negotiation of the Code, which led to its submission for adoption to the Twenty-eighth Session of the FAO Conference. It has been felt useful to annex this section as a reference to the origin and the development of the Code and thus reflect the interest generated and the spirit of compromise of all the parties involved in its elaboration. It is hoped that this will contribute to the promotion of the commitment necessary for its implementation.

2. At various international fora, concern had long been expressed regarding the clear signs of over-exploitation of important fish stocks, damage to ecosystems, economic losses, and issues affecting fish trade - all of which threatened the long-term sustainability of fisheries and, in turn, harmed the contribution of fisheries to food supply. In discussing the current state and prospects of world fisheries, the Nineteenth Session of the FAO Committee

on Fisheries (COFI), held in March 1991, recommended that FAO should develop the concept of responsible fisheries and elaborate a Code of Conduct to this end.

3. Subsequently, the Government of Mexico, in collaboration with FAO, organized an International Conference on Responsible Fishing in Cancûn, in May 1992. The Declaration of Cancûn endorsed at that Conference further developed the concept of responsible fisheries, stating that "this concept encompasses the sustainable utilization of fisheries resources in harmony with the environment; the use of capture and aquaculture practices which are not harmful to ecosystems, resources or their quality; the incorporation of added value to such products through transformation processes meeting the required sanitary standards; the conduct of commercial practices so as to provide consumers access to good quality products".

4. The Cancûn Declaration was brought to the attention of the UNCED Rio Summit in June 1992, which supported the preparation of a Code of Conduct for Responsible Fisheries. The FAO Technical Consultation on High Seas Fishing, held in September 1992, further recommended the elaboration of a Code to address the issues regarding high seas fisheries.

5. The One Hundred and Second Session of the FAO Council, held in November 1992, discussed the elaboration of the Code, recommending that priority be given to high seas issues and requested that proposals for the Code be presented to the 1993 session of the Committee on Fisheries.

6. The Twentieth Session of COFI, held in March 1993, examined general principles for such a Code, including the elaboration of guidelines and endorsed a timeframe for the further elaboration of the Code. It also requested FAO to prepare, on a "fast track" basis, as part of the Code, proposals to prevent reflagging of fishing vessels which affect conservation and management measures on the high seas.

7. The further development of the Code of Conduct for Responsible Fisheries was accordingly carried out in consultation and collaboration with relevant United Nations Agencies and other international organizations including non-governmental organizations.

8. In pursuance of the instructions of the FAO Governing Bodies, the draft Code was formulated in such a way as to be consistent with the 1982 United Nations Convention on the Law of the Sea, taking into account the 1992 Declaration of Cancûn, the 1992 Rio Declaration and the provisions of Agenda 21 of UNCED, the conclusions and recommendations of the 1992 FAO Technical Consultation on High Seas Fishing, the Strategy endorsed by the 1984 FAO World Conference on Fisheries Management and Development, and other relevant instruments including the outcome of the then ongoing United Nations Conference on Straddling Fish Stocks and Highly Migratory Fish Stocks which, in August 1995, adopted an Agreement for the Implementation of the Provisions of the United Nations Convention on the

Law of the Sea of 10 December 1982 Concerning Straddling Fish Stocks and Highly Migratory Fish Stocks.

9. The FAO Conference, at its Twenty-seventh Session in November 1993, adopted the Agreement to Promote Compliance with International Conservation and Management Measures by Fishing Vessels on the High Seas and recommended that the General Principles of the Code of Conduct for Responsible Fisheries be prepared on a "fast track" in order to orientate formulation of thematic articles. Accordingly, a draft text of the General Principles was reviewed by an informal Working Group of Government-nominated experts, which met in Rome in February 1994. A revised draft was widely circulated to all FAO Members and Associate Members as well as intergovernmental and non-governmental organizations. Comments received on the second version of the General Principles were incorporated in the draft Code together with proposals for an alternative text. This document was also the subject of informal consultation with non-governmental organizations on the occasion of the Fourth Session of the United Nations Conference on Straddling Fish Stocks and Highly Migratory Fish Stocks, held in August 1994 in New York.

10. In order to facilitate consideration of the full text of the draft Code, the Director-General proposed to the Council at its Hundred and Sixth Session in June 1994, that a Technical Consultation on the Code of Conduct for Responsible Fishing be organized, open to all FAO Members, interested non-members, intergovernmental and non-governmental organizations, in order to provide an opportunity for the widest involvement of all concerned parties at an early stage of its elaboration.

11. This Technical Consultation took place in Rome from 26 September to 5 October 1994 and a draft for the entire Code and a first draft of technical guidelines to support most of the Thematic Articles of the Code were presented. Following a thorough review of all the Articles of the complete draft Code of Conduct, an Alternative Secretariat Draft was then prepared on the basis of comments made during the discussions in plenary and specific drafting changes submitted in writing during the Consultation.

12. The Consultation was able to review also in detail an alternative draft for three of the six Thematic Articles of the Code, i.e., Article 9 "Integration of Fisheries into Coastal Area Management", Article 6 "Fisheries Management", Article 7 "Fishing Operations", except for those principles which were likely to be affected by the outcome of the ongoing UN Conference on Straddling Fish Stocks and Highly Migratory Fish Stocks. A short Administrative Report was prepared and presented to the FAO Council and to COFI.

13. The Technical Consultation proposed to the Council at its Hundred and Seventh Session, 15–24 November 1994, that the final wording of those principles dealing mainly with high seas issues be left in abeyance pending the outcome of the UN Conference. The Council generally endorsed the proposed procedure, noting that following discussions at the next session of COFI, a final draft of the Code would be submitted to the FAO Council in

June 1995 which would then decide upon the necessity for a Technical Committee to meet in parallel to that Session of the Council in order to elaborate further the detailed provisions of the Code if required.

14. Based upon the substantial comments and detailed suggestions received at the Technical Consultation, the Secretariat elaborated a revised draft of the Code of Conduct for Responsible Fisheries, which was submitted to the Twenty-first Session of the Committee on Fisheries, held from 10 to 15 March 1995.

15. The Committee on Fisheries was also informed that the UN Conference was expected to conclude its work in August 1995. It was proposed that principles left in abeyance in the draft text of the Code could then be reconciled with the language agreed upon at the UN Conference in accordance with a mechanism to be decided upon by the Committee and the Council, before submission of the complete Code for its adoption at the Twenty-eighth Session of the FAO Conference in October 1995.

16. The Committee was informed of the various steps the Secretariat had undertaken in preparing the draft Code of Conduct. The Committee established an open-ended Working Group in order to review the draft text of the Code. The Working Group, which met from 10 to 14 March 1995, undertook a detailed revision of the draft Code in continuation of the work carried out by the Technical Consultation. It completed and approved the text of Articles 8 to 11. In view of the time constraints, the Working Group provided directives to the Secretariat to redraft Articles 1 to 5. It was also recommended that the elements of research and cooperation as well as aquaculture be included in Article 5, General Principles, to reflect issues developed in the Thematic Articles of the Code.

17. The Committee supported the proposal endorsed by the Hundred and Seventh Session of the Council on mechanisms to finalize the Code. The final wording of those principles dealing mainly with issues concerning straddling fish stocks and highly migratory fish stocks, which formed only a small part of the Code, should be re-examined in the light of the outcome of the UN Conference. The Group also recommended that once agreement was reached on the substance, it would be necessary to harmonize legal, technical and idiomatic aspects of the Code, in order to facilitate its final approval.

18. The Report of the open-ended Working Group was presented to a Ministerial Meeting on Fisheries, held on 14 and 15 March 1995, in conjunction with the COFI Session. The Rome Consensus on World Fisheries emanating from this meeting urged that "Governments and international organizations take prompt action to complete the International Code of Conduct for Responsible Fisheries with a view to submitting the final text to the FAO Conference in October 1995".

19. The Hundred and Eighth Session of the Council was presented with a revised version of the Code of Conduct. The Council established an

open-ended Technical Committee, which held its First Session from 5 to 9 June 1995, with a broad regional representation of members and observers. A number of intergovernmental and non-governmental organizations also participated.

20. The Council was informed by the Technical Committee that it had undertaken a thorough review of Articles 1 to 5 including the Introduction. It had also examined, amended and approved Articles 8 to 11. The Council was also informed that the Committee had started the revision of Article 6.

21. The Council approved the work carried out by the Technical Committee and endorsed its recommendation for a Second Session to be held from 25 to 29 September 1995 to complete the revision of the Code once the Secretariat had harmonized the text linguistically and juridically, taking into account the outcome of the UN Conference on Straddling Fish Stocks and Highly Migratory Fish Stocks.

22. A revised version of the Code as approved by the Open-ended Technical Committee at its First Session (5–9 June 1995) and endorsed by the One Hundred and Eighth Session of the Council was issued, both as a Conference document (C 95/20) and as a working paper for the Second Session of the Technical Committee. Elements pending agreement were clearly identified.

23. In order to facilitate the finalization of the entire Code, the Secretariat prepared the document "Secretariat Proposals for Article 6, Fisheries Management, and Article 7, Fishing Operations, of the Code of Conduct for Responsible Fisheries", taking into account the Agreement relating to the Conservation and Management of Straddling Fish Stocks and Highly Migratory Fish Stocks, adopted by the UN Conference in August 1995. The Secretariat also completed proposals for the harmonization of the text on legal and linguistic aspects and made this available to the Committee in three languages for the session (English, French and Spanish).

24. A Second Session of the Open-ended Technical Committee of the Council met from 25 to 29 September 1995, with a wide representation of regions and interested organizations. The Committee, working in a full spirit of collaboration, successfully concluded its mandate, finalizing and endorsing all Articles and the Code as a whole. The Technical Committee agreed that the negotiations of the text of the Code were finalized. An Open-ended Informal Group on Language Harmonization held an additional session and, together with the Secretariat, completed the harmonization on the basis of the text as adopted at the closing session. The Technical Committee instructed the Secretariat to already submit the finalized version as a revised Conference document to the Hundred and Ninth Session of the Council and to the Twenty-eighth Session of the Conference for its adoption. The Council endorsed the Code of Conduct as finalized by the Technical Committee. The Secretariat was requested to prepare the required draft resolution for the Conference, including also a call on countries to ratify, as a matter of urgency, the Compliance Agreement adopted at the last session of the Conference. The Twenty-eighth

Session of the Conference adopted on 31 October 1995, by consensus, the Code of Conduct for Responsible Fisheries and the respective Resolution.

Annex 2

RESOLUTION

THE CONFERENCE

Recognizing the vital role of fisheries in world food security, and economic and social development, as well as the need to ensure the sustainability of the living aquatic resources and their environment for present and future generations,

Recalling that the Committee on Fisheries on 19 March 1991 recommended the development of the concept of responsible fishing and the possible formulation of an instrument on the matter,

Considering that the Declaration of Cancún, which emanated from the International Conference on Responsible Fisheries of May 1992, organized by the Government of Mexico in collaboration with FAO, had called for the preparation of a Code of Conduct on Responsible Fisheries.

Bearing in mind that with the entry into force of the United Nations Convention on the Law of the Sea, 1982, and the adoption of the Agreement for the implementation of the provisions of the United Nations Convention on the Law of the Sea of 10 December 1982 Relating to the Conservation and Management of Straddling Fish Stocks and Highly Migratory Fish Stocks, as was anticipated in the 1992 Rio Declaration and the provisions of Agenda 21 of UNCED, there is an increased need for subregional and regional cooperation, and that significant responsibilities are placed upon FAO in accordance with its mandate,

Recalling further that the Conference in 1993 adopted the FAO Agreement to Promote Compliance with International Conservation and Management Measures by Fishing Vessels on the High Seas, and that this Agreement would constitute an integral part of the Code of Conduct,

Noting with satisfaction that FAO, in accordance with the decisions of its Governing Bodies, had organized a series of technical meetings to formulate the Code of Conduct, and that these meetings have resulted in agreement being reached on the text of the Code of Conduct for Responsible Fisheries,

Acknowledging that the Rome Consensus on World Fisheries, which emanated from the Ministerial Meeting on Fisheries of 14–15 March 1995, urged governments and international organizations to respond effectively to the current fisheries situation, inter alia, by completing the Code of Conduct for

Responsible Fisheries and to consider adopting the Agreement to Promote Compliance with International Conservation and Management Measures by Fishing Vessels on the High Seas:

1. Decides to adopt the Code of Conduct for Responsible Fisheries;

2. Calls on States, International Organizations, whether Governmental or Non-Governmental, and all those involved in fisheries to collaborate in the fulfilment and implementation of the objectives and principles contained in this Code;

3. Urges that special requirements of developing countries be taken into account in implementing the provisions of this Code;

4. Requests FAO to make provision in the Programme of Work and Budget for providing advice to developing countries in implementing this Code and for the elaboration of an Interregional Assistance Programme for external assistance aimed at supporting implementation of the Code;

5. Further requests FAO, in collaboration with members and interested relevant organizations, to elaborate, as appropriate, technical guidelines in support of the implementation of the Code;

6. Calls upon FAO to monitor and report on the implementation of the Code and its effects on fisheries, including action taken under other instruments and resolutions by UN organizations and, in particular, the resolutions adopted by the General Assembly to give effect to the Conference on Straddling Fish Stocks and Highly Migratory Fish Stocks leading to the Agreement for the implementation of the provisions of the United Nations Convention on the Law of the Sea of 10 December 1982 Relating to the Conservation and Management of Straddling Fish Stocks and Highly Migratory Fish Stocks;

7. Urges FAO to strengthen Regional Fisheries Bodies in order to deal more effectively with fisheries conservation and management issues in support of subregional, regional and global cooperation and coordination in fisheries.

UNITED NATIONS **A**

General Assembly

Distr.
GENERAL

A/CONF.164/35
20 September 1995

ORIGINAL: ENGLISH

UNITED NATIONS CONFERENCE ON
STRADDLING FISH STOCKS AND
HIGHLY MIGRATORY FISH STOCKS
Sixth session
New York, 24 July–4 August 1995

STATEMENT OF THE CHAIRMAN, AMBASSADOR SATYA N. NANDAN, ON 4 AUGUST 1995, UPON THE ADOPTION OF THE AGREEMENT FOR THE IMPLEMENTATION OF THE PROVISIONS OF THE UNITED NATIONS CONVENTION ON THE LAW OF THE SEA OF 10 DECEMBER 1982 RELATING TO THE CONSERVATION AND MANAGEMENT OF STRADDLING FISH STOCKS AND HIGHLY MIGRATORY FISH STOCKS

We have just adopted an historic instrument. You deserve hearty congratulations.

The instrument we have adopted is far-sighted, far-reaching, bold and revolutionary. It addresses the problems facing the international community in relation to the fisheries for straddling fish stocks and highly migratory fish stocks for which the Conference was requested to find answers. It takes account of the nature of the stocks and calls therefore for action not only at the national level, but also at the subregional, regional and global levels.

The content of the Agreement constitutes a substantive and effective response to the mandate given to the Conference by the General Assembly in its resolution 47/192 of 22 December 1992. Further, the Conference has recommended to the General Assembly to review developments relating to the conservation and management of straddling fish stocks and highly migratory fish stocks biennially, beginning in 1997. It has urged States to sign the Agreement and to ratify or accede to it. Thus, the Conference has discharged its mandate.

The provisions of the Agreement are practical and realistic. They are detailed, precise and sound and they are firmly based on the principles enshrined in the 1982 United Nations Convention on the Law of the Sea. The Agreement and the Convention are intrinsically linked and are inseparable. At the same time as the Agreement cannot stand without the Convention, it reinforces the foundation laid by the Convention. In many ways, it better secures the future of the Convention by dealing with problems raised in its implementation. This shows the dynamic nature of the process set in train by the elaboration of the Convention.

The link between the Agreement and the Convention is reflected not only in the very title of the Agreement and its preamble, but throughout its substantive provisions. Indeed, the negotiations were premised on the approach taken by all participants that the outcome must be in full accord with and build on the Convention.

The Agreement is built on three essential pillars. First, it sets out principles on which conservation and management of the stocks must be based and establishes that such management must be based on the precautionary approach and the best available scientific information.

The second pillar ensures that the conservation and management measures are adhered to and complied with, and that they are not undermined by those who fish for the stocks. For this purpose, the primary responsibility of the flag State is reaffirmed and the framework for action by States other than the flag States is set out with clear safeguards against abuse.

The third pillar is the provision for peaceful settlement of disputes. While providing for various possibilities of non-binding settlement, in the end result every dispute can be submitted to a court or tribunal for a binding decision.

In essence, this Agreement provides for the conservation and sustainable use of the fish resources in the oceans. In place of conflict, it provides a framework for cooperation in the conservation and management of those resources. It promotes the peaceful use of the oceans, a fundamental principle embodied in the 1982 United Nations Convention on the Law of the Sea which itself is derived from the purposes and principles of the Charter of the United Nations.

In providing for a framework that promotes good order in the oceans and the effective management and conservation of high seas resources, the Agreement, inter alia, establishes detailed minimum international standards for the conservation and management of the two types of stocks; ensures that the measures taken for the conservation and management of those stocks in areas under national jurisdiction and in the adjacent high seas are compatible and coherent; ensures that there are effective mechanisms for compliance and enforcement of those measures on the high seas; and recognizes the special requirements of developing States in relation to conservation and management as well as the development and participation in fisheries for the two types of stocks.

I need not remind the Conference that the Food and Agriculture Organization of the United Nations (FAO) has warned that disastrous social and economic consequences await the entire fishing industry unless fishing fleets are reduced in size, subsidies are eliminated and the activities of fishing fleets are more effectively regulated. The international community has waited with expectation for the outcome of this Conference. It is my considered opinion that the Agreement that has been adopted here for the conservation and management of straddling fish stocks and highly migratory fish stocks provides the necessary basis for the better management of these stocks.

The question might be asked, where would we be without the Agreement that has just been adopted? This is not an easy question to answer, but it is my belief that if we failed to adopt a strong and binding Agreement at this Conference, we would have failed the international community, and in so doing, would have contributed to the further demise of the major international fishery resources. I also believe that failure to agree on a strong and comprehensive regime would have promoted further conflict on the high seas and necessitated and encouraged some States to initiate unilateral action in their frustrated attempts to solve problems that can only be properly addressed multilaterally.

Under the Agreement, the general principles for conservation and management, the application of the precautionary approach and the requirements to set reference levels, the provisions on compatibility of conservation and management measures and the rules on data collection and exchange apply to fisheries within and beyond national jurisdiction. The conservation and management of straddling fish stocks and highly migratory fish stocks must, taking into account their biological unity, be the responsibility of all States concerned in a particular fishery. Improved standards for management are to be applied both within and beyond national jurisdiction. In respect of areas under national jurisdiction, there is an identifiable and accountable authority, that is, the coastal State. The responsibilities of the coastal State are clearly stated in the Convention and these have been further elaborated and reinforced in this Agreement in terms of better management standards and practices that are to be applied.

One of the cornerstones of the Agreement is the provision to ensure compatibility of conservation and management measures throughout the range of stocks. In this sense, the scope of the Agreement is broad enough to embrace resources as a whole, while fully respecting the different jurisdictional responsibilities. No one should escape from the conservation and management principles of the Agreement.

Sound fisheries conservation management requires high-quality data that are comprehensive and available to fisheries managers in a timely manner. The Agreement provides the necessary framework for the collection, provision and exchange of data to ensure proper conservation and management of straddling fish stocks and highly migratory fish stocks.

While acknowledging the consensus reached on the Agreement, we are all very much aware that substantial effort will be required to ensure that its provisions are implemented in a sustained and complete manner. States parties to the Agreement will be required to take specific action at the national level to implement the Agreement. Some States, in particular developing States which lack domestic administrative and financial capacity, will require assistance for this purpose.

The Agreement clearly recognizes the needs of developing States and provides for certain forms of cooperation and the provision of special assistance in order to enable those States to fulfil their obligations. In this connection, international organizations such as the Food and Agriculture Organization of the United Nations will be called upon to provide important technical assistance in the implementation process. Moreover, it is anticipated that FAO will work closely with its own regional fishery bodies and non-FAO fishery bodies as a means of giving the Agreement practical effect.

Subregional or regional fisheries management organizations or arrangements will continue to play a pivotal role in the conservation and management of straddling fish stocks and highly migratory fish stocks. The Agreement gives prominence to those organizations and arrangements as the principal means for the implementation of measures designed to conserve and manage these two types of stocks. The full cooperation of the international community is imperative for this goal to be achieved.

The political leaders who met at the Rio Summit committed themselves to wide-ranging initiatives that would, inter alia, promote the sustainable use of natural resources, including the important and dwindling fish stocks. Consequently, since the 1992 United Nations Conference on Environment and Development, a number of important and complementary initiatives have been launched. These initiatives have the common goal of seeking to secure enhanced conservation and management of fisheries resources and to ensure that those resources, under all circumstances and in all regions of the world, are utilized in a sustainable manner.

We are indebted to the Food and Agriculture Organization of the United Nations for the technical advice it has provided the Conference. Outside our Conference, FAO is in the final stages of completing the Code of Conduct for Responsible Fisheries. I hope that that work will benefit from the results we have achieved here. The Agreement adopted by this Conference and the Code of Conduct will serve to strengthen conservation and management practice for fisheries around the world. The willingness of the international community to commit itself to these initiatives clearly illustrates the concern and goodwill of all States to achieve lasting measures to address the crises being faced in world fisheries.

I am greatly indebted to the Vice-Chairmen who have supported me so ably throughout this Conference. They have provided encouragement and advice at difficult times and made my role as Chairman all the easier.

I wish to pay special tribute to my colleagues from the Pacific - Peniasi Kunatuba, Mary Harwood, Michael Lodge and Talbot Murray. Their assistance to me has been unstinting and selfless. Without them, my own contribution would have been lacking. I wish to acknowledge their outstanding contribution to this Conference.

I must also pay tribute to those from the Secretariat who have assisted me throughout the Conference. I would like to pay particular attention to the Legal Counsel, Mr. Hans Corell, and the Director of the Division for Ocean Affairs and the Law of the Sea, Mr. Jean-Pierre Levy; Mr. Moritaka Hayashi, Secretary of the Conference; to my Secretary, Ms. Cynthia Hardeman; to Ms. Josefa Velasco, Ms. Gabriele Göttsche, and to Messrs Vladimir Jares, Maurice Jorgens and André Tahindro, and the other members of the Secretariat, including those from Conference Services, who have assisted the Conference. I also acknowledge the assistance provided to me by Dr. David Doulman of FAO.

You should feel satisfied and proud of the results which we have achieved together at this Conference. The issues we had to deal with were real and sensitive and needed the urgent attention of the world community. You responded to this challenge in a constructive and practical manner. We have had among us lawyers, fisheries experts, representatives of intergovernmental and non-governmental organizations, including industry and conservation interests. All have had access to the process. Even in the smallest consultations, all have been able to participate and all have actively contributed. We have set a model for the interaction of the various interests involved in diplomatic negotiations.

You have conducted these negotiations in a practical and serious manner, free from rancour and polemics. As could be expected, we began these negotiations with trepidation as to the best way to fulfil our mandate, and as to the form in which the results would best be reflected.

As we became acquainted with the issues and each other's preoccupations, we became ever more convinced of the obvious fact that the problems were common, and also became confident that we could succeed in dealing with them as such. We recognized that it was in our interest to achieve a result which would not allow us to continue "business as usual".

As we went along, individual States became more and more committed to the process. The result we have achieved today reflects a strong common purpose - the long-term sustainability of fishery resources.

As individuals, you have demonstrated your dedication to this purpose. You have served your Governments and your people well, and as citizens of the world, you have earned the gratitude of present and future generations.

Our countries may be dispersed all over the globe, but we are joined together by one ocean. We must protect and preserve the ocean environment and its resources. In this connection, we should recall the origins of this Conference in the Rio Conference on Environment and Development.

We must now proceed to the rapid implementation of this Agreement. Governments must demonstrate their commitment in a tangible manner by signing the Agreement and becoming parties to it as early as possible.

It was a great personal honour for me to have been elected Chairman of the Conference. I deeply appreciate the confidence shown by delegations in electing me to this important office. I have endeavoured to meet your expectations. If I have been inconsiderate in keeping a high pace and late nights, and in driving you hard, it is because I knew that you shared with me the deep sense of commitment to the cause and the goal we set for ourselves. It has been a great pleasure and privilege for me to work with such distinguished and highly competent old and new friends and colleagues. We the veterans of the Third Law of the Sea Conference had a tendency to wax nostalgic about our participation there but we are in turn heartened by the promise and dedication of the new generation and are confident that you will continue the ideals which motivated those of us who were privileged to be involved with the law of the sea.

– – – – – – –

CONVENTION ON THE CONSERVATION AND MANAGEMENT OF HIGH SEAS FISHERY RESOURCES IN THE SOUTH PACIFIC OCEAN

The Contracting Parties,

Committed to ensuring the long-term conservation and sustainable use of fishery resources in the South Pacific Ocean and in so doing safeguarding the marine ecosystems in which the resources occur;

Recalling relevant international law as reflected in the United Nations Convention on the Law of the Sea of 10 December 1982, the Agreement for the Implementation of the Provisions of the United Nations Convention on the Law of the Sea of 10 December 1982 relating to the Conservation and Management of Straddling Fish Stocks and Highly Migratory Fish Stocks of 4 December 1995 and the Agreement to Promote Compliance with International Conservation and Management Measures by Fishing Vessels on the High Seas of 24 November 1993 and taking into account the Code of Conduct for Responsible Fisheries adopted by the Conference of the Food and Agriculture Organisation of the United Nations at its twenty eighth session on 31 October 1995;

Recognising that under international law reflected in the relevant provisions of the above agreements, States have a duty to cooperate with each other in the conservation and management of living resources in the areas of the high seas and, as appropriate, to cooperate to establish sub-regional or regional fisheries organisations or arrangements with a view to taking the measures necessary for the conservation of such resources;

Taking into consideration that, under international law reflected in the relevant provisions of the United Nations Convention on the Law of the Sea of 10 December 1982, coastal States have waters under national jurisdiction within which they exercise their sovereign rights for the purpose of exploring, exploiting, conserving and managing fishery resources and conserving living marine resources upon which fishing has an impact;

Recognising economic and geographical considerations and the special requirements of developing States, in particular the least-developed among them, and small island developing States, and territories and possessions, and their coastal communities, in relation to the conservation, management and sustainable development of fishery resources and equitable benefit from those resources;

Noting the need for regional fisheries management organisations and arrangements to undertake performance reviews in order to assess the degree to which they are attaining their respective conservation and management objectives;

Determined to cooperate effectively to eliminate illegal, unreported and unregulated fishing and the adverse impact that it has on the state of the world fishery resources and the ecosystems in which they occur;

Conscious of the need to avoid adverse impacts on the marine environment, preserve biodiversity, maintain the integrity of marine ecosystems and minimise the risk of long term or irreversible effects of fishing;

Mindful that effective conservation and management measures must be based on the best scientific information available and the application of the precautionary approach and an ecosystem approach to fisheries management;

Convinced that the long-term conservation and sustainable use of fishery resources in the South Pacific Ocean and the protection of the marine ecosystems in which those resources occur may best be achieved by the conclusion of an international convention for that purpose;

Have agreed as follows:

Article 1
DEFINITIONS

1 For the purposes of this Convention:

(a) '1982 Convention' means the United Nations Convention on the Law of the Sea of 10 December 1982;

(b) '1995 Agreement' means the Agreement for the Implementation of the Provisions of the United Nations Convention on the Law of the Sea of 10 December 1982 relating to the Conservation and Management of Straddling Fish Stocks and Highly Migratory Fish Stocks of 4 December 1995;

(c) 'Commission' means the Commission of the South Pacific Regional Fisheries Management Organisation established by Article 6;

(d) 'Convention Area' means the Area to which this Convention applies in accordance with Article 5;

(e) 'Code of Conduct' means the Code of Conduct for Responsible Fisheries adopted by the 28th session of the Conference of the Food and Agriculture Organisation of the United Nations (FAO) on 31 October 1995;

(f) 'fishery resources' means all fish within the Convention Area, including: molluscs; crustaceans; and other living marine resources as may be decided by the Commission; but excluding:

(i) sedentary species in so far as they are subject to the national jurisdiction of coastal States pursuant to Article 77 paragraph 4 of the 1982 Convention;

(ii) highly migratory species listed in Annex I of the 1982 Convention;

(iii) anadromous and catadromous species; and

(iv) marine mammals, marine reptiles and sea birds;

(g) 'fishing' means:

(i) the actual or attempted searching for, catching, taking or harvesting of fishery resources;

(ii) engaging in any activity which can reasonably be expected to result in the locating, catching, taking or harvesting of fishery resources for any purpose;

(iii) transhipment and any operation at sea in support of, or in preparation for, any activity described in this definition; and

(iv) the use of any vessel, vehicle, aircraft or hovercraft, in relation to any activity described in this definition;

but does not include any operation related to emergencies involving the health or safety of crew members or the safety of a vessel;

(h) 'fishing vessel' means any vessel used or intended for fishing, including fish processing vessels, support ships, carrier vessels and any other vessel directly engaged in fishing operations;

(i) 'flag State' means, unless otherwise indicated:

(i) a State whose fishing vessels are entitled to fly its flag; or

(ii) a regional economic integration organisation in which fishing vessels are entitled to fly the flag of a member State of that regional economic integration organisation;

(j) 'IUU fishing' means activities as referred to in paragraph 3 of the FAO International Plan of Action to Prevent, Deter and Eliminate Illegal, Unreported and Unregulated Fishing, and other activities as may be decided by the Commission;

(k) 'nationals' includes both natural and legal persons;

(l) 'port' includes offshore terminals and other installations for landing, transhipping, packaging, processing, refuelling or re-supplying;

(m) 'regional economic integration organisation' means a regional economic integration organisation to which its member States have transferred competence over matters covered by this Convention, including the authority to make decisions binding on its member States in respect of those matters;

(n) 'serious violation' has the same meaning as that set out in Article 21 paragraph 11 of the 1995 Agreement and such other violations as may be specified by the Commission; and

(o) 'transhipment' means the unloading of all or any of the fishery resources or fishery resource products derived from fishing in the Convention Area on board a fishing vessel to another fishing vessel either at sea or in port.

2

(a) 'Contracting Party' means any State or regional economic integration organisation which has consented to be bound by this Convention and for which the Convention is in force.

(b) This Convention applies, *mutatis mutandis*, to any entity referred to in Article 305, paragraph 1 (c), (d) and (e), of the 1982 Convention which becomes a party to this Convention, and to that extent "Contracting Party" refers to any such entity.

Article 2
OBJECTIVE

The objective of this Convention is, through the application of the precautionary approach and an ecosystem approach to fisheries management, to ensure the long-term conservation and sustainable use of fishery resources and, in so doing, to safeguard the marine ecosystems in which these resources occur.

Article 3
CONSERVATION AND MANAGEMENT PRINCIPLES AND APPROACHES

1 In giving effect to the objective of this Convention and carrying out decision making under this Convention, the Contracting Parties, the Commission and subsidiary bodies established under Article 6 paragraph 2 and Article 9 paragraph 1 shall:

(a) apply, in particular, the following principles;

(i) conservation and management of fishery resources shall be conducted in a transparent, accountable and inclusive manner, taking into account best international practices;

(ii) fishing shall be commensurate with the sustainable use of fishery resources taking into account the impacts on non-target and associated or dependent species and the general obligation to protect and preserve the marine environment;

(iii) overfishing and excess fishing capacity shall be prevented or eliminated;

(iv) full and accurate data on fishing, including information relating to impacts on the marine ecosystems in which fishery resources occur, shall be collected, verified, reported and shared in a timely and appropriate manner;

(v) decisions shall be based on the best scientific and technical information available and the advice of all relevant subsidiary bodies;

(vi) cooperation and coordination among Contracting Parties shall be promoted to ensure that conservation and management measures adopted by the Commission and conservation and management measures applied in respect of the same fishery resources in areas under national jurisdiction are compatible;

(vii) marine ecosystems shall be protected, in particular those ecosystems which have long recovery times following disturbance;

(viii) the interests of developing States, in particular the least developed among them and small island developing States, and of territories and possessions, and the needs of developing State coastal communities, shall be recognised;

(ix) effective compliance with conservation and management measures shall be ensured and sanctions for any violations shall be adequate in severity to discourage violations wherever they occur and in particular shall deprive offenders of the benefits accruing from their illegal activities; and

(x) pollution and waste originating from fishing vessels, discards, catch by lost or abandoned gear and impacts on other species and marine ecosystems shall be minimised; and

(b) apply the precautionary approach and an ecosystem approach in accordance with paragraph 2.

2

(a) The precautionary approach as described in the 1995 Agreement and the Code of Conduct shall be applied widely to the conservation and management of fishery resources in order to protect those resources and to preserve the marine ecosystems in which they occur, and in particular the Contracting Parties, the Commission and subsidiary bodies shall:

(i) be more cautious when information is uncertain, unreliable, or inadequate;

(ii) not use the absence of adequate scientific information as a reason for postponing or failing to take conservation and management measures; and

(iii) take account of best international practices regarding the application of the precautionary approach, including Annex II of the 1995 Agreement and the Code of Conduct.

(b) An ecosystem approach shall be applied widely to the conservation and management of fishery resources through an integrated approach under which decisions in relation to the management of fishery resources are considered in the context of the functioning of the wider marine ecosystems in which they occur to ensure the long-term conservation and sustainable use of those resources and in so doing, safeguard those marine ecosystems.

Article 4
COMPATIBILITY OF CONSERVATION AND MANAGEMENT MEASURES

1 The Contracting Parties recognise the need to ensure compatibility of conservation and management measures established for fishery resources that are identified as straddling areas under the national jurisdiction of a coastal State Contracting Party and the adjacent high seas of the Convention Area and acknowledge their duty to cooperate to this end.

2 Conservation and management measures established for the high seas and those adopted for areas under national jurisdiction shall be compatible in order to ensure conservation and management of straddling fishery resources in their entirety. In developing compatible conservation and management measures for straddling fishery resources Contracting Parties shall:

(a) take into account the biological unity and other biological characteristics of the fishery resources and the relationships between the distribution of the resources, the fishing activities for those resources and the geographical particularities of the region concerned, including the extent to which the fishery resources occur and are fished in areas under national jurisdiction;

(b) take into account the respective dependence of the coastal States and the States fishing on the high seas on the fishery resources concerned; and

(c) ensure that such measures do not result in harmful impact on the living marine resources as a whole in the Convention Area.

3 The Commission's initial conservation and management measures shall take due account of, and not undermine the effectiveness of, existing conservation and management measures established by relevant coastal State Contracting Parties in respect of areas under national jurisdiction and by Contracting Parties in respect of their flag vessels fishing in the adjacent high seas of the Convention Area.

Article 5
AREA OF APPLICATION

1 Except as otherwise provided, this Convention applies to waters of the Pacific Ocean beyond areas of national jurisdiction in accordance with international law:

(a) east of a line extending south along the 120° meridian of east longitude from the outer limit of the national jurisdiction of Australia off the south coast of Western Australia to the intersection with the 55° parallel of south latitude; then due east along the 55° parallel of south latitude to the intersection with the 150° meridian of east longitude; then due south along the 150° meridian of east longitude to the intersection with the 60° parallel of south latitude;

(b) north of a line extending east along the 60° parallel of south latitude from the 150° meridian of east longitude to the intersection with the 67° 16′ meridian of west longitude;

(c) west of a line extending north along the 67° 16′ meridian of west longitude from the 60° parallel of south latitude to its intersection with the outer limit of the national jurisdiction of Chile then along the outer limits of the national jurisdictions of Chile, Peru, Ecuador and Colombia to the intersection with the 2° parallel of north latitude; and

(d) south of a line extending west along the 2° parallel of north latitude (but not including the national jurisdiction of Ecuador (Galapagos Islands)) to the intersection with the 150° meridian of west longitude; then due north along the 150° meridian of west longitude to its intersection with 10° parallel of north latitude, then west along the 10° parallel of north latitude to its intersection with the outer limits of the national jurisdiction of the Marshall Islands, and then generally south and around the outer limits of the national jurisdictions of Pacific States and territories, New Zealand and Australia until it connects to the commencement of the line described in paragraph (a) above.

2 The Convention shall also apply to waters of the Pacific Ocean beyond areas of national jurisdiction bounded by the 10° parallel of north latitude and the 20° parallel of south latitude and by the 135° meridian of east longitude and the 150° meridian of west longitude.

3 Where for the purpose of this Convention it is necessary to determine the position on the surface of the earth of a point, line or area, that position shall be determined by reference to the International Terrestrial Reference System maintained by the International Earth Rotation Service, which for most practical purposes is equivalent to the World Geodetic System 1984 (WGS84).

4 Nothing in this Convention shall constitute recognition of the claims or positions of any of the Contracting Parties to this Convention concerning the legal status and extent of waters and zones claimed by any such Contracting Parties.

Article 6
THE ORGANISATION

1 The Contracting Parties hereby agree to establish, maintain and strengthen the South Pacific Regional Fisheries Management Organisation "the Organisation", which shall carry out its functions as set forth in this Convention in order to achieve the objective of this Convention.

2 The Organisation shall consist of:

(a) a Commission;

(b) a Scientific Committee;

(c) a Compliance and Technical Committee;

(d) an Eastern Sub-regional Management Committee;

(e) a Western Sub-regional Management Committee;

(f) a Finance and Administration Committee;

(g) a Secretariat,

and any other subsidiary bodies that the Commission may, from time to time, establish in accordance with Article 9 paragraph 1 to assist it in its work.

3 The Organisation shall have legal personality in accordance with international law and shall enjoy in its relations with other international organisations and in the territories of the Contracting Parties such legal capacity as may be necessary to perform its functions and achieve the objective of this Convention. The immunities and privileges which the Organisation and its officers shall enjoy in the territory of a Contracting Party shall be subject to an agreement between the Organisation and the Contracting Party including, in particular, an agreement between the Organisation and the Contracting Party hosting the Secretariat.

4 The Secretariat of the Organisation shall be in New Zealand or at such other place as may be decided by the Commission.

Article 7
THE COMMISSION

1 Each Contracting Party shall be a member of the Commission and shall appoint one representative to the Commission who may be accompanied by alternative representatives, experts and advisers.

2 The Commission shall elect a Chairperson and a Vice-Chairperson from among the Contracting Parties, each of whom shall serve for a term of two years and shall be eligible for re-election but shall not serve for more than two terms in succession in the same capacity. The Chairperson and Vice-Chairperson shall be representatives of different Contracting Parties.

3 The first meeting of the Commission shall take place no later than 12 months following the entry into force of this Convention. Thereafter the Chairperson of the Commission shall convene an annual meeting, unless the Commission decides otherwise, at a time and location to be decided by the Commission. The Commission shall hold such other meetings as may be necessary to carry out its functions under this Convention.

4 The principle of cost effectiveness shall apply to the frequency, duration and scheduling of meetings of the Commission and its subsidiary bodies.

Article 8
FUNCTIONS OF THE COMMISSION

The Commission shall, in accordance with the objective, principles and approaches, and specific provisions of this Convention, exercise the following functions:

(a) adopt conservation and management measures to achieve the objective of this Convention, including, as appropriate, conservation and management measures for particular fish stocks;

(b) determine the nature and extent of participation in fishing for fishery resources including, as appropriate, for particular fish stocks;

(c) develop rules for the collection, verification, reporting, storing and dissemination of data;

(d) promote the conduct of scientific research to improve knowledge of fishery resources and marine ecosystems in the Convention Area and of the same fishery resources in adjacent waters under national jurisdiction, and, in collaboration with the Scientific Committee, establish procedures for the conduct of fishing for fishery resources for scientific purposes in the Convention Area;

(e) cooperate and exchange data with members of the Commission and with relevant organisations, coastal States, territories and possessions;

(f) promote compatibility of conservation and management measures in the Convention Area, adjacent areas under national jurisdiction and adjacent areas of high seas;

(g) develop and establish effective monitoring, control, surveillance, compliance and enforcement procedures, including non-discriminatory market-related and trade-related measures;

(h) develop processes in accordance with international law to assess flag State performance with respect to the implementation of their obligations under this Convention and adopt proposals, if appropriate, to promote implementation of such obligations;

(i) adopt measures to prevent, deter and eliminate IUU fishing;

(j) develop rules for cooperating non-Contracting Party status under this Convention;

(k) review the effectiveness of the provisions of this Convention and the conservation and management measures adopted by the Commission in meeting the objective of this Convention;

(l) supervise the organisational, administrative, financial and other internal affairs of the Organisation, including the relations among constituent bodies;

(m) guide the Commission's subsidiary bodies in their work;

(n) adopt by consensus the budget of the Organisation, the financial regulations of the Organisation and any amendments thereto, and its rules of procedure, which may include procedures for taking and recording decisions intersessionally;

(o) adopt and amend as necessary any other regulations necessary for the exercise of its functions and those of its subsidiary bodies; and

(p) exercise any other function and take any other decisions that may be necessary for achieving the objective of this Convention.

Article 9
SUBSIDIARY BODIES

1 The Commission may establish other subsidiary bodies, additional to the Scientific Committee, the Compliance and Technical Committee, the Eastern Sub-regional Management Committee, the Western Sub-regional Management Committee and the Finance and Administration Committee as may be required. Such additional subsidiary bodies may be established on a permanent or temporary basis taking into account cost implications.

2 In establishing such additional subsidiary bodies the Commission shall provide specific terms of reference and methods of work, provided always that such specific terms of reference are consistent with the objective and the conservation and management principles and approaches of this Convention and with the 1982 Convention and the 1995 Agreement. Such terms of reference and methods of work may be reviewed and amended as appropriate by the Commission from time to time.

3 All subsidiary bodies shall report, advise and make recommendations to the Commission and contribute to regular reviews of the effectiveness of conservation and management measures adopted by the Commission.

4 In carrying out their functions, all subsidiary bodies shall take into consideration the relevant work of other subsidiary bodies established by the

Commission, and as appropriate the work of other fisheries management organisations and the work of other relevant technical and scientific bodies.

5 All subsidiary bodies may establish working groups. Subsidiary bodies may also seek external advice as required in accordance with any general or specific guidance provided by the Commission.

6 All subsidiary bodies shall operate under the rules of procedure of the Commission unless otherwise decided by the Commission.

Article 10
SCIENTIFIC COMMITTEE

1 Each member of the Commission shall be entitled to appoint one representative to the Scientific Committee who may be accompanied by alternate representatives and advisers.

2 The functions of the Scientific Committee shall be to:

(a) plan, conduct and review scientific assessments of the status of fishery resources including, in cooperation with the relevant coastal State Contracting Party or Parties, fishery resources that straddle the Convention Area and areas under national jurisdiction;

(b) provide advice and recommendations to the Commission and its subsidiary bodies based on such assessments including, as appropriate:

(i) reference points, including precautionary reference points as described in Annex II of the 1995 Agreement;

(ii) management strategies or plans for fishery resources based on such reference points; and

(iii) analyses of conservation and management alternatives, such as the establishment of total allowable catch or total allowable fishing effort at different levels, that estimate the extent to which each alternative would achieve the objective or objectives of any management strategy or plan adopted, or under consideration, by the Commission;

(c) provide advice and recommendations to the Commission and its subsidiary bodies on the impact of fishing on the marine ecosystems in the Convention Area including advice and recommendations on the identification and distribution of vulnerable marine ecosystems, the likely impacts of fishing on such vulnerable marine ecosystems and measures to prevent significant adverse impacts on them;

(d) encourage and promote cooperation in scientific research in order to improve knowledge of the state of fishery resources and the marine ecosystems in the Convention Area including knowledge in relation to fishery resources straddling the Convention Area and areas under national jurisdiction; and

(e) provide such other scientific advice to the Commission and its subsidiary bodies as it considers appropriate, or as may be requested by the Commission.

3 The rules of procedure of the Commission shall provide that where the Scientific Committee is unable to provide its advice by consensus, it shall set out in its report the different views of its members. The reports of the Scientific Committee shall be made publicly available.

4 The Commission, taking into account any recommendations from the Scientific Committee, may engage the services of scientific experts to provide information and advice on the fishery resources and marine ecosystems in the Convention Area and any related matters that may be relevant to the Commission's consideration of conservation and management measures.

5 The Commission shall make appropriate arrangements for the periodic independent peer review of the Scientific Committee's reports, advice and recommendations.

Article 11
COMPLIANCE AND TECHNICAL COMMITTEE

1 Each member of the Commission shall be entitled to appoint one representative to the Compliance and Technical Committee who may be accompanied by alternate representatives and advisers.

2 The functions of the Compliance and Technical Committee shall be to:

(a) monitor and review the implementation of, and compliance with, conservation and management measures adopted under this Convention and provide advice and recommendations to the Commission;

(b) provide such other information, technical advice and recommendations as it considers appropriate or as may be requested by the Commission relating to the implementation of and compliance with the provisions of this Convention and the conservation and management measures adopted, or under consideration, by the Commission; and

(c) review the implementation of cooperative measures for monitoring, control, and surveillance and enforcement adopted by the Commission and provide advice and recommendations to the Commission.

Article 12
EASTERN AND WESTERN SUB-REGIONAL MANAGEMENT COMMITTEES

1 The Eastern and Western Sub-regional Management Committees shall, on their own initiative or at the request of the Commission, develop and make recommendations to the Commission on conservation and management measures, in accordance with Article 20, and on participation in fishing for fishery resources, in accordance with Article 21, for the parts of the Convention Area described in Annex I. Such recommendations shall be consistent with any measures of general application adopted by the Commission and shall require the consent of the coastal State Contracting Party or Parties concerned on the matters on which such consent is required under Article 20 paragraph 4 and Article 21 paragraph 2. Where appropriate the Committees shall make all efforts to coordinate their recommendations.

2 The Commission may by consensus amend Annex I at any time to adjust the geographic coordinates it contains. Such amendment shall take effect from the date of its adoption, or any other date specified in the amendment.

3 The Commission may decide to assign to one Sub-regional Management Committee primary responsibility for developing and making recommendations to the Commission in accordance with this Article for a specific fishery resource even if the range of that resource should extend beyond the part of the Convention Area for which that Committee has responsibilities in accordance with Annex I.

4 Each Committee shall develop its recommendations on the basis of the advice and recommendations of the Scientific Committee.

5

(a) Members of the Commission situated adjacent to the part of the Convention Area for which a Committee has responsibility in accordance with this Article, or whose fishing vessels:

(i) are currently fishing in that area; or

(ii) have fished in that area within the past two years; or

(iii) are fishing for a specific fishery resource assigned to that Committee pursuant to paragraph 3, including in areas under national jurisdiction adjacent to the Convention Area

shall be members of that Committee.

(b) Any member of the Commission that is not a member of a Committee pursuant to subparagraph (a) that gives notice to the Secretariat of an intention to fish within two years of the notice in the part of the Convention Area for which a Committee has responsibility in accordance with this Article, shall become a member of that Committee. If the notifying member of the Commission does not fish in that part of the Convention Area within two years of the notice, it shall cease to be a member of that Committee.

(c) Any member of the Commission that is not a member of a Committee pursuant to subparagraph (a) or (b) may send a representative to participate in the work of that Committee.

(d) For the purposes of this paragraph, "fishing" includes only the activities described in Article 1 paragraph 1 (g) (i) and (ii).

6 The Eastern and Western Sub-regional Management Committees shall make all efforts to adopt their recommendations to the Commission by consensus. If all efforts to reach agreement on a recommendation by consensus have been exhausted, recommendations shall be adopted by a two-thirds majority of the members of the relevant Sub-regional Management Committee. Reports to the Commission may include majority and minority views.

7 The recommendations made in accordance with this Article will be the basis of conservation and management measures and decisions referred to in Articles 20 and 21, respectively, that shall be adopted by the Commission.

8 Any extraordinary costs incurred for the work of either of the Sub-regional Management Committees shall be borne by the members of the relevant Committee.

Article 13
FINANCE AND ADMINISTRATION COMMITTEE

1 Each member of the Commission shall be entitled to appoint one representative to the Finance and Administration Committee who may be accompanied by alternate representatives and advisers.

2 The functions of the Finance and Administration Committee shall be to advise the Commission on the budget, on the time and place of meetings of the Commission, on publications of the Commission, on matters relating to the Executive Secretary and the staff of the Secretariat and on such other financial and administrative matters as may be referred to it by the Commission.

Article 14
SECRETARIAT

1 The Secretariat shall perform the functions delegated to it by the Commission.

2 The chief administrative officer of the Secretariat shall be the Executive Secretary, who shall be appointed with the approval of the Contracting Parties on such terms as they may determine.

3 Any employees of the Secretariat shall be appointed by the Executive Secretary in accordance with such staff regulations as may be determined by the Commission.

4 The Executive Secretary shall ensure the effective functioning of the Secretariat.

5 The Secretariat to be established under this Convention shall be cost effective. The setting up and the functioning of the Secretariat shall, where appropriate, take into account the capacity of existing regional institutions to perform certain technical secretariat functions and more specifically the availability of services under contractual arrangement.

Article 15
BUDGET

1 The Commission, at its first meeting, shall adopt a budget to fund the Commission and its subsidiary bodies, and shall also adopt financial regulations. All decisions on the budget and financial regulations, including decisions relating to the contributions of members of the Commission and the formula for calculating such contributions, shall be taken by consensus.

2 Each member of the Commission shall contribute to the budget. The amount of the annual contributions due from each member of the Commission shall be a combination of a variable fee based on its total catch of such fishery resources as may be specified by the Commission and a basic fee and shall take account of its economic status. For a member of the Commission whose only catch in the Convention Area is that of its territory or territories adjoining the Convention Area the economic status shall be that of the territory concerned. The Commission shall adopt and may amend a formula for the calculation of these contributions which shall be set out in the financial regulations of the Commission.

3 The Commission may request and accept financial contributions and other forms of assistance from organisations, individuals and other sources for purposes connected with the fulfilment of its functions.

4 The Executive Secretary shall submit a draft of the annual budget for the two succeeding financial years to each member of the Commission together with a schedule of contributions, not less than 60 days before the meeting of the Finance and Administration Committee where the Committee will adopt its recommendations to the Commission. In preparing the draft budget the Secretariat shall take full account of the need for cost effectiveness together with the guidance of the Commission as to the meetings of the subsidiary bodies that may be required in the budget year. Each annual meeting of the Commission shall adopt a budget for the succeeding financial year.

5 If the Commission is unable to adopt a budget, the level of contributions to the administrative budget of the Commission shall be determined in accordance with the budget for the preceding year for the purposes of

meeting the administrative expenses of the Commission for the following year until such time as a new budget can be adopted by consensus.

6 Following the annual meeting of the Commission, the Executive Secretary shall notify each member of the Commission of its contribution due as calculated under the formula adopted by the Commission pursuant to paragraph 2 and as soon as possible thereafter each member of the Commission shall pay its contribution to the Organisation.

7 Contributions shall be payable in the currency of the country in which the Secretariat of the Organisation is located, except if otherwise authorised by the Commission.

8 A Contracting Party that becomes party to this Convention during the course of a financial year shall contribute in respect of that financial year a part of the contribution calculated in accordance with the provisions of this Article that is proportionate to the number of complete months remaining in the year from the date that the Convention enters into force for that Party.

9 Unless otherwise decided by the Commission, a member of the Commission that is in arrears with its payment of any monies owed to the Organisation by more than two years shall not participate in the taking of any decisions by the Commission until it has paid all monies owed by it to the Commission.

10 The financial activities of the Organisation shall be conducted in accordance with financial regulations adopted by the Commission and shall be subject to an annual audit by independent auditors appointed by the Commission.

Article 16
DECISION-MAKING

1 As a general rule, decisions by the Commission shall be taken by consensus. For the purpose of this Article, "consensus" means the absence of any formal objection made at the time the decision was taken.

2 Except where this Convention expressly provides that a decision shall be taken by consensus, if the Chairperson considers that all efforts to reach a decision by consensus have been exhausted:

(a) decisions of the Commission on questions of procedure shall be taken by a majority of the members of the Commission casting affirmative or negative votes; and

(b) decisions on questions of substance shall be taken by a three-fourths majority of the members of the Commission casting affirmative or negative votes.

3 When the issue arises as to whether a question is one of substance or not, that question shall be treated as one of substance.

Article 17
IMPLEMENTATION OF COMMISSION DECISIONS

1 Decisions on questions of substance adopted by the Commission shall become binding on the members of the Commission in the following manner:

(a) the Executive Secretary shall promptly notify each decision to all members of the Commission; and

(b) subject to paragraph 2, the decision shall become binding upon all members of the Commission 90 days after the date of transmittal specified in the notification pursuant to subparagraph (a) "the date of notification".

2

(a) Any member of the Commission may present to the Executive Secretary an objection to a decision within 60 days of the date of notification "the objection period". In that event the decision shall not become binding on that member of the Commission to the extent of the objection, except in accordance with paragraph 3 and Annex II.

(b) A member of the Commission that presents an objection shall at the same time:

(i) specify in detail the grounds for its objection;

(ii) adopt alternative measures that are equivalent in effect to the decision to which it has objected and have the same date of application; and

(iii) advise the Executive Secretary of the terms of such alternative measures.

(c) The only admissible grounds for an objection are that the decision unjustifiably discriminates in form or in fact against the member of the Commission, or is inconsistent with the provisions of this Convention or other relevant international law as reflected in the 1982 Convention or the 1995 Agreement.

3 Any member of the Commission that has objected to a decision may at any time withdraw that objection. The decision shall then become binding on that member in accordance with paragraph 1(b) or on the date of the withdrawal of the objection whichever is the later.

4 The Executive Secretary shall promptly notify all members of the Commission of:

(a) the receipt and withdrawal of each objection; and

(b) the grounds for that objection and the alternative measures adopted, or proposed to be adopted, pursuant to paragraph 2.

5

(a) When an objection is presented by a member of the Commission pursuant to paragraph 2, a Review Panel shall be established within 30 days after the end of the objection period. The Review Panel shall be established in accordance with the procedures in Annex II.

(b) The Executive Secretary shall promptly notify all members of the Commission of the establishment of the Review Panel.

(c) If two or more members of the Commission present objections based on the same grounds, those objections shall be dealt with by the same Review Panel, which shall have the membership specified in Annex II paragraph 2.

(d) If two or more members of the Commission present objections on different grounds, those objections may, with the consent of the members of the Commission concerned, be dealt with by the same Review Panel, which shall have the membership specified in Annex II paragraph 2. In the absence of such consent, objections on different grounds shall be dealt with by separate Review Panels.

(e) Within 45 days after its establishment, the Review Panel shall transmit to the Executive Secretary its findings and recommendations on whether the grounds specified for the objection presented by the member or members of the Commission are justified and whether the alternative measures adopted are equivalent in effect to the decision to which objection has been presented.

(f) The Executive Secretary shall promptly notify all members of the Commission of the findings and recommendations of the Review Panel. The findings and recommendations of the Review Panel shall be dealt with and have effect as set out in Annex II.

6 Nothing in this Article limits the right of a member of the Commission at any time to refer a dispute concerning the interpretation or application of this Convention for binding settlement in accordance with the provisions of this Convention relating to the settlement of disputes.

Article 18
TRANSPARENCY

1 The Commission shall promote transparency in decision making processes and other activities carried out under this Convention.

2 All meetings of the Commission and its subsidiary bodies shall be open to all participants and observers registered in accordance with paragraph 4

unless otherwise decided by the Commission. The Commission shall publish its reports and conservation and management measures when adopted and shall maintain a public record of all reports and conservation and management measures in force in the Convention Area.

3 The Commission shall promote transparency in the implementation of this Convention through the public dissemination of non-commercially sensitive information and, as appropriate, facilitating consultations with, and the participation of, non-governmental organisations, representatives of the fishing industry, particularly the fishing fleet, and other interested bodies and individuals.

4 Representatives of non-Contracting Parties, relevant intergovernmental organisations and non-governmental organisations, including environmental organisations and fishing industry organisations with an interest in matters pertaining to the Commission shall be afforded the opportunity to take part in the meetings of the Commission and of its subsidiary bodies, as observers or otherwise as appropriate. The rules of procedure of the Commission shall provide for such participation and shall not be unduly restrictive in this respect. The rules of procedure shall also provide for such representatives to have timely access to all relevant information.

Article 19
RECOGNITION OF THE SPECIAL REQUIREMENTS OF DEVELOPING STATES

1 The Commission shall give full recognition to the special requirements of developing State Contracting Parties in the region, in particular the least developed among them and small island developing States, and of territories and possessions in the region, in relation to the conservation and management of fishery resources in the Convention Area and the sustainable use of such resources.

2 In giving effect to the duty to cooperate in the establishment of conservation and management measures for fishery resources covered by this Convention, the members of the Commission shall take into account the special requirements of developing State Contracting Parties in the region, in particular the least developed among them and small island developing States, and territories and possessions in the region, in particular:

(a) the vulnerability of such developing States and territories and possessions which are dependent on the exploitation of living marine resources, including for meeting the nutritional requirements of their populations or part thereof;

(b) the need to avoid adverse impacts on, and ensure access to fisheries by, subsistence, small-scale and artisanal fishers and women fish workers, as well as indigenous people in such developing States Parties, and territories and possessions; and

(c) the need to ensure that such measures do not result in transferring, directly or indirectly, a disproportionate burden of conservation action onto such developing State Contracting Parties, and territories and possessions.

3 The members of the Commission shall cooperate either directly or through the Commission and other regional or sub-regional organisations to:

(a) enhance the ability of developing State Contracting Parties in the region, in particular the least developed among them and small island developing States, and of territories and possessions in the region, to conserve and manage fishery resources and to develop their own fisheries for such resources;

(b) assist developing State Contracting Parties in the region, in particular the least developed among them and small island developing States, and territories and possessions in the region, to enable them to participate in fishing for fishery resources, including facilitating access to such fishery resources consistent with Article 3 and Article 21; and

(c) facilitate the participation of developing State Contracting Parties in the region, in particular the least developed among them and small island developing States, and of territories and possessions in the region, in the work of the Commission and its subsidiary bodies.

4 Cooperation for the purposes set out in this Article may include the provision of financial assistance, assistance relating to human resources development, technical assistance, transfer of technology, including through joint venture arrangements, and advisory and consultative services. Such assistance shall, *inter alia*, be directed towards:

(a) improved conservation and management of fishery resources through collection, reporting, verification, exchange and analysis of fisheries data and related information;

(b) stock assessment and scientific research; and

(c) monitoring, control, surveillance, compliance and enforcement, including training and capacity-building at the local level, development and funding of national and regional observer programmes and access to technology and equipment.

5 The Commission shall establish a fund to facilitate the effective participation of developing State Contracting Parties in the region, in particular the least developed among them and small island developing States, and, as appropriate, territories and possessions in the region, in the work of the Commission and its subsidiary bodies. The financial regulations of the Commission shall include guidelines for the administration of the fund and criteria for eligibility for assistance.

Article 20
CONSERVATION AND MANAGEMENT MEASURES

1 The conservation and management measures adopted by the Commission shall include measures to:

(a) ensure the long-term sustainability of fishery resources and promote the objective of their responsible utilisation;

(b) prevent or eliminate over-fishing and excess fishing capacity to ensure that levels of fishing effort do not exceed those commensurate with the sustainable use of fishery resources;

(c) maintain or restore populations of non-target and associated or dependent species to above levels at which their reproduction may become seriously threatened; and

(d) protect the habitats and marine ecosystems in which fishery resources and non-target and associated or dependent species occur from the impacts of fishing, including measures to prevent significant adverse impacts on vulnerable marine ecosystems and precautionary measures where it cannot adequately be determined whether vulnerable marine ecosystems are present or whether fishing would cause significant adverse impacts on vulnerable marine ecosystems.

2 The specific conservation and management measures adopted by the Commission shall, as appropriate, include the determination of:

(a) reference points, including precautionary reference points as described in Annex II of the 1995 Agreement;

(b) the actions to be taken if those reference points are approached or exceeded;

(c) the nature and extent of fishing for any fishery resource including the establishment of a total allowable catch or total allowable fishing effort;

(d) the general or specific locations in which fishing may or may not occur;

(e) the periods in which fishing may or may not occur;

(f) the size limits in respect of the catch which may be retained; and

(g) the types of fishing gear, fishing technology, or fishing practices which may be used when fishing.

3 In determining a total allowable catch or total allowable fishing effort for any fishery resource under paragraph 2 (c), the Commission shall take into account the following factors:

(a) the status and stage of development of the fishery resource;

(b) fishing patterns of the fishery resource;

(c) catch of the same fishery resource within areas under national jurisdiction where relevant;

(d) an allowance for discards and any other incidental mortality;

(e) catch of non-target and associated or dependent species and impacts on the marine ecosystems in which the fishery resource occurs;

(f) relevant ecological and biological factors limiting the nature of fishery resources that may be harvested;

(g) relevant environmental factors, including trophic interactions which may have an effect upon the fishery resource and non-target and associated or dependent species; and

(h) as appropriate, relevant conservation and management measures adopted by other intergovernmental organisations.

The Commission shall regularly review the total allowable catch or total allowable fishing effort established for any fishery resource.

4

(a) For a fishery resource that straddles the Convention Area and an area under the national jurisdiction of a coastal State Contracting Party or Parties:

(i) the Commission shall establish a total allowable catch or total allowable fishing effort and other conservation and management measures, as appropriate, for the Convention Area. The Commission and the coastal State Contracting Party or Parties concerned shall cooperate in the coordination of their respective conservation and management measures in accordance with Article 4 of this Convention;

(ii) with the express consent of the coastal State Contracting Party or Parties concerned, the Commission may establish, in accordance with Annex III of this Convention, and as appropriate, a total allowable catch or total allowable fishing effort that will apply throughout the range of the fishery resource; and

(iii) in the case where one or more of the coastal State Contracting Parties does not consent to a total allowable catch or total allowable fishing effort that will apply throughout the range of the fishery resource, the Commission may establish, as appropriate, a total allowable catch or total allowable fishing effort that will apply in the areas of national jurisdiction of the consenting coastal State Contracting Party or Parties and the Convention Area. Annex III will apply, *mutatis mutandis*, to the establishment of this total allowable catch or total allowable fishing effort by the Commission.

(b) In cases covered by subparagraph (a) (ii) or (a) (iii), other complementary conservation and management measures may be adopted so as to ensure sustainable conservation and management of the fishery resource throughout its range. To give effect to this paragraph, such measures may be adopted, in accordance with the principles of compatibility outlined in Article 4, by the Commission for the high seas and the coastal State Contracting Party or Parties concerned for the areas under national jurisdiction; and by the Commission, with the consent of the coastal State Contracting Party or Parties concerned, for measures that will apply throughout the range of the fishery resource.

(c) All conservation and management measures, including a total allowable catch or total allowable fishing effort, adopted by the Commission in accordance with subparagraphs (a) (ii), (a) (iii) and (b) are without prejudice to and do not affect the sovereign rights of coastal States for the purpose of exploring and exploiting, conserving and managing the living marine resources within areas under national jurisdiction in accordance with international law, as reflected in the relevant provisions of the 1982 Convention and the 1995 Agreement, and do not in any other respect affect the Area of application of this Convention established by Article 5.

5

(a) The Commission shall adopt measures to be applied on an emergency basis, in accordance with Article 16, including intersessionally, if necessary, where fishing presents a serious threat to the sustainability of fishery resources or the marine ecosystem in which these fishery resources occur or when a natural phenomenon or human caused disaster has, or is likely to have, a significant adverse impact on the status of fishery resources to ensure that fishing does not exacerbate such threat or adverse impact.

(b) Measures taken on an emergency basis shall be based on the best scientific evidence available. Such measures shall be temporary and must be reconsidered for decision at the next meeting of the Commission following their adoption. The measures shall become binding on the members of the Commission in accordance with Article 17 paragraph 1. Such measures shall not be open to the objection procedure in Article 17 paragraph 2 but may be the subject of dispute settlement procedures under this Convention.

6 The conservation and management measures adopted by the Commission shall be progressively developed and integrated into management strategies or plans that set out the management objectives for each fishery resource, the reference points against which to measure progress in relation to those objectives, the indicators to be used in relation to those reference points and the measures to be taken in response to particular indicator levels.

Article 21
PARTICIPATION IN FISHING FOR FISHERY RESOURCES

1 When taking decisions regarding participation in fishing for any fishery resource, including the allocation of a total allowable catch or total allowable fishing effort, the Commission shall take into account the status of the fishery resource and the existing level of fishing effort for that resource and the following criteria to the extent relevant:

(a) historic catch and past and present fishing patterns and practices in the Convention Area;

(b) compliance with the conservation and management measures under this Convention;

(c) demonstrated capacity and willingness to exercise effective flag State control over fishing vessels;

(d) contribution to the conservation and management of fishery resources, including the provision of accurate data and effective monitoring, control, surveillance and enforcement;

(e) the fisheries development aspirations and interests of developing States in particular small island developing States and of territories and possessions in the region;

(f) the interests of coastal States, and in particular developing coastal States and territories and possessions, in a fishery resource that straddles areas of national jurisdiction of such States, territories and possessions and the Convention Area;

(g) the needs of coastal States and of territories and possessions whose economies are dependent mainly on the exploitation of and fishing for a fishery resource that straddles areas of national jurisdiction of such States, territories and possessions and the Convention Area;

(h) the extent to which a member of the Commission is utilising the catch for domestic consumption and the importance of the catch to its food security;

(i) contribution to the responsible development of new or exploratory fisheries in accordance with Article 22; and

(j) contribution to the conduct of scientific research with respect to fishery resources and the public dissemination of the results of such research.

2 When the Commission establishes a total allowable catch or total allowable fishing effort for any fishery resource pursuant to Article 20 paragraph 4 (a) (ii) or (iii), it may, with the express consent of the coastal State Contracting Party or Parties concerned, also take decisions regarding participation in fishing for that resource throughout its relevant range.

3 In taking decisions under paragraph 2, the Commission shall take into account the historic catch and past and present fishing patterns and practices throughout the relevant range of the fishery resource concerned and the criteria listed in paragraph 1(b) – (j).

4 When the consent of the coastal State Contracting Party or Parties concerned is not provided pursuant to paragraph 2:

(a) the Commission shall take decisions, in accordance with paragraph 1, regarding allocation of the portion of the total allowable catch or total allowable fishing effort established pursuant to Article 20 paragraph 4 (a) (i) that may be taken in the Convention Area; and

(b) the Commission and the coastal State Contracting Party or Parties concerned shall cooperate in accordance with Article 4.

5 In taking decisions under this Article, the Commission may also have regard, as appropriate, to performance with respect to other international fisheries management regimes.

6 The Commission shall, when appropriate, review decisions regarding participation in fishing for fishery resources, including the allocation of a total allowable catch or total allowable fishing effort, taking into account the provisions of this Article and the interests of new Contracting Parties.

Article 22
NEW OR EXPLORATORY FISHERIES

1 A fishery that has not been subject to fishing or has not been subject to fishing with a particular gear type or technique for ten years or more shall be opened as a fishery or opened to fishing with such gear type or technique only when the Commission has adopted cautious preliminary conservation and management measures in respect of that fishery, and, as appropriate, non-target and associated or dependent species, and appropriate measures to protect the marine ecosystem in which that fishery occurs from adverse impacts of fishing activities.

2 Such preliminary conservation and management measures, which may include requirements regarding notification of intention to fish, the establishment of a development plan, mitigation measures to prevent adverse impacts on marine ecosystems, use of particular fishing gear, the presence of observers, the collection of data, and the conduct of research or exploratory fishing, shall be consistent with the objective and the conservation and management principles and approaches of this Convention. The measures shall ensure that the new fishery resource is developed on a precautionary and gradual basis until sufficient information is acquired to enable the Commission to adopt appropriately detailed conservation and management measures.

3 The Commission may, from time to time, adopt standard minimum conservation and management measures that are to apply in respect of some or all new fisheries prior to the commencement of fishing for such new fisheries.

Article 23
DATA COLLECTION, COMPILATION AND EXCHANGE

1 To enhance the information base for the conservation and management of fishery resources, non-target and associated or dependent species and the protection of the marine ecosystems in which those resources occur; and to contribute to the elimination or reduction of IUU fishing and its negative impact on those resources, the Commission shall, taking full account of Annex I of the 1995 Agreement, develop standards, rules and procedures for, *inter alia*:

(a) the collection, verification and timely reporting to the Commission of all relevant data by members of the Commission;

(b) the compilation and management by the Commission of accurate and complete data to facilitate effective stock assessment and ensure that the provision of the best scientific advice is enabled;

(c) the security of, access to and dissemination of data while maintaining confidentiality where appropriate;

(d) the exchange of data among members of the Commission, and with other regional fisheries management organisations, and other relevant organisations including data concerning vessels engaged in IUU fishing, and, as appropriate, concerning the beneficial ownership of such vessels, with a view to consolidating such information into a centralised format for dissemination as appropriate;

(e) the facilitation of coordinated documentation and data-sharing between regional fisheries management organisations, including procedures to exchange data on vessel registers, catch documentation and trade tracking schemes where applicable; and

(f) regular audits of Commission member compliance with data collection and exchange requirements, and for addressing any non-compliance identified in such audits.

2 The Commission shall ensure that data are publicly available concerning the number of vessels operating in the Convention Area, the status of fishery resources managed under this Convention, fishery resource assessments, research programmes in the Convention Area, and cooperative initiatives with regional and global organisations.

Article 24
OBLIGATIONS OF MEMBERS OF THE COMMISSION

1 Each member of the Commission shall, in respect of its fishing activities within the Convention Area:

(a) implement this Convention and any conservation and management measures adopted by the Commission, and take all necessary measures to ensure their effectiveness;

(b) cooperate in furthering the objective of this Convention;

(c) take all necessary measures to support efforts to prevent, deter and eliminate IUU fishing; and

(d) collect, verify and report scientific, technical and statistical data pertaining to fishery resources and marine ecosystems in the Convention Area in conformity with the standards, rules and procedures established by the Commission.

2 Each member of the Commission shall report to the Commission on an annual basis indicating how it has implemented the conservation and management measures and compliance and enforcement procedures adopted by the Commission. In the case of coastal State Contracting Parties, the report shall include information regarding the conservation and management measures they have taken for straddling fishery resources occurring in waters under their jurisdiction adjacent to the Convention Area in accordance with Article 20 paragraph 4 and Article 4. Such reports shall be made publicly available.

3 Without prejudice to the primacy of the responsibility of the flag State, to the greatest extent possible, each member of the Commission shall take measures and cooperate to ensure compliance by its nationals, or fishing vessels owned, operated or controlled by its nationals, with the provisions of this Convention and any conservation and management measures adopted by the Commission, and immediately investigate any alleged violation of such provisions and measures. Members of the Commission shall provide reports on the progress of the investigation to the Commission and relevant members of the Commission at appropriate regular intervals, to the extent permitted by

national law, as well as a final report on the outcome when the investigation is completed.

4 To the extent permitted by its national laws and regulations, each member of the Commission shall establish arrangements for making available to prosecuting authorities of other members of the Commission evidence related to alleged violations of the provisions of the Convention and any conservation and management measures adopted by the Commission, including information available on the beneficial ownership of vessels flying its flag.

5 Each member of the Commission shall fulfil in good faith the obligations assumed under this Convention and shall exercise the rights recognised in this Convention in a manner which would not constitute an abuse of right.

Article 25
FLAG STATE DUTIES

1 Each member of the Commission shall take all necessary measures to ensure that fishing vessels flying its flag:

(a) comply with the provisions of this Convention and the conservation and management measures adopted by the Commission and that such vessels do not engage in any activity which undermines the effectiveness of such measures when operating in the Convention Area;

(b) do not conduct unauthorised fishing within waters under national jurisdiction adjacent to the Convention Area;

(c) carry and operate equipment sufficient to comply with vessel monitoring system standards and procedures adopted by the Commission; and

(d) land or tranship fishery resources caught in the Convention Area in accordance with standards and procedures adopted by the Commission.

2 No member of the Commission shall allow any fishing vessel entitled to fly its flag to be used for fishing in the Convention Area unless it has been authorised to do so by the appropriate authority or authorities of that member of the Commission.

3 Each member of the Commission shall:

(a) authorise the use of fishing vessels flying its flag for fishing in the Convention Area only where it is able to exercise effectively its responsibilities in respect of such vessels under this Convention and in accordance with international law;

(b) maintain a register of fishing vessels entitled to fly its flag and authorised to fish for fishery resources, and ensure that, for all such vessels, such information as may be specified by the Commission is entered in that register;

(c) in accordance with measures adopted by the Commission, investigate immediately and report fully on actions taken in response to any alleged violation by fishing vessels flying its flag of the provisions of this Convention or any conservation and management measure adopted by the Commission. Reporting shall include reports on the progress of the investigation to the Commission at appropriate regular intervals, to the extent permitted by national law, as well as a final report on the outcome when the investigation is completed;

(d) ensure that penalties applicable for such violations are of an appropriate severity, taking into account relevant factors including the value of the catch, to secure compliance, discourage further violations and deprive offenders of the benefits accruing from their illegal activities; and

(e) ensure in particular that, where it has been established, in accordance with its laws, that a fishing vessel flying its flag has been involved in the commission of a serious violation of the provisions of this Convention or of any conservation and management measures adopted by the Commission, the vessel concerned ceases fishing activities and does not engage in such activities in the Convention Area until it has complied with all outstanding sanctions imposed by the member of the Commission in respect of the violation.

4 Each member of the Commission is encouraged to ensure that fishing vessels flying its flag operate in the Convention Area in accordance with applicable international obligations, and with regard to relevant recommendations and guidelines, regarding safety at sea for vessels and their crews.

5 Each member of the Commission shall ensure that fishing vessels flying its flag engaged in or intending to engage in research into fishery resources comply with any procedures established by the Commission for the conduct of scientific research in the Convention Area.

Article 26
PORT STATE DUTIES

1 A port State Contracting Party has the right and duty to take measures, in accordance with international law, to promote the effectiveness of subregional, regional and global conservation and management measures. When taking such measures, a port State Contracting Party shall not discriminate in form or in fact against the fishing vessels of any State.

2 Each member of the Commission shall:

(a) give effect to conservation and management measures adopted by the Commission in relation to the entry and use of its ports by fishing vessels that have engaged in fishing in the Convention Area including, *inter alia*, with respect to landing and transhipment of fishery resources, inspection of fishing vessels, documents, catch and gear on board, and use of port services; and

(b) provide assistance to flag States, as reasonably practical and in accordance with its national law and international law, when a fishing vessel is voluntarily in its ports and the flag State of the vessel requests it to provide assistance in ensuring compliance with the provisions of this Convention and with the conservation and management measures adopted by the Commission.

3 In the event that a member of the Commission considers that a fishing vessel making use of its ports has violated a provision of this Convention or a conservation and management measure adopted by the Commission, it shall notify the flag State concerned, the Commission and other relevant States and appropriate international organisations. The member of the Commission shall provide the flag State and, as appropriate the Commission with full documentation on the matter, including any record of inspection.

4 Nothing in this Article affects the exercise by Contracting Parties of their sovereignty over ports in their territory in accordance with international law.

Article 27
MONITORING, COMPLIANCE AND ENFORCEMENT

1 The Commission shall establish appropriate cooperative procedures for effective monitoring, control and surveillance of fishing and to ensure compliance with this Convention and the conservation and management measures adopted by the Commission including, *inter alia*:

(a) the establishment and maintenance of a Commission record of vessels authorised to fish in the Convention Area, the marking of vessels and fishing gear, the recording of fishing activities, and the reporting of vessel movements and activities by a satellite vessel monitoring system that shall be designed to ensure the integrity and security of near real time transmissions, including through the possibility of direct and simultaneous transmissions, to the Commission and flag State;

(b) an inspection programme for Contracting Parties, both at sea and in port, including procedures for Contracting Parties to board and inspect each others' vessels in the Convention Area, and procedures for notification of inspection vessels and aircraft of Contracting Parties that may participate in the programme;

(c) regulation and supervision of transhipment;

(d) non discriminatory market-related measures, consistent with international law, to monitor transhipment, landings, and trade to prevent, deter and eliminate IUU fishing including, where appropriate, catch documentation schemes;

(e) reporting on violations detected, progress and outcomes of investigations, and enforcement actions taken; and

(f) addressing IUU fishing activities, including by identifying vessels engaging in IUU fishing activities, and by adopting appropriate measures to prevent, deter and eliminate IUU fishing, such as the development of an IUU vessels list, so that owners and operators of vessels engaging in such activities are deprived of the benefits accruing from those activities.

2 The Commission may adopt procedures that enable measures, including trade-related measures in relation to fishery resources, to be applied by members of the Commission to any state, member of the Commission, or entity whose fishing vessels engage in fishing activities that diminish the effectiveness of, or otherwise fail to comply with, the conservation and management measures adopted by the Commission. Such measures should include a range of possible responses so that account can be taken of the reason for and degree of non-compliance and should include, as appropriate, cooperative capacity-building initiatives. Any implementation of trade-related measures by a member of the Commission shall be consistent with that member's international obligations, including its obligations under the Agreement establishing the World Trade Organisation.

3 If, within three years of the entry into force of this Convention, the Commission has not adopted at sea inspection procedures as outlined in paragraph 1 (b), or an alternative mechanism which effectively discharges the obligations of the members of the Commission under the 1995 Agreement and this Convention to ensure compliance with the conservation and management measures adopted by the Commission, Articles 21 and 22 of the 1995 Agreement shall apply among Contracting Parties as if those Articles were part of this Agreement, and boarding and inspection of fishing vessels in the Area, as well as any subsequent enforcement action, shall be conducted in accordance with Articles 21 and 22 of the 1995 Agreement and such additional practical procedures as the Commission may decide are necessary for the implementation of those Articles.

Article 28
OBSERVER PROGRAMME

1 The Commission shall establish an observer programme, within three years of the entry into force of this Convention or such other period as the Commission may agree, to collect verified catch and effort data, other scientific data and additional information related to the fishing activity in the Convention Area, and its impacts on the marine environment. Information collected by the observer programme shall, as appropriate, also be used to support the functions of the Commission and its subsidiary bodies, including the Compliance and Technical Committee. The observer programme shall be coordinated by the Secretariat of the Commission, and shall be organised in a flexible manner which takes into account the nature of the fishery resources

and other relevant factors. In this regard, the Commission may enter into contracts for the provision of the observer programme.

2 The observer programme shall consist of independent and impartial observers that are sourced from programmes or service providers accredited by the Commission. The programme shall be coordinated, to the maximum extent possible, with other regional, sub-regional and national observer programmes.

3 The Commission shall develop the observer programme taking into account advice from the Scientific Committee and Compliance and Technical Committee. The programme shall be operated in accordance with standards, rules and procedures developed by the Commission including, *inter alia*:

(a) arrangements for the placing of observers by a member of the Commission on vessels flying the flag of another member of the Commission with the consent of that member;

(b) levels of coverage appropriate for different fishery resources to monitor and verify catch, effort, catch composition and other details of fishing operations;

(c) requirements for collection, validation and reporting of scientific data and information relevant to the implementation of the provisions of this Convention and the conservation and management measures adopted by the Commission; and

(d) requirements to ensure the safety and training of observers, for observer accommodation while on board the vessel, and to ensure observers have full access to and use of all relevant facilities and equipment on board the vessel in order to perform their duties effectively.

Article 29
ANNUAL REPORT OF THE COMMISSION

1 The Commission shall publish an annual report, which shall include details of decisions taken by the Commission to achieve the objective of this Convention. The report shall also provide information on actions taken by the Commission in response to any recommendations from the General Assembly of the United Nations or the FAO.

2 Copies of the report shall be publicly available and shall be provided to the Secretary-General of the United Nations and the Director-General of the FAO.

Article 30
REVIEWS

1 The Commission shall review the effectiveness of the conservation and management measures adopted by the Commission in meeting the objective

of this Convention and the consistency of such measures with the principles and approaches in Article 3. Such reviews may include examination of the effectiveness of the provisions of the Convention itself and shall be undertaken at least every five years.

2 The Commission shall determine the terms of reference and methodology of such reviews which shall be carried out in accordance with criteria set by the Commission which shall be guided by best international practices and shall include contributions from the subsidiary bodies as appropriate and the participation of a person or persons of recognised competence who is independent of the Commission.

3 The Commission shall take account of the recommendations arising from any such review, including through the appropriate amendment of its conservation and management measures and the mechanisms for their implementation. Any proposals for amendment to the provisions of this Convention arising from any such review shall be dealt with in accordance with Article 35.

4 The results of any such review shall be made publicly available following its submission to the Commission.

Article 31
COOPERATION WITH OTHER ORGANISATIONS

1 The Commission shall cooperate, as appropriate, with other regional fisheries management organisations, the FAO, with other specialised agencies of the United Nations, and with other relevant organisations on matters of mutual interest.

2 The Commission shall take account of the conservation and management measures or recommendations adopted by other regional fisheries management organisations and other relevant intergovernmental organisations that have competency in relation to the Convention Area, or in relation to areas adjacent to the Convention Area or in respect of particular living marine resources including non-target and associated or dependent species, and that have objectives that are consistent with, and supportive of, the objective of this Convention. It shall endeavour to ensure that its own decisions are compatible with, and supportive of, such conservation and management measures or recommendations.

3 The Commission shall seek to make suitable arrangements for consultation, cooperation and collaboration with such other organisations. In particular it shall seek to cooperate with other relevant organisations with the aim of reducing and eventually eliminating IUU fishing.

Article 32
NON-PARTIES

1 Members of the Commission shall exchange information with respect to the activities of fishing vessels engaged in fishing in the Convention Area

that are flying the flags of non-Contracting Parties to this Convention. Members of the Commission shall take measures, individually or collectively, consistent with this Convention and international law to deter activities of such vessels which undermine the effectiveness of conservation and management measures applicable in the Convention Area, and shall report to the Commission any action taken in response to fishing in the Convention Area by non-Contracting Parties.

2 Taking account of Articles 116 to 119 of the 1982 Convention, the members of the Commission, individually or collectively, may draw the attention of any State or fishing entity which is a non-Contracting Party to this Convention to any activity which in the opinion of the member or members of the Commission affects the implementation of the objective of this Convention.

3 Members of the Commission shall, individually or collectively, request non-Contracting Parties to this Convention whose vessels fish in the Convention Area to become party to this Convention or to agree to cooperate fully in the implementation of conservation and management measures adopted by the Commission.

4 Members of the Commission, individually or jointly, shall seek the cooperation of any non-Contracting Party that has been identified as a relevant port State or market State to ensure compliance with the objective of this Convention.

Article 33
RELATION TO OTHER AGREEMENTS

1 Nothing in this Convention shall prejudice the rights, jurisdiction and duties of Contracting Parties under relevant provisions of international law as reflected in the 1982 Convention or the 1995 Agreement.

2 This Convention shall not alter the rights and obligations of Contracting Parties that arise from other agreements compatible with this Convention and that do not affect the enjoyment by other Contracting Parties of their rights or the performance of their obligations under this Convention.

Article 34
Settlement of Disputes

1 Contracting Parties shall cooperate in order to prevent disputes and shall use their best endeavours to resolve any disputes by amicable means which may include, where a dispute is of a technical nature, referring the dispute to an ad hoc expert panel.

2 In any case where a dispute is not resolved through the means set out in paragraph 1, the provisions relating to the settlement of disputes set out in Part VIII of the 1995 Agreement shall apply, *mutatis mutandis*, to any dispute between the Contracting Parties.

3 Paragraph 2 shall not affect the status of any Contracting Party in relation to the 1995 Agreement or the 1982 Convention.

Article 35
AMENDMENTS

1 The text of proposed amendments must be provided to the Executive Secretary at least 90 days in advance of a Commission meeting. The Executive Secretary shall promptly circulate a copy of this text to all members of the Commission.

2 Such proposals for amendment to this Convention shall be adopted by the Commission by a three-fourths majority of the Contracting Parties present and casting affirmative or negative votes. Adopted amendments shall be transmitted by the Depositary to all Contracting Parties without delay.

3 An amendment shall take effect for all Contracting Parties one hundred and twenty days following the date of transmittal specified in the notification by the Depositary of receipt of written notification of approval by three-fourths of all Contracting Parties unless any other Contracting Party notifies the Depositary that it objects to the amendment within ninety days of the date of transmittal specified in the notification by the Depositary of such receipt, in which case the amendment shall not take effect for any Contracting Party. Any Contracting Party which has objected to an amendment may at any time withdraw that objection. If all objections to an amendment are withdrawn, the amendment shall take effect for all Contracting Parties one hundred and twenty days following the date of transmittal specified in the notification by the Depositary of receipt of the last withdrawal.

4 Any State, regional economic integration organisation, or other entity referred to in Article 1 paragraph 2 (b) that becomes a Contracting Party after the adoption of an amendment in accordance with paragraph 2 shall be deemed to be bound by the Convention as amended once that amendment has entered into force in accordance with paragraph 3.

5 The Depositary shall promptly notify all Contracting Parties of the receipt of notifications of approval of amendments, the receipt of notifications of objection or withdrawal of objections, and the entry into force of amendments.

Article 36
SIGNATURE, RATIFICATION, ACCEPTANCE AND APPROVAL

1 This Convention shall be open for signature by:

(a) States, the regional economic integration organisation and the other entities referred to in Article 1, paragraph 2 (b), that participated in the International Consultations on the Establishment of the South Pacific Regional Fisheries Management Organisation; and

(b) any other State or any other entity referred to in Article 1, paragraph 2 (b), that has jurisdiction over waters adjacent to the Convention Area;

and shall remain open for signature for 12 months from the first day of February 2010.

2 This Convention is subject to ratification, acceptance or approval by the signatories.

3 Instruments of ratification, acceptance or approval shall be deposited with the Depositary.

Article 37
ACCESSION

1 This Convention shall be open for accession, after its closure for signature, by any State, regional economic integration organisation or other entity referred to in Article 36 paragraph 1, and by any other State or any other entity referred to in Article 1 paragraph 2 (b) having an interest in fishery resources.

2 Instruments of accession shall be deposited with the Depositary.

Article 38
ENTRY INTO FORCE

1 This Convention shall enter into force 30 days after the date of receipt by the Depositary of the eighth instrument of ratification, accession, acceptance or approval, which shall include ratification, accession, acceptance or approval by:

(a) at least three coastal States adjacent to the Convention Area, which must include representation from both the side of the Convention Area that is east of Meridian 120° West and the side of the Convention Area that is west of Meridian 120° West; and

(b) at least three States that are not coastal States adjacent to the Convention Area and whose fishing vessels are fishing in the Convention Area or have fished in the Convention Area.

2 If within three years of its adoption, this Convention has not entered into force in accordance with paragraph 1, it shall enter into force six months after the deposit of the tenth instrument of ratification, accession, acceptance or approval, or in accordance with paragraph 1, whichever is the earlier.

3 For each signatory which ratifies, accepts or approves this Convention after its entry into force, this Convention shall enter into force for that signatory 30 days after the deposit of its instrument of ratification, acceptance or approval.

4 For each State or regional economic integration organisation which accedes to this Convention after its entry into force, this Convention shall enter into force for that State or regional economic integration organisation 30 days after the deposit of its instrument of accession.

5 For the purposes of this Article, "fishing" includes only the activities described in Article 1 paragraph (g) (i) and (ii).

Article 39
THE DEPOSITARY

1 The Government of New Zealand shall be the Depositary of this Convention and any amendments thereto. The Depositary shall transmit certified copies of this Convention to all signatories and shall register this Convention with the Secretary-General of the United Nations pursuant to Article 102 of the Charter of the United Nations.

2 The Depositary shall inform all signatories of and Contracting Parties to this Convention of signatures and of instruments of ratification, accession, acceptance or approval deposited under Article 36 or 37 and of the date of entry into force of the Convention and of any amendments thereto.

Article 40
PARTICIPATION BY TERRITORIES

1 The Commission and its subsidiary bodies shall be open to participation, with the appropriate authorisation of the Contracting Party having responsibility for its international affairs, to territories in the region that have an interest in fishery resources.

2 The nature and extent of participation by territories shall be provided for by the Contracting Parties in separate rules of procedure of the Commission, taking into account international law, the distribution of competence on matters covered by this Convention and the evolution in the capacity of such territory to exercise rights and responsibilities under this Convention. These rules of procedure shall provide territories with the right to participate fully in the work of the Commission and its subsidiary bodies, except for the right to vote or block consensus on decisions, advice or recommendations.

3 Notwithstanding paragraph 2, all such territories shall be entitled to be present and to speak at the meetings of the Commission and its subsidiary bodies. In the performance of its functions, and in taking decisions, the Commission shall take into account the interests of all participants.

Article 41
WITHDRAWAL

1 A Contracting Party may, by written notification addressed to the Depositary, withdraw from this Convention and may indicate its reasons.

Failure to indicate reasons shall not affect the validity of the withdrawal. The withdrawal shall take effect 1 year after the date of receipt of the notification, unless the notification specifies a later date.

2 Withdrawal from this Convention by a Contracting Party shall not affect the financial obligations of such Contracting Party incurred prior to its withdrawal becoming effective.

3 Withdrawal from this Convention by a Contracting Party shall not in any way affect the duty of such Contracting Party to fulfil any obligation embodied in this Convention to which it would be subject under international law independently of this Convention.

Article 42
TERMINATION

This Convention shall be automatically terminated if and when, as the result of withdrawals, the number of Contracting Parties drops below 4.

Article 43
RESERVATIONS

No reservations or exceptions may be made to this Convention.

Article 44
DECLARATIONS AND STATEMENTS

Article 43 does not preclude a State, regional economic integration organisation or entity referred to in Article 1 paragraph 2 (b), when signing, ratifying or acceding to this Convention, from making declarations or statements, however phrased or named, with a view, *inter alia*, to the harmonisation of its laws and regulations with the provisions of this Convention, provided that such declarations or statements do not purport to exclude or to modify the legal effect of the provisions of this Convention in their application to that State, regional economic integration organisation or entity.

Article 45
ANNEXES

The Annexes form an integral part of this Convention and, unless expressly provided otherwise, a reference to this Convention includes a reference to the Annexes relating thereto.

IN WITNESS WHEREOF, the undersigned Plenipotentiaries, having been duly authorised by their respective Governments, have signed this Convention.

DONE at Auckland this fourteenth day of November, two thousand and nine, in a single original.

Annex I

PARTS OF THE CONVENTION AREA FOR WHICH THE EASTERN AND WESTERN SUB-REGIONAL MANAGEMENT COMMITTEES HAVE RESPONSIBILITIES

1 The Eastern Sub-regional Management Committee shall be responsible for developing and recommending to the Commission conservation and management measures for that part of the Convention Area that lies east of Meridian 120° West.

2 The Western Sub-regional Management Committee shall be responsible for developing and recommending to the Commission conservation and management measures for that part of the Convention Area that lies west of Meridian 120° West.

Annex II

REVIEW PANEL

Establishment

1 A Review Panel to be established in accordance with Article 17 paragraph 5 shall be constituted as follows:

(a) It shall consist of three members appointed from the list of experts in the field of fisheries drawn up and maintained by the FAO pursuant to Annex VIII, Article 2 of the 1982 Convention or a similar list maintained by the Executive Secretary. The list maintained by the Executive Secretary shall be made up from experts whose competence in the legal, scientific or technical aspects of fisheries covered by this Convention is established and generally recognised and who enjoy the highest reputation for fairness and integrity. Each member of the Commission shall be entitled to nominate up to five experts and shall provide information on relevant qualifications and experience of each of its nominees.

(b) The Chairperson of the Commission and the member of the Commission that has presented objection to the decision shall each appoint one member. The name of the member appointed by the objecting member of the Commission shall be included in the notification of the objection to the Executive Secretary pursuant to Article 17 paragraph 2 (a). The name of the member appointed by the Chairperson of the Commission shall be notified to the objecting member of the Commission within 10 days of the expiry of the objection period.

(c) The third member shall be appointed within 20 days of the expiry of the objection period through agreement between the objecting member of the Commission and the Chairperson of the Commission and shall not be a national of the objecting member of the Commission. If there is no agreement within this time period on the appointment of the third member, the appointment shall be made by the Secretary General of the Permanent Court of Arbitration, unless it is agreed that the appointment be made by another person or third State.

(d) The Review Panel is considered to be established on the date that the third member is appointed, and this third member shall chair the Review Panel.

2 If more than one member of the Commission presents an objection to the decision on the same grounds, or where there is agreement pursuant to Article 17 paragraph 5 (d) that objections to the decision made on different grounds may be dealt with by the same Review Panel, the Review Panel shall consist of 5 members from the lists referred to in paragraph 1 (a) and shall be constituted as follows:

(a) One member shall be appointed, in accordance with paragraph 1 (b) by the member of the Commission that presented the first objection, two members shall be appointed by the Chairperson of the Commission within 10 days of the expiry of the objection period, one member shall be appointed by agreement between the subsequent objecting members of the Commission within 15 days of the expiry of the objection period and one member shall be appointed by agreement between all the objecting members of the Commission and the Chairperson of the Commission within 20 days of the expiry of the objection period. If within the latter two time periods as appropriate, agreement cannot be reached on either of the last two appointments, the appointment or appointments on which agreement has not been reached shall be made by the Secretary General of the Permanent Court of Arbitration unless there is agreement that the appointment or appointments be made by another person or third State.

(b) The Review Panel is considered to be established on the date that the final member is appointed. The Review Panel shall be chaired by the member appointed by agreement between all the objecting members of the Commission and the Chairperson of the Commission in accordance with subparagraph (a).

3 Any vacancy on a Review Panel shall be filled in the manner described for the initial appointment.

Functioning

4 The Review Panel shall determine its own rules of procedure.

5 A hearing shall be convened at a place and on a date to be determined by the Review Panel within 30 days following its establishment.

6 Any member of the Commission may submit a memorandum to the Review Panel concerning the objection under review and the Panel shall allow any such member of the Commission full opportunity to be heard.

7 Unless the Review Panel decides otherwise because of the particular circumstances of the case, the expenses of the Review Panel, including the remuneration of its members, shall be borne as follows:

(a) 70 per cent shall be borne by the objecting member of the Commission, or if there is more than one objecting member of the Commission, divided equally amongst them; and

(b) 30 per cent shall be borne by the Commission from its annual budget.

8 The findings and recommendations of the Review Panel shall be adopted by a majority of its members. Any member of the Panel may attach a separate or dissenting opinion. Any decisions on the procedure of the Review Panel shall also be taken by a majority of its members.

9 The Review Panel shall, within 45 days of its establishment, transmit its findings and recommendations to the Executive Secretary in accordance with Article 17 paragraph 5.

Findings and Recommendations

10 The findings and recommendations of the Review Panel shall be dealt with as follows:

Findings of Discrimination

(a) If the Review Panel finds that the decision to which objection has been presented discriminates in form or in fact against the objecting member or members of the Commission and the alternative measures have equivalent effect to the decision to which objection has been presented, the alternative measures shall be deemed to be equivalent to the decision and to be binding on the relevant member or members of the Commission in substitution for the decision.

(b) Subject to subparagraphs (d) and (e), if the Review Panel finds that the decision to which objection has been presented discriminates in form or in fact against the objecting member or members of the Commission and the alternative measures are equivalent in effect to the decision to which objection has been presented, subject to specific modifications, the Review Panel will recommend such modifications. On receipt of the findings and recommendations of the Review Panel the objecting member or members of the Commission shall, within 60 days, modify the relevant alternative measures as recommended by the Review Panel or institute dispute settlement proceedings under this Convention. The alternative measures shall be deemed to be equivalent to the decision to which an objection has been presented when they are modified as recommended by the Review Panel. Such alternative measures shall then be binding on the relevant member or members of the Commission in the modified form in substitution for the decision. If the objecting member or members of the Commission choose to institute dispute settlement proceedings under this Convention then neither the decision nor the modified alternative measures shall be binding on the objecting member or members of the Commission pending decisions made in those proceedings.

(c) Subject to subparagraphs (d) and (e), if the Review Panel finds that the decision to which objection has been presented unjustifiably discriminates in form or in fact against the objecting member or members of the Commission but the alternative measures do not have equivalent effect to the decision to which objection has been presented the objecting member or members of the Commission shall, within 60 days, adopt measures recommended by the Review Panel as equivalent in effect to the decision to which objection has been presented or institute dispute settlement proceedings under this Convention. If the objecting member or members of the Commission adopt the measures recommended by the Review Panel these measures shall be deemed to be binding on the objecting member or members of the Commission in substitution for the decision. If the objecting member or members of the Commission choose to institute dispute settlement proceedings under this Convention then neither the decision nor any measures recommended by the Review Panel shall be binding on the objecting member or members of the Commission pending decisions made in those proceedings.

(d) Where the Review Panel makes findings and recommendations under subparagraphs (b) or (c) the objecting member or members of the Commission may within 30 days from the date of the transmittal of the notification of those findings and recommendations request an extraordinary meeting of the Commission. The Extraordinary Meeting shall be convened by the Chairperson within 45 days of the receipt of any such request.

(e) If the Extraordinary Meeting convened under subparagraph (d) confirms or modifies the recommendations of the Review Panel, the 60 day period under subparagraphs (b) or (c) as appropriate, for the implementation of those findings and recommendations in original or modified form or the institution of dispute settlement proceedings, shall run from the date of the transmittal of the decision of the Extraordinary Meeting. If the Extraordinary Meeting of the Commission decides not to confirm or modify the recommendations of the Review Panel but to revoke the decision to which objection was presented and replace it with a new decision or a modified version of the original decision, the new or modified decision shall become binding on the members of the Commission in accordance with Article 17.

Findings of Inconsistency

(f) If the Review Panel finds that the decision to which objection has been presented is inconsistent with this Convention, or with relevant international law as reflected in the 1982 Convention or the 1995 Agreement, an Extraordinary Meeting of the Commission shall be convened by the Chairperson within 45 days of the notification of the Review Panel's findings and recommendations to reconsider the decision in the light of those findings and recommendations.

(g) If the Extraordinary Meeting of the Commission revokes the decision to which objection has been presented and replaces it with a new decision, or a modified version of the previous decision, the new or modified decision shall become binding on the members of the Commission in accordance with Article 17.

(h) If the Extraordinary Meeting of the Commission confirms its original decision, the objecting member or members of the Commission shall, within 45 days, implement the decision or institute dispute settlement proceedings under this Convention. If the objecting member or members of the Commission choose to institute dispute settlement proceedings under this Convention, the decision shall not be binding on the objecting member or members of the Commission pending decisions made in those proceedings.

Findings of Non-justification of Objection

(i) If the Review Panel finds that the decision to which objection has been presented does not discriminate in form or in fact against the objecting member or members of the Commission and is not inconsistent with this Convention or with relevant international law as reflected in the 1982 Convention or the 1995 Agreement, the objecting member or members of the Commission shall, subject to subparagraph (j), within 45 days implement the decision or institute dispute settlement proceedings under this Convention. If the objecting member or members of the Commission choose to institute dispute settlement proceedings under this Convention the decision shall not be binding on the objecting member or members of the Commission pending decisions made in those proceedings.

(j) If the Review Panel finds that the decision to which objection has been presented does not discriminate in form or in fact against the objecting member or members of the Commission and is not inconsistent with this Convention or with relevant international law as reflected in the 1982 Convention or the 1995 Agreement but that the alternative measures are equivalent in effect to the decision and should be accepted as such by the Commission, the alternative measures shall be binding on the objecting member or members of the Commission in substitution for the decision pending confirmation of their acceptance by the Commission at its next meeting.

Annex III

PROCEDURES FOR THE ESTABLISHMENT AND IMPLEMENTATION OF A TOTAL ALLOWABLE CATCH OR TOTAL ALLOWABLE FISHING EFFORT FOR A STRADDLING FISHERY RESOURCE WHEN APPLIED THROUGHOUT ITS RANGE

1 In accordance with Articles 23 and 24, coastal State Contracting Parties and members of the Commission whose vessels fish for the straddling fishery resource in areas under national jurisdiction or on the high seas in the adjacent Convention Area shall provide all relevant scientific, technical and statistical data with respect to such fishery resources to the Commission for consideration by the Scientific Committee and, as appropriate, the Compliance and Technical Committee.

2 In accordance with Article 10, the Scientific Committee shall assess the status of the straddling fishery resource throughout its range and provide advice to the Commission and the relevant Sub-regional Management Committee on an appropriate total allowable catch or total allowable fishing effort for the resource throughout its range. Such advice should include where possible estimates of the extent to which the establishment of a total allowable catch or a total allowable fishing effort at different levels would achieve the objective or objectives of any management strategy or plan adopted by the Commission.

3 In accordance with Article 12, and on the basis of the advice of the Scientific Committee and any relevant advice of the Compliance and Technical Committee, the relevant Sub-regional Management Committee shall make recommendations to the Commission on a total allowable catch or total allowable fishing effort for the fishery resource throughout its range and appropriate measures to ensure the total allowable catch or total allowable fishing effort is not exceeded.

4 In accordance with Articles 16 and 20, the Commission, on the basis of the recommendations and advice from the Scientific Committee and the relevant Sub-regional Management Committee and any relevant advice of the Compliance and Technical Committee, shall establish a total allowable catch or total allowable fishing effort for the fishery resource throughout its range and adopt appropriate measures to ensure that the total allowable catch or total allowable fishing effort is not exceeded.

5 In relation to the conservation and management of *Trachurus murphyi* (jack mackerel), the Commission shall, in accordance with Article 20, and as appropriate, give primary consideration to establishing a total allowable catch, without prejudice to any other conservation and management measures which it considers appropriate to adopt to ensure the conservation and sustainable use of this fishery resource.

Annex IV

FISHING ENTITIES

1 After the entry into force of this Convention, any fishing entity whose vessels have fished or intend to fish for fishery resources may, by a written instrument delivered to the Depositary, express its firm commitment to abide by the terms of this Convention and comply with any conservation and management measures adopted pursuant to it. Such commitment shall become effective 30 days from the date of receipt of the instrument. Any such fishing entity may withdraw such commitment by written notification addressed to the Depositary. The withdrawal shall become effective 1 year after the date of its receipt, unless the notification specifies a later date.

2 Any fishing entity referred to in paragraph 1 above may by a written instrument delivered to the Depositary, express its firm commitment to abide by the terms of the Convention as it may be amended pursuant to Article 35(3). This commitment shall be effective from the dates referred to in Article 35(3) or on the date of receipt of the written communication referred to in this paragraph, whichever is later.

3 A fishing entity which has expressed its firm commitment to abide by the terms of this Convention and comply with conservation and management measures adopted pursuant to it in accordance with paragraph 1 must abide by the obligations of members of the Commission, and may participate in the work, including decision making, of the Commission in accordance with the provisions of this Convention. For the purposes of this Convention, references to the Commission or members of the Commission include such fishing entity.

4 If a dispute involves a fishing entity which has expressed its commitment to be bound by the terms of this Convention in accordance with this Annex and cannot be settled by amicable means, the dispute shall, at the request of any party to the dispute, be submitted to final and binding arbitration in accordance with the relevant rules of the Permanent Court of Arbitration.

5 The provisions of this Annex relating to the participation of a fishing entity are only for the purposes of this Convention.

CONVENTION ON THE CONSERVATION AND MANAGEMENT OF HIGHLY MIGRATORY FISH STOCKS IN THE WESTERN AND CENTRAL PACIFIC OCEAN

The Contracting Parties to this Convention,

Determined to ensure the long-term conservation and sustainable use, in particular for human food consumption, of highly migratory fish stocks in the western and central Pacific Ocean for present and future generations,

Recalling the relevant provisions of the United Nations Convention on the Law of the Sea of 10 December 1982 and the Agreement for the Implementation of the Provisions of the United Nations Convention on the Law of the Sea of 10 December 1982 relating to the Conservation and Management of Straddling Fish Stocks and Highly Migratory Fish Stocks,

Recognizing that, under the 1982 Convention and the Agreement, coastal States and States fishing in the region shall cooperate with a view to ensuring conservation and promoting the objective of optimum utilization of highly migratory fish stocks throughout their range,

Mindful that effective conservation and management measures require the application of the precautionary approach and the best scientific information available,

Conscious of the need to avoid adverse impacts on the marine environment, preserve biodiversity, maintain the integrity of marine ecosystems and minimize the risk of long-term or irreversible effects of fishing operations,

Recognizing the ecological and geographical vulnerability of the small island developing States, territories and possessions in the region, their economic and social dependence on highly migratory fish stocks, and their need for specific assistance, including financial, scientific and technological assistance, to allow them to participate effectively in the conservation, management and sustainable use of the highly migratory fish stocks,

Further recognizing that smaller island developing States have unique needs which require special attention and consideration in the provision of financial, scientific and technological assistance,

Acknowledging that comp atible, effective and binding conservation and management measures can be achieved only through cooperation between coastal States and States fishing in the region,

Convinced that effective conservation and management of the highly migratory fish stocks of the western and central Pacific Ocean in their entirety may best be achieved through the establishment of a regional Commission,

Have agreed as follows:

PART I
GENERAL PROVISIONS

Article 1
Use of terms

For the purposes of this Convention:

(a) "1982 Convention" means the United Nations Convention on the Law of the Sea of 10 December 1982;

(b) "Agreement" means the Agreement for the Implementation of the Provisions of the United Nations Convention on the Law of the Sea of 10 December 1982 relating to the Conservation and Management of Straddling Fish Stocks and Highly Migratory Fish Stocks;

(c) "Commission" means the Commission for the Conservation and Management of Highly Migratory Fish Stocks in the Western and Central Pacific Ocean established in accordance with this Convention;

(d) "fishing" means:

(i) searching for, catching, taking or harvesting fish;

(ii) attempting to search for, catch, take or harvest fish;

(iii) engaging in any other activity which can reasonably be expected to result in the locating, catching, taking or harvesting of fish for any purpose;

(iv) placing, searching for or recovering fish aggregating devices or associated electronic equipment such as radio beacons;

(v) any operations at sea directly in support of, or in preparation for, any activity described in subparagraphs (i) to (iv), including transhipment;

(vi) use of any other vessel, vehicle, aircraft or hovercraft, for any activity described in subparagraphs (i) to (v)

except for emergencies involving the health and safety of the crew or the safety of a vessel;

(e) "fishing vessel" means any vessel used or intended for use for the purpose of fishing, including support ships, carrier vessels and any other vessel directly involved in such fishing operations;

(f) "highly migratory fish stocks" means all fish stocks of the species listed in Annex 1 of the 1982 Convention occurring in the Convention Area, and such other species of fish as the Commission may determine;

(g) "regional economic integration organization" means a regional economic integration organization to which its member States have transferred competence over matters covered by this Convention, including the authority to make decisions binding on its member States in respect of those matters;

(h) "transhipment" means the unloading of all or any of the fish on board a fishing vessel to another fishing vessel either at sea or in port.

Article 2
Objective

The objective of this Convention is to ensure, through effective management, the long-term conservation and sustainable use of highly migratory fish stocks in the western and central Pacific Ocean in accordance with the 1982 Convention and the Agreement.

Article 3
Area of application

1. Subject to article 4, the area of competence of the Commission (hereinafter referred to as "the Convention Area") comprises all waters of the Pacific Ocean bounded to the south and to the east by the following line:

> From the south coast of Australia due south along the 141° meridian of east longitude to its intersection with the 55° parallel of south latitude; thence due east along the 55° parallel of south latitude to its intersection with the 150° meridian of east longitude; thence due south along the 150° meridian of east longitude to its intersection with the 60° parallel of south latitude; thence due east along the 60° parallel of south latitude to its intersection with the 130° meridian of west longitude; thence due north along the 130° meridian of west longitude to its intersection with the 4° parallel of south latitude; thence due west along the 4° parallel of south latitude to its intersection with the 150° meridian of west longitude; thence due north along the 150° meridian of west longitude.

2. Nothing in this Convention shall constitute recognition of the claims or positions of any of the members of the Commission concerning the legal status and extent of waters and zones claimed by any such members.

3. This Convention applies to all stocks of highly migratory fish within the Convention Area except sauries. Conservation and management measures under this Convention shall be applied throughout the range of the stocks, or to specific areas within the Convention Area, as determined by the Commission.

Article 4
Relationship between this Convention and the 1982 Convention

Nothing in this Convention shall prejudice the rights, jurisdiction and duties of States under the 1982 Convention and the Agreement. This Convention shall be interpreted and applied in the context of and in a manner consistent with the 1982 Convention and the Agreement.

PART II
CONSERVATION AND MANAGEMENT OF HIGHLY MIGRATORY FISH STOCKS

Article 5
Principles and measures for conservation and management

In order to conserve and manage highly migratory fish stocks in the Convention Area in their entirety, the members of the Commission shall, in giving effect to their duty to cooperate in accordance with the 1982 Convention, the Agreement and this Convention:

(a) adopt measures to ensure long-term sustainability of highly migratory fish stocks in the Convention Area and promote the objective of their optimum utilization;

(b) ensure that such measures are based on the best scientific evidence available and are designed to maintain or restore stocks at levels capable of producing maximum sustainable yield, as qualified by relevant environmental and economic factors, including the special requirements of developing States in the Convention Area, particularly small island developing States, and taking into account fishing patterns, the interdependence of stocks and any generally recommended international minimum standards, whether subregional, regional or global;

(c) apply the precautionary approach in accordance with this Convention and all relevant internationally agreed standards and recommended practices and procedures;

(d) assess the impacts of fishing, other human activities and environmental factors on target stocks, non-target species, and species belonging to the same ecosystem or dependent upon or associated with the target stocks;

(e) adopt measures to minimize waste, discards, catch by lost or abandoned gear, pollution originating from fishing vessels, catch of non-target species, both fish and non-fish species, (hereinafter referred to as non-target species) and impacts on associated or dependent species, in particular endangered species and promote the development and use of selective, environmentally safe and cost-effective fishing gear and techniques;

(f) protect biodiversity in the marine environment;

(g) take measures to prevent or eliminate over-fishing and excess fishing capacity and to ensure that levels of fishing effort do not exceed those commensurate with the sustainable use of fishery resources;

(h) take into account the interests of artisanal and subsistence fishers;

(i) collect and share, in a timely manner, complete and accurate data concerning fishing activities on, inter alia, vessel position, catch of target and non-target species and fishing effort, as well as information from national and international research programmes; and

(j) implement and enforce conservation and management measures through effective monitoring, control and surveillance.

Article 6
Application of the precautionary approach

1. In applying the precautionary approach, the members of the Commission shall:

(a) apply the guidelines set out in Annex II of the Agreement, which shall form an integral part of this Convention, and determine, on the basis of the best scientific information available, stock-specific reference points and the action to be taken if they are exceeded;

(b) take into account, inter alia, uncertainties relating to the size and productivity of the stocks, reference points, stock condition in relation to such reference points, levels and distributions of fishing mortality and the impact of fishing activities on non-target and associated or dependent species, as well as existing and predicted oceanic, environmental and socio-economic conditions; and

(c) develop data collection and research programmes to assess the impact of fishing on non-target and associated or dependent species and their environment, and adopt plans where necessary to ensure the conservation of such species and to protect habitats of special concern.

2. Members of the Commission shall be more cautious when information is uncertain, unreliable or inadequate. The absence of adequate scientific information shall not be used as a reason for postponing or failing to take conservation and management measures.

3. Members of the Commission shall take measures to ensure that, when reference points are approached, they will not be exceeded. In the event they are exceeded, members of the Commission shall, without delay, take the action determined under paragraph 1(a) to restore the stocks.

4. Where the status of target stocks or non-target or associated or dependent species is of concern, members of the Commission shall subject such stocks and species to enhanced monitoring in order to review their status and the efficacy of conservation and management measures. They shall revise those measures regularly in the light of new information.

5. For new or exploratory fisheries, members of the Commission shall adopt as soon as possible cautious conservation and management measures, including, inter alia, catch limits and effort limits. Such measures shall remain in force until there are sufficient data to allow assessment of the impact of the fisheries on the long- term sustainability of the stocks, whereupon conservation and management measures based on that assessment shall be implemented. The latter measures shall, if appropriate, allow for the gradual development of the fisheries.

6. If a natural phenomenon has a significant adverse impact on the status of highly migratory fish stocks, members of the Commission shall adopt conservation and management measures on an emergency basis to ensure that fishing activity does not exacerbate such adverse impacts. Members of the Commission shall also adopt such measures on an emergency basis where fishing activity presents a serious threat to the sustainability of such stocks. Measures taken on an emergency basis shall be temporary and shall be based on the best scientific information available.

Article 7
Implementation of principles in areas under national jurisdiction

1. The principles and measures for conservation and management enumerated in article 5 shall be applied by coastal States within areas under national jurisdiction in the Convention Area in the exercise of their sovereign rights for the purpose of exploring and exploiting, conserving and managing highly migratory fish stocks.

2. The members of the Commission shall give due consideration to the respective capacities of developing coastal States, in particular small island developing States, in the Convention Area to apply the provisions of articles 5 and 6 within areas under national jurisdiction and their need for assistance as provided for in this Convention.

Article 8
Compatibility of conservation and management measures

1. Conservation and management measures established for the high seas and those adopted for areas under national jurisdiction shall be compatible in order to ensure conservation and management of highly migratory fish stocks in their entirety. To this end, the members of the Commission have a duty to cooperate for the purpose of achieving compatible measures in respect of such stocks.

2. In establishing compatible conservation and management measures for highly migratory fish stocks in the Convention Area, the Commission shall:

(a) take into account the biological unity and other biological characteristics of the stocks and the relationships between the distribution of the stocks, the fisheries and the geographical particularities of the region concerned, including the extent to which the stocks occur and are fished in areas under national jurisdiction;

(b) take into account:

(i) the conservation and management measures adopted and applied in accordance with article 61 of the 1982 Convention in respect of the same stocks by coastal States within areas under national jurisdiction and ensure that measures established in respect of such stocks for the Convention

Area as a whole do not undermine the effectiveness of such measures;

(ii) previously agreed measures established and applied in respect of the same stocks for the high seas which form part of the Convention Area by relevant coastal States and States fishing on the high seas in accordance with the 1982 Convention and the Agreement;

(c) take into account previously agreed measures established and applied in accordance with the 1982 Convention and the Agreement in respect of the same stocks by a subregional or regional fisheries management organization or arrangement;

(d) take into account the respective dependence of the coastal States and the States fishing on the high seas on the stocks concerned; and

(e) ensure that such measures do not result in harmful impact on the living marine resources as a whole.

3. The coastal State shall ensure that the measures adopted and applied by it to highly migratory fish stocks within areas under its national jurisdiction do not undermine the effectiveness of measures adopted by the Commission under this Convention in respect of the same stocks.

4. Where there are areas of high seas in the Convention Area entirely surrounded by the exclusive economic zones of members of the Commission, the Commission shall, in giving effect to this article, pay special attention to ensuring compatibility between conservation and management measures established for such high seas areas and those established in respect of the same stocks in accordance with article 61 of the 1982 Convention by the surrounding coastal States in areas under national jurisdiction.

PART III
COMMISSION FOR THE CONSERVATION AND MANAGEMENT OF HIGHLY MIGRATORY FISH STOCKS IN THE WESTERN AND CENTRAL PACIFIC OCEAN

SECTION 1. GENERAL PROVISIONS

Article 9
Establishment of the Commission

1. There is hereby established the Commission for the Conservation and Management of Highly Migratory Fish Stocks in the Western and Central Pacific Ocean, which shall function in accordance with the provisions of this Convention.

2. A fishing entity referred to in the Agreement, which has agreed to be bound by the regime established by this Convention in accordance with the provisions of Annex I, may participate in the work, including

decision-making, of the Commission in accordance with the provisions of this article and Annex I.

3. The Commission shall hold an annual meeting. The Commission shall hold such other meetings as may be necessary to carry out its functions under this Convention.

4. The Commission shall elect a chairman and a vice-chairman from among the Contracting Parties, who shall be of different nationalities. They shall be elected for a period of two years and shall be eligible for re-election. The chairman and vice-chairman shall remain in office until the election of their successors.

5. The principle of cost-effectiveness shall apply to the frequency, duration and scheduling of meetings of the Commission and its subsidiary bodies. The Commission may, where appropriate, enter into contractual arrangements with relevant institutions to provide expert services necessary for the efficient functioning of the Commission and to enable it to carry out effectively its responsibilities under this Convention.

6. The Commission shall have international legal personality and such legal capacity as may be necessary to perform its functions and achieve its objectives. The privileges and immunities which the Commission and its officers shall enjoy in the territory of a Contracting Party shall be determined by agreement between the Commission and the member concerned.

7. The Contracting Parties shall determine the location of the headquarters of the Commission and shall appoint its Executive Director.

8. The Commission shall adopt, and amend as required, by consensus, rules of procedure for the conduct of its meetings, including meetings of its subsidiary bodies, and for the efficient exercise of its functions.

Article 10
Functions of the Commission

1. Without prejudice to the sovereign rights of coastal States for the purpose of exploring and exploiting, conserving and managing highly migratory fish stocks within areas under national jurisdiction, the functions of the Commission shall be to:

(a) determine the total allowable catch or total level of fishing effort within the Convention Area for such highly migratory fish stocks as the Commission may decide and adopt such other conservation and management measures and recommendations as may be necessary to ensure the long-term sustainability of such stocks;

(b) promote cooperation and coordination between members of the Commission to ensure that conservation and management measures for highly migratory fish stocks in areas under national jurisdiction and measures for the same stocks on the high seas are compatible;

(c) adopt, where necessary, conservation and management measures and recommendations for nontarget species and species dependent on or associated with the target stocks, with a view to maintaining or restoring populations of such species above levels at which their reproduction may become seriously threatened;

(d) adopt standards for collection, verification and for the timely exchange and reporting of data on fisheries for highly migratory fish stocks in the Convention Area in accordance with Annex I of the Agreement, which shall form an integral part of this Convention;

(e) compile and disseminate accurate and complete statistical data to ensure that the best scientific information is available, while maintaining confidentiality, where appropriate;

(f) obtain and evaluate scientific advice, review the status of stocks, promote the conduct of relevant scientific research and disseminate the results thereof;

(g) develop, where necessary, criteria for the allocation of the total allowable catch or the total level of fishing effort for highly migratory fish stocks in the Convention Area;

(h) adopt generally recommended international minimum standards for the responsible conduct of fishing operations;

(i) establish appropriate cooperative mechanisms for effective monitoring, control, surveillance and enforcement, including a vessel monitoring system;

(j) obtain and evaluate economic and other fisheries-related data and information relevant to the work of the Commission;

(k) agree on means by which the fishing interests of any new member of the Commission may be accommodated;

(l) adopt its rules of procedure and financial regulations and such other internal administrative regulations as may be necessary to carry out its functions;

(m) consider and approve the proposed budget of the Commission;

(n) promote the peaceful settlement of disputes; and

(o) discuss any question or matter within the competence of the Commission and adopt any measures or recommendations necessary for achieving the objective of this Convention.

2. In giving effect to paragraph 1, the Commission may adopt measures relating to, inter alia:

(a) the quantity of any species or stocks which may be caught;

(b) the level of fishing effort;

(c) limitations of fishing capacity, including measures relating to fishing vessel numbers, types and sizes;

(d) the areas and periods in which fishing may occur;

(e) the size of fish of any species which may be taken;

(f) the fishing gear and technology which may be used; and

(g) particular subregions or regions.

3. In developing criteria for allocation of the total allowable catch or the total level of fishing effort the Commission shall take into account, inter alia:

(a) the status of the stocks and the existing level of fishing effort in the fishery;

(b) the respective interests, past and present fishing patterns and fishing practices of participants in the fishery and the extent of the catch being utilized for domestic consumption;

(c) the historic catch in an area;

(d) the needs of small island developing States, and territories and possessions, in the Convention Area whose economies, food supplies and livelihoods are overwhelmingly dependent on the exploitation of marine living resources;

(e) the respective contributions of participants to conservation and management of the stocks, including the provision by them of accurate data and their contribution to the conduct of scientific research in the Convention Area;

(f) the record of compliance by the participants with conservation and management measures;

(g) the needs of coastal communities which are dependent mainly on fishing for the stocks;

(h) the special circumstances of a State which is surrounded by the exclusive economic zones of other States and has a limited exclusive economic zone of its own;

(i) the geographical situation of a small island developing State which is made up of non-contiguous groups of islands having a distinct economic and cultural identity of their own but which are separated by areas of high seas;

(j) the fishing interests and aspirations of coastal States, particularly small island developing States, and territories and possessions, in whose areas of national jurisdiction the stocks also occur.

4. The Commission may adopt decisions relating to the allocation of the total allowable catch or the total level of fishing effort. Such decisions, including decisions relating to the exclusion of vessel types, shall be taken by consensus.

5. The Commission shall take into account the reports and any recommendations of the Scientific Committee and the Technical and Compliance Committee on matters within their respective areas of competence.

6. The Commission shall promptly notify all members of the measures and recommendations decided upon by the Commission and shall give due publicity to the conservation and management measures adopted by it.

Article 11
Subsidiary bodies of the Commission

1. There are hereby established as subsidiary bodies to the Commission a Scientific Committee and a Technical and Compliance Committee to provide advice and recommendations to the Commission on matters within their respective areas of competence.

2. Each member of the Commission shall be entitled to appoint one representative to each Committee who may be accompanied by other experts and advisers. Such representatives shall have appropriate qualifications or relevant experience in the area of competence of the Committee.

3. Each Committee shall meet as often as is required for the efficient exercise of its functions, provided that each Committee shall, in any event, meet prior to the annual meeting of the Commission and shall report to the annual meeting the results of its deliberations.

4. Each Committee shall make every effort to adopt its reports by consensus. If every effort to achieve consensus has failed, the report shall indicate the majority and minority views and may include the differing views of the representatives of the members on all or any part of the report.

5. In the exercise of their functions, each Committee may, where appropriate, consult any other fisheries management, technical or scientific organization with competence in the subject matter of such consultation and may seek expert advice as required on an ad hoc basis.

6. The Commission may establish such other subsidiary bodies as it deems necessary for the exercise of its functions, including working groups for the purpose of examining technical issues relating to particular species or stocks and reporting thereon to the Commission.

7. The Commission shall establish a committee to make recommendations on the implementation of such conservation and management measures as may be adopted by the Commission for the area north of the 20° parallel of north latitude and on the formulation of such measures in respect of stocks which occur mostly in this area. The committee shall include the

members situated in such area and those fishing in the area. Any member of the Commission not represented on the committee may send a representative to participate in the deliberations of the committee as an observer. Any extraordinary cost incurred for the work of the committee shall be borne by the members of the committee. The committee shall adopt recommendations to the Commission by consensus. In adopting measures in relation to particular stocks and species in such area, the decision of the Commission shall be based on any recommendations of the committee. Such recommendations shall be consistent with the general policies and measures adopted by the Commission in respect of the stocks or species in question and with the principles and measures for conservation and management set out in this Convention. If the Commission, in accordance with the rules of procedure for decision-making on matters of substance, does not accept the recommendation of the committee on any matter, it shall return the matter to the committee for further consideration. The committee shall reconsider the matter in the light of the views expressed by the Commission.

SECTION 2. SCIENTIFIC INFORMATION AND ADVICE

Article 12
Functions of the Scientific Committee

1. The Scientific Committee is established to ensure that the Commission obtains for its consideration the best scientific information available.

2. The functions of the Committee shall be to:

(a) recommend to the Commission a research plan, including specific issues and items to be addressed by the scientific experts or by other organizations or individuals, as appropriate, and identify data needs and coordinate activities that meet those needs;

(b) review the assessments, analyses, other work and recommendations prepared for the Commission by the scientific experts prior to consideration of such recommendations by the Commission and provide information, advice and comments thereon, as necessary;

(c) encourage and promote cooperation in scientific research, taking into account the provisions of article 246 of the 1982 Convention, in order to improve information on highly migratory fish stocks, non-target species, and species belonging to the same ecosystem or associated with or dependent upon such stocks in the Convention Area;

(d) review the results of research and analyses of target stocks or non-target or associated or dependent species in the Convention Area;

(e) report to the Commission its findings or conclusions on the status of target stocks or non-target or associated or dependent species in the Convention Area;

(f) in consultation with the Technical and Compliance Committee, recommend to the Commission the priorities and objectives of the regional observer programme and assess the results of that programme;

(g) make reports and recommendations to the Commission as directed, or on its own initiative, on matters concerning the conservation and management of and research on target stocks or non-target or associated or dependent species in the Convention Area; and

(h) perform such other functions and tasks as may be requested by or assigned to it by the Commission.

3. The Committee shall exercise its functions in accordance with such guidelines and directives as the Commission may adopt.

4. The representatives of the Oceanic Fisheries Programme of the Pacific Community and the Inter- American Tropical Tuna Commission, or their successor organizations, shall be invited to participate in the work of the Committee. The Committee may also invite other organizations or individuals with scientific expertise in matters related to the work of the Commission to participate in its meetings.

Article 13
Scientific services

1. The Commission, taking into account any recommendation of the Scientific Committee, may engage the services of scientific experts to provide information and advice on the fishery resources covered by this Convention and related matters that may be relevant to the conservation and management of those resources. The Commission may enter into administrative and financial arrangements to utilize scientific services for this purpose. In this regard, and in order to carry out its functions in a cost-effective manner, the Commission shall, to the greatest extent possible, utilize the services of existing regional organizations and shall consult, as appropriate, with any other fisheries management, technical or scientific organization with expertise in matters related to the work of the Commission.

2. The scientific experts may, as directed by the Commission:

(a) conduct scientific research and analyses in support of the work of the Commission;

(b) develop and recommend to the Commission and the Scientific Committee stock-specific reference points for the species of principal interest to the Commission;

(c) assess the status of stocks against the reference points established by the Commission;

(d) provide the Commission and the Scientific Committee with reports on the results of their scientific work, advice and recommendations in support of the formulation of conservation and management measures and other relevant matters; and

(e) perform such other functions and tasks as may be required.

3. In carrying out their work, the scientific experts may:

(a) undertake the collection, compilation and dissemination of fisheries data according to agreed principles and procedures established by the Commission, including procedures and policies relating to the confidentiality, disclosure and publication of data;

(b) conduct assessments of highly migratory fish stocks, non-target species, and species belonging to the same ecosystem or associated with or dependent upon such stocks, within the Convention Area;

(c) assess the impacts of fishing, other human activities and environmental factors on target stocks and species belonging to the same ecosystem or dependent upon or associated with the target stocks;

(d) assess the potential effects of proposed changes in the methods or levels of fishing and of proposed conservation and management measures; and

(e) investigate such other scientific matters as may be referred to them by the Commission.

4. The Commission may make appropriate arrangements for periodic peer review of scientific information and advice provided to the Commission by the scientific experts.

5. The reports and recommendations of the scientific experts shall be provided to the Scientific Committee and to the Commission.

SECTION 3. THE TECHNICAL AND COMPLIANCE COMMITTEE

Article 14
Functions of the Technical and Compliance Committee

1. The functions of the Technical and Compliance Committee shall be to:

(a) provide the Commission with information, technical advice and recommendations relating to the implementation of, and compliance with, conservation and management measures;

(b) monitor and review compliance with conservation and management measures adopted by the Commission and make such recommendations to the Commission as may be necessary; and

(c) review the implementation of cooperative measures for monitoring, control, surveillance and enforcement adopted by the Commission and make such recommendations to the Commission as may be necessary.

2. In carrying out its functions, the Committee shall:

(a) provide a forum for exchange of information concerning the means by which they are applying the conservation and management measures adopted by the Commission on the high seas and complementary measures in waters under national jurisdiction;

(b) receive reports from each member of the Commission relating to measures taken to monitor, investigate and penalize violations of provisions of this Convention and measures adopted pursuant thereto;

(c) in consultation with the Scientific Committee, recommend to the Commission the priorities and objectives of the regional observer programme, when established, and assess the results of that programme;

(d) consider and investigate such other matters as may be referred to it by the Commission, including developing and reviewing measures to provide for the verification and validation of fisheries data;

(e) make recommendations to the Commission on technical matters such as fishing vessel and gear markings;

(f) in consultation with the Scientific Committee, make recommendations to the Commission on the fishing gear and technology which may be used;

(g) report to the Commission its findings or conclusions on the extent of compliance with conservation and management measures; and

(h) make recommendations to the Commission on matters relating to monitoring, control, surveillance and enforcement.

3. The Committee may establish, with the approval of the Commission, such subsidiary bodies as may be necessary for the performance of its functions.

4. The Committee shall exercise its functions in accordance with such guidelines and directives as the Commission may adopt.

SECTION 4. THE SECRETARIAT

Article 15
The Secretariat

1. The Commission may establish a permanent Secretariat consisting of an Executive Director and such other staff as the Commission may require.

2. The Executive Director shall be appointed for a term of four years and may be re -appointed for a further term of four years.

3. The Executive Director shall be the chief administrative officer of the Commission, and shall act in that capacity in all the meetings of the

Commission and of any subsidiary body, and shall perform such other administrative functions as are entrusted to the Executive Director by the Commission.

4. The Secretariat functions shall include the following:

(a) receiving and transmitting the Commission's official communications;

(b) facilitating the compilation and dissemination of data necessary to accomplish the objective of this Convention;

(c) preparing administrative and other reports for the Commission and the Scientific and Technical and Compliance Committees;

(d) administering agreed arrangements for monitoring, control and surveillance and the provision of scientific advice;

(e) publishing the decisions of and promoting the activities of the Commission and its subsidiary bodies; and

(f) treasury, personnel and other administrative functions.

5. In order to minimize costs to the members of the Commission, the Secretariat to be established under this Convention shall be cost effective. The setting up and the functioning of the Secretariat shall, where appropriate, take into account the capacity of existing regional institutions to perform certain technical secretariat functions.

Article 16
The staff of the Commission

1. The staff of the Commission shall consist of such qualified scientific and technical and other personnel as may be required to fulfil the functions of the Commission. The staff shall be appointed by the Executive Director.

2. The paramount consideration in the recruitment and employment of the staff shall be the necessity of securing the highest standards of efficiency, competence and integrity. Subject to this consideration, due regard shall be paid to the importance of recruiting the staff on an equitable basis between the members of the Commission with a view to ensuring a broad-based Secretariat.

SECTION 5. FINANCIAL ARRANGEMENTS OF THE COMMISSION

Article 17
Funds of the Commission

1. The funds of the Commission shall include:

(a) assessed contributions in accordance with article 18, paragraph 2;

(b) voluntary contributions;

(c) the fund referred to in article 30, paragraph 3; and

(d) any other funds which the Commission may receive.

2. The Commission shall adopt, and amend as required, by consensus, financial regulations for the administration of the Commission and for the exercise of its functions.

Article 18
Budget of the Commission

1. The Executive Director shall draft the proposed budget of the Commission and submit it to the Commission. The proposed budget shall indicate which of the administrative expenses of the Commission are to be financed from the assessed contributions referred to in article 17, paragraph 1 (a), and which such expenses are to be financed from funds received pursuant to article 17, paragraphs 1 (b), (c) and (d). The Commission shall adopt the budget by consensus. If the Commission is unable to adopt a decision on the budget, the level of contributions to the administrative budget of the Commission shall be determined in accordance with the budget for the preceding year for the purposes of meeting the administrative expenses of the Commission for the following year until such time as a new budget can be adopted by consensus.

2. The amount of the contribution to the budget shall be determined in accordance with a scheme which the Commission shall adopt, and amend as required, by consensus. In adopting the scheme, due considerationshall be given to each member being assessed an equal basic fee, a fee based upon national wealth, reflecting the state of development of the member concerned and its ability to pay, and a variable fee. The variable fee shall be based, inter alia, on the total catch taken within exclusive economic zones and in areas beyond national jurisdiction in the Convention Area of such species as may be specified by the Commission, provided that a discount factor shall be applied to the catch taken in the exclusive economic zone of a member of the Commission which is a developing State or territory by vessels flying the flag of that member. The scheme adopted by the Commission shall be set out in the financial regulations of the Commission.

3. If a contributor is in arrears in the payment of its financial contributions to the Commission it shall not participate in the taking of decisions by the Commission if the amount of its arrears equals or exceeds the amount of the contributions due from it for the preceding two full years. Interest shall be payable on such unpaid contributions at such rate as may be determined by the Commission in its financial regulations. The Commission may, nevertheless, waive such interest payments and permit such a member to vote if it is satisfied that the failure to pay is due to conditions beyond the control of the member.

Article 19
Annual audit

The records, books and accounts of the Commission, including its annual financial statement, shall be audited annually by an independent auditor appointed by the Commission.

SECTION 6. DECISION-MAKING

Article 20
Decision-making

1. As a general rule, decision-making in the Commission shall be by consensus. For the purposes of this article, "consensus" means the absence of any formal objection made at the time the decision was taken.

2. Except where this Convention expressly provides that a decision shall be made by consensus, if all efforts to reach a decision by consensus have been exhausted, decisions by voting on questions of procedure shall be taken by a majority of those present and voting. Decisions on questions of substance shall be taken by a three- fourths majority of those present and voting provided that such majority includes a three-fourths majority of the members of the South Pacific Forum Fisheries Agency present and voting and a three-fourths majority of non- members of the South Pacific Forum Fisheries Agency present and voting and provided further that in no circumstances shall a proposal be defeated by two or fewer votes in either chamber. When the issue arises as to whether a question is one of substance or not, that question shall be treated as one of substance unless otherwise decided by the Commission by consensus or by the majority required for decisions on questions of substance.

3. If it appears to the Chairman that all efforts to reach a decision by consensus have been exhausted, the Chairman shall fix a time during that session of the Commission for taking the decision by a vote. At the request of any representative, the Commission may, by a majority of those present and voting, defer the taking of a decision until such time during the same session as the Commission may decide. At that time, the Commission shall take a vote on the deferred question. This rule may be applied only once to any question.

4. Where this Convention expressly provides that a decision on a proposal shall be taken by consensus and the Chairman determines that there would be an objection to such proposal, the Commission may appoint a conciliator for the purpose of reconciling the differences in order to achieve consensus on the matter.

5. Subject to paragraphs 6 and 7, a decision adopted by the Commission shall become binding 60 days after the date of its adoption.

6. A member which has voted against a decision or which was absent during the meeting at which the decision was made may, within

30 days of the adoption of the decision by the Commission, seek a review of the decision by a review panel constituted in accordance with the procedures set out in Annex II to this Convention on the grounds that:

(a) the decision is inconsistent with the provisions of this Convention, the Agreement or the 1982 Convention; or

(b) the decision unjustifiably discriminates in form or in fact against the member concerned.

7. Pending the findings and recommendations of the review panel and any action required by the Commission, no member of the Commission shall be required to give effect to the decision in question.

8. If the review panel finds that the decision of the Commission need not be modified, amended or revoked, the decision shall become binding 30 days from the date of communication by the Executive Director of the findings and recommendations of the review panel.

9. If the review panel recommends to the Commission that the decision be modified, amended or revoked, the Commission shall, at its next annual meeting, modify or amend its decision in order to conform with the findings and recommendations of the review panel or it may decide to revoke the decision, provided that, if so requested in writing by a majority of the members, a special meeting of the Commission shall be convened within 60 days of the date of communication of the findings and recommendations of the review panel.

SECTION 7. TRANSPARENCY AND COOPERATION WITH OTHER ORGANIZATIONS

Article 21
Transparency

The Commission shall promote transparency in its decision-making processes and other activities. Representatives from intergovernmental organizations and non-governmental organizations concerned with matters relevant to the implementation of this Convention shall be afforded the opportunity to participate in the meetings of the Commission and its subsidiary bodies as observers or otherwise as appropriate. The rules of procedure of the Commission shall provide for such participation. The procedures shall not be unduly restrictive in this respect. Such intergovernmental organizations and non-governmental organizations shall be given timely access to pertinent information subject to the rules and procedures which the Commission may adopt.

Article 22
Cooperation with other organizations

1. The Commission shall cooperate, as appropriate, with the Food and Agriculture Organization of the United Nations and with other specialized agencies and bodies of the United Nations on matters of mutual interest.

2. The Commission shall make suitable arrangements for consultation, cooperation and collaboration with other relevant intergovernmental organizations, particularly those which have related objectives and which can contribute to the attainment of the objective of this Convention, such as the Commission for the Conservation of Antarctic Marine Living Resources, the Commission for the Conservation of Southern Bluefin Tuna, the Indian Ocean Tuna Commission and the Inter-American Tropical Tuna Commission.

3. Where the Convention Area overlaps with an area under regulation by another fisheries management organization, the Commission shall cooperate with such other organization in order to avoid the duplication of measures in respect of species in that area which are regulated by both organizations.

4. The Commission shall cooperate with the Inter-American Tropical Tuna Commission to ensure that the objective set out in article 2 of this Convention is reached. To that end, the Commission shall initiate consultation with the Inter-American Tropical Tuna Commission with a view to reaching agreement on a consistent set of conservation and management measures, including measures relating to monitoring, control and surveillance, for fish stocks that occur in the Convention Areas of both organizations.

5. The Commission may enter into relationship agreements with the organizations referred to in this article and with other organizations as may be appropriate, such as the Pacific Community and the South Pacific Forum Fisheries Agency, with a view to obtaining the best available scientific and other fisheries-related information to further the attainment of the objective of this Convention and to minimize duplication with respect to their work.

6. Any organization with which the Commission has entered into an arrangement or agreement under paragraphs 1, 2 and 5 may designate representatives to attend meetings of the Commission as observers in accordance with the rules of procedure of the Commission. Procedures shall be established for obtaining the views of such organizations in appropriate cases.

PART IV
OBLIGATIONS OF MEMBERS OF THE COMMISSION

Article 23
Obligations of members of the Commission

1. Each member of the Commission shall promptly implement the provisions of this Convention and any conservation, management and other measures or matters which may be agreed pursuant to this Convention from time to time and shall cooperate in furthering the objective of this Convention.

2. Each member of the Commission shall:

(a) provide annually to the Commission statistical, biological and other data and information in accordance with Annex I of the Agreement and, in addition, such data and information as the Commission may require;

(b) provide to the Commission in the manner and at such intervals as may be required by the Commission, information concerning its fishing activities in the Convention Area, including fishing areas and fishing vessels in order to facilitate the compilation of reliable catch and effort statistics; and

(c) provide to the Commission at such intervals as may be required information on steps taken to implement the conservation and management measures adopted by the Commission.

3. The members of the Commission shall keep the Commission informed of the measures they have adopted for the conservation and management of highly migratory fish stocks in areas within the Convention Area under their national jurisdiction. The Commission shall circulate periodically such information to all members.

4. Each member of the Commission shall keep the Commission informed of the measures it has adopted for regulating the activities of fishing vessels flying its flag which fish in the Convention Area. The Commission shall circulate periodically such information to all members.

5. Each member of the Commission shall, to the greatest extent possible, take measures to ensure that its nationals, and fishing vessels owned or controlled by its nationals fishing in the Convention Area, comply with the provisions of this Convention. To this end, members of the Commission may enter into agreements with States whose flags such vessels are flying to facilitate such enforcement. Each member of the Commission shall, to the greatest extent possible, at the request of any other member, and when provided with the relevant information, investigate any alleged violation by its nationals, or fishing vessels owned or controlled by its nationals, of the provisions of this Convention or any conservation and management measure adopted by the Commission. A report on the progress of the investigation, including details of any action taken or proposed to be taken in relation to the alleged violation, shall be provided to the member making the request and to the Commission as soon as practicable and in any case within two months of such request and a report on the outcome of the investigation shall be provided when the investigation is completed.

PART V
DUTIES OF THE FLAG STATE

Article 24
Flag State duties

1. Each member of the Commission shall take such measures as may be necessary to ensure that:

(a) fishing vessels flying its flag comply with the provisions of this Convention and the conservation and management measures adopted pursuant hereto and that such vessels do not engage in any activity which undermine the effectiveness of such measures; and

(b) fishing vessels flying its flag do not conduct unauthorized fishing within areas under the national jurisdiction of any Contracting Party.

2. No member of the Commission shall allow any fishing vessel entitled to fly its flag to be used for fishing for highly migratory fish stocks in the Convention Area beyond areas of national jurisdiction unless it has been authorized to do so by the appropriate authority or authorities of that member. A member of the Commission shall authorize the use of vessels flying its flag for fishing in the Convention Area beyond areas of national jurisdiction only where it is able to exercise effectively its responsibilities in respect of such vessels under the 1982 Convention, the Agreement and this Convention.

3. It shall be a condition of every authorization issued by a member of the Commission that the fishing vessel in respect of which the authorization is issued:

(a) conducts fishing within areas under the national jurisdiction of other States only where the fishing vessel holds any licence, permit or authorization that may be required by such other State; and

(b) is operated on the high seas in the Convention Area in accordance with the requirements of Annex III, the requirements of which shall also be established as a general obligation of all vessels operating pursuant to this Convention.

4. Each member of the Commission shall, for the purposes of effective implementation of this Convention, maintain a record of fishing vessels entitled to fly its flag and authorized to be used for fishing in the Convention Area beyond its area of national jurisdiction, and shall ensure that all such fishing vessels are entered in that record.

5. Each member of the Commission shall provide annually to the Commission, in accordance with such procedures as may be agreed by the Commission, the information set out in Annex IV to this Convention with respect to each fishing vessel entered in the record required to be maintained under paragraph 4 and shall promptly notify the Commission of any modifications to such information.

6. Each member of the Commission shall also promptly inform the Commission of:

(a) any additions to the record;

(b) any deletions from the record by reason of:

(i) the voluntary relinquishment or non-renewal of the fishing authorization by the fishing vessel owner or operator;

(ii) the withdrawal of the fishing authorization issued in respect of the fishing vessel under paragraph 2;

(iii) the fact that the fishing vessel concerned is no longer entitled to fly its flag;

(iv) the scrapping, decommissioning or loss of the fishing vessel concerned; and

(v) any other reason,

specifying which of the reasons listed above is applicable.

7. The Commission shall maintain its own record, based on the information provided to it pursuant to paragraphs 5 and 6, of fishing vessels referred to in paragraph 4. The Commission shall circulate periodically the information contained in such record to all members of the Commission, and, on request, individually to any member.

8. Each member of the Commission shall require its fishing vessels that fish for highly migratory fish stocks on the high seas in the Convention Area to use near real-time satellite position-fixing transmitters while in such areas. The standards, specifications and procedures for the use of such transmitters shall be established by the Commission, which shall operate a vessel monitoring system for all vessels that fish for highly migratory fish stocks on the high seas in the Convention Area. In establishing such standards, specifications and procedures, the Commission shall take into account the characteristics of traditional fishing vessels from developing States. The Commission, directly, and simultaneously with the flag State where the flag State so requires, or through such other organization designated by the Commission, shall receive information from the vessel monitoring system in accordance with the procedures adopted by the Commission. The procedures adopted by the Commission shall include appropriate measures to protect the confidentiality of information received through the vessel monitoring system. Any member of the Commission may request that waters under its national jurisdiction be included within the area covered by such vessel monitoring system.

9. Each member of the Commission shall require its fishing vessels that fish in the Convention Area in areas under the national jurisdiction of another member to operate near real-time satellite position-fixing transmitters in accordance with the standards, specification and procedures to be determined by the coastal State.

10. The members of the Commission shall cooperate to ensure compatibility between national and high seas vessel monitoring systems.

PART VI
COMPLIANCE AND ENFORCEMENT

Article 25
Compliance and enforcement

1. Each member of the Commission shall enforce the provisions of this Convention and any conservation and management measures issued by the Commission.

2. Each member of the Commission shall, at the request of any other member, and when provided with the relevant information, investigate fully any alleged violation by fishing vessels flying its flag of the provisions of this Convention or any conservation and management measure adopted by the Commission. A report on the progress of the investigation, including details of any action taken or proposed to be taken in relation to the alleged violation, shall be provided to the member making the request and to the Commission as soon as practicable and in any case within two months of such request and a report on the outcome of the investigation shall be provided when the investigation is completed.

3. Each member of the Commission shall, if satisfied that sufficient evidence is available in respect of an alleged violation by a fishing vessel flying its flag, refer the case to its authorities with a view to instituting proceedings without delay in accordance with its laws and, where appropriate, detain the vessel concerned.

4. Each member of the Commission shall ensure that, where it has been established, in accordance with its laws, that a fishing vessel flying its flag has been involved in the commission of a serious violation of the provisions of this Convention or of any conservation and management measures adopted by the Commission, the vessel concerned ceases fishing activities and does not engage in such activities in the Convention Area until such time as all outstanding sanctions imposed by the flag State in respect of the violation have been complied with. Where the vessel concerned has conducted unauthorized fishing within areas under the national jurisdiction of any coastal State Party to this Convention, the flag State shall, in accordance with its laws, ensure that the vessel complies promptly with any sanctions which may be imposed by such coastal State in accordance with its national laws and regulations or shall impose appropriate sanctions in accordance with paragraph 7. For the purposes of this article, a serious violation shall include any of the violations specified in article 21, paragraphs 11 (a) to (h) of the Agreement and such other violations as may be determined by the Commission.

5. Each member of the Commission shall, to the extent permitted by its national laws and regulations, establish arrangements for making available to prosecuting authorities of other members evidence relating to alleged violations.

6. Where there are reasonable grounds for believing that a fishing vessel on the high seas has engaged in unauthorized fishing within an area under the national jurisdiction of a member of the Commission, the flag State of that vessel, at the request of the member concerned, shall immediately and fully investigate the matter. The flag State shall cooperate with the member concerned in taking appropriate enforcement action in such cases and may authorize the relevant authorities of such member to board and inspect the vessel on the high seas. This paragraph is without prejudice to article 111 of the 1982 Convention.

7. All investigations and judicial proceedings shall be carried out expeditiously. Sanctions applicable in respect of violations shall be adequate in severity to be effective in securing compliance and to discourage violations wherever they occur and shall deprive offenders of the benefits accruing from their illegal activities. Measures applicable in respect of masters and other officers of fishing vessels shall include provisions which may permit, inter alia, refusal, withdrawal or suspension of authorizations to serve as masters or officers on such vessels.

8. Each member shall transmit to the Commission an annual statement of compliance measures, including imposition of sanctions for any violations, it has taken in accordance with this article.

9. The provisions of this article are without prejudice to:

(a) the rights of any of the members of the Commission in accordance with their national laws and regulations relating to fisheries, including the right to impose appropriate sanctions on the vessel concerned in respect of violations occurring within areas under national jurisdiction in accordance with such national laws and regulations; and

(b) the rights of any of the members of the Commission in relation to any provision relating to compliance and enforcement contained in any relevant bilateral or multilateral fisheries access agreement not inconsistent with the provisions of this Convention, the Agreement or the 1982 Convention.

10. Each member of the Commission, where it has reasonable grounds for believing that a fishing vessel flying the flag of another State has engaged in any activity that undermines the effectiveness of conservation and management measures adopted for the Convention Area, shall draw this to the attention of the flag State concerned and may, as appropriate, draw the matter to the attention of the Commission. To the extent permitted by its national laws and regulations it shall provide the flag State with full supporting evidence and may provide the Commission with a summary of such evidence. The Commission shall not circulate such information until such time as the flag State has had an opportunity to comment, within a reasonable time, on the allegation and evidence submitted, or to object as the case may be.

11. The members of the Commission may take action in accordance with the Agreement and international law, including through procedures

adopted by the Commission for this purpose, to deter fishing vessels which have engaged in activities which undermine the effectiveness of or otherwise violate the conservation and management measures adopted by the Commission from fishing in the Convention Area until such time as appropriate action is taken by the flag State.

12. The Commission, when necessary, shall develop procedures which allow for non-discriminatory trade measures to be taken, consistent with the international obligations of the members of the Commission, on any species regulated by the Commission, against any State or entity whose fishing vessels fish in a manner which undermines the effectiveness of the conservation and management measures adopted by the Commission.

Article 26
Boarding and inspection

1. For the purposes of ensuring compliance with conservation and management measures, the Commission shall establish procedures for boarding and inspection of fishing vessels on the high seas in the Convention Area. All vessels used for boarding and inspection of fishing vessels on the high seas in the Convention Area shall be clearly marked and identifiable as being on government service and authorized to undertake high seas boarding and inspection in accordance with this Convention.

2. If, within two years of the entry into force of this Convention, the Commission is not able to agree on such procedures, or on an alternative mechanism which effectively discharges the obligations of the members of the Commission under the Agreement and this Convention to ensure compliance with the conservation and management measures established by the Commission, articles 21 and 22 of the Agreement shall be applied, subject to paragraph 3, as if they were part of this Convention and boarding and inspection of fishing vessels in the Convention Area, as well as any subsequent enforcement action, shall be conducted in accordance with the procedures set out therein and such additional practical procedures as the Commission may decide are necessary for the implementation of articles 21 and 22 of the Agreement.

3. Each member of the Commission shall ensure that fishing vessels flying its flag accept boarding by duly authorized inspectors in accordance with such procedures. Such duly authorized inspectors shall comply with the procedures for boarding and inspection.

Article 27
Measures taken by a port State

1. A port State has the right and the duty to take measures, in accordance with international law, to promote the effectiveness of subregional, regional and global conservation and management measures. When taking such measures a port State shall not discriminate in form or in fact against the fishing vessels of any State.

2. Whenever a fishing vessel of a member of the Commission voluntarily enters a port or offshore terminal of another member, the port State may, inter alia, inspect documents, fishing gear and catch on board such fishing vessel.

3. Members of the Commission may adopt regulations empowering the relevant national authorities to prohibit landings and transhipments where it has been established that the catch has been taken in a manner which undermines the effectiveness of conservation and management measures adopted by the Commission.

4. Nothing in this article affects the exercise by Contracting Parties of their sovereignty over ports in their territory in accordance with international law.

PART VII
REGIONAL OBSERVER PROGRAMME AND REGULATION OF TRANSHIPMENT

Article 28
Regional observer programme

1. The Commission shall develop a regional observer programme to collect verified catch data, other scientific data and additional information related to the fishery from the Convention Area and to monitor the implementation of the conservation and management measures adopted by the Commission.

2. The observer programme shall be coordinated by the Secretariat of the Commission, and shall be organized in a flexible manner which takes into account the nature of the fishery and other relevant factors. In this regard, the Commission may enter into contracts for the provision of the regional observer programme.

3. The regional observer programme shall consist of independent and impartial observers authorized by the Secretariat of the Commission. The programme should be coordinated, to the maximum extent possible, with other regional, subregional and national observer programmes.

4. Each member of the Commission shall ensure that fishing vessels flying its flag in the Convention Area, except for vessels that operate exclusively within waters under the national jurisdiction of the flag State, are prepared to accept an observer from the regional observer programme, if required by the Commission.

5. The provisions of paragraph 4 shall apply to vessels fishing exclusively on the high seas in the Convention Area, vessels fishing on the high seas and in waters under the jurisdiction of one or more coastal States, and vessels fishing in waters under the jurisdiction of two or more coastal States. When a vessel is operating on the same fishing trip both in waters

under the national jurisdiction of its flag State and in the adjacent high seas, an observer placed under the regional observer programme shall not undertake any of the activities specified in paragraph 6 (e) when the vessel is in waters under the national jurisdiction of its flag State, unless the flag State of the vessel agrees otherwise.

6. The regional observer programme shall operate in accordance with the following guidelines and under the conditions set out in article 3 of Annex III of this Convention:

(a) the programme shall provide a sufficient level of coverage to ensure that the Commission receives appropriate data and information on catch levels and related matters within the Convention Area, taking into account the characteristics of the fisheries;

(b) each member of the Commission shall be entitled to have its nationals included in the programme as observers;

(c) observers shall be trained and certified in accordance with uniform procedures to be approved by the Commission;

(d) observers shall not unduly interfere with the lawful operations of the vessel and, in carrying out their functions, they shall give due consideration to the operational requirements of the vessel and shall communicate regularly with the captain or master for this purpose;

(e) the activities of observers shall include collecting catch data and other scientific data, monitoring the implementation of conservation and management measures adopted by the Commission and reporting of their findings in accordance with procedures to be developed by the Commission;

(f) the programme shall be cost effective, shall avoid duplication with existing regional, subregional and national observer programmes, and shall, to the extent practicable, seek to minimize disruption to the operations of vessels fishing in the Convention Area;

(g) a reasonable period of notice of the placement of an observer shall be given.

7. The Commission shall develop further procedures and guidelines for the operation of the regional observer programme, including:

(a) to ensure the security of non-aggregated data and other information which the Commission deems to be of a confidential nature;

(b) for the dissemination of data and information collected by observers to the members of the Commission;

(c) for boarding of observers which clearly define the rights and responsibilities of the captain or master of the vessel and the crew when an observer is on board a vessel, as well as the rights and responsibilities of observers in the performance of their duties.

8. The Commission shall determine the manner in which the costs of the observer programme would be defrayed.

Article 29
Transhipment

1. In order to support efforts to ensure accurate reporting of catches, the members of the Commission shall encourage their fishing vessels, to the extent practicable, to conduct transhipment in port. A member may designate one or more of its ports as transhipment ports for the purposes of this Convention, and the Commission shall circulate periodically to all members a list of such designated ports.

2. Transhipment at a port or in an area within waters under the national jurisdiction of a member of the Commission shall take place in accordance with applicable national laws.

3. The Commission shall develop procedures to obtain and verify data on the quantity and species transhipped both in port and at sea in the Convention Area and procedures to determine when transhipment covered by this Convention has been completed.

4. Transhipment at sea in the Convention Area beyond areas under national jurisdiction shall take place only in accordance with the terms and conditions set out in article 4 of Annex III to this Convention, and any procedures established by the Commission pursuant to paragraph 3 of this article. Such procedures shall take into account the characteristics of the fishery concerned.

5. Notwithstanding paragraph 4 above, and subject to specific exemptions which the Commission adopts in order to reflect existing operations, transhipment at sea by purse-seine vessels operating within the Convention Area shall be prohibited.

PART VIII
REQUIREMENTS OF DEVELOPING STATES

Article 30
Recognition of the special requirements of developing States

1. The Commission shall give full recognition to the special requirements of developing States Parties to this Convention, in particular small island developing States, and of territories and possessions, in relation to conservation and management of highly migratory fish stocks in the Convention Area and development of fisheries for such stocks.

2. In giving effect to the duty to cooperate in the establishment of conservation and management measures for highly migratory fish stocks, the Commission shall take into account the special requirements of developing States Parties, in particular small island developing States, and of territories and possessions, in particular:

(a) the vulnerability of developing States Parties, in particular small island developing States, which are dependent on the exploitation of marine living resources, including for meeting the nutritional requirements of their populations or parts thereof;

(b) the need to avoid adverse impacts on, and ensure access to fisheries by, subsistence, small-scale and artisanal fishers and fishworkers, as well as indigenous people in developing States Parties, particularly small island developing States Parties, and territories and possessions; and

(c) the need to ensure that such measures do not result in transferring, directly or indirectly, a disproportionate burden of conservation action onto developing States Parties, and territories and possessions.

3. The Commission shall establish a fund to facilitate the effective participation of developing States Parties, particularly small island developing States, and, where appropriate, territories and possessions, in the work of the Commission, including its meetings and those of its subsidiary bodies. The financial regulations of the Commission shall include guidelines for the administration of the fund and criteria for eligibility for assistance.

4. Cooperation with developing States, and territories and possessions, for the purposes set out in this article may include the provision of financial assistance, assistance relating to human resources development, technical assistance, transfer of technology, including through joint venture arrangements, and advisory and consultative services. Such assistance shall, inter alia, be directed towards:

(a) improved conservation and management of highly migratory fish stocks through collection, reporting, verification, exchange and analysis of fisheries data and related information;

(b) stock assessment and scientific research; and

(c) monitoring, control, surveillance, compliance and enforcement, including training and capacity- building at the local level, development and funding of national and regional observer programmes and access to technology and equipment.

PART IX
PEACEFUL SETTLEMENT OF DISPUTES

Article 31
Procedures for the settlement of disputes

The provisions relating to the settlement of disputes set out in Part VIII of the Agreement apply, mutatis mutandis, to any dispute between members of the Commission, whether or not they are also Parties to the Agreement.

PART X
NON-PARTIES TO THIS CONVENTION

Article 32
Non-parties to this Convention

1. Each member of the Commission shall take measures consistent with this Convention, the Agreement and international law to deter the activities of vessels flying the flags of non-parties to this Convention which undermine the effectiveness of conservation and management measures adopted by the Commission.

2. The members of the Commission shall exchange information on the activities of fishing vessels flying the flags of non-parties to this Convention which are engaged in fishing operations in the Convention Area.

3. The Commission shall draw the attention of any State which is not a Party to this Convention to any activity undertaken by its nationals or vessels flying its flag which, in the opinion of the Commission, affects the implementation of the objective of this Convention.

4. The members of the Commission shall, individually or jointly, request non-parties to this Convention whose vessels fish in the Convention Area to cooperate fully in the implementation of conservation and management measures adopted by the Commission with a view to ensuring that such measures are applied to all fishing activities in the Convention Area. Such cooperating non-parties to this Convention shall enjoy benefits from participation in the fishery commensurate with their commitment to comply with, and their record of compliance with, conservation and management measures in respect of the relevant stocks.

5. Non-parties to this Convention, may, upon request and subject to the concurrence of the members of the Commission and to the rules of procedure relating to the granting of observer status, be invited to attend meetings of the Commission as observers.

PART XI
GOOD FAITH AND ABUSE OF RIGHTS

Article 33
Good faith and abuse of rights

The obligations assumed under this Convention shall be fulfilled in good faith and the rights recognized in this Convention shall be exercised in a manner which would not constitute an abuse of right.

PART XII
FINAL PROVISIONS

Article 34
Signature, ratification, acceptance, approval

1. This Convention shall be open for signature by Australia, Canada, China, Cook Islands, Federated States of Micronesia, Fiji Islands, France, Indonesia, Japan, Republic of Kiribati, Republic of the Marshall Islands, Republic of Nauru, New Zealand, Niue, Republic of Palau, Independent State of Papua New Guinea, Republic of the Philippines, Republic of Korea, Independent State of Samoa, Solomon Islands, Kingdom of Tonga, Tuvalu, United Kingdom of Great Britain and Northern Ireland in respect of Pitcairn, Henderson, Ducie and Oeno Islands, United States of America and Republic of Vanuatu and shall remain open for signature for twelve months from the fifth day of September 2000.

2. This Convention is subject to ratification, acceptance or approval by the signatories.

3. Instruments of ratification, acceptance or approval shall be deposited with the depositary.

4. Each Contracting Party shall be a member of the Commission established by this Convention.

Article 35
Accession

1. This Convention shall remain open for accession by the States referred to in article 34, paragraph 1, and by any entity referred to in article 305, paragraph 1, subparagraphs (c), (d) and (e) of the 1982 Convention which is situated in the Convention Area.

2. After the entry into force of this Convention, the Contracting Parties may, by consensus, invite other States and regional economic integration organizations, whose nationals and fishing vessels wish to conduct fishing for highly migratory fish stocks in the Convention Area to accede to this Convention.

3. Instruments of accession shall be deposited with the depositary.

Article 36
Entry into force

1. This Convention shall enter into force 30 days after the deposit of instruments of ratification, acceptance, approval or accession by:

(a) three States situated north of the 20° parallel of north latitude; and

(b) seven States situated south of the 20° parallel of north latitude.

2. If, within three years of its adoption, this Convention has not been ratified by three of the States referred to in paragraph 1 (a), this Convention shall enter into force six months after the deposit of the thirteenth instrument of ratification, acceptance, approval or accession or in accordance with paragraph 1, whichever is the earlier.

3. For each State, entity referred to in article 305, paragraph 1, subparagraphs (c), (d) and (e) of the 1982 Convention which is situated in the Convention Area, or regional economic integration organization which ratifies, formally confirms, accepts or approves the Convention or accedes thereto after the entry into force of this Convention, this Convention shall enter into force on the thirtieth day following the deposit of its instrument of ratification, formal confirmation, acceptance, approval or accession.

Article 37
Reservations and exceptions

No reservations or exceptions may be made to this Convention.

Article 38
Declarations and statements

Article 37 does not preclude a State, entity referred to in article 305, paragraph 1, subparagraphs (c), (d) and (e) of the 1982 Convention which is situated in the Convention Area, or regional economic integration organization, when signing, ratifying or acceding to this Convention, from making declarations or statements, however phrased or named, with a view, inter alia, to the harmonization of its laws and regulations with the provisions of this Convention, provided that such declarations or statements do not purport to exclude or to modify the legal effect of the provisions of this Convention in their application to that State, entity or regional economic integration organization.

Article 39
Relation to other agreements

This Convention shall not alter the rights and obligations of Contracting Parties, and fishing entities referred to in article 9, paragraph 2, which arise from other agreements compatible with this Convention and which do not affect the enjoyment by other Contracting Parties of their rights or the performance of their obligations under this Convention.

Article 40
Amendment

1. Any member of the Commission may propose amendments to this Convention to be considered by the Commission. Any such proposal shall be made by written communication addressed to the Executive Director at least 60 days before the meeting of the Commission at which it is to be considered. The Executive Director shall promptly circulate such communication to all members of the Commission.

2. Amendments to this Convention shall be considered at the annual meeting of the Commission unless a majority of the members request a special meeting to consider the proposed amendment. A special meeting may be convened on not less than 60 days notice. Amendments to this Convention shall be adopted by consensus. The text of any amendment adopted by the Commission shall be transmitted promptly by the Executive Director to all members of the Commission.

3. Amendments to this Convention shall enter into force for the Contracting Parties ratifying or acceding to them on the thirtieth day following the deposit of instruments of ratification or accession by a majority of Contracting Parties. Thereafter, for each Contracting Party ratifying or acceding to an amendment after the deposit of the required number of such instruments, the amendment shall enter into force on the thirtieth day following the deposit of its instrument of ratification or accession.

Article 41
Annexes

1. The Annexes form an integral part of this Convention and, unless expressly provided otherwise, a reference to this Convention or to one of its Parts includes a reference to the Annexes relating thereto.

2. The Annexes to this Convention may be revised from time to time and any member of the Commission may propose revisions to an Annex. Notwithstanding the provisions of article 40, if a revision to an Annex is adopted by consensus at a meeting of the Commission, it shall be incorporated in this Convention and shall take effect from the date of its adoption or from such other date as may be specified in the revision.

Article 42
Withdrawal

1. A Contracting Party may, by written notification addressed to the depositary, withdraw from this Convention and may indicate its reasons. Failure to indicate reasons shall not affect the validity of the withdrawal. The withdrawal shall take effect one year after the date of receipt of the notification, unless the notification specifies a later date.

2. Withdrawal from this Convention by a Contracting Party shall not affect the financial obligations of such member incurred prior to its withdrawal becoming effective.

3. Withdrawal from this Convention by a Contracting Party shall not in any way affect the duty of such member to fulfil any obligation embodied in this Convention to which it would be subject under international law independently of this Convention.

Article 43
Participation by territories

1. The Commission and its subsidiary bodies shall be open to participation, with the appropriate authorization of the Contracting Party having responsibility for its international affairs, to each of the following:

American Samoa
French Polynesia
Guam
New Caledonia
Northern Mariana Islands
Tokelau
Wallis and Futuna

2. The nature and extent of such participation shall be provided for by the Contracting Parties in separate rules of procedure of the Commission, taking into account international law, the distribution of competence on matters covered by this Convention and the evolution in the capacity of such territory to exercise rights and responsibilities under this Convention.

3. Notwithstanding paragraph 2, all such participants shall be entitled to participate fully in the work of the Commission, including the right to be present and to speak at the meetings of the Commission and its subsidiary bodies. In the performance of its functions, and in taking decisions, the Commission shall take into account the interests of all participants.

Article 44
Depositary

The Government of New Zealand shall be the depositary of this Convention and any amendments or revisions thereto. The depositary shall register this Convention with the Secretary-General of the United Nations in accordance with article 102 of the Charter of the United Nations.

IN WITNESS WHEREOF, the undersigned Plenipotentiaries, being duly authorized thereto, have signed this Convention.

DONE at Honolulu this fifth day of September, two thousand, in a single original.

ANNEX I. FISHING ENTITIES

1. After the entry into force of this Convention, any fishing entity whose vessels fish for highly migratory fish stocks in the Convention Area, may, by a written instrument delivered to the depositary, agree to be bound by the regime established by this Convention. Such agreement shall become effective thirty days following the delivery of the instrument. Any such fishing entity may withdraw such agreement by written notification addressed to the depositary. The withdrawal shall take effect one year after the date of receipt of the notification, unless the notification specifies a later date.

2. Such fishing entity shall participate in the work of the Commission, including decision-making, and shall comply with the obligations under this Convention. References thereto by the Commission or memb ers of the Commission include, for the purposes of this Convention, such fishing entity as well as Contracting Parties.

3. If a dispute concerning the interpretation or application of this Convention involving a fishing entity cannot be settled by agreement between the parties to the dispute, the dispute shall, at the request of either party to the dispute, be submitted to final and binding arbitration in accordance with the relevant rules of the Permanent Court of Arbitration.

4. The provisions of this Annex relating to participation by fishing entities are solely for the purposes of this Convention.

ANNEX II. REVIEW PANEL

1. In accordance with article 20, paragraph 6, an application for review of a decision of the Commission shall be submitted within 30 days of the adoption of the decision by written notification to the Executive Director. Such notification shall be accompanied by a statement of the grounds upon which the review is sought. The Executive Director shall circulate copies of the notification and the accompanying statement to all members of the Commission.

2. The review panel shall be constituted as follows:

(a) The review panel shall consist of three members appointed in accordance with this Annex from the list of experts in the field of fisheries drawn up and maintained by the Food and Agriculture Organization of the United Nations pursuant to Annex VIII, article 2, of the 1982 Convention or a similar list maintained by the Executive Director;

(b) The member of the Commission submitting the application for review ("the applicant") shall appoint one member, who may or may not be its national. The appointment shall be included in the written notification referred to in paragraph 1;

(c) Where more than one member of the Commission is seeking review of the same decision, such members shall, within 20 days of receipt of the first notification submitted, appoint one member of the panel jointly by agreement, irrespective of the grounds upon which review is sought by each applicant. If the members concerned are unable to reach agreement on the appointment, the appointment shall be made in accordance with subparagraph (f), at the request of any such member;

(d) The chairman of the Commission shall, within 20 days of receipt of the notification referred to in paragraph 1 of this Annex, appoint one member;

(e) The other member shall be appointed by agreement between the member or members of the Commission seeking the review and the chairman of the Commission. They shall appoint the President of the review panel from among those three members. If, within 20 days of receipt of the notification referred to in paragraph 1 of this Annex, the member or members seeking the review and the chairman of the Commission are unable to reach agreement on the appointment of one or more members of the panel to be appointed by agreement, or on the appointment of the President of the review panel, the remaining appointment or appointments shall be made in accordance with subparagraph (f), at the request of any party. Such request shall be made within 10 days of the expiration of the aforementioned 20 day period;

(f) Unless the parties agree that any appointment under subparagraphs (c), (d) and (e) of this paragraph be made by a person or a third State chosen by the parties, the President of the International Tribunal for the Law of the Sea shall make the necessary appointments.

(g) Any vacancy shall be filled in the manner described for the initial appointment.

3. A hearing shall be convened at a place and on a date to be determined by the panel within 30 days following the constitution of the review panel.

4. The review panel shall determine its own procedures, providing for the expeditious conduct of the hearing and assuring to the applicant or applicants full opportunity to be heard and to present its or their case.

5. The Executive Director shall act on behalf of the Commission and shall provide the review panel with sufficient information to enable it to understand the basis upon which the decision was made.

6. Any member of the Commission may submit a memorandum to the review panel concerning the matter under review and the panel shall allow any such member full opportunity to be heard.

7. Unless the review panel decides otherwise because of the particular circumstances of the case, the expenses of the review panel, including the remuneration of its members, shall be borne as follows:

(a) 70 per cent shall be borne by the applicant or, if there is more than one applicant, divided equally among the applicants; and

(b) 30 per cent shall be borne by the Commission from its annual budget.

8. Any decision of the review panel shall be taken by a majority of its members.

9. If the applicant or, where there is more than one applicant, any one of them, does not appear before the review panel, the panel may continue the proceedings and make its findings and recommendations. Absence of an applicant shall not constitute a bar to the review proceedings.

10. The findings and recommendations of the review panel shall be confined to the subject matter of the application and state the reasons on which it is based. It shall contain the names of the members who have participated and the date of the finding. Any member of the panel may attach a separate or dissenting opinion to the finding. The review panel shall not, however, substitute its decision for that of the Commission. The panel shall communicate its findings and recommendations, including its reasons, to the applicant or applicants and the Executive Director within 30 days of the end of the hearing. The Executive Director shall circulate copies of the review panel's findings and recommendations and reasons therefor to all members of the Commission.

ANNEX III. TERMS AND CONDITIONS FOR FISHING

Article 1
Introductory

The operator of every fishing vessel authorized to be used for fishing in the Convention Area shall comply with the following terms and conditions at all times when the vessel is in the Convention Area. Such terms and conditions shall apply in addition to any terms and conditions which may apply to the vessel in areas under the national jurisdiction of a member of the Commission by reason of a licence issued by such member or pursuant to a bilateral or multilateral fisheries agreement. For the purposes of this Annex, "operator" means any person who is in charge of, directs or controls a fishing vessel, including the owner, master or charterer.

Article 2
Compliance with national laws

The operator of the vessel shall comply with the applicable national laws of each coastal State Party to this Convention in whose jurisdiction it enters and shall be responsible for the compliance by the vessel and its crew with such laws and the vessel shall be operated in accordance with such laws.

Article 3
Obligations of the operator in respect of observers

1. The operator and each member of the crew shall allow and assist any person identified as an observer under the regional observer programme to:

(a) embark at a place and time agreed to;

(b) have full access to and use of all facilities and equipment on board which the observer may determine is necessary to carry out his or her duties, including full access to the bridge, fish on board, and areas which may be used to hold, process, weigh and store fish, and full access to the vessel's records including its logs and documentation for the purpose of records inspection and copying, reasonable access to navigational equipment, charts and radios, and reasonable access to other information relating to fishing;

(c) remove samples;

(d) disembark at an agreed place and time; and

(e) carry out all duties safely.

2. The operator or any crew member shall not assault, obstruct, resist, delay, refuse boarding to, intimidate or interfere with observers in the performance of their duties.

3. The operator shall provide the observer, while on board the vessel, at no expense to the observer or the observer's government, with food, accommodation and medical facilities of a reasonable standard equivalent to those normally available to an officer on board the vessel.

Article 4
Regulation of transhipment

1. The operator shall comply with any procedures established by the Commission to verify the quantity and species transhipped, and any additional procedures and measures established by the Commission with respect to transhipment in the Convention Area.

2. The operator shall allow and assist any person authorized by the Commission or by the member of the Commission in whose designated port or area a transhipment takes place to have full access to and use of facilities and equipment which such authorized person may determine is necessary to carry out his or her duties, including full access to the bridge, fish on board and areas which may be used to hold, process, weigh and store fish, and full access to the vessel's records, including its log and documentation for the purpose of inspection and photocopying. The operator shall also allow and assist any such authorized person to remove samples and gather any other information required to fully monitor the activity. The operator or any member of the crew shall not assault, obstruct, resist, delay, refuse boarding to, intimidate or interfere with any such authorized person in the performance of such person's duties. Every effort should be made to ensure that any disruption to fishing operations is minimized during inspections of transhipments.

Article 5
Reporting

The operator shall record and report vessel position, catch of target and non-target species, fishing effort and other relevant fisheries data in accordance with the standards for collection of such data set out in Annex I of the Agreement.

Article 6
Enforcement

1. The authorization issued by the flag State of the vessel and, if applicable, any licence issued by a coastal State Party to this Convention, or a duly certified copy, facsimile or telex confirmation thereof, shall be carried on board the vessel at all times and produced at the request of an authorized enforcement official of any member of the Commission.

2. The master and each member of the crew of the vessel shall immediately comply with every instruction and direction given by an authorized and identified officer of a member of the Commission, including to stop, to move to a safe location, and to facilitate safe boarding and inspection of the vessel, its licence, gear, equipment, records, facilities, fish and fish products. Such boarding and inspection shall be conducted as much as possible in a manner so as not to interfere unduly with the lawful operation of the vessel. The operator and each member of the crew shall facilitate and assist in any action by an authorized officer and shall not assault, obstruct, resist, delay, refuse boarding to, intimidate or interfere with an authorized officer in the performance of his or her duties.

3. The vessel shall be marked and identified in accordance with the FAO Standard Specifications for the Marking and Identification of Fishing Vessels or such alternative standard as may be adopted by the Commission. At all times when the vessel is in the Convention Area, all parts of such markings shall be clear, distinct and uncovered.

4. The operator shall ensure the continuous monitoring of the international distress and calling frequency 2182 khz (HF) or the international safety and calling frequency 156.8 Mhz (channel 16, VHF-FM) to facilitate communication with the fisheries management, surveillance and enforcement authorities of the members of the Commission.

5. The operator shall ensure that a recent and up to date copy of the International Code of Signals (INTERCO) is on board and accessible at all times.

6. At all times when the vessel is navigating through an area under the national jurisdiction of a member of the Commission in which it does not have a licence to fish, and at all times when the vessel is navigating on the high seas in the Convention Area and has not been authorized by its flag State to fish on the high seas, all fishing equipment on board the vessel shall be stowed or secured in such a manner that it is not readily available to be used for fishing.

ANNEX IV. INFORMATION REQUIREMENTS

The following information shall be provided to the Commission in respect of each fishing vessel entered in the record required to be maintained under article 24, paragraph 4, of this Convention:

1. Name of fishing vessel, registration number, previous names (if known), and port of registry;
2. Name and address of owner or owners;
3. Name and nationality of master;
4. Previous flag (if any);
5. International Radio Call Sign;
6. Vessel communication types and numbers (INMARSAT A, B and C numbers and satellite telephone number);
7. Colour photograph of vessel;
8. Where and when built;
9. Type of vessel;
10. Normal crew complement;
11. Type of fishing method or methods;
12. Length;
13. Moulded depth;
14. Beam;
15. Gross register tonnage;
16. Power of main engine or engines;
17. The nature of the authorization to fish granted by the flag State;
18. Carrying capacity, including freezer type, capacity and number and fish hold capacity.

PART V

OTHER SUPPLEMENTARY DOCUMENTS AND MATERIALS

INTERNATIONAL MARITIME ORGANIZATION
4 ALBERT EMBANKMENT
LONDON SE1 7SR

Telephone: 020 7735 7611
Fax: 020 7587 3210

IMO

E

LEG/MISC.6
10 September 2008

IMPLICATIONS OF THE UNITED NATIONS CONVENTION ON THE LAW OF THE SEA FOR THE INTERNATIONAL MARITIME ORGANIZATION

Study by the Secretariat of the International Maritime Organization (IMO)

TABLE OF CONTENTS

INTRODUCTION

This document is intended to provide a comprehensive overview of the work of the International Maritime Organization (IMO) relating to the United Nations Convention on the Law of the Sea ("the Convention" or "UNCLOS"). Originally prepared in 1987 and issued as document LEG/MISC.1, this survey was substantially revised and updated. The present version updates LEG/MISC.5 by reflecting developments that took place from January 2007 to May 2008. It was finalized in consultation with the Division for Ocean Affairs and the Law of the Sea of the United Nations (DOALOS).

Part I includes comments and concepts of relevance in assessing the general legal framework relating to UNCLOS and the work of IMO and its instruments.

Part II provides a detailed analysis of the relationship between UNCLOS and various IMO instruments.

Part III deals with the role of IMO in settling disputes, in the light of the UNCLOS provisions in this area.

In Part IV consideration is given to the scope of IMO activities since the entry into force of UNCLOS and to the possibilities of modifying or extending the Organization's functions and responsibilities.

The annex contains a table showing the relationship between articles of UNCLOS and relevant IMO instruments.

An updated table of the status of all IMO treaty instruments referred to in this document, including those in the annex, can be found on the IMO website (www.imo.org).

The contents of this document complement the information and analysis contained in two publications prepared by DOALOS:

- *Obligations of States Parties under the United Nations Convention on the Law of the Sea and Complementary Instruments* published by the Division for Ocean Affairs and the Law of the Sea, Office of Legal Affairs, of the United Nations; and
- *Law of the Sea Bulletin No.31, part III. Competence of relevant international organizations under the UN Convention on the Law of the Sea.*

PART I

GENERAL FEATURES OF THE RELATIONSHIP BETWEEN UNCLOS AND IMO SHIPPING REGULATIONS

Historical background

Since 1973 the Secretariat of IMO (formerly IMCO) has actively contributed to the work of the Third United Nations Conference on the Law of the Sea (UNCLOS) in order to ensure that the elaboration of IMO instruments conforms with the basic principles guiding the elaboration of UNCLOS.

Overlapping or potential conflict between IMO's work and that of UNCLOS have been avoided by the inclusion in several IMO conventions of provisions which state specifically that their text does not prejudice the codification and development of the law of the sea by UNCLOS or any present or future claims and legal views of any State concerning the law of the sea and the nature and extent of coastal and flag State jurisdiction.

After the adoption of UNCLOS, the IMO Secretariat held consultations with the Office of the Special Representative of the Secretary-General of the United Nations for the Law of the Sea, and later with the Division for Ocean Affairs and the Law of the Sea, Office of Legal Affairs, United Nations, in connection with several matters relating IMO's work to UNCLOS. Even before the entry into force of the Convention in 1994, explicit or implicit references to its provisions were incorporated into several IMO treaty and non-treaty instruments.

The global mandate of IMO

Although IMO is explicitly mentioned in only one of the articles of UNCLOS (article 2 of Annex VIII), several provisions in that convention refer to the "competent international organization" in connection with the adoption of international shipping rules and standards in matters concerning maritime safety, efficiency of navigation and the prevention and control of marine pollution from vessels and by dumping.

In such cases the expression "competent international organization", when used in the singular in UNCLOS, applies exclusively to IMO, bearing in mind the global mandate of the Organization as a specialized agency within the United Nations system established by the Convention on the International Maritime Organization (the "IMO Convention"). The IMO Convention was adopted by the United Nations Maritime Conference in Geneva on 6 March 1948. (The original name of "Inter-Governmental Maritime Consultative Organization" was changed by IMO Assembly resolutions A.358(IX) and A.371(X), adopted in 1975 and 1977 respectively.)

Numerous provisions in UNCLOS refer to the mandate of several organizations in connection with the same subject matter. In some cases, activities set forth in these provisions may involve IMO working in co-operation with other organizations. In order to assist States and to contribute to a better understanding of the implications of the Convention for the organizations and bodies dealing with maritime affairs both within and outside the United Nations system, the Division for Ocean Affairs and the Law of the Sea, Office of Legal Affairs has prepared a table on "Competent or relevant international organizations" in relation to UNCLOS. Published in the Law of the Sea Bulletin No.31, the table lists subjects and articles in the sequence in which they appear in the Convention, together with the corresponding competent organizations.

Article 1 of the IMO Convention establishes the global scope of IMO safety and anti-pollution activities. It also refers to other tasks such as the promotion of efficiency of navigation and the availability of shipping services based upon the freedom of shipping of all flags to take part in international trade without discrimination. Article 59 mentions IMO as the specialized agency within the United Nations system in relation to shipping and its effect on the marine environment. Articles 60 to 62 refer to co-operation between IMO and other specialized agencies as well as governmental and non-governmental organizations, on matters of common concern and interest.

The following facts indicate the wide acceptance and uncontested legitimacy of IMO's universal mandate in accordance with international law:

- 168 sovereign States representing all regions of the world are at present Parties to the IMO Convention and accordingly Members of IMO;
- all Members may participate in meetings of the IMO bodies responsible for drafting and adopting recommendations containing safety and anti-pollution rules and standards. These rules and standards are normally adopted by consensus;
- all States, whether or not they are Members of IMO or the United Nations, are invited to participate in the IMO conferences responsible for adopting new IMO conventions. All IMO treaty instruments have so far been adopted by consensus.

Relationship between UNCLOS and IMO instruments

UNCLOS is acknowledged to be an "umbrella convention" because most of its provisions, being of a general kind, can be implemented only through specific operative regulations in other international agreements.

This is reflected in several provisions of UNCLOS which require States to "take account of", "conform to", "give effect to" or "implement" the relevant international rules and standards developed by or through the "competent international organization" (*i.e.* IMO). The latter are variously referred to as "applicable international rules and standards", "internationally agreed rules, standards, and recommended practices and procedures", "generally accepted international rules and standards", "generally accepted international regulations", "applicable international instruments" or "generally accepted international regulations, procedures and practices".

The following UNCLOS articles and provisions are of particular relevance in this context:

- article 21(2) refers to the "generally accepted international rules or standards" on the "design, construction, manning or equipment" of ships in the context of laws relating to innocent passage through the territorial sea; article 211(6)(c) refers to the "generally accepted international rules and standards" in the context of pollution from vessels; article 217(1) and (2) refers to the "applicable international rules and standards" in the context of flag State enforcement; and article 94(3), (4) and (5) requires flag States to conform to the "generally accepted international regulations, procedures and practices" governing, *inter alia*, the construction, equipment and seaworthiness of ships, as well as the manning of ships and the training of crews, taking into account the "applicable international instruments";
- articles 21(4), 39(2), and by reference article 54 refer to "generally accepted international regulations" in the context of prevention of collisions at sea;
- article 22(3)(a) refers to the "recommendations of the competent international organization" (IMO) in the context of the designation of sea lanes, the prescription of traffic separation schemes, and their substitution. In the same context, articles 41(4) and 53(9) provide for the referral of proposals by States to the "competent international organization" (IMO) with a view to their adoption;
- article 23 refers to the requirements in respect of documentation and special precautionary measures established by international agreements for foreign nuclear-powered ships and ships carrying nuclear or inherently dangerous or noxious substances;
- article 60 and article 80 refer to the "generally accepted international standards established by the competent international organization" (IMO) for the removal of abandoned or disused installations or structures to ensure safety of navigation (paragraph 3); the "applicable international standards" for determination of the breadth of safety zones; the "generally accepted standards" or recommendations of the "competent international organization" (IMO) where the breadth exceeds a distance of 500 metres (paragraph 5); and the "generally accepted international

standards" regarding navigation in the vicinity of artificial islands, installations, structures and safety zones (paragraph 6);

- article 94(3), (4), and (5), which regulates the duties of flag States, and article 39(2), which concerns the duties of ships in transit passage, refer to the "generally accepted international regulations, procedures and practices" for safety at sea and for the prevention, reduction and control of pollution from ships;

- article 210(4) and (6) refers to the "global rules, standards, and recommended practices and procedures" for the prevention, reduction and control of pollution by dumping; article 216(1) refers to the enforcement of such "applicable rules and standards established through competent international organizations or general diplomatic conference";

- article 211 refers to the "international rules and standards" established by "States acting through the competent international organization" (paragraph 1) and "generally accepted international rules and standards established through the competent international organization" (paragraphs 2 and 5) for the prevention, reduction and control of pollution of the marine environment from vessels. Article 217(1) and (2), article 218(1) and (3), and article 220(1), (2) and (3), dealing with enforcement of anti-pollution rules, refer to the "applicable international rules and standards". Articles 217(3) and 226(1) refer to the certificates (records and other documents) required by international rules and standards in the context of pollution control;

- article 211(6)(a), in connection with pollution from vessels, refers to such international rules and standards or navigational practices are made applicable, through the competent international organization (IMO), for special areas;

- article 211(7) requires such "international rules and standards" to include, *inter alia*, those relating to prompt notification to coastal States whose coastline or related interests may be affected by incidents, including maritime casualties, which involve discharges or probability of discharges;

- articles 219 and 226(1)(c) refer to "applicable international rules and standards" relating to seaworthiness of vessels, while article 94(5) refers to "generally accepted international regulations, procedures and practices" governing seaworthiness of ships.

These provisions clearly establish an obligation on UNCLOS States Parties to apply IMO rules and standards. The specific form of such application relies to a great extent on the interpretation given by Parties to UNCLOS to the expressions "take account of", "conform to", "give effect to" or "implement" in relation to IMO provisions. A distinction should be also made between the two main types of IMO instruments that contain such provisions: on the one hand, the recommendations adopted by the IMO Assembly, the IMO Maritime Safety Committee (MSC) and the IMO Marine Environment Protection Committee (MEPC), and on the other the rules and standards contained in IMO treaties.

IMO resolutions

All IMO Member States are entitled to participate in adopting resolutions of the IMO Assembly, the MSC and the MEPC which incorporate recommendations on the implementation of technical rules and standards not included in IMO treaties. These resolutions are normally adopted by consensus and accordingly reflect global agreement by all IMO Members. Parties to UNCLOS are expected to conform to these rules and standards, bearing in mind the need to adapt them to the particular circumstances of each case. Moreover, national legislation implementing IMO recommendations can be applied with binding effect to foreign ships.

Technical codes or guidelines included in the resolutions are frequently made mandatory by incorporation into national legislation. This is, for instance, the case of the International Maritime Dangerous Goods Code (IMDG Code), which came into mandatory effect on 1 January 2004 following the entry into force of amendments to SOLAS chapter VII.

In several cases, codes and guidelines initially contained in non-mandatory IMO resolutions are incorporated at a later stage into IMO treaties. For instance, the International Code for the Construction and Equipment of Ships carrying Dangerous Chemicals in Bulk (IBC Code) has been incorporated into both SOLAS and MARPOL.

IMO treaty instruments

The general obligations established by UNCLOS regarding compliance with IMO rules and standards should, in the case of IMO conventions and protocols, be assessed with reference to the specific operative features of each treaty. These features relate not only to the way in which the rules and standards regulate substantive matters such as the construction, equipment or manning of ships, but also to the procedural rules governing the interrelations between flag and port State jurisdiction in matters such as certificate recognition and enforcement of sanctions following violation of treaty obligations.

The application of IMO treaties should also be guided by the provisions contained in articles 311 and 237 of UNCLOS. Article 311 regulates the relation between the Convention and other conventions and international agreements. Article 237 includes specific provisions on the relationship between UNCLOS and other conventions concerned with the protection and preservation of the marine environment.

Article 311(2) provides that the Convention shall not alter the rights and obligations of States Parties which arise from other agreements, provided that they are compatible with the Convention and do not affect the application of its basic principles. As long as this paramount proviso of compatibility with the basic principles of the Convention is observed, international agreements expressly permitted or preserved by other articles of the Convention will not be affected (article 311(5)).

Article 237(1) establishes that the provisions of part XII of the Convention are without prejudice to the specific obligations assumed by States under previously-concluded special conventions and agreements relating to the protection and preservation of the marine environment, or to agreements which may be concluded in furtherance of the general principles set forth in the Convention. Paragraph 2 provides that specific obligations assumed by States under special conventions with respect to the protection and preservation of the marine environment should be carried out in a manner consistent with the general principles and objectives of the Convention.

Against this background, compatibility between UNCLOS and IMO treaties can be established on the following basis:

- Several provisions of UNCLOS reflect principles compatible with those already included in IMO treaties and recommendations adopted prior to the Convention. In this regard, mention should be made of provisions on collisions at sea, search and rescue of persons in distress at sea, traffic separation schemes, exercise of port State jurisdiction for the protection and preservation of the marine environment, liability and compensation for oil pollution damage and measures to avoid pollution arising from maritime casualties.

- The active participation of the IMO Secretariat at the Third United Nations Conference on the Law of the Sea has ensured that no overlapping, inconsistency or incompatibility exist between UNCLOS and IMO treaties adopted after 1973. In some cases, compatibility has been further ensured by the inclusion in IMO treaties of specific clauses indicating that these treaties should not be interpreted as prejudicing the codification and development of the law of the sea by UNCLOS (see article 9(2) of MARPOL 73/78, article V of STCW 1978, and article II of SAR). A similar provision is included in the Convention on the Prevention of Marine Pollution by Dumping of Wastes and Other Matter, 1972 (London Convention), in respect of which IMO performs secretariat functions. These clauses also stipulate that nothing in these treaties should prejudice present or future claims and legal views of any State concerning the law of the sea and the nature and extent of coastal and flag State jurisdiction. In this way, legal certainty is provided, ensuring that IMO global regulatory activities do not overlap with developments in the field of codification of the law of the sea.

Legal status of IMO treaties in accordance with international law and the Law of the Sea. Consequences for Parties to UNCLOS

The degree of acceptability and worldwide implementation accorded to the rules and standards contained in IMO treaties is paramount in considering the extent to which Parties to UNCLOS should, in compliance with obligations specifically prescribed in the Convention, apply IMO rules and standards. In this regard it should be noted that reference to the obligation for States Parties to the Convention to "take account of", "conform to", "give effect to" or "implement" IMO rules and standards is related to the requirement that these standards are "applicable" or "generally accepted". This means that the degree of international acceptance of these standards is decisive in establishing the extent to which Parties to UNCLOS are under an obligation to implement them.

The criteria for establishing the degree of compliance of the most important IMO treaties with the requirement of general acceptance must in the first place take into account that, since 1982, formal acceptance of the most relevant IMO treaty instruments has increased so greatly that it seems beyond question that these treaties should be accepted and implemented worldwide.

As of 31 August 2008, the three conventions that include the most comprehensive sets of rules and standards on safety, pollution prevention and training and certification of seafarers, namely, SOLAS, MARPOL and STCW Conventions, have been ratified by 158, 147 and 151 States respectively (representing approximately 99% gross tonnage of the world's merchant fleet). Since the general degree of acceptance of these shipping conventions is mainly related to their implementation by flag States, it is of paramount importance to note that States Parties to these Conventions in all cases represent more than 90 per cent of the world's merchant fleet. The effectiveness of this wide implementation is strengthened by the fact that, under the principle of "no more favourable treatment", port States which are Parties to these conventions, respectively, are obliged to apply these rules and standards to vessels flying the flag of non-party States.

Technical rules and standards contained in several IMO treaties can be updated through a procedure based on tacit acceptance of amendments. This procedure enables amendments to enter into force on a date selected by the conference or meeting at which they are adopted unless, within a certain period of time after adoption, they are explicitly rejected by a specified number of Contracting Parties representing a certain percentage of the gross tonnage of the world's merchant fleet.

IMO treaties and amendments to them are normally adopted by consensus.

These facts are decisive in establishing the extent to which any obligation under UNCLOS to comply with generally accepted safety and anti-pollution shipping standards can bind Parties to the Convention even if they are not Parties to the IMO treaties containing those rules and standards. In determining the degree to which such binding character might operate, account should be taken of the following circumstances:

- The degree of compliance with IMO rules tends to vary depending on the interpretation given by UNCLOS Parties to the expressions "give effect to", "implement", "conform to" or "take account of", in respect of IMO rules and standards. Parties should, in each case, assess the context of the UNCLOS provisions establishing obligations in this regard and relate this context to the specific IMO treaty and corresponding rules and standards referred to in UNCLOS.
- The most important consideration in such an assessment seems to be that Parties to UNCLOS should ensure that ships flying their flag or foreign ships under their jurisdiction apply generally accepted IMO provisions regarding safety and prevention and control of pollution. Non-compliance with these IMO provisions would result in sub-standard ships and violate the basic obligations set forth in UNCLOS concerning safety of navigation and prevention of pollution from ships.
- The application by Parties to UNCLOS of IMO rules and standards should be seen as an incentive for them to become Parties to the IMO treaties containing those rules and standards. As Parties to those treaties they would receive specific entitlements in accordance with specific treaty law provisions in each case. Paramount among them would be the value accorded by IMO treaties to certificates issued by Parties. Also important would be the right to participate in any action taken to amend the treaty.

The exercise of State jurisdiction in accordance with IMO instruments

While UNCLOS defines the features and extent of the concepts of flag, coastal and port State jurisdiction, IMO instruments specify how State jurisdiction should be exercised so as to ensure compliance with safety and shipping anti-pollution regulations. The enforcement of these regulations is primarily the responsibility of the flag State. Nevertheless, one of the most important features reflecting the evolution of IMO's work in the last three decades is the progressive strengthening of port State jurisdiction with a view to correcting non-compliance with IMO rules and standards by foreign ships voluntarily in port. Voluntary access to port implies acceptance by the foreign ship of the port State's powers to exert corrective jurisdiction in order to ensure compliance with IMO regulations. The relationship between flag and port State jurisdiction will be further analysed in part II.

An important distinction of a general kind can nevertheless be advanced here: in every IMO treaty the exercise of port State jurisdiction to correct deficiencies in the implementation of rules and standards laid down in these treaties should be distinguished from the power of the port State to impose sanctions. Sanctions can be imposed for violations occurring outside port State jurisdiction and committed by a foreign ship while voluntarily in port. The distinction is especially important in the case of pollution damage. In this regard, the power to impose sanctions conferred by IMO regulations on the port State (notably in the MARPOL Convention) should be related to the scope and characteristics of those jurisdictional powers as regulated by part XII of UNCLOS.

In general, IMO treaties do not regulate the nature and extent of coastal State jurisdiction. Thus, the degree to which coastal States may enforce IMO regulations in respect of foreign ships in innocent passage in their territorial waters or navigating the exclusive economic zone (EEZ) is a subject to be regulated by UNCLOS. The same principle applies to transit passage in straits used for international navigation or to archipelagic sea lane passage in archipelagic waters. (It should be noted that MARPOL includes provisions on monitoring and investigating illegal discharges of harmful substances into the marine environment.)

In one case, coastal State jurisdiction has been regulated by two IMO instruments: the Convention Relating to Intervention on the High Seas in Cases of Oil Pollution Casualties, 1969, and its Protocol Relating to Intervention on the High Seas in Cases of Pollution by Substances Other than Oil, 1973, are international public law treaties which specifically regulate the right of the coastal State to intervene on the high seas in the case of pollution casualties.

The enforcement of routeing measures adopted at IMO also relies primarily on the exercise of coastal State jurisdiction.

Maritime zones and the implementation of IMO regulations

States Parties to IMO treaties are under the obligation to enforce jurisdiction on ships flying their flag, irrespective of the maritime zone where the ships may be. Accordingly, the differences of legal status between the territorial sea, the EEZ and the high seas do not directly influence the way safety and anti-pollution measures on board should be implemented. The proximity of a coast, artificial islands or platforms sometimes modifies such implementation, owing to the different safety and anti-pollution risks existing there rather than the different jurisdictional regimes applicable to the corresponding sea areas.

The existence of maritime zones does become relevant in determining how coastal State jurisdiction should be exercised in connection with the enforcement of routeing measures to be adopted by the Organization.

IMO's general provisions on ships' routeing should in this regard be interpreted together with the corresponding provisions of UNCLOS. The legal status of the different sea zones has also been taken into account in the four IMO Conventions establishing a regime on civil liability and compensation for oil pollution damage (the Civil Liability Convention, the FUND Convention, the HNS Convention, 1996, and the Bunker Oil Convention, 2001). In these conventions, the entitlement of States Parties to file claims for pollution damage depends on where the damage occurred: whether within their territory, the territorial sea, or within the EEZ.

PART II

RELATIONSHIP BETWEEN UNCLOS AND IMO INSTRUMENTS

This part comprises four chapters which deal with the following subjects:

- Safety of navigation
- Prevention and control of marine pollution
- Liability and compensation
- Technical co-operation and assistance for developing countries.

CHAPTER I - SAFETY OF NAVIGATION

1 GENERAL

Several provisions of UNCLOS set up the jurisdictional framework for the adoption and implementation of safety rules and standards. As mentioned in the introduction, IMO's global mandate to adopt international regulations in this regard is acknowledged whenever reference is made to the competent organization through which those regulations are adopted.

Enforcement of IMO regulations concerning construction, equipment, seaworthiness and manning of ships relies primarily on the exercise of flag State jurisdiction. Other areas such as signals, communications, prevention of collisions, ships' routeing, and ship reporting involve the effective exercise of both flag and coastal State jurisdiction. Furthermore, several IMO instruments regulate the degree to which States may enforce corrective measures to ensure that foreign ships voluntarily in port comply with international safety regulations. However, such enforcement is limited to the conditions laid down in the main IMO safety conventions.

UNCLOS establishes the basic features relating to the exercise of flag State jurisdiction in the implementation of safety regulations. It also regulates the extent to which coastal States may legitimately interfere with navigation by foreign ships in different maritime zones for the purpose of ensuring proper compliance with safety regulations.

Flag State jurisdiction

The basic obligations imposed upon the flag State are contained in article 94 of UNCLOS, which requires flag States to take measures for ensuring safety at sea that conform to "generally accepted international regulations, procedures and practices" (article 94(3), (4) and (5)). The following IMO conventions may, on account of their worldwide acceptance, be deemed to fulfil the general acceptance requirement:

- International Convention for the Safety of Life at Sea, 1974 (SOLAS 1974);
- Protocol of 1978 relating to the International Convention for the Safety of Life at Sea, 1974 (SOLAS Protocol 1978);
- International Convention on Load Lines, 1966 (Load Lines 1966);
- International Convention on Tonnage Measurement of Ships, 1969 (TONNAGE 1969);
- Convention on the International Regulations for Preventing Collisions at Sea, 1972 (COLREG 1972);

- International Convention on Standards of Training, Certification and Watchkeeping for Seafarers, 1978 (STCW 1978);
- International Convention on Maritime Search and Rescue (SAR 1979).

IMO resolution A.847(20) entitled *Guidelines to Assist Flag States in the Implementation of IMO Instruments* provides flag States with a means to establish and maintain measures for the effective application and enforcement of the following IMO Conventions: SOLAS 1974, MARPOL 73/78, Load Lines, and STCW 1978. A subsequent IMO resolution A.912(22), which supersedes and revokes resolution A.881(21), provides guidance to assist flag States in the self-assessment of their performance; Assembly resolution A.914(22) provides guidance on measures to further strengthen flag State implementation. Enforcement of IMO safety and anti-pollution provisions has been strengthened by the incorporation into SOLAS of the International Safe Management Code (ISM), under which companies operating ships are subject to a safe management system under the control of the administration of the flag State.

The basic obligations of the flag State in relation to safety of navigation are found in part VII of UNCLOS dealing with the high seas; here, enforcement of international safety regulations relies exclusively upon the effective exercise of flag State jurisdiction. Enforcement of these regulations continues to rely primarily on the exercise of flag State jurisdiction, irrespective of where the ship is sailing.

IMO's Sub-Committee on Flag State Implementation (FSI) was set up in 1992 after the Maritime Safety Committee (MSC) recognized an urgent need to improve maritime safety through stricter and more uniform application of existing regulations following accidents such as those to the **Herald of Free Enterprise**, **Scandinavian Star**, **Doña Paz**, and **Exxon Valdez**. Incidents such as those involving the **Erika** and the **Prestige** have reinforced the importance of the Sub-Committee's activities. Its primary objective is to identify the measures needed to ensure effective and consistent global instruments, including consideration of the special difficulties faced by developing countries. There is agreement in the Sub-Committee that the effectiveness of IMO safety and pollution-prevention instruments depends primarily on the application and enforcement of their requirements by states that are parties to them, and that many had experienced difficulties in complying fully with the provisions of the instruments. To meet the primary objective, the Sub-Committee has been assigned the tasks of identifying the range of flag State obligations emanating from IMO treaty instruments, as well as those areas where flag States have difficulty in fully implementing IMO instruments. The Sub-Committee has also been requested to assess problems relating to actions taken by the states that are parties to IMO instruments in their capacity as port States, coastal States and as countries training and certifying officers and crews.

Since its creation, the FSI Sub-Committee has produced important guidelines and recommendations. Some have been adopted as resolutions by the IMO Assembly, the MSC and the MEPC, others have taken the form of IMO circulars.

The IMO Model Audit Scheme

At its twenty-third session held in November 2003 the IMO Assembly adopted, by resolution A.946(23), the Voluntary IMO Member State Audit Scheme. At its 24 session, held in November-December 2004 the Assembly adopted resolution A.974(24) on *Framework and Procedures for the Voluntary IMO Member State Audit Scheme*. Alongside the audit scheme framework and procedures, the Assembly adopted a Code for the Implementation of Mandatory IMO Instruments, which will provide the audit standard.

The objective of the Scheme is to enhance the performance of Member States in implementing the IMO Conventions relating to maritime safety and prevention of marine pollution. In particular, the scheme addresses issues such as compliance with the *Code for the Implementation of Mandatory IMO Instruments*; enactment, administration and enforcement of laws and regulations; delegation of authority; control and monitoring of the execution of statutory responsibilities; discharge of other obligations and responsibilities by a Member State; capacity building and technical assistance; and the provision of appropriate feedback to the audited Member State and the Organization's membership at large, and into the work of the Organization. The Assembly has decided that the scheme should be developed in such a manner as not to exclude the future possibility of its becoming mandatory.

A further resolution, on Future development of the Voluntary IMO Member State Audit Scheme, requests the Maritime Safety Committee (MSC) and the Marine Environment Protection Committee (MEPC) to review the future feasibility of including, within the scope of the audit scheme, maritime security-related matters and other functions not presently covered and also to identify any implications of broadening the scope of the audit scheme.

In response to the invitation to the IMO and other relevant competent international organizations in General Assembly resolutions 58/240 and 58/14, an inter-agency report has been prepared by senior representatives of international organizations, convened by IMO, on the role of the "genuine link" and the potential consequences of non-compliance with duties and obligations of flag States described in relevant international instruments. This report was submitted to the General Assembly at its 61st session. In resolution 61/222 (paragraph 73), the General Assembly took note of the report.

Since the commencement of audits in September 2006, 20 audits have been successfully conducted by 48 auditors, who have undertaken a total of

61 individual assignments. A further 16 Member States have formally indicated their readiness to be audited.

In this context, the IMO Assembly at its twenty-fifth session held in November 2007 invited IMO Member States to nominate qualified auditors and encouraged IMO Member States that have not yet volunteered for audits to do so as and when they are ready and as early as possible. In its resolution 62/215 of 22 December 2007, the General Assembly welcomed the audits that have been completed pursuant to the Voluntary IMO Member State Audit Scheme and the Code for the Implementation of Mandatory IMO Instruments, and encouraged all flag States to volunteer to be audited.

Coastal State jurisdiction

IMO treaty instruments do not attempt to regulate the jurisdictional power of the coastal State. This is a subject exclusively within the scope of UNCLOS. This Convention provides the enforcement framework for IMO instruments by establishing the degree to which coastal States may legitimately interfere with foreign ships in order to ensure compliance with IMO rules and standards.

Against this background, the following provisions of UNCLOS are relevant to the enforcement of IMO standards by coastal States:

– In its territorial sea, the coastal State may enact laws and regulations relating to innocent passage (article 21(1)), particularly with respect to safety of navigation and the regulation of maritime traffic (article 21(1)(a)). These laws and regulations must conform with the provisions of the Convention and "other rules of international law". The adoption of the IMO conventions referred to above and their consequent incorporation into national legislation entitles coastal States to request that foreign ships in innocent passage through their territorial sea comply with the rules of these conventions, even if the flag State is not party to the relevant instrument.

– Pursuant to article 41(3), the sea lanes and traffic separation schemes which States bordering straits may designate or prescribe must conform to "generally accepted international regulations". On account of their wide acceptance, SOLAS, the General Provisions on Ships' Routeing and COLREG, should be considered as representing the "generally accepted international regulations". As in the case of the territorial sea, foreign ships must comply with the laws and regulations which States bordering straits adopt, including those relating to safety and the prevention, reduction and control of pollution (article 42), even if their flag States are not bound by the treaties containing these regulations. Furthermore, in order to protect bordering States' interests,

UNCLOS has imposed on foreign ships in transit passage the obligation to comply with "generally accepted international regulations, procedures and practices for safety at sea, including the International Regulations for Preventing Collisions at Sea" (article 39(2)(a)). This expression seems to have a wider connotation in that it may cover also non-binding instruments. (It should also be noted that elements of search and rescue are encompassed within the terms of article 39.)

- In accordance with article 35(c), the provisions in the Convention concerning straits used for international navigation (part III) do not affect the legal regime in straits in which passage is regulated by the related long-standing international conventions in force and specifically relating to such straits. These conventions should, however, be implemented with reference to the criteria of compatibility established in article 311 of UNCLOS and referred to in the introductory part of this document.
- Article 54 of UNCLOS extends the application of the provisions of articles 39, 40, 42 and 44 on transit passage to archipelagic sea lanes passage.
- In accordance with article 58(2), the regime of the high seas applies in principle to the EEZ. As will be explained below, coastal States may adopt jurisdictional measures in connection with the implementation of routeing measures.

(See below for further relevant discussion under section 5 on "Ships' Routeing" and section 6 on "Ship Reporting".)

Port State jurisdiction

By contrast to the situation with coastal State jurisdiction, the most important IMO conventions include provisions which regulate the features of port State jurisdiction and the extent to which such jurisdiction should be exercised. It should be noted that, within the context of the implementation of IMO instruments, port State jurisdiction is a concept of an essentially corrective kind: it aims to correct non-compliance or ineffective flag State enforcement of IMO regulations by foreign ships voluntarily in port.

The exercise of port State jurisdiction for the purpose of correcting deficiencies in the implementation of safety rules is established in the main IMO safety conventions, namely, Load Lines 1966, TONNAGE 1969, SOLAS 1974, SOLAS Protocol 1978 and STCW 1978. These treaties regulate the right of the port State to verify the contents of certificates issued by the flag State attesting compliance with safety provisions. They also entitle the port State to inspect the ship if the certificates are not in order or if there are clear grounds to believe that the condition of the ship or of its equipment does not correspond substantially with the particulars of the certificates or if they are not properly maintained. SOLAS provides that the port State may check operational requirements when there are clear grounds for believing that the master or the crew is not familiar with essential shipboard procedure relating to the safety of the ship or procedures set out in the ship's safety management system.

STCW regulates the control of certificates by the authorities of port States that are parties to that Convention, in order to ensure that seafarers serving on board are competent in accordance with the Convention. Measures similar to those referred to in Load Lines and SOLAS can be taken when there are clear grounds to believe that a certificate has been fraudulently obtained, or its holder has not been trained in accordance with the provisions of the Convention, or the ship is being operated in such a manner as to pose a danger to persons, property or the environment.

IMO Assembly resolution A.882(21) on *Procedures for Port State Control* contains a comprehensive set of guidelines on port State control inspections, identification of contraventions and detention of ships. The procedures apply to ships which come under the provisions of SOLAS, Load Lines, STCW, TONNAGE and MARPOL. The resolution also addresses special port State control issues relating to the ISM Code requirements.

2 CONSTRUCTION, EQUIPMENT AND SEAWORTHINESS OF SHIPS

Article 94(3)(a) of UNCLOS imposes upon flag States the obligation to ensure safety at sea on the high seas with regard to the construction, equipment and seaworthiness of ships. A further specification in relation to this obligation is provided in paragraph 4(a) of the same article, which indicates that measures to be taken by flag States must include those necessary to ensure "that each ship, before registration and thereafter at appropriate intervals, is surveyed by a qualified surveyor of ships, and has on board such charts, nautical publications and navigational equipment and instruments as are appropriate for the safe navigation of the ship". Paragraph 5 provides that in taking such measures "each State is required to conform to generally accepted international regulations, procedures and practices and to take any steps which may be necessary to secure their observance". This obligation also applies to the EEZ (article 58(2)). Article 217(2) of UNCLOS extends the scope of article 94(3) to the protection of the marine environment. It requires the flag State to ensure that its vessels are prohibited from sailing until they can proceed to sea in compliance with the requirements of international rules and standards with regard to design, construction and equipment of vessels.

UNCLOS provides in its article 21(2) that the coastal State must not impose on foreign ships in innocent passage through its territorial sea laws and regulations applicable to the design, construction, and equipment of foreign ships "unless they are giving effect to generally accepted international rules or standards". This provision is of paramount importance for the implementation of IMO treaty instruments containing such rules and standards, because it sets a clear limit to the jurisdictional powers of the coastal State. Regulations imposing either additional or more stringent requirements than those regulated in such instruments could potentially violate the rules of innocent passage regulated by UNCLOS. Article 211(6)(c) provides that the additional laws and regulations which the coastal State can adopt for special areas in the EEZ must not require foreign vessels to observe design, construction or equipment standards other than generally accepted international rules and standards.

The generally accepted international regulations, procedures and practices referred to in article 94(5) and the generally accepted international rules and/or standards referred to in article 21(2) are basically contained in the SOLAS and Load Lines Conventions. These rules and standards, together with the anti-pollution rules and standards contained in MARPOL (see chapter II below) are also referred to in articles 211(6)(c), 217(2), and 219.

SOLAS 1974 and the SOLAS Protocol of 1978 regulate minimum standards for the construction, equipment and operation of ships, in regard to aspects such as subdivision and stability, machinery and electrical installations, fire protection, detection and extinction, life-saving appliances and arrangements and radiocommunication. The regulations provide for surveys of various types of ship (oil carriers, gas and chemical tankers, passenger ships, ro-ro ferries, etc.), the issue of documents certifying that the ships meet the required conditions, and the obligation to carry adequate equipment and nautical publications.

Load Lines 1966 determines the minimum freeboard to which a ship may be loaded, including the freeboard of tankers, taking into account the potential hazards present in different climate zones and seasons.

Construction and equipment requirements for the safety of fishing vessels are contained in the 1977 Torremolinos Convention as amended by the 1993 Torremolinos Protocol. Neither the Convention nor its Protocol has entered into force.

The Assembly, at its twenty-fifth session, adopted resolution A.1003(25) on the entry into force and implementation of the 1993 Torremolinos Protocol, which reiterates the need for Governments to consider ratifying, accepting, approving or acceding to the Torremolinos Protocol at the earliest possible opportunity, so that this international Convention covering fishing vessel safety can enter into force. The IMO Assembly remains convinced that the entry into force of the Torremolinos Protocol would make a significant contribution to maritime safety in general (and that of fishing vessels in particular) and also that the continuing and alarmingly high number of fishermen's lives and of fishing vessels reportedly lost every year could be substantially reduced by the global, uniform and effective implementation of the Protocol.

To that end, the Assembly endorsed the decision of the MSC at its eighty-third session, to explore further the legal and technical options to facilitate and expedite the Protocol's entry into force, which were previously recommended by the Joint FAO/IMO *Ad Hoc* Working Group on Illegal, Unregulated and Unreported Fishing and Related Matters.

The IMO Assembly, at its twenty-third session, held in November 2003 decided to include the development of goal-based new ship construction standards ("GBS") in the IMO Strategic Plan to determine new hull construction standards for new ships which are currently largely under the responsibility of classification societies. The standards, once finalized, are intended to ensure that hull standards developed by classifications societies and other recognized organizations conform to the safety goals and functional requirements established by IMO.

Detailed technical work was initiated by the MSC at its seventy-eighth session, held in May 2004, and it was agreed to focus initially on the development of GBS for bulk carriers and oil tankers. The MSC at its 82nd session held in December 2006 progressed its work on the development of GBS for bulk carriers and oil tankers following a five-tier system agreed at the beginning of the work. The MSC has so far approved, in principle, goals (Tier I) and functional requirements (Tier II) for bulk carriers and oil tankers and significantly progressed the development of guidelines for the verification of compliance (Tier III) for bulk carriers and oil tankers with the help of a pilot project on trial application of the Tier III verification process, which started in January 2007 and is still ongoing.

In addition to these conventions, IMO has adopted numerous recommendations, guidelines, and codes concerning the construction, equipment, and seaworthiness of ships. As stated above, while not legally binding, some of these regulations have been widely implemented by the Member States.

"Black box" carriage requirements

Like the black boxes carried on aircraft, Voyage Data Recorders (VDRs) fitted in ships enable accident investigators to review the procedures and instructions pertaining at the moment before an incident and to help identify the cause of any accident. The regulations on VDRs are contained in the revised chapter V (Safety of Navigation) of SOLAS. These regulations require passenger ships and ships other than passenger ships of 3,000 gross tonnage and upwards built on or after 1 July 2002 to be fitted with VDRs. Amendments to chapter V adopted by the MSC in December 2004 require ships constructed before 1 July 2002 to be fitted with a Simplified VDR.

MSC, at its eighty-first session, adopted amendments to resolution A.861(20) on Performance standards for shipborne voyage data recorders and resolution MSC.163(78)) on Performance standards for shipborne simplified voyage data recorders (S-VDRs).

AIS

The revised chapter V also makes it mandatory for certain ships to carry an automatic identification system (AIS). Regulation 19 of the chapter V of SOLAS – Carriage requirements for shipborne navigational systems and equipment – sets out navigational equipment to be carried on board ships, according to ship type. Under this regulation, an AIS should be capable of providing information about the ship automatically to other ships and to coastal authorities.

The same regulation requires an AIS to be fitted aboard all ships of 300 gross tonnage and upwards engaged on international voyages, cargo ships of 500 gross tonnage and upwards not engaged on international voyages and passenger ships irrespective of size built on or after 1 July 2002. It also applies to ships engaged on international voyages constructed before 1 July 2002, according to the following timetable:

- passenger ships, not later than 1 July 2003;
- tankers, not later than the first survey for safety equipment on or after 1 July 2003;
- ships other than passenger ships and tankers, of 50,000 gross tonnage and upwards, not later than 1 July 2004;
- ships other than passenger ships and tankers, of 10,000 gross tonnage and upwards but less than 50,000 gross tonnage, not later than 1 July 2005;
- ships other than passenger ships and tankers, of 3,000 gross tonnage and upwards but less than 10,000 gross tonnage, not later than 1 July 2006; and
- ships other than passenger ships and tankers, of 300 gross tonnage and upwards but less than 3,000 gross tonnage, not later than 1 July 2007.

Ships not engaged on international voyages constructed before 1 July 2002, will have to fit an AIS not later than 1 July 2008. A flag State may exempt ships from carrying an AIS if they are to be taken permanently out of service within two years after the implementation date.

LRIT

The MSC, at its eighty-first session, in 2006 adopted regulation V/19-1 on the Long Range Identification and Tracking of Ships (LRIT) to SOLAS chapter V on Safety of Navigation, together with associated performance standards and functional requirements.

The new regulation is included in SOLAS chapter V on Safety of Navigation. It provides for the introduction of a mandatory requirement for the following ships on international voyages: passenger ships, including high-speed craft; cargo ships, including high-speed craft, of 300 gross tonnage and upwards; and mobile offshore drilling units. The regulation establishes a multilateral agreement for sharing LRIT information for security and search and rescue purposes, amongst SOLAS Contracting Governments, in order to meet the maritime security needs and other concerns of such Governments. It maintains the right of flag States to protect information about the ships entitled to fly their flag, where appropriate, while allowing coastal States access to information about ships navigating off their coasts. The SOLAS regulation on LRIT does not create or affirm any new rights of States over ships beyond those existing in international law, particularly, UNCLOS, nor does it alter or affect the rights, jurisdiction, duties and obligations of States set out in UNCLOS.

Under the new system, ships will be required to transmit the ship's identity, location and date and time of position. There will be no interface between LRIT and AIS. One of the more important distinctions between LRIT and AIS, apart from the obvious one of range, is that, whereas AIS is a broadcast system, data derived through LRIT will be available only to the recipients who are entitled to receive such information. Further, safeguards concerning the confidentiality of those data have been built into the regulatory provisions. SOLAS Contracting Governments will be entitled to receive information about ships navigating within a distance not exceeding 1,000 nautical miles off their coast.

The MSC also adopted *Performance standards and functional requirements for LRIT* and an MSC resolution on *Arrangements for the timely establishment of the long-range identification and tracking system*.

The MSC, at its eighty-second session, agreed to develop the draft technical specifications; update the required technical documents; prepare a technical costing and billing standard for LRIT; consider technical issues and develop technical criteria to be taken into account when establishing the International LRIT Data Centre and the International LRIT Data Exchange; liaise with the IMO Secretariat regarding consistency, security and other aspects of the Data Distribution Plan with the technical specifications; and ensure that the testing documents completely address the Performance Standards.

The MSC, at its eighty-third session, accepted the contingency offer of the United States to host, build and operate, on an interim and temporary basis, the International LRIT Data Exchange (IDE), agreeing that a permanent home should be found for the IDE as soon as possible (within two years from 1 January 2008, subject to a further review by the Committee). An MSC resolution on Establishment of the IDE on an interim basis was adopted.

The LRIT system will consist of the shipborne LRIT information transmitting equipment, the Communication Service Provider(s), the Application

Service Provider(s), the LRIT Data Centre(s), including any related Vessel Monitoring System(s), the LRIT Data Distribution Plan and the IDE. The LRIT Data Centres communicate with each other and exchange information and data though the IDE and thus the IDE has a key and pivotal role in the establishment and functioning of the system.

LRIT information will be provided to Contracting Governments and search and rescue services entitled to receive the information, upon request, through a system of National, Regional, Co-operative and International LRIT Data Centres, using where necessary, the IDE.

The establishment of the interim IDE will allow the LRIT system to be launched on schedule with multiple LRIT Data Centres operating and joined through the IDE.

The MSC, as a result of the work done in relation to various technical aspects of the LRIT system adopted an MSC resolution on *Amendments to the Performance Standards and functional requirements of Long-Range Identification for Tracking for Ships*.

The MSC adopted a resolution on the *Use of Long-range Identification and Tracking Information for Safety and Environmental Purposes*, which notes that use of LRIT information for safety and marine environment protection purposes would add significant value to existing systems by improving knowledge of ships' positions and identity. The resolution states that MSC agrees that Contracting Governments may request, receive and use LRIT information for these purposes.

Carriage requirements for shipborne navigational systems and equipment

Regulation V/19 also provides that an electronic chart display and information system (ECDIS) may be accepted as meeting its chart carriage requirements. The regulation requires all ships, irrespective of size, to carry nautical charts and nautical publications enabling them to plan and display the intended route and to plot and monitor positions throughout the voyage. The ship must also carry back-up arrangements if electronic charts are used either fully or partially.

High-Speed Craft Code 2000

The new International Code for High Speed Craft, 2000 entered into force on 1 July 2002. The Code is mandatory under SOLAS chapter X (Safety measures for high-speed craft). The original HSC Code was adopted by IMO in May 1994, but the rapid pace of development in this sector of shipping required an early revision of the Code. The original Code will continue to apply to existing high-speed craft, while the new text will apply to all HSC built on or after the date of entry into force. The changes incorporated in the new Code are intended to bring it into line with amendments to SOLAS and new recommendations that have been adopted in the past few years – for example, requirements covering public address systems and helicopter pick-up areas. Consequential amendments to SOLAS chapter X (Safety measures for high-speed craft) that refer to the new Code were also adopted.

Construction, fire protection, fire detection and fire extinguishment. New International Code for Fire Safety Systems (FSS Code)

SOLAS chapter II-2 includes requirements applicable to all or specified ship types. The same chapter makes mandatory the Fire Safety Systems (FSS) Code, which includes detailed specifications for fire safety systems.

Prohibition of installation of materials containing asbestos

SOLAS chapter II-1 (Construction – Structure, subdivision and stability, machinery and electrical installations) prohibits the installation of materials containing asbestos on all ships. The regulation states that for all ships, new installation of materials which contain asbestos is prohibited, except for vanes used in rotary vane compressors and rotary vane vacuum pumps, watertight joints and linings used for fluid circulation when at high temperature or pressure there is a risk of fire, corrosion or toxicity, and for supple and flexible thermal insulation assemblies used at temperatures above 1000°C.

Elimination of sub-standard oil tankers

An MSC working group has developed a proposed list of measures designed to eliminate sub-standard ships, which the MSC has agreed to refer to the Organization's sub-committees and to the Marine Environment Protection Committee (MEPC) for general consideration. A revised accelerated phase-out scheme for single-hull tankers, was adopted by MEPC at its 50th session.

Ships operating in ice-covered waters

The MSC, at its seventy-seventh session (2 to 13 December 2002), and the MEPC at its 48th session (7 to 11 October 2002), recognizing the need for recommendatory provisions applicable to ships operating in Arctic ice-covered waters in addition to the mandatory and recommendatory provisions contained in other IMO documents, approved guidelines for ships operating in Arctic ice-covered waters, which are set out in MSC/Circ.1056.

3 MANNING OF SHIPS AND TRAINING OF CREWS

As in the case of construction and equipment, UNCLOS provides in article 94(3)(b) that every State must take the necessary measures to ensure safety at sea with regard to "the manning of ships, labour conditions and the training of crews, taking into account the applicable international instruments". Paragraph 4(b) specifies that such measures must ensure "that each ship is in the charge of a master and officers who possess appropriate qualifications, in particular in seamanship, navigation, communications and marine engineering, and that the crew is appropriate in qualification and numbers for the type, size, machinery and equipment of the ship". Paragraph 4(c) further requires "that the master, officers and, to the extent appropriate, the crew are fully conversant with and required to observe the applicable international regulations concerning the safety of life at sea, the prevention of collisions, the prevention, reduction and control of marine pollution, and the maintenance of communications by radio". Also in connection with these matters, paragraph 5 states that "each State is required to conform to generally accepted international regulations, procedures and practices and to take any steps which may be necessary to secure their observance". Article 217(2) of UNCLOS extends the scope of article 94(3) to protection of the marine environment. It requires the flag State to ensure that its vessels are prohibited from sailing until they can proceed to sea in compliance with the international rules and standards with regard to manning.

Article 21(2) also provides that the coastal State cannot impose on foreign ships in innocent passage in its territorial sea the laws and regulations applicable to manning "unless they are giving effect to generally acceptable international rules or standards". Article 211(6)(c) provides that the additional laws and regulations which the coastal State may adopt for special areas in the EEZ must not require foreign vessels to observe manning standards other than generally accepted international rules and standards.

SOLAS 1974 imposes a general obligation on flag States to ensure, for the purpose of safety of life at sea, the appropriate manning of the ship. Thus, ships must be provided with an appropriate certificate as evidence of the minimum required safe manning (see regulation V/14).

STCW 1978, as amended, contains a comprehensive set of international regulations with regard to training and certification of personnel. This Convention establishes minimum requirements for training, qualifications and seagoing service for masters and officers and for certain categories of ratings, such as those forming part of a navigational watch or engine-room watch on oil, chemical or liquefied gas tankers and passenger ships.

STCW 1978 was revised at the Conference of States Parties held in 1995. The amendments adopted on that occasion addressed the concerns that the STCW Convention was not being uniformly applied and did not impose any strict obligations on Parties regarding implementation; they also generally brought the STCW Convention up to date. One of the major features of the revision involved the adoption of a new STCW Code to which the whole content of the technical regulations was transferred. Part A of the Code is mandatory, while part B is recommendatory. Further, enhanced procedures concerning the exercise of port State control under article X of the STCW 1978 Convention were developed. In addition, the Conference amended chapter I of the STCW Convention, entitled "General Provisions".

Accordingly, States Parties must provide information to IMO concerning the implementation of the Convention's requirements. The Maritime Safety Committee of IMO (MSC) uses this information to identify Parties that are able to demonstrate that they have given full and complete effect to the Convention (*i.e.* the so-called IMO White List which was first issued by the MSC at its seventy-third session in December 2000 and supplemented at its seventy-fourth session in May 2001). The publication of this list marks the end of the first stage of a ground-breaking verification procedure in which, for the first time, IMO has been given a direct role in the implementation of one of its instruments. Finally, the amendments also provide for special conditions for the training and qualifications of personnel on board ro-ro passenger ships. The STCW Convention was further amended in 1997 to add training requirements for personnel on passenger ships other than ro-ro passenger ships, and in 1998 to add a requirement for masters and deck officers to be capable of detecting damage and corrosion in cargo spaces and ballast tanks.

A separate conference running concurrently with the 1995 STCW Conference adopted a new International Convention on Standards of Training, Certification and Watchkeeping for Fishing Vessel Personnel. This Convention represents the first attempt to make safety standards mandatory for the crews of fishing vessels.

In November 1999, the IMO Assembly adopted resolution A.892(21) on *Unlawful Practices Associated with Certificates of Competency and Endorsements*. This resolution was intended to highlight the problem of fraudulent certificates issued in relation to the STCW Convention, and to encourage Member States to take action to eliminate the circulation of such certificates. Research was conducted on behalf of IMO to assess the scope of the problem and to identify possible solutions. The results of this research were brought to the attention of the MSC and considered in more detail by the Sub-Committee on Standards of Training and Watchkeeping (STW). In January 2002, the Sub-Committee developed a list of actions to be undertaken by the Secretariat on unlawful practices associated with certificates of competence. In 2004, the Sub-Committee completed all the actions identified by the Sub-Committee. However, it has still to develop a harmonized format for ancillary certificates providing evidence leading to the award of the certificate of competence. Furthermore, it has yet to develop appropriate anti-fraud training for the personnel responsible for verification based on the established standards for anti-fraud guidelines.

Also in November 1999, the IMO Assembly adopted a new resolution A.890(21) on *Principles of Safe Manning*, which updates and supersedes the resolution on the same subject from 1981 (resolution A.481(XII)). The new resolution is intended to take into account recent developments in the shipping industry, including increased reliance on automated systems and labour-saving devices, and the concern regarding fatigue and other human-element aspects of crew performance. The resolution includes basic principles to be applied in considering the manning levels necessary for safe operation of the ship.

Each ship should be issued with a "minimum safe manning document", specifying the minimum safe manning levels for that particular ship. The document can then be produced for inspection during port State control.

The resolution includes detailed guidelines for the application of safe manning principles and guidance on the contents of the minimum safe manning document, as well as a model format. Annex I on Principles on Manning and Annex II on Guidelines for the Application of Principles on Manning were amended by Assembly resolution A.955(23).

The MSC, at its 81st session, in 2006 adopted amendments to Part A of the STCW Code. The amendments add new minimum mandatory training and certification requirements for persons to be designated as ship security officers (SSOs). The amendments to the STCW Convention and to parts A and B of the STCW Code include *Requirements for the issue of certificates of proficiency for Ship Security Officers; Specifications of minimum standards of proficiency for ship security officers*; and *Guidance regarding training for Ship Security Officers*.

Further amendments to part A of the STCW Code add additional training requirements for the launching and recovery of fast rescue boats. The amendments have been prepared in response to reports of injuries to seafarers in numerous incidents involving the launching and recovery of fast rescue boats in adverse weather conditions. The STCW amendments entered into force on 1 January 2008.

Bearing in mind that more than 10 years had elapsed since its last major revision, the MSC, in 2007, agreed to undertake a comprehensive review of the STCW Convention so as to take into account new and innovative training methodologies, including the use of simulators for training, e-learning, and training related to cargoes of liquefied natural gas, liquefied petroleum gas, oil and chemicals carried by tankers, to ensure that it meets the new challenges facing the shipping industry today and in the years to come. The review is expected to be completed in 2010.

4 SIGNALS, COMMUNICATIONS AND PREVENTION OF COLLISIONS

To ensure safety on the high seas and in the EEZ, the flag State, in its exercise of jurisdiction, must take appropriate measures regarding "the use of signals, the maintenance of communications and the prevention of collisions" (articles 94(3)(c) and 58(2)). These measures must conform to "generally accepted international regulations, procedures and practices", and each State is required to take the necessary steps to secure their observance (article 94(5)). A broad range of standards concerning signals, communications and prevention of collisions has been developed by the MSC and approved by the relevant bodies within the framework of treaty instruments or recommendations. The following paragraphs refer to the provisions of IMO instruments which relate to the subject matter mentioned in article 94(3)(c) of UNCLOS.

Rules on signals

Rules and regulations on signals are found in SOLAS 1974 and COLREG 1972. Under SOLAS regulation V/21, all ships required to carry radio installations shall carry the International Code of Signals. Any other ship which, in the opinion of the Administration, has a need to use it, shall carry it as well. This Code was adopted by the fourth session of the IMO Assembly in 1965, and has since been amended by the MSC on a number of occasions.

Regulations on communications

Rules on communications for safety purposes are contained in chapter IV of SOLAS 1974, which deals with the provision of radiocommunication services by Contracting Governments and provides for the keeping of equipment on board ships for distress and safety purposes as well as for general radiocommunications. The specific technical requirements of radio equipment used for these purposes are defined in the Radio Regulations of the International Telecommunication Union. As a result of amendments to Chapter IV which were adopted in 1988, with a phase-in period to 1999, the Global Maritime Distress and Safety System (GMDSS) became fully effective on 1 February 1999. GMDSS is a worldwide satellite-based network of automated emergency communications for ships at sea. (In part, GMDSS provides for the implementation of article 39(3) of UNCLOS, since one of the key components of this system is the use of international distress radio frequencies by ships, aircraft, and shore-based rescue co-ordination centres.)

MSC, at its eighty-third session in 2007, adopted an amendment to SOLAS chapter IV, to add a new regulation 4-1 on Global Maritime Distress and Safety System (GMDSS) satellite providers. The new regulation provides for the MSC to determine the criteria, procedures and arrangements for the evaluation, recognition, review and oversight of the provision of mobile satellite communication services in the GMDSS. The amendment is expected to enter into force on 1 July 2009.

The MSC also had approved the related draft revised *Criteria for the provision of mobile-satellite communication systems in the GMDSS* which was adopted by the IMO Assembly at its twenty-fifth session in 2007.

Rules on communications are also contained in chapter V of SOLAS, as amended, particularly in regulations 31 and 32 concerning danger messages and in regulation V/9 concerning meteorological services.

At its twenty-second session in November 2001, the Assembly adopted resolution A.918(22) on *Standard Marine Communication Phrases*.

Regulations for the prevention of collisions at sea

Regulations for the prevention of collisions at sea are found in COLREG 1972, which deals with steering and sailing rules, lights and shapes, and sound and light signals. COLREG also regulates the behaviour of ships operating in or near traffic separation schemes. Within the general framework established by the provisions of UNCLOS, COLREG applies to the high seas, the EEZ, the territorial sea, archipelagic waters, straits used for international navigation and archipelagic sea lanes. Rule 1(a) of COLREG provides that the rules apply to "all vessels upon the high seas and in all waters connected therewith navigable by seagoing vessels".

At its twenty-second session, the Assembly adopted resolution A.910(22) by which it adopted amendments to COLREG. The amendments concern:

- whistles and sound signals (Rules 33 and 35);
- action to avoid collision (Rule 8(a)) – to make it clear that any action to avoid collision should be taken in accordance with the relevant rules in the COLREGs;
- amendments with respect to high-speed craft (relating to the vertical separation of masthead lights); and
- amendments in relation to Wing-In-Ground (WIG) craft, including a rule that WIG craft should keep well clear of all other vessels and another rule that WIG craft should exhibit a high-intensity all-round flashing red light when taking off, landing and in-flight near the surface.

UNCLOS requires foreign ships to comply with these regulations while navigating in the territorial sea, in straits used for international navigation, and in archipelagic waters. In this regard the Convention provides that "generally accepted international regulations relating to the prevention of collisions at sea" shall also apply to foreign ships exercising the right of innocent passage through the territorial sea and archipelagic waters (articles 21(4) and 52(1)). In accordance with article 39(2)(a) and article 54, ships exercising the right of transit passage in straits used for international navigation or the right of archipelagic sea lanes passage must comply with the International Regulations for Preventing Collisions at Sea.

5 SHIPS' ROUTEING

Territorial sea

In accordance with UNCLOS, article 22, the coastal State may:

– designate sea lanes and prescribe traffic separation schemes to regulate the innocent passage of ships through its territorial sea, where necessary having regard to the safety of navigation (article 22(1));

– require tankers, nuclear powered ships and ships carrying nuclear or other inherently dangerous or noxious substances or materials to confine their passage to such sea lanes (article 22(2)).

In accordance with article 22(3)(a), coastal States must, in the designation of sea lanes and the prescription of traffic separation schemes, "take into account", *inter alia*, "the recommendations of the competent international organization" (IMO). In the case of sea lanes, the relevant IMO provisions are contained in SOLAS regulation V/8, amended in 1995, and the IMO General Provisions on Ships' Routeing adopted by resolution A.572(14) of the IMO Assembly. Provisions on traffic separation schemes (TSS) are contained in COLREG, rules 1(d) and 10. (In November 1997, the IMO Assembly adopted resolution A.858(20) by which it delegated to the MSC the function of adopting traffic separation schemes and routeing measures other than traffic separation schemes, including the designation and substitution of archipelagic sea lanes.)

SOLAS regulation V/8(j) (see V/10 in the text as amended by MSC in 2000) states that "all adopted ships' routeing systems and actions taken to enforce compliance with those systems shall be consistent with international law, including the relevant provisions of the 1982 United Nations Convention on the Law of the Sea". Bearing in mind the terms of article 22(3)(a) of UNCLOS, regulation V/8 establishes that ships' routeing systems "are recommended for use by, and may be made mandatory for, all ships, certain categories of ships or ships carrying certain cargoes, when adopted and implemented in accordance with the guidelines and criteria developed by the Organization" (IMO). These provisions of UNCLOS and SOLAS and the classes of ships referred to in article 22(2) of UNCLOS are relevant in connection with the work undertaken by IMO and the International Atomic Energy Agency (IAEA) to review the conditions of transport by sea of radioactive material from a safety point of view.

Paragraph (d) of regulation V/8 (see V/10 in the text as amended by MSC 73 in 2000) acknowledges that the initiation of action for establishing a ships' routeing system is the responsibility of the government(s) concerned, which should take into account the guidelines and criteria developed by IMO.

Rules 1(d) and 10 of COLREG define, respectively, the competence of IMO to adopt TSS and the main technical regulations to be followed in this regard. These regulations effectively institute restrictions on navigation in order to ensure safety.

The IMO General Provisions on Ships' Routeing contain conditions for the adoption of routeing measures applicable not only to the territorial sea but also to the EEZ, straits and archipelagic waters. In accordance with paragraph 3.4 of the Guidelines,

> "IMO shall not adopt or amend any routeing system without the agreement of the interested coastal State, where that system may affect:
>
> .1 their rights and practices in respect of the exploitation of living and mineral resources;
>
> .2 the environment, traffic pattern or established routeing systems in the waters concerned;
>
> .3 demands for improvements or adjustments in the navigational aids or hydrographic surveys in the waters concerned."

In direct reference to the case of a territorial sea (paragraphs 3.14 to 3.16), paragraph 3.16 recommends that Governments establishing routeing systems, "no parts of which lie beyond their territorial seas (3.14), should design them in accordance with the criteria established by IMO and submit them to IMO for adoption. Paragraphs 3.15 and 3.16 apply to cases where, for whatever reason", a Government decides not to submit a routeing system to IMO. In such cases Governments should, in promulgating the routeing system to mariners, ensure that there are clear indications on charts and in nautical publications as to what rules apply. Article 22(4) of UNCLOS obliges coastal States clearly to indicate sea lanes and traffic separation schemes on charts to which due publicity must be given.

Straits used for international navigation

In the same way as the coastal State has authority within the territorial sea, States bordering straits are entitled to designate sea lanes and traffic separation schemes or, as appropriate, substitute them in order to promote the safe passage of ships in straits used for international navigation (article 41(1) and (2)). Whereas, in the case of the territorial sea, coastal States are simply required to "take into account" the recommendations of IMO, the implementation of these regulations is made mandatory in the case of States bordering straits. In accordance with the Convention, sea lanes and traffic separation schemes in straits used for international navigation "shall conform to generally accepted international regulations" (article 41(3)). The IMO regulations to be considered in this regard are contained in SOLAS (regulation V/8), for routeing measures other than TSS, COLREG 1972 (rules 1(d) and 10), for TSS, and the *IMO General Provisions on Ships' Routeing* contained in resolution A.572(14), as amended.

UNCLOS further establishes that States bordering straits must present the proposals for the designation of sea lanes and the prescription of TSS, and their substitution, to the competent international organization (IMO) with a view to their adoption (article 41(4)). States bordering straits may enforce TSS and regulations establishing sea lanes only after they have been formally adopted by IMO. However, IMO is empowered to adopt them only if agreed with the States concerned (article 41(4)). Sea lanes and TSS established under article 41 are mandatory for ships in transit passage (article 41(7)).

Article 35(c) of UNCLOS establishes that its provisions on straits used for international navigation do not affect "the legal regime in straits in which passage is regulated in whole or in part by long-standing international conventions in force specifically relating to such straits". This provision should be borne in mind in connection with paragraph (k) of SOLAS regulation V/8:

> "Nothing in this regulation nor its associated guidelines and criteria shall prejudice the rights and duties of Governments under international law or the legal regime of international straits."

With respect to sea lanes and traffic separation schemes through the waters of two or more States bordering straits, the States concerned are required to co-operate in formulating proposals in consultation with "the competent international organization" (IMO) (article 41(5)). SOLAS regulation V/8(f) requires States to formulate joint proposals on the basis of an agreement between them which would be disseminated to the Governments concerned. It is also worth emphasizing that in the case of straits which are excluded from the regime of transit passage by virtue of article 38 of UNCLOS, or straits which lie between a part of the high seas or an EEZ and the territorial sea of a foreign State, the regime of innocent passage applies (article 45).

Archipelagic waters

Several paragraphs in article 53 of UNCLOS regulate the right of archipelagic States to establish sea lanes and TSS, and refer to the role of IMO in this connection:

- Archipelagic States may designate sea lanes suitable for the continuous and expeditious passage of foreign ships through their archipelagic waters and the adjacent territorial sea, and prescribe traffic separation schemes for the purpose of safety of navigation through narrow channels in such sea lanes (paragraphs 1 and 6).
- As in the case of transit passage in straits used for international navigation, sea lanes and TSS within archipelagic waters must conform to "generally accepted international regulations" (paragraph 8).
- Archipelagic States must submit the proposals – including those for substituting sea lanes and TSS – to the "competent international organization" (IMO) for adoption. Proposals may be adopted by IMO only upon agreement with the archipelagic State concerned. Only after adoption by IMO may sea lanes or TSS be designated, prescribed or substituted (paragraph 9).

- Clear indication of the sea lanes and TSS must be provided on charts, to which due publicity must be given (paragraph 10).
- Established sea lanes and traffic separation schemes must be respected by ships during passage through archipelagic sea lanes (paragraph 11).

In November 1997, the IMO Assembly adopted resolution A.858(20) by which it delegated to the MSC the function of adopting traffic separation schemes, and routeing measures other than traffic separation schemes, including the designation and substitution of archipelagic sea lanes. In 1998, the MSC adopted a partial system of archipelagic sea lanes based on a proposal by Indonesia (SN/Circ.200).

EEZ

UNCLOS has no provisions concerning the designation of sea lanes and TSS for the purpose of safety of navigation in the EEZ or on the high seas. Nevertheless, bearing in mind IMO's global mandate, the IMO General Provisions on Ships' Routeing (resolution A.572(14)) contain provisions which can be applied for the adoption of routeing measures beyond the territorial sea. In accordance with paragraph 3.8 a Government proposing a new routeing system or an amendment to an adopted routeing system "any part of which lies beyond its territorial sea should consult IMO so that such system may be adopted or amended by IMO for international use". This provision furthermore recommends that the interested Government should provide all relevant information including, as appropriate, the following additional information:

.1 the reasons for excluding certain ships or classes of ship from using a routeing system or any part thereof;

.2 any alternative routeing measures, if necessary, for ships or certain classes of ship which may be excluded from using a routeing system or parts thereof.

The General Provisions further establish that such a system, when adopted "shall not be amended or suspended before consultation with and agreement by IMO, unless local conditions and the urgency of the case require that earlier action be taken".

Bearing in mind the recommendation in paragraph 3.8 of the General Provisions that proposals for routeing measures beyond the territorial sea should be adopted by IMO, any safety zone established in accordance with article 60(5) of UNCLOS which exceeds 500 metres must be submitted to IMO for adoption.

6 SHIP REPORTING

General principles for ship reporting systems and ship reporting requirements are contained in IMO resolution A.851(20). IMO resolution

A.857(20) contains guidelines for establishing vessel traffic services, including guidelines on recruitment, qualifications and training of VTS operators.

During 1992 and 1993 the Legal Committee and an *ad hoc* informal working group reporting to the Committee considered legal issues regarding the adoption of mandatory ship reporting to VTS, bearing in mind the basic framework established by UNCLOS. These deliberations paved the way for the adoption of a new SOLAS regulation on mandatory ship reporting.

SOLAS regulation V/8-1 (see V/11 in the text of the amendments adopted by the MSC in 2000) enables States to adopt and implement mandatory ship reporting in accordance with guidelines and criteria developed by IMO. The regulation makes it mandatory for ships entering areas covered by ship reporting systems to report to the coastal authorities giving details of sailing plans. Other information may also be required in the case of certain categories of ships and ships carrying certain cargoes. The regulation also provides that:

- All adopted ship reporting systems must be consistent with international law, including the relevant provisions of UNCLOS.
- IMO be recognized as the only international body for developing guidelines, criteria and regulations on an international level for ship reporting systems.
- The initiation of action to establish a ship reporting system must be the responsibility of the Governments concerned. They should, in principle, refer their proposals to the Organization. Governments which do not submit ship reporting systems for adoption by the Organization should, wherever possible, try to conform with the guidelines and criteria developed by the Organization. Resolution MSC.43(64) adopted by the MSC contains such guidelines and criteria.
- The regulation and its associated guidelines and criteria must not prejudice the rights and duties of Governments under international law, or the legal regime of international straits.

Bearing in mind the specific nature and features of VTS, regulation V/8-1(k) (see V/11 in the text of the amendments adopted by the MSC in 2000) adds that the participation of ships in accordance with the provisions of adopted ship reporting systems is free of charge to the ships concerned.

SOLAS regulation V/8-2 (see V/12 in the text of the amendments adopted by the MSC in 2000) deals with vessel traffic services and provides that the use of a VTS may only be made mandatory in sea areas within the territorial sea of a coastal State.

In November 1997, the IMO Assembly adopted resolution A.858(20) by which it delegated to MSC the function of adopting ship reporting systems. MSC established criteria for ship reporting systems in MSC.43(64).

7 PASSENGER SHIPS

Since 2000, a number of IMO bodies have been working on a series of specific tasks and objectives relating to large passenger ship safety. The package of amendments to SOLAS adopted at the 82nd session of the MSC meeting were therefore the result of a comprehensive review of passenger ship safety initiated in 2000 with the aim of assessing whether the current regulations were adequate, in particular for the large passenger ships being built.

The work in developing the new and amended regulations has based its guiding philosophy on the dual premise that the regulatory framework should place more emphasis on the prevention of a casualty from occurring in the first place and that future passenger ships should be designed for improved survivability so that, in the event of a casualty, persons can stay safely on board as the ship proceeds to port.

The amendments include new concepts such as the incorporation of criteria for the casualty threshold (the amount of damage a ship is able to withstand, according to the design basis, and still safely return to port) into SOLAS chapters II-1 and II-2. The amendments also provide regulatory flexibility so that ship designers can meet any safety challenges the future may bring. The amendments include:

- alternative designs and arrangements;
- safe areas and the essential systems to be maintained while a ship proceeds to port after a casualty, which will require redundancy of propulsion and other essential systems;
- on-board safety centres, from where safety systems can be controlled, operated and monitored;
- fixed fire detection and alarm systems, including requirements for fire detectors and manually operated call points to be capable of being remotely and individually identified;
- fire prevention, including amendments aimed at enhancing the fire safety of atriums, the means of escape in case of fire and ventilation systems; and
- time for orderly evacuation and abandonment, including requirements for the essential systems that must remain operational in case any one main vertical zone is unserviceable due to fire.

The amendments are expected to enter into force on 1 July 2010.

In addition to the aforementioned developments on safety of passenger ships, IMO has adopted two treaties on liability and compensation in connection with passenger claims. The 1974 Athens Convention relating to the Carriage of Passengers and their Luggage by Sea establishes limits of liability for claims such as death and injury and loss or damage to passenger's property (luggage and vehicles). The 2002 Protocol to the 1974 Convention (not yet in force) significantly increases these limits and also introduces strict liability and compulsory insurance in connection with passenger claims.

The IMO Assembly, at its twenty-fifth session, adopted a resolution on Guidelines on voyage planning for passenger ships operating in remote areas in response to the growing popularity of cruise ships sailing to new destinations, some of which are at considerable distances from search and rescue facilities. This new IMO initiative comes in the aftermath of the adoption, by the Organization's Maritime Safety and Marine Environment Protection Committees, in December 2002, of Guidelines for ships operating in Arctic ice covered waters.

8 NUCLEAR-POWERED SHIPS AND SHIPS CARRYING DANGEROUS CARGO

Article 22(2) of UNCLOS empowers coastal States to confine the passage of foreign nuclear-powered ships and ships carrying dangerous cargoes in the territorial sea to the sea lanes, which, in accordance with paragraph 1 of the same article, these States are entitled to establish and enforce in respect of ships exercising the right of innocent passage.

The basic precautionary requirements regarding ships' cargo and structure contained in article 22(1) and (2) are complemented by article 23, which specifically addresses the case of foreign nuclear-powered ships and ships carrying nuclear or other inherently dangerous and noxious substances. According to article 23, those ships have a duty, in exercising the right of innocent passage through the territorial sea, to carry the documents and observe the precautionary measures stipulated in "international agreements". Undoubtedly SOLAS is one of these international agreements, in particular its chapter VIII dealing with nuclear ships and chapter VII, which governs the carriage of dangerous goods.

Nuclear ships

According to regulation VIII/10 of SOLAS, a certificate shall be issued to a nuclear ship which complies with the requirements of this Convention. Chapter VIII is supplemented by the Code of Safety for Nuclear Merchant Ships and the Safety Recommendations on the Use of Ports by Nuclear Merchant Ships.

In view of the risk posed by nuclear merchant ships, SOLAS regulation VIII/11 introduces special control measures. In addition to the general powers of control conferred upon port States by regulation I/19, regulation VIII/11 provides that nuclear ships "shall be subject to special control before entering the ports and in the ports of Contracting Governments, directed towards verifying that there is on board a valid Nuclear Ship Safety Certificate and that there are no unreasonable radiation or other hazards at sea or in port, to the crew, passengers or public, or to the waterways or food or water resources". Accordingly, port States are authorized to enforce control measures in respect of foreign vessels in innocent passage through the territorial sea provided these vessels have clearly shown their intention to enter port.

Dangerous goods

Ships carrying dangerous cargo are subject to chapter VII of SOLAS, which regulates safety measures, including safe packaging and stowage, applicable to the carriage of dangerous goods by sea. This chapter is supplemented by several IMO codes, namely:

- the International Code for the Construction and Equipment of Ships Carrying Dangerous Chemicals in Bulk (IBC Code), made mandatory under SOLAS in accordance with regulation VII/10; in view of the importance of its application for the protection of the marine environment the IBC Code has also been made mandatory under MARPOL 73/78;
- the International Code for the Construction and Equipment of Ships Carrying Liquefied Gases in Bulk (IGC Code) (regulation VII/13), made mandatory for Parties to SOLAS under regulation VII/13;
- the International Maritime Dangerous Goods Code (IMDG Code), adopted by IMO in 1965, contains a consistent set of regulations for the transport of dangerous goods by sea. The Code covers such matters as packing, container traffic and stowage, with particular reference to the segregation of incompatible substances. Some sections of the code were made mandatory as from January 2004;
- the Code for the Safe Carriage of Irradiated Nuclear Fuel, Plutonium and High-Level Radioactive Wastes in Flasks on Board Ships (INF Code), applies, in addition to SOLAS and IMDG regulations, to all ships carrying certain high-level radioactive material. In resolution A.790(19), the IMO Assembly requested IMO's technical bodies, in consultation with the IAEA and UNEP, to continue the review of the INF Code. The review of the INF Code under resolution A.790(19) included questions such as route planning, notification to coastal States, and the restriction or exclusion of such ships from particularly sensitive sea areas bearing in mind international conventions in force. A revised Code was adopted by the MSC at its seventy-first session in May 1999. At the same session, the Committee adopted regulations to make the Code mandatory under SOLAS chapter VII. These amendments came into force on 1 January 2001.

9 OFFSHORE INSTALLATIONS

UNCLOS establishes that in the territorial sea, the coastal State may adopt laws and regulations for the protection of facilities and installations in conformity with the Convention and "other rules of international law" (article 21(1)(b)).

Within the EEZ, the Convention (article 56(b)(i)), establishes the scope of coastal State jurisdiction regarding the establishment and use of artificial islands, installations and structures. Article 60 of the Convention reaffirms the exclusive right and jurisdiction of coastal States regarding regulation of the construction, operation and use of offshore facilities. Paragraphs 3 to 7 of the same article address the implications of these activities for the freedom and safety of navigation and regulate the duties of the coastal State in this regard.

Due notice must be given of the construction of offshore facilities and permanent means for giving warning of their presence must be maintained (paragraph 3). The coastal State may, where necessary, establish reasonable safety zones around such artificial islands, installations and structures in which it may take appropriate measures to ensure the safety both of navigation and of the artificial islands, installations and structures (paragraph 4). In accordance with paragraph 7, offshore installations and safety zones around them may not be established where this may cause interference in the use of recognized sea lanes essential to international navigation.

The implications of the establishment of structures and installations in connection with routeing systems and traffic separation schemes is considered in resolution A.572(14) on *General Provisions on Ships' Routeing* referred to above. Paragraph 3.10 of the resolution recommends that Governments ensure, as far as practicable, that oil rigs, platforms and other similar structures are not established within routeing systems adopted by IMO or near their terminations. If the establishment of these installations cannot be avoided, the traffic separation scheme should be amended temporarily in accordance with guidelines given in section 7 of the same resolution. In the case of the establishment of permanent installations within a traffic separation scheme, permanent amendments to the scheme should, if deemed necessary, be submitted to IMO for adoption. IMO resolution A.671(16) on safety zones and safety of navigation around offshore installations and structures recommends Governments to study the pattern of shipping traffic at an early stage in order to assess potential interference with marine traffic passing close to or through resource exploration areas.

In accordance with article 60(3), any installations or structures which are abandoned or disused should be removed to ensure safety of navigation, taking into account any generally accepted international standards established in this regard by the competent international organization. Appropriate publicity must be given to the depth, position and dimensions of any installations or structures not entirely removed. IMO resolution A.672(16) on *Guidelines and Standards for the Removal of Offshore Installations and Structures on the Continental Shelf and in the Exclusive Economic Zone* defines the standards to be followed by the coastal State when making decisions regarding the removal of abandoned or disused installations and structures. Abandoned offshore installations should be removed, except in certain cases. A decision to allow an installation to remain, in whole or in part, on the seabed should take into account the circumstances described in the resolution. This instrument also incorporates and extends the requirement under article 60(3) of UNCLOS to provide "appropriate publicity" for the partial removal. According to resolution A.672(16), notification not only of partial removal but also of non-removal should be forwarded to IMO. IMO may establish that the publicity requirement takes into account the depth, position and dimension of the installations and structures not entirely removed, as provided in article 60(3) of UNCLOS. If the disposal is to be solved by dumping, article III(a)(ii) of the London Convention 1972 may apply. In this regard the Twenty-second Consultative Meeting of the London Convention, 1972, adopted the Specific Guidelines for Assessment of Platforms or other Man-made Structures at Sea, in 2000.

Article 60(4) of UNCLOS provides that States may, when necessary, establish reasonable safety zones around artificial islands, installations and structures "in which it may take appropriate measures to ensure the safety both of navigation and of the artificial islands installation and structures". Paragraph 5 of the same article establishes that the breadth of these safety zones should be determined by the coastal State taking into account "applicable international standards". In principle this breadth must not exceed 500 metres, except as authorized by "generally accepted international standards" or as recommended by the "competent international organization" (IMO). In accordance with article 60(6), ships must respect those safety zones and comply with "generally accepted international standards" concerning navigation in the vicinity of offshore installations and safety zones.

IMO resolution A.671(16) recommends Governments to consider traffic patterns for the assessment of safety zones (recommendation 1(c)). The resolution has an annex containing specific guidelines for coastal and flag States, bearing in mind the requirement to give due notice of the construction of offshore structures and the extent of safety zones established in article 60(5) of the Convention. In this regard, the resolution recalls that coastal States are responsible for the dissemination of information concerning the location of offshore installations or structures and the breadth of safety zones around them. This dissemination should take the form of Notices to Mariners, radio warnings, lights and sound signals, etc. (Nos.1 and 4 of the annex). Permanent installations, structures or safety zones should be shown on all appropriate navigational charts (No.5 of the annex).

In addition, resolution A.671(16) provides international standards for vessels navigating in the vicinity of offshore installations or structures (No.2 of the annex), as required by article 60(6) of UNCLOS. The resolution also calls on coastal States to take action against those responsible for infringement of the regulations on safety zones, or at least to notify flag States, giving detailed evidence of the infringement by their vessels.

In accordance with article 80 of UNCLOS, the provisions of article 60 apply *mutatis mutandis* to artificial islands, installation and structures on the continental shelf.

Mobile offshore units

In November 1999, the IMO Assembly adopted resolution A.891(21) on *Recommendations on Training of Personnel on Mobile Offshore Units (MOUs)*, which provide an international standard for the training of such personnel to ensure that levels of safety and protection of the marine environment are complementary to what is required under the STCW Convention. The resolution addresses all categories of personnel on MOUs, including the maritime crew, special personnel, and visitors.

10 NAVIGATIONAL AIDS AND FACILITIES

As stated above, the coastal State has legislative jurisdiction over innocent passage through the territorial sea with regard to the protection of navigational aids and facilities and other facilities or installations (article 21(1)(b), UNCLOS). The laws and regulations adopted by the coastal State must conform to the provisions of UNCLOS and "other rules of international law", thereby becoming mandatory for all foreign ships (article 21(4), UNCLOS). The obligation of Contracting Governments to arrange for the establishment and maintenance of navigational aids is contained in SOLAS regulation V/14.

UNCLOS adopts a different approach to the establishment and maintenance of navigational and safety aids in the case of transit passage through straits used for international navigation: pursuant to article 43(a), user States and States bordering a strait should co-operate by agreement to establish and maintain in a strait any necessary navigational and safety aids or other improvements to assist international navigation. Whenever any routeing measures are to be established in straits, paragraph 3.3 of the General Provisions on Ships' Routeing requires that, in deciding whether or not to adopt a routeing measure, IMO must consider whether the aids to navigation are adequate for the purpose of the system. Any action leading to the consideration and adoption of instruments of this kind should be taken by IMO as the competent international organization. Furthermore, the regulation in SOLAS V obliging Contracting Governments to arrange for the establishment and maintenance of such aids to navigation as they determine are required (V/14) was revised and renumbered as V/13 in the amendments adopted by the MSC in 2000.

Through the adoption of the Singapore Statement on Enhancement of Safety, Security and Environmental Protection in the Straits of Malacca and Singapore on 6 September 2007, a new framework, in which the littoral States of the Straits of Malacca and Singapore (the Straits) can work together with the international maritime community to enhance navigational safety, security and environmental protection in the Straits, has been formally agreed. It includes a co-operative mechanism on safety of navigation and environmental protection to promote dialogue and facilitate close co-operation between the littoral States, user States, shipping industry and other stakeholders in line with article 43 of UNCLOS. In resolution 62/215 of 22 December 2007, the General Assembly welcomed this progress in regional co-operation and the formal establishment of the Cooperative Mechanism.

In November 1997, the IMO Assembly adopted resolution A.860(20) on *Maritime Policy for a Future Global Navigation Satellite System (GNSS)* and set out the requirements for such a system, including "control by an international civil organization". The system should provide ships with navigational position-fixing throughout the world for general navigation, including navigation in harbour entrances and approaches and other waters in which navigation is restricted. A revision to this policy was approved by the MSC at its 73rd session as a draft Assembly resolution, which was later on submitted to the twenty-second Assembly in 2001. Resolution A.915(22), which revoked resolution A.860(20), updated the user requirements for general navigation and positioning and introduced user requirements for non-general navigation and positioning.

11 RULES ON ASSISTANCE

Duty to render assistance

Under article 98 of UNCLOS, every State must require the master of a ship flying its flag, in so far as he can do so without danger to the ship, the crew, or the passengers, to:

- render assistance to any person found at sea in danger of being lost (paragraph 1(a));
- proceed to the rescue of persons in distress, when necessary (paragraph 1(b)); and
- after a collision, render assistance to the other ship, its crew and its passengers (paragraph 1(c)).

The obligations to render assistance and to proceed to the rescue of persons in distress is contained in two IMO treaty instruments. SOLAS stipulates the general obligation of the master of a ship to proceed, where necessary, with all speed to the assistance of a ship, aircraft, or survival craft in distress (regulation V/10, renumbered as V/33 in the amendments adopted in 2000). The 1989 International Convention on Salvage lays down in article 10 the duty of a ship's master to render assistance to any person at sea in danger of being lost. It further requires States Parties to adopt the necessary measures to enforce this duty.

Under articles 18(2), 45 and 52 of UNCLOS a ship may stop and anchor in the territorial sea of another State if it is necessary for the purpose of rendering assistance to persons or aircraft in danger or distress. Ships in transit passage through straits used for international navigation or in passage through archipelagic sea lanes are allowed to stop in cases of distress (articles 39(1)(c) and 54). It should be noted that article 39(3) concerning the requirement for aircraft to monitor the "appropriate international distress radio frequency" also has relevance to the search and rescue matters that fall within the competence of IMO, such as the Global Maritime Distress and Safety System (GMDSS).

Search and rescue services

UNCLOS requires coastal States to promote, through regional co-operation if necessary, the establishment, operation, and maintenance of a search and rescue service for safety at sea (article 98(2)). SOLAS stipulates the obligation of the master of a ship to proceed, where necessary with all speed, to the assistance of a ship, aircraft, or survival craft in distress (regulation V/10, renumbered as V/33 in the amendments adopted in 2000). Furthermore, SOLAS regulation V/15 (renumbered as V/7 in the amendments adopted in 2000) obliges State Parties to undertake the necessary arrangements for coast watching and the rescue of persons in distress around its coasts.

A specific legal framework for the obligations relating to search and rescue is established in the International Convention on Maritime Search and Rescue, 1979 (SAR). This Convention requires States Parties to establish services for search and rescue of persons in distress, although these are limited to the area around the coasts (rule 2.1.1). For this purpose, SAR includes regulations on the establishment of search and rescue regions within which the coastal State is responsible for the provision of search and rescue services. Parties to SAR are required to co-ordinate their search and rescue services with those of neighbouring States. Unless otherwise agreed between the States concerned, parties should authorize immediate entry into their territorial sea or territory of rescue units of other parties solely for the purpose of searching for the position of maritime casualties and rescuing the survivors of such casualties. In such cases the State requesting entry must transmit to the coastal State full details of the projected mission and the need for it (SAR, chapters 3, 3.1.2 and 3.1.3). SAR regulation 2.1.7 contains a proviso of paramount importance: the delimitation of search and rescue regions "shall not prejudice the delimitation of any boundary between States".

Following the entry into force of the SAR Convention, the world's seas were divided into 13 SAR regions. In most of them, provisional SAR plans have been developed in line with the requirements of the Convention. At present, provisional SAR plans have still to be completed in the Western South Atlantic, Eastern North Pacific, Eastern South Pacific and Mediterranean and Black Seas regions. It should be noted that article 39(3) concerning the requirement for aircraft to monitor the "appropriate international distress radio frequency" also has relevance to the search and rescue matters that fall within the competence of IMO, such as GMDSS.

In May 2004 the MSC agreed to establish an international Search and Rescue Fund as soon as possible to support the establishment and continued maintenance of regional Maritime Rescue Co-ordination Centres (MRCCs) and Maritime Rescue Sub-Centres (MRSCs) along the African coastlines.

Treatment of persons rescued at sea

At its twenty-second session held in 2001, the IMO Assembly adopted resolution A.920(22) on *Review of Measures and Procedures for the Treatment of Persons Rescued at Sea*. The resolution requests IMO bodies to review all relevant IMO instruments to identify any existing gaps, inconsistencies, ambiguities, vagueness or other inadequacies, so that appropriate action can be taken. Work in this area is continuing in co-operation and co-ordination with the Division of Ocean Affairs and the Law of the Sea (DOALOS) of the United Nations Office of Legal Affairs and with other international organizations including the United Nations High Commissioner for Refugees (UNHCR), the United Nations Office on Drugs and Crime (UNODC), the Office of the High Commissioner for Human Rights (OHCHR), and the International Organization for Migration (IOM).

In response to resolution A.920(22), in May 2004 the MSC adopted amendments to the SOLAS and SAR conventions concerning the treatment of persons rescued at sea, and/or asylum seekers, refugees and stowaways. The amendments, which entered into force on 1 July 2006, include:

- SOLAS – chapter V (*Safety of Navigation*) – to add a definition of search and rescue services; to set an obligation to provide assistance, regardless of nationality or status of persons in distress, and mandate co-ordination and co-operation between States to assist the ship's master in delivering persons rescued at sea to a place of safety; and to add a new regulation concerning master's discretion.

- SAR – Annex to the Convention – addition of a new paragraph to chapter 2 (*Organization and co-ordination*) relating to definition of persons in distress, new paragraphs to chapter 3 (*Co-operation between States)* relating to assistance to the master in delivering persons rescued at sea to a place of safety, and a new paragraph to chapter 4 (*Operating procedures*) relating to rescue co-ordination centres' initiation of the process of identifying the most appropriate places to disembark persons found in distress at sea.

The MSC also adopted the "Guidelines on the treatment of persons rescued at sea" with the aim of providing guidance regarding humanitarian obligations and obligations under the relevant international law.

Unsafe practices associated with trafficking of migrants by sea

IMO Assembly resolution A.867(20), on *Combating Unsafe Practices Associated with the Trafficking or Transport of Migrants by Sea*, notes with concern the incidents involving the loss of life resulting from the use of substandard ships for transport of migrants. The resolution invites governments to co-operate and increase their efforts in order to suppress these unsafe practices. Following the adoption of this resolution, the MSC approved MSC/Circ.896 entitled "Interim measures to prevent and suppress unsafe practices associated with the trafficking or transport of migrants by sea".

Reference may also be made in this regard to resolution A.773(18) on *Enhancement of Safety of Life at Sea by the Prevention and Suppression of Unsafe Practices Associated with Alien Smuggling by Ships.*

12 MARINE CASUALTY INVESTIGATIONS

Article 94(7) of UNCLOS provides that the flag State has the duty to conduct an investigation into every marine casualty or navigational incident on the high seas involving a ship flying its flag. This duty applies if the casualty has caused loss of life or serious personal injury, or serious damage to ships, installations, or the marine environment. The investigation has to be conducted by, or before, suitably qualified persons. UNCLOS requires the flag State and the other State involved to co-operate in conducting the investigation. Provisions on penal jurisdiction in matters of collision or any other incident of navigation are contained in article 97 of the Convention. By virtue of article 58(2) of the Convention, articles 94(7) and 97 apply also to marine casualties in the EEZ. While the English text of UNCLOS uses the expressions "marine casualty" in article 94 and "maritime casualty" in article 221, they are probably intended to mean the same thing, since all other language texts of the Convention use the same expression in both articles.

Article 97(2) provides that in disciplinary matters, "the State which has issued a master certificate or a certificate of competence or licence shall alone be competent, after due legal process, to pronounce the withdrawal of such certificates, even if the holder is not a national of the State which issued them". This provision should be considered when maritime administrations take decisions on withdrawal of certificates issued according to STCW.

The obligation of the flag State to conduct an investigation of any casualty occurring to any of its ships is contained in SOLAS regulation I/21, Load Lines, article 23, and MARPOL, article 12. However, these provisions regulate the duty to investigate only for the purpose of determining the need for any changes to each of these treaties, and accordingly include the requirement that Parties provide IMO with appropriate information. Resolutions A.849(20) and A.884(21) elaborate extensively on the duties regulated in UNCLOS for States to co-operate in conducting an inquiry. Resolution A.849(20) notes that the relevant articles of UNCLOS reflect an established international determination to achieve greater investigative co-operation between States, and recommends States to implement the proposed procedures for the conduct of maritime investigations into maritime safety and/or environmental protection. These procedures are set out in the Code for the

Investigation of Marine Casualties and Incidents, including the procedures for consultation, co-ordination, and co-operation in conducting an investigation between flag States and other States having a substantial interest in a maritime casualty. This Code was amended by resolution A.884(21) to include guidelines for the investigation of human factors in marine casualties and incidents.

The Long-Term Work Plan of IMO, recognizing the importance of maritime casualty investigation, includes items such as the role of the human element, casualty statistics and investigations, safe evacuation, and survival and recovery following maritime casualties.

In 2008, the MSC, at its eighty-fourth session, adopted a new Code of International Standards and Recommended Practices for a Safety Investigation into a Marine Casualty or Marine Incident to become mandatory under SOLAS. The new Code provides a common approach for States to adopt in the conduct of marine safety investigations into marine casualties and incidents and promotes co-operation among substantially interested States to contribute to the investigation. It requires a marine safety investigation to be conducted into every "very serious marine casualty". It recommends that a marine safety investigation be conducted into other marine casualties and incidents, by the flag State of any ship involved, if it is considered likely that an investigation would provide information that could be used to prevent future marine casualties and marine incidents.

Fair treatment of seafarers in the event of a maritime accident

The Legal Committee, at its ninety-first session in 2006, adopted the Guidelines on fair treatment of seafarers in the event of a maritime accident.

The Guidelines recommend that they be observed in all instances where seafarers may be detained by public authorities in the event of a maritime accident.

Given the global nature of the shipping industry and the different jurisdictions with which the seafarers may be brought into contact, they need special protection, especially in relation to contact with public authorities. The objective of the Guidelines is to ensure that seafarers are treated fairly following a maritime accident and during any investigation and detention by public authorities and that detention is for no longer than necessary.

The Guidelines give advice on steps to be taken by all those who may be involved following an incident: the port or coastal State, flag State, the seafarer's State, the shipowner and seafarers themselves. The emphasis is on co-operation and communication between those involved and in ensuring that no discriminatory or retaliatory measures are taken against seafarers because of their participation in investigations. All necessary measures should be taken to ensure the fair treatment of seafarers. The implementation of the Guidelines is being monitored by the Legal Committee.

13 ILLICIT ACTS

Several provisions in UNCLOS establish conditions for co-operation among States to suppress illicit acts such as piracy or drug-trafficking.

Piracy

In articles 100 to 107 UNCLOS reaffirms the duty and obligation of every State to act against piracy. The definitions of piracy and pirate ship, the seizure of a pirate ship, and the liability for seizure are the main elements in these provisions that may be of interest to IMO. Articles 105 (on seizure of a pirate ship or aircraft), 110 (on the right of warships to visit a foreign ship on the high seas) and 111 (on the right of hot pursuit) provides a legal basis for responding to attempted acts of piracy. This legal basis applies to the EEZ by virtue of article 58(2).

Some areas of the oceans are still affected by a disturbing number of acts of piracy, giving rise to grave danger to life and to severe navigational and environmental risks. In this connection and mindful of the duty of the States to co-operate in the repression of piracy as stipulated in article 100 of UNCLOS, IMO has adopted among others resolution A.738(18) on *Measures to Prevent and Suppress Piracy and Armed Robbery Against Ships*. The resolution empowers the Maritime Safety Committee to keep this issue under continuous review, and it has accordingly been included in the Long-Term Work Plan. As a result, the IMO Secretariat circulates monthly reports on piracy and armed robbery against ships, and on stowaway cases and illegal migrants, and has explored ways to maintain pressure against all forms of unlawful acts at sea. IMO is also actively promoting regional co-operation in combating piracy through a series of regional meetings and seminars. Additionally, Assembly resolution A.922(22) provides a *Code of Practice for the Investigation of the Crimes of Piracy and Armed Robbery against Ships* and resolution A.923(22) prescribes *Measures to Prevent the Registration of "Phantom" Ships*.

IMO Assembly, at its twenty-fourth session in November-December 2005 adopted a resolution A.979(24) on Piracy and armed robbery against ships in waters off the coast of Somalia. The resolution condemns and deplores all acts of piracy and armed robbery against ships and appeals to all parties, which may be able to assist, to take action, within the provisions of international law, to ensure that all acts or attempted acts of piracy and armed robbery against ships are terminated forthwith; any plans for committing such acts are abandoned; and any hijacked ships are immediately and unconditionally released and that no harm is caused to seafarers serving in them.

Whilst the recommendations set out in resolution A.979(24) continue to be sound and relevant, a review of a number of incidents reported to the Organization appeared to suggest that not all Member States had acted pursuant to it. The Assembly reaffirmed its recommendations and raised, once more, the level of international awareness, especially in view of the risk to human life placed by the continual operation of pirates and armed robbers in the area under review by adopting resolution A.1002(25) on Piracy and armed robbery against ships in waters off the coast of Somalia. The new resolution requests the Transitional Federal Government of Somalia, the Council and the Secretary-General to take appropriate action within their remit; and, in particular, the Maritime Safety Committee to undertake a comprehensive review of the existing guidance provided by the Organization for preventing and suppressing piracy and armed robbery against ships.

In resolution 62/215 of 22 December 2008, the General Assembly expressed deep concern regarding the continuous violent attacks on ships off the coast of Somalia, and welcomed the initiatives supported by IMO and the World Food Programme to strengthen cooperation among States to protect ships, in particular those transporting humanitarian aid, from acts of piracy and armed robbery in that region. In addition, the General Assembly noted the adoption of resolution A.1002(25) on 29 November 2007 by IMO Assembly and encouraged States to ensure its full implementation, and also noted the initiatives taken by the Secretary-General of IMO, following up on resolution A.979(24), to engage the international community in efforts to combat acts of piracy and armed robbery against ships sailing the waters off the coast of Somalia.

In April 2008, IMO convened a sub-regional meeting on piracy and armed robbery against ships in the Western Indian Ocean in Dar es Salaam, Tanzania. The meeting considered a regional agreement on piracy and armed robbery against ships for the Western Indian Ocean area.

On 2 June 2008, the UN Security Council unanimously adopted resolution 1816(2008). Under the terms of this resolution, the Security Council decided that, following receipt of a letter from Somalia to the President of the UN Security Council giving the consent of Somalia's Transitional Federal Government (TFG), States co-operating with the TFG would be allowed, for a period of six months, to enter the country's territorial waters and use "all necessary means" to repress acts of piracy and armed robbery at sea, in a manner consistent with relevant provisions of international law.

The Security Council text was adopted with the consent of Somalia, which itself lacks the capacity to interdict pirates or patrol and secure its territorial waters. It follows a surge in attacks on ships in the waters off the country's coast, including hijackings of vessels operated by the World Food Programme (WFP) and other commercial vessels – all of which posed a threat "to the prompt, safe and effective delivery of food aid and other humanitarian assistance to the people of Somalia", and a grave danger to vessels, crews, passengers and cargo.

Affirming that the authorization provided in the resolution applies only to the situation in Somalia and shall not affect the rights and obligations under the United Nations Convention on the Law of the Sea, nor be considered as establishing customary international law, the Security Council also requested co-operating States to ensure that anti-piracy actions they undertake do not deny or impair the right of innocent passage to the ships of any third State.

While urging States, whose naval vessels and military aircraft operate on the high seas and airspace adjacent to the coast of Somalia to be vigilant, the Security Council encouraged States interested in the use of commercial routes off the coast of Somalia to increase and co-ordinate their efforts to deter attacks upon and hijacking of vessels, in co-operation with the country's Government. All States were urged to co-operate with each other, with IMO and, as appropriate, with regional organizations, and to render assistance to vessels threatened by or under attack by pirates.

Illicit drug-trafficking

UNCLOS (article 108) imposes upon States the duty to co-operate in the suppression of illicit drug-trafficking engaged in by ships on the high seas. Article 58(2) makes this obligation applicable to the EEZ. The problem of drug-trafficking has been considered by IMO within the scope of the amendments introduced in 1990 to the 1965 Convention on Facilitation of International Maritime Traffic (FAL). The standards and recommended practices adopted by FAL are addressed to the public authorities of the Contracting Governments but are applicable only within the jurisdiction of the port State. Measures to suppress illicit traffic in narcotic drugs and psychotropic substances on the high seas and in the exclusive economic zone are addressed in article 108 of UNCLOS and article 17 of the United Nations Convention against Illicit Traffic in Narcotic Drugs and Psychotropic Substances, 1988. Article 17 deals with co-operation among parties under authorization of the flag State to search and board vessels engaged in such illicit traffic. It further provides that, if evidence of involvement in illicit traffic is found, appropriate action can be taken with respect to the vessel, persons, and cargo on board.

IMO Assembly resolution A.872(20) on *Guidelines for the Prevention and Suppression of the Smuggling of Drugs, Psychotropic Substances and Precursor Chemicals on Ships Engaged in International Maritime Traffic* was revised by MSC at its eighty-second session.

Terrorism

A variety of acts of terrorism have also threatened the safety of ships and the security of their passengers and crews. IMO has addressed the request of the General Assembly of the United Nations to contribute to the progressive elimination of international terrorism. The Convention for the Suppression of Unlawful Acts against the Safety of Maritime Navigation, 1988 and the Protocol for the Suppression of Unlawful Acts against the Safety of Fixed Platforms Located on the Continental Shelf, 1988 (SUA

Convention and Protocol) deal with unlawful acts that fall outside the crime of piracy as defined in article 101 of UNCLOS.

The main purpose of the original SUA Convention and Protocol is to ensure that appropriate action is taken against persons committing unlawful acts against ships and fixed platforms located on the Continental Shelf. The SUA Convention and the Protocol list several offences, including the seizure of ships by force; acts of violence against persons on board ships; and the placing of devices on board a ship which are likely to destroy or damage it. It obliges Contracting Governments either to extradite or prosecute those alleged to have committed these offences.

The terrorist attacks of 11 September 2001 on the United States of America prompted a concerted response from IMO, reflected in IMO Assembly resolution A.924(22) on *Review of Measures and Procedures to Prevent Acts of Terrorism which Threaten the Security of Passengers and Crews and the Safety of Ships*. In the resolution the Assembly request the revision of legal and technical measures and considers new ones to prevent and suppress terrorism against ships and to improve security aboard and ashore, in order to reduce the risk to passengers, crews and port personnel on board ships and in port areas and to the vessels and their cargoes.

In response to resolution A.924(22), the Legal Committee of IMO undertook a comprehensive review of the SUA treaties. As a result of this review an International Conference on the revision of the SUA Treaties was convened at IMO in October 2005, at which two Protocols amending the original Convention and Protocol were adopted, namely the 2005 Protocol to the Convention for the Suppression of Unlawful Acts against the Safety of Maritime Navigation, 2005 and the 2005 Protocol to the Protocol for the Suppression of Unlawful Acts Against the Safety of Fixed Platforms Located on the Continental Shelf.

The 2005 Protocols amend the original treaties by broadening the list of offences to include, for example, the offences of using a ship itself in a manner that causes death or serious injury or damage, transporting a biological, chemical or nuclear (BCN) weapon, knowing it to be such, and transporting any equipment, materials or software or related technology that significantly contributes to the design, manufacture or delivery of a BCN weapon, with the intention that it be used for such purpose. It is also an offence to unlawfully and intentionally transport a person on board a ship knowing that the person has committed an offence under the SUA Convention or an offence set forth in any of the conventions listed in the Annex. The 2005 Protocol to the Convention introduces provisions for the boarding of a ship where there are reasonable grounds to suspect that the ship or a person on board the ship is, has been, or is about to be involved in, the commission of an offence under the Convention. The Preamble to the 2005 Protocol to the SUA Convention recalls the importance of UNCLOS and of the customary international law of the sea.

In addition to the amendments to SUA treaties, a completely new regulatory safety regime designed to prevent ships and their cargoes becoming the targets of terrorist activities was considered and adopted at a diplomatic conference in December 2002. The new measures are centred around a proposed International Ship and Port Facility Security Code, part of which has become mandatory through amendments to SOLAS 74. The Code provides the framework for co-operation between governments, government agencies, local administrations and the shipping and port industries to detect security threats and take preventive measures against security incidents affecting ships or port facilities used in international trade.

The most far-reaching of these amendments consists in the introduction of a new SOLAS chapter XI-2 regulating implementation of the International Ship and Port Facility Security Code (ISPS Code). The Code contains detailed security-related requirements for governments, port authorities and shipping companies in a mandatory section (Part A), together with a series of guidelines on how to meet these requirements in a second, non-mandatory section (Part B). Maritime administrations are required to set security levels and ensure the provision of security-level information for ships entitled to fly their flag. Prior to entering a port, or while in a port within the territory of a Contracting Government, a ship shall comply with the requirements for the security level set by that Contracting Government if that security level is higher than the security level set by the Administration for that ship. The role of the master in exercising his professional judgement over decisions necessary to maintain the security of the ship is explicitly confirmed with the proviso that the master shall not be constrained by the company managing the ship, the charterer or any other person.

The new SOLAS regulations require all ships to be provided with a ship security alert system. When activated, the ship security alert system must initiate and transmit a ship-to-shore security alert to a competent authority designated by the Administration, identifying the ship and its location and indicating that the security of the ship is under threat or has been compromised. The system will not raise any alarm on board the ship. The ship security alert system must be capable of being activated from the navigation bridge and at least one other location.

The new regulations also cover requirements for port facilities, obliging Contracting Governments to ensure, *inter alia*, that port facility security assessments are carried out and that port facility security plans are developed, implemented and reviewed in accordance with the ISPS Code. Other regulations cover the provision of information to IMO, the control of ships in port, (including measures such as the delay, detention, restriction of operations – including movement within the port – or expulsion of a ship from port) and the specific responsibility of companies.

The amendments came into force on 1 July 2004.

In May 2004 the MSC approved a Circular on "Guidelines for the Implementation of SOLAS chapter XI-2 and the ISPS Code" which provides guidance on:

- security measures and procedures to be applied at the ship/port interface when either the ship or the port facility do not comply with the requirements of chapter XI-2 and of the ISPS Code;
- security measures and procedures to be applied by a ship which is required to comply with the requirements of chapter XI-2 and the ISPS Code, when it interfaces with an FPSO or an FSU; and
- implementation of the ISPS Code in relation to shipyards.

In 2006, the MSC approved Guidance on voluntary self-assessment by Administrations and for Ship Security (MSC.1/Circ.1193) and Interim Guidance for voluntary self-assessment by Companies and Company Security Officers for Ship Security (MSC.1/Circ.1217).

At its eighty-third session, the MSC began consideration of issues relating to the security aspects of the operation of ships which do not fall within the scope of SOLAS chapter XI-2 and the ISPS Code (including cargo ships of less than 500 gross tonnage which are engaged on international voyages). The Committee agreed that non-SOLAS vessels share the same operational environment as ships which fall within the scope of application of SOLAS chapter XI-2 and the ISPS Code and the operations of the former affect the security of the latter. Thus, it was necessary to address the security aspects of the operation of non-SOLAS ships in a systematic and analytical manner, so as to achieve a tangible enhancement of the global security net which the provisions of SOLAS chapter XI-2 and the ISPS Code were seeking to establish.

At the same session, the MSC also agreed that any guidelines to be developed on this subject should be non-mandatory, and that their application be kept under the purview of the individual Contracting Governments concerned. A correspondence group was established to undertake a study to determine the scope of the issues and threats involved and to develop recommendatory guidelines on measures to enhance maritime security to complement measures required by SOLAS chapter XI-2 and the ISPS Code, which could be utilized by Contracting Governments and/or administrations, at their own discretion.

Stowaways

Resolution A.871(20) of the IMO Assembly contains *Guidelines on the Allocation of Responsibilities to Seek the Successful Resolution of Stowaway Cases*. These guidelines acknowledge that legislation in this area is different from country to country, but establishes some basic common principles based on close co-operation between shipowners and port authorities.

14 OTHER ISSUES

Removal of wrecks

Several provisions in UNCLOS are relevant to the removal of wrecks, including the general obligation on States to protect and preserve the marine environment (article 192). In relation to the territorial sea, article 21(1)(a) provides that a coastal State may adopt laws and regulations, in conformity with the provisions of UNCLOS and other rules of international law, relating to innocent passage through the territorial sea, in respect of the safety of navigation and the regulation of maritime traffic. Article 221(1) of UNCLOS, which codifies basic principles under the Intervention Convention of 1969 and its Protocol of 1973, recognizes the right of a coastal State, pursuant to international law, both customary and conventional, to take and enforce measures beyond the territorial sea proportionate to the actual or threatened damage to protect their coastline or related interests from pollution or threat of pollution following upon a maritime casualty or acts relating to such a casualty, which may reasonably be expected to result in "major harmful consequences".

The scope of the Intervention Convention of 1969, the Protocol of 1973, and article 221(1) of UNCLOS is restricted to casualties of a catastrophic nature likely to cause major harmful consequences to the coastline and related interests of a State. Moreover, the treaties are restricted to damage to coastal or related interests from pollution. Accordingly, these treaties do not empower a coastal State either to intervene generally to remove wrecks in waters beyond the territorial sea in situations where safety of navigation rather than damage from pollution is an issue, or in cases of pollution that does not result in major harmful consequences.

An IMO Conference convened at the United Nations Office (UNON) in Nairobi adopted, on 18 May 2007, the Nairobi International Convention on the Removal of Wrecks, 2007. The Nairobi Convention fills a gap in the existing international legal framework and provides the legal basis for States to remove from their exclusive economic zones, wrecks which pose a hazard to the safety of navigation or to the marine and coastal environments, or both. It will make shipowners financially liable and require them to take out insurance or provide other financial security to cover the costs of wreck removal. It will also provide States with a right of direct action against insurers.

Articles in the Nairobi Convention cover:

- reporting and locating ships and wrecks – covering the reporting of casualties to the nearest coastal State; warnings to mariners and coastal States about the wreck; and action by the coastal State to locate the ship or wreck;
- criteria for determining the hazard posed by wrecks, including depth of water above the wreck, proximity of shipping routes,

traffic density and frequency, type of traffic and vulnerability of port facilities. Environmental criteria such as damage likely to result from the release into the marine environment of cargo or oil are also included;

- measures to facilitate the removal of wrecks, including rights and obligations to remove hazardous ships and wrecks – which sets out when the shipowner is responsible for removing the wreck and when a State may intervene;
- liability of the owner for the costs of locating, marking and removing ships and wrecks – the registered shipowner is required to maintain compulsory insurance or other financial security to cover liability under the convention; and
- settlement of disputes - part XV of UNCLOS, relating to the settlement of disputes, applies, *mutatis mutandis*, if no settlement is possible within 12 months.

The Nairobi Convention also includes an optional clause enabling States Parties to extend the application of certain provisions of this Convention to wrecks located within its territory, including the territorial sea. If a State chooses the opt-in option, it has to notify the Secretary-General accordingly, at the time of expressing its consent to be bound by this Convention or at any time thereafter.

The new Convention will be open for signature from 19 November 2007 until 18 November 2008.

CHAPTER II

PREVENTION AND CONTROL OF MARINE POLLUTION

GENERAL

Article 1 of UNCLOS includes definitions of pollution of the marine environment and dumping. Several other articles refer in general to the rights and obligations of States in relation to protection and preservation of the marine environment and the prevention of marine pollution on the high seas, the EEZ and the territorial sea. These provisions should be read together with those included in part XII, which deals exclusively with the protection and preservation of the marine environment from different sources of pollution. IMO has a mandate as the competent international organization to adopt rules and standards relating to pollution from vessels and pollution by dumping.

Several IMO safety instruments include provisions which also aim at preventing and controlling pollution hazards posed by maritime accidents involving ships. In these provisions the management of safety and pollution risks are interconnected.

Other IMO instruments exclusively regulate anti-pollution measures, irrespective whether the introduction of polluting substances into the sea is the result of an accident involving a ship or from the operational discharges from vessels. In this regard, the following instruments should be noted:

- International Convention for the Prevention of Pollution from Ships, 1973, as modified by the Protocol of 1978 relating thereto (MARPOL);
- Protocol of 1997 to MARPOL concerning the prevention of air pollution from ships;
- International Convention on Oil Pollution Preparedness, Response and Co-operation, 1990 (OPRC);
- Protocol on Preparedness, Response and Co-operation to Pollution Incidents by Hazardous and Noxious Substances, 2000 (HNS Protocol);
- International Convention Relating to Intervention on the High Seas in Cases of Oil Pollution Casualties, 1969 (Intervention Convention);
- Protocol Relating to Intervention on the High Seas in Cases of Marine Pollution by Substances Other Than Oil, 1973 (Intervention Protocol);
- International Convention on the Control of Harmful Antifouling Systems on Ships, 2001 (AFS – will enter into force on 17 September 2008); and

- International Convention for the Control and Management of Ships' Ballast Water and Sediments, 2004 (BWM – not yet in force).

In the case of MARPOL, compliance with the requirement of general acceptance of the anti-pollution rules and standards established in the Convention is shown by the fact that 147 States representing 99% of the world's merchant fleet are parties to this Convention and implement its two mandatory Annexes I and II, which regulate prevention of pollution by oil and noxious liquid substances, respectively. Annexes III (harmful substances in package form), IV (sewage from ships) and V (garbage) are optional. Annex VI, contained in a separate treaty instrument (the 1997 Protocol to MARPOL) contains provisions for the prevention of air pollution from ships. All MARPOL annexes are in force.

Prevention and control of pollution by dumping is regulated by two treaty instruments:

- Convention on the Prevention of Marine Pollution by Dumping of Wastes and Other Matter, 1972 (LC or London Convention);
- Protocol of 1996 to the Convention on the Prevention of Marine Pollution by Dumping of Wastes and Other Matter, 1972 (1996 LC Protocol).

Anti-pollution measures are also the subject of several IMO Assembly resolutions.

Taking into account provisions of UNCLOS, including articles 195 and 211, the MEPC has been considering IMO's role regarding the scrapping of ships or ship recycling, with the intention of reducing pollution from ships in connection with such recycling and reducing the risk to human health at the recycling yards. This is a process involving the International Labour Organization (ILO), the Basel Convention under UNEP, and IMO. For its part, IMO has developed guidelines on ship recycling (resolution A.962(23)) which were adopted by the Assembly in 2003. The three organizations have agreed to continue to co-operate on this issue.

As already indicated in the introductory part to this document, IMO's anti-pollution treaties should be applied with reference to the compatibility criteria established in article 237 of UNCLOS, which refers to obligations under other conventions on the protection and preservation of the marine environment. Paragraph 1 of article 237 establishes that provisions included in part XII are without prejudice to the specific obligations contained in previously concluded treaties; paragraph 2 provides that these treaties should be implemented in accordance with the general principles and objectives of UNCLOS. The application of the compatibility criteria is especially important in connection with the implementation of MARPOL and the London Convention, the two main treaties regulating prevention of pollution from vessels and from dumping which were adopted years before UNCLOS.

Like the provisions related to IMO activities in other parts of UNCLOS, several articles in part XII include references to general rules and standards, namely the operative provisions included not in UNCLOS but in IMO instruments. In some cases, however, UNCLOS contains regulations which are themselves of an operative kind and can thus be implemented in a way similar to IMO rules and standards. One such example is to be found in the provisions on enforcement of port State jurisdiction, and another in the special mandatory measures adopted for certain areas. Such subjects are regulated by both UNCLOS and MARPOL. Provisions in the two treaties therefore complement each other and should be read together in order to ensure proper and uniform implementation.

Article 9(3) of MARPOL requires that jurisdiction be construed in light of international law in force at the time of application or interpretation of MARPOL. Such international law, as set forth in UNCLOS, describes, *inter alia*, the circumstances, safeguards, and geographical zones relating to coastal, flag and port State jurisdiction. Thus, for many Parties to MARPOL, international law influences the enforcement of MARPOL. For ease of reference, MARPOL provisions which are complementary to or require interpretation in light of provisions of UNCLOS are contained in the following table:

MARPOL Section	UNCLOS Section
1(1)	94, 217(1)
4(2)	21(1), 56(1)(b), 211, 220, 228, 231
4(3)	217(7)
5	217(3)
5(2)	217(2)
6	218
7	226(1), 232
9(3)	91, 217, 220, 218
10	287

A VESSEL-SOURCE POLLUTION

1 GENERAL FRAMEWORK

Article 211(1) of UNCLOS lays down a general obligation for States, acting through the competent international organization (IMO) or general diplomatic conference, to establish international rules and standards regarding vessel-source pollution, and to re-examine them from time to time as necessary. As mentioned above, the main IMO treaty in this area is MARPOL. Article 2(2) and (3) of MARPOL includes a definition of "harmful substances" which is entirely compatible with the definition of "pollution of the marine environment" included in article 1(4) of UNCLOS. Both definitions refer to the introduction of substances into the marine environment which results or can result in hazards to human health, harm to resources and hindrance to legitimate uses of the sea. While the definition included in UNCLOS applies to all sources of marine pollution, MARPOL deals only with pollution from vessels and accordingly includes a definition of "discharges" from ships.

In principle, MARPOL deals with operational discharges of harmful substances, namely those related to the normal operation of ships. Six technical annexes regulate preventive measures regarding five main categories of substances, namely, Oil (Annex I), Noxious Liquid Substances in Bulk (Annex II), Harmful Substances Carried by Sea in Packaged Forms (Annex III), Sewage (Annex IV), Garbage (Annex V), and Air Pollution (Annex VI). The Convention includes a Protocol concerning reports on incidents involving harmful substances, which apply to incidents resulting from operational discharges as well as from accidents involving a ship.

In 1997, a Conference of Parties to MARPOL adopted the Protocol of 1997 to amend MARPOL by adding a new Annex VI containing the Regulations for the Prevention of Air Pollution from Ships. The Protocol entered into force on 19 May 2005. Annexes I, II and IV have been revised and are in force. Annex III has also been revised and will enter into force in 2010.

Relationship between flag, port and coastal State jurisdiction

As in the case of IMO safety instruments, the enforcement of MARPOL relies primarily on the exercise of flag State jurisdiction in regard to the construction, design, equipment and manning of ships. MARPOL also includes regulations relating to the inspection of foreign ships voluntarily in port, to ensure that they comply with anti-pollution rules and standards and to prevent the ship from sailing if these requirements are not met. Furthermore, MARPOL entitles port States to institute proceedings in accordance with their law. Provisions on the institution of proceedings in this regard should be read together with the regulations included in article 228 of UNCLOS.

Regulations contained in UNCLOS and MARPOL on the exercise of flag and port State jurisdiction should be related to the UNCLOS provisions dealing with the exercise of coastal State jurisdiction in connection with the enforcement of anti-pollution measures. These provisions regulate the institution of proceedings for violations in respect of foreign ships navigating the jurisdictional waters of the coastal State without voluntarily entering its ports or the port of another State.

Safeguards in connection with proceedings instituted in respect of foreign ships

Section 7 of part XII of UNCLOS contains several provisions which regulate the enforcement powers of both port and coastal States *vis-à-vis* flag States in connection with the institution of proceedings against foreign ships.

Article 225 of UNCLOS provides that States, when exercising measures of enforcement against foreign vessels, shall not endanger the safety of navigation or otherwise create any hazard to a vessel, or bring the vessel to an unsafe port or anchorage, or expose the marine environment to an unreasonable risk.

Inspections

Article 226 declares that inspections shall not unduly delay the vessel and shall be limited to an examination of certificates, records and other documents required by "generally accepted international rules and standards". Article 5 of MARPOL contains provisions on certificates and special rules on ship inspections which apply to foreign vessels voluntarily in port. Regulations on the issue and content of certificates are included in the annexes to this Convention. Article 7 of MARPOL includes the obligation to avoid undue delay to ships.

Article 6 of MARPOL contains regulations on the detection of violations and the procedures to be undertaken by port States. They include detailed requirements on co-operation between the administrations of the port and flag State following the detection of a violation to this Convention committed by a foreign ship. These provisions should be considered bearing in mind article 226(2) of UNCLOS. Resolution A.787(19) on *Procedures for Port State Control* adopted by the IMO Assembly in 1995 contains comprehensive guidelines on port State inspections, identification of contraventions, detention and port and flag State reporting requirements. The guidelines include provisions on the detention of ships.

Protocol I to MARPOL contains provisions regarding reporting on pollution or imminent threat of pollution by the ship to the nearest coastal radio station. Regulation 25 of Annex I and regulation 16 of Annex II oblige ships to establish on-board contingency plans to deal with incidents involving oil or chemical spills from ships.

Institution of proceedings

UNCLOS (article 231) provides that States shall promptly notify the flag State, particularly its diplomatic agents or consular officers and maritime authority, and any other State concerned, of enforcement measures taken against foreign ships. However, with respect to violations committed in the territorial sea, this obligation applies only to such measures as are taken in proceedings. The obligation of port authorities to notify the consul or diplomatic representative and the Administration of the ship concerned of any action against the ship is contained in article 5(3) of MARPOL.

In accordance with article 223 of UNCLOS, States are obliged in the proceedings taken against a vessel to facilitate the admission of evidence submitted by, *inter alia*, the "competent international organization". States are also required to facilitate the attendance at such proceedings of official representatives of the "competent international organization". Those representatives have such rights and duties as may be provided under national law or international law. The appropriate bodies of IMO may find it necessary to consider the procedures and arrangements required to enable IMO to intervene in such proceedings, including the criteria for determining when such an intervention would be appropriate and the procedure for designating the "official representatives" of the Organization, as envisaged in UNCLOS.

Suspension and restrictions on institution of proceedings

UNCLOS regulates special suspension and restriction conditions on proceedings to impose penalties. In accordance with article 228(1), proceedings taken against a foreign ship for violations which occurred beyond the territorial sea of other States must be suspended if the flag State institutes proceedings within six months after the original proceedings were initiated. However, the requirement of suspension does not apply to proceedings which involve major damage to the coastal State or when the flag State has repeatedly disregarded its obligations effectively to enforce the applicable international rules and standards in respect of violations committed by its vessels. The flag State which has taken proceedings is obliged in due course to "make available to the State previously instituting proceedings a full dossier of the case and the records of the proceedings, whenever the flag State has requested the suspension of proceedings in accordance with this article".

Sanctions

UNCLOS distinguishes different types of sanctions to be imposed with respect to violations of applicable laws and international rules and standards relating to vessel-source pollution committed by foreign vessels. If the violation is committed beyond the territorial sea, monetary penalties only may be imposed (article 230(1) of UNCLOS). As an exception, non-monetary penalties are allowed in cases of violations committed by foreign vessels in the territorial sea causing a "wilful and serious act of pollution" (article 230(2) of UNCLOS).

Pollution incidents and emergencies at sea

In accordance with article 198 of UNCLOS, when a State becomes aware of cases in which the marine environment is in danger of being damaged or has been damaged by pollution, it must give immediate notification to other States likely to be affected by such damage and to the competent international organizations. Article 199 provides that the affected States shall co-operate with the competent international organizations, to the extent possible, in eliminating the effects of pollution and preventing or minimizing the damage. States are further required jointly to develop and promote contingency plans for responding to marine pollution incidents.

The OPRC provides a global framework for international co-operation in combating major oil pollution incidents or threats of marine pollution. In article 3(1)(a), the OPRC establishes that each Party shall require that ships entitled to fly its flag have on board a shipboard oil pollution emergency plan. In accordance with articles 5(1)(c) and 3, Parties are required to inform all States concerned and IMO in cases of major oil pollution incidents. Provisions concerning reports on incidents involving harmful substances are also contained in MARPOL, article 8 and Protocol I.

Article 7 of the OPRC further develops the main principles of international co-operation in pollution response. Paragraph 3 provides that, in accordance with applicable international agreements, each Party must take the necessary legal or administrative measures to facilitate the arrival and utilization in and departure from its territory of ships, aircraft and other modes of transport engaged in responding to an oil pollution incident or transporting personnel, cargoes, materials and equipment required to deal with such an incident.

Article 12 on institutional arrangements gives IMO important co-ordinating roles regarding the provision of information, education and training services, technical services and technical assistance.

The Conference on International Co-operation on Preparedness and Response to Pollution Incidents by Hazardous and Noxious Substances, held in London in March 2000, adopted the Protocol on Preparedness, Response and Co-operation to Pollution Incidents by Hazardous and Noxious Substances, 2000. This Protocol entered into force on 14 June 2007.

2 FLAG STATE JURISDICTION

The obligation for flag States to adopt and enforce anti-pollution laws and regulations in compliance with international rules and standards adopted by IMO is included in articles 211(2) and 217 of UNCLOS respectively.

General obligations

In accordance with article 211(2), States must adopt laws and regulations for the prevention, reduction and control of pollution of the marine environment from vessels “flying their flag or of their registry”. Such laws and regulations must at least have the same effect as that of generally accepted international rules and standards (i.e. those contained in MARPOL) established though the competent international organization (IMO).

Article 217 exclusively addresses the enforcement of international rules and standards by flag States, and provides that such enforcement must take place “irrespective of where a violation occurs”.

Design and Equipment

In December 2003, the IMO Marine Environment Protection Committee (MEPC) adopted amendments to MARPOL which had the effect of accelerating the phasing out of single-hull tankers. Under a revised regulation 13G of Annex I of MARPOL, the final phasing-out date for Category 1 tankers (pre-MARPOL tankers) is brought forward from 2007 to 2005. The final phasing-out date for category 2 and 3 tankers (MARPOL tankers and smaller tankers) is brought forward from 2015 to 2010. In addition, the MEPC adopted new regulation 13H, requiring the carriage of heavy grade oil in single-hull tankers to be phased out by 2008.

Manning

In accordance with article 94(4)(c) of UNCLOS, flag States must ensure that the master, officers, and, to the extent appropriate, the crew are fully conversant with and observe the applicable international regulations concerning, *inter alia*, marine pollution.

STCW 78 includes the requirement of special training for masters in charge of oil or chemical tankers. The comprehensive 1995 amendments to this Convention establish a general obligation for the States Parties to ensure that seafarers on board ships are qualified and fit for their duties in connection with the safety of life and property at sea, as well as with the protection of the marine environment. Specific provisions on anti-pollution training not only for the crews of tankers but also for any other ships are contained in the annex to the Convention. Detailed regulations are laid down in the STCW Code.

Prohibition from sailing

In accordance with article 217(2) of UNCLOS, the flag State must ensure that vessels flying its flag or of its registry are prohibited from sailing until they can proceed to sea in compliance with the requirements of the international rules and standards established through the competent international organization (IMO) including those on the design, construction, equipment and manning of vessels. This provision in fact extends the scope of flag State jurisdiction over the design, construction, equipment and manning of vessels regulated in article 94(3) of UNCLOS: not only should this jurisdiction be exerted for the purpose of safety, as stated in this provision, but also in connection with the protection of the marine environment by operation of article 217(2).

Carriage and inspection of certificates

Article 217(3) of UNCLOS provides that States must ensure that vessels flying their flag or of their registry carry on board certificates required by and issued pursuant to international rules and standards established through the competent international organization (IMO). Provisions concerning conditions for the issue of mandatory certificates and the information which these certificates should contain are included in the technical annexes of MARPOL. This Convention also provides for the obligation of the flag State to undertake not only initial surveys as a prerequisite for the issue of certificates but also periodical and intermediate inspections and surveys, in order to verify that the certificates conform with the actual condition of the vessels.

IMO resolution A.997(25), which supersedes the guidelines adopted by resolution A.948(23), takes account of the Harmonized System of Survey and Certification in some of the instruments.

Conditions for the recognition of validity of certificates also addressed in article 217(3) are discussed in section 3 of this chapter.

Investigation of an alleged violation

Article 217(4) regulates the obligation of the flag State to provide for immediate investigation of a violation by its ships of rules and standards established through the competent international organization (IMO), irrespective of where the violation occurred or where the pollution caused by such violation has occurred or has been seen. Likewise, article 4 of MARPOL establishes the obligation of the flag State to institute proceedings as soon as possible with respect to any violation of the requirements of the Convention wherever it occurs, in accordance with its law.

Under article 217(5), the flag State, in order to investigate the violation, may request assistance from other States, which in turn must endeavour to meet such requests. Correlatively, article 217(6) states that flag States must, at the written request of any State, investigate any violation alleged to have been committed by vessels flying their flag. If satisfied that sufficient evidence is available to enable proceedings to be brought in respect of the alleged violation, the flag State must institute proceedings without delay. Several provisions in articles 4 and 6 of MARPOL elaborate in more detail the basic features of the co-operation between the Administration of the flag State and other States Parties. Both UNCLOS (article 217(7)) and MARPOL (article 4(3)) impose upon the flag State the obligation to inform the requesting State and "the competent international organization" (IMO), of the action taken and its outcome. That information must be available to all States. IMO may consider whether special publicity arrangements are needed for these purposes.

Penalties

UNCLOS (article 217(8)) establishes that penalties provided by the laws and regulations of the flag State shall be adequate in severity to discourage violations wherever they may occur. A similar obligation is imposed on States Parties to MARPOL (article 4(4)).

Notification of incidents

Article 211(7) of UNCLOS recommends that international anti-pollution rules and standards should include, *inter alia*, those relating to prompt notification of coastal States whose coastline or related interests may be affected by incidents, including maritime casualties, which involve discharges or probability of discharges. MARPOL (article 8 and Protocol I) contains provisions concerning reports on incidents involving discharge or probable discharge of harmful substances. Article 8 establishes the obligation for States to report without delay to other States likely to be affected by pollution incidents involving harmful substances. In accordance with article I of Protocol I, the master or other person having charge of any ship involved in an incident involving discharges or probable discharges of harmful substances should report the particulars of such incident without delay and to the fullest extent possible. Discharges include not only those resulting from maritime casualties but also those occurring, during the operation of the ship, of oil or noxious liquid substances in excess of the quantity or instantaneous rate permitted under MARPOL. Article V(1) of the Protocol establishes that reports should be made "by the fastest telecommunications channels available with the highest possible priority to the nearest coastal State".

Under article 4 of OPRC, the flag State is responsible for requiring masters to report without delay to the nearest coastal State any event on their ship involving a discharge or probable discharge of oil.

3 PORT STATE JURISDICTION

Several provisions of UNCLOS refer to the jurisdictional powers of States over foreign ships voluntarily in their ports in connection with the implementation of anti-pollution measures. These provisions, which are explicitly extended to offshore terminals of a State, should be considered together with MARPOL regulations relating to the exercise of port State control. IMO resolution A.787(19) on *Procedures for Port State Control*, which has already been referred to in this document, contains a detailed interpretation of applicable IMO rules and standards and includes an explanation of the meaning of basic concepts involved in the exercise of port State jurisdiction, such as "clear grounds" (for believing that violations have taken place), "inspection", and "detention".

General obligations

Article 219 of UNCLOS (Measures relating to seaworthiness of vessels to avoid pollution) establishes that port States shall, as far as practicable, take administrative measures to prevent the sailing of a vessel which has been found to be in violation of "applicable international rules and standards relating to seaworthiness of vessels and thereby threatens damage to the marine environment". The concept of seaworthiness should be understood not only as embracing provisions concerning the design, construction, manning, equipment and maintenance of vessels regulated in IMO safety treaties but also those contained in MARPOL. Bearing in mind the principle of no more favourable treatment contained in article 5(4) of MARPOL, port States which are parties to this Convention are entitled to request compliance with preventive anti-pollution measures therein, also from ships flying the flag of non-parties.

In accordance with article 217(3) of UNCLOS, compliance with anti-pollution rules and standards must be attested by certificates required by and issued pursuant to international rules and standards established through the competent international organization (IMO) or general diplomatic conference. Article 217(3) establishes that these certificates must be accepted by other States as evidence of the condition of the vessels and must be regarded as having the same force as certificates issued by them, unless there are clear grounds for believing that the condition of the vessel does not correspond substantially with the particulars of the certificates. Further rules on the investigation of foreign vessels voluntarily in port are contained in article 226. These regulations reproduce the basic features relating to the inspection of certificates and ships contained in MARPOL, article 5. Paragraph 2 of this article refers to the inspection of certificates regulated in the technical annexes of this Convention.

Both UNCLOS (article 219) and MARPOL (article 5(2)) establish the basic principles governing the detention in port of foreign vessels: port States must ensure that vessels do not sail until they can proceed to sea without representing an unreasonable threat of damage to the marine environment (article 226(1)(c)). However, ships can be granted permission to leave port in order to proceed to the nearest appropriate repair yard. These measures can be taken without prejudice to the right of the port State to impose penalties in accordance with their national law for violation of anti-pollution rules and standards, even if this violation consists solely in the non-observance of preventive measures without any illegal discharge having taken place.

IMO recognizes that the primary responsibility for implementing the regulations provided for in IMO conventions rests with the flag State. However, it also acknowledges the need for port State control (PSC) with a view to promoting more effective implementation of all applicable standards for maritime safety and pollution prevention.

With the foregoing in mind, IMO has adopted a number of resolutions in respect of PSC over the years. In 1995, the 19th IMO Assembly adopted resolution A.787(19) amalgamating guidelines contained in relevant IMO resolutions, with the aim of providing one set of basic guidelines on the conduct of PSC inspections. In 1999 resolution A.882(21), amending the procedures for port State control, was adopted.

Member Governments, through the conduct of PSC inspections at their ports and discussions at IMO, realized that more effective PSC could be conducted by signing regional agreements. Accordingly, the following nine regional PSC agreements have been signed and are currently in operation:

.1 the Paris Memorandum of Understanding on Port State Control (Paris MoU), adopted in Paris on 1 July 1982;

.2 the Acuerdo de Viña del Mar (Viña del Mar or Latin-America Agreement), signed in Viña del Mar (Chile) on 5 November 1992;

.3 the Memorandum of Understanding on Port State Control in the Asia-Pacific Region (Tokyo MoU), signed in Tokyo on 1 December 1993;

.4 the Memorandum of Understanding on Port State Control in the Caribbean Region (Caribbean MoU), signed in Christchurch, Barbados on 9 February 1996;

.5 the Memorandum of Understanding on Port State Control in the Mediterranean Region (Mediterranean MoU), signed in Malta on 11 July 1997;

.6 the Indian Ocean Memorandum of Understanding on Port State Control (Indian Ocean MoU), signed in Pretoria, South Africa on 5 June 1998;

.7 the Memorandum of Understanding for the West and Central African Region (Abuja MoU), signed in Abuja, Nigeria on 22 October 1999;

.8 the Memorandum of Understanding on Port State Control in the Black Sea signed in Istanbul, Turkey on 7 April 2000; and

.9 the Arab States of the Gulf (Riyadh MoU), signed in Riyadh, 2004.

Discharge violations

UNCLOS provisions concerning measures to be taken by port States in the event of discharge in violation of international rules and standards are contained in article 218. Paragraph 1 of this article expressly authorizes port States to institute proceedings in respect of foreign ships voluntarily in their ports in cases where illegal discharges have occurred outside the internal waters, territorial sea or EEZ of the port State. Paragraphs 2, 3 and 4 regulate situations involving requests to the port State from the flag State as well as coastal States regarding discharge violations of applicable international rules and standards. Violations by a foreign ship voluntarily in port which have been committed within the territorial sea or EEZ of a State are dealt with in article 220 of the Convention. In both cases the State into whose port the vessel has voluntarily come should apply MARPOL rules and standards.

Action to be taken in the event of violations of regulations on discharges are contained in article 6(2) of MARPOL. This provision establishes that ships to which the Convention apply may, in any port of a Party, be subject to inspection by officers appointed or authorized by that Party "for the purposes of verifying whether the ship has discharged any harmful substances in violation of the provisions of the regulations". Other provisions in the same article deal with communications with the Administration of the flag State and other States affected by the violation, as well as the rules governing institution of proceedings.

Reception facilities

As previously noted, article 211 lays down a general obligation for States to co-operate in the establishment of international rules and standards regarding pollution from ships. The main international treaty implementing this obligation is MARPOL 73/78, which sets out requirements for port reception facilities, and all parties to the Convention are obliged to provide reception facilities for ships calling at their ports. The requirement for such reception facilities is especially necessary in "special areas" where, because of the vulnerability of these areas to pollution, more stringent discharge restrictions have been imposed. MARPOL 73/78 also provides that these reception facilities should, in each case, be "adequate" for the reception of wastes from ships without causing undue delay to the ships using them.

However, while ships are subject to both survey and certification by the flag State Administration and port State control, the responsibility for providing reception facilities is a matter only for port States, and progress in this regard has not been satisfactory. In order to address the matter, IMO has developed a number of guidelines, the most recent of which have been published as a "Comprehensive Manual on Port Reception Facilities". The manual provides guidance on matters such as waste management strategy, type and quantity of ship-generated wastes, planning, choice of location, collection and treatment, financing and cost recovery, and co-operation of port and ship requirements. IMO has also provided technical assistance over many years to a large number of countries in the form of seminars, symposia and workshops, mostly at the regional level. Progress has been made in certain parts of the world. It is apparent, however, that, in some oil producing regions, the situation with regard to the provision of reception facilities is not improving.

The provision of adequate reception facilities worldwide is a matter of extreme complexity which involves the shipping industry, port operators, oil and chemical companies and Governments. A satisfactory solution to the shortage of reception facilities in many parts of the world has yet to be found. It is widely recognized that, if this problem is to be satisfactorily resolved, it will be necessary to address the economic as well as the technical aspects of this issue.

At its forty-fourth session in March 2000, the MEPC adopted "Guidelines for ensuring the adequacy of reception facilities" (resolution MEPC.83(44)).

The MEPC, at its fifty-fifth session in October 2006, approved an Action Plan to tackle the alleged inadequacy of port reception facilities. The Plan contains a list of proposed work items to be undertaken by IMO with the aim of improving the provision and use of adequate port reception facilities, including items relating to reporting requirements; provision of information on port reception facilities; identification of any technical problems encountered during the transfer of waste between ship and shore and the standardization of garbage segregation requirements and containment identification; review of the type and amount of wastes generated on board and the type and capacity of port reception facilities; revision of the *IMO Comprehensive Manual on Port Reception Facilities*; and development of a *Guide to Good Practice on Port Reception Facilities*. With regard to regional arrangements, the Committee agreed to recognize them as a means to provide reception facilities in light of the MARPOL requirements, taking into account the benefit of having such regional arrangements in place.

Undue delay to ships

UNCLOS (article 226(1)(a)) provides that States must not delay a foreign vessel longer than is essential for the purposes of investigating violations of international rules and standards. MARPOL (article 7(1)) establishes that port States should make all possible efforts to avoid a ship being unduly detained or delayed in connection with such investigations.

Special provisions on single-hull tankers

In December 2003, IMO adopted a revised, accelerated phase-out scheme for single-hull tankers, along with other measures including an extended application of the Condition Assessment Scheme (CAS) for tankers and a new regulation banning the carriage of Heavy Grade Oil (HGO) in single-hull tankers.

The amendments to the International Convention for the Prevention of Pollution from Ships, 1973, as modified by the Protocol of 1978 thereto (MARPOL 73/78) were adopted at the fiftieth session of IMO's Marine Environment Protection Committee (MEPC) and entered into force on 5 April 2005, under the tacit acceptance procedure.

4 COASTAL STATE JURISDICTION

Routeing measures

Article 211(1) of UNCLOS prescribes that States, acting through the competent international organization or general diplomatic conference, shall promote the adoption of routeing systems designed to minimize the threat of accidents which might cause pollution of the marine environment, including the coastline and related interests of coastal States. As mentioned in the previous chapter dealing with safety of navigation, IMO is the competent international organization for developing guidelines and regulations on ships' routeing systems, and comments made under that chapter apply to the prevention of marine pollution. In this regard, mention should be made of new SOLAS regulation V/8, (a) and (j) (see V/10 in the text of SOLAS chapter V as amended by MSC in 2000). According to paragraph (a), ships' routeing systems should also be established bearing in mind the need to protect the marine environment. Paragraph (j) requires that routeing systems comply with UNCLOS.

The General Provisions on Ships' Routeing (resolution A.572(14) adopted by the IMO Assembly in 1985) were amended in 1995 by the insertion of new paragraphs 3.6 and 3.7, which deal with routeing systems for the protection of environmentally sensitive areas. Paragraph 3.6 establishes the criteria to be taken into account when considering the adoption of a routeing system for the protection of the marine environment. Paragraph 3.7 sets limits for the adoption of routeing systems. In accordance with this paragraph IMO should not adopt a system that would impose unnecessary constraints on shipping, or establish an area to be avoided that would impede the passage of ships through an international strait. In November 1997, the IMO Assembly adopted resolution A.858(20) by which it delegated to the MSC the function of adopting traffic separation schemes and routeing measures other than traffic separation schemes, including the designation and substitution of archipelagic sea lanes.

Territorial sea

In accordance with article 21(1) of UNCLOS the coastal State may adopt rules and regulations "in conformity with the provisions of this Convention and other rules of international law, relating to innocent passage through the territorial sea in respect of … (f) the preservation of the environment of the coastal State and the prevention, reduction and control of pollution thereof". In this connection, article 211(4) establishes that coastal States may "in the exercise of their sovereignty within their territorial sea, adopt laws and regulations for the prevention, reduction, and control of marine pollution from foreign vessels, including vessels exercising the right of innocent passage". This provision is complemented by a reference to the need not to hamper innocent passage of foreign vessels. The regulatory powers of the coastal State in this regard are limited in accordance with article 21(2): in the case of anti-pollution measures, laws and regulations adopted by the coastal State shall not apply to the design, construction, manning, or equipment of foreign ships unless they are giving effect to generally accepted international rules and standards, in this case also to those contained in MARPOL.

Article 220(2) of UNCLOS regulates the right of intervention of the coastal State in the territorial sea in connection with the violation of international rules and standards for the prevention, reduction and control of pollution from vessels, namely those rules and standards adopted at IMO. In accordance with article 220(5), the coastal State may undertake physical inspection of a vessel navigating in its territorial sea where there are clear grounds for believing that such vessel has committed a violation of the international rules and standards for the prevention, reduction and control of pollution from vessels while navigating in the EEZ of the coastal State. Where evidence so warrants, the coastal State may institute proceedings, including detention of the vessel in accordance with its laws.

Exclusive Economic Zone

Article 56(1)(b)(iii) of UNCLOS provides that in the EEZ the coastal State has jurisdiction with regard to the protection and preservation of the marine environment. In exercising this jurisdiction the coastal State is empowered to enact laws and regulations for the prevention, reduction, and control of vessel-source pollution in the EEZ. Such laws and regulations must, in accordance with article 211(5) of UNCLOS, conform to and give effect to "generally accepted international rules and standards established through the competent international organization" (IMO).

Several provisions of UNCLOS regulate the rights of the coastal State in cases of violations to international anti-pollution rules and standards committed in the EEZ by vessels navigating either in the EEZ or the territorial sea:

- If there are clear grounds for believing that such a violation has taken place, the State may, in accordance with article 220(3), require the vessel to give information regarding its identity and port of registry, its last and next port of call and other relevant information required to establish whether a violation has occurred.
- If there are clear grounds for believing that a vessel has committed a violation resulting in a substantial discharge causing or threatening significant pollution of the marine environment, the coastal State may, in accordance with article 220(5), undertake physical inspection of the vessel for matters related to the violation if the vessel has refused to give information or if the information supplied by the vessel is manifestly at variance with the evident factual situation, and if the circumstances of the case justify such inspection.
- Article 220(6) establishes that if there is "clear objective evidence" that a vessel has committed a violation resulting in a discharge causing major damage or threat of major damage to the coastline or related interest of the coastal State, or to any of its resources of the territorial sea or the EEZ, the State may, provided that the evidence so warrants, institute proceedings, including detention of the vessel.

Intervention in case of a major incident beyond the territorial sea

Article 221(1) recognizes the rights of States, "pursuant to international law, both customary and conventional, to take and enforce measures beyond the territorial sea proportionate to the actual or threatened damage to protect their coastline or related interests, including fishing, from pollution or threat of pollution following upon a maritime casualty … which may reasonably be expected to result in major harmful consequences".

This provision echoes the main features of the right of intervention by the coastal States regulated by the Intervention Convention of 1969 and its Protocol of 1973, in respect of incidents involving, respectively, a major discharge of oil or of substances other than oil. These treaties refer solely to the right of intervention on the high seas because the concept of EEZ was not known at the time of their adoption. Following the entry into force of UNCLOS, the regulations on the right of the coastal State laid down in both IMO treaties should be considered as applicable both to the EEZ and to the high seas.

Special mandatory measures

In accordance with article 211(6) of UNCLOS the coastal State may adopt special mandatory measures for the prevention of vessel-source pollution in certain clearly defined areas of its EEZ. To justify the adoption of such measures, evidence must indicate that the existing international rules and standards are inadequate for the special circumstances of the area concerned. The area must be clearly defined and the adoption of special measures must be required for recognized technical reasons in relation to the oceanographical and ecological conditions, as well as the utilization or protection of the resources and the particular character of the traffic of the area concerned.

Article 211(6)(a) and (b) includes specific conditions for the adoption of special mandatory measures:

- the coastal State should conduct appropriate consultations through the "competent international organization" (IMO) with other States concerned. It should also submit a communication to IMO for special mandatory measures, supported by scientific and technical evidence and information on reception facilities;
- IMO, within 12 months of receiving the communication, shall determine whether the conditions in the proposed area justify the adoption of special mandatory measures;
- following a decision by IMO, the coastal State may adopt laws and regulations implementing such international rules and standards or navigational practices as are made applicable, through the organization (IMO), for special areas. These laws shall not become applicable to foreign vessels until 15 months after the submission of the communication to the organization (IMO);
- the coastal State must publish the limits of the area where the special mandatory measures are to be enforced.

In accordance with article 211(6)(c) the coastal State may enact for the same area additional laws and regulations on discharges or navigational practices. However, these laws and regulations must not require foreign vessels to observe design, construction, manning or equipment standards other than generally accepted international rules and standards. If the coastal State intends to adopt additional laws and regulations it must notify the organization (IMO) thereof at the time it submits the communication referred to above.

In accordance with article 220(8) of UNCLOS, the provisions on enforcement contained in article 220(3) to (7) also apply to the enforcement of national laws and regulations implementing special mandatory measures pursuant to article 211(6).

Special areas and particularly sensitive sea areas (PSSAs)

Special mandatory requirements for certain areas regarding the prevention of operational discharges of harmful substances are contained in Annexes I, II, and V of MARPOL. Guidelines for the designation of Special Areas under MARPOL are formulated in resolution A.927(22) on guidelines for the designation of special areas and the identification of particularly sensitive sea areas adopted by the IMO Assembly in 2001. Annex VI - Regulations for the Prevention of Air Pollution from Ships, establishes certain sulphur oxide (SOx) Emission Control Areas with more stringent controls on sulphur emissions.

A comparison between areas requiring special mandatory measures mentioned in article 211(6) of UNCLOS and provisions on special areas under MARPOL indicates that, while the former are restricted in jurisdictional scope to the EEZ, the MARPOL special area provisions cover enclosed or semi-enclosed areas which may include parts of the territorial sea, the EEZ and the high seas.

While MARPOL special requirements apply only to the discharge of harmful substances, article 211(6) of UNCLOS does not contain any specification as to the kind of measures that may be taken.

To date, 10 special areas have been designated under MARPOL Annex I (Mediterranean Sea, Baltic Sea, Black Sea, Red Sea, "Gulfs" area, Gulf of Aden, Antarctic area, North West European Waters, Oman area of the Arabian Sea, Southern South African waters). One special area has been designated under Annex II (Antarctic area), eight special areas have been designated under Annex V (Mediterranean Sea, Baltic Sea, Black Sea, Red Sea, "Gulfs" area, North Sea, Antarctic area (south of latitude 60 degrees south), Wider Caribbean region including the Gulf of Mexico and the Caribbean Sea). Owing to the absence of adequate reception facilities, some of those areas have not yet taken effect. Two SO_x Emission Control Areas have been designated under Annex VI (Baltic Sea, North Sea).

The Assembly, at its twenty-fourth session, adopted revised Guidelines for the Identification and Designation of Particularly Sensitive Sea Areas (PSSAs) (resolution 982(24)). A PSSA is an area that needs special protection through action by IMO because of its significance for recognized ecological, socio-economic, or scientific attributes where such attributes may be vulnerable to damage by international shipping activities. An application for PSSA designation should contain a proposal for an associated protective measure or measures aimed at preventing, reducing or eliminating the threat or identified vulnerability. Associated protective measures for PSSAs are limited to actions that are to be, or have been, approved and adopted by IMO, for example, a routeing system such as an area to be avoided.

The guidelines provide advice to IMO Member Governments in the formulation and submission of applications for the designation of PSSAs to ensure that, in the process, all interests – those of the coastal State, flag State, and the environmental and shipping communities – are thoroughly considered on the basis of relevant scientific, technical, economic, and environmental information regarding the area at risk of damage from international shipping activities.

In order to ensure the proper development, drafting and submission of proposals in accordance with the Guidelines, the MEPC approved a revised guidance document for the preparation of PSSAs proposals at its fifty-fourth session.

The following 12 PSSAs have been designated to date: the Great Barrier Reef (Australia); the Sabana-Camagüey Archipelago (Cuba); Malpelo Island (Colombia); the sea around the Florida Keys (United States of America); the Wadden Sea (Denmark, Germany, the Netherlands); Paracas National Reserve (Peru); Western European Waters (Belgium, France, Ireland, Portugal, Spain and the United Kingdom); Extension of the existing Great Barrier Reef PSSA to include the Torres Strait (Australia and Papua New Guinea); Canary Islands (Spain); the Galapagos Archipelago (Ecuador); the Baltic Sea area (Denmark, Estonia, Finland, Germany, Latvia, Lithuania, Poland and Sweden); and the Papahānaumokuākea Marine National Monument (United States of America)

States bordering straits used for international navigation and archipelagic States

Article 42(1)(b) of UNCLOS empowers States bordering straits used for international navigation to adopt laws and regulations relating to transit passage through the strait in respect of the prevention, reduction and control of pollution, by giving effect to "applicable international regulations regarding the discharge of oil, oily wastes and other noxious substances in the strait". National legislation adopted in this regard must not discriminate among foreign ships or have the practical effect of impairing the right of transit passage (article 42(2)). In accordance with article 39(2)(b), ships in transit must comply with "generally accepted international regulations, procedures and practices for the prevention, reduction and control of pollution from ships", namely MARPOL and other relevant IMO instruments.

UNCLOS (article 43(b)) provides that user States and States bordering straits should by agreement co-operate for the prevention, reduction and control of vessel-source pollution. There are currently no specific international instruments regulating this matter. Thus, IMO may consider whether adoption of international regulations in this regard may be necessary.

By virtue of article 54 of UNCLOS, the rights and obligations of flag and coastal States regarding the prevention, reduction and control of pollution in accordance with applicable international regulations regarding the discharge of oil, oily wastes and other noxious substances in international straits apply *mutatis mutandis* to archipelagic sea lane passage.

UNCLOS includes a specific provision on the enforcement powers of States bordering straits used for international navigation. Under article 233 of UNCLOS, States bordering straits are entitled to take enforcement measures against ships in transit passage only if the ship has committed a violation of the laws and regulations referred to in article 42(1)(a) and (b) of UNCLOS causing or threatening major damage to the marine environment of the straits. In such a case, the enforcement measures taken by the bordering State are subject to the safeguards of part XII, section 7 of UNCLOS.

B DUMPING AT SEA OF WASTES AND OTHER MATTER

General

UNCLOS includes a definition of "dumping" in article 1(5). Article 210 contains regulations specifically related to the prevention, reduction and control of pollution by dumping. The obligation for States to adopt laws and regulations and to take other measures that may be needed to prevent, reduce and control pollution of the marine environment by dumping is contained in paragraphs 1 and 2. In accordance with paragraph 6 such laws, regulations and measures shall be no less effective in preventing, reducing and controlling such pollution than the "global rules and standards".

In this connection, article 210(4) imposes upon States the obligation to endeavour to establish global and regional rules and standards and recommended practices and procedures to prevent, reduce and control pollution by dumping. Such provisions should be adopted through "competent international organizations or diplomatic conference". The reference in the plural to international organizations indicates that in this case the task of IMO at global level can be complemented by regulatory activities undertaken under the auspices of other organizations. Co-operation between IMO and other organizations has been implemented, especially in connection with the adoption of regional agreements.

The international global and regional framework which has been established in this regard consists of several treaties and agreements. At a global level, anti-pollution measures are contained in the Convention on the Prevention of Marine Pollution by Dumping of Wastes and Other Matter, 1972 (London Convention, 1972), as periodically amended by decisions of its Contracting Parties. In 1996 the Contracting Parties to the London

Convention adopted the Protocol to the Convention on the Prevention of Marine Pollution by the Dumping of Wastes and Other Matter, 1972 (1996 LC Protocol) which comprehensively and substantially amends the parent convention. Eventually, the 1996 LC Protocol will replace the Convention.

Since 1977, IMO has been responsible for the performance of secretarial functions such as the organization and servicing of the Consultative Meetings of the Contracting Parties to the London Convention and other subsidiary bodies reporting to the Consultative Meetings. Similar functions, as well as depositary functions, are regulated in the 1996 LC Protocol. The Protocol further expands the tasks of IMO by assigning to the Organization, *inter alia*, the duties of providing advice on implementation and, subject to availability of adequate resources, collaborating in environmental assessments and co-operating with competent international organizations concerned with the prevention and control of pollution. The Protocol assigns IMO the roles of co-ordination and co-operation regarding technical co-operation activities in the field of training, and access to and transfer of environmentally sound technologies and know-how to developing countries. The 1996 LC Protocol entered into force in March 2006.

The Contracting Parties to the London Protocol, at their first meeting held in London from 30 October to 3 November 2006, adopted amendments to the 1996 LC Protocol. The amendments regulate the sequestration of CO_2 streams from CO_2 capture processes in sub-seabed geological formations.

Parties also agreed that guidance on the means by which sub-seabed geological sequestration of carbon dioxide can be conducted should be developed as soon as possible. This will, when finalized, form an important part of the regulation of this activity.

This means that a basis has been created in international environmental law to regulate carbon capture and storage (CCS) in sub-seabed geological formations, for permanent isolation, as part of a suite of measures to tackle the challenge of climate change and ocean acidification, including, first and foremost, the need to further develop low carbon forms of energy. In practice, this option would apply to large point sources of CO_2 emissions, including power plants, steel and cement works.

The Meeting of Contracting Parties, at its twenty-ninth session in 2007, adopted "Specific Guidelines for Assessment of Carbon Dioxide Streams for Disposal into Sub-seabed Geological Formations". The Guidelines will be kept under review and updated in five years' time, or earlier, as warranted in light of new developments. These Guidelines complement the 2006 amendments on CO_2 sequestration in sub-seabed geological formations under resolution LP.1(1).

A Legal and Technical Working Group on Transboundary CO_2 Sequestration Issues was also established by the twenty-ninth Consultative Meeting of Contracting Parties to the London Convention to analyze all realistic scenarios by which CO_2 streams intended for sequestration in sub-seabed geological formations are collected, treated, transported and sequestered, in cases involving transboundary movements of CO_2 streams. The Group met from 25–27 February 2008 and considered whether and how the transboundary movement of CO_2 for and during sub-seabed sequestration in geological formations relates to Article 6 of the London Protocol, and whether an amendment to this provision was necessary. The recommendations of the Working Group will be considered at the thirtieth session of the Meeting of Contracting Parties to the London Convention and the third meeting of the Parties to the London Protocol. An amendment to Article 6 of the London Protocol was proposed regarding the "Export of wastes and other matter" to include an exception to the prohibition of export of wastes in the case of transboundary movements, including migration of CO_2 streams, for disposal provided, *inter alia*, that there is a consent of the receiving State, and that the disposal is made in compliance with the requirement of annex 2 of the London Protocol.

In its resolution 62/215 of 22 December 2007, the General Assembly welcomed the decision of the twenty-ninth Consultative Meeting of Contracting Parties to the London Convention and second meeting of the Parties to the London Protocol, which endorsed the June 2007 "Statement of concern" on large scale fertilization by the Scientific Groups of the London Convention and Protocol; recognized that it was within the purview of each State to consider proposals on a case-by-case basis in accordance with the London Convention and Protocol; urged States to use the utmost caution when considering proposals for large-scale ocean fertilization operations; and took the view that, given the present state of knowledge regarding ocean fertilization, such large-scale operations were currently not justified.

Relationship with UNCLOS

Bearing in mind the provisions relating to the need prescribed in article 237 of UNCLOS for compatibility between this Convention and environmental treaties, the Eleventh Consultative Meeting of Contracting Parties agreed in 1988 that there were "no fundamental inconsistencies" between UNCLOS and the London Convention 1972. At their Seventeenth Consultative Meeting held in 1994, the Contracting Parties expressed their opinion that States Parties to UNCLOS would be legally bound to adopt laws and regulations and take other measures to prevent, reduce and control pollution by dumping. In accordance with article 210(6) of UNCLOS, these laws and regulations must be no less effective than the global rules and standards contained in the London Convention.

The Seventeenth Consultative Meeting further noted that States which are Parties to both UNCLOS and the London Convention 1972 could be called upon to carry out specific obligations assumed by them under UNCLOS. In compliance with a decision taken at the meeting, the Secretary-General of IMO wrote to States Parties to UNCLOS which are not Parties to the London Convention 1972, drawing attention to their obligations relating to the provisions concerning the prevention of marine pollution by dumping, and the objectives and achievements of the London Convention 1972.

In its resolution 62/215 of 22 December 2007, the General Assembly encouraged States that have not yet done so to become parties to the 1996 London Protocol.

Relationship with regional agreements

Article VIII of the London Convention encourages Contracting Parties with common interests in a given geographical area to enter into regional agreements consistent with the Convention "for the prevention of pollution, especially by dumping", taking into account characteristic features of the region's marine environment. The contents of these agreements should be consistent with those of the Convention. Non-parties to these regional agreements, although not legally bound by them, should endeavour to act consistently within them. Regional agreements compatible with the London Convention have been concluded within the framework of the Regional Seas Programme developed by the United Nations Environment Programme (UNEP). The implementation of this programme has resulted in the adoption of several regional conventions and protocols, some of which include provisions concerning the prevention of marine pollution by dumping. This is the case of the Mediterranean Sea Convention, the South Pacific Convention and the Black Sea Convention. The South East Pacific Convention also includes provisions regarding the prevention of marine pollution by disposal of radioactive wastes at sea.

Flag State jurisdiction

Article 216(1)(b) of UNCLOS requires the flag State to enforce with regard to vessels flying its flag or vessels or aircraft or its registry the laws and regulations adopted in accordance with the Convention and applicable international rules and standards adopted through the competent international organizations or diplomatic conference for the prevention, reduction and control of pollution of the marine environment by dumping. The London Convention (article VII(1)(a)) requires each Contracting Party to apply the measures required to implement the Convention to vessels and aircraft registered in its territory or flying its flag.

The application of the London Convention to all sea areas is established by way of interpretation of the definition of "sea" included in article 1 of the Convention, which makes the global rules and standards contained therein applicable to all marine waters other than the internal waters of States. Bearing in mind decisions which had already been taken and implemented by Contracting Parties, the 1996 Protocol extends the concept specifically to include the seabed and the subsoil thereof, to the exclusion of sub-seabed repositories accessed only from land.

Coastal State jurisdiction

According to UNCLOS (article 210(5)), dumping within the territorial sea and the EEZ or onto the continental shelf must not be carried out without the express prior approval of the coastal State. The coastal State is required by article 216(1) of UNCLOS to enforce laws and regulations adopted in accordance with the Convention and applicable international rules and standards established through the competent international organizations or diplomatic conference for the prevention, reduction and control of pollution of the marine environment by dumping. The Eleventh Consultative Meeting of Contracting Parties agreed that a Party could apply the London Convention 1972 not only in its territorial waters, as specifically stated in this Convention, but also in the EEZ.

The London Convention contains specific regulations establishing the conditions which coastal States should follow in the granting of permits for dumping in their jurisdictional waters. Annex I to the Convention includes a list of substances the dumping of which is entirely forbidden. Substances which are part of the list contained in Annex II require a prior special permit from the coastal State. The dumping of all other substances not listed in either Annex I or II requires a prior general permit. This system is decisively reversed by the 1996 LC Protocol which establishes a general prohibition on dumping of all wastes and other matter, except for those belonging to one of the seven categories listed in Annex 1 to the Protocol, namely dredged material, sewage sludge, fish waste or material resulting from industrial fish processing operations, vessels and platforms or other man-made structures, inert, inorganic geological material, organic material of natural origin and bulky items comprising unharmful materials. These wastes or other matter may be considered for dumping provided they do not contain levels of radioactivity greater than *de minimis* (exempt) concentrations as defined by the IAEA.

C OTHER SOURCES OF MARINE POLLUTION

Air pollution

Within the framework of articles 212(3) and 222 of UNCLOS, IMO is competent to establish global rules and standards applicable to vessels on the prevention and control of marine pollution from or through the atmosphere. States must adopt national laws in this field, taking account of internationally agreed rules and standards (UNCLOS (article 212(1)). In this regard, States must take account, *inter alia*, of relevant IMO regulations. States are further under obligation to enforce their laws and regulations and to implement applicable rules and standards adopted internationally.

In September 1997 a Conference of Parties to MARPOL held in September 1997 adopted the Protocol of 1997 to amend the International Convention for the Prevention of Pollution from Ships, 1973 as modified by the Protocol of 1978 relating thereto. This new Protocol incorporates into

MARPOL Annex VI entitled Regulations for the Prevention of Air Pollution from Ships.

The Conference also invited the MEPC to consider what CO_2 reduction strategies may be feasible in light of the relationship between CO_2 and atmospheric pollutants, especially NO_x, since NO_x emissions may exhibit an inverse relationship to CO_2 reductions. Annex VI entered into force on 19 May 2005.

IMO Assembly resolution A.963(23) on *IMO Policies and Practices Related to Reduction of Greenhouse Gas Emissions from Ships* urges the MEPC to identify and develop mechanisms to achieve the limitation or reduction of greenhouse gases emissions from international shipping and keep the matter under review.

MEPC, at its fifty-fourth session approved two circulars aimed at assisting implementation of MARPOL Annex VI:

- The MEPC Circular on *Bunker Delivery Note and Fuel Oil Sampling*, clarifies how to comply with regulation 18, which places requirements on ship owners and fuel oil suppliers in respect of bunker delivery notes and representative samples of the fuel oil received and on Parties to the 1997 Protocol to regulate the bunker suppliers in their ports. The circular urges all Member States, both Parties and non-Parties to the 1997 Protocol, to require fuel oil suppliers in their ports to comply with the requirements and to raise awareness of the necessity to enhance implementation and enforcement of regulation 18 of Annex VI.
- The MEPC circular on *Notification to the Organization on ports or terminals where volatile organic compounds (VOCs) emissions are to be regulated* notes that regulation 15 of Annex VI requires Parties to inform the Organization of their intention to introduce requirements for the use of vapour emission control systems and to notify the Organization of ports and terminals under their jurisdiction where such requirements are already in force. However, many terminals are implementing or operating such practices without notification to the Organization. The Committee shared the concern that, since there is no circulation of such information, it is difficult for owners and operators to prepare for these changes at ports and terminals. The circular reiterates that Parties to the 1997 Protocol are required to notify the Organization without delay with information on ports and terminals under their jurisdiction at which VOCs emissions are or will be regulated, and on requirements imposed on ships calling at these ports and terminals. Any information received by the Organization on the availability of vapour emission control systems will be circulated through MEPC circulars so that owners and operators will have up-to-date information on current and future requirements for the utilization of such systems.

With regard to the work on reduction of green house gas emissions from ships, the MEPC, at its fifty-sixth session, confirmed the need to update the 2000 IMO GHG Study, and agreed on a timeframe, scope and terms of reference for that purpose. The study, it agreed, should cover current global inventories of GHGs and relevant substances emitted from ships engaged in international transport; any methodological aspects and future emission scenarios; identify progress made to date in reducing GHG emissions and other substances; identify possible future measures to reduce emissions of GHGs and undertake a cost benefit analysis, including environmental and public health impacts, of options for current and future reductions in GHG emissions and other relevant substances from international shipping. Finally, it should identify the impact of emissions from shipping on climate change.

MEPC at its fifty-seventh session approved proposed amendments to the MARPOL Annex VI regulations to reduce harmful emissions from ships.

The main changes would be a progressive reduction in sulphur oxide (SO_x) emissions from ships, with the global sulphur cap reduced initially to 3.50% (from the current 4.50%), effective from 1 January 2012; then progressively to 0.50%, effective from 1 January 2020, subject to a feasibility review to be completed no later than 2018.

The revised Annex VI will allow for an Emission Control Area to be designated for SO_x and particulate matter, or NO_x, or all three types of emissions from ships, subject to a proposal from a Party or Parties to the Annex which would be considered for adoption by the Organization, if supported by a demonstrated need to prevent, reduce and control one or all three of those emissions from ships.

IMO is working expeditiously with the aim of adopting in 2009 a legally biding instrument that actually reduces the CO_2 emission from international shipping and its impact on climate change and ocean acidification.

Pollution from seabed activities

Article 208(1) of UNCLOS provides that coastal States shall establish national laws for the control of marine pollution from seabed activities including artificial islands, installations and structures under national jurisdiction. These laws shall be no less effective than "international rules, standards and recommended practices and procedures" which may be established through "competent international organizations" on a global or regional level (UNCLOS article 208(2) and (5)). States shall also enforce their national legislation and take other measures necessary to implement "applicable international rules and standards" established through competent international organizations (UNCLOS, article 214).

IMO has contributed to the establishment of global rules and standards for the prevention and control of this type of pollution. Regulation 21 in Annex I of MARPOL contains special requirements for drilling rigs and other platforms. The Code for the Construction and Equipment of Mobile Offshore Drilling Units, 1989 (MODU Code), recommends design criteria, construction standards and other safety measures for mobile offshore drilling units so as to minimize not only risks to such units and to the personnel on board, but also environmental risks which could arise from a collision between vessels and offshore installations and structures. In this regard, IMO resolution A.671(16) establishes recommendations on safety of navigation around offshore installations and structures.

MARPOL applies to pollution from "fixed or floating platforms" other than pollution resulting from the "release of harmful substances directly arising from the exploration, exploitation and associated offshore processing of seabed mineral resources" (article 2). In this regard Annex I, regulation 21 lays down special oil discharge requirements for drilling rigs and other platforms.

Both the London Convention (article IV(1)(c)) and the 1996 Protocol (article 1.4.3) exclude governance of "disposal of wastes" directly arising from seabed activities. In article 1.4.3 of the 1996 Protocol, this exclusion was extended to "storage of wastes" to address the storage of excess gas produced in offshore wells and the need to avoid an inadvertent prohibition of this practice.

Harmful aquatic organisms in ballast water

The IMO Council convened a diplomatic conference on ballast water management in February 2004, at which the International Convention for the Control and Management of Ships' Ballast Water and Sediments was adopted. The Convention will enter into force 12 months after ratification by 30 States representing 35% of world merchant shipping tonnage. To date 12 countries representing 3.46% of the world tonnage have become contracting States.

The MEPC, at its fifty-fifth session, in 2006, adopted the following guidelines, which are part of a series developed to assist in the implementation of the (BWM Convention).

- ballast water exchange design and control standards (G11);
- design and construction to facilitate sediment control on ships (G12);
- designation of areas for ballast water exchange (G14);
- sediment reception facilities (G1); and
- ballast water reception facilities (G5).

The MEPC, at its fifty-sixth session, adopted three sets of guidelines for additional measures regarding ballast water management, including emergency situations (G13), risk assessment under regulation A-4 of the BWM Convention (G7) and ballast water exchange in the Antarctic Treaty Area.

IMO resolution A.1005(25) Application of the International Convention for the Control and Management of Ships' Ballast Water and Sediments,

2004 was adopted to provide certainty and confidence in the application of the BWM Convention, thereby assisting shipping companies, ship owners, managers and operators, as well as the shipbuilding and equipment manufacturing industries, in the timely planning of their operations. The resolution addresses concerns over implementation of the Convention for vessels constructed in 2009, given the uncertainties as to whether type-approved technology would be immediately available for these ships. It allows for certain new ships built in 2009 to be exempted, if such technologies are not available, and calls on States, which have not yet done so, to ratify, accept, approve or accede to the Convention as soon as possible.

Harmful effects of the use of anti-fouling paints for ships

Since 1988, the MEPC has been considering measures to reduce the harmful effects of the use of "anti-fouling" paint which are intended to keep organisms such as barnacles from clinging to ships hulls, but which disperse an active substance that contaminates the marine environment and can damage or destroy biological systems (such as oyster beds). In 1999, the Assembly adopted resolution A.895(21) on *Anti-Fouling Systems Used on Ships*. This resolution called for a ban on the use of certain compounds in anti-fouling systems by 2008, and called on the MEPC to develop a legally-binding instrument to this effect. The MEPC subsequently prepared a text of a draft International Convention on the Control of Harmful Anti-fouling Systems on Ships. This convention was adopted by a diplomatic conference held in October 2001.

Following accession by Panama on 17 September 2007, the Convention had been ratified by 25 States, with a combined 38.11 per cent of world merchant shipping tonnage, and will therefore enter into force on 17 September 2008. As of 31 August 2008, the Convention has been ratified by 33 States, with a combined 52.55 per cent of world merchant shipping tonnage.

Ship recycling

MEPC has been considering IMO's role regarding the scrapping of ships or ship recycling, with the intention of reducing pollution from ships in connection with such recycling and reducing the risk to human health and the environment at recycling yards. This issue concerns the International Labour Organization (ILO), the Basel Convention under UNEP, and IMO. In this respect, IMO developed guidelines on ship recycling which were adopted by the Assembly in 2003 (resolution A.962(23)). These guidelines seek to encourage recycling as the best means to dispose of ships at the end of their operating lives, provide guidance in respect of the preparation of ships for recycling and minimising the use of potentially hazardous materials and waste generation during a ship's operating life, foster inter-agency co-operation, and encourage all stakeholders to address the issue of ship recycling.

MEPC, at its fifty-third session, in 2005 approved amendments to the IMO Guidelines on Ship Recycling.

MEPC also agreed that the IMO should develop, as a high priority, a new instrument on recycling of ships with a view to providing legally binding and globally applicable ship recycling regulations for international shipping and for recycling facilities. It is anticipated that the instrument will be adopted in the biennium 2008–2009.

CHAPTER III

LIABILITY FOR POLLUTION DAMAGE

Article 235(2) of UNCLOS regulates the obligation for States to ensure that "recourse is available in accordance with their legal systems for prompt and adequate compensation or other relief in respect of damage caused by pollution of the marine environment by natural or juridical persons under their jurisdiction". Paragraph 3 provides that, with the objective of assuring prompt and adequate compensation in respect of damage caused by pollution of the marine environment, where appropriate, States shall co-operate in the development of international law setting out criteria and procedures for payment of adequate compensation, such as compulsory insurance or compensation funds.

These provisions should be considered in connection with several treaty instruments adopted by IMO prior to, and after the adoption of, UNCLOS in the field of liability and compensation for damage related to the carriage of oil and other hazardous and noxious substances by sea. These instruments are:

- International Convention on Civil Liability for Oil Pollution Damage, 1969, and the 1992 Protocol thereto (the Civil Liability Convention or CLC);
- International Convention on the Establishment of an International Fund for Compensation for Oil Pollution Damage, 1971, and the 1992 Protocol thereto (the FUND Convention);
- International Convention on Liability and Compensation for Damage in Connection with the Carriage of Hazardous and Noxious Substances by Sea (HNS), 1996;
- International Convention on Civil Liability for Bunker Oil Pollution Damage, 2001;
- Protocol of 2003 to the International Convention on the establishment of an International Fund for Compensation for Oil Pollution Damage, 1992.

The 1969 Civil Liability Convention establishes a system of strict liability for the shipowner and the obligation to contract compulsory third-party liability insurance to cover for limits of compensation for damage caused by spill of heavy crude oils transported as cargo.

The 1971 Fund Convention regulates the constitution and functioning of an international fund in charge of providing compensation (the IOPC Fund) additional to that paid by the shipowner under the Civil Liability Convention whenever this compensation proves to be insufficient. The fund also pays compensation in some cases where the compensation to be paid by the shipowner is not available.

Both the Civil Liability and the Fund Conventions were amended by the Protocols of 1992 which entirely supersede the original parent treaties and increase the limits of compensation. The original treaties, as amended, are now widely known as the 1992 Civil Liability Convention and the 1992 Fund Convention, respectively.

The CLC 69 and 71 Fund Convention applied to damage occurring in the territorial sea of States Parties. The Protocols of 1992 extend the scope to cover damage occurring in the EEZ.

The IMO Legal Committee, at its 82nd session in 2000, considered a request to increase the limitation amounts set out in the 1992 Protocol to the 1969 Civil Liability Convention (1992 CLC) and the compensation limits set out in the 1992 Protocol to the 1971 International Oil Pollution Compensation Fund Convention (1992 Fund Convention). Utilizing the tacit acceptance procedure for the first time, the Committee adopted two resolutions amending the 1992 Protocols by increasing the limits in each of them by 50.37%. The amendments entered into force on 1 November 2003.

In May 2003 a Conference of Parties to the 1992 Fund Convention adopted a Protocol establishing an International Oil Pollution Compensation Supplementary Fund, 2003. This supplementary scheme seeks to ensure that victims of oil pollution damage are compensated in full for their loss or damage and alleviate the difficulties faced by victims in cases where there is a risk that amount of compensation available under the 1992 Liability and 1992 Fund Conventions will be insufficient to pay established claims in full. The accession to the supplementary scheme is open only to the Contracting States to the 1992 Fund Convention. Following ratification by Spain, on 3 December 2004, the entry into force conditions of the 2003 Protocol have been met (ratification by at least eight States, which have received a combined total of 450 million tons of contributing oil). The new Fund entered into force on 3 March 2005.

The HNS Convention regulates the strict liability of the shipowner and the obligation to contract compulsory third party liability insurance to cover for limits of compensation for damage caused by accidental spills of hazardous and noxious substances other than heavy crude oil and bunker fuel oil carried as cargo. The same treaty also regulates the constitution and functioning of an HNS Fund similar to the IOPC Fund. This treaty is not yet in force.

The HNS Convention has a geographical scope of application similar to the 1992 Civil Liability and Fund Conventions in respect of pollution damage. Accordingly, it regulates compensation for pollution damage occurred within the territorial sea and the EEZ. Damage other than pollution damage, for instance death and injury incurred on board as a result of explosions involving HNS substances, has a universal scope of application. In such cases, compensation is regulated regardless of the sea zone where the incident at the source of the damage took place.

In March 2001, IMO adopted a new International Convention on Civil Liability for Bunker Oil Pollution Damage, 2001, which will establish a liability and compensation regime for spills of oil carried as fuel in ships' bunkers once it enters into force on 21 November 2008. The convention is modelled on the 1992 International Convention on Civil Liability for Oil Pollution Damage. As of 31 August 2008, the Convention has 25 States Parties comprising 39.92% of gross tonnage.

CHAPTER IV

TECHNICAL CO-OPERATION ASSISTANCE TO DEVELOPING COUNTRIES

General

Parts XII, XIII and XIV of UNCLOS provide for co-operation among States, either directly or through competent international organizations, in the field of marine pollution, marine scientific research, and marine technology. Some of these provisions refer in particular to co-operation by means of assistance to developing countries. The Convention on the International Maritime Organization (article 43(a)) provides that IMO shall, through its Technical Co-operation Committee, consider any matter within its scope concerned with "the implementation of technical co-operation projects funded by the relevant United Nations Programme for which the Organization acts as the executing or co-operating agency or by funds-in-trust voluntarily provided to the Organization …".

Within the framework of the Integrated Technical Co-operation Programme (ITCP), other IMO committees work with the IMO Secretariat and the Technical Co-operation Committee to identify developing countries' needs for assistance in strengthening their institutional, legal, managerial, scientific, technical and training capacities to implement the global rules and standards contained in the treaty and non-treaty instruments adopted by IMO in the following areas:

– maritime safety and related aspects of shipping and ports;

– marine environmental protection;

– maritime legislation;

– facilitation of international maritime traffic.

MARPOL, the 1972 London Convention and its 1996 Protocol, OPRC and STCW contain provisions designed to encourage technical co-operation among Parties.

A PROTECTION AND PRESERVATION OF THE MARINE ENVIRONMENT

Article 197 of UNCLOS prescribes that States must co-operate on a global or regional basis, directly or through competent international organizations, in formulating and elaborating international rules, standards and recommended practices and procedures for the protection and preservation of the marine environment, taking into account characteristic regional features. IMO, together with other organizations, co-operates in the Regional Seas Programme of the United Nations Environment Programme (UNEP). In particular, IMO has played a key role in establishing regional arrangements for combating marine pollution. Also significant is IMO's participation in and contribution to the Group of Experts on the Scientific Aspects of Marine Environmental Protection (GESAMP), which brings together several United Nations agencies for the expert consideration and the undertaking of appropriate studies on scientific aspects of marine pollution. IMO provides administrative secretariat services to GESAMP.

Article 202 establishes the duty of States, directly or through the competent international organizations, to promote scientific and technical assistance to developing States for the protection and preservation of the marine environment. The scope of the assistance covers activities such as training of scientific personnel, supply of necessary equipment and facilities, and advice for research. The duty of technical assistance also includes appropriate assistance for the minimization of the effects of major incidents which may cause serious marine pollution, and the preparation of environmental assessments. In accordance with article 203, developing States should be granted preference by international organizations in the allocation of appropriate funds and technical assistance and the utilization of their specialized services.

In compliance with these UNCLOS provisions, article 17 of MARPOL on promotion of technical co-operation establishes that Parties must, in consultation with IMO and other international bodies, with assistance and co-ordination by the Executive Director of the United Nations Environment Programme, promote support for those Parties that request technical assistance for training, monitoring and supply of equipment and facilities for the reception of wastes, encouragement of research and the facilitation of other measures and agreements to prevent or mitigate pollution of the marine environment by ships. A similar provision is included in article IX of the London Convention in connection with the disposal and treatment of waste and other measures to prevent or mitigate pollution caused by dumping.

IMO continues to provide assistance to many developing countries – at the national, regional and global levels – for the effective implementation of its Conventions dealing with the prevention of marine pollution. Such activities include technical and legal advisory services, training of administrative personnel and ship surveyors and inspectors, and the development of plans for the reception and management of ship-generated wastes. Among the principal regional or global activities carried out by IMO in these fields, the following may be cited: (a) a GEF/World Bank/IMO programme entitled "Wider Caribbean Initiative on Ship-generated Wastes" carried out during 1994–1998; (b) a five-year GEF/UNDP/IMO Regional Programme on Building Partnerships for Environmental Management in the East Asian Seas (PEMSEA), which started in October 1999; (c) a three-year GEF/UNDP/IMO project on removal of barriers to the effective implementation of ballast water control and management measures in developing countries, which commenced in May 2000; and (d) a one-year GEF/WB/PDF Block B grant, which started in March 2001, for the preparation of a project for the development of a regional marine electronic highway in the East Asian Seas with a first phase in the Straits of Malaysia and Singapore.

Article 8 of the OPRC contains the agreement of the Parties to co-operate directly or through IMO and relevant regional organizations in the promotion and exchange of results of research and development programmes related to oil pollution preparedness and response, including technologies and techniques for the minimization and mitigation of the effects of oil pollution and for restoration of the marine environment. In accordance with article 9, Parties undertake to provide support to those Parties that request technical assistance in respect of training, availability and transfer of the relevant technology, equipment and facilities, and other measures to prepare for and respond to oil pollution incidents. Article 10 establishes that Parties must endeavour to conclude bilateral or multilateral agreements implementing arrangements concerning oil pollution preparedness and response. In accordance with article 12, IMO is given the tasks of facilitating the provision of assistance and advice to States establishing national or regional response capabilities and in connection with major oil pollution incidents.

As part of the development of regional systems in preparedness, response and co-operation in the event of accidental marine pollution, regional contingency plans were prepared and approved for the Black Sea, South Asia and North-West Pacific regions. The same process is being developed in the Mediterranean region, the Sea and Gulf of Aden, and the Central and Western Africa region. The IMO has signed an agreement with UNOPS as executing agency for the United Nations Development Programme's Caspian Environment Programme (CEP), in which IMO and UNOPS/CEP wish to implement activities relating to the preparation and development of the national and regional contingency plans for the Caspian Sea countries.

Regional co-operation under the Emergency Protocol to the Abidjan Convention was revitalized through the organization in the year 2000 of a joint IMO/UNEP meeting of national experts and of an IMO/IPIECA regional workshop aiming to adopt a plan of action for the development of regional co-operation for preparedness and response to accidental marine pollution.

In 1994, IMO and the Port Management Association of Eastern and Southern Africa (PMAESA) developed a strategy and action plan for the protection of the marine environment in Eastern and Southern Africa. This strategy is now under review and will in future be implemented by IMO, PMAESA, the Southern Africa Transport and Communication Commission (SATCC) and the Common Market for Eastern and Southern Africa (COMESA).

In the Wider Caribbean region, the Regional Marine Pollution Emergency Information and Training Centre (REMPEITC-Carib) has been formally established in Curaçao as a Regional Activity Centre within the framework of the Caribbean Environment Programme. A Memorandum of

Understanding between the Netherlands Antilles, UNEP and IMO was signed in September 2002 in that connection. The Centre provides advice and hands-on support to the countries and territories of the region on matters concerning the prevention of marine pollution, response and control activities when pollution has in fact occurred, as well as civil liability and compensation issues.

Within the framework of the North-West Pacific Action Plan, the Marine Environmental Emergency Preparedness and Response Regional Activity Centre (MER/RAC) has been established in the Republic of Korea. In July 2000 the Korean Research Institute of Ship and Ocean Engineering/ Korean Ocean Research and Development Institute, UNEP and IMO signed a Memorandum of Understanding aiming at establishing long-term co-operation with MER/RAC.

Article 13 of the 1996 London Convention Protocol obligates Parties to promote technical co-operation and assistance in connection with access to and transfer of environmentally sound technologies and corresponding know-how, in particular to developing countries and countries in transition to market economies. IMO is assigned specific functions of co-ordination in this regard.

Articles 200 and 201 of UNCLOS deal with the duty of co-operation in the promotion of studies, research programmes and exchange of information and data acquired about marine pollution, and the establishment of scientific criteria for international regulations. In this context, IMO has supported the organization of three global Research and Development Forums on matters concerning oil pollution of the seas. Articles 204 to 206 contain provisions on co-operation regarding the monitoring and assessment of the environmental impact of pollution. IMO's contribution to the work of GESAMP should again be mentioned in this regard.

B TRAINING

Co-operation requirements for training of seafarers in the field both of safety of navigation and the prevention and control of marine pollution are addressed in article XI(1) of STCW 78, as amended, which regulates the obligation for Parties to promote, in consultation and with the assistance of IMO, support for those parties which request technical assistance for the training of personnel, the establishment of institutions for the training of seafarers, the supply of equipment and facilities for training institutions, the development of adequate training programmes and the facilitation of measures and arrangements to enhance qualifications of seafarers. The article includes the provision that this assistance should be performed preferably on a national, subregional or regional basis, "to further the aims and purposes of the Convention, taking into account the special needs of developing countries". In compliance with this requirement IMO provides worldwide assistance for maritime training institutes in charge of providing basic training for seafarers in accordance with STCW.

The Organization has sponsored a series of seminars and workshops around the world to promote implementation of the 1995 STCW amendments. Venues for these seminars include Ghana, Kenya, Malta, Namibia, South Africa, Tanzania and Tunisia. At the same time, the IMO model courses have been revised to bring them up to date with the new certification requirements.

Maritime training institutes under the auspices of IMO

Within the framework of its technical co-operation programme, IMO is particularly active in the development of human resources to provide maritime administrations, especially those in developing countries, with the know-how required to comply with international rules and standards.

Under the auspices of IMO, three global educational institutions have been created. The World Maritime University (WMU) in Malmö, Sweden, offers Master of Science degree courses plus professional development courses in maritime safety administration, general maritime administration and environmental protection, shipping management, port management and maritime education and training. The IMO International Maritime Law Institute (IMLI) in Malta offers a one-year advanced course at postgraduate level leading to the degree of Master of Laws. The IMO International Maritime Academy (IMA) in Trieste, Italy, offers students the opportunity to attend seminars and short courses at the Academy based on a range of IMO model courses. These courses contain precise and up-to-date information on a wide range of particular issues related to safety of navigation and prevention of marine pollution.

C MARINE SCIENTIFIC RESEARCH

Article 242 of UNCLOS places upon States and competent international organizations the general obligation to promote international co-operation in marine scientific research for peaceful purposes. In article 243, States and international organizations are required to co-operate through the conclusion of bilateral and multilateral agreements to create favourable conditions for the conduct of marine scientific research in the marine environment. In accordance with article 244, publication and dissemination of information on proposed major programmes and their objectives as well as knowledge resulting from marine scientific research relies on States and competent international organizations. MARPOL, article 17, expressly provides for the obligation to promote technical assistance for the encouragement of research. The 1996 Protocol to the London Convention includes in article 14 a new provision on scientific and technical research related to pollution by dumping. This provision deals with the duty of Parties to promote such research and to facilitate information on scientific and technical activities and programmes, and on impact assessment.

Scientific research installations

In accordance with article 261 of UNCLOS, the deployment and use of any type of scientific research installation or equipment shall not constitute an obstacle to established international shipping routes. Article 262 provides that such installations or equipment shall bear identification markings and shall have adequate internationally agreed warning signals to ensure safety at sea, taking into account rules and standards established by competent international organizations.

IMO would appear to be the most appropriate body for developing international rules and standards on warning signals for such installations and equipment to ensure safety at sea. Such elaboration may need to be undertaken in consultation with other international organizations concerned, such as the International Civil Aviation Organization (ICAO), the International Telecommunication Union (ITU), the International Mobile Satellite Organization (Inmarsat), the Inter-governmental Oceanographic Commission (IOC), the International Hydrographic Organization (IHO) and the International Association of Lighthouse Authorities (IALA).

D DEVELOPMENT AND TRANSFER OF MARINE TECHNOLOGY

Among the objectives of the development and transfer of marine technology listed in article 268 of UNCLOS mention is made of "the development of human resources through training and education of nationals of developing States ...". Article 269(a) includes among the measures to achieve these objectives the establishment of programmes of technical co-operation "for the effective transfer of all kinds of marine technology to States which may need and request technical assistance in this field", and to developing States which have not been able to establish or develop their own technological capacity. The OPRC, articles 8(1) and 9(2), and the 1996 LC Protocol, article 13(5), make specific reference to the transfer of technology within the framework of technical co-operation activities to be promoted in order to comply with the objectives and provisions of both treaties.

PART III

SETTLEMENT OF DISPUTES

Role of IMO in the Special Arbitration Procedure

According to article 1 of Annex VIII of UNCLOS, disputes concerning the interpretation or application of the articles of the Convention relating to "navigation, including pollution from vessels and by dumping" may be submitted to a special arbitral procedure provided for in that annex. Under article 2 of the same Annex the members of the special arbitral tribunal to deal with such disputes should be selected preferably from a list of experts established and maintained by IMO or by the appropriate subsidiary body to which IMO has delegated this function. In compliance with article 2 of Annex VIII of UNCLOS, IMO has invited all States Parties to the Convention at the moment of its entry into force and each State becoming Party thereafter, to nominate two experts to be included in the list of experts in the field of navigation, including pollution from vessels and by dumping. In response to this invitation, several States have nominated such experts. For a listing of the experts who have been nominated by Governments, see the website of the Division for Ocean Affairs and the Law of the Sea, Office of Legal Affairs, United Nations at www.un.org/Depts/los.

In accordance with article 289 of UNCLOS, experts in the list established in accordance with article 2 of Annex VIII in connection with special arbitration procedures may also be selected to assist proceedings by courts or tribunals in connection with disputes related to navigation and pollution from vessels and by dumping.

Jurisdiction of courts or tribunals

The jurisdiction of court or tribunal referred to in article 287 of UNCLOS over disputes concerning the interpretation or application of the Convention also extends to the interpretation or application of an international agreement related to the purposes of the Convention, which is submitted to it in accordance with the agreement (UNCLOS, article 288). Reference to the possibility for the Parties concerned to use the dispute settlement procedures of UNCLOS is included in article 16 of the 1996 LC Protocol. A similar provision is contained in the Nairobi International Convention on the Removal of Wrecks, 2007 (see part II, chapter I of this document).

In accordance with Annex VI, article 22 of UNCLOS, the International Tribunal for the Law of the Sea may exercise jurisdiction over disputes concerning the interpretation or application of related treaties already in force, if all the parties to the treaty so agree. Agreements in this regard may be concluded by parties to IMO treaties in connection with any dispute regarding their interpretation or application.

Procedures in respect of violation of international anti-pollution rules and standards

Under article 223 of UNCLOS a State which institutes proceedings against a foreign vessel in respect of violations of international or national laws and regulations on marine pollution prevention is required to take measures to facilitate the hearing of witnesses and the admission of evidence submitted by, *inter alia*, "the competent international organization" (IMO). Such a State is also required to facilitate the attendance of such proceedings by "official representatives" of that organization, who shall have such rights and duties as may be provided for under national or international law.

The appropriate bodies of IMO may find it necessary to consider the procedures and arrangements required to enable IMO to intervene in such proceedings, including the criteria for determining when such an intervention would be appropriate and the procedure for designating the "official representatives" of the Organization.

Article 297(1) of UNCLOS specifies the situations where compulsory dispute settlement procedures entailing binding decisions, as established in section II of part XV, apply also to disputes concerning the interpretation or application of the Convention with regard to the exercise by a coastal State of sovereign rights and jurisdiction. One such situation concerns the allegation that a coastal State has acted in contravention of specified international rules and standards for the protection and preservation of the marine environment which are applicable to the coastal State and which have been established by the Convention or through a "competent international organization" (IMO) (article 297(1)(c)).

PART IV

THE IMPLEMENTATION OF IMO FUNCTIONS AND RESPONSIBILITIES IN THE LIGHT OF THE ENTRY INTO FORCE OF UNCLOS

General

Throughout this document an assessment has been provided of the existing functions and responsibilities of IMO within the general framework of international law as reflected in UNCLOS. Appropriate reference has been made to areas in respect of which IMO's tasks could be expanded following the entry into force of the Convention.

This part endeavours to identify any such areas in order to determine whether there is a need for IMO to modify its work or to extend the scope and purpose of its international regulations or procedures or to provide clearer or additional guidelines to States or other entities in implementing the provisions of the Convention.

Documentary and special precautionary requirements in respect of nuclear-powered ships and ships carrying nuclear or other inherently dangerous or noxious substances

Bearing in mind article 23 of UNCLOS, and the adoption of amendments to SOLAS chapter VII to make the INF Code mandatory, IMO may consider the adoption of multilateral agreements in relation to additional matters such as emergency preparedness and response arrangements in the event of an accident involving cargoes subject to the INF Code.

Routeing measures

IMO could extend its present role in connection with the provisions of UNCLOS relating to the establishment of international rules and standards concerning routeing measures. In this regard, consideration may be given to identifying or establishing, as necessary, in addition to existing IMO Guidelines on ships' routeing:

- the recommendations which coastal States must take into account in prescribing traffic separation schemes or designating sea lanes in their territorial sea;
- the international regulations to which traffic separation schemes and sea lanes within straits used for international navigation and in archipelagic waters must conform;
- the procedures to be followed by coastal States wishing to refer proposals for traffic separation schemes or sea lanes in international straits or archipelagic waters to IMO for consideration and

adoption, including procedures and arrangements to facilitate co-operation between two or more States in respect of sea lanes or traffic separation schemes through the waters of such States.

Construction, operation and use of artificial islands, installations and structures in the exclusive economic zone, and the removal of such installations and structures

IMO may consider the adoption of applicable international standards for determining the breadth of safety zones, as prescribed in article 60(5) of UNCLOS.

Procedures and requirements for bonding or other appropriate financial security in respect of vessels detained by a coastal or port State

Article 220(7) of UNCLOS obliges a coastal State which has detained a vessel for a violation of international regulations, or national laws, as appropriate, to allow the vessel to proceed if the vessel has complied with the requirements for bonding or other appropriate financial security and the coastal State is bound by the procedures establishing the requirements in question. The obligation for States to order the release of a ship upon provision of adequate financial security to cover for the liability of the shipowner is regulated in a number of IMO liability treaties, namely:

- the Convention on Limitation of Liability for Maritime Claims, 1976 (article 13);
- the Protocol on Limitation of Liability for Maritime Claims, 1996;
- the International Convention on Civil Liability for Oil Pollution Damage, 1969 and the 1992 Protocol thereto (article VI);
- the International Convention on Liability and Compensation for Damage in Connection with the Carriage of Hazardous and Noxious Substances by Sea, 1996 (article 10); and
- the International Convention on Civil Liability for Bunker Oil Pollution Damage, 2001.

Article 220 also states that the appropriate procedures may be established through "the competent international organization" (IMO). Consideration may, therefore, be given to the possible establishment of procedures on provision of bonds or financial security and a suitable mechanism for establishing such procedures. In this regard it should be noted that article 292 of the Convention provides for a procedure under which an application may be made by or on behalf of the flag State of a vessel, if it is alleged that the vessel is being detained in contravention of the requirement of the Convention for prompt release, following the posting of a reasonable bond or other financial security. The existence of international procedures in this regard will, accordingly, be of some importance in the implementation of the dispute settlement arrangements in part XV of the Convention.

Role of IMO in proceedings against foreign vessels

Bearing in mind the provisions on jurisdiction (article 288) and the possibility for IMO to submit evidence and/or send official representatives to attend proceedings instituted in connection with pollution incidents (article 223), the appropriate bodies of IMO may consider the procedures and arrangements required to enable IMO to intervene in such proceedings, including the criteria for determining when such an intervention would be appropriate and the procedure for designating the "official representatives" of the Organization, as envisaged in the Convention.

Prevention of harmful consequences to vessels and the marine environment as a result of the exercise of enforcement powers by States

Article 225 of UNCLOS provides that States, when exercising measures of enforcement against foreign vessels, shall not endanger the safety of navigation or otherwise create any hazard to a vessel, or bring the vessel to an unsafe port or anchorage, or expose the marine environment to an unreasonable risk. Article 226 declares that States shall not delay a foreign vessel longer than is essential for purposes of the investigations provided for in the Convention. The article lays down the conditions and limits of physical inspections of a vessel, and provides for the release of the vessel, whether absolutely or on conditions, as may be appropriate. Paragraph 2 of article 226 provides that States must co-operate to develop procedures for "the avoidance of unnecessary physical inspection of vessels at sea".

To the extent that it may be considered that any of the procedures envisaged in article 226(2) should be developed on the international plane, IMO would be the appropriate forum for that purpose. In this connection, reference may be made to the provisions in article 6 of MARPOL 73/78 relating to detection of violations and enforcement of the convention. Consideration may be given to whether these provisions provide an appropriate or suitable basis for the elaboration of the necessary international procedures in this regard.

Prevention of interference by marine scientific research installations or equipment with safety of navigation

Article 261 of UNCLOS states that the deployment and use of any type of scientific research installations or equipment shall not constitute an obstacle to established international shipping routes. Article 262 states that such installations or equipment shall bear identification markings and "shall have adequate internationally agreed warning signals to ensure safety at sea and the safety of air navigation, taking into account rules and standards established by competent international organizations". IMO would appear to be the most appropriate body for developing the international rules and standards to ensure safety at sea. Any work in this area needs to be undertaken in consultation with other international organizations concerned such as the International Civil Aviation Organization (ICAO), the International Telecommunication Union (ITU), the International Maritime Satellite Organization (INMARSAT), the Intergovernmental Oceanographic Commission (IOC), the International Hydrographic Organization (IHO) and the International Association of Lighthouse Authorities (IALA).

Possible role of IMO in the facilitation of appropriate publicity with respect to measures for the safety of navigation and the prevention of marine pollution

A number of articles of UNCLOS impose on States and other entities the obligation to provide publicity with regard to legislative or other measures taken by them, and to publicize information which may become available to them relating to safety of navigation or the prevention of pollution of the marine environment from vessels or by dumping. This publicity is to make States, seafarers and other interested persons aware of the measures or information in question and thus enable them to take appropriate and necessary steps either to prevent infringements of the laws and regulations, or to avoid any dangers which may be presented in particular situations. It is, therefore, essential that the publicity be given in a manner that ensures that the information provided will in fact reach those who are likely to be affected. In some cases the States or other entities required to provide publicity are also enjoined to make the information available to IMO. Even in cases where reference has been made to another body or bodies, some IMO involvement may be necessary, or at least helpful.

The articles of the Convention relating to "publicity", in respect of matters of possible interest to IMO, include the following:

- **Article 21(3):** The coastal State is required to give due publicity to its laws and regulations for the regulation of innocent passage in its territorial sea. The same provision applies to the laws and regulations relating to transit passage in straits used for international navigation (article 42(3)).
- **Article 22(4):** The coastal State is required to indicate clearly the sea lanes and traffic separation schemes in its territorial sea on charts to which "due publicity" is to be given. The same applies under article 41(6) in relation to transit passage in straits used for international navigation and under article 53(10) in respect of archipelagic sea lane passage.
- **Article 24(2):** The coastal State is required to give publicity to any danger to navigation within its territorial sea of which

the State has knowledge. (The same obligation is imposed on States bordering straits used for international navigation under article 44.)

- **Article 41(2):** Publicity should be given by States bordering straits used for international navigation in respect of sea lanes and traffic separation schemes adopted in such straits. The same obligation is imposed by article 53(7) in respect of sea lanes and traffic separation schemes in archipelagic waters.

- **Article 52(2):** An archipelagic State is required to give publicity in respect of suspensions of innocent passage in its archipelagic waters. Suspensions of innocent passage in the territorial sea must take place only after having been duly published (article 25(3)).

- **Article 60(3):** The coastal State is required to give publicity in respect of the depth, position and dimensions of installations or structures in its exclusive economic zone which are not entirely removed. (The same requirements apply in respect of similar installations in the continental shelf, article 80.)

- **Article 60(5):** The coastal State is required to give publicity in respect of the extent of safety zones established around artificial islands, installations or structures in its exclusive economic zones. (The same requirement applies to safety zones on the continental shelf, article 80.)

- **Article 211(3):** A coastal State which establishes particular requirements for the prevention, reduction and control of pollution of the marine environment as a condition for the entry of foreign vessels into its ports or internal waters or for a call at its offshore terminals, must give due publicity of such requirements.

- **Article 211(6):** A State which establishes special mandatory measures for marine pollution prevention in a clearly defined area of its exclusive economic zone (paragraph 6, subparagraphs (a) and (b)); or adopts additional laws and regulations (paragraph 6, subparagraph (c)), must give due publicity to such measures.

- **Article 217(7):** A flag State is required to provide IMO with information in respect of action taken by it against a vessel flying its flag for violations of rules and standards adopted through IMO. IMO is required to make such information "available to all States".

In respect of all these provisions, it appears clear that the required publicity objective will be effectively achieved only if the information in question reaches the States, authorities, entities and persons that are intended to be guided by the information. IMO maintains the most direct and continuing contact with the authorities of States concerned with safety of navigation and the prevention of vessel-source pollution. Accordingly the purpose of the publicity is likely to be served by some IMO involvement. To the extent that this involvement is considered necessary and appropriate, it may be useful to consider suitable arrangements by which the Organization may assist or co-operate with the States or international organizations concerned in ensuring that the publicity given by them will in fact reach the destinations for which it is intended.

IMO's involvement or co-operation in enhancing the effective dissemination of information on maritime safety and pollution prevention measures may even extend to cases in which responsibility for the publicity concerned may have been assigned to specific States or organizations by the Convention. For example, several articles of the Convention, in requiring that States give due publicity to legislation or other measures adopted by them, also stipulate that the information should be deposited with the Secretary-General of the United Nations, who is the depositary of the Convention itself. In line with its normal practice in this regard, it must be assumed that the Secretariat of the United Nations will make information deposited with it available to all States concerned. But even in such cases, there may be a need for IMO's involvement in the further dissemination of information, particularly where the information in question may be of significance to ships' personnel or other persons operating in the marine environment who are required to take such information into account in order to safeguard safety or prevent pollution. IMO may therefore find it useful to consider how it might usefully co-operate with or assist the United Nations in making sure that the information will reach ships and other persons which may be in closer contact with IMO.

For example, article 147 of the Convention lays down certain conditions for the erection, emplacement and removal of installations used for carrying out activities in the Area, i.e. "the seabed and ocean floor and sub-soil thereof, beyond the limits of national jurisdiction". One of the conditions is that such installations should not interfere with the use of recognized sea lanes essential to international navigation. It is also provided that permanent means for giving warnings of their presence must be maintained, and safety zones shall be established around the installations, but in a way that does not impede "the lawful access of shipping to particular maritime zones or navigation along international sea lanes" (article 147(2)).

Also under article 16(2), States are required to give due publicity to the charts showing the baselines for measuring the breadth of their territorial sea, or the lists of geographical co-ordinates of points. Copies of such charts or lists are to be deposited with the Secretary-General of the United Nations. Similar requirements apply in respect of archipelagic baselines under article 47(9), in respect of the exclusive economic zone under Article 75. There is a similar provision regarding the continental shelf (article 84(2)). The primary responsibility for preparing and publicizing these charts will fall on the States concerned, but IMO may be in a position to assist in cases where it is deemed that the information may be of relevance to maritime safety or pollution prevention. There is no doubt that some of the information to be publicized under these articles of the Convention can be of considerable relevance to flag States, shipowners and other persons involved in international shipping that will need the information in order fully to discharge their responsibilities and international obligations in respect of safety of navigation and pollution prevention. Accordingly, IMO has a legitimate interest in the most effective dissemination of the information involved. For the purposes of facilitating this effective dissemination of information, IMO may find it necessary or useful to establish mechanisms suitable for channelling, in particular cases, information to the authorities, institutions or persons directly affected. Any such involvement of IMO will, of course, be in full consultation with the Secretariat of the United Nations or other intergovernmental organizations concerned, or individual States, as appropriate. It is essential that any role that IMO may play should be such that it does not create unnecessary duplication or proliferation of information and communications on the same subject. Therefore, care should be taken to organize matters in such a way that all concerned recognize clearly that the role of IMO is complementary to the functions of the States, national institutions or international organizations concerned, and not in any way to be regarded as substitutes for those functions.

The development and transfer of marine technology and international co-operation

The basic objectives of international co-operation, as spelt out in articles 202 and 268, and especially the development of human resources through training and education for nationals of developing countries are already part of the fundamental aims of IMO and its Technical Co-operation Programme, as provided for in the IMO Convention and in the relevant decisions of the Organization's intergovernmental bodies. In implementing these aims, IMO may find it useful to expand the scope of the specific arrangements and measures suggested or envisaged in the relevant articles of UNCLOS, particularly those relating to the transfer of technology and the provision of assistance to developing countries in the maritime field.

Further avenues of co-operation among international organizations

Article 278 enjoins the competent international organizations to take all appropriate measures to ensure, either directly or in close co-operation among themselves, the effective discharge of their functions and responsibilities. In accordance with its Constitution and pursuant to decisions of its governing organs, IMO has established co-operative and fruitful arrangements for collaboration with the United Nations and the other agencies and organizations within the United Nations system. However, IMO has continued to explore appropriate avenues to promote and facilitate further co-operation with all international organizations whose activities may affect, or be affected by, the measures taken by the Organization with regard to matters dealt with by the Convention. Effective and co-ordinated liaison will also be needed with the International Seabed Authority and the International Tribunal for the Law of the Sea. Any such liaison and co-operation will be subject to the relevant provisions of UNCLOS, and in accordance with the view of the IMO Assembly that IMO might provide "advice and assistance" to the Preparatory Commission for the International Seabed Authority "on matters falling within the competence of IMO". The Tribunal and the IMO exchanged notes in July 2002 reconfirming the desire to maintain regular contact and co-operation.

Other possible roles for IMO in connection with the implementation of UNCLOS

In addition to the new or modified functions and responsibilities directly or indirectly imposed on IMO by UNCLOS, it may be necessary to consider what other possible roles, if any, may legitimately be played by IMO in connection with implementation of the provisions of the Convention that deal with matters within the field of competence of IMO, particularly the provisions whose interpretation or application may be assisted by work within IMO. Reference may be made in this connection to the articles of the Convention that relate to safety at sea and the prevention of marine pollution, since many of these articles refer to or presuppose the existence of international regulations and standards adopted by IMO and by reference to which States may implement the principles in UNCLOS.

As indicated above, many articles of UNCLOS stipulate that the powers and obligations of States are to be exercised or discharged by reference to "generally accepted" or "applicable" international regulations and standards. In some cases, the Convention expressly states that the international rules or regulations involved are those established by "the competent international organization" (IMO) or by "general diplomatic conference". Furthermore, in many other cases the Convention does not specify the rules and regulations that are deemed to be "generally accepted" or "applicable". It would therefore be necessary for the appropriate bodies of IMO to consider what guidelines IMO can usefully provide to States in this regard.

***

ANNEX

PROVISIONS OF UNCLOS RELEVANT TO THE INSTRUMENTS AND WORK OF IMO

INNOCENT PASSAGE IN THE TERRITORIAL SEA

(rules applicable to all ships)

Articles of UNCLOS	Subject-Matter	Specific provisions on the subject-matter	Relationship between UNCLOS and IMO instruments	Relevant IMO instruments	Comments/ recommendations
21	Laws and regulations of the coastal State relating to innocent passage	Paragraph 1: Matters concerning which the coastal State is entitled to adopt laws and regulations including safety of navigation, regulation of maritime traffic, protection of navigational aids and facilities, prevention of marine pollution (also article 211(4))	Reference to "rules of international law"	SOLAS Load Lines COLREG STCW MARPOL	
		Paragraph 2: Laws and regulations on design, construction, manning or equipment	Reference to "generally accepted international rules or standards"	SOLAS Load Lines MARPOL STCW	

Articles of UNCLOS	Subject-Matter	Specific provisions on the subject-matter	Relationship between UNCLOS and IMO instruments	Relevant IMO instruments	Comments/ recommendations
		Paragraph 4: Laws and regulations on prevention of collisions	Reference to "generally accepted international regulations relating to the prevention of collisions at sea"	COLREG	
22	Sea lanes and traffic separation schemes in the territorial sea	Paragraph 2: Nuclear-powered ships and ships carrying dangerous cargo			
		Paragraph 3: Duty of coastal States in establishing sea lanes and traffic separation schemes	Reference to the recommendations of the "competent international organization"	SOLAS (regulation V/10) COLREG (rules 1(d) and 10)) Res. A.572(14)	IMO is the competent international organization.
		Paragraph 4: Duty to indicate sea lanes and traffic separation schemes on charts and duty of publicity		Res. A.572(14)	Additional work may be undertaken as regards PSSA/ special area requirements. (See Art 211.)

Articles of UNCLOS	Subject-Matter	Specific provisions on the subject-matter	Relationship between UNCLOS and IMO instruments	Relevant IMO instruments	Comments/ recommendations
23	Foreign nuclear-powered ships and ships carrying nuclear or other inherently dangerous or noxious substances	Documentary requirements and special precautionary measures	Reference to "international agreements"	SOLAS (chapters VII and VIII) Code of Safety for Nuclear Merchant Ships IMO/IAEA Safety Recommendations on the Use of Ports by Nuclear Merchant Ships IMDG Code IBC Code IGC Code INF Code	
24	Duties of the coastal State	Paragraph 2:	IMO's field of competence (safety of navigation) SOLAS V/4 Res. A.706(17)		

Articles of UNCLOS	Subject-Matter	Specific provisions on the subject-matter	Relationship between UNCLOS and IMO instruments	Relevant IMO instruments	Comments/ recommendations
27	Criminal jurisdiction on board a foreign ship	Criminal activity	Prevention of unlawful acts against the safety of navigation	SUA SUA Protocol	Consider possible roles of IMO in prevention of terrorist acts against ships.

STRAITS USED FOR INTERNATIONAL NAVIGATION
(transit passage)

Articles of UNCLOS	Subject-Matter	Specific provisions on the subject-matter	Relationship between UNCLOS and IMO instruments	Relevant IMO instruments	Comments/ recommendations
39	Duties of ships and aircraft during transit passage through straits used for international navigation (applicable also to archipelagic sea lanes passage according to articlc 54)	Paragraph 2: Compliance with international regulations on safety at sea and prevention and control of pollution from ships	Reference to "generally accepted international regulations, procedures and practices", "including the International Regulations for Preventing Collisions at Sea"	SOLAS COLREG Load Lines STCW MARPOL	

Articles of UNCLOS	Subject-Matter	Specific provisions on the subject-matter	Relationship between UNCLOS and IMO instruments	Relevant IMO instruments	Comments/ recommendations
41	Sea lanes and traffic separation schemes in straits used for international navigation	Paragraph 3: Duty of States bordering straits in establishing sea lanes and traffic separation schemes	Reference to "generally accepted international regulations"	SOLAS V/8 (renumbered V/10 in 2000 amendments) COLREG (rules 1(d) and 10) Res. A.572(14)	
		Paragraph 4: Duty to refer proposals concerning sea lanes or traffic separation schemes to the competent international organization	Reference to the "competent international organization"	SOLAS V/8 (renumbered as V/10 in 2000 amendments) COLREG (rules 1(d) and 10) Res. A.572(14)	IMO is the competent international organization.
		Paragraph 5: Duty for States bordering straits to co-operate in formulating proposals for sea lanes or traffic separation schemes	Reference to the "competent international organization"	SOLAS V/8 (renumbered as V/10 in 2000 amendments)	IMO is the competent international organization.

Articles of UNCLOS	Subject-Matter	Specific provisions on the subject-matter	Relationship between UNCLOS and IMO instruments	Relevant IMO instruments	Comments/ recommendations
		Paragraph 6: Duty to indicate sea lanes and traffic separation schemes on charts and duty of publicity		Res. A.572(14) SOLAS V/8 (renumbered as V/10 in 2000 amendments)	
42	Laws and regulations of States bordering straits relating to transit passage (applicable also to archipelagic sea lanes passage according to article 54)	Paragraph 1: Matters concerning which the coastal State is entitled to adopt laws and regulations	Reference to the "generally accepted international regulations" on matters concerning safety at sea as provided in article 41, and to "applicable international regulations" within the scope of marine pollution	SOLAS COLREG Load Lines STCW MARPOL	
43	Navigational and safety aids and other improvements and the prevention, reduction and control of pollution	Duty of user States and States bordering straits to co-operate by agreement	IMO's fields of competence (navigational aids and vessel-source pollution)	SOLAS V/14 (renumbered V/13 in 2000 amendments) Res. A.857(20)	

Articles of UNCLOS	Subject-Matter	Specific provisions on the subject-matter	Relationship between UNCLOS and IMO instruments	Relevant IMO instruments	Comments/ recommendations
44	Duties of States bordering straits (applicable also to archipelagic sea lanes passage according to article 54)	Publicity in respect of dangers to navigation	IMO's field of competence (safety of navigation)	SOLAS V/2 (renumbered as V/4 in 2000 amendments) Res. A.706(17)	

ARCHIPELAGIC STATES
(archipelagic sea lane passage)

Articles of UNCLOS	Subject-Matter	Specific provisions on the subject-matter	Relationship between UNCLOS and IMO instruments	Relevant IMO instruments	Comments/ recommendations
53	Right of archipelagic sea lanes passage	Paragraph 8: Duty of archipelagic States in establishing sea lanes and traffic separation schemes	Reference to "generally accepted international regulations"	SOLAS V/8 (renumbered as V/10 in 2000 amendments) COLREG (rules 1(d) and 10)	

Articles of UNCLOS	Subject-Matter	Specific provisions on the subject-matter	Relationship between UNCLOS and IMO instruments	Relevant IMO instruments	Comments/ recommendations
				Res. A.572(14) Res. A.858(20) MSC.72(69)	
		Paragraph 9: Duty to refer proposals concerning sea lanes or traffic separation schemes to the competent international organization	Reference to the "competent international organization"	SOLAS V/8 (renumbered as V/10 in 2000 amendments) COLREG (rules 1(d) and 10) Res. A.572(14) Res. A.858(20) MSC.72(69)	IMO is the competent international organization.
		Paragraph 10: Duty to indicate sea lanes and traffic separation schemes on charts and duty of publicity		SOLAS V/8 (renumbered as V/10 in 2000 amendments) Res. A.572(14) Res. A.858(20) MSC.72(69)	IMO is the competent international organization.

EXCLUSIVE ECONOMIC ZONE

Articles of UNCLOS	Subject-Matter	Specific provisions on the subject-matter	Relationship between UNCLOS and IMO instruments	Relevant IMO instruments	Comments/ recommendations
60	Artificial islands, installations and structures in the EEZ	Paragraph 3: Duty to remove abandoned or disused artificial islands, installations or structures, and duty of publicity with respect to their partial removal	Reference to "generally accepted international standards" established by the "competent international organization"	Res. A.672(16) London Convention (article III, and annex 17)	Notification of partial removal but also of non-removal should be forwarded to IMO.
		Paragraph 4: Safety zones around artificial islands, installations or structures	IMO's field of competence (safety of navigation)	Res. A.671(16)	Consider whether the provisions of res. A.671(16), particularly No.1(b), are compatible with article 60(4) of UNCLOS.

Articles of UNCLOS	Subject-Matter	Specific provisions on the subject-matter	Relationship between UNCLOS and IMO instruments	Relevant IMO instruments	Comments/ recommendations
		Paragraph 5: Breadth of safety zones, and duty of publicity with respect to the extent of safety zones	Reference to "applicable international standards" and to "generally accepted international standards" or as recommended by the "competent international organization"	Res. A.671(16)	The coastal State is responsible for the dissemination of information.
		Paragraph 6: Navigation in the vicinity of artificial islands, installations, structures and safety zones	Reference to "generally accepted international standards"	Res. A.671(16)	
		Paragraph 7: Non-interference with recognized sea lanes essential to international navigation	IMO's field of competence (safety of navigation)	Res. A.671(16) Res. A.572(14)	

CONTINENTAL SHELF

Articles of UNCLOS	Subject-Matter	Specific provisions on the subject-matter	Relationship between UNCLOS and IMO instruments	Relevant IMO instruments	Comments/ recommendations
80	Artificial islands, installations and structures on the continental shelf				Same as in relation to article 60 of UNCLOS.

HIGH SEAS

Articles of UNCLOS	Subject-Matter	Specific provisions on the subject-matter	Relationship between UNCLOS and IMO instruments	Relevant IMO instruments	Comments/ recommendations
91 and 92	Nationality of ships and status of ships	Registration of ships	Prevention of unlawful acts against safety of navigation	SUA SUA Protocol Intervention 1969 Intervention Prot 1973	
94	Duties of the flag State (applicable also to the EEZ as far as compatible with the EEZ regime according to article 58(2))	Paragraph 1: Flag State jurisdiction with respect to administrative, technical and social matters			

Articles of UNCLOS	Subject-Matter	Specific provisions on the subject-matter	Relationship between UNCLOS and IMO instruments	Relevant IMO instruments	Comments/ recommendations
		Paragraph 3: Measures to ensure safety at sea on the following matters:	Reference to "generally accepted international regulations, procedures and practices" according to article 94(5)	SOLAS Load Lines COLREG MARPOL STCW STCW-F	1. The flag State must, as appropriate, comply with non-binding IMO instruments (Res. A.739(18), A.740(18), A.741(18)). 2. IMO rules and standards represent the minimum requirements *vis-à-vis* flag State jurisdiction.
		(a) Construction, equipment and seaworthiness of ships	As above	SOLAS Load Lines SFV MARPOL A.961(23)	
		(b) Manning of ships	Reference to "applicable international instruments"	STCW STCW-F SOLAS A.955(23)	

Articles of UNCLOS	Subject-Matter	Specific provisions on the subject-matter	Relationship between UNCLOS and IMO instruments	Relevant IMO instruments	Comments/ recommendations
		(c) Signals, communications and prevention of collisions	Reference to "generally accepted international regulations, procedures and practices" according to article 94(5)	SOLAS COLREG Code of Signals	
		Paragraph 4: The above measures shall include the following:	As above		
		(a) Survey of ships and duty to carry charts, nautical publications, instruments and equipment	As above	SOLAS MARPOL A.948(23) A.952(23)	
		(b) Technical qualification of the master, officers, and crew	Reference to "applicable international regulations"	SOLAS STCW STCW-F	
		(c) Qualification of the master, officers, and crew in maritime law	Reference to "generally accepted international regulations, procedures and practices" according to article 94(5)	SOLAS STCW STCW-F A.947(23) MSC.209(81)	

Articles of UNCLOS	Subject-Matter	Specific provisions on the subject-matter	Relationship between UNCLOS and IMO instruments	Relevant IMO instruments	Comments/ recommendations
		Paragraph 7: Duty of the flag State to conduct an investigation of any casualty occurring to its ships	IMO's field of competence	SOLAS (regulation I/21) Load Lines (art. 23) MARPOL art. 6(4) and art. 12 Res. A.637(16)	1. The duty to investigate under relevant IMO regulations is limited to the purpose of determining the need for any changes to the pertinent convention.
98	Duty to render assistance	Paragraph 1: Duty of the master to render assistance to persons and ships	IMO's field of competence	Salvage SOLAS V/33	
		Paragraph 2: Duty of the coastal State to promote search and rescue services	IMO's field of competence	SAR SOLAS V/7 GMDSS	
100	Piracy	Duty of States to co-operate in the repression of piracy	IMO's field of competence (navigational and environmental risk	Res. A.738(18) Res. A.979(24)	
108	Illicit traffic in narcotic drugs or psychotropic substances	Duty of co-operation for the suppression of illicit drug-trafficking			

THE AREA

Articles of UNCLOS	Subject-Matter	Specific provisions on the subject-matter	Relationship between UNCLOS and IMO instruments	Relevant IMO instruments	Comments/ recommendations
142	Rights and legitimate interests of coastal States	Right of coastal States to take proportionate measures beyond the territorial sea to avoid pollution resulting from or caused by any activities in the Area		Intervention Convention 1973 Intervention Protocol	
163	Organs of the Council (International Seabed Authority)	Paragraph 13: Each Commission may consult any competent organ of the United Nations or of its specialized agencies	Reference to the specialized agencies of the United Nations		IMO is a specialized agency of the United Nations.

PROTECTION AND PRESERVATION OF THE MARINE ENVIRONMENT

Articles of UNCLOS	Subject-Matter	Specific provisions on the subject-matter	Relationship between UNCLOS and IMO instruments	Relevant IMO instruments	Comments/ recommendations
196	Use of technologies or introduction of alien or new species	Duty of States to take measures to prevent, reduce and control pollution of the marine environment resulting use of technologies or introduction of alien or new species which may cause significant and harmful changes	IMO field of competence (environmental risk)	BWC	
197	Co-operation on a global or regional basis	Duty of States to co-operate on a global or regional basis directly or through competent international organization, in elaborating international anti-pollution standards	Reference to "competent international organizations"	Res. A.964(23)	IMO is a competent international organization.
198	Notification of imminent or actual damage	Duty of States to notify other States and the competent international organizations in cases or imminent or actual damage	Reference to "competent international organizations"	OPRC OPRC PROT 2000	IMO is a competent international organization.
199	Contingency plans against pollution	Duty of affected States and the competent international organizations to co-operate in eliminating the effects of pollution and preventing or minimizing damage	Reference to "competent international organizations"	OPRC OPRC PROT 2000 MARPOL Annex I, reg.	IMO is a competent international organization.

Articles of UNCLOS	Subject-Matter	Specific provisions on the subject-matter	Relationship between UNCLOS and IMO instruments	Relevant IMO instruments	Comments/ recommendations
				26 & Annex II, reg. 16	
200	Studies, research programmes and exchange of information and data	Duty of States to co-operate through competent international organizations, for the purpose of promoting studies, undertaking programmes of scientific research and encouraging the ex-change of information and data	Reference to "competent international organizations"	AFS, 2001	IMO is a competent international organization.
201	Scientific criteria for regulations	Duty of States to co-operate through competent international organizations in establishing appropriate scientific criteria for the formulation of international anti-pollution standards	Reference to "competent international organizations"		IMO is a competent international organization.
202	Scientific and technical assistance to developing States	Duty of States to provide scientific and technical assistance to developing States for the protection and preservation of the marine environment	Reference to "competent international organizations"	IMO convention and specific treaty obligations under	1. IMO is a competent international organization.

Articles of UNCLOS	Subject-Matter	Specific provisions on the subject-matter	Relationship between UNCLOS and IMO instruments	Relevant IMO instruments	Comments/ recommendations
				MARPOL, London Convention, OPRC, OPRC PROT 2000, STCW	2. IMO's programme for technical co-operation and assistance for developing States.
203	Preferential treatment for developing States	Granting of preferential treatment to developing States by international organizations	Reference to "international organizations"		IMO may take these guidelines into account when implementing the duty of technical assistance.
204 to 206	Monitoring and environmental assistance	Monitoring of the risks or effects of pollution, publication of reports, assessing potential effects of activities	Reference to "competent international organizations"		IMO's participation and contribution to GESAMP.

Articles of UNCLOS	Subject-Matter	Specific provisions on the subject-matter	Relationship between UNCLOS and IMO instruments	Relevant IMO instruments	Comments/ recommendations
208 (also article 214 with respect to enforcement)	Pollution from seabed activities and from artificial islands, installations and structures subject to national jurisdiction	Establishment by States, through competent international organizations, of international regulations	Reference to "competent international organizations"	Res. A.671(16) Res. A.672(16) OPRC OPRC PROT 2000	Partly covered in MARPOL 73/78, Annex I, reg. 21. Further regulation of offshore activities is under discussion (but not agreed at this time). Pollution directly arising from exploration/ exploitation is however not the direct concern of IMO, the Organization may contribute to the establishment of international regulations.

Articles of UNCLOS	Subject-Matter	Specific provisions on the subject-matter	Relationship between UNCLOS and IMO instruments	Relevant IMO instruments	Comments/ recommendations
210	Pollution by dumping	Paragraph 4: Adoption by States, through the competent international organization, of global rules, standards and recommended practices and procedures	Reference to "competent international organizations"	London Convention Resolution of the Consultative Meetings of Contracting Parties, LC Protocol, 1996	1. IMO is a competent international organization. 2. The Consultative Meeting concluded that there were no fundamental inconsistencies between UNCLOS and the London Convention.
211	Pollution from vessels	Paragraph 1: Adoption by States, through the competent international organization, of international rules and standards concerning vessel-source pollution, and promotion of routeing systems to minimize marine pollution	Reference to the "competent international organization"	MARPOL SOLAS V/8 (renumbered as V/10 in 2000 amendments) Res. A.572(14) Res. A.858(20) AFS, 2001 Res. A.962(23)	IMO is the competent international organization for establishing international rules and standards on vessel-source pollution.

Articles of UNCLOS	Subject-Matter	Specific provisions on the subject-matter	Relationship between UNCLOS and IMO instruments	Relevant IMO instruments	Comments/ recommendations
		Paragraph 2: Duty of flag States to adopt laws and regulations on vessel-source pollution	Reference to "generally accepted international rules and standards established through the competent international organization"	MARPOL	1. IMO is the competent international organization. 2. National legislation shall have at least the same effect as MARPOL, which represents the minimum standards for flag States.
		Paragraph 3: Duty of States to give due publicity and to communicate to the competent international organization their particular port entry requirements	Reference to the "competent international organization"		1. IMO is the competent international organization.
		Paragraph 5: Adoption by coastal States of laws and regulations for the prevention of vessel-source pollution in their EEZ conforming to generally accepted international rules and standards established through the competent international organization	Reference to "generally accepted international rules and standards established through the competent international organization"	MARPOL	IMO is the competent international organization for establishing international rules and standards concerning vessel-source pollution.

Articles of UNCLOS	Subject-Matter	Specific provisions on the subject-matter	Relationship between UNCLOS and IMO instruments	Relevant IMO instruments	Comments/ recommendations
		Paragraph 6: Particular, clearly defined area for the prevention of vessel-source pollution in the coastal State's EEZ		MARPOL A.982(24) SOLAS COLREG	MEPC 46(2001) revised the guidelines for designation of Special Areas under MARPOL 73/78 and guidelines for the identification and designation of Particularly Sensitive Sea Areas.
		Paragraph 6(a) Requirements and procedures to obtain recognition of a particular, clearly defined area	Reference to "consultations through the competent international organization with any other States concerned"		IMO is the competent international organization.

Articles of UNCLOS	Subject-Matter	Specific provisions on the subject-matter	Relationship between UNCLOS and IMO instruments	Relevant IMO instruments	Comments/ recommendations
		Paragraph 6(c) Additional laws and regulations for the particular, clearly defined area on discharges or navigational practices	Reference to "generally accepted international rules and standards" on the design, construction, manning or equipment of ships	SOLAS Load Lines MARPOL STCW	The generally accepted international regulations represent the highest standards.
		Paragraph 7: International rules and standards under article 211 include those relating to notification to coastal States in cases of incidents or maritime casualties	This paragraph complements article 211(1)	MARPOL (article 8) and Protocol I OPRC (article 4)	IMO is the competent international organization for establishing international rules and standards concerning prompt notification of coastal States affected by pollution incidents.

Articles of UNCLOS	Subject-Matter	Specific provisions on the subject-matter	Relationship between UNCLOS and IMO instruments	Relevant IMO instruments	Comments/ recommendations
212	Pollution from or through the atmosphere	Paragraph 1: National legislation must take into account internationally agreed regulations	Reference to "internationally agreed rules, standards and recommended practices and procedures"	MARPOL Annex VI (1997) (with the development of an IMO strategy for the emission of climate gases from ships)	IMO is competent for establishing global rules and standards.
		Paragraph 3: Establishment of global and regional rules, standards through competent international organizations	Reference to "competent international organizations"	A.963(23)	
216	Enforcement with respect to pollution by dumping	Enforcement of national legislation and applicable international regulations adopted through competent international organizations	Reference to "applicable international rules and standards" established through "competent international organizations"	London Convention	IMO is a competent international organization.

Articles of UNCLOS	Subject-Matter	Specific provisions on the subject-matter	Relationship between UNCLOS and IMO instruments	Relevant IMO instruments	Comments/ recommendations
217	Flag State enforcement	Paragraph 1: Duty of flag States to ensure compliance by their vessels with international regulations	Reference to the “applicable international rules and standards, established through the competent international organization”	MARPOL	1. IMO is the competent international organization for establishing rules and standards on vessel-source pollution. 2. The flag State shall enforce MARPOL “as far as applicable”.
		Paragraph 2: Prohibition of sailing	Mention of the international rules and standards referred to in paragraph 1 including those of design, construction, equipment and manning of ships	SOLAS Load Lines MARPOL STCW	As above.

Articles of UNCLOS	Subject-Matter	Specific provisions on the subject-matter	Relationship between UNCLOS and IMO instruments	Relevant IMO instruments	Comments/ recommendations
		Paragraph 3: Carry and inspection of certificates	Mention of the international rules and standards mentioned in paragraph 1	MARPOL	As above.
		Paragraph 4: Investigation and institution of proceedings with respect to an alleged violation	Reference to “rules and standards established through the competent international organization”	MARPOL (article 4)	IMO is the competent international organization for establishing rules and standards on vessel-source pollution.
		Paragraph 7: Duty of flag States to inform the competent international organization of the action taken	Reference to the “competent international organization”	MARPOL (article 4)	IMO is the competent international organization.

Articles of UNCLOS	Subject-Matter	Specific provisions on the subject-matter	Relationship between UNCLOS and IMO instruments	Relevant IMO instruments	Comments/ recommendations
218	Port State enforcement	Paragraph 1: Investigations and proceedings by the port State against a vessel within its port or offshore terminal with respect to a discharge violation outside its jurisdictional waters	Reference to discharges in violation of "applicable international rules and standards established through the competent international organization"	MARPOL	1. IMO is the competent international organization for establishing international regulations on ships' discharges. 2. The port State may enforce MARPOL "as far as applicable" to that State.
219	Measures relating to seaworthiness of vessels to avoid pollution	Duty of States to take administrative measures on vessels within their port or offshore terminal in violation of seaworthiness standards and thereby threatening pollution damage	Reference to "applicable international rules and standards relating to seaworthiness of vessels"	MARPOL SOLAS Load Lines COLREG STCW	

Articles of UNCLOS	Subject-Matter	Specific provisions on the subject-matter	Relationship between UNCLOS and IMO instruments	Relevant IMO instruments	Comments/ recommendations
220	Enforcement by coastal States	Paragraph 1: Institution of proceedings by the coastal State against a vessel within its port or offshore terminal with respect to any violation occurred in its territorial sea or EEZ Paragraph 7: Duty of the coastal State to allow the vessel to proceed if the vessel assures compliance with requirements for bonding or other financial security	Reference to "applicable international rules and standards for the prevention, reduction and control of pollution from vessels". Reference to the "competent international organization"	MARPOL	The coastal State may enforce MARPOL "as far as applicable" to that State. IMO is the competent international organization.
221	Measures to avoid pollution arising from maritime casualties	Right of States to take proportionate measures beyond the territorial sea to avoid pollution arising from maritime casualties		Intervention Convention 1973 Intervention Protocol	
222	Enforcement with respect to air pollution	Duty of States to adopt laws and regulations to implement applicable international rules and standards established through competent international organizations concerning air-pollution	Reference to "applicable international rules and standards established through competent international organizations"	Annex VI to MARPOL	IMO is a competent international organization.

Articles of UNCLOS	Subject-Matter	Specific provisions on the subject-matter	Relationship between UNCLOS and IMO instruments	Relevant IMO instruments	Comments/ recommendations
223	Institution of proceedings	Submission of evidence and attendance of official representatives at the proceedings taken against a vessel	Reference to "competent international organization"		IMO is a competent international organization.
226	Investigation of foreign vessels	Avoidance of unnecessary physical inspection of vessels and limits of such inspection	Reference to "generally accepted international rules and standards" and to "applicable laws and regulations or international rules and standards"	MARPOL	
228	Suspension and restrictions on institution of proceedings	Special suspension and restriction conditions on proceedings to impose penalties	Reference to applicable international rules and standards relating to vessel-source pollution	MARPOL	
230	Monetary penalties and the observance of recognized rights of the accused		Reference to applicable international rules and standards relating to vessel-source pollution	MARPOL	

Articles of UNCLOS	Subject-Matter	Specific provisions on the subject-matter	Relationship between UNCLOS and IMO instruments	Relevant IMO instruments	Comments/ recommendations
231	Notification to the flag State and other States concerned			MARPOL article 5(3)	
233	Safeguards with respect to straits used for international navigation	Right of States bordering straits to take enforcement measures against foreign ships which have violated safety and anti-pollution standards, causing or threatening damage to the marine environment of straits	Reference to "the laws and regulations referred to in article 42, paragraph 1(a) and (b)"		
235	Responsibility and liability	Duty of co-operation for the development of inter-national law on responsibility and liability for the assessment of and compensation for damage and the settlement of disputes		CLC Convention and Protocols Fund Convention and Protocols HNS Convention Bunkers Convention (2001)	

Articles of UNCLOS	Subject-Matter	Specific provisions on the subject-matter	Relationship between UNCLOS and IMO instruments	Relevant IMO instruments	Comments/ recommendations
237	Obligations under the conventions on the protection and preservation of the marine environment	Non-prejudice clause and duty of consistency of special conventions with UNCLOS	Reference to the conventions on the protection and preservation of the marine environment	MARPOL London Convention Intervention OPRC CLC FUND HNS	IMO conventions on the protection of the marine environment reflect principles compatible with UNCLOS.

MARINE SCIENTIFIC RESEARCH

Articles of UNCLOS	Subject-Matter	Specific provisions on the subject-matter	Relationship between UNCLOS and IMO instruments	Relevant IMO instruments	Comments/ recommendations
242–244	International Co-operation	Promotion of international co-operation, publication and dissemination of information and knowledge	Reference to "competent international organizations"	MARPOL 1996 Protocol to the London Convention	IMO is a competent international organization.

Articles of UNCLOS	Subject-Matter	Specific provisions on the subject-matter	Relationship between UNCLOS and IMO instruments	Relevant IMO instruments	Comments/ recommendations
261	Non-interference with shipping routes	The deployment and use of any type of scientific research installations or equipment must not interfere with established international shipping routes			
262	Identification markings and warning signals	Duty to place identification markings on installations or equipment and to use adequate warning signals to ensure safety of navigation	Reference to "rules and standards established by competent international organizations"		IMO may be the most appropriate body for developing international rules and standards on warning signals. (Resolutions A.671(16) and A.672(16) on offshore installations have some relevance.)

DEVELOPMENT AND TRANSFER OF MARINE TECHNOLOGY

Articles of UNCLOS	Subject-Matter	Specific provisions on the subject-matter	Relationship between UNCLOS and IMO instruments	Relevant IMO instruments	Comments/ recommendations
268	Basic objectives		Reference to "competent international organizations"		The pertinent objectives of the transfer of technology are part of the ITCP.
269 to 272	Measure and arrangement to achieve the basic objectives		Reference to "competent international organizations"		IMO may refer to some of the specific arrangements and measures envisaged in UNCLOS.
275 to 277	National and regional marine scientific and technological centres		Reference to "competent international organizations"		

SETTLEMENT OF DISPUTES

Articles of UNCLOS	Subject-Matter	Specific provisions on the subject-matter	Relationship between UNCLOS and IMO instruments	Relevant IMO instruments	Comments/ recommendations
288	Compulsory procedures entailing binding decisions	Jurisdiction of courts or tribunals	Reference to the "interpretation or application of an international agreement related to the purposes of this Convention"	1996 Protocol to the London Convention	The 1996 Protocol to the London Convention is the only IMO convention which permits parties to use the dispute settlement procedures of UNCLOS.
292	Prompt release of vessels and crews	Submission by the flag State to a court or tribunal for release of a vessel or its crew if the detaining State has not complied with provisions for prompt release of the vessel or its crew upon the posting of a bond or financial security			

Articles of UNCLOS	Subject-Matter	Specific provisions on the subject-matter	Relationship between UNCLOS and IMO instruments	Relevant IMO instruments	Comments/ recommendations
297	Limitations on applicability of section 2 (dealing with compulsory procedures entailing binding decisions)	Paragraph 1(c): Disputes concerning the interpretation or application of UNCLOS arising from an alleged contravention by a coastal State of specified anti-pollution standards shall be subject to the compulsory procedures entailing binding decisions established in section 2	Reference to applicable "international rules and standards for the protection and preservation of the marine environment" which have been established "through a competent international organization"	MARPOL London Convention	In certain cases, IMO anti-pollution standards may be subject to compulsory procedures entailing binding decisions.

FINAL PROVISIONS

Articles of UNCLOS	Subject-Matter	Specific provisions on the subject-matter	Relationship between UNCLOS and IMO instruments	Relevant IMO instruments	Comments/ recommendations
311	Relationship to other conventions and international agreements	UNCLOS shall not alter international agreements compatible with the Convention or expressly permitted by the Conventions' provisions		IMO's treaties and other international regulations	

ANNEXES

Articles of UNCLOS	Subject-Matter	Specific provisions on the subject-matter	Relationship between UNCLOS and IMO instruments	Relevant IMO instruments	Comments/ recommendations
Annex VI article 22	Competence of the International Tribunal for the Law of the Sea	Reference of disputes subject to other agreements	Reference to “a treaty or convention already in force and concerning the subject-matter covered by this Convention”	IMO treaties in force related to the purposes of UNCLOS	Parties to the treaty may agree to have recourse to the Tribunal.
Annex VIII article 2	List of experts	List of experts in the field of navigation, including pollution from vessels and by dumping	Reference to the “International Maritime Organization”		

EVOLUTION OF THE MODERN LAW OF THE SEA

Date	Event	Comment (n.b.: some links are broken to fit into cell)
1494	Treaty of Tordesillas	Oceans divided between them by Spain and Portugal http://en.wikipedia.org/wiki/Treaty_of _Tordesillas
1609	Hugo Grotius, *Mare Liberum*	http://socserv.mcmaster.ca/econ/ugcm/3ll3/ grotius/Seas.pdf Later edition published in 1633
1635	John Selden, *Mare Clausum*	Later editions published in 1652 and 1663. David J. Padwa, 54 Am. J. Int'l L. 156 (1960)
1884	Convention for the Protection of Submarine Cables	LOS Convention arts. 58(1), 79, 112–115 http://www.austlii.edu.au/au/other/dfat/ treaties/1901/1.html 43 parties
1888	Suez Canal Convention adopted	Convention respecting the Free Navigation of the Suez Canal, Constantinople, 29 October 1888, 171 CTS 241 http://www.mfa.gov.eg/MFA_Portal/en-GB/ Foreign_Policy/Treaties/Convention+Respecti ng+the+Free+Navigation+of+the+Suez+Mariti me+Canal.htm
1894	Definition of the regime of the territorial sea	L'Institut de Droit International, Tableau Gènèral des Resolutions (1873–1913), pp 176–189 (NY:OUP 1920) (in French) [JX24. I43 1913]
1895	ILA study on the territorial sea	"Territorial Waters," International Law Association, Report of the Seventeenth Conference Held at Brussels, October 1–4, 1895, pp 102–116 (1986) [JX24.I5 vol. 17 1895]
1910	Salvage Convention adopted	International Convention for the Unification of Certain Rules relating to Assistance and Salvage at Sea, Brussels, 23 September 1910, 103 BFSP 434, http://www.admiraltylawguide .com/conven/salvage1910.html

Date	**Event**	**Comment** (n.b.: some links are broken to fit into cell)
1917	Gulf of Fonseca Case decided	Historic bay El Salvador v. Nicaragua, Central American Court of Justice http://www.worldcourts.com/cacj/eng/ decisions/1917.03.09_el_salvador/
1919	International Labor Organization (ILO) established	Peace Treaty of Versailles, articles 387–399 http://net.lib.byu.edu/~rdh7/wwi/versa/versa12 .html http://www.ilo.org/global/lang–en/index.htm
1926	Slavery Convention adopted	Slavery Convention, Geneva, 25 September 1926, 60 LNTS 253 http://www2.ohchr.org/english/law/slavery.htm 161 parties as at 6 December 2009
1927	The *Lotus* case decided	PCIJ, Ser. A 10, http://www.icj-cij.org/pcij/ serie_A/A_10/30_Lotus_Arret.pdf
1927	Schückling Report on territorial sea	"Territorial Waters," Report of the subcommittee on questionnaire no. 2, Committee of Experts for the Progressive Codification of International Law, Report to the Council of the League of Nations on Questions Which Appear Ripe for International Regulation, Communication C.196.M.70.1927.V, pp. 289–75, L/N Pub. V.Legal.1927.V.1 [JX1261.L45]
1930	Hague Codification Conference	Draft articles on TS not agreed upon. 66 participant countries. League of Nations, Conference for the Codification of International Law [1930], vol. II, pp. 223–420 (S. Rosenne ed. 1975) [JX1261.R672 1930]; Hunter Miller, The Hague Codification Conference, 24 Am. J. Int'l L. 674, 686–693 (1930)
1935	The *I'm Alone* arbitration decided	Hot pursuit. LOS Convention, art. 111 Canada v. United States, III RIAA 1613; 29 Am. J. Int'l L. 326–331 (1935), http://www.jstor.org/sici?sici= 0002-9300 (193504)29%3A2%3C326%3ACOTBS %22%3E2.0.CO%3B2-S

Date	**Event**	**Comment** (n.b.: some links are broken to fit into cell)
1936	Montreux Convention adopted	Convention regarding the Regime of the Straits, Montreux, 20 July 1936, 173 LNTS 2113, http://www.turkishpilots.org.tr/ingilizcedernek/DOCUMENTS/montro.html LOS Convention, art. 35(c)
1942	First continental shelf boundary treaty	UK (Trinidad & Tobago) – Venezuela (Gulf of Paria), Limits in the Seas No. 11, http://www.state.gov/g/oes/ocns/c16065.htm
1944	International Convention on Civil Aviation (ICAO) adopted	LOS Convention, arts. 39.3, 54 http://www.icao.int/
1945	UN Charter adopted	http://www.un.org/aboutun/charter/
1945	Truman Proclamation on the U.S. continental shelf	First coastal State claim to the continental shelf. Proclamation 2667: Policy of the United States With Respect to the Natural Resources of the Subsoil and Sea Bed of the Continental Shelf. http://www.oceanlaw.net/texts/truman1.htm; http://www.presidency.ucsb.edu/ws/index.php?pid=12332 LOS Convention, article 76–77
1945	Truman Proclamation on fisheries	Proclamation 2668–Policy of the United States with respect to coastal fisheries in certain areas of the high seas http://www.presidency.ucsb.edu/ws/print.php?pid=58816
1945	Food and Agriculture Organization (FAO) founded	LOS Convention Annex VIII art. 2.2 www.fao.org
1946	International Convention for the Regulation of Whaling (ICRW) adopted	LOS Convention arts. 65, 87, 116, 120 http://www.iwcoffice.org/
1947	ICAO Convention enters into force	190 parties as at July 2007

Date	**Event**	**Comment** (n.b.: some links are broken to fit into cell)
1948	ICRW enters into force	88 parties (as amended) as at 3 December 2009
1948	Convention on the International Maritime Consultative Organization (IMCO) adopted	Name subsequently changed to International Maritime Organization (IMO) www.imo.org
1949	ICJ decides *Corfu Channel Case*	United Kingdom v. Albania, 1949 ICJ 4 http://www.icj-cij.org/docket/index.php?p1=3 &p2=3&k=cd&case=1&code=cc&p3=4
1952	Brussels Penal Jurisdiction Convention adopted	International Convention for the Unification of Certain Rules relating to Penal Jurisdiction in Matters of Collision or Other Incidents of Navigation, 439 UNTS 233 Reverses rule of the *Lotus* case
1952	Brussels Civil Jurisdiction Convention adopted	International Convention on Certain Rules concerning Civil Jurisdiction in Matters of Collision, 439 UNTS 217
1954	IMO adopts Intervention Convention	International Convention for the Prevention of Pollution of the Sea by Oil, London, 12 May 1954, 327 UNTS 3 http://www.admiraltylawguide.com/conven/ oilpol1954.html
1956	Protocol to ICRW adopted	http://www.iwcoffice.org/commission/ convention.htm
1956	Supplemental Slavery Convention adopted	Supplementary Convention on the Abolition of Slavery, the Slave Trade and Institutions and Practices similar to Slavery, Geneva, 7 September 1956, 266 UNTS 3. 123 parties as at 6 Dec. 2009 http://www.unhchr.ch/html/menu3/b/30.htm
1956	International Law Commission work on codification and progressive development of the law of the sea concluded	Adopted draft conventions on the territorial sea and the contiguous zone, high seas, continental shelf, fisheries, and optional protocol on dispute settlement http://www.un.org/law/ilc/ Work began in 1944

Date	**Event**	**Comment** (n.b.: some links are broken to fit into cell)
1958	First UN Conference on the Law of the Sea	Conventions on the Territorial Sea and the Contiguous Zone, the High Seas, the Continental Shelf, Fishing and Conservation of the Living Resources of the High Seas, and dispute settlement protocol adopted. 86 participants. http://www.intfish.net/treaties/ index1.htm
1958	IMCO Convention enters into force	LOS Convention Annex VIII art. 2(2). 168 parties as at 30 November 2009 representing 97% of world's merchant shipping by tonnage. www.imo.org
1959	Antarctic Treaty adopted	402 UNTS 71; http://www.scar.org/treaty/at _text.html
1960	Second UN Conference on the Law of the Sea	No agreement on the maximum breadth of the territorial sea
1960	Intergovernmental Oceanographic Commission (IOC) established	LOS Convention Annex VIII art. 2.2. http://ioc.unesco.org/iocweb/index.php
1961	Antarctic Treaty entered into force	47 parties http://www.ats.aq/devAS/ats_parties .aspx?lang=e
1962	Convention on the High Seas enters into force	63 parties as at 4 December 2009 http://untreaty.un.org/ilc/texts/instruments/ english/conventions/8_1_1958_high_seas.pdf
1964	Convention on the Territorial Sea and the Contiguous Zone enters into force	52 parties as at 4 December 2009 http://untreaty.un.org/ilc/texts/instruments/ english/conventions/8_1_1958_territorial_sea .pdf
1964	Convention on the Continental Shelf enters into force	58 parties as at 4 December 2009 http://untreaty.un.org/ilc/texts/instruments/ english/conventions/8_1_1958_continental _shelf.pdf
1965	IMO adopts Facilitation Convention	Convention on Facilitation of International Maritime Traffic, with annex, London April 9, 1965, 591 UNTS 265

Date	Event	Comment (n.b.: some links are broken to fit into cell)
1966	IMO adopts Load Lines Convention	International Convention on Load Lines, London, April 5, 1966, 640 UNTS 133; http://images.io.gov.mo/bo/i/99/50/dlar-49209-69-eng.pdf LOS Convention 94.5
1967	UNGA establishes Ad Hoc Sea Bed Committee	UNGA resolution A/Res/2340 (XXII) http://daccessdds.un.org/doc/RESOLUTION/GEN/NR0/236/75/IMG/NR023675.pdf?OpenElement
1967	1965 IMO Facilitation Convention enters into force	114 parties as at 30 November 2009 representing 90% of world's merchant shipping by tonnage
1968	1966 Load Lines Convention enters into force	159 parties as at 30 November 2009 representing 99% of world's merchant shipping by tonnage
1969	IMO adopts Tonnage Convention	International Convention on Tonnage Measurement of Ships, London June 23, 1969, TIAS 10490, http://www.admiraltylawguide.com/conven/tonnage1969.html
1969	IMO adopts Intervention Convention	International Convention relating to Intervention on the High Seas in Cases of Oil Pollution Casualties, 29 November 1969, TIAS 8068, http://www.austlii.edu.au/au/other/dfat/treaties/1984/4.html LOS Convention art. 221
1969–2007	IMO adopts liability and compensation conventions	LOS Convention art. 235.3 www.imo.org; http://www.admiraltylawguide.com/interconv.html#MP
1969	UNGA Resolution 2574D (XXIV)	Question of the reservation exclusively for peaceful purposes of the sea-bed and the ocean floor, and the subsoil thereof, underlying the high seas beyond the limits of present national jurisdiction, and the use of their resources in the interests of mankind (Moratorium resolution) http://daccessdds.un.org/doc/RESOLUTION/GEN/NR0/257/08/IMG/NR025708.pdf?OpenElement

Date	**Event**	**Comment** (n.b.: some links are broken to fit into cell)
1970	UNGA Resolution 2749 (XXV)	Declaration of Principles Governing the Sea-bed and the Ocean Floor, and the Subsoil Thereof, beyond the Limits of National Jurisdiction http://daccessdds.un.org/doc/RESOLUTION/GEN/NR0/350/14/IMG/NR035014.pdf?OpenElement
1970	UNGA resolution 2750 (XXV)	Reservation exclusively for peaceful purposes of the sea-bed and the ocean floor, and the subsoil thereof, underlying the high seas beyond the limits of present national jurisdiction and use of their resources in the interests of mankind, and convening of a conference on the law of the sea http://daccessdds.un.org/doc/RESOLUTION/GEN/NR0/350/15/IMG/NR035015.pdf?OpenElement
1972	IMO adopts COLREGS convention	Convention on the International Regulations for Preventing Collisions at sea, London Oct. 20, 1972, LOS Convention arts. 21.4, 39.2(a), 94.3(c) www.imo.org; http://www.admiraltylawguide.com/conven/collisions1972.html
1972	IMO adopts London Dumping Convention	Convention on the Prevention of Marine Pollution by Dumping of Wastes and Other Matter, December 29, 1972, LOS Convention arts. 1(5), 210, 216 See http://www.imo.org/home.asp?topic_id=1488; http://www.admiraltylawguide.com/conven/dumping1972.html
1972	UN Environment Program established	LOS Convention Annex VIII art. 2.2 http://www.unep.org/
1973	UNCLOS III convened	In New York for procedural matters pursuant to UNGA resolution 3067 (XXVIII). http://daccessdds.un.org/doc/RESOLUTION/GEN/NR0/281/39/IMG/NR028139.pdf?OpenElement
1974	UNCLOS III convened	In Caracas for fist substantive negotiations pursuant to UNGA resolution 3067 (XXVIII). http://daccessdds.un.org/doc/RESOLUTION/GEN/NR0/281/39/IMG/NR028139.pdf

Date	**Event**	**Comment** (n.b.: some links are broken to fit into cell)
1974	IMO adopts SOLAS Convention	International Convention for the Safety of Life at Sea, 1974, with annex, London November 1, 1974, TIAS 9700 LOS Convention arts. 39.2(a), 94.3(a), 94.4(a), 94.4(c), 94.5, 98.1(c), 194.3(c), 262 http://www.austlii.edu.au/au/other/dfat/treaties/1983/22.html
1974	SOLAS regulation V/8 (routeing); IMO General Provisions on Ships' Routeing	LOS Convention arts. 22, 53.8
1975	1969 Intervention Convention enters into force	86 parties as at 30 November 2009 representing 74% of world's merchant shipping by tonnage
1975	London Dumping Convention enters into force	86 parties as at 30 November 2009 representing 67% of world's merchant shipping by tonnage
1975	Informal Single Negotiating Text (ISNT) of a law of the sea convention issued at UNCLOS III in NYC	A/CONF.62/WP.8 and WP.9
1976	Revised Single Negotiating Text (RSNT) issued in New York	A/CONF.62/WP.8/Rev.1 and WP.9/Rev.1
1977	Informal Composite Negotiating Text (ICNT) issued in New York	A/CONF.62/WP.10 and Add.1
1977	1972 COLREGS enters into force	153 parties as at 30 November 2009 representing 98% of world's merchant shipping by tonnage

Date	**Event**	**Comment** (n.b.: some links are broken to fit into cell)
1978	IMO adopts MARPOL amendments & Annexes I, II, III, IV and V	Protocol of 1978 relating to the International Convention for the Prevention of Pollution from Ships, 1973, with annexes LOS Convention arts. 211, 217, 218, 219, 220 http://www.austlii.edu.au/au/other/dfat/treaties/1988/29.html
1978	IMO adopts STCW	International Convention on Standards of Training, Certification and Watchkeeping for Seafarers, London July 7, 1978 LOS Convention arts. 94.4(b), 94.4(c), 94.5 http://www.admiraltylawguide.com/conven/stcw1978.html
1978	IMO adopts LC amendments	LOS Convention arts. 1(5), 210, 216 http://www.admiraltylawguide.com/conven/protodumping1996.html
1979	IMO adopts International Convention on Maritime Search and Rescue (SAR) Convention	TIAS 11093 LOS Convention art. 98 http://www.admiraltylawguide.com/conven/searchrescue1979.html
1979	ICNT/Rev.1 issued in Geneva	A/Conf.62/WP.10/Rev.1
1980	1974 SOLAS Convention enters into force	159 parties as at 30 November 2009 representing 99% of world's merchant shipping by tonnage
1980	ICNT/Rev.2 issued in New York	A/Conf.62/WP.10/Rev.2
1980	Informal Draft Convention on the Law of the Sea issued in Geneva	A/Conf.62/WP.10/Rev.3
1981	IMO adopts Chapter VIII to SOLAS Regulations on civilian nuclear ships	LOS Convention art. 23

Date	Event	Comment (n.b.: some links are broken to fit into cell)
1981	Draft Convention on the Law of the Sea issued in Geneva	A/CONF.62/L.78
1982	LOS Convention adopted (April 30) and opened for signature (December 6–10)	119 delegations signed the Convention http://www.un.org/Depts/los/convention_ agreements/convention_overview_convention .htm
1982	1969 Tonnage Convention enters into force	150 parties as at 30 November 2009 representing 99% of world's merchant tonnage
1983	MARPOL 73/78 and Annexes I and II enter into force	150 parties as at 30 November 2009 representing 99% of world's merchant shipping by tonnage
1983	1973 Intervention Protocol enters into force	53 parties as at 30 November 2009 representing 49% of world's merchant shipping
1983–1994	Preparatory Commission met	
1984	1978 STCW Convention entered into force	153 parties as at 30 November 2009 representing 99% of world's merchant shipping by tonnage
1985	1979 SAR Convention enters into force	96 parties as at 30 November 2009 representing 60% of world's merchant shipping by tonnage
1986	UN Convention on Conditions for Registration of Ships adopted	LOS Convention arts. 91, 92.1, 94.2(a) Not in force. http://www.admiraltylawguide .com/conven/registration1986.html
1988	Vienna Drug Convention adopted	UN Convention against Illicit Traffic in Narcotic Drugs and Psychotropic Substances, Vienna December 29, 1988 LOS Convention arts. 27.1(d), 108 http://www.unodc.org/unodc/en/treaties/ illicit-trafficking.html http://www.unodc.org/documents/treaties/ treaty_adherence_convention_1988.pdf

Date	Event	Comment (n.b.: some links are broken to fit into cell)
1988	MARPOL Annex V (garbage) enters into force	139 parties as at 30 November 2009 representing 97% of world merchant shipping
1988	IMO adopts SUA Convention and Fixed Platforms Protocol	Convention for the Suppression of Unlawful Acts against the Safety of Maritime Navigation, Rome March 10, 1988 http://www.imo.org;
1989	IMO adopts International Convention on Salvage	London April 28, 1989 http://untreaty.un.org/English/UNEP/salvage _english.pdf http://www.jus.uio.no/lm/imo.salvage .convention; http://www.admiraltylawguide .com/conven/salvage1989.html 1989/doc.html LOS Convention art. 303(3)
1989	IMO resolution A.672(16) on removal of platforms adopted	LOS Convention art. 60.3
1989	IMO resolution A.671(16), Safety Zones and Safety of Navigation Around Offshore Installations and Structures adopted	LOS Convention art. 60.6
1990	1988 Vienna Drug Convention enters into force	184 parties as at 4 December 2009
1990	IMO adopts International Convention on Oil Pollution Preparedness, Response and Cooperation (OPRC)	London November 30, 1990 http://fletcher.tufts.edu/multi/texts/BH981.txt; http://www.admiraltylawguide.com/conven/ oilpolresponse1990.html LOS Convention art. 211

Date	Event	Comment (n.b.: some links are broken to fit into cell)
1990–1994	UN Secretary-General's Informal Consultations	on resolving difficulties with Part XI
1991	UNGA adopts first oceans resolution	http://www.un.org/Depts/los/general_assembly/general_assembly_resolutions.htm
1991	Antarctic Treaty Environmental Protection Protocol adopted	Protocol on Environmental Protection, Madrid, 4 October 1991, 450 UNTS 169; http://www.ats.aq/index.php?acc=6&updateUser=3
1992	MARPOL Annex III enters into force	150 parties as at 30 November 2009 representing 99% of world's merchant shipping
1992	1988 SUA Convention and Protocol enter into force	156 parties to SUA Convention at 30 November 2009 representing 95% of world's merchant shipping 145 parties to SUA Protocol as at 30 November 2009 representing 90% of world's merchant shipping
1992	ICJ decides Gulf of Fonseca case	Case concerning the Land, Island and Maritime Frontier Dispute (El Salvador v. Honduras, Nicaragua intervening) http://www.icj-cij.org/docket/index.php?p1=3&p2=3&k=0e&case=75&code=sh&p3=4
1993	60th instrument of ratification or accession of LOS Convention deposited	LOS Convention art. 308.1
1993	Commission on Sustainable Development (CSD) established	Review agenda 21, chapter 17 on oceans http://www.un.org/esa/sustdev/index.html
1993	FAO adopts compliance agreement	Agreement to Promote Compliance with International Conservation and Management Measures by Fishing Vessels on the High Seas, Rome November 24, 1993 http://www.fao.org/Legal/treaties/012t-e.htm

Date	**Event**	**Comment** (n.b.: some links are broken to fit into cell)
1994	UNGA adopts Part XI Agreement	Agreement relating to the Implementation of Part XI of the UN Convention on the Law of the Sea http://www.un.org/Depts/los/convention_agreements/convention_overview_part_xi.htm
1994	LOS Convention entered into force	LOS Convention art. 308.1 160 parties as at 9 November 2009
1994	IMO adopts SOLAS regulation XI/4 and MARPOL Annexes I/11, II/16.9 and V/8 on port state control on operational requirements	LOS Convention arts. 73.2, 219, 220.7, 226, 292
1995	Global Plan of Action for the protection of the marine environment from land-based activities adopted	LOS Convention arts. 207, 213 http://www.gpa.unep.org/
1995	UN Fish Stocks Agreement adopted	Agreement for the Implementation of the Provisions of the UN Convention on the Law of the Sea relating to the Conservation and Management of Straddling Fish Stocks and Highly Migratory Fish Stocks, with annexes, New York August 4, 1993 LOS Convention arts. 63, 64, 73, 116–119 http://www.un.org/Depts/los/convention_agreements/convention_overview_fish_stocks.htm
1995	FAO Code of Conduct for Responsible Fisheries adopted	LOS Convention arts. 63, 64, 73, 116–119 http://www.fao.org/DOCREP/005/v9878e/v9878e00.htm

Date	**Event**	**Comment** (n.b.: some links are broken to fit into cell)
1995	International Seabed Authority becomes operational	LOS Convention Part XI as amended by the 1994 Agreement. http://www.isa.org.jm/
1995	IMO adopts revised STCW annex	http://www.uscg.mil/stcw/stcw-code-intro.htm
1995	1990 OPRC enters into force	100 parties as at 30 November 2009 representing 68% of world's merchant shipping by tonnage
1996	IMO adopts London Convention Protocol	LOS Convention arts. 1(5), 210, 216 See http://www.imo.org/home.asp?topic_id=1488; http://www.admiraltylawguide.com/conven/ amendprotomarpol1996.html
1996	1988 Salvage Convention enters into force	58 parties as at 30 November 2009 representing 49% of world's merchant shipping by tonnage
1996	1994 Part XI Agreement enters into force	138 parties as at 9 November 2009
1996	UNSG issues first annual report on oceans and law of the sea (SPLOS/6)	LOS Convention art. 319.2(a) http://www.un.org/Depts/los/general _assembly/general_assembly_reports.htm
1996	ITLOS becomes operational	LOS Convention art. 287.1(a) and Annex VI http://www.itlos.org/
1997	ITLOS decides first case	The M/V *Saiga* (No.1) http://www.itlos.org/start2_en.html
1997	CLCS holds first session	LOS Convention art. 78.8 and Annex II http://www.un.org/Depts/los/clcs_new/ clcs_home.htm
1997	IMO adopts MARPOL Annex VI on air pollution from ships	Cf. LOS Convention arts. 212, 222 http://www.admiraltylawguide.com/conven/ protomarpol1997.html

Date	**Event**	**Comment** (n.b.: some links are broken to fit into cell)
1998	IMO's General Provisions on Ships Routeing amended to include a new Part H on the Adoption, designation and substitution of archipelagic sea lanes	LOS Convention art. 53.9 IMO resolution MSC.72(69); SN/Circ.200 www.imo.org/
1998	1991 Antarctic Environmental Protocol enters into force	32 parties http://www.ats.aq/devAS/ats_parties .aspx?lang=e
1999	First annual UN Ad-hoc Informal Consultative Open-ended Process on Oceans and the Law of the Sea (UNICPOLOS)	http://www.un.org/Depts/los/consultative _process/consultative_process.htm
1999	FAO adopts three International Plans of Action	International Plan of Action for Reducing Incidental Catch of Seabirds in Longline Fisheries International Plan of Action for the Conservation and Management of Sharks International Plan of Action for the Management of Fishing Capacity http://www.fao.org/fi/website/
1999	IMO adds to SOLAS Regulations Chapter VII Part D and adopts as mandatory 1993 International Code for the Safe Carriage of Packaged	LOS Convention art. 23 www.imo.org

Date	**Event**	**Comment** (n.b.: some links are broken to fit into cell)
	Irradiated Nuclear Fuel, Plutonium and High-Level Radioactive Wastes on Board Ships (INF Code), effective 1 January 2001	
2000	UN adopts Convention Against Transnational Organized Crime and Protocols re Trafficking in Persons and Smuggling of Migrants	TOC and protocols adopted by UNGA as A/ RES/55/25, 15 Nov 2000 http://www.unodc.org/unodc/en/treaties/CTOC .html
2001	FAO adopts IPOA-IUU Fishing	International Plan of Action to Combat Illegal, Unregulated and Unreported Fishing LOS Convention arts. 116, 117 http://www.fao.org/fi/website/ FIRetrieveAction.do?dom=org&xml=ipoa _IUU.xml
2001	UN 1995 Fish Stocks Agreement enters into force	73 parties as at 9 November 2009
2001	Russia makes first submission to CLCS	LOS Convention art 76 http://www.un.org/Depts/los/clcs_new/ submissions_files/submission_rus.htm
2001	ILC draft articles on state responsibility	LOS Convention art. 31, 235.1 ember http://untreaty.un.org/ilc/texts/ instruments/ english/commentaries/ 9_6_2001.pdf
2003	UN OCEANS established	Coordination of UN specialized agencies and other UN bodies. http://www.oceansatlas.org/ www.un-oceans.org/Index.htm

Date	**Event**	**Comment** (n.b.: some links are broken to fit into cell)
2003	FAO Compliance Agreement enters into force	39 parties as at 8 September 2009
2003	MARPOL Annex IV (sewage) enters into force	124 parties as at 8 September 2009 representing 82% of world's merchant shipping
2003	2000 TOC enters into force	151 parties as at 4 December 2009 http://www.unodc.org/unodc/en/treaties/ CTOC/signatures.html
2003	TOC Trafficking in persons protocol enters into force	135 parties as at 4 December 2009 http://www.unodc.org/unodc/en/treaties/ CTOC/countrylist-traffickingprotocol.html
2004	TOC Smuggling of migrants protocol enters into force	122 parties as at 4 December 2009 http://www.unodc.org/unodc/en/treaties/ CTOC/countrylist-migrantsmugglingprotocol .html
2004	OPRC HNS Protocol adopted	http://www.admiraltylawguide.com/conven/ noxious1996.html
2005	MARPOL Annex VI (air pollution from ships) enters into force	57 parties as at 30 November 2009 representing 84% of world's merchant shipping by tonnage
2005	IMO adopts Protocols to 1988 SUA Convention	LOS Convention art. 110. http://www.state.gov/t/isn/trty/81727.htm Not in force. First treaty with comprehensive shipboarding regime 10 States have consented to be bound by 2005 SUA Protocol 8 States have consented to be bound by 2005 SUA Platforms Protocol as of 30 November 2009. 12 consents to be bound by 2005 SUA Protocol needed to bring into force
2006	ILO adopts consolidated Maritime Labor Convention	LOS Convention art. 94.3(b) Not in force as at 4 December 2009. 5 ratifications as of 10 February 2009 http://www.ilo.org/ilolex/cgi-lex/convde .pl?C186

Date	**Event**	**Comment** (n.b.: some links are broken to fit into cell)
2006	IMO adopts MARPOL Annex IV (sewage) regulation 13 on port State control on operational requirements	LOS Convention arts. 73.2, 219, 220.7, 226, 292 Effective 1 August 2007
2006	London Convention Protocol enters into force	37 parties as at 30 November 2009 representing 32% of world's merchant shipping by tonnage
2006	UN Fish Stocks Agreement Review Conference begins	http://www.un.org/Depts/los/convention _agreements/review_conf_fish_stocks.htm
2006–2007	IAEA reviews international regulations for the safe transport of radioactive material and associated guidance	LOS Convention art. 23
2007	IMO adopts Nairobi Wreck Removal Convention	Not in force
2008	2001 Bunkers Convention enters into force	47 parties as at 30 November 2009 representing 79% of world's merchant shipping
2008	2001 Anti-Fouling Systems Convention enters into force	40 parties as at 30 November 2009 representing 68% of world's merchant shipping
2009	Hong King Ship Recycling Convention adopted by IMO	Hong Kong International Convention for the Safe and Environmentally Sound Recycling of Ships, 2009 Text at IMO document SR/CONF/45

Date	**Event**	**Comment** (n.b.: some links are broken to fit into cell)
2009	FAO adopts Agreement on Port State Measures to Prevent, Deter and Eliminate IUU Fishing	25 Nov. 2009. Text at ftp://ftp.fao.org/docrep/ fao/meeting/018/k6339e.pdf
2010	IMO diplomatic conference to adopt	Amendments to STCW Convention and Code
2010	IMO diplomatic conference to adopt	Draft Protocol to International Convention on Liability and Compensation for Damage in connection with the Carriage of Hazardous and Noxious Substances by Sea, 1996
2010	UN Fish Stocks Agreement Review Conference resumes	http://www.un.org/Depts/los/convention _agreements/review_conf_fish_stocks.htm

September 29, 2010

LAW OF THE SEA CONVENTION: SOURCES AND IMPLEMENTATION

LOS Convention Provision	**Competent International Organization; International Rule or Standard**
Preamble, last paragraph (CIL)	The *Paquete Habana*, 175 U.S. 677 (1900)
arts. 1(5), 210, 216	London Dumping Convention 1972; 1996 Protocol
arts. 5–13 (baselines)	*Anglo-Norwegian Fisheries Case*, 1951 ICJ 116 (merits), http://www.icj-cij.org/docket/files/5/1809.pdf; *Bahrain v. Qatar*, 2001 ICJ 1, 103 (merits) para. 212, http://www.icj-cij.org/docket/files/87/7027.pdf
art. 10 (bays)	*Gulf of Fonseca Case (El Salvador/Nicaragua)*, Central American Court of Justice, 1917; *Case concerning the Land, Island and Maritime Frontier Dispute (El Salvador/Honduras, Nicaragua intervening)*, 1992 ICJ 351
arts. 17–21 (innocent passage)	*Corfu Channel Case* (UK v. Albania), 1949 ICJ 1 (merits), http://www.icj-cij.org/docket/files/1/1645.pdf; US-USSR Joint Statement on a Uniform Interpretation of Rules of International Law Governing Innocent Passage, Sept. 1989, http://findarticles.com/p/articles/mi_m1079/is_n2152_v89/ai_8355265/pg_38
arts. 21.4, 39.2(a), 94.3(c)	IMO COLREGS, 1972
art. 23	SOLAS Chapter VIII; INF Code, 1993; IAEA resolution GC(50)10.B, www.iaea.org/About/Policy/GC/GC50/GC50Resolutions/English/gc50res-10_en.pdf
arts, 22.3, 41.4	IMO General Provisions on Ships' Routeing (GPSR)
art. 27	*Lotus*, 1927, PCIJ, Ser. A 10; ILC draft LOS article 20
arts. 27.1(d), 108	Vienna Drug Convention, 1988
arts. 31, 42.5, 110.3, 111.8, 235.1, 304	ILC draft articles on state responsibility, 2001

LOS Convention Provision	Competent International Organization; International Rule or Standard
arts. 32, 95, 96	Sovereign immunity provisions collected in Roach & Smith, U.S. Responses to Excessive Maritime Claims, 2d ed. 1996, at 466–478
arts. 39.2(a), 94.3(a), 94.4(a), 94.4(c), 94.5, 98.1(c), 194.3(c), 262	IMO SOLAS Convention, 1974
art. 35(c)	Bosporus & Dardanelles, Montreux Convention, July 20, 1936, 173 LNTS 213; Strait of Magellan, Argentina-Chile Boundary Treaty, 1881, art. V; Åland's Hav and Baltic Straits
art. 37	e.g., Bab el Mandeb, Bonifacio, Gibraltar, Hormuz, Lombok, Malacca, Singapore, Sunda, Northeast, Northwest and Windward Passages
art. 38(1)	Tanzania Straits (Zanzibar Channel, Mafia Strait); Strait of Messina
arts. 39.2(b), 42.1(b)	MARPOL 73/78
arts. 39.3, 54	Convention on International Civil Aviation, Chicago 1944, Annex 2, Rules of the Air, as amended
art. 45.1(b)	Head Harbor Passage; Bahrain-Saudi Arabia Passage; Bahrain-Qatar Passage; Strait of Tiran; Khowr Abd Allah
art. 53.9	Archipelagic sea lanes: IMO GPSR Part H, 1998
arts. 63, 64, 73, 116–119	UN Fish Stocks Agreement, 1995
art. 60.3	IMO resolution A.672(16), 19 Oct. 1989, Guidelines and Standards for the Removal of Offshore Installations and Structures on the Continental Shelf and in the EEZ
art. 60.5	Development of criteria for larger safety zones. NAV 56 (2010) decided there was no demonstrated need at present to establish safety zones larger than 500 meters around artificial islands, structures or installations in EEZ or to develop guidelines to do so. NAV 56/20, para. 14.15. MSC 88 invited to approve SN circular on Guidelines for safety zones and safety of navigation around offshore installations and structures

LOS Convention Provision	**Competent International Organization; International Rule or Standard**
art. 60.6	IMO resolution A.671(16), Safety Zones and Safety of Navigation Around Offshore Installations and Structures
art. 61	FAO, Regional Fishery Management Organizations (RFMOs)
arts. 63, 64	RFMOs; 1995 Fish Stocks Agreement
arts. 65, 87, 116, 120	International Whaling Commission, 1946
arts. 73.2, 292	The *Camouco* Case (Panama v. France); The *Monte Confurco* Case (France v. Seychelles), ITLOS, 2000; The *Hoshinmaru* Case and the *Tomimaru* Cases (Japan v. Russia), ITLOS, 2007. www.itlos.org/start2_en.html
arts. 73.4, 219	IMO Port state control on operational requirements, 1994
art. 76.8, Annex II	Commission on the Limits of the Continental Shelf
arts. 76.1, 77	Truman Proclamation 2667, Sept., 28, 1945, http://www .oceanlaw.net/texts/truman1.htm
arts. 79, 112–115	Convention on the Protection of Submarine Cables, 1884, http://www.austlii.edu.au/au/other/dfat/treaties/1901/1 .html
art. 83 (delimitation)	*North Sea Continental Shelf Case* (FRG v. Denmark; FRG v. Netherlands), 1969 ICJ 1 (judgment), http://www .icj-cij .org/docket/files/52/5561.pdf
art. 91, 92, 94 (nationality of ships)	*Lauritzen v. Larsen*, U.S. Supreme Court, 345 U.S. 571 (1952)
art. 94.3(b)	ILO Maritime Labor Convention, 2005, http://www.ilo .org/ilolex/english/convdisp1.htm
arts. 94.4(b), 94.4(c), 94.5	IMO Standards of Training and Certification of Watchkeepers, 1978
art. 94.5	IMO Load Lines Convention, 1966
art. 97	Reverses rule of *Lotus*, 1927, PCIJ, Ser. A 10, http://www .icj-cij.org/pcij/serie_A/A_10/30_Lotus_Arret.pdf
art. 98(1)	SOLAS regulation V/10; IMSAR Manual
art. 98(2)	IMO Search and Rescue Convention, 1979

LOS Convention Provision	**Competent International Organization; International Rule or Standard**
art. 99	1956 Supplementary Convention on the Abolition of Slavery, the Slave Trade and Institutions and Practices similar to Slavery, http://www.unhchr.ch/html/menu3/b/30.htm
arts. 100–107	ILC 1956 draft articles on the law of the sea, articles 38–45
art. 109	Radio Regulations
art. 111	The *I'm Alone* Case (Canada v. United States), III RIAA 1613, 1935
arts. 116, 117	FAO IPOA-IUU Fishing, 2001
Part XI and Annex II	Modified by Part XI Implementing Agreement, 1995
arts. 124–132	Convention on Transit Trade of Land-locked States, 1965 http://www.austlii.edu.au/au/other/dfat/treaties/1972/4.html
arts. 202–203	Stockholm Conference (UN Conference on Human Environment, 1972), Principle 6 of General Principles for Assessment and Control of Marine Pollution, Conference Report, Annex III, at 73
arts. 207, 213	Montreal Guidelines, UNEP GC Decision 13/18/II, May 24, 1985; GPA land-based sources marine pollution, 1995
art. 208.5, 214	SPREP Convention, art. 8; Cartagena Convention, art. 8
art. 209, 215	See www.isa.org.jm
arts. 210, 216	London (Dumping) Convention and Protocol; SPREP Convention, art. 10; Cartagena Convention, art. 6
art. 211.7	IMO OPPRC Convention, 1990
arts. 211, 217, 218, 219, 220	IMO MARPOL Convention, 1973/78; GPSR
arts. 212, 222	SPREP Convention, art. 9; Cartagena Convention, art. 9 Cf. MARPOL Annex VI, 1996
art. 221	IMO Intervention Convention, 1969
art. 235.3	IMO liability and compensation conventions, 1969–2007
art. 236	MARPOL art. 3.3
art. 237	MARPOL and regional environmental protection agreements

LOS Convention Provision	Competent International Organization; International Rule or Standard
Part XIII – marine scientific research	IOC/UNESCO http://ioc.unesco.org/iocweb/index.php
Part XIV – marine technology	IOC/UNESCO IOC Criteria and Guidelines for the Transfer of Marine Technology, http://ioc3.unesco.org/abelos/index.php?option=com_content&task=view&id=27&Itemid=42
art. 287.1(a) and Annex VI	See www.itlos.org
art. 290.1	The M/V *Saiga* (Case No. 2), (St. Vincent and the Grenadines v. Guinea), ITLOS 1999
art. 290.5	The *MOx Plant* Case (Ireland v. United Kingdom), ITLOS 2001; Permanent Court of Arbitration, 2 July 2003 (www.pca-cpa.org/PDF/OSPAR%20Award.pdf); EC & UK v. Ireland & Sweden, European Court of Justice, 30 May 2006 (http://curia.eu.int)
art. 303.2	UNESCO Convention for the Protection of Underwater Cultural Heritage and annexed rules. http://unesdoc.unesco.org/images/0012/001232/123278e.pdf
art. 303.3	IMO Salvage Convention, 1979
art. 319.2(a)	UNSG annual report on oceans and law of the sea www.un.org/Depts/los
Annex VIII art. 2.2.	www.fao.org; www.imo.org; http://ioc.unesco.org/iocweb/index.php; http://www.unep.org/

TABLE OF COMPARABLE PROVISIONS:

1982 LAW OF THE SEA CONVENTION WITH THE 1958 GENEVA CONVENTIONS ON THE TERRITORIAL SEA AND THE CONTIGUOUS ZONE (TSC), CONTINENTAL SHELF (CSC), HIGH SEAS CONVENTION (HSC), FISHING AND CONSERVATION OF THE LIVING RESOURCES OF THE HIGH SEAS (FISHING) AND OPTIONAL PROTOCOL ON DISPUTE SETTLEMENT

1982 LOS CONVENTION	1958 GENEVA CONVENTIONS
Article #	Article #
Part I. Introduction	
1. *Use of terms and scope*	—
Part II. Territorial Sea and Contiguous Zone	TSC
Section 1. General Provisions	
2. *Legal status of the territorial sea, of the air space over the territorial sea and of its bed and subsoil.*	1–2
Section 2. Limits of the Territorial Sea	
3. *Breadth of the territorial sea*	—
4. *Outer limit of the territorial sea*	6
5. *Normal baseline*	3
6. *Reefs*	—
7. *Straight baselines*	4
8. *Internal waters*	5
9. *Mouths of rivers*	13
10. *Bays*	7
11. *Ports*	8
12. *Roadsteads*	9
13. *Low-tide elevations*	11
14. *Combination of methods for determining baselines*	—
15. *Delimitation of the territorial sea between States with opposite or adjacent coasts*	12.1
16. *Charts and lists of coordinates*	4.6, 9, 12.2

1982 LOS CONVENTION	**1958 GENEVA CONVENTIONS**
Section 3. Innocent Passage in the Territorial Sea	
Subsection A. Rules Applicable to All Ships	
17. *Right of innocent passage*	14.1
18. *Meaning of passage*	14.2–.3
19. *Meaning of innocent passage*	14.4–.5
20. *Submarines and other underwater vehicles*	14.6
21. *Laws and regulations of the coastal State relating to innocent passage*	17
22. *Sea lanes and traffic separation schemes*	—
23. *Foreign nuclear-powered ships and ships carrying nuclear or other inherently dangerous or noxious substances*	—
24. *Duties of the coastal State*	15
25. *Rights of protection of the coastal State*	16.1–.3
26. *Charges which may be levied upon foreign ships*	18
Subsection B. Rules applicable to Merchant Ships and Government Ships Operated for Commercial Purposes	
27. *Criminal jurisdiction on board a foreign ship*	19
28. *Civil jurisdiction in relation to foreign ships*	20
Subsection C. Rules Applicable to Warships and Other Government Ships Operated for Non-Commercial Purposes	
29. *Definition of warships*	HSC 8.2
30. *Non-compliance by warships with the laws and regulations of the coastal State*	TSC 23
31. *Responsibility of the flag State for damage caused by a warship or other government ship operated for non-commercial purposes*	—
32. *Immunities of warships and other government ships operated for non-commercial purposes*	22
Section 4. Contiguous Zone	
33. *Contiguous zone*	24.1–.2

1982 LOS CONVENTION	1958 GENEVA CONVENTIONS
Part III. Straits used for International Navigation	
34.–44.	—
45. *Innocent passage*	16.4
Part IV. Archipelagic States	
46.–54.	—
Part V. Exclusive Economic Zone	
55.–59.	—
60. *Artificial islands, installations and structures in the exclusive economic zone*	CSC 5.2–.6
61.–75.	—
Part VI. Continental Shelf	CSC
76. *Definition of the continental shelf*	1
77. *Rights of the coastal State over the continental shelf*	2
78. *Legal status of the superjacent waters and air space and the rights and freedoms of other States*	3, 5.1
79. *Submarine cables and pipelines on the continental shelf*	4
80. *Artificial islands, installations and structures on the continental shelf*	5.2–.6
81. *Drilling on the continental shelf*	—
82. *Revenue sharing beyond 200 nautical miles*	—
83. *Delimitation of the continental shelf with respect to the exploitation of the continental shelf beyond 200 nautical miles*	6.1–.2
84. *Charts and lists of geographical co-ordinates*	6.3
85. *Tunnelling*	7
Part VII. High Seas	HSC
Section 1. General Provisions	
86. *Application of the provisions of this Part*	1
87. *Freedom of the high seas*	2
88. *Reservation of the high seas for peaceful purposes*	—

1982 LOS CONVENTION	**1958 GENEVA CONVENTIONS**
89. *Invalidity of sovereignty over the high seas*	2
90. *Right of navigation*	4
91. *Nationality of ships*	5
92. *Status of ships*	6
93. *Ships flying the flag of the UN, its specialized agencies and the IAEA*	7
94. *Duties of the flag State*	10
95. *Immunity of warships on the high seas*	8.1
96. *Immunity of other ships used only on government non-commercial service*	9
97. *Penal jurisdiction in matters of collision or any other incident of navigation*	11
98. *Duty to render assistance*	12
99. *Prohibition of the transport of slaves*	13
100. *Duty to co-operate in the repression of piracy*	14
101. *Definition of piracy*	15
102. *Piracy by a warship, government ship or government aircraft whose crew has mutinied*	16
103. *Definition of a pirate ship or aircraft*	17
104. *Retention or loss of the nationality of a pirate ship or aircraft*	18
105. *Seizure of a pirate ship or aircraft*	19
106. *Liability for seizure without adequate grounds*	20
107. *Ships and aircraft which are entitled to seize on account of piracy*	21
108. *Illicit traffic in narcotic drugs or psychotropic substances*	—
109. *Unauthorized broadcasting from the high seas*	—
110. *Right of visit*	22
111. *Right of hot pursuit*	23
112. *Right to lay submarine cables and pipelines*	26
113. *Breaking or injury of a submarine cable or pipeline*	27
114. *Breaking or injury by owners of a submarine cable or pipeline of another submarine cable or pipeline*	28

1982 LOS CONVENTION	**1958 GENEVA CONVENTIONS**
115. *Indemnity for loss incurred in avoiding injury to a submarine cable or pipeline*	29
Section 2. Conservation and Management of the Living Resources of the High Seas	Fishing
116. *Right to fish on the high seas*	1.1
117. *Duty of States to adopt with respect to their nationals measures for the conservation of the living resources of the high seas*	1.2
118. *Co-operation of States in the conservation and management of living resources*	1.2
119. *Conservation of the living resources of the high seas*	2
120. *Marine mammals*	—
Part VIII. Regime of Islands	
121. *Regime of Islands*	HSC 10
Part IX. Enclosed or semi-enclosed seas	
122. *Definition*	—
123. *Co-operation of States bordering enclosed or semi-enclosed seas*	—
Part X. Right of Access of Land-Locked States to and from the Sea and Freedom of Transit	HSC
124. *Use of terms*	3
125. *Right of access to and from the sea and freedom of transit*	—
126. *Exclusion of application of the most-favored-nation clause*	—
127. *Customs duties, taxes and other charges*	—
128. *Free zones and other customs facilities*	—
129. *Co-operation in the construction and improvement of means of transport*	—
130. *Measures to avoid or eliminate delays or other difficulties of a technical nature of a technical in traffic in transit*	—

1982 LOS CONVENTION	1958 GENEVA CONVENTIONS
131. *Equal treatment in maritime ports*	3
132. *Grant of greater transit facilities*	—
Part XI. The Area	
133.–191.	—
Part XII. Protection and Preservation of the Marine Environment	
192.–237.	—
Part XIII. Marine Scientific Research	
238.–265.	—
Part XIV. Development and Transfer of Marine Technology	
266.–278.	—
Part XV. Settlement of Disputes	
279.–299.	Optional Protocol
Part XVI. General Provisions	
300.–304.	—
Part XVII. Final Provisions 305.–320.	—

www.ingramcontent.com/pod-product-compliance
Lightning Source LLC
Chambersburg PA
CBHW071403230926
51846CB00001B/5